PROPHECY IN ANCIENT ISRAEL

by

J. LINDBLOM

FORTRESS PRESS
PHILADELPHIA
MCMLXXIII

© BASIL BLACKWELL 1962
FIRST PRINTED OCTOBER 1962
REPRINTED APRIL 1963
REPRINTED JULY 1965
REPRINTED FEBRUARY 1973

PRINTED IN GREAT BRITAIN

CONTENTS

iii

CONTENTS

iv

PREFACE

My researches into Old Testament prophecy have been carried on over a period of nearly forty years. In 1934 I published in Swedish a work entitled *Profetismen i Israel,* in which I summed up the results of my studies up to that time. The present volume, however, is an entirely new work and has hardly a single sentence in common with its predecessor. In particular, I have in the intervening years considerably modified my views on the composition of the prophetic literature.

It is impossible to cover the vast range of works on prophecy; and I am aware that a number of important studies are not included in my Bibliography. It is a matter of particular regret to me that I have been unable to take account of the literature which has appeared during the past few years. My typescript had been completed in 1958; but causes beyond my control have considerably delayed publication.

To the Revd. Professor G. W. Anderson I owe a deep debt of gratitude for the trouble he has taken to improve my English, for assistance in the proof-reading, and for a number of valuable suggestions regarding the subject matter. Without his help this book would never have appeared in print. Professor Gillis Gerleman, my successor on the chair of Old Testament Exegesis, has been of invaluable assistance to me in many ways, for which I am deeply grateful to him. I also tender my sincere thanks to the publisher. Through the publication of my work in English by an English publishing house I have been enabled to present my conclusions to a circle of readers beyond the bounds of Scandinavia.

Lund, March, 1962   J. LINDBLOM

In this reprint the text remains unchanged apart from the correction of a few misprints. I have also appended to the Bibliography a selection of recent works which are relevant to my treatment of the subject and also some earlier items which were not included in the original bibliography.

Lund, March 1963   J. LINDBLOM

CHAPTER ONE

RELIGIO-HISTORICAL SURVEY: PROPHETS OUTSIDE ISRAEL

1. GENERAL REMARKS

When most people speak of prophets, they think of the prophets of ancient Israel, whose work and utterances are familiar to us from the Scriptures of the Old Testament. The modern study of the psychology and history of religion, however, has shown that prophets are found in many provinces of the world of religion, in modern as well as in ancient times. Among men and women who can be characterized as *homines religiosi* we distinguish a special type which can be called *the prophetic type*. What are the characteristics of this prophetic type?

It is often said that the prophet is a person who has the gift of fore-telling the future. The word 'prophet' itself seems to support this definition. Yet, as has been shown, *pro* in the Greek term *prophētēs* does not mean 'before' but 'forth'.[1] Thus the Greek term indicates that the prophet is a preacher, a *forth*teller rather than a *fore*teller. In reality men and women who belong to the prophetic type have been, in the first place, persons who have had something to proclaim, something to announce publicly (their message has of course frequently also been about future events).

Thus the first thing we have to say about the prophets is that they are *homines religiosi*. The prophet is not in himself a politician, a social reformer, a thinker, or a philosopher; nor is he in the first place a poet, even though he often puts his sayings in a poetical form. The special gift of a prophet is his ability to experience the divine in an original way and to receive revelations from the divine world. The prophet belongs entirely to his God; his paramount task is to listen to and obey his God. In every respect he has given himself up to his God and stands unreservedly at His disposal.

There are *homines religiosi* to whom religious experiences as such are the essence of their religious life. Personal communion with God, prayer, devotion, moral submission to the divine will are the principal traits in their religious attitude. That which distinguishes a prophet from other *homines religiosi* is that he never keeps his experiences to himself; he always feels compelled to announce to others what he has

[1] See Fascher, ΠΡΟΦΗΤΗΣ. *Eine sprach- und religionsgeschichtliche Untersuchung*, pp. 4 ff.

I

seen and heard. The prophet is a man of the public word. He is a speaker and a preacher.

The prophet is an inspired man. He claims to share in a particular divine inspiration. He always refers to another who stands behind him and tells him what he must say. A mighty power deals with him and speaks through him. The prophet knows that his thoughts and words never come from himself: they are given him. The philosopher works in the laboratory of the intellect. His task is to combine various thoughts in a logical connection, and from given premises to draw the right conclusions. The prophet does not philosophize, does not muse or speculate; his privilege is to receive, to receive thoughts, visions, and words as wonderful gifts from heaven. The prophet is, in short, a proclaimer of divine revelations.

In this respect the prophet plainly differs from the religious teacher or pedagogue who methodically instructs his pupils according to didactic rules. The prophet is compelled by the spirit; and he knows no other rules than the force and the guidance of the divine impulse.

As one compelled by the divine power, the prophet lives under a divine constraint. He has lost the freedom of the ordinary man and is forced to follow the orders of the deity. He must say what has been given him to say and go where he is commanded to go. Few things are so characteristic of the prophets, wherever we meet them in the world of religion, as the feeling of being under a superhuman and supernatural constraint.

In the experience of inspiration and the feeling of necessity and constraint there is a kinship between the prophet and the poet. The prophet, as we have said, is not in himself a poet; but from a psychological point of view there is a great similarity between the two types. The poet, too, often speaks of inspiration and of a sort of abnormal force which compels him to write. Of course, not all the poets are inspired or even pretend to be inspired. Plato and Aristotle distinguished between poets who worked rationally and methodically and others who composed their verses in a state of mania. But many poets of all ages have been familiar with this peculiar state of irresistible inspiration which, for instance, characterized Æschylus, of whom it was said that he composed his tragedies as in a state of intoxication.[2]

The English-speaking reader of this book has no need to be instructed about the essence of poetical inspiration. He can study this phenomenon in the masterpieces of great English poets. When, for instance, William Blake in *Milton* calls upon the muses—'Muses who inspire the Poet's

[2] See further Inge, *Christian Mysticism*, pp. 14 f.

Song'—these are not empty words. For Blake, as for countless modern poets, inspiration from a higher power outside himself was a wonderful, ineffable fact. Likewise Hesiod said that the muses had inspired him with a divine song to celebrate things of the past and things of the future (*Theogonia, vv.* 31 f.).

Friedrich Nietzsche's sister has given us the most remarkable information concerning the origin of the famous book by her brother *Also sprach Zarathustra*. During his rambles in the mountains, thoughts and ideas overwhelmed him with such vehemence that he could hardly take them down in his note-book. Of the inspiration itself Nietzsche gives an extremely interesting account. If he had preserved a spark of superstition, he would have imagined that he was only an incarnation, a mouthpiece, a medium of mighty celestial powers. He describes this experience as a true revelation. One hears, but does not seek. One receives, but does not ask who is the giver. The ideas come just like flashes of lightning, with compelling power, unsought, and not at will.[3]

Nietzsche's description of inspiration is unequalled; but countless other testimonies point in the same direction. We have a fine account by the Austrian poet Grillparzer of the composition of the play *Die Ahnfrau*. Ideas and verses poured forth without his own initiative. He had only to write them down as soon as they were given him. In a fortnight the whole tragedy was completed.

In such a state of inspiration the poet distinguishes between himself and 'another', who really is the active partner. Grillparzer writes:

> Du nennst mich Dichter, ich bin es nicht!
> Ein anderer sitzt, ich fühl's, und schreibt mein Leben;
> und soll die Poesie den Namen geben,
> statt Dichter fühl' ich höchstens mich Gedicht.

The great Swedish poet Esaias Tegnér writes in the dithyrambic part of the poem *Svea*: 'A deity seizes me. A God dwells in the Song.' Alfred de Musset says: 'One does not work, one listens. It is as if an unknown one were speaking in the ear.' The Russian novelist Gogol says: 'A wonderful work is to be brought to maturity in my soul. My eyes stream with tears for gratitude. Such an inspiration cannot originate from a human being.'

The renowned French painter Eugène Delacroix is a good witness to a similar experience: 'Dieu est en nous. C'est lui sans doute qui fait

---

[3] This description of inspiration can be read, for instance, in *Also sprach Zarathustra* (Anhang).

l'inspiration dans les hommes de génie et qui les enchante au spectacle de leurs propres productions.'[4]

An inspired poet is not in himself a prophet, but from a psychological point of view we have much to learn from the descriptions of what the poet experiences in the divinely endowed moments of highest inspiration. This feeling of personal passivity and absolute dependence on a higher power is extremely typical of the 'prophets', too, wherever we meet them in various parts of the world.

When inspiration strongly intensifies it turns into ecstasy. Ecstasy belongs to the psychical phenomena the definition of which has varied from time to time and from one author to another. Sometimes the etymology of the word has been followed. Then ecstasy has been defined as a mental state in which one has a feeling that the soul leaves the body and goes off to distant regions, and the bond with this world is temporarily cut off. However, this definition is too narrow. Phenomena which are commonly called ecstatic are not always combined with such a conception of the relation between soul and body as is here described; they also appear in connection with other more or less violent alterations in the ordinary spiritual life.

The term 'ecstasy' has also been used to denote the culminating point of religious experience whereby perfect union with God is realized in direct though ineffable experience. Ecstasy in this sense is often described in the works of the great mystics from Plotinus to Eckhart. This *unio mystica* as an act of the highest grace, according to the estimate of the mystics themselves, is a special kind of ecstasy. But firstly, many mystics have had ecstatic experiences without having attained the highest degree of perfect absorption in the divinity, wherein the human personality is dissolved and merged in God; and secondly, ecstatic phenomena are not necessarily associated with religion at all. For this reason it is necessary to find a wider definition, a definition which covers the whole field of experiences which are usually called ecstatic.

Modern psychologists rightly take the term 'ecstasy' in a wider sense. Following scholars such as Weidel, Hauer, Leuba, Evelyn Underhill, and many others, who have thoroughly studied ecstatic experience, I prefer to define ecstasy as an abnormal state of consciousness in which one is so intensely absorbed by one single idea or one single feeling, or by a group of ideas or feelings, that the normal stream of psychical life is more or less arrested. The bodily senses cease to function; one becomes impervious to impressions from without; consciousness is exalted above the ordinary level of daily experience; unconscious mental

---

[4] See further, for instance, Ribot, *Essai sur l'imagination créatrice*[7].

impressions and ideas come to the surface in the form of visions and auditions. Consequently ecstasy can rightly be described as a kind of monoideism. Such ecstasy is, of course, not peculiar to religious men. Any person so predisposed, who concentrates upon one idea or feeling, easily passes into a sort of trance, however trivial the idea may be which gains possession of his consciousness. Ecstasy in this sense merely indicates the presence of certain abnormal psycho-physical conditions, an alteration of the normal equilibrium, a shifting of the threshold of consciousness. Of course the worth of ecstasy depends entirely on the objective value of the dominating idea or feeling.[5]

In religious ecstasy, consciousness is entirely filled with the presence of God, with ideas and feelings belonging to the divine sphere. The soul is lifted up into the exalted region of divine revelation, and the lower world with its sensations momentarily disappears. There are various means to induce such a mental rapture: intoxication of different kinds, fasts, flagellation, dancing, music and so on. On a higher level, prayer and meditation are well-known means of attaining ecstatic experiences. Ecstasy in this sense can be communicated by direct contagion. In the history of religion there have been many instances of psychical epidemics.

It must be kept in mind that ecstasy has many degrees. There is an ecstasy which involves a total extinction of the normal consciousness, a complete insensibility and anaesthesia. There is also an ecstasy which approximates to a normal fit of absence of mind or intense excitement. This observation is very important for the study of the psychology of the prophets. Inspiration or psychical exaltation is characteristic of all men and women who belong to the prophetic type. But this inspired exaltation has in the prophets a tendency to pass over into a real ecstasy of a more or less intense nature, lethargic or orgiastic.

[5] Weidel, 'Zur Psychologie der Ekstase', ZRP, ii, 1908, pp. 190 ff.; Hauer, Die Religionen; Leuba, The Psychology of Religious Mysticism, pp. 204 ff.; Underhill, Mysticism[12]. I fully agree with the definition, with reference to Mantegazza (Die Ekstase des Menschen), given by the German psychiatrist Jacobi in his study Die Ekstase der alttestamentlichen Propheten (Grenzfragen des Nerven- und Seelenlebens, 108), p. 47: 'Beim Ekstatiker ist die Aufmerksamkeit so auf einen einzigen Punkt des Bewusstseins konzentriert, dass alle übrigen Formen der äusseren und inneren Empfindung, die nicht mit jenem in Beziehung stehen, verblassen. Die Gedanken und Gefühle strömen derart in einem einzigen Punkt zusammen, dass alle nicht dorthin gerichteten Eindrücke der Aussen- und Innenwelt verschwinden'. In Record and Revelation, ed. by H. Wheeler Robinson, Porteous says rightly that ecstasy is 'the appropriate term to apply when an overmastering emotion of whatsoever kind produces a state of exaltation or stupefaction in which the mind is obsessed by a single idea or group of ideas to the exclusion of all other ideas, or one or more of the senses are abnormally stimulated, with accompanying suspension of the other bodily functions', p. 228. Ecstasy is taken in a similar sense by Hölscher in Die Profeten, and by Robinson in Prophecy and the Prophets in Ancient Israel. For the discussion about the essence of ecstasy see also J. Ridderbos, Profetie en ekstase. Zaehner, Mysticism, Sacred and Profane, adduces many examples of profane ecstasy.

In the foregoing it has been established that the following attributes are characteristic of the prophetic class among *homines religiosi*. They are entirely devoted, soul and body, to the divinity. They are inspired personalities who have the power to receive divine revelations. They act as speakers and preachers who publicly announce what they have to say. They are compelled by higher powers and kept under divine constraint. The inspiration which they experience has a tendency to pass over into real ecstasy.

One further attribute may be added: the special call. A prophet knows that he has never chosen his way himself: he has been chosen by the deity. He points to a particular experience in his life through which it has become clear to him that the deity has a special purpose with him and has designated him to perform a special mission. The call often takes him by surprise. He sometimes offers resistance, but is vanquished by the deity and makes an unconditional surrender. The call has the character of a supernatural experience. It exceeds all human reason. It is often accompanied by physical and psychical phenomena. The call is frequently met with fear and trembling; but it is always regarded as an act of divine grace.

This is what we have to say in general terms about the prophetic type in the world of religion. We now mention some instances of prophets in the general sense. They may be taken from various periods, regions, and levels of religion. They represent different degrees of religious development. But I hope that through such a survey light may also be thrown on the prophets of the Old Testament, who constitute a group of prophetic personalities, though with its quite unique characteristics.

2. PRIMITIVE PROPHECY

At the lowest state of religious development we find the *shamans* among the Arctic, and particularly Ural-Altaic peoples. Shamanism has been described with great accuracy by many investigators in modern as well as in older times.[6] The chief task of the shamans is to mediate

---

[6] Radloff, *Aus Sibirien*; Stadling, *Through Siberia* and *Shamanismen i norra Asien*; Wasiljew, *Übersicht über die heidnischen Gebräuche, Aberglauben und Religion der Wotjaken*; Donner, *Bei den Samojeden in Sibirien*; Holmberg-Harva, *Die religiösen Vorstellungen der altaischen Völker* and *Die religiösen Vorstellungen der Mordwinen*; Eliade, *Le chamanisme et les techniques archaïques de l'extase*. Phenomena closely related to the shamanism of Russia and North Asia are also to be found among the Indians in America, the Lapps in Fenno-Scandinavia and, in bygone times, among the northern peoples from which the Icelandic Sagas originate. See Strömbäck, *Sejd. Textstudier i nordisk religionshistoria*, esp. pp. 108 ff.

between the spirits and the human world. To fulfil this purpose they have to establish a special communication with the realm of the spirits, either by making journeys into the regions of the spirits or by coercing the spirits to come to them or even enter into them. In this way they elicit secrets from the spirits in order to reveal them to men. With the aid of the spirits the shamans cure sicknesses, effectively perform sacrifices and other cultic rites, execute magical functions, and, obtaining through conversation with spirits and gods a knowledge superior to that of ordinary men, they divine and communicate oracular messages.

These messages usually have a poetical, mysterious and obscure form and must consequently be interpreted by specially competent persons standing around the shaman. Often the shaman himself does not know what he is saying, neither does he remember it when the state of possession has passed. Therefore bystanders must store up in their memory what the shaman has announced.

The psychical experiences of the shaman manifest themselves as a kind of ecstasy. Ecstasy is the proof of his communion with the spirits and gives him a sensational authority and an immense power over men. When officiating the shaman is dressed in special clothes and is preferably sitting in darkness. The ecstasy is induced and intensified with the aid of the troll-drum and various artificial stimuli. Abnormal bodily and psychical phenomena accompany the ecstasy.

The shaman has become a shaman through a special call. Natural predisposition, sometimes of a hereditary nature, prepares him for his life as a shaman. He does not choose his way himself, a higher power designates him to his future office. The shaman is regarded as chosen by the godhead, and the divine command is not to be defied. There is no escape from his fate. Every attempt to evade revenges itself through sickness and death.

Already at this primitive stage of religious life we easily discern several features characteristic of the type which we have called the prophetic type: the consciousness of having received a special call, the constraint exercised by spiritual powers, the ecstatic phenomena, and finally the ability to hear divine secrets, and the duty of pronouncing oracular messages from the spiritual world.

Akin to the shamans, at least psychologically, are the *kahins* and *dervishes* in the Arab world. Of course, the differences in religion and culture are considerable, but the general behaviour of the shamans on the one hand and the kahins and dervishes on the other is very similar.

In Arabian paganism the kahin represented the prophetic type at a relatively primitive stage.[7] A kahin was a 'seer' or soothsayer whose task it was to communicate oracles and divinations. They frequently performed this task in a state of ecstatic exaltation. This mental state was held to have a divine origin, as was also the inspiration of the bedouin poets. The kahin was considered to be a mouthpiece of the divine power which was speaking in him or through his mediation. In the ecstatic state of mind the deity spoke through the kahin in the first person and the kahin could consequently address himself in the second person. He adopted an objective attitude to himself and spoke of his own poems and revelations as if it were another person who had obtained them. The inspiration was assigned to the jinn, the indeterminate, impersonal spirits. Sometimes the relation between the kahin and the spirit was considered as demonic possession. Sometimes the spirit was thought of as a more personal being, who communicated to his friend what he had learned in the celestial regions, whispering it to him in his ear.

The messages of the kahin were usually presented in an artistic form: brief sentences formulated in a sort of rhymed prose.

The kahins enjoyed great authority in their tribes. They were consulted in all affairs of special significance. They often acted as judges. Chieftains frequently kept their own kahins to give them advice in critical situations. Kahins played an important role as leaders of campaigns against hostile tribes. But the kahins were also resorted to in quite trivial matters. They were expected to interpret dreams, reveal thefts, discover lost objects, know where strayed camels were to be found, etc. Usually they were rewarded for their services according to the circumstances of the applicant. Particularly outstanding kahins were called on also from distant tribes. It goes without saying that the prayer of a kahin was held to be particularly effective and that a kahin was expected to have the faculty of performing miracles.

As sacred persons the kahins were also attached to the cult of various gods and could occasionally function as sacrificial priests. In particular they did so in connection with divination and the pronouncement of oracles. Cultic rites such as circumambulation (*ṭawāf*) served to induce and intensify the ecstatic state of mind.

The activities of the dervishes are one of those ways in which Islam

[7] Wellhausen, *Reste arabischen Heidentums*[2], pp. 134 ff.; Goldziher, *Abhandlungen zur arabischen Philologie*, I, *passim*; Andrae, *Mohammed. The Man and his Faith*, pp. 36 ff.; Haldar, *Associations of Cult Prophets among the Ancient Semites*, pp. 161 ff.; Pedersen, 'The Rôle played by Inspired Persons among the Israelites and the Arabs', *SOTP*, pp. 127 ff.

satisfies the need for a more intimate communion with the deity than the public religion offers.[8]

The religion of the dervishes is a religion of training, the end of the religious exercises being ecstasy. In order to induce ecstasy the dervishes utilize detailed methods and ceremonies, among which mental contemplation, reiteration of the divine name, the Moslem creed, or other formulas, prayers, silent or audible, and recitation of certain chapters of the Koran play a substantial role. Furious exclamation of the syllable *hū* frequently forms the climax of the religious excitement. Rudolf Otto sees in this howling an outlet of the feeling of the *numinosum*.[9]

In the Occident the terms 'howling dervishes' and 'dancing dervishes' are often used. Methodical motions of the body are an integral part of the ritual: whirling dances, circular movements, convulsive bending of the head and the upper part of the body, and other fervid efforts ending in religious delirium and subsequent exhaustion.

There are many different orders of dervishes. In several orders music and intoxication by various drugs, especially hashish, are used to induce the ecstatic state. Fasts, holding one's breath, and similar exercises are popular means of attaining to the desired mental state. In this way the dervish proceeds to reach the highest state of religious life and to be drawn nearer to God and the spiritual world.

An important characteristic of the organization of the dervishes is the role played by the spiritual guide, called 'shaikh'. As a rule there is a shaikh in each coenobium or convent, *takiyyah*, where dervishes belonging to the same association assemble for common exercises under his guidance. The brethren often lodge in the *takiyyah* and have their common meals there. There are different types of dervishes. Some of them live as hermits; others are peripatetic; others are craftsmen, shopkeepers, and so on, and appear only occasionally in the convent. Again a number of the dervishes live constantly in the convent, not unlike the monks in the monasteries of the west, though less bound by rules and vows. Married dervishes living in their own quarters are not uncommon. Many dervishes, but by no means all, are mendicants.

The task of the shaikh, or *mukaddam*, is to conduct the religious exercises and by means of them to stimulate the disciples to ecstatic raptures. He exercises a mighty spiritual power on the disciples. The shaikh also possesses the greatest authority among them and among pious Moslems in general.

Every well-educated dervish, and above all the shaikh, is expected to

---

[8] Brown, *The Darvishes or Oriental Spiritualism*; Macdonald, art. 'Derwish' in *EI*.
[9] Otto, *Aufsätze das Numinose betreffend*, pp. 11 f.

be able to perform actions beyond the power of ordinary men. They have the reputation of curing diseases, of having significant dreams and visions, and of possessing the faculty of interpreting dreams, of foreseeing coming events, of revealing secrets, of influencing an absent individual for a good or evil purpose, and of knowing what is happening in distant places. Being inspired by the deity, the dervishes are expected to possess supernatural knowledge and to be able to give advice to those who consult them.

The dervishes and their shaikhs have sometimes played an important role in public affairs. The Janissaries in Constantinople had members of the Bektashi order lodging in their barracks in order to make use of their spiritual powers. Through them they hoped to gain victory and honour. They also used them more or less as army chaplains. Outstanding shaikhs have often exercised a considerable influence on princes and sultans who accepted their advice.[10]

The dervishes, themselves often deeply religious men, are energetic and successful missionaries for the Islamic religion and for the glory of Allah.[11]

The different orders and associations are distinguished by varying attire and equipment. One thing, however, is common to all dervishes: religious inspiration which passes over into ecstasy. Inasmuch as they also pronounce prophecies and messages from the spiritual world they may justly be included in the prophetic type in the world of religion.

The most characteristic features of the dervishes are, however, the training for ecstasy and ecstatic experiences, the organization in associations, the influence of the shaikh on his disciples, and, finally, the authority which the dervishes possess in society. On these points we observe a considerable similarity at least to the early prophets of the Old Testament.

Alois Musil, the well-known Czech orientalist and explorer, has given us a most valuable description of the life and customs of the *Rwala bedouin*, a famous tribe of northern Arabia. Among these bedouin, he tells us, there exists a class of male and female seers called *ahl as-sirr*, owners of secrets.[12] They claim to enjoy God's special protection, and are held to be able to cure diseases, discover what is hidden, have significant dreams, foretell future events, and pronounce oracles. These faculties are all regarded as gifts of *islām*, the intimate contact with God, with

---

[10] Jacob, *Beiträge zur Kenntnis des Derwisch-Ordens der Bektaschis*.

[11] Guillaume, *Prophecy and Divination*, strongly emphasizes the religious side of the inner life of the dervishes; pp. 298 f., 304.

[12] Musil, *The Manners and Customs of the Rwala Bedouins*, pp. 400 ff.

which they claim to be privileged above ordinary men, and which manifests itself as inspiration or ecstasy.

The Rwala believe in spirits, jinn, belonging to the earthly world. The jinn are usually thought of as evil and malevolent beings, and are highly feared as injuring and harming men in various ways. Men possessed by such uncanny spirits are very unhappy and eagerly seek the help of magicians in order to be delivered. With these earthly and evil beings the *ahl as-sirr* have nothing to do. They ascribe their special gifts to a celestial spirit, called *malak*, who is regarded as a messenger from Allah, announcing to the seer Allah's will and thoughts. As Allah's spokesman and mouthpiece the *malak* is called *munâbi*. Musil describes the appearance of the *munâbi* in the following way: 'As a rule the *munâbi* appears in the shape of a rider seated on a white mare. He tells the seer what to proclaim in Allah's name, and woe to him should he say something different from what the angel told him, for the angel would kill him on the spot. The *munâbi* simply says, "O So-and-So, this or that is going to happen; this or that thou wilt proclaim; this or that do." Besides the angel the seer's ancestors also appear to him in the night between Thursday and Friday, instructing him how to behave. Yet neither the angel nor the ancestors ever appear without a thorough preparation on the part of the seer.'

Through the appearance of the angel the seer gets into an exalted state of mind; ecstasy comes upon him. This psychic state is supported by means of music, violent bodily movements, and other performances. In all this the seer is assisted by his disciples, who are taught all the external performances which must be displayed if the *munâbi* is going to appear, as Musil says. When the ecstatic rapture has passed, extreme exhaustion sets in, and the seer can do nothing further.

The seer is regarded as a very powerful man. Accordingly, his assistance is sought after; but he is also feared. Because of the seers' avarice they are sometimes objects of scorn and even hatred. Musil relates a story of a chieftain who was greatly incensed against both the seers and their disciples because of their inordinate greed and was once heard to say, 'Oh, may Allah rid me of you all. If you have enough, you disturb everybody's rest by your music and your foolery; if you are hungry, there is no being rid of you, you beggars.' On hearing this the insulted sorcerers called a meeting, and one of them cursed the chieftain in the name of all present. A few days later the chief was dead.

One cannot read this without remembering the utterance of Micah, the Hebrew prophet, concerning the false prophets of his time: 'Thus says the Lord concerning the prophets who lead my people astray, who, when they have something to bite with their teeth, announce peace, but, when one puts nothing into their mouths, prepare war against him.'[13]

On the other hand the Rwala ecstatics have exercised a great influence in their tribes. They are believed to give good advice concerning campaigns and other public affairs.

The *ahl as-sirr* among the Rwala bedouin belong decidedly to the prophetic type. Pronouncement of oracles is one of their central functions. The oracles are conceived of as messages from God through the mediation of a celestial spirit. They receive their supernatural knowledge in a state of mind which may justly be called ecstasy, using the word in the wider sense. This mental exaltation is evoked by means of stimulating and exciting performances of various kinds. They play an important role in the public life of their tribes, and are both highly esteemed and feared or even despised.

3. MOHAMMED

When Mohammed appeared his compatriots regarded him as a kahin, even though he himself refused this title. Like most originators in the religious field he claimed a place of his own. What the jinn was to the kahin, the angel was to Mohammed. The angel, sent to him from Allah, had, of course, more important revelations to communicate than the low-born jinn.[14]

There is no doubt that Mohammed was in fact an ecstatic; and, as a proclaimer of inspired messages, he deserves the name of prophet in our sense. His fundamental call, prepared by meditations in Mount Hira, had the form of an ecstatic vision. Tradition concerning this occurrence is confused and contradictory; but according to modern researches the call of Mohammed can be described in the following way. The vision was accorded to him in the open air and by daylight. He saw a being, splendid and majestic, which infused him with a feeling of solemnity and veneration. He stood before a messenger from heaven and the highest God; here was something that surpassed the jinn which were in the habit of taking possession of the ordinary seers and poets. The celestial messenger approached Mohammed and imparted to him a communication which probably implied the mission to be a prophet and an apostle of Allah.

[13] Mic. iii. 5.
[14] For the following cf. Andrae, *Mohammed*. Zimmerli, *Der Prophet im Alten Testament und im Islam*, points to many similarities between Mohammed and the Old Testament prophets: ecstasy, consciousness of being sent by God as a messenger to men, the duty of proclaiming a given message and of issuing warnings or exhortations to repentance, amendment, and conversion, announcement of doom and salvation, etc.

There is no ground for calling in question the genuineness of this vision, or for doubting that Mohammed was, in fact, a visionary and an individual predisposed to ecstatic experiences.

Tradition has much to tell about his ecstatic raptures. When the violent inspiration came upon the Prophet he wrapped himself in blankets, his face grew dark, he fell on the ground as if he had been drunk, and roared like a camel. His brow was beaded with sweat.

That which was revealed to him in the moments of inspiration he clothed in a form which clearly distinguished the celestial communications from ordinary human speech. The Prophet's messages, at least in the early period, resembled in form the oracles of the kahins and followed the pattern of rhymed, or rhythmic and rhymed, prose. Later on the sayings became less inspired, less spontaneous, and more like productions of reflection and consideration. The artistic form was replaced by unimaginative prose. The sacred book of the Mohammedans, the Koran, is the collection of the Prophet's revelations, clearly giving evidence of several different degrees of inspiration.

The fundamental call through which, as through an act of grace, Mohammed was accorded the consciousness of having been chosen a messenger of Allah, the inspiration, sometimes passing over into ecstasy, in which he received celestial revelations, and finally the messages pronounced to men and little by little written down and collected by believers, are all features which recall the prophets of the Old Testament. It may be added that the preaching of an imminent judgement and the exhortation to repentance were also characteristic of the Arabian Prophet as well as of the prophets of Ephraim and Judah notwithstanding the fact that, in the content of their preaching, the difference between Mohammed and the Israelite prophets was much greater than the resemblance.

4. SLEEPING PREACHERS IN FINLAND

The prophetic type of *homines religiosi* is not confined to special religions or special races; it is represented in all parts of the world and, as I am inclined to maintain, in all religions. Jewish mysticism shows several examples of this type.[15] The same holds good of Christianity in all ages. It suffices only to mention phenomena such as prophets and inspired men in the early Church, a great number of the medieval mystics, above all figures such as Joan of Arc, St. Catherine of Siena, St. Catherine of Genoa, and Savonarola, ranters and Quakers in

[15] See, for instance, Scholem, *Major Trends in Jewish Mysticism²*; Ysander, *Studien zum B'eštschen Ḥasidismus.*

England, the prophets of the Cévennes in France, 'die Inspirierten' in Germany, the Crying Voices in Sweden, the Pentecostal movement and other ecstatic revivalists in both the New and the Old World, etc.[16] I should like to restrict my investigation to two examples of Christian ecstasy of the prophetic type because they are only little known outside the countries to which they belong and yet very well suited to throw light upon the subject of our present investigation: I mean the so-called Sleeping Preachers in Finland, and St. Birgitta (Bridget) of Sweden.

In Finland popular piety has produced a number of men and women of the ecstatic-prophetic type; and from the middle of the eighteenth century up to our own day we know a good deal about them and can study them in detail.[17] We call them sleeping preachers, ecstatic speakers, or trance-preachers. They all have in common the ability, linked with certain psychic and pathological peculiarities, to fall into ecstasy and in this state to deliver sermons which are regarded by themselves and their listeners as God's word to men. Most of these trance-preachers have been women; but some have been men. Frequently they have been subject to hysteria, ailing, somewhat eccentric, and harassed by existence; but their message has often been completely reasonable and religiously valuable and edifying. Any abnormality that may have been present has been a predisposition to the actual ecstasy, but has not necessarily set its stamp on the thought-content of the ecstatic sermons. Rather, one has the impression, in studying these persons and their words, that in the ecstasy, they have developed beyond themselves and have given from within far more and far more valuable teaching than one might have expected from their education and general intellectual equipment.

A good example of these Finnish trance-preachers, and one whom psychologists have studied carefully, is Karolina Utriainen (born 1843). Series of her sermons have even been reproduced in print from gramophone records. She was called at the age of nine to preach the Word. The call came to her in a trance that lasted almost a whole day. She said herself that it was a dream; *we* say that it was a typical ecstatic vision. She looked into heaven, her eyes were blinded by the glory, and she fell to the ground. In the vision she saw Christ Himself, who showed her a

[16] Cf. Alphandéry, 'Prophètes et ministère prophétique dans le moyen-âge latin', *RHPh.*, xii, 1932, pp. 334 ff.; Achelis, *Die Ekstase, passim*.
[17] See Akiander, *Historiska upplysningar om religiösa rörelserna i Finland i äldre och senare tider*, esp. vol. III; Voipio, 'Observations on Somnambulic Preaching', *The Scandinavian Scientific Review*, 1923, nr. 2, pp. 93 ff., and *Sleeping Preachers. A Study in Ecstatic Religiosity (AASF*, B; 75, 1); Puukko, 'Ekstatische Propheten mit besonderer Berücksichtigung der finnisch-ugrischen Parallelen', *ZAW*, liii, 1935, pp. 23 ff; Lindblom, 'Ecstasy in Scandinavian Christianity', *ET*, lvii, 1946, pp. 236 ff.

book and commanded her to preach. She described her vision as follows: 'The Lamb came to me, lifted me up and said, "Fear not, little friend; as I have chosen you to carry out my commands, I have by this vision wished to confirm my words to you, and to support you in the temptations which will be laid upon you. If you reject the way I show you in my speech and in this vision, your place will be the deepest in the lake which will burn for ever and ever . . . But if you follow my counsel, you shall, even if you fall, rise up to fight the good fight. Then a high seat will be given you in my kingdom." Then He gave me a great book, written with golden letters, and ordered me to preach the gospel of peace. And then I awakened out of my dream.'

This experience inaugurated for the nine-year-old girl a long life with frequent attacks of ecstasy and preaching-fits. The preacher, however, was not restricted to announcing a 'gospel of peace', as was commanded in her vision. She was frequently compelled to make a powerful appeal for repentance. She caused a tremendous sensation; and many were of the opinion that the end of this world was approaching.

The ecstatic raptures were accompanied by curious psychic and physical symptoms. An eye-witness describes these symptoms in this way: 'A chill crept over her limbs and small red dots appeared on her skin. Her heart began to throb violently and she felt a tingling sensation in her arms. A morbid glitter was seen in her eyes, and her face became pale. A weak shiver and giddiness attacked her. Everything darkened and suddenly the preacher threw herself backwards. She moistened the fingers of her right hand with her lips and made with the hand a great arc just as if she were turning a page in a very large book. Then with a terribly distended chest, and in a voice loud enough to fill a medium-sized church, she began to speak. Her legs were always stiff and inflexible, and the skin apparently senseless and dripping with sweat. Once the attack was over, she wakened without any conspicuous symptoms, beyond the fact that she had completely forgotten what she had said during the trance. Of the visionary elements which presented themselves at the very outset there persisted only a faint recollection.'

Perhaps the most remarkable, at all events the most varied, figure among Finland's trance-preachers was Helena Konttinen (1871-1916).[18] Her call came, as it were, in different stages. After her really remarkable conversion-vision, she first had a call to speak in 'a supernatural state', as she says, to various individuals and reveal their sins. The following is her description of this call.

---

[18] On this woman there is a special monograph in Swedish: Sarlin. *En profetissa i våra dagar*, from which the following references are taken.

'I saw a wonderful radiance, and in it a figure whose glory I cannot describe. As I had been greatly depressed about my own state, and uneasily asked if I was on the right way, the figure said about this, "You shall not be anxious and uneasy, for I am your Saviour." He looked at me from above with such indescribable love, then rose still higher, then appeared indistinct and disappeared. But the radiance remained, and in it were revealed two angels who placed a large book before me. The radiance of the Saviour was brighter than that of the angels, and when He appeared, a veil was laid before my eyes. In this large book there were written in shining letters records of the lives of different people. The angels turned to the place where N. N.'s life was described, and ordered me to read it . . . About fifteen minutes later I began to talk in a state of trance. The whole of that person's life now came out . . . Every trick was revealed, also much that he had to admit that no one but God knew anything about.' With that the dam was broken, and Helena's ecstatic, condemnatory speeches about various persons had free course. They afterwards continued during Helena's remaining ten years of activity, and were of course an important reason for the influence this prophetess acquired over the people she came in touch with, and whom her words reached.

The actual initiation into the public exercise of the calling of a prophetic preacher followed a month or two later. One day, after a long period of sickness, fasting, and ecstasy, Helena had a revelation of the Saviour, who told her she should begin to talk to people about true amendment, and always go where she had it laid on her to go in her supernatural state. She also had to write down on a long strip of paper with gilt edges (this is still in the vision) all the Bible texts on which she was to preach in her future life when in a state of ecstasy. She further received a list of texts on which she was to preach in the normal waking state. When she had learnt this, and various other things that had to do with the prophetic calling, she had to promise inviolable obedience and to confirm her promises by oath. A sensitive discernment is revealed in the fact that these promises were to be made not merely in the ecstastic state, but also in her normal condition; and this she did.

The lives of these ecstatics after their call were mostly devoted to ecstatic preaching. In certain cases the gift of preaching was not life-long, but lasted only a limited time. Some produced only a few trance-sermons. Others preached at set times and at regular intervals. Helena Konttinen preached both in ecstasy and in the normal state. She knew the difference between the two very well. The preaching usually alternated with prayers and hymns. To use a modern term, her preaching was composed in various 'literary categories'. Some of the ecstatic experiences had significance only for the ecstatics themselves. Then they received enlightenment and messages that concerned them alone, their personal life, or their vocation as preachers. In such cases we can say that these preachers give us typical examples of prophetic confessions.

Preaching was not their only gift. We have just heard about Helena Konttinen's ability to see through people and reveal secrets in their lives. We often hear of such things in the lives of visionaries both here and elsewhere. Prophecies about things to come are not unusual. But the ecstatics are also able to give information about the present, earthly, profane life.

The ability to cure the sick is also ascribed to them, as well as gifts such as clairvoyance, telepathy, and power of suggestion. It need hardly be said that religious revivals and phenomena connected with mass-suggestion resulted from their activity. It has been observed that the gift of ecstatic preaching never appears alone, but is accompanied by other supernatural powers.

The existing descriptions of the ecstatic experiences made by the Finnish trance-preachers sometimes indicate that the symptom which we call 'the secondary personality' is well-known to them. Helena feels that she is in heaven, but at the same time she sees herself down on earth. The Helena who is caught up in an ecstasy can distinguish herself from the normal Helena of everyday life. In referring to herself as in the ecstatic state she prefers to use the third person, a phenomenon which we find in many of the visionary ecstatics. The Apostle Paul does this when in 2 Cor. xii. 2 ff. he describes an ecstatic experience in this way: I know a man in Christ—this man was caught up into Paradise and heard things that cannot be told.[19]

Feelings of compulsion and supernatural constraint are often mentioned. Helena 'is commanded' to do this and that, go here or there. The commands are accompanied by visions and auditions in which the contents of the commands are communicated. The commands are often given aloud by the ecstatic to himself or herself, another symptom of differentiation of the personality. The compulsion may be felt as severe suffering. Then comes the temptation to evade it. But disobedience has its revenge. Anguish, anxiety, mental and bodily illness are the results

[19] The medieval mystic Alpais de Cudot has given a very concrete and vivid description of such a cleavage of the personality. Her soul left the body, taking it off as a garment. She regarded the body lying motionless in the bed. The soul enjoyed gazing at the body, for it was lovely and beautiful, touched it, and lifted it up; Buber, *Ekstatische Konfessionen*, pp. 54 ff. A similar description is related on p. 112, but in this case the sight evoked feelings of dislike and aversion.

of opposition. In particular, punishment is certain when the command to warn a sinner is neglected. 'It was my lot to drink the fire of God's wrath,' says Helena. 'I myself always had to do the very same wrong action that the other person had done, and for which I had to rebuke him.'

A study of the Finnish trance-preachers reveals to us many traits common to all representatives of the ecstatic-prophetic type. First we have to observe the importance of the special call through which the prophetic life of these visionaries was initiated. They all point to a basic event in their lives through which it was revealed to them that they were chosen from above to perform a special task among men. This task consisted, in the first instance, in the mission to proclaim to men the thoughts and the will of God that were revealed to them. Sometimes the principal revelation was connected with the presentation of a book in which it was written what they had to announce to men. From that time the visionaries felt themselves chosen by God, living under a divine constraint, and forced to go where God ordered them to go and say what God had commanded them to say. The life of such an elect person was, in effect, the life of a prophet. One very marked characteristic of these prophets was the consciousness of standing under God's particular protection; but they also had the experience of anguish and of mental and bodily illness when they were disobedient and refused to fulfil their mission. It is, finally, a prophetic characteristic that, throughout their lifetime, or for longer or shorter periods, they had recurring ecstatic experiences, accompanied by abnormal physical or psychical symptoms.

5. St. Bridget of Sweden

There is a great gulf between the Finnish trance-preachers of our days and the great Swedish fourteenth-century saint, Birgitta (as she is called in Sweden).[20] The Finnish ecstatic preachers were active among simple Finnish peasants gathered in smoky, smelly huts in remote

---

[20] There exists a vast literature on Birgitta. It may here suffice to mention some of the more recent studies; Westman, *Birgitta-Studier*, 1911; Lindblom, *Die literarische Gattung der prophetischen Literatur*, 1924, pp. 19 ff.; Fogelklou, *Birgitta²*, 1955; Schmid, *Birgitta och hennes uppenbarelser*, 1940; Brilioth in *Svenska kyrkans historia*, II, 1941, pp. 177 ff. In English; Wordsworth, *The National Church of Sweden*, 1911, pp. 123 ff.; Jørgensen, *Saint Bridget of Sweden*, 1954; Redpath, *God's Ambassadress St. Bridget of Sweden*, 1947. For the Revelations of Birgitta I have used an edition printed in Munich 1680. Of the so-called *Revelationes extravagantes*, i.e., revelations added to the first collection, a critical text exists, ed. by Hollman 1956. For the complete titles see Bibliography. A new, complete translation into modern Swedish began to be published in 1957.

districts of out-of-the-way Finland. Birgitta lived out in the great world, in quite other circles and circumstances. She was a lady of noble birth and lived in permanent contact with prominent persons of learning. Bishops, kings, noblemen, and even the Holy Father in the chair of St. Peter listened to her words and messages of uncompromising, peremptory command. At the court and the seats of the nobility she was as much at home as in the study. The activity of the Finnish trance-preachers had a limited importance for the popular pietistic movement in Finland. Birgitta was important for the whole of Christendom. The former were simple, uneducated, peasant women of not particularly great intellectual attainment. Birgitta had talent, refinement, and a certain amount of real learning. She felt and saw widely.

However, there are also many similar traits which justify our grouping them together within the type of prophetic *homines religiosi*, which is the object of the present investigation. In both cases we hear of revelations of Heaven and Hell and the spheres of spiritual life, of descriptions of sin and exhortations to penitence and amendment of life, of convincing and comforting speeches about God's grace and forgiveness, of visions and ecstasy and other supernormal powers and gifts, of the communication of messages of various kinds, received by religious inspiration and based on revelations from the divine world, of a feeling of being called, overwhelmed, and compelled by God, and of the consciousness of being in God's service and under His special protection.

Birgitta was born about 1303 and died in Rome in 1373. Her parents belonged to the most prominent Swedish families of that time and she always preserved a full consciousness of her dignity. She is the most outstanding representative of Swedish medieval piety; and at the same time she occupies one of the foremost places in the history of Swedish literature. The vast collection of her *Revelations*, about 700 in number, written both in Latin and in Swedish, is a first-rate source for the study of her personal piety as well as of her prophetic activity.

Birgitta belongs to the long series of Christian mystics who flourished particularly in the later Middle Ages. In the *Revelations* we are sometimes told of the interior communion between Birgitta and Jesus Christ; and, in accordance with an important trend of medieval mysticism, she presents herself as the bride and Christ as her bridegroom. Once we hear Christ saying to Birgitta, the bride, 'Your heart will be in my heart and will be inflamed with my love, just as dry brushwood is easily kindled by fire. In this way your soul will be filled by me, and I shall dwell in you, so that all temporal things become bitter to you, and all

carnal voluptuousness like poison. You will rest in the bosom of my
Divinity, where there is no carnal voluptuousness, but only spiritual
pleasure and delight.'[21]

It is not difficult to find in Birgitta's *Revelations* expressions of such
mystical experiences. But it is remarkable, and very characteristic of
this mystic, that utterances like this are relatively rare in comparison
with expressions of a consciousness of another kind, namely that of
being chosen not to abide in her own world of blessedness and inner
spiritual pleasures, but to go out into the external world and there work
for the salvation of men. In this she appeared as a prophetess.

There is a spiritual laziness, Jesus says to Birgitta in a revelation, in
which a religious man, feeling the sweetness and grace of His Spirit,
prefers resting alone in this sweetness to going out to help others. 'As
one who has abundance of terrestrial goods does not use them for
himself alone, but gives them out to others, so My words and My grace
may not be concealed but must be imparted to others, so that they too
may be edified.'[22]

The will of Jesus Christ is that the bride shall love the bridegroom
above all things and want nothing else but Him. The bride has, however,
to work and labour in His service, whereupon she may rest with Him.[23]
Birgitta is told that visions are accorded her not for her own sake, but
for the benefit of others.[24] She calls herself a poor runner carrying the
letters of a great lord (*ego sum ad modum vilis cursoris, qui portat literas
magni domini*).[25] She is told that Christ's Spirit will show her where to
go and what to say; she must not fear anything but Him. She must go
gladly, speak boldly, and always feel secure, because her Lord will stand
at her side.[26] In Birgitta's prophetic career there are many examples of
courageous obedience. Her venturesome removal to Rome was occasioned by a vision in which she received this command: 'Go to Rome
and stay there until you have seen the pope and the emperor and
committed my words to them.' The Latin relation of this far-reaching
occurrence runs concisely and pregnantly: *Vade Romam et manebis ibi,
donec videas papam et imperatorem, et illis loqueris ex parte mea verba,
quae tibi dicturus sum. Venit igitur sponsa Christi Romam anno aetatis
suae XLII.*[27]

Like other markedly prophetic personalities, Birgitta was able to
point back to an inaugural vision at the beginning of her prophetic
career. It took place shortly after the death of her husband. As so often,

[21] *Rev.* i, 1.   [22] *Rev.* ii, 14.
[23] *Rev.* i, 2.   [24] *Rev.* vii, 13, 27.
[25] Westman, op. cit., p. 141, notes 1 and 2.   [26] *Rev.* iv, 77.
                    [27] *Rev. extrav.* 8.

we read of an ecstatic fit, with a heavenly voice and a wonderful light. Christ said to her, 'I speak to you not only for your own sake, but for the salvation of all Christians . . . You shall be My bride and My mouthpiece, and you shall hear and see spiritual things.'[28] 'I have chosen you and taken you as My bride to show you My divine mysteries, since it so pleases me.'[29] In such phrases her consciousness of a special calling took form, and through them it is vouched for as genuinely prophetic.

The call conferred on Birgitta the consciousness that she was chosen by God in a special sense. She frequently speaks of this privilege. Her appearance at that time was the testimony of a special divine grace. The King (Magnus Ericsson, King of Sweden) may realize what grace is conferred on his kingdom through the fact that Christ speaks to Birgitta. She goes so far as to maintain that her appearance, as it were, means a new epoch in history. As a vessel consists of three parts, world history has three ages: the first from Adam to Jesus Christ, the second from Christ to the time of Birgitta; the third is characterized by Birgitta's preaching to the world.

From the moment of her call, Birgitta was under the power of divine compulsion. After that she did not go her own ways, but God's. She is overpowered by Him who has sent her on her way. She is only a vessel into which Christ pours His wine, and from which others may afterwards drink. She seeks zealously for words to express her nothingness before God and the greatness of her task. She is 'a little ant', 'a gnat', 'an ass', 'a nothing'. As a reward she enjoys the perpetual protection of God. For God remains with her, and no one can resist Him.

It is characteristic of Birgitta that the feeling of compulsion was in the first place of an ethico-religious nature. So it was with St. Paul, when he exclaimed, 'Woe to me if I do not preach the gospel' (1 Cor. ix. 16). But in the compulsion to obedience there was also a certain amount of psychic compulsion as in all visionaries and ecstatics.

The psycho-physical element in her religious experiences appears fairly in descriptions of the ecstatic experiences which served to mediate her religious inspiration. Birgitta herself tells of this in several places. God puts her body to sleep, not in a bodily sleep (she is particularly anxious to emphasize that), but in a spiritual rest. At the same time the powers of the body weaken, a kind of weight comes upon it, and she is deprived of the use of her senses (*alienata a sensibus*). But the soul feels rather as if awakening out of sleep, and strengthened and enlivened to see and hear.[30] She frequently declares that in such trances

---

[28] *Rev. extrav.* 47. [29] *Rev.* i, 2.
[30] *Rev.* iv, 77 and *passim.*

she is waking, not sleeping (*vigilans non dormiens*).[31] What she experiences fills her mostly with joy. 'How pleasant are Thy words,' she exclaims. The soul swallows God's words like the most precious of meats. She is at once satisfied and hungry; satisfied because she will not have anything other than this, hungry because her taste for more increases unceasingly.[32] When Birgitta received the rule for Vadstena Nunnery, she felt as if all the powers of her body would be exhausted, while the soul began to see and hear.[33] Another time she says: 'A person watching in prayer [so she refers to herself] fell into rapture. The power of the body seemed to cease, but her heart was inflamed. Her soul was comforted, was strengthened by divine strength, and her mind was filled with spiritual understanding.'[34]

The psychic exaltation was reflected in the physical. We read of violent palpitation and other internal movements. Sometimes she felt as if the hand of God gripped hold of her breast.

She finds a classic expression for the overwhelming richness of revelation in her account of how she received the Nunnery rule. 'God, the creator of all things, with His blessed mouth announced all the words of this rule so wonderfully and in so short a time to me, unworthy person, that I cannot describe it to anyone. Nor is it possible for anyone to comprehend, without bodily similitude, how so many words could be spoken or understood in so very short a time. For it was as if one had had in a vessel a number of precious things of various kinds, and then tipped them all at once out of the vessel, and as if one looking on should in a moment distinguish each of the things from the others, and they should remain before him just so long that he could pluck up each separately into his lap.'[35]

We also have descriptions of her ecstasies by other persons. Her father-confessor Alphonso says, 'I myself, God is my witness, have several times seen our lady, sometimes sitting, sometimes lying prone, altogether sunk in prayer and, as if unconscious, deprived of the use of the bodily senses, caught away in spiritual ecstasy, without seeing or hearing anything of what was going on at the place where she was in body. When she recovered consciousness, she told me, unworthy man, and the other confessors about the visions she had had and God's great mysteries and hidden things.'[36]

Her daughter Catherine has testified that she sometimes saw Birgitta stand plunged in silent meditation and contemplation, quite absorbed, caught away from the senses of the body, and lifted up in ecstasy.

[31] *Rev.* iv, 139.   [32] *Rev.* iv, 77.   [33] *Regula Salvatoris* 1.
[34] *Rev.* iv, 139.   [35] *Reg. Salv.* 29.   [36] *Epistola solitarii* 4.

These visionary states often left behind them a feeling of strong psychic elevation. After Birgitta had received the Nunnery rule her heart, she says, was lifted up in so much warmth and profound joy, that it could not have gone on long without breaking with joy. 'Like a bladder very full of air was my heart for some days, until I had revealed and reckoned all the articles and words of this rule to a pious friend of God, who rapidly put it all together in writing. When it was all written down, I felt my heart and my body slowly return to their natural state.'[37]

The revelations and visions imparted to this Saint were generally prepared by prayer and meditation. She received the Nunnery rule when absorbed in prayer. Christ sometimes appeared to her while she was praying. She says that the visionary experiences came to her while 'watching in prayer and having been lost in contemplation'. Once it happened during a journey that she began to pray while riding on horseback, whereupon she fell into a trance and was deprived of the use of her senses.[38]

Birgitta calls every inspiration she received in a supernormal state of mind a 'revelation', as other medieval mystics do. A revelation may be a vision in the proper sense or an audition; but it may also be an inspiration of purely intellectual ideas, an inspiration with a content of abstract thought. Accordingly, the extensive literature that Birgitta has given us contains, alongside actual visions, long chapters of purely dogmatic content or with ethical exhortations to individuals or to humanity. But whatever the content is, the Saint apprehends all that she has to say, not as her own words, but as God's words, which God has given her as a messenger from Him, called to pass them to mankind. In accordance with her Christian belief in its Roman Catholic form, the revelations came to her as words from God, Christ, the Virgin Mary, or one of the saints of the Church. Once she tells us that she saw a book in heaven, the words of which were living and spoke to her, revealing spiritual things.[39]

In spite of the numerous descriptions of ecstatic fits and trances in the life of Birgitta, it would be a mistake to maintain that all her revelations were received in ecstasy in the strict sense. Of course many are based on true ecstatic raptures, but many others were experienced in a state of normal prayer or contemplation. Her mental states varied greatly. From a trance, she could easily pass over into a normal psychic state; and, passing from a normal state of mind, she could suddenly experience what she calls *elevatio mentalis*, developing into real ecstasy. It is evident that she sometimes actively sought a revelation. When she

[37] *Reg. Salv.* 29.   [38] *Rev.* v, Prologus.   [39] *Rev.* viii, 48.

received the different parts of a revelation known as *Sermo angelicus*, she had in advance placed herself at a table with paper and pen in hand, in order to write like an ordinary author. Prepared in this manner, she waited for the angel of the Lord, who then appeared before her and distinctly dictated what she must write. Birgitta seldom or never used artificial means for inducing a trance. Often it was only with difficulty that she could find the right words. In such cases she becomes verbose and wearisome. One cannot entirely absolve her from the *prurigo loquendi* which the Paris theologian Jean Gerson criticizes in the prophets and prophetesses of his age.

Even in productions of pure reflection and rational consideration, Birgitta uses the stylistic forms of revelations received in trance. This is a phenomenon common to all visionaries, including Mohammed and the Old Testament prophets. Therefore it is not always easy to distinguish between the genuine ecstatic revelations and the purely literary products of an ordinary kind.

We are told that Birgitta was endowed with gifts of a supernormal nature. She had a remarkable ability to see through men and find out secrets. She felt even with her external senses how matters stood when she met a good and pious or an evil person. She was sensible of a delicious scent when she stood before a holy man and had a taste of sulphur in her mouth when a malefactor came near her. She had the gift of foresight and prediction. A few cases of exorcism and of the healing of sick persons are also related in the literature. That she was a great spiritual guide for many people and had a great spiritual power over men and women is incontrovertibly testified. Finally, she was reputed to possess the gift of powerful intercession for others.

Sometimes the revelations were written down by Birgitta herself. *Sermo angelicus* is a good example of this mode of procedure. If she wrote in Swedish, she ordered one of her confessors to translate the Swedish text into Latin, after which she compared the Latin text with her own notes. She was anxious that the latter should be in full accordance with that which she had written herself. Nothing must be added, nothing taken away. Of the Nunnery rule she tells us that she dictated its contents to a friend of God, who wrote it down from her dictation, as rapidly as he could. This was frequently her practice, particularly when she was weak or ill. She dictated what she saw or heard to a secretary, often in a state of high exaltation, solemnly, as if reading from a book. One of her confessors translated into Latin, whereupon she scrupulously checked the correctness of what had been written. Revelations referring to particular individuals were immediately sent to them.

In all that has been said above about the Swedish saint, she has been presented to us as a true prophet. She shows in her personality and her life all the features that we have regarded as characteristic of the prophetic type of *homines religiosi*. Her prophetic nature is still more evident in the extraordinarily important tasks which she knew that she was chosen to perform. She constantly intervened in the public life of the age in which she lived, and with an astonishing perspicacity as well as an indomitable courage she rebuked immorality and godlessness wherever she found them. In her own country she sternly rebuked the King, the nobility, and the haughty and wanton ladies of her own class. On the other hand she encouraged the King to start a war against the Russians and to present to herself an estate for founding a nunnery in Vadstena. After her removal to Rome, she proclaimed stern judgement upon the inhabitants of that depraved city, filled as it was with 'toads and vermin', as she says. Her words were written on fly-sheets, which then circulated among the population, exciting a violent hatred against her person. On the other hand, she made intercession for the same city: *excellentissima et sanctissima urbs Roma*. She lamented the decline and degeneracy of the city: *O Roma, Roma, muri tui dirupti sunt, ideo portae tuae sunt sine custodia . . . Clerus et populus, qui sunt murus Dei, disperguntur ad faciendum utilitatem carnis . . . O si cognosceres dies tuos, O Roma, fleres utique et non gauderes.*[40]

During her pilgrimage to Jerusalem she visited Naples and Cyprus and was strongly impressed with the sinfulness of these places. She had a revelation concerning the people of Naples in which she rebuked them because they had despised God's commandments and thrown away their God *tamquam virus abominabile*, and vomited Him out of their mouth *velut rem putridam*. Then she announced the punishment to come: *Sicut facit piscator, qui videns pisces in aqua ludentes in delectatione et jucunditate sua, et tunc ipse mittit hamum in mari et extrahit capiendo pisces vicissim . . . sic ego faciam inimicis meis in peccato perseverantibus.*[41] In the same manner she rebuked the population of Cyprus, the capital of which, Famagusta, she likened to Gomorrah: 'O people of Cyprus, listen to my words. If you will not repent, I will eradicate you and your descendants from the kingdom of Cyprus. And thereafter I will plant new plants in this kingdom of Cyprus, which shall fulfil my commandments and love me with all their heart.' We are told that Birgitta herself recited this revelation in Famagusta before the King and the Queen of Cyprus, and the whole royal council.[42]

The protracted war between England and France in the fourteenth

[40] *Rev.* iii, 27.   [41] *Rev.* vii, 27.   [42] *Rev.* vii, 19.

century was to her a grave evil; and she sent a message summoning the two kings in the name of Christ to make peace.

Two concerns in particular filled her heart. The one was to persuade the Pope to confirm the order of Nuns which she desired to found, and also to win the support of the Emperor Charles IV for this enterprise. The other was to bring the popes from Avignon back to Rome. She wrote to Pope Clement VI, urging him to break the fetters of his Babylonian captivity and to return to the true capital of the Church. It was in order to achieve these desires that she went personally to Rome and stayed there until her death. It may be that she personally transmitted a revelation to Urban V, and we know with certainty that she sent different revelations to the popes who lived in exile in Avignon, all with the intention of bringing to an end the scandal of the Babylonian captivity of the popes.

Bishop John Wordsworth in his book, *The National Church of Sweden*, rightly says of the Swedish saint, 'She was throughout filled with a moral purpose like that of the Old Testament prophets, whose language she often recalls to us.'[43] I am inclined to add that, among all the representatives of the prophetic type outside Israel, there are few who have so great an affinity with the prophets of the Old Testament as Birgitta of Sweden.

6. PROPHETS IN GREECE

Hitherto we have been occupied with prophetic phenomena belonging to times and civilizations distant from the prophets of the Old Testament. Now we turn to seek examples of the prophetic type in the neighbourhood of ancient Israel. Two regions may here be taken into account: first the Greek world, then the ancient Near East.

When the Greek translators of the Old Testament chose the word *prophētēs* as a rendering of the Old Testament term *nābî'*, they must have thought of something that was common to the Greek *prophētēs* and the Hebrew *nābî'*. Presumably they did not think that there was any linguistic kinship between the two words. In the time of the Greek translators the linguistic significance of the word *nābî'* was as obscure as it is to us. For what reason was the Greek term *prophētēs* chosen?

Since the Septuagint came into existence in Egypt, one might be tempted to suppose that the translators adopted a term current in Egypt. We know that one of the many priestly classes in the Egyptian temples was called 'prophets'. It is very difficult to characterize exactly

---

[43] Wordsworth, op. cit., p. 127.

the different sacral officials in Egypt and determine their functions, because the texts dealing with these matters are often very obscure and confused. So much seems to be certain, namely that the Greeks frequently used the word 'prophet' to designate one among the priests whose task it was to interpret and formulate the communications imparted through signs and symbols by gods to men. The Egyptian sanctuaries were also to some extent places where oracles were given. The priest who in the temple of Amon announced to Alexander that he was adopted as a son of this god is called 'prophet' in the relevant texts.[44]

However, it is not very likely that the Jewish translators borrowed a title from the pagan hierarchy in Egypt to designate men of God such as Moses, Isaiah, Jeremiah, etc. It is much more probable that they took over the title from a more general Greek mode of expression.

The word *prophētēs* is used in the Greek in many connections. The poets are called prophets of the Muses, the philosophers prophets of nature. Men spoke of prophets of public opinion and prophets of truth, of reason. Preachers and propagators of different philosophical schools were called prophets. We are told of the prophets of Epicurus, of Pyrrho, etc. Everyone who had something to announce publicly was called a prophet. Sometimes prophets were regarded as interpreters of philosophical doctrines, sayings of the poets, divine words and oracles.[45]

But the Greeks were also familiar with men and women who were endowed with the gift of divine inspiration, whether they were expressly called prophets or not. The Pythia in Delphi as well as the Sibyls are described as divinely inspired persons or ecstatics. Their task was to impart, in an ecstatic state of mind, divine messages or oracles. It is ecstasy that distinguishes them from the soothsayers, who obtained their knowledge by means of signs and omens. It is said that the Pythia was put into a trance by means of vapour rising up from the earth or by water from the sacred spring. Possibly this was only a popular belief. But it must be regarded as a fact that she imparted her oracles in a state of ecstasy, while the priests afterwards expressed them in a suitable form.[46]

In the *Agamemnon* of Æschylus Cassandra is depicted as a true prophetess and is also expressly called *prophētēs*. She is seized by Apollo and impelled by his divine power. She has the gift of exercising prophetic functions (τέχναι ἔνθεοι). She says what the god wills, acts

[44] See Otto, *Priester und Tempel im hellenistischen Ägypten;* Fascher, op. cit., pp. 76 ff.
[45] Fascher, op. cit., pp. 11 ff.
[46] Nilsson, *Geschichte der griechischen Religion,* I², pp. 170 ff.; Amandry, *La mantique apollinienne à Delphes.* Other figures belonging to the large prophetic genus are mentioned in Rohde, *Psyche³,* II, pp. 89 ff.

according to his commands, and, as in somnambulism, goes where he leads. When overwhelmed by the god, she passes from her normal mental state into ecstasy. She has visions and utters oracles (χρησμοί) of the greatest importance. She trembles like a wild beast in a snare and appears to those about her to be mad. The leader of the chorus says to her: 'Thou art borne on the breath of God, thou spirit wild' (φρενομανής τις εἶ θεοφόρητος). She feels the power of Apollo as something sweet (πνέων χάριν), but at the same time as something awful: 'Oh, Oh! Agony, Agony! again the awful pains of prophecy (ὀρθομαντείας πόνος δεινός) are on me, maddening as they fall.' It might be objected that Cassandra is only a poetic figure; but this figure would surely not have been created if the poet had not known similar personages in real life.[47]

Plato is our best informant concerning prophets and inspired men and women in ancient Greece. In the *Phaedrus*, Plato deals in detail with the phenomena of ecstasy and inspired oracular utterance. He says that in reality the greatest of blessings come to us through madness (διὰ μανίας) when it is sent as a gift from the gods. He calls the Pythia in Delphi a prophetess (προφῆτις) and maintains that both she and the priestesses at Dodona by their madness have conferred many splendid benefits upon Greece. The gift of prophetic inspiration is also attributed to the Sybil and many others. Inspired persons also had the power to foretell future events. Plato knows of divination and soothsaying by the observation of birds and other signs; but he argues that prophecy is superior to augury. Madness, when it comes from God, is superior to sanity, which is of human origin. Elsewhere in the dialogues Plato mentions the phenomenon of divine inspiration. Inspired men are called by him men of God, men possessed by God (ἐνθουσιάξοντες), who without the aid of human reason utter important things. They are seized by the divinity (κατεχόμενοι) and do not themselves know what they say, deprived as they are of ordinary understanding and being only mouthpieces of God.[48]

The divine inspiration of religious men and women is in Plato's opinion analogous to the poet's inspiration. He speaks of a kind of possession that comes from the Muses. This possession takes hold of a gentle and pure soul, arouses it and inspires it to songs and other poetry. But he who without the divine madness comes to the doors of the Muses, confident that he will be a good poet by art, meets with no

---

[47] The translations are taken from Murray, *The Oresteia, translated into English Rhyming Verse.*
[48] Cf. Fascher, op. cit., pp. 66 ff.

success, and the poetry of the sane man vanishes into nothingness before that of the inspired madmen.

Plato's statements about prophets and prophetic endowment are so lucid and so exhaustive as to make further reference to Greek literature superfluous. We may therefore leave out of consideration statements by Plutarch, Iamblichus, etc. But reference must be made to one other writer, Philo of Alexandria.

It is very interesting to observe that, in speaking of the Old Testament prophets, Philo uses words and expressions directly taken from Greek thought. A prophet is, according to Philo, a man possessed by God (θεοφόρητος); he preaches words inspired by God (θεσπίξει); he says nothing of his own, but, being seized by God (κατεχόμενος) and being in an ecstatic state of mind (ἐνθουσιῶν), he does not himself comprehend what he says. All the words that he utters proceed from him as if another were prompting him. The prophets are interpreters of God, who uses their faculties as instruments in order clearly to display what He chooses.[49] And further, in another passage: 'A prophet does not utter anything whatever of his own, but is only an interpreter, another suggesting to him all that he utters; he is enraptured and in an ecstasy (ἐνθουσιᾷ); his own reasoning power has departed and has quitted the citadel of his soul, while the divine spirit has entered in and taken up its abode there, playing the instrument of his voice in order to make clear and manifest the prophecies that the prophet is delivering.'[50]

Philo's description of what a true prophet is is exceptionally clear and acute and might very well be taken as a characterization of the prophetic type in the world of religion as a whole.

7. Prophets in the Ancient Near East

The authors of the books of Kings were cognizant of the existence of ecstatic prophets in the Semitic world outside Israel. The god of Carmel (perhaps fused with Baal Shamem, Baal of Heaven) had his prophets. So had Asherah and the Tyrian Melkart.[51]

Now we are in possession of literary documents which give evidence of the existence of such prophets in different parts of the ancient Near East. The story of Wen-Amon's journey to Phoenicia (about 1100 B.C.), related in the famous Golenischeff Papyrus, contains an episode that witnesses to the existence of prophetic phenomena in ancient Phoenicia.[52]

[49] Philo, De specialibus legibus, i, 65.
[50] Ibid., iv, 49.
[51] 1 Kings xviii; 2 Kings x. See Eissfeldt, Der Gott Karmel; Alt, Das Gottesurteil auf dem Karmel.
[52] ANET², pp. 25 ff.

Wen-Amon was an official at a temple of the God Amon, who was sent by the Egyptian King to Byblos in order to procure timber for the ceremonial barge of Amon-Re. For certain reasons he was not well received by the Prince of Byblos. The Prince sent to him saying, 'Get out of my harbour.' Wen-Amon answered, 'If you have a ship to carry me, have me taken to Egypt again.' The story goes on to relate that, while the Prince was making an offering to his gods, the god seized one of his youths (probably a court page) and made him possessed. In this state the youth said to the Prince, 'Bring up the god [i.e., Amon-of-the-Road, a travelling Amon, an idol to make a mission successful], bring the messenger who is carrying him. Amon is the one who sent him out; he is the one who made him come.' The determinative of the word 'possessed' shows a human figure in violent motion, obviously in a prophetic frenzy. In such a state of mind (typical of all prophetic personalities) the boy uttered an oracle containing a divine order to the Prince.

Among the documents found by Professor Parrot in ancient Mari in Mesopotamia there are some which contain very remarkable notices about oracles and prophetic men and women from this region. A cuneiform tablet, deciphered and interpreted by Professor G. Dossin, refers to men and women whose task it was to 'give answers', i.e., impart divine oracles. Because there is no hint of signs and omens of any kind, we have probably to think of oracles obtained in a state of inspiration. The oracles are referred to as revelations by Adad of Kallassu and Adad of Aleppo. Through the oracles the gods proclaim their will in different respects. Noteworthy is the declaration by Adad of Kallassu that he has raised the dynasty of Zimrilim, resolved to bless it if it is obedient to the will of the god and to punish it if it rejects his commands.

On other tablets, transcribed and translated by von Soden, the god Dagan is the god who inspires. A prophet transported by Dagan in an ecstasy utters an oracle ordering that sacrifices must be offered to Yaḥdunlim, the king's dead father. The term used for 'prophet' here is *muḫḫūm*. A similar oracle about sacrifices is found on another tablet. A third oracle contains a command to construct a city gate.[53]

[53] See Lods, 'Une tablette inédite de Mari, intéressante pour l'histoire ancienne du prophétisme sémitique', *SOTP*, pp. 103 ff. (treating a text published by Dossin); von Soden, 'Verkündung des Gotteswillens durch prophetisches Wort in den alt-babylonischen Briefen aus Mari', *WO*, 1950, pp. 397 ff.; Noth, 'History and the Word of God in the Old Testament', *BJRL*, xxxii, 1949/50, pp. 194 ff.; de Liagre Böhl, 'Profetisme en plaatsvervangend lijden in Assyrië en Israël, *NTT*, iv, 1949-50, pp. 81 ff.; N. H. Ridderbos, *Israëls Profetie en 'Profetie' buiten Israël* (*Exegetica*, II: 1); Neher, *L'essence du prophétisme*, pp. 24 ff.

The term used here, *muḥḥūm*, is the same as *maḥḥū* mentioned in some Accadian texts. This word means 'frenzied', 'one out of his senses', which exactly corresponds to the term 'ecstatic', or one possessed by a god, one whom a god has seized, one who is affected by the breath of a god. A *maḥḥū* had the power to communicate oracles. The god spoke through him as through his mouthpiece. 'I am struck down as a *maḥḥū*, I bring forth what I do not know', such a prophet declares. The *maḥḥū* groups were as a rule attached to the sanctuaries.[54]

It is not my task here to gather all possible traces of 'ecstatic-prophetic' activities in the ancient world. I would only present a series of typical examples in order to throw light upon the religio-historical type that we have called 'the prophetic type'. In other regions of the ancient Near East, as among the Hittites, in Ugarit, in Hamath, etc., the ecstatic communication of oracles may well have been practised as well as the observation of omens, incubation, and sacrificial and other methods of divination. But the traces are so scanty and in part so uncertain that we must wait for new discoveries of texts before we can make positive statements which are likely to contribute to a comprehensive study of the prophetic type.[55]

Considerable obscurity also surrounds a figure such as Zarathustra, often called the Iranian prophet. The eminent French authority in this field, Duchesne-Guillemin, sees in him a parallel to the prophets of Israel. He says about him: 'His passionate and exclamatory preaching is animated throughout by the presence of a god whom he incessantly entreats and beseeches, and who reveals himself. It recalls the tone of the prophets of Israel, from which, however, it differs. Zoroaster knows that God speaks through his mouth. He sometimes doubts his own mission as a prophet, but only to ask his god at once to strengthen his certainty. For at bottom he has confidence in Ahura Mazdah. He has recognized him in a series of visions as the Holy Lord, and this holiness is not the terrible holiness of Jehovah. "Speak to me", he says to the Wise Lord, "as friend to friend. Grant us the support which friend would give to friend." '[56] He further says that Zarathustra had the consciousness of being chosen by Ahura Mazdah and sent as his messenger to men. The doctrine he preaches is revealed to him by God. He lives in permanent communion with God and has entirely surrendered himself and his life to God.[57]

[54] Haldar, op. cit., pp. 21 ff.
[55] See Götze in *Kulturgeschichte des alten Orients*, III, 1² (*HA*, III, 1, 3: 3, 1), pp. 146 ff; *ANET*², pp. 394 f., 396. Haldar, op. cit., pp. 74 ff., and the critical remarks by Ridderbos, op. cit., pp. 13 ff.
[56] Duchesne-Guillemin, *The Hymns of Zarathustra*, pp. 6 f.
[57] The same author, *Zoroastre. Étude critique avec une traduction commentée des Gâthâ*, p. 144.

The well-known Swedish orientalist Nyberg also sees in Zarathustra a prophet, a bearer of the divine word, an announcer of a divine message to men, revealed to him by Ahura Mazdah. He was a visionary and received his vocation in a visionary experience, although of a more intellectual nature. Nyberg emphasizes strongly the ecstatic elements in Zarathustra's prophetic personality and life. He sees in him a professional ecstatic, who employed technical methods, a leader of groups of professional ecstatics with regulated functions in their tribe. This is disputed by Duchesne-Guillemin. It may be that Nyberg exaggerates Zarathustra's relationship with shamans and dervishes. But granted that he was a visionary, he was surely an ecstatic too. At all events, modern research indicates that Zarathustra displays a number of traits which are characteristic of the prophetic type in the history of religion.[58]

8. Conclusion

In the foregoing we have been confronted with a peculiar and varied world of figures, named and unnamed. They have been presented here in order to make clear what we mean by the prophetic type in religious and psychological terms. They have been taken from different domains and different stages of religious development. Our aim has been to get a background for the treatment of Israelite prophecy which follows. But before continuing the investigation which is the object of this book it would be suitable to make some remarks concerning the foregoing exposition and draw some conclusions from the material collected above.

It is evident that the prophetic phenomena are not peculiar to particular races, peoples, countries, or religions. They are to be found everywhere in the religious world and at all stages of religious development. It is true that ecstasy is contagious between individuals; but it is not accurate to say that ecstasy or prophecy in itself is commonly borrowed by one people from another. These phenomena have arisen in different regions quite independently. The prophetic endowment is deeply rooted in human nature; what may be borrowed from other quarters is the behaviour and the forms, in a word, the external manifestations. This observation will be of importance when we discuss prophecy in Israel in its relation to prophetic phenomena in the surrounding world.

Common to all representatives of the prophetic type here depicted is the consciousness of having access to information from the world above and experiences originating in the divine world, from which ordinary

[58] Nyberg, *Die Religionen des alten Iran*, esp. pp. 264 ff.

men are excluded. They all speak of a particular contact with the supernormal world, by which they have been subjected to influences from that world, not vouchsafed to other men. Such an influx into a human soul from the divine world we call *inspiration*, and the power to receive such influences we call *the inspirational predisposition*.

With regard to the contact which is claimed with the divine world, two types can be distinguished. Characteristic of the one type is the consciousness that the deity itself, or the divine substance, takes its abode within man, penetrates him, acts and speaks in him, so that the divine *ego* dominates and more or less pushes out the human *ego*. Typical of the other category is that there is a distinction between the self and the divinity. The divinity does not enter the human *ego*, but stands outside it. The subject does not say that the divinity penetrates him, but that the divinity comes to him, appears to him, speaks to him, affects him with its powers, seizes him, or that he has fellowship with the divinity, has intercourse with it, and is influenced by it. In both cases we are justified in speaking of inspiration in the general sense, as we have done above. Modern psychologists of religion, e.g., Tor Andrae, distinguish between *possession* and *inspiration proper*, or *personal inspiration*.[59] Then possession corresponds to the first type here depicted, inspiration proper, or personal inspiration to the second.

Possession plays a less important part in the experience of prophetic personalities than might be supposed. At the lower stages of religious development it is often very difficult to define the limits between possession and inspiration proper. The shamans pretend to have been allowed to make journeys into the regions of the spirits and to find out their secrets, but sometimes they believe that the spirits enter themselves and take possession of them.[60] The kahins among the pre-Islamic Arabs were said to be possessed by a *jinn*, but in the time of Mohammed intercourse with the *jinn* was regarded as a more personal relation.[61] When the deity is conceived of as a personal being, possession is forced into the background. The Rwala seers think that Allah speaks to them by means of a special *malak*, messenger, but there is no suggestion that this *malak* takes possession of them. If a revelation of St. Birgitta begins in this way: 'I am the Creator of heaven and earth', this does not mean that Birgitta feels herself to be identical with the Creator; it only means that at this moment she reproduces the words of God in the form of direct speech, as she heard them in her ecstasy. This distinction between

[59] Andrae, *Mystikens psykologi*, pp. 89 ff. On possession studied from a psychological and psychiatric point of view see Oesterreich, *Die Besessenheit*.
[60] See the works of Holmberg-Harva mentioned above.
[61] Andrae, *Mohammed*, p. 36.

possession and personal inspiration may be kept in mind when we come
to analyse the religious experiences of the Israelite prophets.

Possession and personal inspiration have often been confused because
the symptoms of both are to a certain extent similar in nature. Both
personal inspiration and possession may be connected with a number of
sensational phenomena of a psycho-physical nature, such as automatisms
of various kinds, ecstatic raptures, split personality, and so on. The
inspired person may be conceived of, like the possessed person, as a
mouthpiece of the deity. The deity may speak in the first person
through the mouth of the personally inspired man as well as through
the mouth of one possessed. These similarities should not prevent us
from holding fast the principal difference between the two types of
intercourse with the deity to which we have just referred.

Inspiration has been described above in the terms which the inspired
persons would themselves have used. In the technical language of
psychology it might be described rather differently, thus: the characteristic of inspiration in a general sense is that certain ideas, images,
emotions, impulses from the subconscious, subliminal, unconscious,
co-conscious self (whichever term may be used) arise in the mind so
spontaneously and so independently of reflection and meditation, that
the inspired person feels as though his ideas were coming not from
himself, but from another realm, and are given him by a power other
than himself. If the inspiration is of a religious nature this 'other power'
is identified with the deity, and 'the other realm' with the supernatural
or heavenly world.[61a]

Inspiration has many degrees, according to the force and the intensity
of the influx from the other world. It always has the character of the
irruption of something new, of a revelation in the strict sense. But it
does not always come suddenly; it is often prepared for in different
ways, and appears as a result of a more or less conscious process.
Inspiration is sometimes instantaneous; but very often it lasts for a
shorter or longer time. It takes diverse forms. Sometimes the inspired
person loses entirely the sense of any connection between himself and
the inspired ideas: he says expressly that they come from God, not
from himself. Both Plato and Philo lay stress upon this side of the
inspirative experiences. Sometimes reflection and meditation play a
more or less vital part. The vast revelation in which Birgitta of Sweden
depicts the buildings of the convent at Vadstena is presented as a
revelation from the heavenly world; but there is no doubt that the

[61a] See, for instance, Pratt, *The Religious Consciousness*, chapter III, 'Religion and
the Subconscious', pp. 45 ff.

curiously detailed plans and outlines were to a great extent the products of conscious reflection and calculation. A symptom of such a co-operation between the supernatural power and the human subject is the alternation of the divine *ego* and the human *ego* in the reproduction of the revelations.

A clear distinction cannot be drawn between inspiration and ecstasy. Inspiration is the more general term. Inspiration appears as mental excitement and exaltation in general. I prefer to use the term ecstasy when the inspiration has grown so strong that the inspired person has lost full control of himself. The normal current of mental life is interrupted. The ordinary mental faculties, and sometimes the physical powers, are put out of function. Ecstasy is a psycho-physical detachment, arising from a one-sided concentration on a dominant fact. Ecstasy is a sort of psychic paralysis except for the one point at which a dominating idea or complex of ideas, or an intense feeling, powerfully captivates the attention. To be inspired is to be filled with and seized by a new and surprising mental content. Ecstasy is a similar state of mind intensified to such an extent that the normal psychic, or even physical, powers are thrown out of gear.

Ecstasy, too, has many degrees, from absolute psychic unconsciousness and psycho-physical anaesthesia to a state of mind which approaches normal mental abstraction. Ecstasy is not a state of mind which may be sharply delimited, but represents a scale of higher or lower degrees of psychic detachment. In analysing prophetic personalities it must always be kept in mind that inspiration and ecstasy have many degrees and many manifestations. Also in the same personality diversities can be found owing to different circumstances. What can at all events be maintained is that the prophets receive their revelations in a state of inspiration which has a tendency to pass into ecstasy. The prophet always has a predisposition to ecstasy, even if he does not actually experience ecstasy in its most typical form.

Inspiration and ecstasy do not represent a static but a dynamic state of mind. The essential element is the stimulation of the mental life so that experiences occur which do not belong to everyday life. In order to avoid employing terms which are liable to be misunderstood, I use the term 'revelatory state of mind' for a mental state in which the prophetic personalities obtain their revelations, in order to emphasize that this state oscillates between ordinary mental exaltation and abnormal ecstasy in the strict sense. The term 'revelation' itself is taken from the medieval visionary mystics, who so described that which was given them in their moments of bliss. Revelations and visions are certainly not restricted to those whom we designate as 'mystics'. Not every prophet is a mystic (none of the Israelite prophets was a mystic), but every prophet has the gift of receiving revelations in the condition which we call 'the revelatory state of mind'.

Revelations received in the revelatory state of mind are of various kinds. Nearly all formal stylistic categories occur. We meet with messages communicated in specific situations, exhortations, admonitions, denunciations, predictions, prayers, poetry, songs of praise, dogmatic expositions, etc. Sometimes thoughts and ideas are revealed, sometimes things are seen or heard. The former experience may be described as an intellectual illumination within the soul, the latter as visual and auditory revelation.

It is impossible to distinguish sharply between visual and auditory revelations. Visual and auditory elements are very often intermingled in the same revelation, and both categories are usually described as 'visions'. Visions play an outstanding part everywhere in the life of the prophets, but there are different kinds which must be recognized, if we are to understand the psychological background of the revelations and the expression of them in literary form. The medieval theologians after Augustine, and sometimes the visionaries themselves, distinguish between three types of revelation: corporeal, imaginative, and intellectual. In the corporeal revelation the visionary believes that he sees and hears by means of the natural senses, with all the characteristics of ordinary sensation. In the imaginative revelation the visionary sees with 'the eye of the soul', while the natural senses are put out of function. The intellectual revelations are the influx into the mind of thoughts and ideas of a more or less theoretical nature. The fourteenth-century English mystic, Julian of Norwich, says that what was revealed to her came to her in three ways: firstly by 'bodily sight', secondly by 'spiritual sight', 'the spiritual eye', or 'inward sight', thirdly by 'words formed in her understanding' or 'inward teaching'.[62]

Of course it would be a mistake to confine the investigation of prophetic revelations within this scheme. There are more varieties than the theologians, and the mystics themselves, are aware of.

In psychological discussions of the prophets the term 'hallucination' is often used. Hölscher, for instance, in his important book on the Israelite prophets, designates the visions of the Old Testament prophets in general as hallucinations. The Temple vision of Isaiah, in connection with which he received his prophetic call, was, according to Hölscher, a hallucination, though composed of elements familiar to the prophet from tradition and local circumstances.

[62] Julian of Norwich, *Revelations of Divine Love*[13], pp. 21, 110, 134, 167, etc.

However, before using the term, it is necessary to determine what a 'hallucination' is. Modern psychologists define hallucination as a false perception in which the origin of the stimulus is either organic or imaginative. Hallucination, they say, has all the characteristics of an ordinary sensation, without being evoked by an exterior object. It is an essential characteristic of hallucination that the subject has the impression that what he sees, hears, and sometimes also feels, is perceived by the physical senses and has actual existence in space, though in fact no real object corresponds to it. In this, hallucination differs from 'illusion', which is a misinterpretation of a sensation produced by an object actually present to the senses, while in hallucination there is no object at all. Thus hallucination corresponds very well to what the medieval mystics called corporeal revelations. How such purely subjective perceptions really arise is open to dispute, because of our deficient knowledge of the mental and physiological processes of the human organism. To the student of the psychology of the prophets this side of the matter is of little interest, whereas a clear understanding of the general nature of hallucination is of fundamental importance.

Modern psychologists of religion strongly emphasize the complex nature of what they call hallucination. On one side it does not take its rise in any outward object, on the other it has all the characteristics of an ordinary sensation. In order to accentuate the similarity of the hallucination with a real sensation, they speak of 'sensible hallucinations', 'optical hallucinations', 'sensorial hallucinations', etc.

Experiences of a hallucinatory nature are not uncommon among prophetic personalities. They are to be found more at the lower than at the higher stages. They are usual among the Finnish trance-preachers, but less usual in the life of Birgitta of Sweden. The eminent authority on the life and the revelatory literature of this saint, K. B. Westman, mentions only a very small number of hallucinations in the life of Birgitta. As a seven-year-old girl she beheld the Virgin Mary giving her a crown, sometimes she saw Christ in the host, finally she had a hallucination of Christ while lying on her deathbed.[63]

But by far the greatest number of 'visions' related by the prophetic personalities cannot be described as hallucinations in the strict sense. They are of another kind and must be more accurately analysed because they play an outstanding role in Old Testament prophecy.

The prophetic personalities very often relate visionary experiences in which they have seen things not with their physical eye, but, as they

[63] Westman, op. cit., p. 85; cf. Delacroix, *Études d'histoire et de psychologie du mysticisme*, p. 427.

say, 'with the eye of the soul' or 'the inward eye'. These visions resemble
hallucinations in that they are not evoked by an exterior object in the
sensible world; but they differ from hallucinations in being conceived
by the visionaries themselves as having nothing at all to do with the
corporeal senses. Birgitta says that in her visions she is deprived of the
use of her senses, but her soul is enlivened to see and hear. In this
respect these visions remind us of the products of imagination in the
poets, artists, musicians, and others who are capable of an exalted
inspiration, or of memory-pictures and dreams. It is characteristic of
these visions that the images beheld are more diffuse, nebulous, and
more difficult to describe than the hallucinations proper. They are more
fantastic, floating, and airy. Not being limited by space and time, they
are conceived of as belonging to the other world, the invisible regions,
the sphere of the supernatural and divine, in which their objects have
their real existence. Such visions are typical not only of the prophets,
but also of the religious men and women we call 'mystics'. In the
mystical literature we find countless descriptions of such visions. They
are described as at the same time distinct and indistinct, clear and vague,
concrete and diffuse. The famous Spanish saint Teresa often had visions
of Jesus Christ. 'Now and then,' she says of her visions of Christ, 'it
seemed to me that what I saw was an image, but most frequently it was
not so. I thought it was Christ Himself judging by the brightness in
which He was pleased to show Himself. Sometimes the vision was so
indistinct, that I thought it was an image; but still, not like a picture,
however well painted, and I have seen a good many pictures. It would
be absurd to suppose that the one bears any resemblance whatever to
the other, for they differ as a living person differs from his portrait,
which, however well drawn, cannot be life-like, for it is plain that it is
a dead thing.' In another place she says that the vision passes as quickly
as a flash of lightning, 'yet this most glorious picture makes an impression on the imagination that I believe can never be effaced until the
soul at last sees Christ to enjoy Him for ever. Although I call it a
"picture", you must not imagine that it looks like a painting; Christ
appears as a living person, who sometimes speaks and reveals deep
mysteries.'[64]

Julian of Norwich says that she sees 'within her soul' and 'with a
spiritual sight'. Of this she says in a passage, 'I cannot nor may not
shew it as openly nor as fully as I would. But I trust in our Lord God
Almighty that He shall of His goodness, and for your love, make you
take it more spiritually and more sweetly than I can or may tell it.' And

[64] Underhill, op. cit., pp. 288 f.

further, 'For the bodily sight, I have said as I saw, as truly as I can; and for the words, I have said them right as our Lord shewed them to me; and for the spiritual sight, I have told some deal, but I may never fully tell it: and therefore of this sight I am stirred to say more, as God will give me grace.'[65]

The visions here described correspond to some extent to what Kandinsky calls 'pseudo-hallucinations'.[66] However, Kandinsky's statement that the pseudo-hallucinations lack the feeling of objectivity and reality is not applicable to the visions in our sense, the visionary does not question that what he sees and hears is something real, though belonging to another world, a world quite different from the world which is accessible to the physical senses. Our 'visions' correspond rather to 'the imaginative visions' of the medieval theologians and mystics.

An appropriate term for visions of this kind is just 'imaginative' or 'imaginary visions'. As 'imaginary' they differ from the hallucinations proper with their plainly sensory and corporeal character; as 'visions' they differ from all ordinary sensory perceptions in having their objects in 'the invisible world'. Within the imaginary visions (we may call them simply 'visions', because the visionaries themselves often use this term to describe quite different sorts of visionary experiences) we can distinguish between different groups, according to the contents of what is revealed to the visionaries. If words and voices preponderate in a revelation we speak of 'auditory visions' or 'auditions'; if the visual elements predominate we have to do with 'visual visions' or visions proper. In certain prophetic persons the visual elements prevail, in others the auditory. In the first case we have to suppose a visual, an 'eidetic', predisposition, in the second an auditory one, both based on natural aptitude. However, the visual and the auditory elements are often combined together in the same revelation.[67]

To illustrate the character of an audition or auditory vision I would recall what was said above about how the Nunnery rule was revealed to St. Birgitta. God, she says, announced with His mouth all the words of the rule so wonderfully and in so short a time, that it was impossible for her to describe it to anyone. It was as if one had in a vessel a number of precious things of various kinds, and then tipped them all at once out of the vessel, and as if one looking on should in a moment distinguish

[65] *Revelations*, pp. 172, 21, 178.
[66] Kandinsky, *Kritische und klinische Betrachtungen im Gebiete der Sinnestäuschungen.* Hänel, *Das Erkennen Gottes bei den Schriftpropheten*, uses the expression 'halluzinatorische Wahrnehmung'. 'Hallucination' and 'hallucinatory' are, however, not appropriate terms for this experience.
[67] On these terms cf. Andrae, *Mystikens psykologi*, pp. 228 f.

each of the things from the others, and they should remain before him just so long that he could pluck them up each separately into his lap.[68]

St. Teresa says that the divine words uttered to her were very distinctly formed; but by the bodily ear they were not heard. 'They are', she goes on, 'much more clearly understood than if they were heard by the ear. It is impossible not to understand them, whatever resistance we may offer . . . The words formed by the understanding effect nothing, but when our Lord speaks, it is at once word and work . . . The human locution is as something we cannot well make out, as if we were half asleep; but the divine locution is a voice so clear, that not a syllable of its utterance is lost. It may occur, too, when the understanding and the soul are so troubled and distracted that they cannot form one sentence correctly, that yet grand sentences, perfectly arranged, such as the soul in its most recollected state never could have formed, are uttered.'[69] It is told of Teresa that her life was governed by such voices and divine words obtained in her revelations. They advised her in small things as in great. Often they interfered with her plans, ran counter to her personal judgement, and commanded such things as appeared imprudent or impossible.

Many revelations of a predominantly visual character are related in the mystical literature. I take an example from Suso's life, which seems to be exceptionally illuminating. The vision is described by Suso himself in this way: 'It happened one morning that the servitor saw in a vision that he was surrounded by a troop of heavenly spirits. He therefore asked one of the most radiant amongst these princes of the Sky to show him how God dwelt in his soul. The angel said to him, "Do but fix your eyes joyously upon yourself and watch how God plays the game of love within your loving soul." And he looked quickly, and saw that his body in the region of his heart was pure and transparent like crystal; and he saw the divine Wisdom peacefully enthroned in the midst of his heart, and she was fair to look upon And by her side was the soul of the servitor, full of heavenly desires, resting lovingly upon the bosom of God, who had embraced it, and pressed it to His heart.'[70]

Westman has estimated the number of the visual visions among Birgitta's revelations at 10 per cent of the whole (about seven hundred).[71] One of the most characteristic is reproduced by the saint in this way:

To a person, waking in prayer and not sleeping (*vigilanti in oratione et non dormienti*) was shown in a spiritual vision (*in spirituali visione*) a

---

[68] Cf. above, p. 22
[70] Underhill, op. cit., p. 286.
[69] Underhill, op. cit., pp. 275 f.
[71] Westman, op. cit., p. 83.

palace of incomprehensible magnitude. In the palace appeared innumerable men and women wearing white and radiant clothes. There a judgement-seat was erected, on which someone like the sun was sitting. A virgin stood at the side of the seat with a crown on her head. All together sang the praise of the sunlike one who was sitting on the seat. Then she saw a black, horrible in appearance, enraged and crying in a loud voice. In the front of the seat another figure appeared, a knight in arms, tranquil and modest. In the midst a human soul was standing, waiting for the judicial decision. A regular trial was performed, the black playing the role of a prosecutor, the knight acting as defender. A crowd of evil spirits filled the air, resembling sparks emitted from fire, craving the soul as their own property. Now the virgin intervened concealing some mysterious objects under her mantelet. A little church came in sight, and in the church some monks were found. Also other saints, men and women, appeared, all imploring mercy on the soul. A voice was heard from the judgement-seat declaring that, thanks to the intercession of the saints, this soul should be saved. Then the evil spirits all ran away.'[72]

If in a revelation form, colour, contour dominate, we call such a revelation a 'pictorial' one; if an action, or a course of events, is presented to the inward eye, we may speak of a 'dramatic vision'; if the visionary himself plays a conspicuous role in that which happens in the vision, the vision is 'autodramatic'.

We have here taken into consideration only the visual and the auditory elements of the prophetic revelations. There can also be experiences of taste, smell and contact or touch. This must of course be reckoned with, though such phenomena are relatively rare, compared with the visual and the auditory elements of the revelations.

Sometimes the visions of the prophetic persons have a symbolic character. The different traits of what is shown refer to spiritual facts and are to be interpreted with regard to their deeper significance. The vision of St. Birgitta related above is a characteristic example of such symbolic visions. Typically enough the reproduction of this vision is followed by an interpretation, such as is usual in connection with allegories and parables. The palace means heaven, the figures wearing white clothes mean the saints of the Church and the angels; the sun is Christ, the black man signifies the devil, the knight the guardian angel of the human soul, etc.

There is a special group of visions in which a real object is apprehended by the senses, but linked with an interpretation conceived by the visionary as given him in a revelation from above. I call visions of

[72] *Rev.* iv, 7.

this kind 'symbolic perceptions'. The symbolic perceptions differ from
the hallucinations in that the object beheld is real and actual. In contrast
to the visions proper (the imaginary visions) the object of the symbolic
perceptions belongs to the visible, not to the invisible world and is so
understood by the visionary himself. The object is apprehended by the
physical senses, but the interpretation has a revelatory character.

One example from the life of Suso may serve as a good illustration of
this kind of revelation. Early in the morning, after mass, Suso was
sitting in his monastery cell pondering over all the calumnies to which
he was exposed. Suddenly he heard a voice commanding him to open
the window and look out. So he did and became aware of a dog running
round in the cloister with a rag in his mouth, jumping up and down,
biting the rag, which he tossed to and fro. Then Suso heard someone
saying within his soul, 'Like the rag in the mouth of the dog, you are
thrown to and fro in the mouth of your brethren. But since it must be
so, you must resign yourself to your fate. As the rag is silent in being
ill-treated, you have to do the same.'[73] This occurrence looks like a vision,
with several characteristics of a vision, but it was not a real vision that
Suso then experienced. The dog was an actual one and the rag was a
real rag, which is made evident by the fact that Suso took care of the
rag and kept it in his cell as a precious treasure in memory of this event.
But through its significance the occurrence was so to speak sublimated.
It became a symbolic perception of a revelatory character. In the Old
Testament prophets we shall find several examples of this kind.

From the visions proper and the symbolic or sublimated perceptions
we must distinguish what the medieval mystics called *figurata locutio*,
the figurative speech. The visionary is given mental pictures, imaginary
creations, originating in the normal imaginative power, but conceived
of as revealed by God. These 'revelatory fancies', or 'literary visions',
as we may call them, do not imply an ecstasy, even though they are
based on inspiration. They resemble the ecstatic visions in that they
are without an object in the sensible world; but while in the vision
proper the visionary is of the opinion that he beholds something that is
actual in the invisible world, this is not the case with those who receive
the revelatory fancies. They know that the figures originate in their
imaginative faculty, though they assert that they are inspired by God.
They serve to illustrate thoughts and ideas of the prophets and mystics,
and provide them with impressive symbols. Suso says in *Horologium
sapientiae: Visiones quoque in sequentibus contentae non sunt omnes
accipiendae secundum literam, licet multae ad literam contigerint, sed est*

[73] Seuse, *Deutsche Schriften*, pp. 55 f.

figurata locutio. And in *Büchlein der ewigen Weisheit* he tells us about visions which are not genuine visions but only similes.[74]

Revelatory fancies which form a coherent tale and demand to be interpreted in detail may be called 'revelatory allegories'. The classification made above will be of good service to us in dealing with the prophets of the Old Testament.

As was said above, inspiration and ecstasy are often connected with some accessory phenomena of a psycho-physical nature, strongly diverging from the behaviour of ordinary man. Such phenomena were found among the shamans, dervishes, and the Rwala seers, but also among the Finnish trance-preachers and the medieval visionaries. They are either manifestations of an abnormally intensified activity in the form of violent bodily movements, dancing, jumping, leaping, shouting, etc., or symptoms of an unnatural passivity: paralysis, anaesthesia, torpor, etc. We may speak of orgiastic phenomena and of lethargic phenomena, corresponding to psycho-physical excitation on the one side and to somnambulistic apathy on the other.

In certain cases these phenomena are of a preparatory nature. They are brought about by the visionary himself in order to prepare himself for the ecstatic state he aspires to attain. We remember how carefully the Rwala seers prepared themselves for the encounter with the *malak*. They were accompanied by a little group of disciples, whose task it was to support them in their preparatory performances. Everywhere in the reports from the life of inspired men and women, we hear of several methods for evoking ecstatic raptures: dancing and other bodily movements, but also music, self-mutilation, the use of narcotic drugs and intoxicating liquors. These are all familiar practices which need not be further described.

In other cases such phenomena are symptoms of an ecstasy already begun. The psychic dominant has already carried out its function. The balance of the mental life is disturbed and self-control has been lost. Bodily or mental impulses have been disengaged. Now automatisms of several kinds set in, the organizing and controlling forces of every sound soul being made ineffective.

Typical of all prophetic personalities is the feeling that what they have to say is given them from above, that they are only mouthpieces of another, speaking to them and through them. The actual source of their preaching is an alien person, not the preacher himself, just as the poet says: I myself do not compose, another composes within me. But frequently the visionary distinguishes between two persons representing

[74] Ibid., p. 186.

himself, the one being his everyday *ego*, the other the extraordinary *ego*, which is the subject of the supernatural experiences. In the visionary experiences this *alter ego* replaces the everyday *ego*, this latter *ego* having so to speak been removed from its ordinary position. The extraordinary *ego* beholds the invisible things, hears the voices, receives the revelations, has intercourse with the divinities, makes journeys into supernatural regions. Everyday man does not recognize himself in such wonderful experiences. He finds his unexpected accomplishments in the blessed moments so exceptional, so unexampled, so surpassing his normal faculty, that he cannot help ascribing them to an alien person actually playing the role of his extraordinary and better *ego*.

It is very common in all visionary life for the visionary, when speaking of himself as making the extraordinary experiences, to use the third person instead of the first. St. Birgitta in her revelations calls herself 'the bride', 'the bride of Christ', etc. The Finnish trance-preacher Helena Konttinen says simply 'Helena'. Suso calls himself 'the servitor' or 'the pupil'. Similarly, in 2 Cor. xii, the Apostle Paul speaks of himself as having been elevated into heaven, as if it were another person.

Sometimes the extraordinary *ego* places itself at the side of the everyday *ego*, and then a colloquy between them may take place. Or the extraordinary *ego* may stand in its elevated position gazing upon the everyday *ego*, as if it were quite another person. While in heaven, playing the role of the extraordinary *ego*, in front of God's throne, Helena Konttinen sees herself lying in the cottage on earth. She sees mouth and hands moving, and at the same time she knows that she is in heaven.

This doubling of personality in men and women of the visionary type must not be confused with the phenomena of depersonalization and cleavage of personality which belong to the mental diseases based on hysteria and schizophrenia. They are intimately connected with the specifically visionary states and caused by the observation that in the vision man experiences and brings about things quite alien to the everyday *ego*. Generally the mentioning of double personalities takes place in connection with the reflection on, or the reproducing of, the vision in question, but at times the doubling occurs within the vision itself, as in the case of Helena Konttinen. Of course, this doubling can in some measure be conditioned by personal humility before the supernatural powers thanks to whom the visionary was endowed with his unexampled experiences, but there is no doubt that the feeling of being two individuals is principally derived from the visionary experiences themselves.

We have seen above that people belonging to the prophetic type always have a feeling of coercion and constraint, a feeling of not being free to act and talk, but of being in the service of a higher power and being subjected to an alien force. Ribot points out this feeling in the creative geniuses, using the terms 'nécessité' and 'la fatalité de la création'. The constructive men of genius, he says, are conscious of having a peculiar task to perform, so that on no account are they allowed to fail. They judge as infidelity every attempt to desert or alter their way of living. They are forced, as Ribot says, by an 'impulsion irrésistible'.[75] Precisely the same is true of the inspired men and women in the field of religion.

Already at the primitive stages, e.g., in shamanism, this feeling of necessity is very conspicuous. We find it again in more refined forms in the inspired men and women at a higher stage of cultural and religious development. They are servitors of God, runners carrying the letters of a mighty lord, messengers from a great king, mouthpieces by which God speaks, instruments by means of which God acts. To fail or desert would be a crime, but also something that brings its own revenge in both the external and the inner life. It happens that they feel tempted to slip away, but immediately they begin to yield to this temptation they become victims of anguish and agony, pains and torments. Then they turn back, submit to the yoke and begin to walk the ordered way again.

This feeling of coercion and constraint in the prophetic personalities depends on two facts: the initiatory call and their experiences when they are in the inspired or ecstatic state of mind.

To begin with the latter, the visionary experiences imply an influx in consciousness of visual pictures, auditory impressions, intellectual ideas of such a surprising and overwhelming nature, that the inspired person feels quite passive and is convinced that an alien person or irresistible force has taken possession of him. He describes this experience by means of expressions indicating acts of force, at times external to himself. He says that a hand seizes him by his shoulder, that someone grasps him within his chest. He is unable to resist and feels enslaved by his own experiences. Such experiences produce, of course, a feeling of being under constraint. This feeling becomes still more intense if in the revelation one is given commands to go now one way now another, act thus or thus, speak this or that, which is extremely common in the life of the prophets. Frequently the prophets tell us about orders they have received, voices they have heard, instructions which have been communicated to them, all of which were irresistible. It goes without saying

[75] Ribot, op. cit., p. 123.

that such experiences create feelings of coercion, dependency and subservience.

Most prophets speak of their prophetic profession as being based on a special call or vocation. In some cases the prophetic calling is hereditary. To be a member of a certain family implies *eo ipso* a call.[76] To the shamans external and interior signs and omens often serve as an indication that a certain individual is destined to be a shaman. Sometimes education and training within an association of prophets play an important role. At the higher stages the call has a more personal character. A person obtains an inner certitude of a religio-ethical nature that he is chosen by God to be His messenger to men and perform a particular task given him from above. In this case the call is often connected with experiences of a mysterious nature: auditions, visions, etc. Mohammed is a good example of this kind of prophetic call. The same is true of St. Birgitta of Sweden and particularly of the Old Testament prophets.

In the light of all that has been said above, a prophet may be characterized as *a person who, because he is conscious of having been specially chosen and called, feels forced to perform actions and proclaim ideas which, in a mental state of intense inspiration or real ecstasy, have been indicated to him in the form of divine revelations.*

This survey prepares us for a closer study of the Israelite prophets.

---

[76] So with the kahins; see Pedersen in *SOTP*, p. 136.

CHAPTER TWO

SUPERNORMAL EXPERIENCES AND GENERAL ACTIVITIES OF THE PRIMITIVE PROPHETS IN ANCIENT ISRAEL

1. ECSTASY AND OTHER EXTRAORDINARY PHENOMENA

The term 'primitive prophets' is not used here in any derogatory sense, but simply to indicate the earliest phase of Old Testament prophecy, as it is known to us from the oldest traditions, preserved in the Books of Samuel and the Kings. Old Testament scholars frequently use the term 'nebiism' to denote this stage of Israelite prophecy. But since prophets of later epochs are also called $n^e\underline{b}\hat{\imath}\hat{\imath}m$ it is very unfitting to use the word 'nebiism' for a special form of prophecy. As we shall see below, moreover, the affinity between the earlier prophets and the prophets of later times is so great that it would be very misleading to reserve the term $n^e\underline{b}\hat{\imath}\hat{\imath}m$ for the first group of prophets. It is often said that the distinctive feature of the older prophecy is ecstasy. But ecstasy is also found in the later prophets. If there is a difference (and there is), it is not an absolute difference, but consists only in the frequency and the character of the ecstasy. It is true that the 'classical' prophets from Amos to Malachi are prophets of a different type from those of the time of Saul, and different, too, from Elijah or Elisha, but this difference must be defined in other terms, as will be shown below.

The relation of primitive prophecy to classical prophecy cannot be characterized by means of terms such as 'nebiism' or 'ecstasy'. It must be carefully analysed and described in precise detail. That is what we shall try to do in what follows.

Ecstatic prophets appear for the first time, in the reliable records of Israel, in connection with the election of Saul as a king over Israel (we disregard for the present the curious narrative in Num. xi, which we shall consider later, about the seventy elders who were seized by the spirit of prophecy in the desert).[1] But we have no sufficient foundation for assuming that there were no prophets before the days of Samuel and Saul. That the rise of nebiism in Israel should for instance hang together with the political situation during the Philistine oppression of

---

[1] See, e.g., Meek, *Hebrew Origins*, pp. 145 ff. Jepsen, *Nabi*, emphasizes the significance of the destruction of the sanctuary in Shiloh and of the initiative of Samuel for the rise of ecstatic prophecy in Israel.

Israel in that time and the national feeling aroused by this affliction is a baseless surmise. Of the beginnings of prophecy in Israel we know nothing. The question whether it is an indigenous phenomenon in Israel or was derived from outside will be discussed later.

The nature of ecstasy and the distinction between orgiastic and passive (lethargic) ecstasy have been discussed in the preceding chapter. The first reference to prophets in Israel in 1 Sam. x. 5 ff. presents us with the orgiastic type. On his way to Gibeah Saul met a band of prophets, of whom it is said that they were in prophetic ecstasy (*miṭnabbe'îm*). Saul, too, coming across them, fell into ecstasy, *v.* 10. His behaviour in the ecstatic state is described in xix. 22-24: he stripped off his clothes, and fell down, and lay naked all that day and all night. This ecstasy was of the collective kind and contagious. It was through contact with the ecstatic band that Saul himself fell into ecstasy. How effective the ancient narrator imagined the contagious power of the ecstasy to be, we can see from what he tells us about the messengers whom Saul sent to take David. Three times messengers were sent; but all the three groups fell into ecstasy at the mere sight of a company of ecstatic prophets. Another example of collective ecstasy is offered by the narrative in 1 Kings xxii about the four hundred prophets who, on the eve of the attack against Ramoth-gilead, were assembled before the kings of Israel and Judah. It is said that they raged in ecstasy before the kings (*v.* 10).

An instance of orgiastic ecstasy occurs also in the story about Elijah, which relates how the prophet ran before Ahab's chariot the long way from Mount Carmel to Jezreel. That this was done in an ecstasy is evident. It is said that 'the hand of Yahweh' came upon Elijah, which in the prophetic narratives is an expression for an ecstatic fit (1 Kings xviii. 46).

We have also examples of a passive trance. When Elisha visited Damascus, Hazael came to see him in order to seek an oracle about Ben-hadad's sickness. Elisha said to him, 'Go, say to him, "You shall surely recover," but Yahweh has shown me that he shall certainly die.' Then the tale goes on: He (i.e., Elisha) fixed his gaze and stared steadily at him (i.e., Hazael), and he, the man of God, burst into tears. Hazael asked him, 'Why does my lord weep?' Elisha answered, 'Because I know the evil that you will do to Israel.' It seems certain that the fixing of the gaze and the staring refer to the behaviour of Elisha. To apply the expressions to Hazael is unnatural and at variance with Hebrew narrative style. What the narrator means us to understand is that the prophet, falling into a trance, had a vision in which he saw with his 'inward eye', as clairvoyants do, the harm which Hazael would later do to Israel. Throughout the world prophetic persons are reputed to be endowed with the gift of clairvoyance, thought-reading and telepathy. It is something like this that is attributed to Elisha in this story.[2]

Thus, Yahweh did not work upon the prophets in vehement ecstasies only, but also in passive states of mind. I think that this is what the narrative of Elijah on Mount Horeb in 1 Kings xix. 11-13 is intended to demonstrate. Yahweh was not in the hurricane, not in the earthquake, not in the fire, but in the light breath of air. This legend does not condemn orgiastic ecstasy, but aims at defending the more tranquil forms of divine revelation.

Many examples of foreseeing, foretelling, and clairvoyance are related in connection with the primitive prophets. They are of course to some extent legendary, but at any rate they indicate the faculties which at that early period a prophet was held to possess. Similarly pure legends often tell us important things about the situation and the milieu in which their heroes appear.

A man of God, i.e., a prophet, came in consequence of a divine revelation from Judah to Bethel, just as King Jeroboam was standing by the altar to burn a sacrifice. The man cried out in inspiration against the altar and said, 'O altar, altar, thus says Yahweh, "Behold, a son shall be born to the house of David, Josiah by name, and upon you he shall sacrifice the priests of the high places, who burn sacrifices upon you, and he shall burn men's bones on you" ' (1 Kings xiii. 1-2).[3] The wife of Jeroboam, disguised so that her identity might be concealed, visited the prophet Ahijah in Shiloh, seeking an oracle about her son who was sick. When Ahijah, who was blind, heard the sound of her feet he knew that it was the queen and foretold that her son would die (1 Kings xiv). Elijah predicted a lengthy drought (xvii. 1) and the death of King Ahaziah (2 Kings i. 2 ff.). Elisha knew where the Syrian troops had concealed themselves (vi. 9); he knew the words that the Syrian king spoke in his bedroom (vi. 12); he saw, heard, and recognized men who were approaching before their arrival (vi. 32); he foretold a famine

[2] 2 Kings viii. 7 ff. This story illustrates what Guillaume has to say in *Prophecy and Divination* about 'the second sight'. Second sight, says Guillaume, is a universal phenomenon, and he quotes a number of examples from various parts of the world (pp. 115 ff.). However, the second sight is not quite the same as the gift of receiving visions proper. A person who has the second sight claims to see actual events that occur at a distance in space and time; the visionary sees figures and scenes of a purely imaginary nature, pictures which belong to 'the invisible world', usually the super-mundane, celestial world.
[3] The utterance of this prophet is of course based on the events after they had happened. It is consequently a *vaticinium ex eventu*. But the story is interesting as showing what in ancient times was expected of a prophet.

to come upon the land for seven years (viii. 1); he knew in advance that
the Syrian king would die and that Hazael would be his successor on
the throne (viii. 10, 13). He also saw in spirit how Gehazi hurried after
Naaman and how Naaman turned from his chariot to meet him (v. 26).
He saw where water was to be found in the desert (iii. 16 f.).[4] The
members of the prophetic guilds in Bethel and Jericho knew in advance
as well as Elisha himself that Elijah was to be taken away on the same
day (2 Kings ii. 3 ff.). Similarly Elijah heard the rushing sound of rain
before it came. His posture, crouching down to the earth with his face
between his knees, is typical of seers and clairvoyants (1 Kings xviii.
41 f.).

It was regarded as quite normal that a prophet should know all
secrets. Elisha himself was astonished that he had not known of the
death of the Shunammite's son. The prophet says, 'Yahweh has hidden
it from me and has not told me' (2 Kings iv. 27). This notice is of
particular interest as saying that such mysterious knowledge was not
regarded in Israel as a magical art, but as founded on special revelations
from Yahweh.

Ecstatics are for the most part visionaries. Some visionary experiences
of a pictorial nature (see above, p. 41) received by early prophets are
preserved in tradition. Of the prophet Micaiah, a contemporary of
Ahab, it is related that he saw in a vision all Israel scattered on the
mountains like sheep without a shepherd. And he heard Yahweh saying,
'These have no master; let them return each to his home in peace.'
Very characteristic of a prophetic vision is the vision of the heavenly
world given to the same prophet: He saw Yahweh sitting on his throne
and all the host of heaven standing by him on his right hand and on his
left. He saw the spirit coming forth and standing before Yahweh saying
that he would deceive Ahab so that he might go up and fall at Ramoth-
gilead (1 Kings xxii). In the grossly legendary story about Elisha and
the Syrian king in 2 Kings vi a beautiful vision is related. While the
city where Elisha dwelt was surrounded by the Syrian army, Elisha
and his servant saw the mountain full of horses and chariots of fire
around Elisha.

Ecstasy never comes alone. All ecstatics are expected to have the
faculty of miracle-working. The same is true of the primitive prophets
in ancient Israel. A prophet can ensure that a very little supply does

---

[4] Probably the story of Elisha and the water in 2 Kings iii. 9 ff. was originally a story
of a seer's finding water in the desert, a story with countless analogies among desert-
dwellers. In tradition the story became a narrative about a divine wonder foretold by
the prophet, or even a wonder executed by the prophet through the effective power
of Yahweh's word.

not fail. With trifling provisions he provides a meal for a multitude of people. At his command a little oil in a flask fills many vessels. He makes dead men live, poisonous food innocuous, bad water sound, and iron float. On his word men are struck with leprosy and blindness, and fire comes down from heaven. Even his dead body has a wonderful effect. A dead man revives when touching the bones of a prophet. On the whole it is regarded as an advantage to be buried in the grave of a prophet. Sometimes the prophetic miracles bear a great resemblance to primitive magic. Elisha ordered Joash, king of Israel, to take bow and arrows and lay his hand upon the bow. Then the prophet put his own hands upon the king's hands in order to make the magic action still more effective, whereupon the king shot towards the east to secure victory over Syria. After that the king was told to take the arrows and strike on the ground. He struck three times and stopped. The prophet was angry with him and said, 'You should have struck five or six times, then you would have struck down Syria to a finish. But now you will strike Syria only three times.' Elijah and Elisha struck the waters of the Jordan with the prophetic mantle and divided them so that the prophets could pass over.[5]

A prophet sometimes performed his miraculous acts by external means. Everything that belonged to him was, so to speak, charged with power. Even his clothes possessed power, e.g., Elijah's mantle.[6] But more frequently it is said that the prophet worked by means of his word. The prophetic word was thought of as charged with energy and power. The prophetic word was an effective and a creative word. Words which to a modern mind seem to be mere predictions were in fact creative words. In the thought of ancient Israel the spoken word was also a deed. The Hebrew word dābār often does duty for action as well as for word.[7] There are many examples of such creative words in the miracle narratives related above. This is the reason why prophets who announced prosperity or success were highly appreciated and favoured,

[5] 1 Kings xiii. 31; xvii. 9 ff.; 2 Kings i. 10; ii. 8, 14; iv. 4 ff., 40 f., 42 ff.; v. 27; vi. 5 ff., 18; xiii. 14 ff., 21.

[6] Among the external means we may include Elisha's staff, which Gehazi laid upon the face of the son of the Shunammite (2 Kings iv. 29 f.). Further, the living body of a prophet made a dead corpse living (iv. 34 f.). An iron axe which had fallen into the water was made to float by means of a stick (vi. 6), and a handful of meal made noxious food sound (iv. 38 ff.). Such methods for carrying out extraordinary deeds are used in all quarters of the world and are well known to every student of primitive culture and religion.

[7] For the idea of the powerful word in Ancient Orient see Dürr, Die Wertung des göttlichen Wortes. For primitive stages see Guillaume, op. cit., pp. 19 ff., and passim. See further, e.g., Pedersen, Israel, I-II, pp. 167 f.; Repo, Der Begriff 'Rhēma', I, pp. 59 ff., with many literary references. Repo speaks pertinently of the dynamism of the word, pp. 59 ff.

while prophets who foretold ill fortune were feared and hated. Consequently it is quite natural that the King of Israel should say of the
prophet Micaiah, 'I hate him, for he never prophesies good concerning
me, but only evil', and put him into prison (1 Kings xxii. 8, 27). Likewise Elijah was persecuted by Ahab because he was regarded as one
who brought disaster on Israel (xviii. 17).

The effective power of prophetic words was increased by peculiar
actions by which they were frequently accompanied. These actions were
symbolic. They illustrated dramatically what the prophets had to
proclaim. But they were more than that. Just as the words had a creative
effect, so had the actions. In the famous scene in 1 Kings xxii the
prophet Zedekiah made for himself horns of iron and said, 'Thus says
Yahweh, "With these you shall gore the Syrians until they are destroyed."' Of the same nature is the action with the bow and the arrows
in the narrative about Elisha and Joash related above. The striking with
the arrows on the ground is at the same time a symbol and a creative
act. It is to be observed that the Hebrew word for 'strike' (hikkâh) is
also used of 'defeating' enemies.

Another story of the same kind is told in 1 Kings xi. 29 ff. The
prophet Ahijah the Shilonite tore his new mantle into twelve pieces
and gave ten of them to Jeroboam, thus symbolizing that Jeroboam
should have ten of the Israelite tribes to reign over as a king.[8]

We are also told of actions in which the illustrative element pre-
ponderates over the effective. They are, so to speak, parables in action.
An example of this kind of parabolic action is given in the narrative in
1 Kings xx. 35 ff. Ahab of Israel was at war with Ben-hadad, the king
of Syria. Ahab vanquished the Syrians but spared Ben-hadad. This

---

[8] That the mantle was *new* is more than a picturesque detail in the narrative. The
new mantle being clean and undefiled was better fitted for an extraordinary magical-
religious use than an old mantle would have been. With salt in a new bowl Elisha
made bad water wholesome, 2 Kings ii. 19 ff. The linen loin-cloth in Jer. xiii, which
had not been put in water, was better adapted for its purpose than an old one. A
new song, a new name are more powerful than an old song and an old name. Yahweh's
ark was conveyed upon a new cart, 2 Sam. vi. 3. In 1 Sam. vi. 7 the ark was conveyed
upon a cart, drawn by two cows upon which a yoke had never been. Cf. Deut.
xxi. 3. Among primitive peoples the new thing plays a prominent role. For magical
purposes the Berbers in Morocco use new bowls and pipkins, earthenware pots which
have not been used before, new lamps, water from new wells. Milk intended for
magical purposes must be offered on a new tray. Words from the Koran written in a
new plate have a particular effect (Westermarck, *Ritual and Belief in Morocco*; see
Index). Such ideas depend on primitive conceptions of taboo and magical power.
The twelve pieces of the mantle refer of course to the traditional twelve tribes of the
Israelite people. The ten pieces given to Jeroboam symbolize the northern kingdom,
consisting of ten tribes. Of the two remaining tribes one, Judah, would be reserved
for the dynasty of David. The twelfth tribe is not mentioned at all as, at an early stage
of history, having ceased to exist as an independent tribe (Simeon). There is no reason
for changing the text.

generous action awoke opposition from the prophetic circles. Now follows a curious episode. A prophet belonging to a prophetic band let another prophet strike him so that he received a wound. The wounded prophet went and waited for the king beside the road disguising himself with a bandage over his eyes, thus concealing the fact that he was a prophet. As the king was passing by, he cried to the king and told him this fictitious story: In the battle somebody had brought a man to him and ordered him to keep the man. If by any means the captive escaped, then his guard must lose his life or pay a talent of silver. The captive did escape. Then the king answered, 'Such is your verdict: you yourself have decided it.' Then the prophet announced to the king this word from Yahweh: 'Because you have let go out of your hand the man who was under my ban of destruction, therefore your life shall go for his life and your people for his people.'

The prophet intended, of course, that the wound should give the king the impression that he was just coming from the battlefield. Thus the story was made more credible and effective. This little scene would do more than mere verbal denunciation to make the king recognize the nature of his own conduct *vis-à-vis* the Syrian king and feel himself to be judged.

The resemblance between this story and Nathan's narrative of the poor man's lamb in 2 Sam. xii is striking. The difference is that Nathan's narrative was a pure parable, while the passage 1 Kings xx. 35 ff. contains a parable in action.

Another significant prophetic action is the sign or token (*môpēt, 'ôt*). While King Jeroboam was burning the sacrifice on the altar in Bethel, a prophet appeared pronouncing an oracle of doom against the high places and their priests. As a sign of the veracity of this prophecy, the altar would split and the ashes would be poured out. So it happened (1 Kings xiii. 3 ff.).

It is very interesting to note that belief in the creative power of prophetic words and actions survived to a late period. In his praise of the forefathers Sirach celebrates amongst others the prophet Elijah: 'The prophet Elijah arose like fire, and his word burned like a torch. He brought a famine upon them, and made them few by his zeal. By the word of the Lord he shut up heaven; in the same way he brought down fire three times . . . Who can glory like you? You who raised one who was dead, from death, and from Hades, by the word of the Most High; who brought kings down to destruction', etc. (xlviii. 1 ff.). And then concerning Elisha: 'Nothing was too wonderful for him . . . in his life he did signs, and after his death he worked wonders.'

There is no doubt a magical element in the activities of the early prophets, as they were conceived of by their contemporaries and described by the old narrators. However, it would be wrong to make too much of the magical character of their words and acts. The distinctive character of Hebrew belief in God led to a more personal mode of thought, which counterbalanced, and indeed overcame, the magical element. Yahweh Himself stood behind the prophets and worked through them; and their results were attained not through mysterious impersonal forces alone, but through prayer and personal intercession.

King Jeroboam of Israel attempted to arrest the prophet from Judah because he had prophesied against the altar in Bethel. But his hand, which he stretched out against the prophet, withered up, so that he could not draw it back to himself. Then the king said to the man of God, 'Entreat now the favour of Yahweh, your God, and pray for me that my hand may be restored to me.' So the man of God entreated the favour of Yahweh, and the king's hand was restored to him again (1 Kings xiii. 4 ff.). The son of the widow in Zarephath was restored to life in response to the prayer of Elijah (xvii. 20 ff.). On Mount Carmel the fire of Yahweh descended and consumed the burnt-offering of Elijah after the prophet had prayed fervently to his God (xviii. 36 ff.). Elisha prayed to Yahweh when he was about to recall the son of the Shunammite to life (2 Kings iv. 33). Apparently magical acts were sometimes combined with prayer to Yahweh. After Elisha had taken the mantle of Elijah, he struck the waters of the Jordan and prayed saying, 'Where now is Yahweh, the God of Elijah?' Then the waters were divided, so that Elisha could pass over (ii. 13 f.). Surrounded by enemies Elisha prayed and said, 'Strike now this people with blindness.' And Yahweh struck them with blindness. In the same way their eyes were subsequently opened (vi. 18 ff.).

To understand the character of primitive prophecy it is of great importance to analyse carefully the nature of the divine influence which was the cause of the mysterious knowledge, the effective words, the visions, and the miraculous actions of the prophets. The ancient narrators do not use any standardized formula for describing the divine inspiration. Sometimes they simply say that Yahweh Himself spoke to the prophet. 'Yahweh said' to Ahijah (1 Kings xiv. 5). 'As Yahweh lives,' said Micaiah, 'what Yahweh says to me, that I will speak' (xxii. 14). The prophet Ahijah confirms his prophecy concerning the house of Jeroboam with this formula: 'For Yahweh has spoken it' (xiv. 11). The son of Jeroboam died and was buried 'according to the word of Yahweh,

which He spoke by His servant Ahijah, the prophet' (xiv. 18).[9] The
oracles of the prophets are frequently introduced with the formula
'thus says Yahweh' (xx. 13, etc.).[10] Others begin with 'Hear the word
of Yahweh' (2 Kings vii. 1). It may be that such phrases are employed
in imitation of the usage of the later prophets. But at any rate they
correspond well to the general conception of divine inspiration in the
older traditions. The same is true of the formula 'Yahweh's word came
to the prophet' (1 Kings xii. 22).[11] A prophet speaks as one who utters
a word from Yahweh revealed to him (xx. 35). King Jehoshaphat said
concerning Elisha, 'Yahweh's word is with him' (2 Kings iii. 12).
Yahweh's word is in the mouth of a prophet (1 Kings xvii. 24). When a
man resorted to a prophet to obtain an oracle, it was said that he went
to 'inquire (dāraš) for Yahweh's word' (1 Kings xxii. 5; 2 Kings i. 16).

Consequently the divine word plays a dominating role in the descriptions of the divine influence upon the prophets.[12] It may be said that the
divine word and the divine saying are the most characteristic terms for
expressing the content of a prophetic revelation. To have received
Yahweh's word is the same as to have received a revelation. The divine
'word' is the mysterious knowledge, the inner inexplicable certainty, the
wonderful insight into divine and human affairs which a prophet
receives in the hours of inspiration. The reason why the terms 'word'
and 'speak' are used, is that the prophets really sometimes had ecstatic
or inspirational experiences in which they heard a divine voice speaking
to them. What is recorded of Samuel in the sanctuary in Shiloh, must
have occurred many times: Yahweh called Samuel; then Samuel
answered, 'Speak, for thy servant is listening.' Then Yahweh said, etc.
(1 Sam. iii. 10 f.).[13] It is sometimes said that the prophet *saw* that which
was revealed to him. The mysterious knowledge was something that
Yahweh let him see, or that Yahweh showed him. Elisha told
Hazael that Yahweh 'had shown' him (hir'anî) that Ben-hadad
should die (2 Kings viii. 10). And further, in the same story: 'Yahweh
has shown me that you are to be king over Syria,' said Elisha (v. 13).

Thus 'hearing' and 'seeing' were both expressions for the reception
of the mysterious knowledge, for the revelation of the divine word. This

[9] Cf. 1 Sam. iii. 12; 1 Kings xv. 29; xvi. 12; xvii. 16.
[10] 1 Kings xx. 28; xxi. 19; xxii. 11; 2 Kings iii. 17; vii. 1; ix. 6.
[11] 1 Kings xiii. 20; xvi. 1; xvii. 2; xxi. 17.
[12] In tradition, word and prophecy were so intimately combined that the scarcity
of prophets was described as the infrequency of Yahweh's word (1 Sam. iii. 1). To be
a prophet was the same as to receive revelations of Yahweh's word (iii. 7).
[13] That Yahweh's word in prophetic inspiration could really be heard by the 'inward
ear' of the prophets is evident also from some passages in the Psalter: lxxxi. 6;
lxxxv. 9, etc.

double mode of expression certainly depends on the fact that visual and auditory elements were intimately combined in the revelations. Persons of the prophetic type explain their inspired knowledge as derived from revelatory experiences which are partly visual and partly auditory. They tell us of voices heard and visions seen; in one case the voices predominate, in another the visions proper.[14]

As we have seen, the Old Testament traditions do not contain many detailed descriptions of visions experienced by the early prophets. Occasionally it is recorded that an angel, *mal'āk*, appeared as an intermediary between Yahweh and the prophet. The anonymous prophet at Bethel says in 1 Kings xiii. 18, 'I too am a prophet as you are; and an angel spoke to me by the word of Yahweh,' etc. When Elijah was in the desert an angel touched him and said to him, 'Arise, eat.' And Yahweh's angel returned a second time and touched him and said, 'Arise, eat, for the journey will be too great for you' (xix. 5 ff.). Here the appearance of the angel seems to have occurred in a dream, because it is said that the prophet lay sleeping under the broom bush. In other cases it appears that the angel was seen in a trance. While the messengers from Ahaziah were on the way to Elijah Yahweh's angel spoke to the prophet, 'Arise, go up to meet the messengers and say to them,' etc. (2 Kings i. 3). In the narrative about the commander and Elijah in 2 Kings i. 13 ff. Yahweh's angel said to Elijah, 'Go down with him, do not be afraid of him.'

As we know, there are countless references in the Old Testament literature to appearances of angels. They are, of course, often only artificial, legendary elements, employed to express intervention of Yahweh on this earth without infringing His celestial sublimity, whether the angel is conceived of as a real being different from Yahweh or only as some sort of representation of Yahweh.[15] But it is not very likely that the idea of angelic appearances would have emerged, if visions of angels in dreams or ecstasies had not sometimes really occurred. There is, consequently, reason to assume that the early prophets occasionally had visions of angels not unlike the *malak-munâbi* with whom the Rwala seers claim that they have communications, or

---

[14] The author of the passage 1 Sam. iii. 21-iv. 1 wants to present Samuel as an outstanding prophet. If the text is correct he says that Yahweh showed Himself to Samuel revealing Himself by His word. Then the prophetic word of Samuel came to all Israel. Thus prophecy, divine word, and vision inseparably belong together.

[15] For the idea of Yahweh's angel, see, e.g., Johnson, *The One and the Many in the Israelite Conception of God*, pp. 32 ff. The 'angel' is an example of the oscillation between the One and the Many in the conception of God. The 'angel' illustrates the 'extension of the personality', which, according to Johnson, played so great a part in Hebrew thinking.

the angel who appeared before Mohammed in the vision in which he received his call.[16]

It remains to examine the other expressions used to describe the way in which supernormal experiences were obtained: the spirit of Yahweh and the hand of Yahweh.

In the narrative about Saul and the prophets of Gibeah we are told that the spirit, $rûah$, of Yahweh affected Saul, so that he fell into ecstasy like the ecstatic prophets. The context shows clearly that the $rûah$ was also the motive power in the prophetic band (1 Sam. x. 6 ff.). The same occurred in Ramah (xix. 18 ff.). There, we are told, the messengers of Saul fell into ecstasy because the $rû^ah$ of God came upon them. This occurred three times. Finally Saul himself came to Ramah. There the $rû^ah$ of God came upon him, too, and he fell into violent ecstasy. In the remarkable vision of the prophet Micaiah in 1 Kings xxii the $rûah$ is presented as the power which inspired the prophets, whether to tell lies or to tell truth. When in ecstasy a prophet suddenly disappears and departs to another place, it is said that he is taken away by the spirit of Yahweh (xviii. 12).[17]

It ought to be observed that in the oldest traditions of the early prophets $rû^ah$ is taken into account only as the motive power in orgiastic ecstasies. Under the influence of $rû^ah$ a man was 'changed into another man' (1 Sam. x. 6). When only predictions and proclamations of one kind or another are in question the 'word', $dābār$, plays a role analogous to that of the $rû^ah$ in ecstatic experiences of a more violent nature. The idea of $rû^ah$ as the cause of ecstasy is a heritage from still more primitive times, when ecstatic men and women were thought of as possessed by and filled with spirits. In the Old Testament narratives, however, $rû^ah$ is never regarded as a being independent of Yahweh.[18] The spirit is always Yahweh's spirit, a more or less substantial *dynamis*, a force emanating from Yahweh;[19] the spirit is always sent by Yahweh and runs Yahweh's errands. For this reason it is wrong to suggest that $rû^ah$ was regarded as a spirit analogous to the spirits of the shamans or the jinn of the pre-Islamic Arabs; nor is there any question of possession

[16] See above, pp. 11 f.

[17] Also in later tradition the spirit was regarded as a general power of inspiration in the prophetic personalities of ancient times: 1 Chron. xii. 19; 2 Chron. xv. 1 ff.; xx. 14 ff.; Neh. ix. 30.

[18] Johnson characterizes the spirit as an 'extension' of Yahweh's personality, op. cit., p. 19.

[19] In the narrative of Micaiah and the four hundred prophets in 1 Kings xxii the spirit is thought of as a person. But here the personification and the individualization of the spirit depend on the fact that the spirit appears in a vision. In the vision the spirit is seen as a person; in reality the spirit in the mouth of the prophets again becomes a *dynamis* (vv. 22 f.).

in the proper sense of the word, as in the narratives of the demons in the gospels. The *rûᵃḥ* affects the prophet, but it is always thought of as a means by which Yahweh Himself works in human life, and can never be isolated or separated from Yahweh.

There are a few references to 'Yahweh's hand' in connection with the abnormal experiences of the primitive prophets. When the prophet Elijah girded up his loins and ran before Ahab's chariot to the entrance of Jezreel, it is said that Yahweh's hand, *yaḏ yahwêh*, came upon him (1 Kings xviii. 46). When during an expedition against Moab the Israelite army could get no water in the desert and Elisha was asked to help, he ordered a musician to be brought, and then, we are told, Yahweh's hand came upon him (the usual effect of the stimulus of music); and so, in a trance, he saw where water was to be found (2 Kings iii. 15).[20]

What we read about the Israelite prophets in such passages fully corresponds to what ecstatic men and women the world over have had to say about the psycho-physical phenomena which accompany their ecstatic fits. The Finnish trance-preachers say that somebody seizes them by the shoulder, that an invisible hand is put upon their forehead and their breast, etc. St. Birgitta of Sweden tells us that in the ecstasy she felt as if the hand of God were grasping her within her breast.[21] The idea of a hand seizing or grasping one from without is a very appropriate expression indeed for the feeling of a psycho-physical convulsion or cramp so common in ecstatic experience. The prophets understood very well that the hand was Yahweh's; they knew that the power that seized them came from Yahweh and not from any other. Yahweh's hand and Yahweh's *rûᵃḥ* are substantially identical in their effect. They are both expressions for the divine power which is effective in ecstatic experience.[22]

In Israelite prophecy ecstasy was produced by the power of Yahweh. Did the early prophets know how to evoke ecstasy by exterior means? Wherever ecstasy is developed as the culmination of religious experience external methods are deliberately used in order to evoke and intensify ecstasy. These methods are manifold and vary according to different levels of cultural and religious development. As we learned in the first chapter of this book, diverse narcotic and intoxicating drugs and drinks

---

[20] For this story see what was said above. For the 'hand' see further Hempel, *Gott und Mensch im Alten Testament*², p. 17; *ZAW*, lxv, 1953, p. 158.

[21] See above, p. 22.

[22] Of course the term 'Yahweh's hand' can also be used to express Yahweh's power in a more general sense: Ex. ix. 3; Deut. ii. 15; iii. 24; xxvi. 8; Judges ii. 15; 1 Sam. v. 6 f., 9, 11; vii. 13, etc.

were used in order to attain the ecstatic state desired. Frequently fasting and various kinds of mortification were used; likewise perpetual reiteration of suggestive words and formulas or persistent staring at a certain object. The medieval mystics often speak about the efficacy of meditation and contemplation in preparation for ecstatic experience.[23]

The Phoenician prophets of Baal who contended with Elijah on Mount Carmel slashed themselves with swords and lances until blood gushed out upon them and so worked themselves into a prophetic ecstasy. Similar usages are known from different quarters of the world. Did the Israelite prophets also execute such bloody rites? In the opinion of the present writer the passage 1 Kings xx. 35 ff. cannot be adduced as an example of self-wounding. Here the wounds are meant to indicate that the prophet in question comes direct from the battlefield. But the reference in Zech. xiii. 2 ff. to the abolition of debased prophecy in the Messianic age shows that self-wounding was practised by prophets in Israel at least during certain periods. It shall come to pass on that day, the text runs, that when someone says to a prophet, 'What are these wounds on your breast?' He will answer, 'I was wounded in the house of my companions.'[24]

Music seems to have been the most prominent means of evoking ecstasy among the early Old Testament prophets. The prophets in Gibeah whom Saul met after having been anointed by Samuel came from the high place to the music of diverse instruments, tambourines, flutes, harps, etc., while in the ecstatic state. Elisha asked for music when he needed help to attain the state of ecstasy in which he saw where water was to be found in the desert.

Light is thrown on such narratives by what Musil has to tell about the ecstatic seers among the Rwala bedouin. Some of the disciples who accompany the seers have the duty of beating drums and of playing on various instruments. When the seer wishes to be visited by the angel (munâbi) he exhorts his followers to play. After a little while the ecstasy comes on and the angel appears. In this connection we remember the role which drums played among the shamans in Siberia, and tambourines and flutes among the bacchantes in Thrace.

Dancing is not directly mentioned in connection with the Israelite prophets. But when we recall the dancing of the Baal prophets on Mount Carmel and the importance of dancing in the Israelite cult, we are entitled to assume that the primitive prophets also used dancing

[23] See above, p. 23, and Hölscher, *Die Profeten, passim*. The above-mentioned book of Achelis also contains abundant material.
[24] Cultic self-wounding is sometimes mentioned in other connections: Jer. xvi. 6; xli. 5; Deut. xiv. 1. See also Hos. vii. 14 if the true reading is *yitgôdādû* (cf. *BH*).

to evoke ecstasy. It is very likely that the prophets in Gibeah came dancing from the high place to the tones of rhythmic music.[25]

The visionary experiences, as we have seen, are generally ascribed to influence from Yahweh. A clairvoyant experience is described in a more primitive manner in the story about Elisha and Naaman in 2 Kings v. After Elisha had cleansed Naaman from his leprosy but declined remuneration from him, Gehazi, Elisha's servant, ran after Naaman and asked for a present. When he came back to his master, Elisha said to him, 'Where have you been, Gehazi?' Gehazi answered, 'Your servant has not been away anywhere.' Then Elisha said, 'Did not my heart go there when a man turned from his chariot to meet you?' We have here a fine example of the belief that the soul of a person, his second *ego*, can detach itself from the normal *ego* and depart for distant goals. It is noteworthy that the second *ego* is here called 'the heart'. The heart is, as we know, a common Hebrew designation for what we should call the soul. Further, the general character of the statement may be observed. Elisha saw 'a man' turning from his chariot. This corresponds very well to the indistinctness and vagueness of such cases of clairvoyance.[26]

A man endowed with supernatural gifts was called 'a man of God', *'îš 'elōhîm*. In this phrase 'of Elohim' is not a possessive genitive; it implies first and foremost a qualification. The man of God is so called because divine qualities are bestowed upon him. In modern Morocco one would say that such a person was possessed of *baraka*.[27] Moses is called 'man of God' (Deut. xxxiii. 1; Josh. xiv. 6), King David likewise (2 Chron. viii. 14; Neh. xii. 24). An angel in the guise of a human being is conceived of as 'a man of God' (Judges xiii). A renowned seer, such as Samuel, is 'a man of God' (1 Sam. ix. 6 ff.). Very often this title is given to the prophets, particularly Elijah (1 Kings xvii. 18, 24; 2 Kings i. 10) and Elisha (2 Kings iv. 7, 9, 21; viii. 2 ff., 11; xiii. 19). Elisha is even called 'a holy man of God' (2 Kings iv. 9).[28]

The Hebrew expression *'îš 'elōhîm* corresponds to the term *amēl-ili* in Mesopotamia. There this term refers to the priest or prophet as a man of god in a special sense, as his possession, having also in himself

[25] See further Oesterley, *The Sacred Dance*, and on this Haldar, *Associations*, pp. 58 ff., with more material.
[26] For the Hebrew conception of the heart, *lēb*, see Pedersen, *Israel*, I-II, pp. 102 ff. and *passim* (see Indexes). The idea of the soul's going free from the human body is very common in primitive cultures. The best examples are offered by shamanism. But in the higher cultures too this primitive idea is occasionally found. So for instance in Greece: Rohde, *Psyche*[2], II, p. 92. What is said of the 'heart' of Elisha is not in accordance with general Hebrew psychology, but is to be regarded as a survival from a more primitive stage of development.
[27] See Westermarck, op. cit., I, pp. 148 ff.
[28] Other examples: 1 Sam. ii. 27; 1 Kings xii. 22; xiii. 1.

something of the divine nature, so that the god can employ him as an instrument through which he speaks.[29] It may be that in Mesopotamia *amēl-ili* was a designation for a person belonging to the temple staff, but among the Israelites 'a man of God' was not necessarily attached to a sanctuary as is evident from the examples mentioned above. Neither Elijah nor Elisha, neither David nor the angel of Judges xiii belonged to a temple staff. The name only indicated that the individual who was bearer of the name was vouchsafed divine qualifications in an extraordinary degree. It goes without saying that such a man was equipped in a special fashion to be a messenger from God; but the chief stress lay upon his sharing in the divine attributes. The fact that *'îš yahwêh* never occurs is a noteworthy fact, which has been much discussed. In my opinion the reason for it is that *'elōhîm* was a more general designation for the deity and therefore better suited to qualify an individual, while Yahweh as a proper name was less appropriate for this purpose. An expression such as *'îš yahwêh* in Hebrew would only have meant that an individual was thought of as being in Yahweh's possession, a servant in a Yahweh sanctuary, or a messenger from Yahweh.

A prophet, being a man of God, brings good fortune (*šālôm* or *berākâh*) with him. The Shunammite woman, whose son Elisha had restored to life, departed, according to the word of Elisha, and sojourned in the land of the Philistines during the seven years of famine in Palestine. When the woman returned, she went to appeal to the king for her house and her field. She arrived just when Gehazi, the servant of Elisha, was relating to the king all the great things that Elisha, the man of God, had done. 'My lord, O king', said Gehazi, 'this is the woman, and this is her son, whom Elisha restored to life.' Then the king restored to her all that was hers. A person so blessed must also be an object of the king's favour (2 Kings viii. 1 ff.).[30]

But a visit of a prophet could also be feared as a dangerous event. The woman of Zarephath was afraid of Elijah and said to him, 'What have I to do with you, O man of God? You have come to me to make my iniquity known and so to kill my son' (1 Kings xvii. 17 f.). A prophet, being a man of God, was expected to be able to see through a person, find out his secret sins, and then bring punishment upon him. Of countless inspired men and women belonging to the prophetic type similar things are narrated. St. Birgitta for instance was a great discoverer

---

[29] Haldar, *Associations*, pp. 29 f., 126 ff.

[30] The idea of the blessing that follows a prophet lies in my opinion behind the petition of a prophet to be buried in the grave in which another prophet was buried. If a catastrophe should come upon the land, then the bones of the prophet would be saved (1 Kings xiii. 31).

and revealer of secret sins and her rebukes and punishments were highly feared.

Prophets as 'men of God' were sacrosanct. It was dangerous to offend them. Not only were their oracles as words from God absolutely binding, and woe to those who disobeyed them or called their veracity in question (1 Kings xx. 35 f.; 2 Kings vii. 17 ff.); but also their own persons were sacred and must not be insulted or injured. This is illustrated by the following narrative. Once, when Elisha was passing by, some small boys came out of a city and jeered at him and said, 'Go up, you baldhead! Go up, you baldhead!' When he turned around and saw them, he cursed them in Yahweh's name. Then two she-bears came out of the wood and mangled forty-two of the boys (2 Kings ii. 23 f.). The story of the disobedient prophet from Judah in 1 Kings xiii shows that even the wild beasts respected the prophets. A lion slew him, but remained standing beside the dead body without eating it.

As men of God, seized by Yahweh's hand, affected by His spirit, and bearers of Yahweh's word the prophets lived under divine constraint. We have seen in the first chapter of this book that this sense of coercion was one of the most characteristic features among the psychic experiences of the prophets. The prophets *must* go where Yahweh commanded them to go, do what they were ordered to do, say what Yahweh bade them to say. The anonymous prophet from Judah in 1 Kings xiii declined to stay with the king to take refreshment or to accept any present. He *must* go away. He answered the king, 'If you were to give me half of your house, I would not go with you, nor would I eat bread or drink water in this place. For so it was charged me by the word of Yahweh, saying, "You shall neither eat bread nor drink water, nor return by the way that you came." ' Then he went another way and did not return by the way that he came to Bethel.

In obedience to God a prophet must go even the most curious ways, as we see, e.g., from the stories about Elijah and Elisha. Elijah was sent hither and thither, often without knowing the reason for it. Very instructive in this respect is the story narrated in 2 Kings ii. He was sent to Bethel, then to Jericho, then to the Jordan. So rapid could the removals be, that it was believed that they were the direct result of Yahweh's rûªḥ. After Elijah was taken up into heaven, it was supposed that Yahweh's rûªḥ had taken him up and cast him upon some mountain or into some valley. In 1 Kings xviii. 7 ff. we are told that Obadiah met Elijah, for whom Ahab had long been searching. But he would not report to Ahab that Elijah was there because he was afraid that Yahweh's rûªḥ would transport the prophet to some place unknown to him. Similar legends about prophetic personalities were told even in late times. In the apocryphal story of Bel and the Dragon it is narrated of the prophet Habakkuk that the angel of the Lord took hold of the crown of his head, and lifted him up by his hair and with the speed of the wind set him down in Babylon, right over the lion's den, where Daniel was.[31]

A prophet was conscious of having been sent (*šālûᵃḥ*) by God (1 Kings xiv. 6). Accordingly he must obey even when he was sent on difficult errands. But as God's messenger he always stood under God's protection. Elijah did not become a victim of Ahab's persecution. In the desert he was provided with food in a wonderful manner. Horses and chariots of fire were sent to assist Elisha. But if a prophet was disobedient, he was severely punished. The prophet from Judah was killed by a lion because he had rebelled against Yahweh's command (1 Kings xiii).

This legend is also of great significance because it raises a problem which was of great importance in the prophetic experience. If two revelations contradict each other, what is to be done? If one prophet has received a word from God contrary to that received by another prophet, which revelation is the true one? Similar problems have confronted prophets in all parts of the world. The contradiction between two different revelations is only another form of the greatest of all the problems that the visionaries have to solve: Is this revelation really from God? Is this revelation genuine and true? The story of the two prophets in 1 Kings xiii circulated within prophetic circles because it provided a precedent, indicating how such a problem was to be solved.

At Yahweh's command a man of God came from Judah to Bethel in order to pronounce a curse upon the altar. Jeroboam, the king, was about to arrest him, but his hand withered. In response to the prayer of the prophet the king's hand was restored. The prophet was invited by the king to come to him and take refreshment and receive a reward. But the man of God would not go, for he was charged by a revelation from Yahweh that he should neither eat bread nor drink water, nor return by the same way as he came to Bethel. Now there lived in Bethel an aged prophet, who was consequently a man of great authority. This prophet went after the man of God and finding him said to him, 'Come home with me and eat bread.' The prophet from Judah replied, 'I am not permitted to return with you.' The aged prophet protested and said, 'I, too, am a prophet as you are; and an angel has spoken to me at the command of Yahweh, saying, "Bring him back with you to your

---

[31] Acts viii. 39 resembles these stories. After having baptized the Ethiopian eunuch Philip was hurried away by the Spirit, and the eunuch saw no more of him.

house".' (But this was a lie.) So the man of God returned with him.
Now, when they were sitting together, the aged prophet received a
genuine revelation; and he cried out, 'Thus says Yahweh, "Since you
have disobeyed Yahweh's word, your body shall not come to the grave
of your fathers."' After he had departed a lion met him on the way and
slew him. This happened because, as the narrative runs, he had rebelled
against Yahweh's word.

The object of this story was to give this lesson: when a revelation
that you have received is contradicted by the revelation of another
prophet, you have to obey the divine voice that you have heard yourself.
The revelation of another may be untrustworthy. It is not prudent to
rely on it.

The prophetic life is based upon a prophetic call. Great prophetic
personalities such as Isaiah, Jeremiah, Ezekiel, Zarathustra, Mohammed, St. Birgitta and many others expressly refer to a particular
event by which they have obtained the certainty of being chosen by
God to enter His service as His messengers and mouthpieces. The call
itself generally takes the form of a vision of a fundamental nature. At
the lower levels of prophetic experience we seldom hear of a special
call of a more elevated kind. Among the shamans and dervishes some
conventionally fixed signs, or a predisposition to ecstasy, are sufficient
to indicate that a certain individual is a prophet.

Do the oldest Israelite traditions record anything about experiences
of a special prophetic call? There are in fact two narratives which
may be mentioned in this connection; they both belong to the Elisha
cycle. In 1 Kings xix. 19 ff. we are told that Elijah came across Elisha,
the son of Shaphat, as he was ploughing behind twelve yoke of oxen.
Then Elijah came over to him and threw his mantle upon him. Elisha
took a yoke of oxen and slaughtered them, and using the ox-yoke to
boil their flesh, he gave it to the people to eat. Then he went after Elijah
and became his attendant. This little story tells us how Elisha became a
prophet. It came about by the initiative of another prophet, Elijah,
who transferred the gift of prophecy to him by throwing upon him the
prophetic mantle, which shared the mysterious power of its bearer. The
slaughtering of the oxen meant in fact a sacrifice and the eating of their
flesh, a cultic meal. Consequently the call consisted of two actions: the
transferring of the mysterious power from one prophet to another by
investiture with the prophetic mantle, and, secondly, the sacrifice and
the cultic meal.

The ceremonies may of course have varied. In 1 Kings xix. 16
anointing is mentioned. In 2 Kings ii. 9-14, which in some measure

may be regarded as a parallel to the narrative in 1 Kings xix. 19 ff., Elisha similarly assumed Elijah's mantle, charged as it was with power; and he tore his own garments in two pieces. I think the last action symbolizes the break with the former life. In its present form the narrative has another meaning. It does not recount the principal call of Elisha, which was related before, but tells us how Elisha became a sort of successor to Elijah as a prophetic authority of the highest degree and, in particular, the leader of a prophetic order. This is expressed through the petition of Elisha: 'Let me inherit a double share of your spirit',[32] and the utterance of the members of the prophetic order who were at Jericho: 'The spirit of Elijah rests upon Elisha'; whereupon they went to meet him and bowed to the earth before him.

After having received the call the prophet was no longer his own; he belonged body and soul to Yahweh, accredited (ne'emān) as he was by Yahweh as a prophet (1 Sam. iii. 20). From the moment of his call he lived under Yahweh's constraint, and in all that he uttered and undertook as a prophet he was compelled by Yahweh. He was obliged in everything to obey the command of Yahweh. If disobedient he was severely punished. But if he remained steadfast in obedience, he stood under the protection of Yahweh, as is shown by many features, particularly in the Elijah cycle.

2. The Primitive Prophets in Ancient Israelite Society

According to the Old Testament records prophets played a very important role in the social life of Ancient Israel.

There was, to begin with, a large number of them, dispersed over the whole country. King Ahab of Israel once assembled prophets to the number of about four hundred men (1 Kings xxii. 6). On another occasion a group of fifty prophets is mentioned (2 Kings ii. 7). Because of the persecution of the Yahweh prophets by Ahab and Jezebel, Obadiah is said to have taken a hundred prophets and hidden them in a cave (1 Kings xviii. 4). Colonies of prophets lived in Gibeah of Elohim, Ramah, Bethel, Jericho, Gilgal, Samaria, etc.

The prophets lived together in guilds, which we shall study later on; but they often travelled about on various errands. They were easily recognized because of their general behaviour and singular attire. The Buddhist monks are recognizable by mantle, girdle, begging bowl, and other accoutrements. The dervishes have their curiously shaped caps,

[32] For the double share cf. Deut. xxi. 17, the direction that the first-born son shall have a double portion of the inheritance.

flags, and rosaries. The primitive prophets of ancient Israel also had their distinctive marks: a peculiar garment, a sort of stigma, and tonsure. Elijah wore a sheepskin or goatskin as his mantle and a leathern loin-cloth (2 Kings i. 8). Later Isaiah wore next to his skin a *śak̯*, i.e., a sack-cloth, woven of goat or camel hair (Isa. xx. 2), which in later times seems to have replaced the garment of skin. Even in post-exilic times the hairy mantle was characteristic of a prophet (Zech. xiii. 4). According to the gospels John the Baptist wore a cloth woven of camel hair and had a leathern loin-cloth around his waist (Matt. iii. 4).

Many scholars are of the opinion that this clothing in its various forms originated in cultic customs. Hölscher in his work on the Israelite prophets points to the fact that in ancient cults the priests often wore skins of animals that were used for sacrifices. He believes that the clothing of the prophets was originally the bull-skins in which the priests of the Phoenician-Canaanite Baal, the bull god, wrapped themselves.[33]

This theory is connected with the view that primitive Israelite prophecy was derived solely from Canaanite religion and was an essentially alien phenomenon amongst the Hebrews. If this theory means that ecstatic prophecy in Israel was in itself a loan from the Canaanites, there is no ground for such a hypothesis. As has been demonstrated in the first chapter of this book, ecstasy and ecstatic prophecy are not restricted to specific peoples; they appear everywhere in the world, irrespective of race and culture. It can never be proved that prophetic ecstasy was not indigenous in Israel as well as in other peoples throughout the world. But might not a genuine Hebrew movement have borrowed forms and customs from the pagan world? This possibility must be admitted; but it is scarcely likely that the Yahweh prophets in Israel, zealous as they were for the genuine Yahwistic faith and cult, adopted from a foreign religion features so markedly pagan as the bull skins of the Baal priests. In the opinion of the present writer another explanation is more plausible, namely that the skin and the hairy mantle derive their origin from a nomadic usage, well known among the inhabitants of the desert.

Skins or hairy clothes have always formed part of the clothing of desert-dwellers. Cloaks woven of goat or camel hair are common today among the bedouin of the Syrian-Arabian deserts. But the skin is also used. The bedouin of the Sinai peninsula protect themselves against the winter cold by means of a skin hung over their shoulders. The Arabian hunter tribe Sleb uses cloaks of gazelle skin reaching to the feet and covering the whole body. Musil relates that in the winter time a

---

[33] Hölscher, op. cit., pp. 145 f.

sheepskin coat is worn by the Rwala bedouin instead of the mantle.[34] According to the story of Paradise, our first ancestors wore skin garments (Gen. iii. 21). Primitive customs survive in religious practice long after they have been abandoned in everyday life. In particular they are cherished by people who claim a special degree of holiness. In ancient Israel the Rechabites continued to live in tents long after the settlement in Canaan. It is reasonable to suppose that the primitive clothing of the prophets was one expression of their protest against higher culture in general.

That the primitive prophet had as a distinctive sign a mark or stigma on his forehead seems to be evident from the narrative in 1 Kings xx. 35 ff. A prophet was commanded by Yahweh to go to meet King Ahab and pronounce a judgement upon him, because he had set his enemy, the Syrian king, at liberty. The prophet waited for the king by the way, disguising himself with a bandage over his eyes. Then he hastily took the bandage away from his eyes, and the king recognized him as one of the prophets. Consequently the man must have had a mark on his forehead by which it was clear that he was a prophet.

In different parts of the world incisions or marks painted on the skin may indicate that a person belongs to a certain deity, sect, tribe, clan, or caste. Slaves and soldiers were so marked to show to whom they belonged. In the Old Testament the most notorious example is the mark which Yahweh put upon Cain to prevent anyone from killing him. Modern scholars are agreed that this mark is conceived of as a Yahweh sign, probably distinguishing the tribe of the Kenites, of which Cain was the *heros eponymus*.[35] There are reasons for believing that the mark on the forehead of the Yahweh prophets was just such a Yahweh sign, perhaps a *tāw*, which letter originally had the form of a cross. According to Ezek. ix. 4, a mark, a *tāw*, was to be set upon the foreheads of the men who sighed and cried for all the abominations that were done in the midst of Jerusalem. When the apostates were struck dead no one on whom the mark was would be touched. In Isa. xliv. 5 it is said that in the age to come proselytes will have a mark on their hands to show that they belong to Yahweh, the God of Israel.[36] Thus it is likely that in the earliest period, at all events, the Yahweh prophets bore this Yahweh stigma as a mark of their dedication to Yahweh, and, at the same time, to distinguish them from the Baal prophets, who probably bore the sign of their god.

[34] Lindblom, *Genom öknen till Sinai*, p. 115; Eisler in *Le monde oriental*, xxiii, 1929, pp. 48 ff. (esp. p. 80); Musil, op. cit., pp. 120 f.
[35] Eisler, op. cit., pp. 50 f.
[36] Cf. Ex. xiii. 16; Deut. vi. 8; xi. 18.

There is at least one passage in the Old Testament which indicates that the members of the prophetic guilds wore a tonsure on their heads. In 2 Kings ii. 23 f. we read the story of Elisha and the jeering boys. The boys shouted after him, 'Go up, you baldhead! Go up, you baldhead!' Legends do not make much of individual peculiarities of their heroes, such as baldness; they prefer to deal with more general features. This is true not least of Hebrew narrative style. If Elisha's baldness was a ritual tonsure, the mockery of the boys was directed at his character as a prophet. It is a well-known fact that in ancient Israel the prophets were, on occasion, despised as well as revered.

The shaving of the head by priests, monks, and other holy men is a usage found in many different parts of the world. We remember the ancient Egyptian priests, the priests of Isis in the Hellenistic age, the priests and hierodules of the Tyrian Melkart, the Buddhist monks, and the religious in the Roman Church. This usage depends originally on the conception of the significance of the hair which is current at a more primitive stage of civilization, not least in the Semitic world.

According to primitive thought the hair represents its owner more effectively than anything else, and is one of the parts of the human organism in which the life force is most concentrated. Many curious usages become intelligible once this is realized. Even in our times, this conception of the hair and the usages connected with it may be studied in Arabic-speaking countries, for instance in Morocco. Hair placed in a sanctuary or laid on a holy object brings power to the owner. Hair offered to a saint or a spirit confers benefits on him who offers it. Tufts of hair are used as magic means in order to coerce spirits and divinities. Hair cuttings are carefully hidden away lest evil-disposed men or spirits should get hold of them and thereby cause danger to the owner. Because hair is very susceptible to taboo infection, it must be shaved off in situations where dangers of a religious or magical character are thought to be present. This is done with newborn children and as a mourning rite when there is a corpse in the house. But hair may also be deposited on the grave to establish contact between the living and the dead.[37] Ideas and usages like these are well known in all parts of the world and every period of history.

Among holy men and women there are many examples of the custom that the hair must be allowed to grow long and hang loose, and also of the shaving of the hair. For the *nāzîr* in ancient Israel it was prescribed that no razor was to be used on his head as long as his vow to be a nazirite held. In modern Morocco a pilgrim is not allowed to have his

37 Westermarck, op. cit., *passim* (see index, s.v. 'Hair').

hair cut. It is unnecessary to adduce further examples. According to what has just been said about the significance of the hair, this usage can be explained in different ways. The idea of the importance of the integrity of man in a physical sense undoubtedly played a considerable part in this connection. On the other hand, the cutting of the hair, or a part of the hair at least, can be thought of as a sacrifice of something particularly valuable—hair offerings are well known from ancient Greece, Rome, Syria, Arabia, etc. Sacrifice of the hair as representing the whole man can quite simply be conceived of as a substitute for sacrifice of the owner himself or as an outward sign of his entire surrender to the deity. But many different motives may have been blended in the development of the usage in question.

In the light of these analogies from the history of religion it must be regarded as very probable that the early prophets really wore ritual tonsure. Of course, it is not necessary to assume that it was adopted by all prophets at all times. The emergence of the great prophets may have brought about many changes in the outward appearance, as well as in other things.

The early prophets were normally united in associations or guilds. They lived together in common dwelling-houses (which may be termed coenobia) and had their meals together.[38] The members of a prophetic guild were called *bᵉnê hannᵉbî'îm*. At their head was a leader who functioned as a sort of paterfamilias.[39] He played an important role and enjoyed great authority. He could have a special servant at his disposal (Elisha had a servant, Gehazi by name); but all the members of the association must obey him when he assigned them their tasks. In fact we often hear of prophets travelling on various errands in different parts of the country, far from the coenobium in which they normally lived. Sometimes they appeared in groups or bands, accompanied by music and raving in ecstasy. It seems that the leader had to train the members of the guild in ecstatic exercises and ecstatic practice and also instruct them in matters belonging to true Yahwistic religion and cult. The term used is that the members of the guild 'were sitting before' the leader (2 Kings iv. 38). We are told that when Saul's

---

[38] There is a lively description of life in a coenobium in 2 Kings iv. 38 ff.

[39] Possibly he was called 'father', *'āḇ* (cf. 2 Kings ii. 12), thus corresponding to the shaikh or *muḳaddam* of the dervishes and the *mḳaddem* of the religious fraternities in modern Morocco. (Westermarck, op. cit., I, pp. 183 ff.). In this connection also the title *mᵉḇakkēr* may be recalled, which occurs in the Damascus Document and in the Manual of Discipline from the Qumran cave. See for instance Rowley, *The Zadokite Fragments and the Dead Sea Scrolls*, pp. 36 f. Buber, *Hasidism*, p. 90, says that the zadik of the hasidic movement was surrounded by a ring of disciples, the real place of tradition, in which the imparting of the teaching from generation to generation took place.

messengers came to Ramah in order to take David, they saw a group of prophets prophesying in ecstasy with Samuel 'standing before them' as their conductor. Saul, too, was seized by the spirit and raved in ecstasy 'before Samuel' (1 Sam. xix. 20, 24).[40]

However, the organization seems to have been rather loose. We hear of prophets who were married and had families (2 Kings iv). An aged prophet lived in Bethel, in possession of his own house and in the midst of his family (1 Kings xiii). Another prophet, whose name was Ahijah, lived in Shiloh in his own house (xiv). It is clear that Elijah was in some way connected with the prophetic associations, but he worked in entire independence of them and is represented in tradition as one who went his own way and carried out his own tasks. This looseness of organization in the prophetic guilds, this liberty to follow one's own course must be kept in mind when we consider the later prophets and their manner of living.

The resemblance between the prophetic associations in ancient Israel and the dervish associations in the Islamic world has often been noted. As we have seen in the first chapter, the dervishes were also well organized; they lived together in coenobia and had their common meals. They were under the guidance of a shaikh who conducted religious exercises in order to evoke ecstasy. But there were also dervishes who had only a loose connection with the coenobia, were married, lived in their own houses, and did their own work. The analogy of the dervish associations supports the essential correctness of the Old Testament traditions concerning the manner of life of the early Hebrew prophets and helps us to a better understanding of the available records. Admittedly the narratives are to a large extent legendary. What is told of the prophets is often conventional or coloured by later tendencies, thoughts and ideas. There are also doublets in the narratives, for instance in those about Elijah and Elisha. But in its general features the tradition is trustworthy and in a high degree useful for the study not only of the early prophets, but also of the later stages of the development of Israelite prophecy.

The paramount task of the early prophets in Israelite society was to

---

[40] The opinion which has sometimes been advanced that *benê hannebî'îm* means that the prophetic associations consisted of the sons of prophetic fathers, and that, accordingly, the prophetic profession was hereditary, has no philological support. The Hebrew expression simply means that the person in question belonged to the category of prophets. Cf. the similar expressions *benê hārakkāhîm, benê hassōrepîm, benê 'elōhîm*, etc. The term *'ab* is a title of honour; 2 Kings vi. 21; xiii. 14; cf. viii. 9. That the prophetic profession may on occasion have passed from father to son is quite another matter. There is, however, no convincing evidence of this in the Old Testament.

deliver oracles. The special relationship to God which was characteristic of the prophets, their gift of ecstasy, and their position as men of God made them, in the eyes of their compatriots, qualified to receive revelations from God, words and messages from Yahweh. In every age the faculty of receiving revelations and of uttering true oracles has been one of the most conspicuous elements in the endowment of men and women of the prophetic type. It was because they possessed this faculty that the prophets of Israel were respected and sought after by their contemporaries. Men went to the prophet to 'inquire (*dāraš*) of Yahweh' or to 'inquire for the word of Yahweh',[41] or to 'seek a word from the prophet'.[42] Not only the common people, but also kings and queens, high officials and deputations of elders went to the prophets to obtain oracles.[43] In the older narratives we read of oracles being sought in various crises of individual or national life, e.g., to discover whether a patient will recover from an illness or to ascertain the result of a campaign. But oracles might be sought, and were in fact uttered, in any situation, provided that payment was made for the service rendered. When Jeroboam's wife went to the prophet Ahijah to ask him about the sickness of her son, she took with her ten loaves of bread, some cakes, and a jar of honey (1 Kings xiv. 3). When Ben-hadad, the king of Syria, had fallen ill, he sent Hazael to meet Elisha and inquire of God through him. So Hazael, it is told, went to meet the prophet and brought a present with him, all kinds of goods of Damascus, forty camel loads (2 Kings viii. 7 ff.). The present was an immense one; but it was a king of Syria who sent it, and, since the oracle of a prophet was conceived of as a powerful word, mighty in its efficacy, it was necessary to bring effective influence to bear on him.

The prophets did not only communicate oracles when asked for them; impelled by the divine influence which directed their actions they sometimes also did so unasked. The prophet Ahijah, the Shilonite, met Jeroboam on the road from Jerusalem, and as they were alone in the field, Ahijah took the mantle that he wore and tore it into twelve pieces. He then bade Jeroboam take ten pieces for himself and said, 'Thus says Yahweh, the God of Israel, "Behold, I am about to tear the kingdom from the hand of Solomon and will give you ten tribes; but he shall have one tribe for my servant David's sake"',' etc. (1 Kings xi. 29 ff.).[44] Another prophet, whose name was Shemaiah, addressed an

[41] 1 Kings xxii. 5, 8; 2 Kings i. 3, 6, 16; viii. 8; xxii. 13, 18.
[42] 1 Kings xiv. 5; xxii. 7.
[43] Gen. xxv. 22 f.; Josh. ix. 14; 1 Kings xiv. 1 ff.; xxii. 5 ff.; 2 Kings i. 2 ff.; iii. 11; vi. 32; viii. 8 ff., etc.
[44] For this passage see above, p. 52, note 8.

oracle to Rehoboam, the king of Judah, and his people in these words: 'Thus says Yahweh, "You shall not go up to fight against your brothers, the Israelites; return every man to his house for this thing is from me" ' (xii. 22 ff.). One day when King Jeroboam went up to the altar which he had made in Bethel to perform a sacrifice, a prophet from Judah came to Bethel and cried out against the altar saying, 'O altar, altar, thus says Yahweh, "Behold, a son shall be born to the house of David, Josiah by name, and upon you he shall sacrifice the priests of the high places who burn sacrifices upon you, and he shall burn men's bones on you" ' (xiii. 1 ff.). There are, of course, many legendary traits in narratives of this kind (in the last example the Deuteronomistic hand is evident); but notwithstanding this fact, such narratives show what was expected from the prophets in early times, and how the ancient narrators imagined the appearance and the activities of the prophets. In general we may take it that the picture is accurate.

Elijah did not wait to be asked for oracles; he appeared, as a rule, quite unexpectedly, on his own initiative, or rather by divine command, proclaiming what was given him from the Lord. The same is true of the anonymous prophet in 1 Kings xx. 35 ff., who waited for the king by the way, and, as the king was passing by, proclaimed his oracle to the king. 'A man of God' (a prophet) came to Eli and uttered an oracle of judgement (1 Sam. ii. 27 ff.).

It is characteristic of all men and women who belong to the prophetic type, wherever they appear all over the world, that they evoke different and contrary impressions among people who are witnesses of their activities. The dervishes in Islam are at the same time admired and despised. The shamans in Siberia are both venerated and feared. In Finland people listen eagerly to the sermons delivered by the trance-preachers; but at the same time they smile scornfully at their curious behaviour. Birgitta of Sweden was highly respected, praised, and honoured; but at the same time she inspired not only fear but also hatred in her own country as well as in Rome during her long stay in the papal city. This is not surprising. The words and actions of the prophets necessarily produce varying reactions in those who hear and witness them. We are all disposed to listen with pleasure to agreeable and encouraging words, but feel ill at ease when hearing something disagreeable or threatening. Most people feel disgust at, or contempt for, phenomena which seem alien, odd, and shocking. But when men believe in the effective power of words uttered and actions done, they will be still more offended by what appears to them to be ill-omened and dangerous, or pleased by what is thought to bring good fortune and success.

The prophets were regarded as 'men of God'; they lived in the presence of God and experienced the divine power. They had about them an air of sanctity, something of what Rudolf Otto calls *numinosum fascinosum et tremendum*. Men were moved to awe and wonder by what they said and did under divine influence. The narrator of the translation of Elijah in 2 Kings ii shows a fine sense of the numinous character of this event. Elijah and Elisha went down to Bethel. Then the members of the prophetic association at Bethel came out to Elisha and said to him, 'Do you know that today Yahweh is about to take away your master?' Elisha answered, 'Yes; I know; keep silence.' Hugo Gressmann has given an admirable commentary on this passage: The hour of parting has come. The destiny of Elijah is to be fulfilled. Everybody knows what is about to happen; but nobody speaks about it openly because it is a divine secret which is concealed in their hearts, just as the monks on Mount Athos keep to themselves their visionary experiences. Scarcely a whisper is heard; there is a sense of awe like that which prevails in a room where someone is about to die.[45]

Even kings and princes paid the greatest respect to the prophets, seeing in them men who could influence profoundly both them and their peoples. When Hazael came to Elisha in Damascus, he said to him, 'Your son Ben-hadad, king of Syria, has sent me to you.' He calls Elisha 'my lord' and himself his 'servant' (2 Kings viii. 9, 12 f.). When Elisha was stricken by the illness of which he was to die, Joash, the king of Israel, went down to him, and wept over him saying, 'My father, my father! The chariots of Israel and its horsemen!' (xiii. 14). When Obadiah, who was a high official at Ahab's court, met Elijah, he fell on his face and said, 'Is it you, my lord Elijah?' (1 Kings xviii. 7). A commander of the Israelite army fell on his knees before Elijah and said to him, 'O man of God, I pray you, let my life, and the lives of these fifty servants of yours, be precious in your sight' (2 Kings i. 13).

But the prophets were also feared because of their ability to see even what people had thought and done in secret. The widow of Zarephath feared the presence of Elijah when her son fell ill. 'What have I to do with you', she said, 'O man of God? You have come to me to make my iniquity known and to kill my son!' (1 Kings xvii. 17 f.). The mere appearance of Samuel filled the elders of Bethlehem with fear (1 Sam. xvi. 4). Ahab persecuted Elijah because he feared him as one who brought distress on Israel and rebuked the king for his trespasses; and he hated him as his worst enemy. Micaiah was put in prison and fed with bread and water because he had foretold the defeat of Israel and the death of Ahab

[45] *SATA²*, II, 1, p. 284.

at Ramoth-gilead (2 Kings xxii. 27). As bearers of the powerful words of Yahweh the prophets were always regarded as dangerous persons.

The external appearance of the prophets, their general behaviour, their abnormal, uncontrolled manner of speaking often made an unfavourable impression on bystanders. A prophet came to Jehu in the camp at Ramoth-gilead in order to anoint him king over Israel. When Jehu came out the officers said to him, 'Why did this mad fellow come to you?' Jehu answered, 'You know the fellow and his talk.' There is contempt in the officers' question as well as in Jehu's answer (2 Kings ix. 11). The proverbial expression, 'Is Saul also among the prophets?' (1 Sam. x. 11 f.) implies that behaviour like that of the prophets was beneath a man of good family. The question uttered by one of those who witnessed Saul's behaviour in the midst of the raving prophets ('and who is their father?') suggests that the prophets were despised as of lowly and obscure origin.

There is no doubt that the early prophets played an important role in the religious life of their people. They were 'prophets of Yahweh,' in contrast to the prophets of the Baal, and wore the sign of Yahweh on their foreheads. As we shall see later on, they took an active part in the Yahweh cult. In crucial times, when the genuine Yahweh religion was menaced by foreign cults, for instance in the time of Ahab and Jezebel, the prophets of Yahweh were even more prominent as defenders of Yahweh, the God of Israel, against Baal, the Phoenician god. This applies first and foremost to Elijah, the outstanding figure among the early prophets. The old records tell us that Elijah rebuked Ahab to his face because he had forsaken the commands of Yahweh and had gone after the Baal (1 Kings xviii. 18). He repaired the altar of Yahweh on Mount Carmel, which had been torn down, and re-established the Yahweh cult on this mountain, which had belonged alternately to Israel and to the kingdom of Tyre. The legendary narrative in 1 Kings xviii preserves the memory of his success in his fight for Yahweh in this region.[46] There can be little doubt that what is true of Elijah is true in a less degree of the other Yahweh prophets, too. That the prophets appeared at times as defenders of the old social order and the traditional moral standards is evident from the well-known narrative of Naboth's vineyard (1 Kings xxi).

There are many indications that the early prophets also intervened in politics. Visionaries and ecstatics of the prophetic type have always been exploited by kings, chieftains, and other political leaders to serve

---

[46] For this question see Alt, 'Das Gottesurteil auf dem Karmel' in *Kleine Schriften*, II, pp. 135 ff., and *Der Stadtstaat Samaria*; Galling, 'Der Gott Karmel und die Ächtung der fremden Götter' in the *Alt Festschrift*; Eissfeldt, *Der Gott Karmel*.

their interests. We have seen above (Chapter One) that dervishes of the Bektashi order played a conspicuous part in the Ottoman army. The advice of outstanding shaikhs was eagerly sought by the sultans. The same is said of the kahins in Arabia. They were often used as leaders of campaigns against hostile tribes. A strong personality like Birgitta of Sweden, exercised or endeavoured to exercise, a great influence on public affairs in her own country, and also on the European politics of her time, and not least on the popes, cardinals, and bishops of the Roman Church and the political problems which confronted this church during the fourteenth century.

During a campaign which Jehoram of Israel and Jehoshaphat of Judah made against the Moabites, Elisha followed the army. When water was lacking, Elisha in ecstasy pointed out where water was to be found, and thus he supplied water for the army and the livestock that followed it (2 Kings iii). In the same manner many kahins brought success to leaders of raids in the Arabian deserts. Before beginning the campaign against Ramoth-gilead the kings Ahab and Jehoshaphat asked the prophets for an oracle to know whether they should go to war or not (1 Kings xxii). After the separation of the northern tribes from Judah, a prophet, whose name was Shemaiah, received a revelation and proclaimed an oracle in these words: 'Thus says Yahweh, "You shall not go up to fight against your brothers, the Israelites; return every man to his house"' (xii. 24). Elisha seems to have been one of the driving forces in Jehu's revolution. By order of Elisha a prophet anointed Jehu the commander-in-chief of the Israelite army, to be king instead of Jehoram (2 Kings ix). By means of a magic rite the dying Elisha secured for King Joash victory over the Syrians (xiii). An anonymous prophet gave Ahab good advice during the war against the Syrians (1 Kings xx). The role played by an Israelite prophet in connection with the succession to the throne in Damascus (1 Kings xix. 15; 2 Kings viii. 7 ff.), though legendary, is a good example of the functions attributed to a prophet in the early period.

Being a sovereign ruler over all his subjects, the king had command over the prophets too. The king could summon them in order to consult them and ask them for oracles. Before the beginning of the campaign against Ramoth-gilead King Ahab assembled the prophets and asked them whether he should go to battle against the Syrians or forbear. To be quite sure the king also commanded Micaiah, the son of Imlah, to appear before him and prophesy.

But we read also of prophets who had a more permanent relationship to the king and seem to have belonged to his ordinary staff; we may call them 'court prophets'. In the history of King David two such court prophets are mentioned: Gad and Nathan. Gad is expressly called 'David's seer'; he was then bound to the king in a particular manner (2 Sam. xxiv. 11; 1 Chron. xxi. 9; 2 Chron. xxix. 25). Gad is also called *nābî'* (1 Sam. xxii. 5), and in 2 Sam. xxiv. 11 we meet the complete title 'Gad, the prophet, David's seer'. It seems as if 'seer' (*hōzêh*) in this connection was a title belonging to a public functionary at the royal court. That this functionary was also called 'nabi' means that David had taken his 'seer' from the circle of the nabis of his time. To call Gad 'David's prophet' would have been impossible. At the time when the author of the Deuteronomistic historical work wrote down the old traditions the difference between the terms 'prophet' and 'seer' was effaced. In 2 Kings xvii. 13 the prophets and seers are taken together as one homogeneous group, at the end of the same verse summarily labelled as 'prophets'. To the problem of the seers I shall return later on.

Nathan is regularly called 'nabi', and his position in David's entourage clearly shows that he was a public functionary and a court prophet as well as Gad. He is mentioned together with Zadok, the priest, and Benaiah, one of the commanders-in-chief, and men of the body-guard of the king (1 Kings i. 8, 10). In the struggle in connection with the succession to the throne he played an outstanding part and was present at the ritual enthronement of Solomon (1 Kings i). In the tragic story of David and Bathsheba he appeared before the king as a zealous champion of righteousness and traditional moral standards like Elijah in the story of Ahab and Naboth's vineyard.

Being a prophet at David's court Nathan played a part in matters connected with the cult at the palace. In 2 Sam. vii it is expressly said that he played an outstanding part as David's counsellor when the king was planning to build a temple for the Yahweh cult in Jerusalem. The historicity of this chapter has been strongly contested by Mowinckel. This scholar regards the narrative as a theological-aetiological legend, devised to account for the fact that David did not build any temple for Yahweh. According to Mowinckel the chapter contains a late tradition presupposing the existence of the temple of Solomon and embodying the ideas of the New Year festival.[47] Other scholars, e.g., Martin Noth, defend the historicity of the chapter in all essentials.[48]

[47] See *SEÅ*, xii, 1947, pp. 220 ff.; *He That Cometh*, pp. 100 f.; Widengren, *Sakrales Königtum im Alten Testament und im Judentum*, pp. 59 ff. Cf. also Kraus, *Die Königsherrschaft Gottes im Alten Testament*, pp. 35 ff.

[48] Noth, *Überlieferungsgeschichtliche Studien*, I, pp. 64 f.; *History of Israel*, pp. 220, 224, 194; *Gesammelte Studien zum Alten Testament, passim;* see 'Register der Bibelstellen'. Cf. also Herrmann, 'Die Königsnovelle in Ägypten und in Israel', and, earlier, Rost, *Die Überlieferung von der Thronnachfolge Davids.*

The chapter tells in fact of two different interventions by Nathan. First we have an oracle referring to the building of a temple, secondly the prediction of the continuance of David's dynasty. The two parts of the narrative in its present literary form are linked together by means of the 'house' motif. Yahweh will not have a house, but He will make David a house; the kingdom of David will be established before Yahweh for ever.

What is said about Solomon, his building of a temple, and his personal life bears the impress of a *vaticinium ex eventu*. The prediction concerning the continuance of the Davidic dynasty seems to be based on a liturgical formula associated with the ritual celebration of the kingdom of David. But what is said about the building of a temple planned by David and the part played by Nathan in this connection may very well be an authentic historical record. David had built a palace for himself (2 Sam. v. 11). Nothing could be more natural than that he should also wish to build a temple for Yahweh, who till now had had to rest content with a simple tent for His ark, and that he should consult his court prophet Nathan about the matter. In the ancient Orient no temple was built without the assent of a divine oracle delivered by a priest or a prophet. It is very interesting to observe that it is said that Nathan at first approved the plan, but after a special revelation felt himself obliged to reject it. There are many examples of the fact that prophets have had to alter their own opinion as a result of a more distinct revelation from the deity.

According to tradition Gad was already in attendance on David when he was an outlaw and gave good advice in critical situations (1 Sam. xxii. 5). Later he was David's prophetic counsellor during his reign, as we are told in 2 Sam. xxiv. The building of the altar to Yahweh on the top of the hill of Zion came about as a consequence of an oracle communicated by Gad in his capacity as David's court prophet. This notice also shows the importance of the early prophets for the cult. Like Nathan, Gad also gave the king moral guidance (xxiv. 11 ff.).

In two passages we are told that the extension of David's kingdom to include the northern tribes was foretold by a prophetic oracle: 2 Sam. iii. 9 f. and v. 2. No such oracle is to be found in the historical narratives; but, in the view of the present writer, we have this oracle in the prophecy concerning Judah in the so-called 'Blessing of Jacob' in Gen. xlix: 'The sceptre shall not depart from Judah, nor the commander's staff from between his feet until he comes to Shiloh' etc. (*v.* 10).[49]

[49] For the following cf. Lindblom in *SVT*, I, 1953, pp. 78 ff., and the critical remarks by Eissfeldt in *SVT*, IV, 1957, pp. 138 ff.

'The Blessing of Jacob' is a specimen of a literary type which we may call 'the tribal poem'. Here we have to do with a mixed composition. Epigrams of a more popular nature, with a stamp of folk-lore, and prophetic oracles about the different Israelite tribes alternate with one another. The poet formulates a series of oracles, but he adds numbers of epigrams, taken, no doubt, from popular epigrammatic poetry. The typical oracles prove that the poem is the work of a prophet. An analysis of the different sayings makes it clear that the poem is a mixture of predictions and descriptions of historical facts, and that as a whole it presupposes a certain historical situation. Two of the Israelite tribes play a prominent role in the poem: Judah and Joseph. The tribe of Judah is the seat of a kingdom. The king of Judah is promised hegemony over the other Israelite tribes. In addition an empire including foreign nations is predicted for him. Joseph is praised for valour and staying power in battle. He is in possession of old and venerable cult centres, and thus enjoys a religious superiority, but there is no mention at all of a kingdom in his territory.

The historical situation which is evident in these sayings corresponds admirably to the situation during the seven years and six months when David was king in Judah and resided in Hebron. The main object of the poem was, it seems to me, to foretell to David that his kingdom would not be limited to the tribe of Judah, but would also include the northern tribes. Shiloh must then be regarded as a representative of these northern tribes. Shiloh was in fact one of the oldest and most important places in the territory of Ephraim. Above all it was a central cultic site and even after its destruction was rich in historical associations and sacred memories.

Apparently one of King David's court prophets at Hebron composed the so-called 'Blessing of Jacob', foretelling a great future for David and his kingdom, and at the same time aiming at gaining for David the sympathy of the proud northern tribes.

One of the most debated problems concerning Israelite prophecy is that of the relation of the prophets to the sanctuaries and the cult which was performed at them.

Since the pioneering researches of Mowinckel in the third volume of his *Psalmenstudien: Kultprophetie und prophetische Psalmen* (1923), the discussion has continued. Mowinckel himself drew our attention to the prophetic oracles and other prophetic utterances in the Psalms. From the frequent occurrence of such prophetic sayings in liturgical texts Mowinckel concluded that prophets were a normal part of the permanent staff of the Jerusalem temple at least. This connection of the prophets with the cult originated, according to Mowinckel, in circumstances which already prevailed in the earliest phase of prophecy. Of the early prophets Mowinckel says that they formed free associations, but with an intimate connection with the cult.[50] Professor Aubrey Johnson follows in Mowinckel's footsteps. He, too, emphasizes the connection of the prophets with the cult and contends that such a connection may be traced from the very beginning. Like the prophets of Baal the Israelite prophets were, according to Johnson, certainly not to be regarded as individuals working independently; they were, as the phrase goes, associated 'either permanently or temporarily' with different sanctuaries throughout the country.[51]

Johnson occupies an intermediate position between Mowinckel and the Swedish scholar Alfred Haldar, who lays still more stress upon the cultic character of the prophets. They belonged, Haldar maintains, just like the Mesopotamian prophets, to the cult associations and performed their functions in the cult. The nabi, he says, was a cult functionary in the strict sense of the term.[52]

Obviously this question calls for further examination.

There can be no doubt that there were intimate connections between the early prophets and the cult. The band of prophets whom Saul met had just come down from the bāmâh, the place of worship (1 Sam. x. 5). Here they had obviously exercised certain cultic functions. In 1 Sam. i-iv.1a Samuel is described as priest and prophet in one person. He was educated in the sanctuary of Shiloh, and it is said that he was ministering, $m^e\check{s}\bar{a}r\bar{e}t$, in the service of Yahweh 'before' Eli, i.e., under the supervision of Eli, the chief priest (1 Sam. iii. 1). But at the same time Samuel is explicitly called a prophet of Yahweh, since Yahweh revealed Himself to him in Shiloh (iii. 20 f.). Whether or not the account which the sources give of Samuel is historical, the combination of priest and prophet in one person was felt by the narrators to be quite normal and appropriate. Elijah re-established the Yahweh altar on Mount Carmel which had been destroyed in favour of the Phoenician cult of the god of Mount Carmel.[53] Later on we meet Elisha on Carmel, certainly functioning at the restored sanctuary (2 Kings iv. 25). We find prophets living on places well known as ancient cult centres: Samaria, Bethel, Gilgal, Jericho, Ramah. The Shunammite woman set

[50] Cf. Mowinckel, *Offersang og sangoffer*, pp. 308 ff. Eng. transl., *The Psalms in Israel's Worship*, Ch. xii.
[51] Johnson, *The Cultic Prophet in Ancient Israel*.
[52] Haldar, *Associations of Cult Prophets*. For this question see also Rowley in *JSS*, i, 1956, pp. 338 ff., with many references to the literature of the subject.
[53] See above, p. 74.

out to seek the prophet Elisha at the sanctuary on Mount Carmel. Her husband raised objections since it was neither new moon nor sabbath. On festival days the prophets were to be found at the sanctuaries performing their cultic duties. At other times they were travelling throughout the country.

As we have seen above, the court prophets were, as such, also engaged in the cult, because the king himself was responsible for the official cult and took part in cultic acts. As a prophet attached to David's court, Nathan was consulted when the king intended to build a temple for Yahweh in Jerusalem. Gad commanded David in the name of the Lord to rear an altar to Yahweh on the threshing-floor of Araunah. Nathan took an active part in the cultic ceremonies which were connected with the enthronement of Solomon. According to 2 Chron. xxxv. 15 (admittedly a late passage), prophets were responsible for the organization of certain levitical duties in the temple.

Mowinckel has shown that in later times members of the Levite class appeared as prophets, and that, in particular, the temple singers were often endowed with prophetic gifts. As a result of the penetrating researches of this scholar there can be little doubt that prophets belonged to the permanent staff of the Jerusalem temple. It is to these prophets that we owe the prophetic psalms in the Psalter, the prophetic oracles which are included in many of them, and also the psalms which are contained in the prophetic books (e.g., Hab. iii). It is possible that several of these psalms belong to the post-exilic period, but most of them are doubtless from the earlier period. The statement in Ps. lx. 8 (cviii. 8): 'God has spoken in his sanctuary,' is not an empty phrase but a simple statement of fact. What God has spoken is without doubt an oracle delivered by a temple prophet.[54]

However, from several passages in the old narratives we get the impression that the prophets were not always bound to the sanctuaries and the cult, but lived their own life apart from the sacred places. The aged prophet in Bethel who is mentioned in 1 Kings xiii had a house of his own, to which he invited the wandering prophet from Judah. The prophet Ahijah lived at Shiloh in his private house (xiv). The same is true of the prophet whose widow, being in a precarious situation, was helped by Elisha (2 Kings iv). As we have seen above, Elijah sometimes exercised typical cultic functions; but for the most part he wandered from place to place performing activities which had nothing to do with the cult. What we do know is that the prophets often lived

[54] Prophetic voices are directly or indirectly heard in Psalms such as ii, vi, xii, xx, xxi, xxxi, xlv, l. lx, lxxii, lxxv, lxxxi, lxxxii, lxxxv, lxxxvii, lxxxix, xci, xcv, cviii, cx.

together in monasteries or coenobia just like the Arabian dervishes in their *takiyyah*. There they had their common meals and were trained in ecstatic practices under the direction of an especially gifted ecstatic leader.

Scholars who have discussed the question of the relation of the early prophets to the sanctuaries have often used very general expressions which convey little. Hölscher, for instance, contents himself with the statement that besides the priests the prophets belonged to the cultic staff of the sanctuaries 'in a certain sense'.[55] It is necessary to make clear what belonging to the ordinary cultic staff really implied. There can be little doubt that people who belonged to the ordinary staff had their maintenance from the sanctuary to which they were attached. They got their food from the sacrifices, and at the larger sanctuaries at least there were also lodgings at their disposal.

Persons who belonged to the royal court are said to be allowed to eat bread at the king's table. This was for instance the privilege of Meribbaal, Jonathan's son (2 Sam. ix. 7; xix. 28), the sons of Barzillai the Gileadite (1 Kings ii. 7), Jehoiachin at the court of the Babylonian king Evil-merodach (2 Kings xxv. 29), and Daniel and his friends at the court of Nebuchadnezzar (Dan. i).[56] We are told that a group of prophets of the Phoenician Baal and the Asherah ate at Jezebel's table (1 Kings xviii. 19). Priests and Levites had their maintenance from the sacrifices and the offerings brought by the people to the sanctuary. Also, according to the Deuteronomic law, the priests from the high places were to have an equal share with the other priests (Deut. xviii. 6 ff.). It was at all times a general rule that persons who performed tasks in the sanctuary had their maintenance from the sanctuary.[56a] The Apostle Paul asks the Corinthians, 'Do you not know that those who are employed in the temple service get their food from the temple?' (1 Cor. ix. 13). Amaziah, the priest of Bethel, saw in Amos a cult prophet of the ordinary type and treated him as such. When he told Amos to go away to the land of Judah and there eat bread, i.e., there earn his living, by prophesying, the meaning of his words was that Amos should attach himself to any sanctuary in Judah and there get his maintenance (Am. vii. 12).

If the early prophets in Israel 'belonged to the cultic staff' at different sanctuaries, this would have implied that they, like the priests, had their

---

[55] Hölscher, *Die Profeten*, p. 143.

[56] The phrase 'use the salt of the palace' in Ezr. iv. 14 is to be taken in a symbolic sense as expressing loyalty to and friendly feelings towards the king and his government (cf. Rudolph in *HAT*). Originally it no doubt had a more realistic import.

[56a] About the term *millū'îm* as an expression for the maintenance of the priests see Noth, *Amt und Berufung im Alten Testament*, p. 8.

maintenance from the sanctuary where they worked. We have, however, seen above that this was by no means always the case. The picture of the life of the early prophets given in the old narratives is incontestably not homogeneous. There are different types and classes of them.

A thorough investigation of the traditions shows that a typical feature of the early prophetic movement was the common life in the coenobia. Their chief business was engaging in ecstatic exercises and delivering oracles in a state of inspired exaltation. No doubt they lived on the gifts which they received in return for the oracles they gave.

As we have seen, the prophets were consulted as ecstatic oracle-givers not only by common people but by kings and high officials. Some of them were even firmly attached to the royal court; they 'ate at the king's table', that is to say, they were maintained as part of the royal household.

It may, further, be taken as certain that some prophets were part of the cultic staff at the sanctuaries and were maintained by them like the sacrificial priests and other cultic functionaries. We know that this was so in the temple at Jerusalem. Why should not the same practice have been followed at other cult centres?[57]

Not all of the prophets belonged to associations, either coenobitic or cultic. Besides the organized prophets and the court prophets there were also prophets who lived a life of their own. They had their own houses and lived in the midst of their families. Examples of such private prophets have been cited above. We call them 'free prophets'.

Finally, there existed prophetic personalities who at times belonged to some association and at other times lived as free prophets. Samuel is a good example. He is also represented as a priest, a fact which proves that there was no definite dividing-line between priests and nabis. Priestly and prophetic qualities could very well be combined in the same person.

Prophets who were not professionally attached to the different sanctuaries had, notwithstanding, a more or less intimate connection with

[57] Jepsen, *Nabi*, pp. 159 ff., holds that there was an essential difference between prophecy in the Northern Kingdom and in Judah. He is right in pointing out that there is no mention in the sources of court prophets in the strict sense in Northern Israel; but the argument from silence is not cogent here. After the division of the kingdom we hear nothing of court prophets in Jerusalem either; but this does not prove that they had ceased to exist. The earliest traditions make it clear that there was an intimate connection between the prophets and the cult in Northern Israel. Recent study of the relation between prophets and priests shows that it is wrong to make as sharp a distinction as Jepsen does. His thesis that the prophets in Northern Israel were exclusively coenobitic prophets, as we have called them, is not convincing. In my view such passages as Hos. iv. 5; ix. 8; Am. vii. 10 ff. make it evident that there was a connection between prophets and priests, ecstatics and cultic life, in Northern Israel, as there was in Judah.

the cultic life of their people. They often appeared at the sanctuaries and conferred on the cultic acts a particular sanctity and power. The ecstatic frenzy was regarded as a proof of the active presence of the divinity. We may take it that in some circumstances they even performed priestly functions. Through their presence the religious enthusiasm of the cultic assembly was mightily increased. But attendance at the cultic ceremonies was of great importance for the prophets themselves. The sacrificial rites, the music, the cultic cries, the religious excitement of the crowd, all helped to evoke and stimulate the ecstatic state.

Accordingly, there were in ancient times different, but not necessarily mutually exclusive, groups of prophets: coenobitic prophets, court prophets, sanctuary prophets, free prophets, and prophets of a mixed type. That this was so was owing to the fact that the ecstatic disposition and the ability to deliver oracles were the constitutive elements in the prophetic endowment. This endowment could of course be utilized for different purposes and in different connections and positions.

This is the picture that tradition gives us of the social life of the early prophets in Israel. It seems sounder to base our reconstruction on notices which are preserved to us in the Old Testament than quite simply to apply evidence from Mesopotamia to Israel, where the development was in many respects on different lines.

3. Seers and Prophets. The Figures of Samuel and Balaam

Throughout the world there are men and women who maintain that they know secret things, hidden from common people, and are regarded by other people as being possessed of the gift of divination and soothsaying. Their special ability is essentially based on a supernormal perspicacity (or far-seeing), external signs and omens, dreams, and trances.

In a Swedish parish (Åsele) in the south of West Bothnian Lapland there is a tradition which runs:

People had assembled at a farm to receive the judge, for there was to be a 'thing'. It was winter and blowing up for a whirling snow-storm, so that the roads were being snowed up. The judge therefore was later than expected, and they were growing impatient, wondering why he did not turn up. In the cottage by the fire-side sat an old Lapp. People knew that he was a diviner, and a man said to him, 'You may as well try and find out where the judge is.' After much begging and praying, the Lapp promised to make an attempt. But he wanted to be alone, and no one was to disturb him. He went into the back-room. As he stayed there for quite a long time, someone peeped in through the door-chink. He then saw the Lapp lying on the bed, looking like one dead. After a while he came out, looking very tired, and merely said, 'He will be here in two hours.' Exactly two hours later the judge arrived, took off his fur coat, and greeted those present. But when he saw the Lapp, he was greatly astonished. 'How did you come here?' he said. 'We met you two hours ago on the Great Swamp and asked you about the way, didn't we?'[58]

Alois Musil in his above-mentioned book on the manners and customs of the Rwala bedouin tells us about men and women who in ways which are often inexplicable are able to tell of hidden things of the past, the present, or the future. They sometimes utilize exterior means, for instance, the position of objects cast about at random. Such a soothsayer is supposed to be able to inform people concerning a strayed camel or a lost boy. He always receives a reward, great or small, for the service done. Musil relates some very curious stories about such soothsayers and their successes.[59]

Westermarck in his great work about the life of the Berbers and Arabs in Morocco has much to tell concerning divination and soothsaying in these regions.[60] There people are very anxious to attain information in mysterious ways concerning matters they do not know, but they are eager to find out. Since the spirits are regarded as all-knowing, it is to them primarily that people address themselves to obtain the knowledge wanted. Thus the inquirers get to know for instance whether an absent friend is dead, or whether he lives and is in good health. By means of certain ceremonies they force the spirits to ascertain what will happen in the future to themselves, whether a sick person will recover, etc., but also where buried treasure is to be found. Divination by sacrificial animals plays a great role in Morocco. The movements and the general behaviour of the sacrificial animals are carefully observed. People read their fortune in the sacrificial blood and the intestines of a slaughtered animal. In various ways the slaughtered animal is supposed to tell whether the year will be good or bad, whether there will be rain or drought, etc. Dreams are also supposed to bring real information. The Berbers believe that during sleep the soul is

---

[58] This story, which for a long time was transmitted orally, was written down by my colleague E. Arbman, Professor of the History of Religion in Stockholm. It is now reproduced in print by Professor Arbman in: Å. Hultcrantz, *Primitiv religion och magi.*
[59] Musil, op. cit., pp. 404 ff.
[60] Westermarck, op. cit., I, pp. 148 ff., 158 ff.; see further Index, s.vv. 'Divination', 'Dreams'.

absent from the body; what has been seen in a dream is a reality and not an illusion. But, above all, there are men and women who are supposed to be in possession of the gift of divination in a particular degree and to be able to tell what is happening in distant places. It is believed that they are capable of seeing behind as well as ahead; they can see the whole world as though it were laid out on the palm of their hand. They are able to predict future events and to give advice to those who consult them. To these men and women is ascribed a super-natural force, *baraka*, in abundant measure, which renders them capable of practising the profession of a 'seer'. A famous seer is often invited even from far countries. It is taken for granted that a seer obtains a reward for the service done, a sum of money or something else.

It is a well-known fact that the 'seer', *bārū*, played an important role in ancient Mesopotamia. The verb *bārū* means 'to see', 'to behold'. Accordingly the *bārū* is a man who has the power of seeing in a special sense; thus the notion *bārū* nearly corresponds to the Hebrew *rō'êh*. Our knowledge of the character and activities of the Mesopotamian seers has been augmented by much useful research on the subject carried out during the past half-century.[61] Obviously the Sumero-Accadian seers were intimately connected with the temple cult. They formed a particular class amongst the temple priests, and they may quite correctly be called '*bārū* priests'.

The chief function of the *bārū* priests was to communicate knowledge concerning the future. Since that which is going to happen in the future is hidden from common men, the seers are thought to be able to reveal secrets. As future events depend on the will of the gods, the seers are regarded as discoverers of the will of the gods, and what they have to tell is called answers, messages, or oracles of the gods. But the 'seeing' of the *bārū* priests was not confined to future events, they possessed generally 'the secret knowledge of heaven and earth'. The means used by the *bārū* priests were primarily of a technical nature, consisting in observation of oil and water in a cup, the way in which objects fall when thrown, the entrails of sacrificial animals, celestial phenomena, the movements of animals, the flight of birds, etc. Dreams were also regarded as revealing secrets and were interpreted by seers. A divine revelation given to the seer by such means is sometimes called 'the word of God'. The deity speaks to the diviner, and thus the diviner becomes a mediator between God and man. The seer's task is to inquire for divine answers. His questioning of the deity is expressed by the verb *ša'ālu*,

---

[61] See for instance Guillaume, *Prophecy and Divination*, and Haldar, *Associations of Cult Prophets*. The latter book in particular is abundant in literary references.

ask. Even though the methods of the *bārū* priests were for the most part of a more technical nature, they could on occasion receive the divine answer by intuitive knowledge without the aid of external omens, even in a state of trance. Scholars have rightly emphasized that the distinction between *bārū* priests and ecstatics was not so great that the one could not perform the functions of the other. To summarize: the Sumero-Accadian 'seer' had the power to impart secret knowledge. His methods were essentially technical, but occasionally he received his visions in a trance or in dreams. It seems likely that the Mesopotamian seers were generally attached to the cult and formed a special class within the temple staff.

An interesting passage in the book of Ezekiel gives us a vivid picture of the practice of divination: the king of Babylon stands at the fork of two roads using methods of divination: he shakes the arrows, he consults the teraphim, he inspects the liver (xxi. 26). Here we meet with three significant terms: *ḳesem*, divination, *šā'al*, inquire, consult, and *rā'âh*, see, inspect. During his sojourn in Babylonia the Second Isaiah witnessed the arts of the Babylonian *bārū* priests. With scorn he addresses the inhabitants of Babylon: 'You have wearied yourself with your many counsellors; now let them stand up and save you' (Isa. xlvii. 13).

Also from the West-Semitic area we have some traces of the existence of 'seers'. In the well-known inscription of King Zakir of Hamath, the king tells us that in a critical situation he had received a divine answer through 'seers': 'Be'elshamayn spoke to me through seers and through diviners.'[62] In the Ras Shamrah texts there are references to dream oracles and to divination by the flight of birds.[63]

Among the pre-Islamic Arabs the kahins, whom we have described above as belonging to the prophetic type, showed many traces which remind us of the typical 'seers'. They were also expressly called 'seers'. When engaged in 'seeing' they covered themselves with a veil. They acted as interpreters of dreams and finders of camels and other lost objects. They were consulted about various enterprises, particularly before the beginning of raids and wars, and were believed to be able to detect criminals. For these services they accepted rewards, great or small. Famous kahins were sent for from foreign countries. The kahin had—as we have seen—several of the typical marks of the prophet. Thus in the kahin 'seer' and 'prophet' were united in the same person. There is clear evidence that they occasionally exercised priestly functions and

[62] *ANET²*, p. 501.
[63] Haldar, op. cit., pp. 79 ff.

belonged to the temple staff. The Arabian kahin was seer, prophet, priest, and even judge in the same person.[64]

In the Old Testament diviners of various kinds are often mentioned, who obviously belong to the 'seer' class described above, but were mostly regarded as illegitimate from the point of view of the Yahweh religion. Terms used for such diviners are *ḥōzêh, yidde'ōnî, ḳōsēm, me'naḥēš, me'ônēn, môrêh*. The etymology of these words is in several cases rather obscure; but *yidde'ōnî* seems to signify one who knows secrets; *môrêh*, one who gives directions or oracles; *ḥōzêh* is, of course, one who sees or finds out hidden things (in Mic. iii. 7 *ḥōzîm* stands parallel to *ḳōs'mîm*, diviners).

There are a few indications of the methods used by the diviners. From 1 Sam. xxviii and Isa. viii. 19 we may conclude that some of them were believed to be able to bring up dead men from Sheol or to be mouthpieces of the ghosts, pronouncing their oracles and counsels in a chirping and gibbering tone. Divination from the movements and sounds of trees is possibly presupposed in the name Elon-meonenim (Judges ix. 37). An instance of a legitimate tree oracle is described in 1 Sam. v. 24, which resembles the pagan divinatory methods. The practices described in Ezek. xxi. 26 are mentioned above: arrows shaken, teraphim consulted, liver inspected. Of Joseph it is said that he understood how to obtain cup oracles (Gen. xliv. 5, 15). Such cup oracles are common everywhere. Dreams also played an important role among the practices of the diviners, as can be seen from Jer. xxvii. 9; xxix. 8; Zech. x. 2, etc.

The Old Testament authors regard these diviners in general as belonging to a foreign and pagan world. They were to be found among the Philistines (1 Sam. vi. 2; Isa. ii. 6), in Babylonia (Isa. xliv. 25; Ezek. xxi. 26), in Egypt (Isa. xix. 3). But first and foremost such diviners were characteristic of the paganism of the Canaanites. Divination was one of the practices because of which the pre-Israelite inhabitants of Palestine were conquered (Deut. xviii. 9 ff.). Being intimately connected with the pagan culture of Canaan and the religion of the Baal, the diviners were detested and condemned by the religious leaders of Israel, as can be seen, for instance, in the laws of the books of Leviticus and Deuteronomy. A true Israelite was forbidden to resort to them and consult them. To have something to do with them was regarded as apostasy. He who ran after them defiled himself; Yahweh would cut off such a person from His people. The diviner through whom a ghost was believed to speak must be stoned. It is recorded that Josiah

---

[64] See above all Wellhausen, *Reste arabischen Heidentums*[2], pp. 134 ff.

put away all the diviners from the land of Israel (2 Kings xxiii. 24). During the reign of Manasseh diviners obtained an immense influence (xxi. 6). But even in the days of Isaiah they were an important factor in public life. This prophet mentions them along with guardsmen, soldiers, judges, prophets, and elders (Isa. iii. 2) 'Diviner' was even used as an abusive term (lvii. 3). In particular Jeremiah and Ezekiel treat false prophets and diviners alike. Sometimes they are even identified (Jer. xxvii. 9; xxix. 8; Ezek. xiii. 9, 23, etc.; Mic. iii. 6 f.). It is taken for granted that the diviners will be exterminated in the Messianic age (Mic. v. 11). The reason for the abhorrence of diviners was first and foremost their pagan origin and further the consciousness that a true Israelite should consult only Yahweh and listen to His words through the true prophets (Deut. xviii. 14 ff.).

However, Israelite tradition knows also of divination which was not opposed to the Yahweh religion. The ancient narrator has no objection to make against the fact that Joseph practised cup divination (Gen. xliv). During the war against the Philistines King David acted in accordance with a tree oracle (2 Sam. v). Such instances prove that certain forms of divination were occasionally felt as compatible with the Yahweh religion. In the latter case Yahweh Himself stood behind the message given by the foliage of the trees. When David had inquired of the Lord concerning the attack against the Philistines, Yahweh said, 'When you hear the sound of marching in the tops of the balsam trees, make haste, for at that moment Yahweh has gone forth before you to smite the camp of the Philistines.'

Such phenomena are evidence of the well-known fact that primitive religious usages are often adopted at higher levels of religion and combined with ideas of a more advanced kind. They are accepted as legitimate elements, and their lower origin is forgotten. We have already noted that even Yahwist prophets display on occasion traits derived from lower forms of divination (1 Kings xviii. 41 ff.; 2 Kings iii. 16; v. 26).

Divination by means of the Urim and Thummim was the affair of the priests proper. But the method in itself did not differ much from what is known of the usages of seers in various parts of the world.

I hope that the above is a fairly clear picture of what 'seeing' is in a religio-historical sense. The seer is a man who has the gift of seeing and revealing things hidden from common people, the chief media being second sight, dreams, and trances. But external methods of various kinds are also abundantly used.

Now the question arises whether there existed in Israel, besides the priests who used the Urim and Thummim, people who practised divination *professionally*, i.e., whether there existed 'seers' (in the religio-historical sense of the word) who were approved by true Yahweh believers.

The very word 'seer', *rō'êh*, is used of Samuel in 1 Sam. ix and 1 Chron. ix. 22; xxvi. 28; xxix. 29. In addition the priest Zadok is called 'seer' in 2 Sam. xv. 27. The text of this passage is uncertain, but it seems possible that Zadok is here called a 'seer' corresponding to the Accadian *bārū*, because he divined by means of the priestly oracle. Finally, a man whose name was Hanani is called 'seer' in 2 Chron. xvi. 7, 10. But there is nothing in what is told of him that recalls the appearance and the behaviour of a seer. Hanani's type is definitely prophetic, and 'seer' is here exactly synonymous with 'nabi' (cf. Isa. xxx. 10).

To understand the seer type in ancient Israel we must examine the narrative about Samuel. The chief source for our knowledge of Samuel as a seer is the old narrative in 1 Sam. ix. The first we hear of him is that he knew and could reveal secrets. Saul, the son of Kish, was in search of some asses which his father had lost. After a lengthy journey he called on Samuel, the seer, in order to get to know where the asses were. Further, we are told that he was a 'man of God', i.e., a man endowed with divine gifts; he was held in honour, and all that he spoke was sure to prove true. He was to be offered a quarter of a shekel as his fee for providing the required information about the lost asses. The men encountered the seer on the way to the high place, where the people were about to join in a sacrificial meal. Samuel was prepared for the encounter with Saul because on the previous day Yahweh had revealed to him that Saul would come. Now Samuel was told by Yahweh that Saul was the man of whose coming he had been informed. The seer told Saul that the asses had been found. He even knew that they had been lost three days previously. At the high place Samuel acted as cultic leader and blessed the sacrifice. Finally, at the command of Yahweh he anointed Saul king of Israel. In what follows there are further examples of Samuel's ability to foresee events. Later on we find the same Samuel presiding over an assembly of prophets as leader of their ecstatic exercises (ch. xix).

Leaving out of consideration the possibly or certainly fictional traits in the narrative of Samuel, it is clear that he is regarded as a man who was renowned for his supernormal ability to see and reveal secrets, and to foresee future events, and was also paid for his services. Being a holy man, a 'man of God', he was also employed to execute cultic acts, and was on occasion able to conduct the ecstatic exercises of the nabis. The description is that of an ordinary diviner of the seer type. Since the narrator was a true Yahweh believer, he naturally regarded the special gifts of the seer as depending on an exceptional endowment from Yahweh. We are not told *how* this seer obtained his mysterious knowledge; only that Yahweh had 'uncovered his ear' and 'answered' him, i.e., imparted to him what he saw and knew. In accordance with similar descriptions of the activities of the seers, we are justified in supposing that the narrator thought of dreams or a supernormal perception as the basis of the divine communications.

Another word used for a seer is *ḥōzêh*. The two words *rō'êh* and *ḥōzêh* are synonyms. It is impossible to establish any distinction in meaning between them. Perhaps there existed a dialectal difference. But about this we know nothing with certainty. The prophet Gad is called King David's *ḥōzêh* (2 Sam. xxiv. 11); but what is told of Gad indicates that he is rather conceived of as a 'nabi' than a 'seer'. It seems to me that *ḥōzêh* in this connection is used as an old-fashioned title to mark Gad's position at the court of David. It was, of course, impossible to call him 'David's nabi' (cf. 1 Chron. xxv. 5). In accordance with a later mode of expression, *ḥōzêh* is often used as equivalent to nabi (2 Kings xvii. 13; Isa. xxix. 10; xxx. 10; Am. vii. 12; Mic. iii. 6 f., and in several passages of the books of Chronicles).[64a] From the passages where the term *ḥōzêh* is met with nothing can be concluded concerning the function of a seer in the strict sense.

In one passage, Josh. xiii. 22, Balaam is designated as a *ḳōsēm*, one of the many words which are used in the Old Testament for a diviner. In exegetical literature this Balaam is often called a 'seer'. It is necessary to examine this figure in detail.

Like many kahins in the Arabian world, Balaam was called from a foreign country to do his service in a precarious situation (Num. xxii-xxiv). His task was to pronounce a curse against the Israelite tribes which were about to attack Moab. King Balak was convinced that a word from Balaam had an effective power either to create blessing or to paralyse an enemy, making him impotent and ineffective. The message of Balak runs: 'Come and curse this people for me; for they are too strong for me; perhaps I may be able to defeat them and drive them out of the land; for I know that he whom you bless is blessed and he whom you curse is cursed.' The messengers brought appropriate

---

[64a] Any difference in meaning between the two verbs is difficult to maintain. For this problem see, for instance, Hänel, *Das Erkennen Gottes bei den Schriftpropheten*, pp. 7 ff.; Jepsen, *Nabi*, pp. 43 ff.; Johnson, *The Cultic Prophet*, pp. 13 ff.; Ehrlich, *Der Traum im AT*, pp. 4 ff.

remuneration with them. Balaam was not disposed to give an answer immediately. He waited for a divine communication during the following night through a dream. He was prohibited from performing the task because the people against which he was asked to pronounce a curse was a people filled with $b^e r\bar{a}k\hat{a}h$, blessing, i.e., power of success and resistance. The invitation from Balak was repeatedly renewed. At last Balaam went away, but declared that he had no power of himself to speak; it was only 'the word that God put in his mouth' that he could speak.

Then sacrificial rites were performed in order to draw the divinity near and to strengthen Balaam's power of cursing. Balaam went aside on the camel track[65] to spy for an omen. He received it: 'the Lord put a word in Balaam's mouth,' as the narrator says. Balaam was forced to pronounce a blessing instead of the expected curse. 'I must be careful to speak what the Lord puts in my mouth,' he said.

The same scene recurred time after time. The last time Balaam did not go in search of omens ($n^e h\bar{a}\check{s}im$); he knew of himself what God expected him to say. When he saw Israel grouped into their tribes, the spirit of God came upon him, and again he pronounced an oracle of blessing over Israel. The words by which the last oracles concerning Israel are introduced are highly interesting: 'The oracle of Balaam, the son of Beor, the oracle of the man with the eye opened,[66] the oracle of him who hears the words of God and is acquainted with the knowledge of the Most High; who has visions from Shaddai, falls prostrate and has the eyes open' (xxiv. 3 f., 15 f.).[67] Reproached by Balak because he had pronounced a blessing instead of a curse, he answered that he could not violate the instructions of Yahweh to do either good or bad of his own will. 'It is only what Yahweh tells me that I can speak,' (v. 13).

Those are the essential features of the figure of Balaam, as it is depicted to us in tradition. Balaam is manifestly presented to us as a kahin, such as existed in ancient Arabia. We find in the figure of Balaam many traits which recall the characteristics of the prophets of

---

[65] So Köhler in *LVT*.

[66] The verb *šāṭam* has in New Hebrew and Aramaic the sense 'unseal', 'open'. In *VT*, iii, 1953, pp. 78 f., Allegro refers to an Arabic stem meaning 'to be austere'. Accordingly he thinks that Balaam is here designated as 'the unrelenting or the grim-faced one' (A. Ehrlich previously: 'with the malicious eye'). However, in Num. xxii ff. Balaam is not a wicked man. On behalf of Yahweh he blessed Israel. In the verses in question he is only characterized as a typical seer-prophet. He has opened eyes, i.e., he has visions and sees secret things. The translation 'with shut eyes' (cf. *BH*) is inappropriate in a general description of the seer in his visionary capacity. Zorell in *Lexicon Hebraicum et Aramaicum Veteris Testamenti* accepts the translation 'open' for *šāṭam*, in our passage.

[67] For the text in xxiv. 4 see *BH*.

the Old Testament and other parts of the world, but there are also features typical of the 'seers' in the strict sense, such as we have described above.

Words pronounced by Balaam were regarded as inspired by the divinity and having a creative power. A curse spoken by him was effective in the same measure as a blessing pronounced. The inspiration was ascribed to the effect of the spirit; it is said in a phrase typical of the prophetic terminology that the *rûᵃḥ* of God came upon him (xxiv. 2). Then the words which he spoke were no more his own, but the words of Yahweh; they were words which Yahweh had 'put in his mouth'. He was endowed with the gift of hearing words from the divinity, having visions from God, and participating in supernatural knowledge. Balaam stood under divine constraint. He was incapable of doing or saying anything except as he was directed. Before acting he must wait for a command from Yahweh; the command given he must obey. All that reminds us of men and women of the prophetic type.

However, in the figure of Balaam there are also features typical of a seer in the strict sense. He receives his mysterious knowledge by means of dreams and omens of different kinds. He lies prostrate on the ground and sees secret things by his inward eye, opened towards the hidden world. All that is in accordance with what is recorded of typical seers the world over.

Then the author in Josh. xiii. 22 is right in calling Balaam a *ḳōsēm*, a diviner. In consideration of the prophetic traits he could also have called him a *nābî'*. Comprising in the same person the qualities of a seer and those of a nabi, Balaam, as he is pictured in tradition, clearly belongs to the kahin type. Characteristically enough, like the most famous kahins, Balaam was called from a foreign country to pronounce his fateful words and was promised a generous reward for the service done.

The cultic performances executed in connection with the activity of Balaam have many analogies in the narratives of both the seers and the prophets. By means of such cultic performances the support of the deity was secured and the supernormal power of the diviner and the prophet augmented.

Scholars have endeavoured to carry through a detailed analysis of different sources in the narrative of Balaam. The common literary distribution of the narrative matter between two literary sources, the Yahwist and the Elohist, has also affected the understanding of the figure of Balaam. It is maintained that there are two conceptions of the personality of Balaam, one more naive and popular, the other more 'theologically' coloured. On the whole in the present narrative Balaam is thought to have been transformed from a professional 'seer' into a 'man of God' and a prophet in a higher sense.[68]

It may be that different traditions are combined in the present narrative about Balak and Balaam, it is possible, too, that there were some variations in the picture of the seer-prophet; but from a religio-historical point of view there is no ground for splitting up the personage of Balaam into two or more quite different figures. As we have seen, Balaam shows traits both of a seer in the strict sense and of a prophet; but such a combination of seer and prophet is very common in the religious world.

It is not easy to draw a definite dividing-line between the 'seer' and the 'prophet' either in the pagan world or in ancient Israel. There are scholars who even maintain that there did not exist any difference at all between 'seers' and 'prophets' in Israel. The 'seers' were in fact nabis. 'Nabi' was the general name; the nabis were called 'seers' as executing the special function of 'seeing'.[69] On the other side Hölscher says that 'seers' and 'prophets' originally had nothing to do with one another. Characteristic of the prophets was ecstasy, the divine inspiration; characteristic of the 'seers' was the faculty of receiving knowledge concerning secret things in the present or in the future by other means, such as nocturnal visions or dreams, external omens, ghosts, and spirits.[70]

I hope that what has been said above has proved that neither of these two standpoints is quite justifiable. Above all it is a mistake to suppose that ecstasy was confined to the prophets. It is often told of the 'seers' that they received their supernormal knowledge in a state of ecstasy or trance, though commonly of a lethargic nature. What is correct in Hölscher's statement is that the most characteristic methods of the seers for obtaining supernormal knowledge were dreams and external omens, to which we may add second sight and extraordinary sagacity. This becomes quite clear from a careful study of the religio-historical facts.

[68] See Mowinckel in *ZAW*, xlviii, 1930, pp. 233 ff.; Eissfeldt in *ZAW*, lvii, 1939, pp. 212 ff.; Noth, *Überlieferungsgeschichte des Pentateuch*, pp. 81 ff.

[69] Junker, *Prophet und Seher in Israel*, reduces the difference between 'seer' and 'prophet' to a minimum. Even during the oldest times, he says, there was no definite difference between them. Many 'seers' came, he maintains, from the circles of the nabis. Junker underestimates the non-ecstatic methods of the 'seers' because he does not relate the Israelite seers to the general religio-historical type. Junker rightly draws attention to the two names 'seer' and 'prophet'. But he draws no clear conclusion from this fact (pp. 77 ff.).

[70] Hölscher, *Die Profeten*, pp. 125 ff.

From a psychological and religio-historical point of view the 'seer' can appropriately be described in the following way: Seer is a man or a woman who claims to possess the faculty of knowing things that are concealed from ordinary men. The chief methods used by the seer are dreams, extraordinary perspicacity, clairvoyance, communications from ghosts and spirits, and, finally, external signs and omens. Sometimes the seers also obtain their extraordinary knowledge in a psychic state of ecstasy or trance. Characteristic of the prophets are ecstasies of various kinds, based on a direct contact with the divine world or the divine power ('the spirit of God'), a supernormal state of mind in which divine revelations are communicated in the form of visions and auditions. Being overwhelmed by God the prophet feels himself compelled to proclaim publicly what he has seen or heard. Nevertheless the prophet may occasionally use the methods and do the work of a seer.

Briefly one could also say that a seer's general function was, by using different methods, to see things of various kinds on this earth hidden from common men; the main function of a prophet was, filled with or touched by the divinity, to receive revelations from the other world and utter them as oracles to men. The dividing-line between a seer and a prophet can not be drawn sharply. Both could on occasion execute the same functions.

Balaam was a foreigner from a pagan country, but Samuel was a genuine Israelite. The former figure shows, at any rate, that the Israelite traditionists were quite familiar with the seer type. It is also to be observed that Balaam is thought of as a mouthpiece of Yahweh: he utters what has been whispered (*ne'um*) to him by Yahweh. The figure of Samuel proves, no doubt, that there existed in olden times seers in Israel. For the rest the traces of professional seers in the Old Testament are very scarce. The name *'ēlôn môrêh*, the Soothsayer-terebinth, given to a holy tree (Gen. xii. 6; Deut. xi. 30) in all probability arises from the fact that seers used to sit there imparting to people their directions. Deborah, as she is described in Judges iv-v, has several features recalling a seer (see below, p. 96, note 71). Answers from God such as are reported for instance in 1 Sam. x. 22 (that Saul had hidden himself among the baggage) or Judges i. 2 (that Judah should go up first against the Canaanites) were most likely delivered by seers. We have heard above that seers could be appointed at the royal court. The very term *ḥōzêh*, so common in the Old Testament as equivalent to *nābî'*, points in the same direction. So does the term *ne'um* used for oracles, originally belonging to the old seer terminology.

Obviously the old-fashioned seer gradually gave way to the prophets.

One reason for the disappearance of the seers in Israel was the theocentric nature of the Yahweh religion; another was the fact that the functions of the seers fell into disrepute because of their resemblance to analogous phenomena in Canaanite paganism. The polemics of the prophets and the laws against pagan soothsaying and divination necessarily threw an air of ignominy even over the activities of the Israelite seers. Their proceedings were then regarded as illegitimate and incompatible with the true Yahweh religion.

This development involving the disappearance of the seers in the strict sense and their replacement by the prophets is observed by the author of the well-known remark in 1 Sam. ix. 9: 'Formerly in Israel, when a man went to inquire of God, thus he said, "Come, let us go to the seer"; for he who is now called a prophet was formerly called a seer.' It is not very likely that this remark indicates merely a change in the mode of expression; it rather implies an observation concerning historic facts: in earlier times there existed in Israel professional seers in the strict sense; now they no longer exist; their functions in Israelite society as explorers of secret things are now taken over by the prophets.

4. HISTORICAL REMARKS

The narratives about the early prophets in the Old Testament are so filled with legendary material that it is very difficult to reconstruct with certainty the historical facts. Everywhere in the world men and women who give the impression of being in possession of extraordinary gifts, particularly of a divine nature, stimulate men's fancy and give birth to fanciful stories and legendary tales. This is true of the medieval saints as well as of seers and prophets of every kind. It is characteristic of the legendary literature that the same motifs and ideas frequently recur in different connections and, further, that the same story is told in identical form or with slight variations of different personalities. Legends are by nature migratory stories.

In the historical books there is mention of many prophets, named or anonymous, of whom we can say nothing or very little with any certainty. There is no reason to call in question the historicity of Nathan and Gad, the court prophets of David, although, as we have seen above, not all that has been related of them is authentic (cf. above, pp. 75 ff.). The same is true of Ahijah in the days of Jeroboam, Micaiah in the days of Ahab and Jehoshaphat, and Shemaiah, who pronounced an oracle to Rehoboam, prohibiting the blood-feud between Judah and the northern tribes. It is impossible here to scrutinize the traditions of such figures in detail.[71]

It is of greater interest to examine more important personalities such as Elijah and Elisha.[72] The narratives of these prophets are, as we know, rich in legendary traits, miracle anecdotes and so on. Many of them are doublets, typical migratory stories, which still further reduces their historical value. Of both Elijah and Elisha it is told that they abundantly furnished a widow with oil, both raised, approximately in the same manner, a boy from the dead, both were in a wonderful way saved from bodies of warriors coming to capture them. Elijah as well as Elisha played an outstanding role during a great famine in the country. According to tradition both of them were engaged in Jehu's revolt against Joram and Hazael's conspiracy against Ben-hadad, the Syrian king. Both were honoured with the name 'the chariots of Israel and its horsemen'.

It is difficult to fix with certainty historical details in the life of Elisha. He seems to have been called to be a prophet by Elijah and to have continued Elijah's work; he stood in intimate connection with the prophetic guilds, and played a part in the revolutionary proceedings of Jehu.

As regards Elijah we are better informed. During Ahab's reign Elijah was a champion of Yahweh against the cult of the Tyrian Melkart, and to him we must assign the re-establishment of the Yahweh cult on Mount Carmel. He stepped into the breach for old Israelite customs and morals (the story of Naboth!), announced doom on the house of Ahab and the apostates of Israel, and incited his followers to a merciless persecution of the priests and prophets of the Phoenician Baal. He derived his origin from the steppes of Gilead and lived for long periods in the wilderness. He was always on the tramp, suddenly appearing and suddenly disappearing, now frightened, pursued and fleeing, now honoured. He had good relations with the associations of prophets, but acted for the most part independently and of his own accord. He called

[71] Unhistorically Abraham is called a prophet in Gen. xx. 7, Moses in Deut. xviii. 15; xxxiv. 10; Hos. xii. 14, Miriam in Ex. xv. 20. 'Prophet' in these passages is not a precise term, but taken in a loose sense, referring to a supernormal endowment. Deborah is in Judges iv. 4 called a prophetess, but her historical position is not quite clear because it is impossible to distinguish between the oldest tradition and later additions to it; cf. Jepsen, *Nabi*, p. 151, note 2. I agree with Hölscher in believing that Deborah originally belonged rather to the old seer type. She used to sit under a holy tree delivering her directions. Like an Arabian kahina she incited Barak to the fight against Sisera, and, following the army, supported its enterprises by her incantations (cf. Hölscher, op. cit., pp. 120 f.).

[72] For the problem of the historicity of the narratives of Elijah and Elisha see for instance Jepsen, *Nabi*, pp. 68 ff. The last attempt to give a historical representation of Elijah, on the basis of a literary-critical analysis, is Fohrer, *Elia*.

Elisha to be a prophet and entrusted him with the task of continuing his mission.

That Samuel occupied an outstanding position in Israel in the days of Saul and David is clear. He played an active part in connection with the events which brought Saul to the throne. He was the prophetic guide of the king and endeavoured to keep him in the right way, in accordance with old Israelite customs, but he was finally unsuccessful and found himself in hopeless conflict with Saul. Then he anointed David king over Israel. Holding, in all probability, no official position, but combining in his person the functions of seer, prophet, priest, and judge, Samuel was in his time a religious and political leader of the greatest importance, working in virtue of his personal authority.[73]

The complicated literary and traditio-historical nature of the story of Balaam makes it difficult to fix any historical facts with regard to his personality. Perhaps Balaam (an Aramean?) was originally a widely known figure of the kahin type, whose personality was combined by the old Israelite narrators with the early history of Israel. The oracles attributed to the pagan seer and prophet are of varying dates. They had originally nothing to do with the Israelite invasion of the territory of Moab in the thirteenth century B.C. The value of the Balaam story does not lie in the authenticity of what is told about him, but in the description of a kahin and his activities as they were imagined in the early period. As we have seen above, the Balaam story contains many valuable details illustrating the activity and behaviour of a kahin. A careful examination of them is certainly more profitable than hypotheses about the historicity of the material presented in the present sources.[74]

Far more interesting is the question of the historical origin of ecstatic prophecy in ancient Israel. All the leading scholars who have dealt with ancient Israelite prophecy have raised this question: from where is this phenomenon to be derived? The common opinion is that Israelite ecstatic prophecy derived its origin from outside and that Israel took over this phenomenon from the Phoenician-Canaanite world.

In *Die Profeten* Hölscher strongly emphasizes the foreign origin of Israelite prophecy. In a special section entitled: 'Die kanaanäische

---

[73] A precise office might be attributed to Samuel if Kraus were right in assuming the existence of a particular office of a 'Bundesmittler', functioning at the central sanctuary during the early history of Israel. Kraus thinks that Samuel was possibly such a 'Bundesmittler'. At any rate Kraus is right in warning against the tendency to assign different functions of the personality of Samuel to different traditions. It is clear that in his time he was a charismatic leader in Israel with the highest authority; Kraus, *Gottesdienst in Israel*, pp. 65, 111.

[74] The historicity of the Balaam story is discussed by Mowinckel and Noth in the works mentioned above.

Herkunft des israelitischen Ekstatikertums', Hölscher presents a series of reasons for the derivation of ancient Israelite prophecy from Canaanite culture. A comparison of the ecstatic movement among the Israelites, he says, with similar phenomena in the neighbouring religions shows that parallels to the ecstatic prophecy in ancient Israel are to be found only in the territories of Syria and Asia Minor. Ecstatic prophecy is, according to this scholar, not indigenous on purely Semitic ground, i.e., in the desert, but flourishes in regions where culture and probably also race are neither purely Semitic nor purely non-Semitic. Consequently the Israelites must have taken over ecstatic phenomena from their Canaanite neighbours. Hölscher lays stress upon the fact that ecstatic prophecy is found only in the northern tribes, more influenced as they were by Canaanite religion and culture, not among the southern tribes, which preserved more faithfully the old nomadic customs.[75]

After more recent investigations of a religio-historical and psychological nature the ideas presented by Hölscher are hardly tenable. Ecstatic phenomena and movements are not confined to particular races, peoples, or countries; they flourish all over the world. I think that this is evident from the introductory chapter of this book. Ecstasy with its manifestations is a general human phenomenon and based not on peculiarities of races and peoples but on personal predisposition in individuals.[76] That exterior conditions may support and favour such predispositions is a different matter. The existence of ecstatics, maḫḫus, in the Accadian religion, proves that a limitation such as Hölscher suggests is not justified. Nor was ecstatic prophecy confined to the northern regions. In 1 Kings xiii we hear of a prophet from Judah; there existed a prophetic guild in Jericho (2 Kings ii. 5 ff.), and the ecstatic sheep-breeder Amos of the eighth century was from the farthest south of Palestine, living just on the border of the desert.

Moreover, what is meant by the statement that ecstatic prophecy derived its origin from outside? Ecstatic predisposition and ecstasy itself cannot be 'borrowed' from other quarters like clothing and customs, words and technical inventions; ecstasy can arise by suggestion and psychic contagion, but not through cultural influence of an external

---

[75] Hölscher, op. cit., pp. 140 ff. For the following cf. also Lindblom in the *Eissfeldt Festschrift*, 1957, pp. 89 ff.

[76] Similarly Ridderbos, *Profetie en ekstase*, p. 88: 'De godsdienstige ekstase is van ouds voorgekomen in de meest uiteenloopende cultuurkringen.' Junker expresses the same opinion in *Prophet und Seher in Israel*, pp. 102 ff.; cf. Skinner, *Prophecy and Religion. Studies in the Life of Jeremiah*, p. 1; Albright, *From the Stone Age to Christianity*[2], p. 231. The problem of race and ecstasy is discussed by Walz in *ZAW*, lix, 1942/43, pp. 111 ff. This author overstates considerably the significance of race for the phenomena of ecstasy, inspiration, and revelation. See also Achelis, *Die Ekstase in ihrer kulturellen Bedeutung*.

sort. This does not of course exclude the possibility that certain outward forms may be taken over from one quarter to another. As regards the ecstatic prophecy of ancient Israel the phenomenon in itself may very well be indigenous, while for instance the oracle formula: 'Thus says (Yahweh)', is borrowed from the neighbouring culture. The origin of the term *nābî'* is not yet fully clear, but it seems to be a term taken over from another language.[77] The intimate connection of the prophets with the cult at the old Canaanite high places must have influenced their behaviour in certain directions, for instance as regards musical practices. Why should not men and women endowed with the gift of visionary seeing and ecstatic prophesying have existed in Israel already at a primitive stage as well as among the Rwala bedouin and the Berbers and Arabs of North Africa today?

Alfred Jepsen shares Hölscher's opinion that ecstatic prophecy was borrowed from the Canaanites.[78] He takes, however, one step further. He tries to prove that ecstatic prophecy emerged in a definite historical situation in ancient Israel. In earlier times Yahweh spoke to men for instance through dreams, but above all through the ephod oracle. Ecstatic prophecy came into existence under Canaanite influence because the ephod oracle, which was attached to the central sanctuary, was not accessible to ordinary men. Alongside the priestly class there now arose a new class of oracle-givers, namely the nabis. After the destruction of the sanctuary in Shiloh the nabis obtained a new authority and an unprecedented influence. In fact, according to Jepsen, Samuel was the man who by virtue of his authority imparted to Israel the knowledge that the oracles of the nabis were revelations from Yahweh in the same measure as the priestly oracles at the sanctuary.

It seems that Jepsen builds too much upon the notices about the prophets in the present sources. It is true that bands of ecstatic prophets are mentioned first during the days of Samuel, but there is nothing that indicates that they were not organized long before. The distinction made by Jepsen between Israelite nabis who were authorized as Yahweh prophets and nabis who were not is hardly justifiable. Prophets in Israel were Yahweh prophets, thought of as impelled by Yahweh's spirit, if they were not prophets of the Baal. On the whole Jepsen's theories seem rather doctrinaire. History does not proceed along such strictly rational lines.

From the passages where Abraham, Moses, Miriam, and Deborah are called prophets nothing can be concluded about the earliest history of Israelite prophecy. When these personalities are called prophets, the

[77] See below.   [78] Jepsen, *Nabi*, pp. 143 ff.

term *nāḇî'* is taken in a more general sense and refers to their position as men standing in an extraordinarily close communion with God.[79]

The same is true of the curious chapter Num. xi. In this chapter different traditions are more or less intimately combined. There is a tradition about the quails which were gathered by the people and eaten until they became loathsome to them. Then we have a tradition about the manna. Both these traditions have parallels in Ex. xvi. Further there are aetiological explanations of two place names: *taḇ'ērâh* and *ḳiḇrôṭ hatta'ᵃwâh*, designating two stations on the route of the Israelites through the desert. In addition two significant stories are incorporated in the narrative: the story of the seventy elders and the story of Eldad and Medad prophesying in the camp. The story of the elders belongs to the group of narratives in the old sources which aim at explaining the origin of important social institutions in ancient Israel. Other similar examples of this group are the narrative of the appointment of judges in Ex. xviii. 13 ff. (Deut. i. 16 ff.) and that of the ordaining of chieftains and captains in Ex. xviii. 21, 25 (Deut. i. 15).

The institution of elders played an important part in the social life of Israel during all epochs of Israelite history. According to tradition there were already elders among the Israelites in Egypt (Ex. iii. 16 ff.), and, in fact, nothing prevents us from assuming that the institution of elders in its origins was pre-Mosaic. There were elders even among the captives in Babylonia (Ezek. viii. 1; xiv. 1), in the post-exilic community (Ezr. x. 8 ff.), and among the Jews in the time of the New Testament, as is evident from many passages in the Gospels and the Acts of the Apostles. Beside the firmer organization during the monarchic period the old-fashioned institution of the elders played a considerable role. Mention is made of elders of single villages and cities, of tribes or groups of tribes; of Judah or Zion, of Gilead, of Israel, in the sense of the northern tribes, and of Israel as a whole. The task of the elders was to judge and to give decisions in disputed cases in general; further to represent the people in matters which were important for the community as a whole. There are traces of a delegation of seventy elders, who in special cases represented the entire corporation of the elders. According to Ex. xxiv. 1, seventy of the 'elders of Israel' went up to Mount Sinai together with Moses and Aaron, Nadab and Abihu. In the temple vision of Ezekiel (ch. viii) the prophet saw seventy of 'the elders of the house of Israel' standing in front of the abominable images worshipping the pagan idols. We do not know with certainty what was the task of the seventy elders; there is, however, reason to

[79] See above, p. 96, note 71.

suppose that they represented the whole of Israel in certain affairs which concerned all the tribes, possibly, in particular, at the common functions of the amphictyony. Perhaps the elders whom Joshua assembled at Shechem according to Josh. xxiv. 1 were precisely this delegation of the seventy elders.

The origin of this institution of the seventy elders is what the aetiological narrative in Num. xi. 16-17, 24-25 seeks to explain; and it explains it in this way: The burden of the riotous people became too heavy for Moses. Then he was commanded by the Lord to gather seventy of the elders of Israel and bring them to the tent of meeting. He did so, and placed them round about the tent. Then the Lord withdrew some of the spirit that was upon Moses and put it upon the seventy elders, and as soon as the spirit came upon them they fell into ecstasy; but this never occurred again.[80] And so Moses obtained helpers who shared the burden of the people with him.

The following appears to be the point of this narrative. The seventy elders, who must have played a considerable role in the administrative organization of Israel, were an institution founded by Moses. The seventy elders received a portion of the spirit which Moses himself possessed, just as Elisha according to 2 Kings ii. 9-15 was endowed with a portion of the spirit of Elijah. A symptom of their sharing in the spirit of Moses was a fit of ecstasy, but thereafter ecstasy was something alien to them. Thus the narrative seeks to emphasize the high authority of the institution of the seventy elders and at the same time distinguish them as a civil and administrative class from the class of the ecstatic nabis.

Intimately combined with this narrative is the succeeding story of Eldad and Medad. Two men, Eldad and Medad by name (the names meaning 'beloved by God' seem to be symbolical), who belonged to those chosen—they were among those registered, it is said—did not go out to the tent; but the spirit came upon them, too, and rested upon them, so that they were in ecstasy in the camp. A youth ran and told Moses. Joshua the attendant of Moses said, 'Put a stop to them!' But Moses answered, 'Are you jealous on my account? O that all the people of Yahweh were prophets, that Yahweh would put His spirit upon them.'

In this narrative the professional nabis as enjoying the privilege of a permanent possession of the spirit are placed alongside the seventy

[80] $we^{l}\bar{o}$' $y\bar{a}s\bar{a}p\hat{u}$ means: 'they did so no more'. The equipment with spirit was momentary; it belonged to the inauguration of the institution of the seventy, when ecstasy was something alien to them. To change the verb into $y\bar{a}s\hat{u}p\hat{u}$ would destroy the very sense of the saying (cf. Vulg.: *nec ultra cessaverunt*)

elders as a class deriving its origin from Moses. There was an opposition against them, but Moses rejected the remonstrants and defended the ecstatics, expressing the wish that all the people might be prophets. Thus this narrative aetiologically explains the origin of the estate of the nabis as a legitimate class in Israelite society and gives them incontestable authorization.[81]

This story of Eldad and Medad is of great value as an aetiological narrative showing the high estimation of the ecstatic prophecy in certain circles. It cannot be utilized as a historical record and has nothing to teach us about the real origin of ecstatic prophecy. The first beginning of ecstatic prophecy in Israel is as obscure as the 'beginning' of such phenomena elsewhere. Nothing forbids the supposition that Yahweh had his prophets among the Israelite nomads in the desert as well as among the settled population in Canaan, even though the first historically reliable notices of them appear in the narratives of Samuel.

Notwithstanding the fact that the ecstatic phenomenon in itself is indigenous, terms and forms may be borrowed from other quarters. The very term *nābî'* and the denominatives *nibbâ'* and *hitnabbê'*, both meaning 'be in ecstasy' or 'pronounce prophetic oracles', are not genuine Hebrew words, but taken over from the surrounding cultural world. The Hebrew equivalent to *nābî'* is 'man of the spirit' (*'îš hārûaḥ*, Hos. ix. 7) or simply 'man of God' (*'îš 'elōhîm*). The very meaning of the word *nābî'* is still obscure. Several scholars derive the word from the Accadian *nabū*, 'call', 'proclaim'. Even so the question remains whether the form is to be taken in an active or a passive sense. In the former case *nābî'* will mean 'speaker', in the latter case it will mean 'a called one' (called by God or by the spirit), 'one who has a vocation'. Personally I am inclined to prefer the latter sense.[82] Perhaps new inscriptions from the Near East will throw more light upon this problem.

The same is true of the term for the dwelling-place of the prophetic guilds. The very form is uncertain. It is transmitted in the forms *nāyôt, nāwôt*, or *nwyt* (*nāwît* or *nāwyat*), 1 Sam. xix. 18 ff.; xx. 1. The word seems to be cognate with the Hebrew *nāwêh*, 'place to stay at',

---

[81] In his article 'Die falschen Propheten' in *ZAW*, li, 1933, pp. 109 ff., von Rad deals with the narrative of Num. xi (pp. 115 f.). von Rad is right in seeing in the story of the elders an aetiological narrative. But he seems to be wrong in thinking that the narrative refers to two groups of prophets: the organized cult prophets and the free prophets. In fact two quite different institutions are aetiologically explained in Num. xi: the institution of the seventy among the elders and ecstatic prophecy, not two different classes of prophets.

[82] See Albright, *From the Stone Age to Christianity*[2], p. 231; Johnson, *The Cultic Prophet*, pp. 24 f., note 8.

'abode'. At all events it is probably the Hebrew equivalent to the Arabic *takiyyah*, the assembling house of the dervishes.

The oracle formula *kôh 'āmar yahwêh*, 'thus says Yahweh', was commonly used by the early prophets as an introduction to their oracles and from them inherited by the classical prophets. This formula was no invention by the Hebrew prophets, but belonged to the oracular terminology of the ancient world.[83] There are many examples from Mesopotamia as well as from Egypt of oracle sayings formulated in an analogous way, uttered by different gods concerning different affairs.

The old oracle formula 'thus says X' can be traced back along several lines. It was used to introduce the content of public proclamations and edicts indicating the person from whom the proclamation or the edict proceeded. A number of proclamations introduced by the formula in question are preserved in royal inscriptions from Mesopotamia and later from Persia. From the Old Testament we may recall the edict of Cyrus concerning the release of the deported Jews in Ezr. i. 2 and 2 Chron. xxxvi. 23: 'Thus says Cyrus, the king of Persia' (*kôh 'āmar kōreš melek pāras*).

The formula was also used in letters. Countless letters from the ancient Near East, preserved in the Amarna collection, in Assyrian and Babylonian inscriptions, in new published letters from Mari, in Persian letters reproduced by ancient historians, etc., commence in this way: 'X says to X' or 'X says this to X', or 'thus says X to X'. Similar introductions of letters are known from Egypt, too. Late examples of this oriental epistolary style are provided by the letters to the churches of Asia Minor in Rev. ii: 'Thus speaks he who holds the seven stars,' etc.; 'thus speaks the first and the last,' etc.

The formula generally employed in public proclamations and letters was also used as an introduction to messages brought from one person to another. In the Old Testament there are a good many examples of this stylistic peculiarity. Jacob sent ahead messengers to his brother Esau commanding them as follows: 'Thus shall you say to my lord Esau, "Thus says your servant Jacob"', etc. (Gen. xxxii. 4 f.). Balak, the king of Moab, sent chieftains to Balaam, who said to him, 'Thus says Balak, "Let nothing hinder you from coming to me"' (Num. xxii. 15 f.). Jephthah sent messengers to the king of the Ammonites to say to him, 'Thus says Jephthah, "Israel did not take away the land of Moab"' (Judges xi. 14 f.). Benaiah brought a message from King Solomon to Joab with the following words: 'Thus says the king, "Come out"' (1 Kings ii. 30). Ben-hadad sent messengers to Ahab to say to

[83] For the following see Lindblom, *Die literarische Gattung*, pp. 102 ff.

him, 'Thus says Ben-hadad, "Your silver and your gold are mine"'
(xx. 2 f.)[84]

When using the oracle formula 'thus says Yahweh', the prophets
claimed to be considered as authoritative messengers from Yahweh
bringing forth a divine proclamation. The certainty of being sent by
God is everywhere a characteristic element in the self-consciousness
of men and women who belong to the prophetic type. The oracle
formula used by the Hebrew prophets was borrowed by them from the
surrounding cultural world, like some other features belonging to the
outward appearance and organization of the Hebrew ecstatics. Whether
the old oracle formula originated in the royal proclamations or in the
style used in letters or that employed in messages, is impossible to decide
and of little significance.

[84] See further Ex. v. 10; Num. xx. 14; Josh. xxii. 15 f.; 2 Kings i. 11; xviii. 28 f.;
xix. 2 f.; 2 Chron. xxxii. 9 f. In the book of Exodus Moses frequently appears before
Pharaoh as a messenger from Yahweh saying, 'Thus says Yahweh', etc.: v. 1; x. 3;
xi. 4. Cf. passages where the angel of Yahweh appears as a messenger from Yahweh:
Ezek. xliii. 18; Zech. iii. 6 f. See above all Köhler, *Deuterojesaja stilkritisch untersucht*,
pp. 102 ff.

CHAPTER THREE

THE SUPERNORMAL EXPERIENCES AND GENERAL ACTIVITIES OF THE CLASSICAL PROPHETS

1. THE CLASSICAL PROPHETS AND PRIMITIVE PROPHECY

By 'the classical prophets' I mean those prophets (also known as the canonical prophets) who worked in Israel from the eighth century onwards to the time when prophetic inspiration died out in Israel, or, at all events, left no considerable record in tradition. The first of this series of prophets is Amos, the sheep-breeder from Tekoa, the last is the prophet traditionally known as Malachi. They have this in common, that their preaching was concentrated on the ideas of the rejection and the eventual re-establishment of Israel, the elect but sinful people of Yahweh, and, further, that their messages made such a strong impression on their contemporaries, that they were carefully preserved in tradition and sooner or later written down. Thus we have excellent material for a scientific study of these personalities; but the literary character of the books which bear their names is such that they must be handled with critical care.

It is unquestionable that this group of prophets must also be treated as *prophets* or nabis in the strict sense. It would be a serious mistake to dissolve the connection between these prophets and those whom we have called above the primitive or early prophets.

First, many of the classical prophetic personalities are expressly called 'prophets' and their activity 'prophesying'. They are even classed by themselves or by their disciples with the Yahweh prophets of earlier times, and, in fact, they considered themselves as belonging to the same general category of inspired men as their rivals, the so-called 'false prophets', although both their relation to Yahweh and the contents of their preaching were different. Secondly, an analysis of the psychic peculiarities of these prophets shows incontrovertibly that they belong to the general religio-historical type which we have called prophetic, and that their psychological experiences resemble those of the early prophets. This latter point will be worked out in detail in the following examination of the psychological material in which our prophetic books abound.

Scholars who are inclined to dissolve the ties between the ecstatics of earlier times and the later prophets of judgement and reform reduce to a minimum the supernormal experiences of the latter, mistakenly in my view. I hope to show that in the prophetic books there is ample evidence that, in spite of certain differences and individual modifications, the later prophets belong to the same general type as the primitive prophets, which, of course, is quite consistent with the fact that the preaching of the great classical prophets is on a higher level than the oracles of the primitive prophets.

The attempt to minimize the supernormal experiences of the great prophets usually arises from a desire to defend the genuine religious and moral elements in the religion of these prophets. Those who take this line maintain that modern studies of the prophets which favour the psychological approach detract from the personal religion of the prophets. Though this may be true of some such studies it is not true of the best of them. Hermann Gunkel, one of the foremost of those who adopt this approach, often speaks emphatically of the religious feeling of the prophets. They are entirely filled with zeal for God and His cause. They share in Yahweh's wrath and love and feel themselves bound to His will, because He has laid hold upon them.[1]

If the term 'ecstasy' is to be applied to the prophetic experience, it is essential that it should be clearly defined. If ecstasy is understood as the well-known mental state in which the *ego* fully loses the consciousness of itself and becomes completely absorbed in the Divine, in the so-called *unio mystica*, there can be no talk of ecstasy in connection with the Israelite prophets. Psychologists also use the term ecstasy, however, in another sense, denoting a mental state in which human consciousness is so concentrated on a particular idea or feeling that the normal current of thoughts and perceptions is broken off and the senses temporarily cease to function in a normal way. In the first chapter of this book we have mentioned examples of this form of ecstasy, which may also be called 'concentration ecstasy'.

If the prophetic ecstasy were to be characterized as a real *unio mystica*, this would of course lead to a depreciation of the personalistic religion of the prophets. Ecstasy in the other sense is not in any way at variance with personal religion. To use the language of religious experience, God can speak to men during a state of ecstasy as well as during a state of prayer. It is a fact that men whose awareness of the external world is temporarily inhibited can have religious experiences and receive divine revelations and spiritual impulses which by far surpass what can be given in a normal state of mind. The value of

[1] See Additional Note I.

religious preaching is not dependent on the psychological conditions associated with it, but on its content.

Scholars who hold that the emergence of the canonical prophets marks a radical break in the history of the prophetic movement lay stress on the fact that Amos, the first of them, expressly denies that he is a prophet. In the well-known scene at Bethel (Am. vii), when Amaziah, the priest, said to Amos, 'O seer, flee away to the land of Judah, and there earn your living by working there as a prophet,' Amos replied, 'I am no prophet, I am no member of a prophetic association, but I am a herdsman and a dresser of sycamores,' etc. In these words Amos seems to deny outright that he was a nabi, and accordingly it is argued that Amos introduced a quite new epoch in the history of inspired men in Israel.

However, it is clear that the difference between Amos and the earlier nabis was not a radical one. He was connected with them by many ties. In tradition he was regarded as a prophet. Amaziah called him a seer, hōzêh. 'Seer' and 'prophet' were at that time identical. His activity was described as 'prophesying', i.e., his appearance and his actions were those of a nabi. The redactor of the Book of Amos calls its contents 'words which he saw', i.e., prophetic revelations. Amos himself represents Yahweh's command in the moment of his call in this way: 'Go, speak as a prophet to my people Israel.' When he says, 'When the Lord Yahweh speaks, who can but prophesy?' (iii. 8), he no doubt has in mind himself and his personal experiences. His messages frequently have the form of oracles, introduced by the usual oracle formula: "Thus says Yahweh'. They were based on revelations from God. As divine words they were regarded as having an effective power. Amaziah said that the land was unable to endure all his words. The feeling of divine constraint and compulsion is expressed in his words: 'When the lion roars, who does not fear? When the Lord Yahweh speaks, who can but prophesy?' (iii. 8). A series of real visions received by Amos is preserved in tradition. A real vision is always based upon ecstasy of one form or another.

Thus Amos may appropriately be described as an ecstatic. In what follows we shall often have occasion to return to Amos and to an analysis of his words and his activity, especially to his significant dialogue with the priest of Bethel and the references there made to his call and his relation to the cult and the nabis of his time. This preliminary outline of his work may, I hope, have shown that it is not possible to isolate Amos from the earlier prophets. All the features mentioned above connect him intimately with them. When he denied that he was a prophet he cannot have meant that there was no connection at all between himself and the professional nabis. His words must be understood in another sense, as will become clear later in our discussion of his call and his attitude to the cult.

Nevertheless, Amos undoubtedly represents a new phase in the history of Israelite prophecy, but this is evident primarily in the content of his preaching. Psychological and external factors are of subordinate importance in this connection.

In what follows we shall examine the psychological experiences and the work of the classical prophets in order to determine those characteristics which they have in common. There are, of course, many differences between the individual prophets; and they should not be regarded as conforming in every detail to a single pattern. In some of them the supernormal features are more marked than in others; and this is a factor which we must take into consideration.

This part of the present study owes much to the researches of other scholars who have worked in this field, notably Duhm, Gunkel, Hölscher, Mowinckel, T. H. Robinson, Guillaume, Lods, and Kuhl.

2. The Prophets as Recipients of Divine Revelations. The Divine Word

Nothing is more characteristic of the classical prophets in Israel, nothing is more central in their life and work than their privilege of receiving revelations from Yahweh. The prophets belong unmistakably to the 'visionary type' of *homines religiosi*, of which we have countless examples in many different countries and periods, not least in medieval Christendom, where this type can be most profitably studied. The term 'revelation' is here used rather than 'vision', because it is more general and comprehensive. The word 'vision' suggests something that is literally shown and seen, whereas the content of a revelation may be apprehended by hearing, or may consist simply in thoughts and ideas which come into the mind of the inspired person. In the prophetic literature no definitive dividing-line is drawn between visions, auditions, and inspired ideas in general. Everything which came to a prophet in the inspired state may be called 'vision'. But to the modern reader the more general word 'revelation' is indubitably less misleading than the word 'vision' with its specific association with sight.

All that a prophet has to proclaim, based on divine revelation, is regarded by him as something that Yahweh has spoken to him. It is held to be a 'word' (*dābār*) from Yahweh. This becomes apparent from the manner in which the prophets designate their messages, particularly from the formulas by which they introduce and conclude them.

One of the most common of these is the typical oracle formula 'thus says Yahweh', which, as we have seen above, was also used by the primitive prophets. Its origin in ancient oriental terminology has been demonstrated above.[2] When a prophet speaks it is not really he who speaks but Yahweh. It is stated expressly that Yahweh speaks 'through' the prophet.[3] Therefore a prophetic message is frequently introduced by the formula: 'Hear the word of Yahweh'. The content of a prophetic oracle can be designated as a *maśśā'*, an utterance, a proclamation of Yahweh.[4] It is said that 'Yahweh's word comes' to a prophet, which means that he is receiving a revelation from Yahweh. Frequently we meet with expressions such as: 'Yahweh says' or 'has said' to the prophet. Isaiah exhorts heaven and earth to listen because Yahweh speaks.[5] Finally a prophetic utterance is characterized as a word of Yahweh by means of the technical formula *ne'um yahwêh*, which appears countless times in the prophetic literature. Every oracle can be described as a *ne'um yahwêh*, perhaps 'a whispering' of Yahweh, or even simply as a 'word' of Yahweh.[6]

The formulas 'Yahweh has spoken' or 'I, Yahweh, have spoken' (with several variations) are used when the importance and the reliability of a prophetic utterance are to be particularly emphasized.[7]

The chief mission of the prophets was to carry Yahweh's words to their people. Yahweh had charged them with His words.[8] The prophet Ezekiel is commanded to speak Yahweh's words to the people, whether they listen or refuse to listen (iii. 10 f.). Jeremiah sought indefatigably to convey Yahweh's word to his people, but it only brought him scorn and derision (xx. 8). All the prophets, from ancient times to his own time, were sent by Yahweh in order that they should carry Yahweh's words to Israel. The sending of the prophets early and late meant an uninterrupted sending of the divine word (xxix. 19).

If the message of a prophet is called Yahweh's word, this means:

[2] See above, p. 103. For the use of this and the following formulas and their significance as pointing to real revelations in the book of Jeremiah see the very detailed investigations in Wildberger, *Jahwewort und prophetische Rede bei Jeremia*.

[3] Isa. xx. 2; Jer. xxxvii. 2; l. 1; Hag. i. 1, 3; ii. 1; Zech. vii. 7; Mal. i. 1. The Hebrew term here used is *beyaḏ*.

[4] Jer. xxiii. 33; Zech. ix. 1; xii. 1; Mal. i. 1 (cf. 2 Kings ix. 25). With reference to a prophetic oracle in general the term stands Isa. xiii. 1; xiv. 28; xv. 1; xix. 1, etc.

[5] Isa. i. 2.

[6] For the use of this formula see Rendtorff in *ZAW*, lxvi, 1954, pp. 27 ff.

[7] Isa. xxi. 17; xxii. 25; xxiv. 3; xxv. 8; xl. 5; lviii. 14; Ezek. v. 15, 17; xvii. 21, 24; xxxvii. 14, etc.

[8] Cf. the expression *debāray 'aśer ṣiwwîṯî* in Zech. i. 6. Similarly Jer. xiv. 14; Deut. xviii. 18.

Yahweh speaks to the prophet, the prophet hears what Yahweh says, and then he pronounces what he has heard to the listening people. Thus Yahweh says to Ezekiel, 'All my words that I shall speak to you receive in your heart and hear with your ears. And go to the exiles, to the children of your people, and speak to them', etc. (iii. 10 f.). Isaiah says that he has 'heard' from Yahweh a sentence of decisive destruction (xxviii. 22). Another prophet says, after having received a vision concerning the downfall of Babylon, 'What I have heard from Yahweh Zebaoth, the God of Israel, I have made known to you' (Isa. xxi. 10).

Jeremiah knows that what is spoken by him is an utterance of 'the voice (ḳôl) of Yahweh' (xxxviii. 20). This is also the people's belief. Yahweh sends His words through the prophet, and then the people are willing to obey 'the voice of Yahweh', their God (xlii. 6). From the day of the Exodus from Egypt until the present day Yahweh has appealed to His people saying, 'Listen to my voice' (xi. 7). To listen to the words of a prophet is the same as to listen to Yahweh's voice (Hag. i. 12).

This thought is expressed even more realistically in passages which include the phrase 'the mouth of Yahweh'. The true prophet speaks what comes from 'Yahweh's mouth'; the false prophet pronounces the visions of his own heart, and not what comes from 'the mouth of Yahweh' (Jer. xxiii. 16). Ezekiel must warn the people whenever he hears a word from Yahweh's mouth (iii. 17). So clear is the prophet's awareness of the voice of Yahweh that it is described in terms of physical hearing. Isaiah introduces an oracle in the following way: 'Yahweh Zebaoth has let Himself be heard in my ears' (v. 9); and in another passage: 'Yahweh has revealed Himself in my ears' (xxii. 14).[9]

Like the early prophets, the classical prophets were resorted to by those who wanted information from Yahweh. It is said that King Zedekiah sent messengers to Jeremiah in order to 'ask' (dāraš) him (Jer. xxxvii. 7). But what was really sought was not an answer from the prophet, but a word from Yahweh. Once the king sent for Jeremiah and asked him secretly, 'Is there any word from Yahweh?' (xxxvii. 17). Other significant expressions are the following: 'inquire of Yahweh for us' (Jer. xxi. 2); 'to ask (šā'al) Yahweh's mouth' (Isa. xxx. 2). The prophet is asked, 'What is the utterance (maśśâ') of Yahweh?' (Jer. xxiii. 33). One who comes to ask for an oracle has to say, 'What has

---

[9] It is interesting to note that the same or a similar terminology was used by the Gatha community in ancient Iran. Here the inspired seer hears and speaks words from Vohu Manah's tongue. Vohu Manah speaks through him. One prays to Ahura Mazdāh: 'Tell us this, Mazdāh, through the tongue of thy mouth'. Of the adherents of the Drugs it is said that they speak with their own tongues, etc. See Nyberg, *Die Religionen des alten Iran*, pp. 164 ff.

Yahweh answered?' ('*ānâh*) or, 'What has Yahweh spoken?' (xxiii. 35, 37). People who resort to a prophet in this way say to each other, 'Come and hear what the word is that comes forth from Yahweh' (Ezek. xxxiii. 30). The prophet promises to tell to those who ask him for an oracle whatever answer Yahweh may give (Jer. xlii. 4). When the prophetic voice is silent and revelations are not given, it is said that Yahweh does not answer; there is no answer from God (Mic. iii. 4, 7).

Yahweh Himself calls the prophetic word *His* word. In the vision by which Jeremiah was called to be a prophet Yahweh says to him, 'Behold, I put My words in your mouth' (i. 9). On another occasion Yahweh says to Jeremiah, 'Behold, I am making My words in your mouth a fire and this people wood' (v. 14). To an anonymous prophet, or rather to the people of the age to come, Yahweh says, 'My words which I have put in your mouth, shall not depart from your mouth,' etc. (Isa. lix. 21).[10] And to Ezekiel, 'I appoint you a watchman to the house of Israel; and whenever you hear a word from My mouth, you shall warn them from Me' (iii. 17). In Zech. i. 6, Yahweh asks, 'Did not My words and My statutes with which I charged My servants, the prophets, overtake your fathers?' And in Deutero-Isaiah Yahweh says of the prophetic predictions, 'The former things I foretold of old, they issued from My mouth, and I announced them' (Isa. xlviii. 3).

That the prophets brought Yahweh's word to their people is also expressed in the assertion that they prophesied 'in Yahweh's name'.[11] One who carried a message on behalf of another was said to speak 'in the name' of whoever had sent him. This is said of Jeremiah as a prophet sent by Yahweh (xxvi. 16). But in the prophetic terminology the formula signifies primarily that the prophets expressly claimed to speak in Yahweh's stead.[12] The true prophet always speaks 'in Yahweh's name', i.e., he refers to his relation to Yahweh; he claims to be inspired by Yahweh or by the spirit of Yahweh and says that the words which he utters come from Yahweh. The meaning of the phrase 'in Yahweh's name' is clear in a passage in Jeremiah which refers to the false prophets: It is lies which the prophets prophesy in My name. I neither sent them,

[10] The expressions 'the mouth of your seed' and 'the mouth of your seed's seed' tell, in my opinion, in favour of the view that these words are addressed to the people, and not to an individual prophet. The people are thought of as being in possession of the divine word while they have the prophets in their midst. The transition from the third to the second person is not unusual in a revelatory speech.

[11] This formula is particularly frequent in the book of Jeremiah: xi. 21; xiv. 14 f.; xx. 9; xxiii. 25; xxvi. 9, 16, 20; xxvii. 15; xxix. 9, 21, 23; xliv. 16; cf. Zech. xiii. 3; Deut. xviii. 19 ff.

[12] For the use of the formula 'in Yahweh's name' see Heitmüller, '*Im Namen Jesu*'; Grether, *Name und Wort Gottes im Alten Testament*; Bietenhard, art. ὄνομα in *TWBNT*, V.

nor commissioned them, nor spoke to them' (xiv. 14). Also the false prophets refer to Yahweh in their preaching, but this claim is dishonest and baseless. They are wrong in so using the name of Yahweh. Yahweh has not sent them, and their inspiration does not come from Yahweh. They are in fact inspired by the Baal and should actually say that they preach the Baal's words. What is meant is that these prophets were intimately connected with the syncretistic cult at the high places, which was the source of their inspiration.[13] The claim that the Yahweh prophets were actually thought of as sent by Yahweh and as messengers from Yahweh is frequently made. Haggai for instance is emphatically called 'the messenger of Yahweh', entrusted with the message of Yahweh (i. 13). The name of the last canonical prophet, Malachi, designates this prophet as a messenger of Yahweh.

In the time of the classical prophets the identity of Yahweh's word and the words of a true prophet was self-evident and indisputable. Later, however, in the post-exilic period we meet with expressions which show that men were aware of a possible distinction between Yahweh's word and a prophet's own words. This may account for the curiously formed utterance in Hag. i. 12: 'So Zerubbabel, the son of Shealtiel, and Joshua, the son of Jehozadak, the high priest, and all the remnant of the people, listened to the voice of Yahweh, their God, and the words of the prophet Haggai, inasmuch as Yahweh, their God, had sent him.'[14]

That the prophets are in possession of the divine word depends on the fact that they are admitted to the *sôd* of Yahweh. In the Old Testament *sôd* means in the first place consultation, then a group of men consulting together, and finally a decision, plan, or purpose, which is the result of consultation. Even in modern times a traveller in the Arabian deserts cannot fail to observe how, now and then, some of the men in the caravan go aside for consultations concerning the way to go, water supply, payment, etc. A raid against a hostile tribe must of course be prepared by careful and penetrating deliberation and consultation. In the Old Testament we find a typical example of a *sôd* in the story of Joseph and his brothers in Gen. xxxvii. 18 ff. When the brothers saw the boy Joseph in the distance, they began to form a plan for making away with him. Some of them wanted to kill him and then throw him into a pit. Reuben would not shed any blood; he proposed that they should throw Joseph into the pit alive. This was decided. Thereupon, when a caravan of Ishmaelites passed by, Judah proposed that they

---

[13] See Jer. ii. 8; xxiii. 13, where the formula *babba'al* occurs.
[14] So Sellin in *Das Zwölfprophetenbuch*, II.

should sell Joseph to the Ishmaelites. The brothers agreed. This was a characteristic *sôḏ*. The term could have been applied to the brothers when they conferred together, to the act of consultation, and to the decision which was its outcome. This well illustrates what is meant by the *sôḏ* of Yahweh.

According to Jeremiah, Yahweh says of the false prophets, 'If they had stood in My *sôḏ* [i.e., My council], they had preached My words to My people' (xxiii. 22). The original idea behind this is that Yahweh has consultations with the divine beings who surround Him in heaven (cf. Gen. i. 26; 1 Kings xxii. 19 ff.; Job i. 6 ff.). In this heavenly council plans were made for the actions of Yahweh on earth. If the false prophets had taken part in these consultations, they would have had Yahweh's words, thoughts, and decisions to announce to the people. The same thought occurs in Jer. xxiii. 18: 'Which of them has stood in the council of Yahweh, so that he could perceive His word?'[15] Amos says in a famous passage in which he speaks of his prophetic consciousness, 'Surely, the Lord Yahweh does nothing without revealing His *sôḏ* [i.e., what He has planned and decided] to His servants the prophets' (iii. 7).

Thus the words of the prophets are words which they have heard directly from Yahweh. So great is the privilege of the true prophets, so high their mission, that Yahweh does nothing at all that He has not first revealed to the prophets. In the prophetic passages the idea of the *sôḏ* of Yahweh is presumably spiritualized and metaphorical. But originally it was of course realistically meant.

The medieval mystics said that *lingua divinitatis* was speaking in them. The true Yahweh prophet accused the false prophet of conceitedly using his own tongue (Jer. xxiii. 31), while he himself was conscious of being Yahweh's mouth. Jeremiah heard Yahweh saying, 'If you return, I will let you stand again before Me; and if you bring forth what is precious, without anything base, you shall be as My mouth' (xv. 19). The same prophet knew that in the significant vision at the beginning of his career Yahweh had put His words in his mouth (i. 9). From this very moment he was sure that Yahweh's word was 'with him' (xxiii. 28).[16]

The relation between Yahweh as the author of the divine word and the prophet as the mouth of Yahweh is very clearly illustrated by the

---

[15] This passage refers to the false prophets. The text is doubtful. *wᵉyēre'* and *wᵉyišma'* seem to be doublets, as is suggested by the text of the LXX, which presupposes *wᵉyēre'* only. 'To *see* words' is in accordance with Hebrew idiom, particularly in the prophetic literature (cf. Isa. ii. 1; Am. i. 1, etc.). *wᵉyišma'* is to be regarded as an explanatory gloss.

[16] Hebr. *'ittô*: he was in possession of Yahweh's word.

relation between Moses and Aaron described in Ex. iv. 15 f. Moses was commanded by Yahweh to speak to Aaron and put the words in his mouth. 'Aaron', Yahweh said to Moses, 'shall speak for you to the people; he shall serve as a mouth to you, and you shall act the part of God to him.' What Aaron is here in relation to Moses, every prophet is in relation to Yahweh.

Thus the true prophets are conscious of being mouthpieces of Yahweh and nothing else. They are nothing but channels for the stream of revelation. What they have to bring forth is not their own words (they would be worthless), but only the precious divine word which has been put in their mouth.

Underlying all these conceptions of the divine word is the idea of the objective nature of this divine word, so characteristic of the prophetic consciousness. We have referred to the experience of Jeremiah, when in his first vision he heard Yahweh saying, 'See, I put My words in your mouth.' Such was also the experience of Ezekiel, though he describes it in a more picturesque manner, appropriate to his peculiar temperament. In his inaugural vision he saw a hand stretched out to him, and in the hand was a scroll covered with writing on both sides; words of lamentation, mourning, and woe were written on it. Then the prophet was ordered to eat the scroll; and he opened his mouth and heard the divine voice saying to him, 'Eat and digest this scroll.' Thus the prophet was prepared to preach the words of God to the house of Israel.

This sense of the objective nature of the inspired word leads us straight to the heart of the psychology of inspiration and has countless analogies in the prophetic consciousness as well as in the inspiration of the great poets.

It is impossible to understand the role played by the prophets in Israelite society without realizing that the divine word pronounced by them in exhortation, warning, and judgement was not only descriptive, but also effective and creative.

Precisely because it was a divine word from Yahweh's own mouth the prophetic word was a word with effective power. In Sumerian and Accadian texts we frequently find the idea that the words uttered by a deity were powerful and creative.[17] Words were means by which the gods exercised their power in the world. In every publication of Accadian hymns we find passages where the word of a particular deity is praised for its effective and creative power. The same idea was current in ancient Israel. By His word Yahweh made the heavens and the earth.

---

[17] For the idea of the effective power of the divine word see above, pp. 51 ff.

Yahweh said, 'Let there be light!' and there was light (Gen. i. 3). 'By Yahweh's word the heavens were made and by the breath [$r\hat{u}^a h$] of His mouth all their host' (Ps. xxxiii. 6). 'He spoke, and it came to be. He commanded, and it stood there' (v. 9). The connection of the word with the breath or the spirit of Yahweh may be noticed. This connection was characteristic of the prophets, too, as will be shown below. In a typical cultic hymn all created things are exhorted to praise Yahweh: 'Let them praise the name of Yahweh! For He commanded and they were created' (Ps. cxlviii. 5). Also Yahweh's everyday activities in nature are ascribed to the effectiveness of His word: 'He sends forth His command to the earth; His word runs with speed. He gives snow like wool; He scatters hoar-frost like ashes' (cxlvii. 15 f.). In human life, too, Yahweh's word exercised its effective power: 'When they cried to Yahweh in their trouble, He delivered them from their distress. He sent forth His word to heal them and to free their life from the grave' (cvii. 19 f.).[18]

This idea of the active force of the divine word survived until late times. In the Wisdom of Solomon the destroying angel who slew the first-born in Egypt is identified with the hypostatized word of Yahweh: 'When peaceful silence enveloped everything and night was midway of her swift course, Thy all-powerful word leaped from heaven, from the royal throne, a stern warrior, into the midst of the doomed land, carrying as a sharp sword Thy undisguised command', etc. (Wisd. xviii. 14 ff.).

In the Wisdom literature the role of the powerful divine word is usually taken over by the figure of Wisdom,[19] and in rabbinical literature we often meet with the idea of the creative *memra*. The Torah, too, is sometimes spoken of as a form of the divine word, partaking in its active power. Obedience to the Torah has its recompense, and disobedience to it brings punishment; but it is also said that the Torah itself produces effects in human life. We read for instance in Ps. cxix. 50 f.: 'This is my comfort in my affliction, that Thy word revives me. The arrogant have scoffed at me bitterly, but I have not turned away from Thy Torah.'

There is no essential difference between Yahweh's word and Yahweh's voice (*kôl yahwêh*). Always when Yahweh's voice is heard a creative effect is produced. Especially in the cultic hymns Yahweh's voice is glorified for its power. One of the finest examples is to be found in Ps. xxix: 'The voice of Yahweh is powerful, the voice of Yahweh is majestic. The voice of Yahweh breaks the cedars, Yahweh shatters the

[18] More examples in Dürr, *Die Wertung des göttlichen Wortes*, pp. 38 ff.
[19] See Ringgren, *Word and Wisdom*, pp. 157 ff.

cedars of Lebanon', etc. Further: 'He utters His voice and the earth melts' (xlvi. 7). Originally 'Yahweh's voice' was, of course, the thunder; later it referred more generally to the powerful commands of Yahweh in His government of the world.

Here a few words may be said about the passage on Yahweh's voice in Am. i. 2. The passage runs: 'When Yahweh roars from Zion and utters His voice from Jerusalem, the pastures of the shepherds mourn and the top of Carmel withers.' It has been suggested that this verse is a sort of motto to the whole book. Another view is that the word is a summarizing and anticipatory description of the afflictions with which the prophet threatens the nations in the next following series of oracles. I think that the introductory words aim at glorifying the voice of Yahweh in a more general sense. It is a fragment taken from a cultic hymn and placed here in order to prepare and evoke the appropriate emotional response to all the oracles which follow. Joel iv. 16, a parallel to the passage in Amos, is consequently not a quotation from Amos, but taken from the same liturgy. With a slight variation the same word occurs a third time, namely in Jer. xxv. 30: 'Yahweh roars from on high, from his holy habitation He utters His voice.'[20]

The cultic explanation of Am. i. 2 is supported by the fact that there are many Accadian cultic hymns similarly devoted to glorifying the power of the divine voice or the word uttered by a god. Thus we read in a hymn to the Moon-God: 'When thy word drifts along in heaven like the wind it makes rich the feeding and drinking of the land./When thy word settles down on the earth green vegetation is produced./Thy word makes fat the sheepfold and the stall; it makes living creatures widespread./Thy word causes truth and justice to be, so that the people speak the truth.'[21]

But the divine word has also a destructive effect. We read in a hymn to Marduk: 'Thy word is a lofty net which over heaven and earth thou spreadest out./Unto the sea it turns, the sea takes fright./Unto the marsh it turns, the marsh laments./To the flood of Euphrates it turns:/ the word of Marduk stirs up the bottom./Lord, thou art lofty, who equals thee?' And, finally, in a hymn to Nergal: 'His word makes the people sick, the people it makes weak./His word when it goes on high the land makes sick./His word when it goes below destroys the land.'[22]

Was the introductory liturgical fragment in Am. i. 2 placed there by

---

[20] Similarly Bentzen in *OTS*, VIII, 1950, pp. 85 ff.
[21] *ANET*², p. 386.
[22] Cumming, *The Assyrian and Hebrew Hymns of Praise*, pp. 90 f. Other examples in the book by Dürr mentioned above.

Amos himself or is it a later addition? It is impossible to answer this question with certainty, but it seems most likely that the word was inserted when the revelations of Amos were used in the cult. In my view the so-called doxologies in the later chapters of Amos are also liturgical additions of a similar kind.[23]

The ancient Israelites also thought of the human word as an effective power. There was to them an intimate connection between the soul of a man and the word uttered by him. The power of a strong soul was infused into the word uttered by its owner. A blessing or a curse pronounced on another person created good fortune or misfortune in his bodily and mental life.[24] That the word of Yahweh, the almighty God, was a powerful word in the highest degree, was self-evident to the ancient Israelites. That the words of the prophets of Yahweh, the mouthpieces and messengers of the omnipotent God, were filled with creative power was likewise self-evident to them. The following examples from the prophetic literature are of particular interest.

One of the finest instances of the effect of the powerful divine word is this utterance by Deutero-Isaiah: 'As the rain comes down, and the snow from heaven, and returns not thither without having watered the earth and made it bring forth and sprout, giving seed to the sower and bread to the eater, so shall My word be that goes out of My mouth—it shall not return to Me fruitless without having done the things that I pleased and accomplishing the purpose for which I sent it' (Isa. lv. 10 f.).

There is no essential difference between the word as an expression of the active power of Yahweh and the divine word pronounced by the prophets. In this respect Yahweh's word and the words of the prophets are one and the same. The words of the prophets were divine words and thus they shared the active power of Yahweh. The same prophet who uttered the sublime words quoted above about the divine word says of the efficacy of his own words: 'He made my mouth like a sharp sword . . . ; He made me a polished arrow' (xlix. 2).

The prophet Jeremiah in his inaugural vision heard Yahweh saying, 'See, I put My words in your mouth; this day I give you commission over the nations and kingdoms to root up and to pull down, to build and to plant' (i. 9 f.).[25] Here it is said that Jeremiah's message, whether of judgement or of salvation, would be not only a statement about doom

[23] Am. iv. 13; v. 8 f.; ix. 6. Similarly Weiser in his commentary on Amos in *ATD*.
[24] See Pedersen, *Israel*, I-II, pp. 167 f.
[25] The words 'to destroy and to overthrow' are somewhat awkward in this passage and seem to have been inserted here by a writer who remembered the phraseology of xviii. 7; xxiv. 6; xxxi. 28.

or salvation, but also a power which really created ruin or prosperity
for the nations. We may compare two other striking sayings: 'Behold,
I am making My words in your mouth a fire, and this people wood,
and the fire shall devour them' (Jer. v. 14); and: 'Is not My word
burning like fire, or like a hammer that breaks rocks in pieces' (Jer.
xxiii. 29).[26]

Jeremiah's fateful oracle, hurled in the face of the false prophet
Hananiah, is followed immediately by the terse statement of its fulfilment: '"This very year you shall die; for you have uttered rebellion
against Yahweh." That very year, in the seventh month, the prophet
Hananiah died' (Jer. xxviii. 16 f.). Here the oracle is certainly not
thought of only as a prediction, but as a word of power which really
killed Hananiah. There is no need to question the historicity of this
episode. The prophets spoke of the divine power of the word; a modern
psychologist speaks of suggestion. The practical result is in both cases
the same. Hananiah died, and the oracle of disaster against him proved
to be true.

The famous vision of the bones in the valley related in Ezek. xxxvii
gives us another interesting example of the idea of the powerful word.
Ezekiel was commanded to prophesy over the dry, lifeless bones. Then
he said to the bones, 'Thus says Yahweh, "Behold, I am causing breath
to enter you, and you shall live. I will put sinews upon you, and will
clothe you with flesh, and cover you with skin."' And as Ezekiel prophesied, there was a sound, and there followed a rustling, and the bones
came together, and, finally, at the word of the prophet, breath came into
them all together, obviously by the power of the divine word acting
through the mouth of the prophet.

The active power of the divine word is reflected in several realistic
expressions connected with the prophetic preaching. When a prophetic
word was heard, it was as if a catastrophe had happened, as if a thunder-
bolt had struck the earth, as if a blow had fallen on men. Hosea, seeing
that his people will not repent, says in Yahweh's stead, 'Therefore I
hew them by the prophets, I slay them by the words of My mouth'
(vi. 5). Isaiah begins one of his revelations thus: 'The Lord sends a word
against Jacob, and it lights upon Israel' (ix. 7). Deutero-Zechariah says
that Yahweh's word has come into the land of Hadrach and has found
its resting-place in Damascus (Zech. ix. 1). Here the divine word is
almost identical with the divine judgement itself, just as the divine
voice (ḳôl) in Isa. xxx. 30 f., where Yahweh's voice and the blow of
Yahweh's arm stand as parallels.

[26] Read kōwēh for kôh; cf. BH.

The vision in which Zechariah saw a roll flying over the land is particularly illuminating. This roll contained the words of a curse upon the sinners in the land, and it was sent forth that it might enter the house of the thief and the house of him who swore falsely by Yahweh's name, and settle in the midst of his house and consume it with its woodwork and its stonework (v. 1-4). This description reflects old ideas of the magic writing which acts *ex opere operato*. With this we may compare the law in Num. v. 11 ff. about the ordeal applied to a woman suspected of unfaithfulness. The priest had to write down certain curses and then wash them off into water. Then he had to make the woman drink the water; if the woman was guilty, the water would produce painful and unpleasant effects; if she was not guilty, the water would do her no harm.

A similar idea occurs in the curious passage in Jer. li. 61 ff. about the scroll the contents of which were to be read aloud in Babylon. A stone was then to be tied to the scroll and it was to be thrown into the Euphrates. This story obviously presupposes ultimately the idea of a writing filled with power, which exercised its disastrous effect in the midst of the doomed land.[27] Such magical usages are common among more primitive peoples. It is for instance known that the bedouin of the Syrian deserts write down formulas or verses from the Koran on scraps of paper, which are then burnt, and a sterile woman has to inhale the smoke; or the paper is dissolved in water, which then is given to the woman to drink.[28]

Magical ideas of this kind are of course alien to the great prophets. In their opinion Yahweh Himself was working in His words. The magical colouring is only superficial. The essential element is the belief of the prophets in the power of Yahweh, the almighty God.

Since the prophetic word was a word of effective power, menacing words uttered by a prophet were felt as a real evil and a grave affliction for a people or a country. After having heard the terrible oracles of

[27] Since the curses on Babylon were recited when no one was present to hear them, the throwing of the scroll into the Euphrates cannot have been merely symbolic. A symbolic action presupposes spectators. The idea is that both the recitation of the curses and the sinking of the scroll were intended to bring about the downfall of Babylon. The words of *v.* 64 are to be conceived as a curse accompanying the sinking of the stone, not as an interpretation of a symbolic action. We should, however, note the prayer (*v.* 62) which precedes the action. The magical character of the action is confined to the outward form. The active force is, according to the prophetic view, Yahweh's will. There is no cogent reason for questioning the historicity of the narrative.

[28] Müller, *En Syrie avec les bédouins*, p. 273. More examples in Canaan, *Aberglaube und Volksmedizin im Lande der Bibel*, pp. 116 ff. See also Fohrer, *Die symbolischen Handlungen der Propheten*, p. 34. The law of Num. v. 23 f. obviously describes an action of this kind.

Amos against Israel and her king, Amaziah, the priest of Bethel, sent
to Jeroboam, the king, saying, 'Amos has conspired against you in the
midst of the house of Israel. The land cannot *endure all his words*'
(Am. vii. 10).

Because the prophets not only *foretold* calamities, but also *created*
calamities, it was logical enough that they were both hated and feared.
They were persecuted; and attempts were made to kill them. Amos and
Jeremiah both provide good examples of the hostility which the prophets
had to suffer.

At the same time the prophets were regarded as being sacrosanct and
inviolable, just because their words were not human words, but divine
words filled with sanctity. It was dangerous to do violence to them, to
defy them, or to obstruct them. When Amaziah, the priest, tried to
prevent Amos from prophesying in Bethel and told him to quit the
country, the menaces of the prophet against the people took the form
of an oracle of doom against the priest personally; and when Hananiah,
the false prophet, had taken the yoke from the neck of Jeremiah and
broken it, and had turned his prophecy into its reverse, he was struck
down by the disastrous oracle: 'This very year you shall die.'

Just as an oracle of doom was regarded as creating misfortune, an
oracle of peace was regarded as creating good fortune. This belief caused
people to call on the prophets to intercede with God and supplicate
Him to give a favourable oracle. This was, of course, the intention of
King Zedekiah, when he sent to Jeremiah to consult him (Jer. xxxvii.
3 ff.), though in fact the outcome was not what he expected.[29]

Because the prophetic word was claimed to be the word of Yahweh,
the omnipotent God, it was a word worthy of attention throughout the
world. When heaven, earth, and mankind are exhorted to listen to the
proclamations of Isaiah or Micah (Isa. i. 2; Mic. i. 2), it is not for the
sake of Isaiah or Micah, but because the word they have to utter is of
divine origin; and such a word was of importance not only for Israel,
but also for the whole creation. Deutero-Isaiah calls upon the coastlands and the far nations to listen to him in silence when he unfolds the
plans and designs of Yahweh and His actions in world-history (Isa.
xli. 1; xlix. 1); and Jeremiah summons the nations and the whole earth
to hear what Yahweh has determined for His apostate people (vi. 18 f.).
Thus Yahweh's word penetrates as far as His rule reaches.

Before ending this section we must briefly consider the psychological
background of the reception of the word of Yahweh. The idea was that

[29] The verb *hitpallēl*, *v.* 3, means here, 'pray for a favourable oracle,' as is evident
from *v.* 7.

Yahweh spoke to the prophet, and that the prophet heard the voice of Yahweh. What did this hearing imply?

It is tempting to apply to it the term 'audition', which is so common in the psychology of religion. If by 'audition' is meant a hearing with the 'inward ear' in the ecstatic experience, then it is not wholly appropriate to the prophetic hearing of the divine voice. Instances of such ecstatic audition may, of course, have occurred, for instance, when the hearing is included in an ecstatic vision. In the inaugural visions of the prophets visual and auditory elements are mingled together. We are also justified in speaking of an 'audition' when the hearing as such is described by expressions which point to an ecstatic experience. When Isaiah says that Yahweh spoke to him, while 'the hand' grasped him strongly (viii. 11), he is, no doubt, describing an ecstatic experience; and therefore the term 'audition' in the above sense is appropriate.[30]

But in most cases there can be no talk of auditions in the strict sense. The idea of hearing is only a means of describing the inspiration by which the high ideas emerged in the soul of the prophet, and is used because of the conviction that all that was given the prophet, was given him from God and did not originate in the man himself.

What is true of the Old Testament prophets is also true of the medieval visionaries. Many of their so-called 'auditions' are not auditions in the strict sense, but simply refer to inspiration of a general kind or are purely literary productions. In this respect there is no difference between the Israelite prophets and the Christian visionaries.[31]

It is curious that the prophets are said not only to have *heard* Yahweh's word, but to have *seen* it. The prophetic revelations are regarded as visions, even when nothing is 'seen' in our sense. The prophetic *words* of Amos are something that he had *seen* (i. 1). The eschatological prophecy in Isa. ii on the mountain of Yahweh is described as a *word* that Isaiah *saw*. Jeremiah speaks of the *words* that Yahweh had let him *see* (xxxviii. 21).[32] The prophets are frequently called 'seers', never 'hearers'. This mode of expression undoubtedly arises in part from the feeling of an intimate connection between the classical prophets and the 'seers' of old times,[33] and also in part from the fact that the real visions were

[30] Cf. Isa. v. 9; xxii. 14; Ezek. ix. 1, 5.

[31] Andrae in his above-mentioned admirable book on the psychology of mysticism seems to me to exaggerate on this point the difference between the medieval visionaries and the Israelite prophets (pp. 254 ff.). His statement (p. 256) that the inspiration of the prophets was predominantly auditory, while the medieval revelation literature is visionary or eidetic, is hardly tenable; cf., for instance, the revelations of Birgitta, which for the most part are unquestionably auditory.

[32] Cf. Isa. i. 1; xiii. 1; xxx. 10; Hab. i. 1; ii. 2, etc.

[33] This is particularly emphasized by Knight, *The Hebrew Prophetic Consciousness*, p. 44.

considered as an essential element in the prophetic experience. Finally
it is to be noted that the Israelites did not accurately distinguish between
the various kinds of sensation. The verb 'see' could be applied to hearing
as well as to the reception of any sort of mental impression.[34]

To the real auditions we shall return in the next section.

3. ECSTATIC VISIONS AND AUDITIONS

Like their predecessors the classical prophets were endowed with the
gift of receiving revelations from the divine world. Indeed, they themselves make this claim. Thus the term 'revelation' in this connection is
not used in its dogmatic sense, nor is an opinion expressed about the
reality which lies behind the claim. Our point of view is a historical and
psychological, not a dogmatic one.

Because the revelations were conveyed through perceptions, thoughts,
and ideas which were then expressed in words, we are justified in using
the term 'revelation' also for the verbal, we might say, the literary
expressions of what had been revealed. All such prophetic revelations
have this in common that they are apprehended in a state of inspiration,
which may be experienced in different degrees from real ecstasy to a condition which is almost indistinguishable from the normal state of mind.

The contents of the revelations vary widely. We find among them
sermons and admonitory addresses, announcements of doom and
punishment, lyric poems, prayers, hymns, parables, dialogues, monologues, short oracles, didactic sentences, predictions, messages, letters,
etc. Neither the prophets themselves nor their contemporaries regarded
these as ordinary literary productions, but as inspired by God and
revealed to the prophets in a supernatural way. Accordingly, we may,
for the sake of brevity, appropriately apply the term 'revelation' always
when a prophet speaks *qua* prophet.

We now proceed to examine two groups of prophetic revelations
which are of great psychological interest: visions (i.e., revelations
experienced in the form of visual perceptions) and auditions (i.e.,
revelations experienced in the form of auditory perceptions). It will be
well at the outset to define our terms by recapitulating briefly part of
what was said in Chapter One.

By 'vision' and 'audition' we understand visual and auditory perceptions received in trance or ecstasy, or in a mental state approximating
thereto. These perceptions are not caused by any object in the external
world, but arise within the soul. He who sees and hears often says that

[34] See Pedersen, *Israel*, I-II, p. 100.

he sees by his 'inward eye' and hears by his 'inward ear'. What appears to him is not the external world, but the invisible, the divine world, the doors of which are closed to everyday consciousness, but open to men who are in 'the supernatural state of mind', in the holy hours when it pleases God to reveal His secrets to human beings.[34a]

It is necessary to distinguish carefully between ecstatic 'visions' and 'auditions' on one side and 'hallucinations' on the other. A hallucination is a visual, auditory, or other sensory perception which does not correspond to any objective reality in the external world, but (and here it differs from vision and audition) is thought to be apprehended by the bodily senses and has all the characteristic features of a real perception, although it does not correspond to any external reality.

At the higher stages of religious development hallucinations are not very common.[35] Taking hallucination in its proper sense and in its rigorously restricted meaning, I could not with confidence describe any of the extraordinary perceptions of the classical prophets of the Old Testament as hallucinations. It is of course possible that some of the curious experiences of Ezekiel were hallucinatory. Neurotic and hysterical traits are more evident in him than in the other prophets. Perhaps the taste of honey which he felt in his mouth, as he ate the scroll (iii. 1 ff.), was of a hallucinatory nature. The same may have been true of his awareness of the hand which on different occasions grasped him (muscular hallucination). But at all events the great majority of the prophetic visions are ecstatic visions in the sense indicated above.[36]

Hölscher and other scholars have described the bulk of the prophetic visions as hallucinations.[37] The ground for this mistake (for it is a mistake) is that these scholars do not distinguish between hallucinations and what have been called 'pseudo-hallucinations', or, according to our terminology, 'ecstatic visions'. Once the distinction is made between the 'outward eye' and the 'inward eye', the 'outward ear' and the 'inward ear' (as in the medieval visionaries) it is much more appropriate to say that the supernatural visual experiences of the prophets were ecstatic visions than that they were hallucinations.

It would likewise be a mistake to maintain that the majority of the prophetic visions were only products of the creative imagination

[34a] The term 'revelation' in the above sense was common among the medieval visionaries. The literary works of Birgitta of Sweden, for instance, are called 'Revelationes celestes sanctae Birgittae'.

[35] Cf. Andrae, op. cit., pp. 220 ff.

[36] Interesting examples of various kinds of hallucination are to be found in Schneider, *Die Erlebnisechtheit der Apokalypse des Johannes* with abundant literary references.

[37] Hölscher *Die Profeten*, pp. 35 ff.

comparable with poetry. The visions of the Israelite prophets must be studied in the light of the modern psychology of *religion*, and it would be a serious blunder to isolate them as something entirely unique and not connect them with similar phenomena elsewhere in the religious world. Those scholars who are content to inquire how the prophets *themselves* regarded their visions are neglecting the task of studying the visions *scientifically* in the proper sense of the word, i.e., objectively, in the light of the history and psychology of religion.[38]

It is not difficult to establish the general characteristics of the ecstatic visions. There is in them something irrational and ineffable, something which transcends normal, everyday experience, opening the doors of the supernatural world as they do. Though what the visionary sees may be described vividly and in detail, there is a looseness and lack of structural connection. Time and space seem not to matter, and scenes change rapidly as in dreams.[39]

Among the ecstatic visions we may distinguish between two groups. In one group the attention is directed simply to the objects or figures which are seen. We may call such visions *pictorial visions*. In the other group the essential element is the action. The stress lies upon what the persons who appear in the vision undertake and do. Different figures appear and play their parts as in a drama. Such visions may be called *dramatic visions*. This distinction (as we have seen before) may be applied to the experiences of visionaries wherever they appear in the religious world.

A typical example of a pictorial vision is the inaugural vision of Ezekiel. Our attention is held captive by the wonderful throne, the four creatures, the wheels, the firmament stretched out above the heads of the creatures, and finally, sitting on the throne, the supermundane Being who is described vaguely but impressively. But there is also a dramatic element. A hand was stretched out to the prophet, and in the hand was a scroll which the prophet ate. This detail is the most significant in the whole vision because it contains the call of the prophet to his mission; but in the general structure of the vision the pictorial elements predominate.

The description of this vision is very instructive. We notice how difficult it was for the visionary to render in a comprehensible manner what he had seen in his ecstasy. It is quite useless to attempt to get all the details in order, for instance, to determine how the wheels and the

[38] On these points I follow other lines than, for instance, Hänel in *Das Erkennen Gottes bei den Schriftpropheten* (cf. 'Die Aufgabe', pp. 1 ff.).

[39] For the structure of the visions see, for instance, Sister in *MGWJ*, lxxviii, 1934, pp. 399 ff.

creatures were constructed in relation to each other. What Ezekiel saw in his vision was not a coherent and clearly outlined picture. The description is only a feeble attempt to reproduce something that in itself was ethereal and ineffable. The content of an ecstatic vision is always mysterious, unnatural, and unlike normal perceptions. As we have said above, there is a close affinity between an ecstatic vision and a dream.

It is significant that the prophet constantly uses comparisons instead of direct statements. He saw the semblance of four creatures; the soles of their feet resembled the sole of a calf's foot; in the midst of the creatures was an appearance like burning coals of fire resembling torches; the construction of the wheels was as if one wheel were within another; above the firmament was the semblance of a throne, and so on. Such a mode of expression corresponds exactly to the manner in which we describe a dream.

Like a dream, a vision is composed of different elements taken from the world of normal experience, but often caricatured and combined in a strange and unreal unity. The same is true of this vision of Ezekiel. Behind the individual elements we recognize the cherubs of the Babylonian temples and palaces, 'the molten sea' in the sanctuary of Jerusalem, the burning coals of the altar, etc., all, however, transformed in a fanciful way.

Rendering in human words what he had seen in his vision, the prophet inevitably rationalized certain features in some measure, interpreted them, and gave them an allegorical explanation, so that the reader should have an impression of Yahweh's omnipotence, omnipresence, and all-seeing eye.[40] The passage which follows after the description of the vision in ii. 3 ff. does not of course belong to the original vision. Here the prophet reflects on and expresses in rational terms the message which he has been called to deliver. This is also true of the parallel in iii. 4 ff. We must always distinguish carefully between what was originally seen or heard by a prophet and what was subsequently announced. This distinction is typical of all the prophetic revelations and has an important bearing on the interpretation of the prophetic texts.[41]

The vision of the bones in the valley in Ezek. xxxvii is another example of a pictorial vision. The prophet saw a valley which was full of dry bones. At the prophet's command there was a movement among the bones; a sound was heard, then followed a rattling, and the bones came together, bone to its bone. Sinews and flesh came upon them. At

---

[40] Cf. Bertholet in *HAT*, p. 7.

[41] The importance of the rational elaboration of the visionary experiences is pointed out by Mowinckel in *Act. Or.*, xiii, 1935, pp. 264 ff.

the prophet's further command breath came into the bones, and they became living beings which stood upon their feet. These were the original elements of this vision. In addition there seems to have been a dialogue between the prophet and Yahweh concerning the bones. In the actual narrative certain features have been considerably worked over in the light of subsequent reflection. This is particularly true of the colloquial elements and, above all, of the interpretation which follows the vision.

The majority of the visions in the book of Amos are also pictorial visions: the locusts consuming the grass of the land; the fire which devoured the great Ocean and was about to devour Yahweh's land; Yahweh Himself, standing upon a wall, with a plumb-line in His hand, and, finally, the total ruin of the temple in Bethel. In the last two visions the traces of subsequent reflection are particularly marked. The extended description of the total annihilation of the apostate people in ix. 2-4 is, of course, formed by the prophet in connection with the vision, but does not belong to the vision proper. The colloquial elements in some of the visions are certainly original. In the visions of the medieval visionaries dialogues between the visionary and God are very common.[42]

In the vision of the plumb-line, the question 'What do you see, Amos?' and the prophet's answer form a stylistic feature which probably belongs to the subsequent formulation of the visionary dialogue. The same question together with the following answer also appears in the vision of the basket of summer fruit in ch. viii, and later in Jeremiah's visions of the twig of an almond tree and of the pot blown upon in Jer. i, and of the baskets of figs in Jer. xxiv. 1 ff. Finally it occurs in Zech. v. 1 ff., the vision of the flying scroll. This peculiar formal method of expression is not fully explained. In the opinion of the present writer it is a reminiscence from the didactic practice of the old wisdom schools, where we can suppose the teacher to have been in the habit of pointing to an object in nature and connecting it with his instruction about spiritual matters in order to illustrate and elucidate them.[43]

In this connection the description of the return of chaos in Jer. iv. 23 ff. is worth mentioning, since it has often been misunderstood by commentators.

[42] The text of the vision of the plumb-line in Am. vii. 7 f. is somewhat uncertain. In the MT Yahweh Himself stands upon a wall with a plumb-line in His hand. In the text proposed in *BH*, in accordance with the Septuagint, a man holds the plumb-line. If the MT is accepted, the vision must be considered as an ecstatic vision in which Yahweh is seen by the prophet just as in ix. 1. If the amended text is followed, the passage records a symbolic vision. I think that the MT may be retained as quite acceptable except for the words *hômat 'anāk* (see *BH*). Other explanations are presented by Hempel in *Die Mehrdeutigkeit der Geschichte als Problem der prophetischen Theologie*, p. 32, note 4.

[43] See further Lindblom in *SVT*, III, 1955, pp. 192 ff.

> I looked at the earth, and lo, there was chaos;
> at the heavens, and their light was gone.
> I looked at the mountains, and lo, they were quaking;
> and all the hills swayed to and fro.
> I looked, and lo, there was no man,
> and all the birds of the air had flown.
> I looked, and lo, the garden land was a desert,
> and all its cities were ravaged
> before Yahweh, before His fierce anger.

The clue to the correct understanding of this passage is the fact that the picture of the destruction given here applies to the universe and not only to the land of Judah. The latter comes into consideration first in *v.* 27: 'For thus says Yahweh, "The whole land shall be a desolation."' The description of the destruction of the universe is a symbolic representation of the destruction of the land of Judah. But the picture of chaos does not give the impression of being merely figurative. It reads like something that the prophet has seen either in his excited fancy or in an ecstatic vision. I prefer to explain the picture as a real vision. The picture of the destroyed cosmos as a pattern of the destruction of the land of Judah is not what we should expect as a product of normal imagination. Everything becomes clear if we realize that it was in a real vision that the prophet saw the chaotic disorder in the world, and that he then interpreted this vision as alluding to the devastation of Judaea. In the visionary literature we often meet descriptions of such symbolic or parabolic visions followed by an interpretation. The Old Testament itself contains other examples of this kind of vision. One of the best is Ezekiel's vision of the dry bones in the valley which became living bodies. That vision is likewise followed by an explanation indicating that everything that happened in the vision alluded to the re-establishment of the Jewish people.

Thus it is not correct to say that this passage (Jer. iv. 23 ff.) contains an eschatological or apocalyptic prophecy. As we have tried to show, the chaos picture serves to illustrate what is soon to happen in Judaea, not something that will happen in the world in the remote future. Thus there is no reason for denying the authenticity of the passage in question. It may very well be Jeremianic.[44]

A vision of a marked dramatic character is the inaugural vision of

---

[44] Cf. Lindblom in *St.Th.*, vi, 1952, pp. 79 ff. (esp. p. 84). Gressmann found cosmic eschatology in the above passage from Jeremiah (*Der Ursprung der israelitisch-jüdischen Eschatologie*, p. 147). Volz, in his commentary, regarded it as apocalyptic. Frost, *Old Testament Apocalyptic*, says that the passage in question is 'eschatological in the absolute sense' and probably not Jeremianic (pp. 53 f.).

Isaiah related in Isa. vi. It is most likely that the prophet experienced this vision when standing in one of the courts of the temple in Jerusalem. Yahweh Himself appeared to him as the kingly God of heaven, sitting on His heavenly throne, filling the whole universe with His majesty; only the skirts of His royal mantle filled the temple. Spatial limits are often transcended in this way in ecstatic visions as in dreams. Yahweh was accompanied by the seraphim, mythical, heavenly beings of fire and light, partly animal and partly human. Though we are not told how many of them there were, it is probable that there were two, corresponding to the two figures who were in attendance upon the king in Accadian usage. It may be remembered that the cherubim in the interior of Solomon's temple were two in number. The *Trisagion* sung by the seraphim was no doubt a formula in the temple ritual. The shaking of the thresholds and the smoke which filled the house are features of the theophany, the smoke being a cover for the divine majesty, as often in the Bible. We remember for instance what is told in connection with the placing of the ark in the temple of Solomon (1 Kings viii. 10 f.), that a cloud filled Yahweh's house, for the glory of Yahweh was in the house. When Isaiah experienced the theophany, he was overwhelmed with fear, because no man can see God and live.[45]

Now the dramatic elements increase. One of the seraphim flew to the prophet with a red-hot stone in his hand, which he had taken from the altar, probably the incense-altar. He touched the prophet's mouth in order to cleanse his lips from sin. Then the prophet heard Yahweh's voice saying, 'Whom shall I send, and who will be My messenger?' whereupon Isaiah said, 'Here am I, send me.' Then follows the content of the message that the prophet had to bring forth to his people. The core of it was an original element of the vision, but, as almost always happens, this core was elaborated in subsequent reflection. We shall return to this vision and its literary reproduction in a following section, where we are dealing with the call of the prophets.

The vision of the downfall of Babylon which is reproduced in Isa. xxi is another example of a dramatic vision. This vision presupposes the rise of Babylon as a world-capital, the subjugation of the Jewish people by the Babylonian empire, and the imminent attack on Babylon by the Persians (historical events which took place 100 to 150 years after the life-time of Isaiah), and is in later times incorporated into the collection of the Isaianic revelations. The vision bears traces of being a genuine ecstatic vision, but comes from an anonymous prophet.

The visionary hears a noise, like the noise of whirlwinds which sweep

---

[45] See further Engnell, *The Call of Isaiah*; Béguerie in *LD*, 14, pp. 11 ff.

through the Negeb.[46] It comes from the desert, i.e., the Syrian desert beyond which Babylonia is situated. He sees with his inward eyes the work of plunder and devastation. He hears a cry of command: 'Go up, O Elam, lay siege, O Media!' and further: 'Now I will bring all the groaning [i.e., of the oppressed Jews] to an end.' Then he sees tables laid out, mats spread, men eating and drinking. Suddenly a command is heard: 'Arise, O princes, anoint the shields!'

In close connection with this vision another vision comes, which is not really a new vision, but only another phase of the same sequence of visionary events. There is a sudden change of scene, such as we often experience in dreams. Now the visionary, at the command of God, stations a watchman to announce what he sees. If he sees a train of chariots, teams of horses, a train of asses, a train of camels, he must pay close heed. Then the watchman cries, 'On my watch-tower, O Lord, I stand continually by day; and at my guard-post I am stationed night after night. Behold, now there come chariots with their horsemen, teams of horses.' Further the watchman cries, 'Fallen, fallen is Babylon; and all the images of her gods are shattered to the earth.'

Here we have a reproduction of a typical ecstatic vision with all its ardour and excitement, its high-strung agitation and dramatic tension. The scenes change, the roles are altered. The pictures change like the pieces of glass in a kaleidoscope. Visual and auditory impressions abruptly succeed each other. The vague indications and the indistinct contours are very characteristic. 'Something' comes, 'something' is heard. Undetermined figures appear, voices are heard—we do not know from where. The speaking and acting persons suddenly alternate in a peculiar manner.

The second phase of the vision contains a feature of the greatest interest to the student of prophetic psychology. The watchman whom the prophet was ordered to station is not called 'a watchman', but 'the watchman'. It has been questioned who this watchman was. In the light of modern psychology the watchman is identical with the visionary himself when he was transported into the other world. The prophet distinguishes between himself as ordinary man and himself when rapt away. The rapt personality is observed and spoken of by the prophet in his normal state of mind as if this rapt personality were quite another

[46] *yām* is probably the remains of some word from the root *hmh*, which the text originally contained. The first colon of the poem must be completed by one word, probably a verb. The superscription is derived from *miḏbār* in the second line. Dhorme in *Recueil*, pp. 301 ff., retains the words *miḏbar yām* and thinks that they correspond to the well-known Accadian expression 'the Land of the Sea', meaning the land on the Persian Gulf (Babylonia).

person. Now we are enabled to understand why this watchman is called '*the* watchman', and why he is later called 'the seer' (*v.* 8).[47] The watchman sees exactly the same as the prophet himself would have seen. The watchman plays, in a word, entirely the same role as the prophet. In his being on guard continually night and day the prophet's own expectant attitude towards the events of the time is reflected. Consequently we have here to do with the curious phenomenon which in the first chapter of this book we have called the phenomenon of 'the secondary personality'. Other examples were there given of similar peculiar experiences undergone by men and women of the visionary type.[48]

In this vision we also learn what the prophet felt when he had his vision. He calls the vision a 'stern' one. His loins are filled with anguish; pangs have seized him like those of a woman in travail. He is tortured so that he cannot hear, terror-stricken so that he cannot see. His mind reels, shuddering assails him. The twilight he waited for was turned into trembling.

This description of the prophet's emotional experiences was of course added when the vision was subsequently formulated. In a vision as well as in a dream the emotional life is often excited to the uttermost, but the description of the feelings comes subsequently.

By saying that the longed-for twilight was turned into trembling, the prophet possibly gives us to understand that the vision came to him in the evening.

The phenomenon of 'the secondary personality' is not very common among the Israelite prophets. A further example is to be found in the book of Isaiah, namely in xxi. 11. The prophet (possibly Isaiah) hears in an audition a voice coming from Seir (Edom.) The voice asks what hour of the night it is. The prophet answers in typical oracle style, 'Morning comes, but also night', i.e., events alternate, the circumstances of the time are obscure and untransparent. If you would know more, then—come again! The prophet is called 'watchman' by the mysterious voice; but speaking of himself in the third person he also calls himself 'the watchman', the watchman consequently being his *alter ego*, his secondary personality.

The passage in Jer. xxv. 15 ff. on the cup of wine is keenly discussed by the commentators. The prophet is ordered to take from Yahweh's hand a cup of wine and make all the nations to whom Jeremiah was to be sent drink it, so that they should drink and reel and be crazed like madmen. Jeremiah took the cup from the Lord's hand and made all

---

[47] For '*aryêh* I read *rō'êh*.
[48] For this vision see further Scott in *VT*, ii, 1952, pp. 278 ff.

nations drink as he was ordered. Then a number of peoples are enumerated who had to drink from the cup. Obviously the narrative of this incident has been considerably expanded. The series of peoples has been increased and interpretative remarks have been added; but at all events a core remains which compels us to ask: what is this narrative dealing with? There are only two alternatives: either the narrative is only a literary parable, or it is a reproduction of a vision. The central role which the prophet himself plays in that which happens and the absence of all expressions which usually characterize a comparison speak in favour of the fact that we here have to do with a real vision, and, moreover, with a vision of a markedly dramatic character. Like the chaos vision in Jer. iv. 23 ff., this vision has a symbolic significance. The cup of wine symbolizes the wrath of Yahweh revealed in His terrible punishment of the nations. The reeling symbolizes the ruin of the nations considered as the result of the divine destructive force.[49]

Akin to the narrative of the cup of wine is the narrative of the linen loin-cloth in Jer. xiii. The prophet was commanded to buy a linen loin-cloth and put it on his loins without letting water touch it. The new and untouched loin-cloth was better fitted to its purpose than an old one.[50] He did so. Then he received a new order. He must arise and go to the Euphrates and hide the loin-cloth there in a crevice of the rock. The prophet did what he was commanded to do. A long time after his return to his own country the prophet was again ordered to go to the Euphrates and take out the loin-cloth from its hiding-place. He went a second time to the Euphrates and dug out the loin-cloth only to find that the loin-cloth was ruined and good for nothing.

How is this narrative to be explained? It is impossible to suppose that the narrative is a literal description of actual events. We cannot imagine that Jeremiah in his real life again and again went to the distant region of the Euphrates. Some scholars have maintained that the river in question was not the Babylonian Euphrates, but a wadi in the neighbourhood of Jerusalem or Anathoth. Such an interpretation is, however, quite without foundation. In the Bible the Hebrew *pᵉraṭ* always signifies the well-known Mesopotamian river and nothing else. The highly dramatic tenor of the description of what the prophet did at Yahweh's command becomes more comprehensible if we assume that it depicts his actual experiences in an ecstatic vision than if we interpret it purely as a piece of allegorical fiction.

[49] Ringgren in *SEÅ*, xvii, 1952, pp. 19 ff., thinks that the motif of the cup of wine symbolizing Yahweh's doom upon the nations has its origin in ancient Semitic cultic usages.
[50] See above, p. 52, note 8.

This vision has also a symbolic meaning. It must be interpreted as an allegory. The precious loin-cloth folded around the loins of the prophet means the people of Israel, joined by election to her God. The destruction of the loin-cloth in the crevice of the Euphrates refers to the ruin of the Jewish people in the Babylonian exile, regarded as a punishment for the apostasy of the people. Three ideas find expression in the vision: the election of the people, its rejection by Yahweh, and its destruction through the Babylonian exile. It is difficult to suppose that those who in the days of Jeremiah heard the account of this vision could have understood it in another way. The interpretation given in vv. 8-11, though Deuteronomically coloured, expresses exactly the same ideas. It is often said that Jeremiah's view of the deported Jews in this vision contradicts the view expressed in the vision of the two baskets of figs in ch. xxiv, but this supposed contradiction disappears if we assume that the two visions are from different times. The vision of the loin-cloth is readily intelligible in the times of King Jehoiakim (cf., for instance, xxv. 1-11). The vision of the baskets of figs presupposes the deportation in the reign of King Jehoiachin, a quite different situation.[51]

Of visionary voyages from one place to another there are many examples. Of Mohammed, for instance, it is told that he made a nocturnal voyage from Mecca to Jerusalem, and Ezekiel was more than once transported in visions from Babylonia to Palestine.

Jeremiah's inaugural vision (ch. i) must likewise be classified as a dramatic vision. This vision contains a theophany, but there are few descriptive details. The auditory elements preponderate. Jeremiah seems to have been less visually disposed, less apt for 'eidetic imagery',

---

[51] Scholars disagree about the meaning of this vision. Volz was of the opinion that the point of the allegory was the information that the exile would last *for a long time*. But the long time is a necessary element in the vision to account for the fact that the loin-cloth became entirely destroyed. Rudolph thinks that the vision is intended to depict the moral decay of the Israelite people under the political and religious influence of Assyria and Babylonia during the period of the monarchy. But this idea could have been better illustrated than by the transporting of the loin-cloth to the Euphrates. Besides, the alteration of the text in vv. 9 and 10 proposed by Rudolph (cf. *BH*) seems to be rather gratuitous. Weiser declares that the main point lies in the fact that the prophet fetched the loin-cloth from the Euphrates, indicating the return of the Jews from the exile. But in the vision nothing is said about the fetching of the loin-cloth from Babylonia to Judaea. It is only said that the prophet dug and took it out from the crevice where it was hidden, in doing which he established the fact that it was entirely ruined. Baumann in *ZAW*, lxv, 1953, pp. 77 ff., holds that the vision is intended to depict the surrendering of the people to the power of the Babylonian gods and its disastrous consequences for the national life. The prophet is warning the people of this danger. But all this could have been much better symbolized than by the transport of the cloth and the voyage of Jeremiah to Euphrates. Because of the contrast between this passage and the passage of the two baskets of figs in ch. xxiv, Welch rejects the authenticity of the whole passage xiii. 1-11; *Jeremiah. His Time and his Work*, pp. 160 f.; for this supposed contradiction see above.

as the psychologists say, than, for instance, Ezekiel. The narrative of the call of Jeremiah begins with an audition: Yahweh said to him, 'Before I formed you in the womb I elected you, and before you were born I consecrated you. I appointed you a prophet to the nations.' As often happens in prophetic visions there is a dialogue between Yahweh and the visionary. Then comes the pictorial and dramatic element, although rather meagre: Yahweh stretched forth His hand and touched Jeremiah's mouth saying, 'Behold, I now put My words in your mouth.' At this point there is a resemblance between the inaugural vision of Jeremiah and that of Ezekiel. But in its pictorial structure Ezekiel's vision by far surpasses that of the earlier prophet.

Perhaps the most dramatic of all the visions reproduced in the prophetic literature of the Old Testament is the magnificent vision of Ezekiel which is described in ch. viii-xi of his book.

This vision has not been transmitted to us in its original form; it has obviously been extensively revised. This is not the place to discuss the text in its details (for this task I must refer to the commentaries); many things are, moreover, so obscure and confused as to defy all explanation. The principal features of the original vision are the following.

On a certain day the prophet was sitting in his house, with the elders of Judah sitting before him. There the hand of Yahweh fell upon him, i.e., he fell into ecstasy. He was aware of a heavenly being, appearing as a figure of fire and lustre. This figure reached out something which had the shape of a hand, and caught the prophet by a lock of his hair. The prophet was lifted up by a spiritual power (in reality identical with the heavenly being) between earth and heaven and brought, in the vision, to Jerusalem. Coming to the sanctuary he saw Yahweh in His glory, and at His command he went from one place to another to see the abominations which filled the temple. First he saw 'the image of jealousy' (a cult object which we are unable definitely to identify). Then he dug through a wall and saw inside the wall all sorts of loathsome forms of reptiles and beasts together with idols of various kinds. Seventy of the elders of Israel were standing in front of the pictures worshipping them with incense-offering. In other places he saw women weeping for Tammuz and men worshipping the sun.

Now a change of scene takes place. Judgement is executed upon the apostates. Six men appear furnished with murderous implements. A writer sets marks upon the foreheads of the righteous among the people. The rest are slain without mercy. Blazing coals from the sanctuary are scattered over the city.

There is another change of scene. The prophet is lifted up by the spiritual power and brought to the east gate of the sanctuary. There he sees twenty-five men, evil leaders of the people, among them Pelatiah. Against them the prophet pronounces a terrible oracle of doom. Impressed by this prophecy Pelatiah falls down dead. The prophet is terrified by this effect of his words and falls upon his face and cries aloud saying, 'Ah God Yahweh, wilt Thou make a complete end of the remnant of Israel?'

Parallel with this course of events another series of occurrences runs through the same vision, namely the gradual moving off of the glory of Yahweh. At the beginning of the massacre in the city the glory of Yahweh went up from the cherubim to the threshold of the temple building. From there the glory was brought by the cherubim through the air to the door of the east gate of the temple. Finally the cherubim lifted their wings, and the glory of Yahweh rose from the midst of the city and stood upon the mountain east of the city, i.e., the Mount of Olives. At last the prophet in the vision was brought back to the exiles in Babylonia. Then, it is said, the vision vanished away.

The vision of Ezekiel here related is one of the finest examples of ecstatic visions in the Old Testament. It has all the remarkable characteristics of a true vision.

The prophet's falling into ecstasy is described by an expression familiar from the early prophetic narratives: 'the hand of Yahweh' fell upon him. At the end of the description the passing of the ecstasy and the disappearing of the vision are expressly indicated: the vision vanished away, as the words run. What the prophet sees transcends normal human experience: the visionary sees the Deity and other heavenly beings. Yahweh in His glory moves from place to place. The vagueness of the objects perceived is noteworthy: there was an appearance of a man, an appearance of fire, something shaped as a hand was stretched out, etc. The dialogue between God and the visionary is a familiar feature in many descriptions of visionary experiences in the Bible and elsewhere. The vision is of course built up from elements which were already present in the consciousness of the prophet. Most of them were well known to the prophet from experience (details in the description of the sanctuary recall the structure of the pre-exilic temple); others were products of the visionary imagination. The episode of Pelatiah is commonly misunderstood. As Pelatiah himself was part of what was seen in the vision, so was his death. In this incident there is no indication of clairvoyance or of something that really happened as an effect of the suggestive power of the prophet. The death of Pelatiah happened in the vision; how or when it actually took place cannot now be established. The discrepancy between this scene and that of ix. 5 ff. and x. 2 (the massacre in Jerusalem) is not surprising in an ecstatic vision such as this. The keenly discussed question where the prophet was living when he had this vision (in Jerusalem or Babylonia) is irrelevant so far as the content of the vision is concerned. If he was in Jerusalem, the references to his transit from Babylonia to Jerusalem and from Jerusalem back to Babylonia must, of course, be explained as secondary additions. To this question we shall return in a following chapter (pp. 261 ff.).

The analysis of the great temple vision in Ezek. xl-xlviii as well as of the so-called night visions of Zechariah may suitably be made in connection with our treatment of the literary visions. Now we pass on to a brief discussion of the existence of *ecstatic auditions* among the prophetic revelations.

There are countless utterances introduced by formulas like these: Yahweh said, Yahweh has spoken, the prophet preaches what he has heard from Yahweh, Yahweh has revealed something in the ears of the prophet, etc. There are also narratives in which the prophet says that he hears voices, the noise of people, the din of arms, words of commands, etc. How are such expressions to be understood? On this point scholars disagree. Some of them think that these are only stylistic formulations; others maintain that behind the bulk of them there lie ecstatic experiences. But generalization is unwise. Every instance must be interpreted on the evidence available.

We are justified in speaking of ecstatic auditions when the auditory formulas occur in contexts where for other reasons an ecstatic experience must be assumed. If we have to do with a vision of an ecstatic character which contains auditory perceptions, these perceptions must be judged as ecstatic auditions. Nobody can be doubtful about the ecstatic nature of the inaugural vision of Isaiah. The visual elements are predominant, but there are several auditory perceptions, too. There is the sound of the singing of the seraphim; there is the utterance of the seraph who cleansed the prophet's lips, there is, finally, the voice of Yahweh.

The same is true of the initial visions of Jeremiah and Ezekiel. Auditory elements are mingled with visual elements. Practically all the visions analysed in the foregoing contain auditory elements. But if there are, admittedly, auditory elements in the visions, we may suppose that there are ecstatic auditions independent of the visions proper. That such is the case, is evident from the texts.

Isa. viii. 11 contains an utterance of Yahweh received by the prophet while 'the hand' grasped him, i.e., in a state of ecstasy. When there is particular emphasis on the actuality of the voice it is natural to assume that an audition is recorded; so, e.g., when it is said in Isa. v. 9 that Yahweh spoke in the ears of the prophet, or in xxii. 14 that Yahweh has revealed Himself in his ears. These expressions are comparable with similar expressions in the ecstatic vision in Ezek. viii-xi: 'He cried in my ears with a strong voice' (ix. 1); 'He said in my ears' (ix. 5), etc.

In many cases it is impossible to decide whether we have to do with real auditions or only with fanciful expressions of a poetical nature, e.g., Isa. xvii. 12: 'Ah! the roaring of many peoples, that roar like a roaring of seas', etc. Personally I am inclined to assume that no ecstatic experience underlies this sublime poetry. This is also true of the wonderful oracle uttered by Isaiah to the Ethiopian ambassadors in Isa. xviii: 'Thus has Yahweh said to me, "I will look on quietly in my dwelling-place, like shimmering heat in sunshine" ', etc. The descriptions at the beginning of the Book of Jeremiah of the enemy from the north with their numerous auditory elements must also be regarded as inspired poetry cast in the form of revelations. The prophet hears the advance of the hostile armies, the sound of trumpets, exclamations and crying in his own country, etc.

In numerous passages impulses in the domain of the will or the feeling are regarded as auditory perceptions. A prophet feels an inner prompting to do or say this or that. Such a prompting he often takes as an order from Yahweh, saying that Yahweh has spoken to him. Yahweh said to Isaiah, 'Go out to meet Ahaz, you and your son Shear-jashub' (vii. 3). Yahweh said to him, 'Take a great tablet and write upon it', etc. (viii. 1). Hosea tells us, 'Yahweh said to me, "Go, love a woman, a lover of other men and an adulterous one" ', etc. (iii. 1).

In the book of Jeremiah such commands from Yahweh are particularly common.[52] Because of the intimate communion with Yahweh which was so characteristic of the prophets, such impulses are regarded by them as something that they have heard from Yahweh. They think and feel in this way because they live constantly in the world of revelation.

Not only orders from Yahweh are considered as auditory perceptions, but also illumination of different kinds which the prophets receive concerning their inner life, especially their relation to God. Jeremiah in particular describes his inner experiences, his struggle with different religious problems and problems belonging to his prophetic calling in the form of dialogues between himself and Yahweh. The solution of a problem often comes in the form of an utterance of Yahweh heard by

[52] Jer. vii. 1 f.; xvi. 1; xviii. 1; xix. 1; xxxii. 6 f., etc,

the prophet. The so-called prophetic confessions in Jeremiah contain many examples of such a mode of expression.

A great many discourses and sermons of the prophets are described as in some sense auditions. In most cases there can be no question of ecstatic auditions in a proper sense; the auditory form is only an expression of the fact that what the prophets had to say was regarded by them as given by Yahweh.

Finally there are several passages where the auditory form is only of a stylistic nature. The great vision of Ezekiel in xl-xlviii is for the most part of a purely literary character and may be described as a fictitious vision. Consequently the auditory elements that it contains must generally be considered as stylistic formulations. In the real visions dialogues between Yahweh and the visionary are not unusual; but in several cases the prophets have reproduced their visions after some reflection on their experience, in doing which they often utilize the auditory form as a purely stylistic device.

To sum up, numbers of the so-called 'auditions' in the prophetic revelations are exalted poetry, or even fictitious literary productions and nothing else. In other cases they are expressions of an inner awareness that the prophet stands under Yahweh's command and is an object of divine impulses. A small minority are real auditions, i.e., auditions received in an ecstatic experience.

4. Symbolic Perceptions

In the preceding section we have dealt with genuine visions and auditions, i.e., visions and auditions of an ecstatic nature. Now we pass on to another group of prophetic experiences, namely visions which in the first chapter of this book have been called 'symbolic perceptions'.

It is characteristic of a symbolic perception that it has a real, objective foundation in the material world; that which is seen is, however, conceived of as something particularly significant and interpreted as a symbol of another, higher reality.

The genuine vision and the symbolic perception have this in common that they are both regarded as given by God to provide insight into the spiritual world, thus playing an essential role in the life of him who has the favour of receiving them. Further, both are connected with inspiration, the supernormal mental state which makes it possible for men to assign a supernatural significance to what they see. Because they have the form of visions, the symbolic perceptions have often been confused with, and interpreted as, ecstatic visions.

The differences are, however, equally manifest. The vision proper
has no basis in outward reality; the symbolic perception is an observation of a real object in the material world. The former is an insight into
the invisible world by 'the inward eye', the latter is an apprehension of
a material object by the bodily eye; only through divine illumination
does the object perceived become a revelation of invisible realities. The
content of a vision is, finally, something supermundane, something
beyond space and time; the primary content of a symbolic perception
is temporal, material, everyday.

All over the world men are in the habit of using exterior things as
revelations of secrets. Everywhere omens and portents have played a
great role in human life. Auguring from the flight of birds, from the
movements and cries of birds and beasts, from the behaviour of
sacrificial animals and the appearance of their entrails is well known in
all quarters of the world. The conditions which it presupposes are
technical skill and traditional methods.

Students of life and customs among modern Arabs have observed
various methods of drawing omens and important indications from
purely occasional phenomena. The appearance of a water-seller with
water confined in his skin can under certain circumstances indicate that
someone is in prison. A raven croaking three times in succession
indicates that someone will die after three days. A person carrying a
burden indicates that a child is unborn but waited for. A male sparrow
noticed in this connection shows that the child is a male child,
etc.[53]

Such prognostications from everyday phenomena have a certain
resemblance to what we have called symbolic perceptions. There is,
however, a great difference. In the last mentioned cases the divination
is throughout trivial, secular, and fortuitous. The symbolic perceptions
among the Old Testament prophets are connected with revelations
from the divine world. Yahweh stands behind them, Yahweh arranges
them; and what they reveal has a deeply religious significance.

More akin to the relations of symbolic perceptions in the prophetic
literature is the story of the dog and the rag in the life of Suso, which
was told in the first chapter of this book (p. 42). There an occasional
and trivial occurrence acquires a great religious significance because the
pious friar was a divinely inspired man and was able to interpret what
he saw entirely in spiritual terms.

An example of symbolic perception is the 'vision' of the basket of
summer-fruit (perhaps ripe figs) upon which Amos's eye fell one day

[53] Guillaume, op. cit., pp. 118 f., and *passim*.

(viii. 1 f.). What the prophet saw in this moment became to him an indication of the end which was impending over Israel. The connection between the summer-fruit and the end is based on a pun: 'summer-fruit' is in Hebrew ḳayiṣ, 'end' is ḳēṣ, two words which sounded very alike in a Hebrew ear. The idea of the end of Israel was regarded by Amos as a revelation from God coming to him through the medium of the basket of summer-fruit. Therefore he says, 'Thus Yahweh, the Lord, showed me.' So the seeing of the basket took the form of a vision. But in the strict sense this seeing was not a vision. The object seen was throughout trivial and had nothing in it of the characteristics of an ecstatic vision. The question, 'What do you see, Amos?' and the following answer belong to the reproduction of 'the vision', not to 'the vision' itself. This is a stylistic form probably taken from the didactic methods used in the Wisdom schools.[54]

One day when Jeremiah was walking in the field he noticed a twig of an almond tree which captured his attention. We may imagine that he walked in prophetic reverie. He pondered over the problem if his preaching of doom really would be fulfilled, or if he would one day be put to shame before his people. We know that the prophet was later frequently concerned with this problem. Whilst gazing upon the twig, the Hebrew name of an almond tree, šāḳēḏ, became actualized to him. The name šāḳēḏ led him to the idea of something that watched—'watch' is in Hebrew šāḳaḏ. This association of ideas came to him as an answer to the question he was just pondering. Had not Yahweh let him see this almond tree in order to show him that He at all events would watch over the accomplishment of His words spoken by His prophets? This occurrence, too, has the form of a vision and is introduced by the common revelatory formula, 'Yahweh's word came to me, saying.' The whole had for the prophet the character of a revelation. The trivial impression was by inspiration from God lifted up to a higher level. The everyday observation was sublimated, carried over into the divine and supernatural sphere. In short, we have here a typical 'symbolic perception'. Also in this 'vision' the didactic Wisdom formula is used (Jer. i. 11 f.).[54a]

Another example of the same group of visions is the 'vision' of the cauldron in Jer. i. 13 f. Jeremiah was absorbed by thoughts concerning the judgement to come. How would the punishment come to pass, and through whom? Palestine also was affected by the rumour of the

[54] See above, p. 126.
[54a] Williams (in *A Stubborn Faith*, pp. 91 ff.) refers the almond twig in an original fashion to Aaron's rod in Num. xvii.

upheavals in the northern countries where various peoples strove for power. Would the catastrophe come upon Judah from those quarters? Pondering over such questions Jeremiah's attention was drawn to a cauldron placed upon a flaming fire blown upon by the wind, a cauldron of which it is said in the narrative that its face was turned to the north. This expression is somewhat obscure. But everything becomes clear if we realize that the cauldron was sunk down in an open air hearth of stones or bricks forming a circle round it, but open towards the north, from where the wind blew on the fuel consisting of wood or dry thorns.[55] The face of the cauldron is thus a somewhat inexact expression for the face of the hearth in which the cauldron was placed. The cauldron on the fire blown upon from the north gave the prophet an answer to his questions. From the northern countries the judgement was to come upon Judah, the apostate nation. Here the common sight of the wind blowing from the north upon a cauldron standing on its hearth was a fact from which the prophet drew the significant omen. As arranged by Yahweh this phenomenon together with its interpretation became to the prophet a revelation from God. It was reproduced by him as a vision and cast in the usual didactic form.

The present writer is of the opinion that the two baskets of figs which, according to ch. xxiv, Jeremiah saw in front of the temple like-wise were real baskets upon which the eyes of the prophet chanced to fall. Several scholars think of a vision seen in ecstasy; but in the light of what has been said above I think it most likely that the baskets of figs belong to the same category as the almond twig and the cauldron in Jeremiah and the baskets with summer-fruit in Amos. One basket contained fresh and good figs, delicious as early figs, the other rotten and uneatable figs. The two baskets with their contents became to the prophet a revelation from Yahweh. He saw in them symbols of the two parts of his people, on one hand the exiled Jews, on the other those who were left behind in the homeland. With the former Yahweh was well pleased, upon the latter His wrath rested. The former were destined to be bearers of the new age, the latter would be struck with destructive judgement. It was significant to the prophet that he saw the baskets against the background of the temple. There is no hint that they were destined for offering (that is in fact out of question). He says only that the baskets were placed just there. The objects seen were things of everyday occurrence, but standing side by side against the background of the temple building they became to the inspired prophet

---

[55] See Dalman, *Arbeit und Sitte in Palästina*, VII, fig. 98. See further Lindblom in *ZAW*, lxviii, 1956, pp. 223 f., and Duhm, *Das Buch Jeremia*, ad loc.

the basis of a highly important revelation. Here again the didactic formula is used.[56]

Finally we must consider the passage about the potter in Jer. xviii. One day Jeremiah went down to the potter's house and found him engaged in work on the wheels. Whenever the vessel at which he was working became spoiled, he changed it into another vessel, such as seemed suitable in the potter's own eyes. The observation of this procedure in the potter's shop suggested to the prophet the idea of the sovereignty of Yahweh in His dealing with His people. Here, too, the providential character of the occurrence is strongly emphasized. It is said that the prophet was ordered by Yahweh to arise and go down to the potter's house, to obtain there a message from Yahweh. The whole is regarded as a revelation, as appears from the introductory words: 'The word that came to Jeremiah from Yahweh.'

The symbolic perceptions resemble in some measure what the psychologists call illusions, but must not be confused with them. In illusions something real is seen, but what is seen is transformed by error, either by a hyper-sensitive imagination or by a hallucinatory procedure in the brain. In the symbolic perception again the object seen is not changed in the apprehension of the observer, but is interpreted by a more or less spontaneous act of reflection. That which is seen is not perverted into something else, but becomes a symbol of ideas of a higher character. For this reason we may speak of sublimated or symbolic perceptions. I have not found any illusions proper in the Old Testament prophets.

5. Literary Visions

The symbolic perceptions could be described as in some sense pseudo-visions. There is also another group of visual pictures which could be called pseudo-visions, although of another nature. Without being in ecstasy, although in an exalted state of mind, a prophet receives an inspiration in the form of a visual creation of the imagination. What the prophet produces in such a psychic state resembles the products of visual poetry; but the prophetic imagery differs from the products of the poets in so far as it appears in the form of revelations given by God.

[56] It may be mentioned that both Rudolph and Weiser are of the opinion that this is an ecstatic vision. That the figs are *compared* with early figs is only intended to emphasize the good quality of the figs. Welch sees in the vision a pure allegory, but he rightly lays stress upon the connection of the fig-baskets with the temple (op. cit., pp. 160 f.).

I have called such creations of the prophetic imagination 'revelatory fancies'.[57] Another suitable term for them is 'literary visions'.

When the medieval visionaries speak of *figurata locutio*, in which their writings are so abundant, they mean approximately the same as we here call 'revelatory fancies' or 'literary visions'.

The descriptions in Jeremiah of the enemy from the north are not ecstatic visions, but typical revelatory fancies.

> Behold, he comes up like clouds,
> his chariots like a whirlwind;
> his horses are swifter than eagles—
> woe to us, for we are ruined (iv. 13).

> (Thus says Yahweh:)
> Behold, a people is coming from the north land;
> a mighty nation is stirring from the ends of the earth.
> They lay hold on bow and javelin;
> they are cruel and pitiless.
> The sound of them is like the roaring sea;
> and they ride upon horses—
> arrayed every man for the battle,[58]
> against you, O daughter of Zion!

> We have heard the report of it,
> and our hands fall helpless;
> anguish lays hold on us,
> pain like that of a woman in travail.
> Go not out to the fields,
> nor walk on the way!
> For there is the sword of the enemy,
> terror all around.
> O daughter of my people, gird on sackcloth,
> and wallow in ashes;
> take up mourning, as for an only son,
> wailing most bitter!
> For suddenly will come
> the despoiler upon us (vi. 22-26).

If these examples resemble visual visions, the little poem of Rachel's lamentation is in the form of an audition:

[57] Lindblom, *Profetismen i Israel*, pp. 93, 266 ff., and in *Studia Theologica* (Riga), I, pp. 22 ff.
[58] I read *'ārûḳ 'îš;* cf. Gen. xl. 5; Ex. xvi. 29.

(Thus says Yahweh:)
Hark! in Ramah is heard lamentation,
bitter weeping!
It is Rachel weeping for her children,
refusing to be comforted
for her children,
because they are not (xxxi. 15).

A splendid specimen of this genre is the poem of Jeremiah about the battle of Carchemish (ch. xlvi). Here the picture is in the form of a dramatic vision.

Other examples of literary visions are the poems of the advancing Assyrians in Isaiah, the *maśśā'* on Moab in Isa. xv, the picture of the capture of Nineveh in the book of Nahum, etc. Such passages (there are several examples of this genre in the prophetic literature) are poetical compositions, but with the character of revelations. Accordingly, we may apply to them the term 'revelatory fancies'.

Why do we not regard such poems as ecstatic visions? First of all they are not presented to us as visions in the strict sense but as oracles. They are introduced by the usual oracle formulas and sometimes expressly called *maśśā'* or even *māšāl*. Further, the visionary style is not accurately adhered to; the pictures often glide into other types of prophetic preaching: exhortation, lamentation, announcement of doom, hymn. Finally, the descriptions of this kind are as a rule more realistic and less fanciful than ecstatic visions usually are. The conscious reflection of the author is more evident.

The so-called night visions of Zechariah offer a special problem. There are eight of them: four riders reporting that the earth is at peace, Yahweh having not yet begun His planned Messianic work; four horns representing the world-powers and four blacksmiths who are coming to break them down; the man with a measuring-line in his hand going to measure Jerusalem but being informed that Jerusalem of the future can have no walls on account of the multitude of men and cattle; the high priest Joshua dressed in dirty garments and accused by Satan is vindicated by Yahweh and clothed in festal and clean garments; the golden candlestick with seven lamps and two olive trees at the side thereof symbolizing Yahweh, the all-seeing God, and Joshua and Zerubbabel as His servants; the flying roll, a symbol of the curse which strikes the evil-doers in the land; the woman within the ephah-measure representing the wickedness which is to be taken forth from the land; the four chariots going out to the four quarters of the earth, probably indicating the return of the dispersed Jews to the homeland.[59]

What the prophet here describes is given the form of ecstatic visions. The first vision is introduced by these words: 'Last night I saw.' Most of the following visions are introduced by one or other of the phrases, 'I lifted my eyes and saw', or 'he showed me'. In one case a very interesting phrase is used, namely in the introduction to the vision of the candlestick: 'The angel who was talking with me waked me again like a man who is waked from his sleep.' This expression does not mean that the prophet had been sleeping and now awoke; he *compares* his transition from one state of mind to another with the awakening from sleep. As a man, when awakening, sees the light and the shapes of the day, Zechariah, when passing into the ecstatic state of mind, saw figures and shapes appearing from the invisible, spiritual world. Similar descriptions of the revelatory experiences are common among the medieval visionaries. St. Birgitta says that God frequently rouses her soul as from sleep to see and hear in a spiritual way. The mystic says that, while the soul is making its orison, it sometimes feels its spiritual sense suddenly awakening; it becomes conscious of the presence of God in a way quite new. Very many utterances of this sort can be quoted.[59a]

Now the question arises whether these 'visions' really are ecstatic visions or have only been given the form of visions. The latter is of course conceivable. As we have seen above, the prophets often give their inspired utterances the form of visions. The introductory phrases mentioned above, particularly some of them, seem, however, to tell in favour of the other explanation. But there are several facts which tell against it, at least so far as certain of the visions are concerned. A number of the visions entirely lack the characteristics of genuine visions. In the descriptions of the 'visions' the visionary features are often very scanty and fragmentary. The visionary pictures are not completed. We miss the conclusion which should have accomplished and rounded off the scene. Irrespective of the fact that the descriptions of the visions in most cases are confused by extended explanations of an allegorical nature, oracles by the prophet from different times, and secondary additions, the visions have given the interpreters much trouble, precisely because of their fragmentary character.

Four of the visions are noteworthy exceptions: the flying roll, the

---

[59] For the night visions see, besides the well-known commentaries, Rignell, *Die Nachtgesichte des Sacharja*, with abundant bibliographical references, and later Galling in *VT*, ii, 1952, pp. 18 ff.

[59a] Pratt, op. cit., p. 392.

woman within the ephah-measure, the clothing of the high priest in clean clothes, and, above all, the candlestick with the two olive trees at its side.

These four visions (including the Joshua vision) have this in common that they are all pictorial, completed, and do not need any additions to be fully intelligible. They have all the characteristics of genuine ecstatic visions. Their contents are highly fanciful, unreal, irrational, and unreflective. The introductory phrase with which the vision of the candlestick begins points decidedly to the fact that we have here an ecstatic vision. Saying that he was roused *again* the prophet possibly indicates that the preceding vision also was an ecstatic one.[60]

The present writer suggests the following solution of the problem of the night visions in the Book of Zechariah. Four of the eight visions are visions in a strict sense, namely those mentioned above.[61] The others are products of the imagination of the prophet, although he was in a state of inspiration. He wanted to complete the genuine series with a number of 'visions' in order to give a more comprehensive picture of the Messianic age which in his opinion was about to dawn. One cannot say that what came into his mind was particularly excellent. The fundamental idea of the genuine visions is the new Messianic community in its cultic and national organization, and the moral and ritual cleansing necessary for its realization.[62] In the four literary visions, as we consequently may call them, the prophet, in addition, intended to depict the waiting for the wonderful events, the crushing of the hostile nations, the future immensity of the Messianic capital, and the return of the dispersed Jews.[63]

In the visionary literature we find many examples of such a combination of genuine visions and literary visions, in which the reflection of the visionary played a more marked part. The Apocalypse of John is a fine specimen of this sort in our Bible. The Revelations of Birgitta and many other medieval visionaries consist to a great extent of literary

[60] For the vision of the candlestick see Rost in *ZAW*, lxiii, 1951, pp. 216 ff. For i t structure see the figure on col. 348 in Galling, *Biblisches Reallexikon*.

[61] That they were seen in one single night (i. 7 f.) is curious, but not impossible. There are analogies in the visionary literature. Julian of Norwich had fifteen 'shewings' from four o'clock till after nine in the same morning (*Rev.*, xix, p. 164).

[62] I think that the high priest was cleansed as a representative of the whole community. So Horst in *HAT* and Rignell, op. cit., pp. 100 ff. If this is taken as a genuine vision, there is no ground for excluding it from the original series. In literature of this sort it is not advisable to lay too much stress upon matters of form (against Jepsen in *ZAW*, lxi, 1945/48, pp. 95 ff., Elliger, Galling, etc.).

[63] The prophetic words linked to the visions surely belong to different times; but I see no cogent reason for going against the assertion of the prophet that he saw the visions at the beginning of the reign of Darius. For the more precise point of time see the discussion in Jepsen's article.

visions combined with genuine ones. The visionary in the book of Zechariah was stimulated by his ecstatic visionary experiences to create new fanciful visions expressing his ideas concerning the heavenly secrets of the age to come. The very order of the visions in the present book may of course be owing to the man who has given the book of Zechariah its present form.

Here we have been interested only in the psychological aspect of the problem of the night visions. For the exegetical questions reference may be made to special treatises and the commentaries.

In the second part of the Book of Zechariah, the so-called Deutero-Zechariah, we meet with a passage which in all probability should be assigned to the same category, namely the description of the shepherd and the sheep, xi. 4-16+xiii. 7-9.[64] A prophet receives the divine command to be a shepherd of a flock which is to be slaughtered and to be badly treated by sellers and buyers. He took over the charge and took for himself two rods, called 'Grace' and 'Union'. The shepherd got weary of his task, abandoned the flock to destruction, and broke the rods. Wages were weighed out to him, a ridiculous sum: thirty shekels of silver, which he threw to the metal founder.[65] Then the prophet was ordered to be a bad shepherd of the flock. As such he had to be killed, whereupon the flock would be scattered. Only a small part would be rescued.

That these happenings occurred in reality is out of the question. Of an ecstatic vision one would expect more pictorial detail and less reflection. The picture has all the characteristics of a literary vision of a pronounced allegorical nature. Thus it may be classed among the category which we have called 'revelatory allegories'. The interpretation is rendered a little difficult because of the fact that later hands have applied the original text to specific historical events (e.g., the three shepherds in xi. 8) and because of the blend at different points of allegory and interpretation, which is common in descriptions of this kind.

What the allegory means is the following. The Jews are in a miserable situation. They are ill-treated by evil rulers. The nation is itself stubborn

---

[64] While xiii. 7-9 seems to be a continuation of xi. 4-16, the passage xi. 17 gives the impression of being an interpolation by a later hand to serve as a substitute for the original passage, after it had been removed from there and placed after xiii. 6. Sellin holds that xiii. 7 ff. refers to the good, not to the bad shepherd. The killing of the bad shepherd, says Sellin, is already spoken of in xi. 17; and the bad shepherd could not be called Yahweh's shepherd and fellow. Yet xi. 17 is in all probability an interpolation (see further below, pp. 275 f.), and the man who was charged with the task of a bad shepherd was in *the vision* the prophet himself; in this capacity he could appropriately be called Yahweh's shepherd and fellow.

[65] So rightly Elliger. Cf. Köhler in *Lexicon*, s.v. *yāsar*.

and not even worthy of a good leader. Yahweh's covenant with all the peoples is broken. So is the bond between the Jews and their northern neighbours in Samaria. Severe judgement is imminent. A cruel tyrant will rise in the land. He will be killed and the nation itself will be destroyed. Only a small remnant will be saved.[66]

I think it most probable that the great vision of Ezekiel in ch. xl-xlviii concerning the new temple, the new city, and the new land is to be judged in a similar way. The visionary frame of the whole is manifest. Not all the details, however, can have been seen in ecstasy. But the introduction to the whole section points so palpably to a basic ecstatic experience as to make it very unlikely that this is only a literary form. It is stated that on a certain day 'Yahweh's hand' came upon the prophet; in divine visions he was transferred to the land of Israel and found himself set on a high mountain, where something like the structure of a city was raised. The expression 'divine visions' is also used in the undoubtedly ecstatic vision in Ezek. viii-xi (viii. 3; cf. xi. 24). Thus my thesis concerning the great temple vision of Ezekiel is that the prophet, after having been transferred in ecstasy to Mount Zion, saw the future city and the future temple in their general contours in an ecstatic vision. The vision of the glory of Yahweh in xliii. 2 f. seems also to be an ecstatic experience. After the passing of the ecstatic rapture the prophet worked out all the details contained in the nine chapters, giving to all that emerged in his imagination and reflection the form of a long series of visionary experiences linked to the basic ecstatic visions. Most of the 'visions' in Ezek. xl-xlviii are consequently to be classified as literary visions.

A very interesting parallel to the great temple vision of Ezekiel is the immense 'vision' of St. Birgitta in her *Regula Salvatoris*. The Swedish visionary 'saw' in all details the Nunnery in Vadstena, the church with its altars, ornaments, etc., the garments of the nuns, the lodgings and garments of the various functionaries, the holy ceremonies, and so on. Obviously most of what she 'saw' must be regarded as 'literary visions', but the exceptionally concrete and lively description of the ecstatic experience in the introduction to the revelation of the Nunnery rule makes it difficult to deny that an ecstatic rapture gave the first impulse.

Visions of various kinds (ecstatic visions, symbolic perceptions, or literary visions) played a central role in the religious life of the prophets. It seems that the prophets themselves as well as their contemporaries

---

[66] I agree with Elliger in *ATD* in his general conception of the picture of the shepherd as a literary product of an allegorical character. On certain details I follow my own line.

regarded their visionary endowment as the essential element in their prophetic equipment. Like the early prophets, the later prophets are frequently called 'seers'. 'Prophet' and 'seer' stand as synonyms (Isa. xxix. 10; xxx. 10; Am. vii. 12). To be a prophet and to have visions are almost the same (Ezek. xxi. 34; Joel iii. 1). In the book of Hosea it is said that Yahweh speaks to the prophets and gives many visions (xii. 11). Deutero-Zechariah in his experience of the decay of prophecy in his time says that in the future age it shall come to pass that the prophets will each be ashamed of his visions when he prophesies (xiii. 4). In the Book of Lamentations a poet complains of the fact that the prophets do not receive any visions from Yahweh (ii. 9).

The prophetic oracles and messages can in general be called visions irrespective of whether they really are, or have simply been given the literary form of visions. The words of the prophets are called 'vision words' (Ezek. xii. 23). The collections of the revelations of Amos, Isaiah, Micah, Nahum, Obadiah are described as visions. Individual oracles, too, can be called 'visions' irrespective of their general character: Isa. xiii. 1; xxix. 11; Jer. xxxviii. 21; Hab. ii. 2 f.

6. THE PROPHETS AS YAHWEH'S MESSENGERS.
THE PROPHETIC ORACLES AND SERMONS

Many visionaries in different religions have preferred a life of solitude. They have sought the seclusion of the cell in order to enjoy, to their own benefit, their inexpressible revelations and their intercourse with the invisible world. The Israelite prophets, on the contrary, knew that they were called to be messengers of Yahweh to His people. They could have said, like St. Birgitta of Sweden, 'I am there not for my own sake, but for the salvation of others.' The prophets were conscious of the fact that they were called and sent to proclaim a divine message. Their task was to utter oracles and to bring to their people an urgent communication from God about sin and repentance, judgement and salvation.

A prophet's first task was to open his soul for divine revelations and receive messages from the invisible world. Then it was his duty to impart them to men. Fortunately many situations are related in the prophetic literature which illustrate how the prophets communicated their revelations to individuals and to assemblies of men.

The prophet Jeremiah was sitting in his house. Jerusalem was besieged by the army of Nebuchadnezzar. Within the city there was distress and fear. Must the city fall, or was there a possibility of deliverance? King Zedekiah sent to the prophet two trusted men to require an oracle from Jeremiah: 'Inquire of Yahweh on our behalf,' they said. They wanted to know whether Yahweh would come to their help or not. The prophets were traditionally oracle-givers; and this function was never abandoned during the whole history of prophecy. Jeremiah immediately received a 'word', i.e., a revelation from Yahweh and formulated an oracle introduced by the common formula, 'Thus says Yahweh.' His answer to the messengers from the king was that they should say to the king, 'Thus says Yahweh, the God of Israel, "I Myself will fight against you. And I will smite the inhabitants of this city with a great pestilence. And I will give Zedekiah into the hand of Nebuchadnezzar" ' (xxi. 1 ff.).

As is often the case in the prophetic writings, the original oracle has been edited and somewhat enlarged. But there is no doubt about the essential content of the original oracle.

On a later occasion the same occurred once more. The Babylonian army had raised the siege of Jerusalem because of the advance of Pharaoh Hophra's army. King Zedekiah sent messengers to Jeremiah to request an oracle because of the altered situation. Jeremiah received a revelation and gave this answer, 'Pharaoh's army, which is advancing to your aid, will return to the land of Egypt; and the Chaldeans will come back to fight against this city; they will take it and burn it' (xxxvii. 3 ff.).

Once the king sent for Jeremiah and asked him secretly in his palace whether any word had come from Yahweh, i.e., whether he had received a revelation. Jeremiah said, 'There is one. You shall be given into the hand of the king of Babylon' (xxxvii. 17).

It happened sometimes that the revelation asked for did not come instantly, but after a longer or shorter time of waiting. After the fall of Jerusalem those who still remained in the land wanted to emigrate to Egypt. But first they would make sure that this was the will of Yahweh. They went to the prophet Jeremiah to receive an oracle from him about their plan. At the end of ten days Jeremiah received a revelation: the people should stay in their own land and not emigrate. This oracle was, however, not obeyed (xlii. 1 ff.).

Of Ezekiel the following story is told. On a certain day he was sitting in his house. The elders of Judah were sitting before him, obviously in order to acquaint themselves with what was to be revealed to the prophet. Suddenly Yahweh's hand fell upon him, i.e., he fell into ecstasy. In a vision he was transported to Jerusalem. There he saw the pagan ceremonies which were exercised in the temple and the terrible judgement which was executed on the apostates. This event is precisely dated (Ezek. viii ff.).[67]

Several stories with similar contents are told in the book of Ezekiel. A general picture of the interest which people could show in the revelations of the prophets is given in xxxiii. 30 ff. Ezekiel's fellow-countrymen talk of him by the walls and at the doors of the houses, and say to one another, 'Come, and hear what the oracle is that comes from Yahweh!' They come to the prophet and sit before him; they listen to his words, but they do not take them to heart. The prophet is to them like a singer of love songs, who sings with a beautiful voice, and is able to play well on his instrument. They listen but will not obey. This passage illustrates very well the great role which a prophet could play among his people, but at the same time how his oracles could fall on deaf ears and be entirely fruitless.[68]

Thus there was a custom that people approached the prophets in order to receive oracles from them. Sometimes the revelation came in the presence of the inquirers; sometimes it had come in advance and was now communicated to them; sometimes it followed some time after. That was exactly how it was done in the days of the earlier prophets.

Frequently the prophets themselves took the initiative in communicating a revelation. Something had happened which had caused the revelation and led them to impart it to others. One day Jeremiah went off to the royal palace and pronounced an oracle to the king and his officials. They should do justice and righteousness. If they did not listen to his words, this splendid palace would become a desolation (xxii. 1 ff.).[69] Isaiah went out to meet King Ahaz and communicated to him the oracle about the futile alliance of the hostile kingdoms, Syria and Ephraim (vii). He appeared quite unexpectedly before Shebna, the king's steward, who was just visiting his magnificent tomb, hewn in the rock, and hurled this oracle in his face: 'Yahweh will toss you away like a ball into a spacious land. There shall you die, and there shall your splendid chariots go, you shame of your master's house!' (xxii. 15 ff.). According to the historical part of the book of Isaiah this prophet was not only sent for by King Hezekiah, but also went, on his own initiative, to the king to give an oracle (xxxvii f.) Haggai went to Zerubbabel and announced to him an oracle about the coming of the Messianic age and the choice of Zerubbabel to be king of the new kingdom (ii). Jeremiah

---

[67] For the text see the commentaries.
[68] For the text see, for instance, Bertholet in *HAT*.
[69] The original oracle is reproduced in *vv*. 6 f.

pronounced an oracle to Ebed-melech, who had drawn him out of the cistern: on the day of the conquest of the city he would be rescued (xxxix. 15 ff.).

Oracles were also sent to foreign peoples as answers to political proposals. Messengers coming from Philistia in order to persuade Judah to take part in political actions against Assyria received the following oracle announced by Isaiah: 'Yahweh has founded Zion, and in her the afflicted of His people shall find refuge' (xiv. 32). An oracle was also given to ambassadors from Ethiopia who came on a similar errand. Isaiah answered, 'Thus has Yahweh said to me, "I will look on quietly in My dwelling-place, like the shimmering heat in sunshine."' But when time comes for Him to act, then He will intervene with power (xviii).[70]

It was mentioned above that revelations could come after a time of waiting. They could also fail to come. Elders who were apostate were refused when they asked Ezekiel for an oracle (Ezek. xiv. 1 ff.). A prophet who delivered oracles to idol-worshippers among the Israelites would be severely punished (*vv.* 9 f.). It could happen that the situation was quite obscure. When asked for an oracle the prophet did not receive any revelation. The ambassadors from Edom in Isa. xxi. 11 f. were told that the historical situation was utterly obscure. If they wished to know more, they should come again.

An oracle already given could be replaced by another if the situation altered. Yahweh's thoughts and plans were not unchangeable. Yahweh did not deal with men in a mechanical way, but according to their behaviour. He judged the unrepentant sinners, but was merciful towards those who repented. This was illustrated by the description of the farmer's methods in Isa. xxviii. 23 ff. (cf. Jer. xviii). Bearing this in mind we can understand Isaiah's words when King Hezekiah was taken ill. First Isaiah came to the king and uttered this oracle: 'Thus says Yahweh, "Set your house in order, for you shall die, and not recover."' Then Hezekiah turned his face to the wall and prayed to Yahweh. Thereafter Isaiah received a second oracle and went again to the king with this oracle: 'Thus says Yahweh, "I have heard your prayer; I have seen your tears; behold, I will add fifteen more years to your life, and I will deliver you and this city from the hand of the king of Assyria and will hold My shield over this city'" (2 Kings xx; Isa. xxxviii).

[70] In the opinion of the present writer this oracle deals with world judgement. The parable of the vineyard contained in *vv.* 5 f. shows how when the time has come Yahweh's judgement occurs unexpectedly and mercilessly. Neither the Assyrians nor the Ethiopians are specifically thought of as wrongdoers. The object of the judgement is all mankind. See further Lindblom in *St. Th.*, vi, 1952, pp. 79 ff. (esp. pp. 90 f.).

There are suggestions that prayer was used as a preparation for the reception of oracles. In Jer. xxxvii. 3 and xlii. 2, 20, where the prophet was asked for oracles, the common term *dāraš* is not used, but *hitpallēl*, 'pray', 'intercede for'. After praying the prophet received the oracle requested.[71]

The oracles of the prophets were mostly given a peculiar form. They were as a rule briefly and rhythmically worded. This is the case with oracles all the world over. They were often intentionally obscure and ambiguous. An oracle in Isa. xxi. 12 runs: 'Morning comes, but also night.' Amos, using the same style, says that Israel will be carried into exile beyond Damascus (v. 27). Jeremiah speaks in oracular style of the enemy from the north. The prophetic utterances in Isa. vii are intentionally ambiguous. They are all characterized by a peculiar vague allusiveness which from a modern point of view makes them hard to interpret. 'The young woman,' he says mysteriously, 'shall conceive and bear a son,' etc. The oracles were as a rule introduced by special phrases such as 'thus says Yahweh' (the formula of messages and royal proclamations), 'hear the word of Yahweh' (the rhetorical formula), 'thus has Yahweh said to me' (the revelation formula), 'whispering (*neʾum*) of Yahweh' (the old seer formula), etc.

Accordingly, there is in the giving and the formulation of the oracles an intimate connection between the earlier and the later prophets.

Very often we find the prophets presenting themselves as speakers in public, pronouncing their oracles or delivering their sermons. They appear in places where people assemble and proclaim their revelations. They turn up everywhere where an audience is to be found: in streets (Jer. xi. 6), in the gates of the cities (xvii. 19), in the royal palace (xxii), in the sanctuaries (Am. vii; Jer. vii; xix. 14), etc.

Sometimes there was a specific and concrete cause of the intervention of a prophet. During the siege of Jerusalem King Zedekiah and the inhabitants of Jerusalem had made a covenant that all Hebrew slaves should be liberated, but after the retreat of the Chaldeans and the approach of the Egyptian army they had broken the covenant and brought back the slaves. Now Jeremiah received a revelation and pronounced a terrible punishment because of this crime: 'Since you have not listened to me in regard to the proclamation of liberty to one another, behold, I am making for you, is the oracle of Yahweh, a proclamation of liberty to sword, pestilence, and famine,' etc. (xxxiv. 8 ff.). When the people delayed the erection of the temple after the end

[71] So Mowinckel, *Die Erkenntnis Gottes bei den alttestamentlichen Propheten*, pp. 27 f.

of the exile, Haggai made a public speech exhorting them to begin the work immediately (ch. i).

However, the majority of the discourses of the prophets in the present prophetic books were not evoked by special causes. They were caused by the apostasy and the sins of the people in general. Thus the prophets appear as ordinary but inspired preachers of repentance and heralds of doom or bliss.

We are justified in assuming that the bulk of the utterances reproduced in the prophetic books were really delivered as public speeches or sermons. Frequently the term 'cry', 'exclaim' (Hebr. *ḳārā'*) is employed (Jer. ii. 2; iii. 12; vii. 2; Zech. i. 14). Once a prophet is commanded 'to cry by his throat and not hold back' (Isa. lviii. 1). Hosea is exhorted: 'Set a trumpet to your mouth' (viii. 1). We may usually conclude that an oracle or a sermon was publicly proclaimed if it is introduced by a statement that Yahweh ordered the prophet to go and say this or that, even when it is not expressly said that the command was carried out. Such a phrase indicates that the sermon in question was based upon a revelation. But many prophetic utterances which lack such an introduction were, of course, nevertheless proclaimed publicly. We feel tempted to seek for a concrete situation even when the actual text does not allude to it, because it was forgotten when the prophetic books got their present form, or there was no particular interest in preserving for the future the historical situation. Of course such attempts must often be mere guesswork and rather hypothetical.

Many prophetic utterances have the form of speeches without being speeches in the strict sense. We find such fictitious speeches particularly in Ezekiel, but also in other prophets. Ezekiel was commanded to make a speech to all birds of the air and all beasts of the field (xxxix. 17). This speech is embedded in a speech addressed to Gog. Another time he prophesied against the mountains of Israel, exactly as if he had spoken to men: 'O mountains of Israel, hear the word of Yahweh. Thus says the Lord Yahweh to the mountains and the hills, the ravines and the valleys' (vi. 1 ff.)[72] He spoke to the land of Israel: 'Thus says the Lord Yahweh to the land of Israel, "An end has come, nay the end has come, upon the four corners of the land. Now has the end come upon you. I will send my anger against you" ', etc. (vii. 2 f.). We can hardly imagine that Ezekiel once assembled all the false prophets of Israel and prophesied doom against them (xiii. 1 ff.). When a prophet

---

[72] The fictitious character here becomes particularly manifest through the fact that the prophet suddenly turns towards the people of Israel and later even speaks about this people in the third person.

directly addresses foreign nations, such a speech must be regarded as a fictitious speech. So for instance Isa. xli. 1 f.: 'Listen to me in silence, you coastlands,' etc. (an introduction to a proclamation of the appearance of Cyrus).[73]

Ezekiel used a special formula for introducing such a fictitious speech: 'Yahweh said, "Set your face towards".'[74] Possibly the prophet occasionally made a gesture which is indicated in this formula, but in general we must assume that the fictitious speeches were not delivered in their present form, but communicated to people in another way.

All that the prophets saw and heard in their visions was as a rule publicly disclosed. Ezekiel says that he told the exiles all that Yahweh had shown him (xi. 25). That in many cases the prophetic speeches are not transmitted to us in their original form is another matter. We have frequently only brief accounts or summaries, not to mention the fact that many of the original speeches have been worked over by the disciples of the prophets, the collectors, and the redactors of the prophetic books.

As in public speeches, the prophetic utterances frequently begin with a call to the hearers to come and listen, to gather together, to draw near to the speaker: 'Rise up, hear my voice'; 'come hither'; 'draw near to listen, attend'; 'assemble and listen'; 'ho! everyone, come' (a formula taken from the cries of the street traders in eastern towns and villages). Sometimes the speeches begin with a 'silentium!': 'Keep silence and listen to me.' Very common is this exhortation to listen: 'Hear!' The book of Isaiah begins: 'Hear, O heavens, and give ear, O earth.'[75]

Sometimes the prophets chose to appear as poets or minstrels rather than speakers or preachers. It is not quite out of the question that on occasion they conveyed their message in song. When Isaiah recited the song of Yahweh's vineyard (ch. v), he stood before his audience as a popular poet or singer, to whom people liked to listen in the streets and the gates:

> Let me sing of my loved one,
> a song of my beloved of his vineyard, etc.[76]

[73] Other good examples are Jer. xxxi. 10 (announcement of the redemption of Israel) and Isa. xlix. 1 (a prophetic confession).

[74] Ezek. iv. 3, 7; vi. 2; xiii. 17; xx. 46; xxi. 7; xxv. 2; xxviii. 21; xxix. 2; xxxv. 2; xxxviii. 2. Possibly the formula had originally a magical significance; cf. Fohrer in *HAT*. The same phrase is frequently utilized in the Ugaritic texts to indicate the person to whom a speech or a message is addressed, someone to whom a visit is to be paid, etc. (Driver, *Canaanite Myths and Legends*, pp. 89, 91, 103, 105, 107).

[75] Some examples: Isa. xxxii. 9; xxxiv. 1; xli. 1; xlviii. 14, 16; lv. 1; lvii. 3. See further Lindblom in the *Buhl Festschrift*, 1925, pp. 112 ff.

[76] For a better understanding of this song see the sound remarks made by Bentzen in *AfO*, iv, 1927, pp. 209 ff.

Amos announces in v. 1 f. the judgement upon his people in the form of a dirge (*ḳînâh*). The lament for the princes of Israel in Ezek. xix is expressly called a dirge. So are the laments over Tyre (xxvii), over the king of Tyre (xxviii. 11 ff.), and over Pharaoh of Egypt (xxxii. 2 ff.). Ezekiel is exhorted to raise a lament (*nâhâh*) over Egypt (xxxii. 18 ff.). An anonymous prophet takes up a taunt-song (*mašâl*) against the king of Babylon, dealing with his coming to Sheol (xiv).

Of course, such poems embedded in the prophetic sermons were not necessarily sung; the prophets might only have imitated in them familiar methods of reciting popular songs of various kinds.

A great many rhetorical and literary types are represented in the utterances of the prophets in accordance with the different themes which are dealt with. There are exhortations to repentance, reproaches, announcements of judgement, threats against the apostates in Israel and against pagan nations, words of consolation and promises for the future. There are woe and satire, scorn and lamentation, hymns and prayers, monologues and dialogues, judicial debating, utterances formulated after a ritual pattern, descriptions of visions and auditions and confessions of personal experiences of different kinds. There are letters and messages, short oracles and extended sermons, historical retrospects, confessions of sin, decisions in cultic matters, parables and allegories, similes and sententious phrases of wisdom, lyric poetry of various kinds, and discussions of religious and moral problems.

In recent years particular attention has been paid to the so-called liturgies in the prophetic literature. A liturgy is a ritual dialogue between God and the cultic assembly, the original *Sitz im Leben* of which was in the cult. The great pioneer in this field was the famous German scholar, H. Gunkel. Such liturgies, or imitations of liturgies, have been found in Isa. xxxiii, Mic. vii. 7-20, and in the books of Habakkuk and Nahum. In other sections of the prophetic books such liturgies have been identified with more or less probability. The present author has tried to show that in Isa. xxiv-xxvii, we have to do with a cantata performed because of the capture of Babylon by Xerxes in 485 B.C. Whether the ritually formulated passages in the prophetic literature were really performed in connection with the cult or are only to be regarded as imitations made by the prophets is still an open question.[77]

[77] During recent decades the style of the prophetic utterances has attracted increasing attention among scholars. Pioneering monographs were Baumgartner, *Die Klagege-dichte des Jeremia* (*BZAW*, 32, Giessen, 1917); Köhler, *Deuterojesaja* (*Jesaja* 40-55) *stilkritisch untersucht* (*BZAW*, 37, Giessen, 1923). The 'Gattungsforschung' founded by Gunkel has also been of the utmost moment for the study of the prophetic literature. For the so-called prophetic liturgies see Gunkel in *ZAW*, xlii, 1924, pp. 177 ff., and *ZS*, ii, 1924, pp. 145 ff.; Humbert in *ZAW*, xliv, 1926, pp. 266 ff.; Balla in *RGG²*

All these various forms of speech are presented as revelations from God. It is said that Yahweh has spoken the words uttered, or that the words have come from Yahweh. A letter written by Jeremiah to the exiles in Babylonia begins: 'Thus says Yahweh Zebaoth, the God of Israel, to all the exiles whom I carried into exile from Jerusalem to Babylon,' etc. (xxix). As we have frequently emphasized in the foregoing, this is what distinguishes the prophetic utterances from utterances of ordinary men: a prophet never speaks in his own name, but always in the name of God and on God's behalf. Even if the oracle formulas are not actually inserted, the prophetic words are conceived of as divine words, as words inspired by God.

The primary form of a prophetic utterance was, as we know, the oracle. The original oracles were short, concise, pregnant, and formulated in a peculiar fashion. A number of such oracles are to be found in the prophetic books. But, as we have seen above, the prophets also used the oracle form for utterances which were not oracles in the strict sense. It may be said that the old oracle form disintegrated and that the utterances of the later prophets are mostly pseudo-oracles, which, of course, does not mean that they are not thought of as direct revelations from God. These pseudo-oracles vary considerably in content. From the point of view of the content a prophetic pseudo-oracle may resemble a modern address or sermon of an admonitory or even a markedly didactic type.[78]

As a teaching about the will and the ways of God, the utterances of the prophets could be called *tôrâh*. The prophetic 'words' and the prophetic 'torah' sometimes stand as synonyms. Isaiah says in a well-known passage, 'Hear the word of Yahweh, you rulers of Sodom; listen to the torah of our God, you people of Gomorrah!' (i. 10). Jeremiah threatens with terrible punishment all those who do not listen to God by following the torah which He had set before them and by heeding the words of the prophets (xxvi. 4 f.; cf. vi. 19). Zechariah rebukes his people because they made their minds unresponsive so that

---

[78] Sometimes an oracle in the strict sense is preserved and embedded in a more extended prophetic discourse. This discourse is so to speak built up around the short oracle. So for instance Jer. vii. 14 (xxvi. 6); xx. 3 ff. Such oracles may appropriately be called 'embryonic' or 'germinal oracles'; so Scott in *VT*, ii, 1952, pp. 278 ff.

II, 1928, cols. 1556 f.; Sellin, *Einleitung*[5], 1929, p. 120. Kapelrud, 'Cult and Prophetic Words', *St. Th.*, iv, 1951/52, pp. 5 ff., emphasizes that the prophets had to use cultic terms in order to be better understood by their audience. For wisdom phrases see Lindblom in *SVT*, III, 1955, pp. 102 ff., and for Isa. xxiv-xxvii see my book *Die Jesaja-Apocalypse*. A general survey of the stylistic questions is to be found in Hempel, *Die althebräische Literatur und ihr hellenistisch-jüdisches Nachleben*, pp. 56 ff.

they could not hear the torah and the words which Yahweh had sent by His Spirit, through the former prophets (vii. 12). The testimony and the torah of the prophet Isaiah is sealed within his disciples (viii. 16). Israel is a rebellious people who will not hear the torah of Yahweh and say to the prophets, 'You shall not prophesy to us right things' (xxx. 9 f.). The apostate people are accused of having scorned the torah of the Lord of hosts and having spurned the word of the Holy One of Israel (v. 24). The prophet thinks here, of course, of the preaching of the true prophets. The enemies of the true prophets, priests and false prophets, ask ironically: 'Whom will he teach [yôrêh] knowledge?' (Isa. xxviii. 9), which proves that the prophets were also regarded by them as teachers of torah.

In this respect the great prophets arrogated to themselves the function of the priests, who were the real custodians of torah and also were regarded by the prophets as authentic transmitters of torah. Probably the prophets directly adopted from the priests the very term torah.[79] In controversy with the priests they accused them of having mismanaged and neglected their important task and yet claimed to be the true imparters of the torah of Yahweh. This we can learn, for instance, from the preaching of Hosea. In older times at least there was a difference between the torah of the priests and the torah of the classical prophets. An important part of the priestly torah was to impart direction in cultic matters, while the essential content of the torah of the prophets was an instruction of a religious and ethical nature. This difference between the priestly and the prophetic torah was of course essentially reduced in so far as the prophets were attached to the sanctuaries as cultic prophets, or otherwise particularly interested in cultic matters. How prophets of this class functioned, is to be seen for instance from the narrative in Zech. vii about the discussion concerning the fast in the fifth month and, likewise, from the passage Ezek. xliii. 11 f., where the prophet is commanded to make known to the people the tôrôt which were available for the new temple. Further, the false prophet was designated by the classical prophets as a teacher (môrêh), but as one who teaches lies (Isa. ix. 14).

There are many stages from the short oracles to the extended sermons with a didactic character. Moreover, the prophetic revelations are, as we have seen above, of the most varied character. Among them we can distinguish two main types: one group consists in revelations

[79] See further Östborn, Tōrā in the Old Testament, pp. 127 ff. The positive co-operation of priests and prophets is emphasized by Welch, Prophet and Priest in Old Israel. Cf. also Plöger in ZAW, lxiii, 1951, pp. 179 ff.

which by their very nature were intended to be made public; the revelations of the other group had, from the point of view of their content, reference only to the prophet himself. In all these cases the problem arises: how was it that these revelations were brought to the knowledge of the public?

First of all we must recall that in the opinion of the prophets everything which had the character of a revelation was a word from God and for this reason did not belong to the prophet alone, but was the property of all men. In this men and women belonging to the prophetic type differ essentially from many visionaries of a more individualistic and mystic type.

When examining the oracle-giving of the prophets we pointed out that several possibilities must be taken into account. The same is true of the more extended revelations.

A prophet is sitting in his house, or is standing in the sanctuary, or is walking in the open. He falls into ecstasy or simply feels strongly inspired by God. He receives a revelation, whether a vision, poem, or speech. From the moment of his call he was conscious of not being his own, but a servant of others. For this reason he feels prompted to go out and make his revelation known to people. Under the impress of the inspiration he gives form and shape, usually an artistic one, to what he has received, and then he is ready to communicate it to men. I think that this was what usually happened.

Or again, the prophet is seized by ecstasy in public. He receives a revelation, which may be suggested by the sight of a certain person or a crowd of men, or by something that has happened. A speech pours out from the well-spring of inspiration in the same moment as it is delivered. The public speeches frequently made by the prophets before an assembly of men, in the streets, in the courts of the sanctuaries or the royal palace, were in many cases conceived in the same instant as they were delivered. In these cases the inspired revelation, the composing and the uttering of the speech occurred simultaneously.

Finally we may realize that an idea or an outline was given to the prophet in the form of a revelation on the basis of which the prophet afterwards delivered a speech. Perhaps such a revelation had the form of a short oracle, which became the nucleus of the subsequent sermon. An oracle of this kind has been appropriately called an embryonic or germinal oracle.[80]

As regards the phrases which often introduce the revelatory speeches and indicate that a prophet was ordered to go and say this or that to the

[80] See above, p. 156, note 78.

people or a named person, we must take into account that they frequently may have been formed and inserted by the collectors and redactors. It was generally thought that all that was said and done by the prophets was arranged beforehand by God, who in all situations directed the ways of the prophets and told them what to say.

Owing to the actual condition of the prophetic texts it is of course in most cases impossible definitely to decide whether a prophetic utterance has arisen in one way or another.

A good many of the utterances of the prophets are preserved to us in their original form. This is particularly true of those which have a rhythmical and poetical form. In other cases we have only shorter or longer reports or summaries. A third group bears traces of being worked over by later hands. In many cases it is now impossible to distinguish between the authentic words of the prophets and words put in their mouths by their disciples, by later reciters or readers of the prophetic texts, for instance in connection with the cult, and, lastly, by the collectors and redactors of the actual prophetic books.

In the study of the prophetic texts we must always keep in mind that the revelations of the prophets have been transmitted to us by oral or written tradition. This tradition was in both forms a living tradition exposed to changes and modifications either unintentional or deliberate in accordance with the taste of different times and the needs of different situations. But it would be an exaggeration to maintain that because of this fact it would be unjustified and useless to seek in the prophetic literature for authentic utterances of the prophets. The historian cannot simply abstain from going behind tradition in order to discover the original facts upon which tradition is built up. It is indeed possible to attain good results if we become aware of the factors which may have influenced the development of tradition. In many cases we cannot now establish the *ipsissima verba* of a prophet; we must be content with the authentic ideas. But this also is a worthwhile result. As we have said before, our prophetic books frequently supply us with summaries and reports of the prophetic utterances instead of verbatim reports. But even this does not prevent us from surmising the essential content of what the prophet said on a certain occasion. The sceptical attitude of some scholars towards the possibility of establishing what Amos, Hosea, Isaiah, etc., really said is undoubtedly exaggerated.

How was it that the utterances of the prophets were preserved and handed down to posterity? This question has been keenly discussed in recent years. Every student in this field knows the main lines of this discussion, and it is unnecessary to give here a detailed account of all the different standpoints. I simply state the view which my own researches and those of others have led me to adopt.[81]

Several of the prophetic sayings were from the outset given such a form as to be easily kept in mind by the hearers. I think particularly of two groups: the short oracles and the smaller lyrical poems. The oracles on Damascus and Samaria and their kings pronounced by Isaiah (vii. 8 f.), or the oracle on Immanuel (vii. 14), or the answer given to the ambassadors from Edom: 'Morning comes, but also night' (xxi. 12) once heard could not be forgotten. From Jer. xxvi. 17 f. we see how a prophetic oracle delivered a century ago is literally cited by Jewish authorities. The same is true of poems such as that of the vineyard (Isa. v.), the dirge of the fallen virgin, Israel (Am. v. 1 f.), the epigram uttered by Jeremiah against Judah: 'Can the Ethiopian change his skin, or the leopard his spots? Then may you also do good, who are trained to do evil' (xiii. 23). Such sayings were easily remembered and transmitted from generation to generation.

But this was not possible in all cases. Discourses of a more elaborate and developed character could not easily be remembered for a long time. A very lengthy sermon, even if in rhythmical form, could not be remembered word for word after the first hearing. And what of sayings and narratives which were never delivered as public speeches, but were of an intimate and personal nature and concerned only the prophet himself and his intimate friends?

Here we have to take into account the role played by the inner circles which surrounded the prophets, their true adherents, their friends, their disciples. In all the records about visionaries, wherever we have to do with people who have had the faculty of receiving revelations, we hear of friends, disciples, fathers confessor who have aided them with the recording and the conservation of their revelations in one fashion or another.[82] In addition we may remember that in the Orient teachers have always gathered around themselves disciples in greater or smaller numbers to receive their instruction and pass on their ideas.[83]

Now we know that at least two of the Old Testament prophets had such friends and disciples. Jeremiah, who otherwise lived a solitary life, had at his side Baruch, his friend and secretary. But the best example is the circle around Isaiah mentioned in Isa. viii. 16 ff. Those who belonged to this circle are expressly called 'disciples' (*limmûḏîm*)

---

[81] See Additional Note II.

[82] See above, pp. 24, 69.

[83] Mowinckel in particular has pointed out the importance of the disciples of the prophets for transmission of the prophetic words. See *Profeten Jesaja* and *Jesaja-disiplene*, and many later works.

and 'sons' (yᵉlāḏîm) of the prophet, whom Yahweh had given him. It is highly probable that other prophets, too, were surrounded by disciples, even if there is no direct mention of it. However, I think that it is very likely that the disciples (limmûḏîm) mentioned in Isa. l. 4 are disciples of the prophets. They are presented as anxious to hear and trained to speak.[84] With such disciples the prophet compares himself when he says that he is a disciple of Yahweh who receives divine revelations. When Amaziah, the priest of Bethel, accused Amos of having conspired (ḳāšar) against the king, he presumably thought of Amos amid the circle of his disciples. A conspiracy presupposes more than one man (vii. 10). Are the disciples of Amos perhaps referred to in the difficult passage iii. 13? It runs: 'Hear and testify [seriously assure] in the house of Jacob that on the day when I punish Israel for its offences, I shall inflict punishment upon the altars of Bethel,' etc. In every commentary this question is put: Who are addressed here? Whom does the prophet exhort to listen and convey the terrible message to the people of Israel? No satisfactory answer is given. I think that the prophet is addressing his own disciples. It is they who are summoned by him to listen intently to the oracle and repeat it among the people.[85]

We are justified in assuming that as a rule the classical prophets were surrounded by a circle of disciples who had attached themselves to the great prophetic personalities, regarding them as their teachers and masters. These circles were then a continuation of the prophetic guilds of earlier times, the members of which were called bᵉnê hannᵉḇî'îm. The main business of those early bᵉnê hannᵉḇî'îm seems to have been exercises in the art of ecstasy and oracle-giving. Among the disciples of Isaiah, Jeremiah, and other prophets of the classical type, methodical training in ecstasy presumably played a minor role. These disciples occupied themselves with other and more important matters.

Isa. viii. 16 ff. is very instructive in this respect. The prophet says here that he will bind up the testimony and seal his teaching among his disciples. In the opinion of the present author this is figuratively

---

[84] Notice the expressions used: lišmōaᶜ kallimmûḏîm and lᵉšôn limmûḏîm.

[85] Nowack thought of the inhabitants of the palaces mentioned in iii, 9; similarly Cripps in his Commentary on Amos. Guthe in HSAT was of the opinion that the passage is a secondary addition, the persons addressed being the Gentiles mentioned in v. 9, or Jews of a later time summoned against the Samaritans. Sellin thought of the prophet's hearers in general and changed the text reading 'Jeroboam' instead of 'Jacob'. Other explanations are to be found in more recent commentaries. Robinson in HAT thinks of the whole of mankind; similarly Neher in Amos. Weiser thinks of those rich merchants who had their establishments in Samaria and Damascus; etc. There is, then, wide disagreement on this point. The utterance is of course very obscure, but like many other prophetic words it is fragmentary and no longer in its original context.

spoken. Like a man who binds up a scroll and seals it with seals, so that it cannot be read by everybody, the prophet in a certain historical situation felt obliged not to speak publicly, but to entrust his message to his disciples to be preserved by them.[86] To this utterance another is linked, a word addressed to the disciples: when anxious people come and ask them to inquire of spirits and ghosts, they have only to turn away the superstitious oracle-seekers and point to the catastrophe to come.[87] I shall have occasion to return to this passage later on.

If we have correctly interpreted the passages adduced above, the following account may be given of the functions of the disciples of the prophets.

The occupation of the disciples consisted in the first place in receiving instruction from their prophetic leaders concerning the religious and moral principles of their preaching. They had to be initiated into the 'knowledge of God', da'at yahwêh. Further, they had to listen intently to what the prophet told them concerning his prophetic experiences. The disciples were the first to be entrusted with the 'confessions' of the prophets and such revelations as were not intended for immediate public recitation. They had also by diligent repetition to learn by heart the revelatory speeches of the prophet and so preserve them, that they might be accurately transmitted to following generations. A right disciple's ear and tongue (Isa. l. 4) were highly valued. The ability to learn by heart and preserve in memory has always been highly developed in the Orient. But examples are also found in other cultures. Individual Finnish Rune-singers of the nineteenth century could without difficulty

---

[86] Jones in *ZAW*, lxvii, 1955, pp. 226 ff., sees rightly that 'testimony' and 'torah' are synonyms and refer to the teaching of Isaiah. But in my opinion he is wrong in maintaining that the words about the sealed scroll are to be understood literally.

[87] The exegesis of *vv.* 16 ff. presents many difficulties. With *BH* and many critics I regard the two verbs in *v.* 16 as absolute infinitives indicating the decision of the prophet for the present to entrust his message to his disciples only. Concerning *vv.* 19-20 there is no agreement as to the demand made by the oracle-seekers and the answer given by the disciples. Some critics think that the demand is expressed in *v.* 19a and the answer in 19b (Duhm, Procksch, Herntrich in *ATD*); others are of the opinion that 19b also belongs to the words of the oracle-seekers (Guthe, Cheyne, Buhl, Kissane, Hoschander, *The Priests and Prophets*, p. 361). Bentzen is undecided on this point. In my opinion *v.* 19 as a whole reproduces the supposed demand of the oracle-seekers, which is ironically formulated by the prophet (notice the expressions 'that chirp and murmur' and 'the dead on behalf of the living'). Consequently *'am* is not Israel, but people in a general sense. *'elōhâw* does not refer to Yahweh, but to the spirits of the dead. Cf. also *La Bible de Jérusalem*: 'Cette réponse [comprising the second half of *v.* 19] est probablement ironique. Isaïese moque du peuple qui préfère consulter les nécromanciens plutôt que le prophète.' I explain *haddābār hazzêh* in *v.* 20 as referring to the utterance of the visitors in *v.* 19b. In a coming time of fathomless distress, when the people will be forsaken by their king and their God, the visitors will have still more reason for inquiring of the spirits of the dead. Then the words *lᵉtôrâh wᵉlitᵉ'ûdâh* must be regarded as a marginal gloss saying that *vv.* 16 ff. concern the important theme *tôrâh* and *tᵉ'ûdâh*.

recite ten thousands of verses without the help of written texts. Probably they sometimes recited prophetic oracles and sermons before the people. From Isa. viii. 19 it is evident that the prophetic disciples themselves were active in delivering oracles. For this reason they had to be taught to deliver right oracles. In certain circumstances the disciples of the prophets had to write down and collect revelations of the prophets and other communications made by them.

The problem of the preserving of the prophetic revelations cannot be solved without taking into consideration the activities of the disciples of the prophets. For most of the prophetic literature which has been transmitted to us we are above all indebted to the disciples of the prophets. They learnt from the prophets, they listened to what they said, they stored up in their memory and sometimes put down in writing what they had heard. One generation transmitted its precious treasure to the next (as has always been the custom in the Orient), until the time came when first the collectors of larger collections and later the redactors of the books commenced their operations.

Did not the prophets themselves put down in writing their experiences and inspired revelations? We may conclude from many passages in the prophetic literature that a number of revelations may have been written down by the prophets themselves. As has been rightly pointed out, ancient Palestine was the seat of an ancient scribal culture.[88] Material of various kinds was recorded in writing: letters, political or private, annals and diaries, lists and catalogues of different sorts, laws, purchase-deeds, historical narratives, songs, and poems. The prophets were quite familiar with the practice of writing. In Isa. xxix. 11 it is said that the prophetic revelations have become to the people like the words of a scroll that is sealed. In xxxiv. 4, a prophet says that the heavens will roll up like a scroll. That prophetic oracles and revelations could be written down is indirectly proved by what is said in the narrative of the inaugural vision of Ezekiel. A hand was stretched out to the prophet, in the hand was a scroll covered with writing on both sides; words of lamentation, mourning, and woe were written on it. Without doubt this scroll is thought of as a scroll containing prophetic revelations of various kinds.

But there are also several explicit references. Isaiah wrote upon a tablet these words: 'Spoil hastens. Booty hurries' (viii. 1). The same prophet was commanded to write down a revelation that it might be a testimony for ever (xxx. 8). Jeremiah was ordered to write down some of his revelations (xxx. 2). Further it is told of Jeremiah that he

---

[88] Cf. above all Widengren, *Literary and Psychological Aspects of the Hebrew Prophets*, pp. 57 ff.

once wrote on a scroll a record of all the trouble that was to come upon Babylon. This book was to be brought to Babylonia by Seraiah, the quarter-master, read aloud by him, and then thrown into the Euphrates (li. 60 ff.). Ezekiel was commanded to record in writing the description of the new temple which is contained in ch. xl-xlviii of his book (xliii. 11). The prophet Habakkuk was likewise commanded to write down a certain revelation that it might be read as a witness of the reliability of the prophetic word (ii. 2 f.).

As we have already seen, Baruch wrote at Jeremiah's dictation the revelations which the prophet had uttered. It is not said whether it was by his own hand or by the hand of a secretary that Jeremiah wrote the letter to the captives in Babylon which contained his revelations concerning their life in exile and their liberation (ch. xxix). The main point is that a letter was written on Jeremiah's initiative.

Of course these passages do not say anything more than that on particular occasions the prophets themselves (or by the hand of another) wrote down specific revelations. Without doubt they were in the first place speakers; and it was only in special circumstances that they wrote. More often, no doubt, the disciples afterwards put in writing what they had heard and seen. It would not be correct to say that the prophetic revelations were orally handed down for many years, and then, at a subsequent period, recorded in writing. We must, in fact, allow for the existence of both oral and written transmission from the beginning, though it may be that the former predominated in the earliest period.

What prompted the prophets to take measures to preserve their revelations for the future? First, they regarded their experiences and utterances as Yahweh's word. Being divine words, the prophetic sayings had significance and validity for all times. Secondly, through being written down or orally repeated they could always perform their task of influencing their readers or hearers, to arouse the dormant, judge the sinners, console the afflicted, give directions for the future, and predict what was to come. Thirdly, if a prophecy was written down, its truth and the trustworthiness of the prophet could be verified by the course of events; people could be aware that the word of God was reliable and that a prophet had been in the midst of them, a phrase used by Ezekiel.[89]

The manner in which the prophetic revelations, and episodes from the lives of the prophets, were handed down accounts for the form in which they survive in our present prophetic books. There are many obscure passages, many discrepancies, many doublets, many gaps, and many additions. Several revelations have been placed under different

[89] Isa. viii. 1 f.; xxx. 8; Hab. ii. 2 f.; Ezek. ii. 5; xxxiii. 33.

names. Such phenomena are much easier to explain if we adopt a traditio-historical point of view than a purely literary one.

When in later times the prophetic revelations were more methodically collected and brought together in books, material of various kinds was available: oracles and poems which circulated orally among the people, oral tradition conserved within the circles of disciples, written documents deriving from the prophets themselves or their disciples. How all this material was later put together into collections and books, such as we have today, will be demonstrated in a later chapter.

7. SYMBOLIC ACTIONS

According to tradition the early prophets frequently acted in unusual ways in order to drive home the oracles they uttered. In the presence of the kings of Israel and Judah the prophet Zedekiah made for himself horns of iron and said, 'Thus says Yahweh, "With these you shall gore the Syrians until they are destroyed."' Elisha told the king of Israel to shoot with bow and arrows in the direction of Syria in order to secure victory over Syria.[90] Numbers of similar actions are ascribed to the later prophets, too.

Let us begin with the familiar and much debated marriage of Hosea.[91] Of this we have two accounts, one related in the third person (i. 2-9), the other related in the first person (iii. 1-3). According to the first narrative Yahweh ordered Hosea to espouse an adulteress and have children born of an adulteress.[92] He married Gomer, the daughter of Diblaim. She bore him a son who by the command of Yahweh was called Jezreel, indicating that Yahweh would soon demand from the house of Jehu 'the blood of Jezreel', i.e., the massacre of the royal family as recorded in 2 Kings ix f. Then Gomer bore a daughter who was called *lô' ruḥāmâh*, 'She, who-is-unpitied', symbolizing that Yahweh would not have pity upon the house of Israel. Finally she bore a son to whom was given the name *lô' 'ammî*, 'Not-my-people', demonstrating that Yahweh had rejected His people.

Apart from the addition concerning Judah in *v.* 7[93] the narrative rings

[90] 1 Kings xxii. 11; 2 Kings xiii. 14 ff.
[91] A detailed analysis of the narratives of the marriage of Hosea with numerous references to the older literature is given in my book *Hosea literarisch untersucht*. See further the more recent article by Rowley 'The Marriage of Hosea', *BJRL*, vol. 39, 1956, pp. 200 ff.
[92] The root *znh* signifies fornication in a general sense or even adultery in the strict sense. Here the latter is meant, as is evident from the expression *yaldê zᵉnûnîm* of the children born after the marriage.
[93] It is generally held that *v.* 7 is a secondary interpolation reflecting Jewish interests. See the commentaries.

true: the marriage with Gomer, the birth of the three children, and the symbolic names given them, one indicating the doom over the dynasty, two indicating the broken covenant between Yahweh and His people. The preamble in *v.* 2 saying that Hosea was commanded by Yahweh to marry an adulteress and have children born of an adulteress is to be explained in accordance with the usual prophetic narrative style. Every action and every utterance by a prophet with a prophetic significance was regarded as ordered by Yahweh in advance and occurring on a divine initiative. Many examples of this have been given above. In the introductory words the subsequent happenings are anticipated. The description of the woman may therefore be regarded as proleptic. If this were not the case, not only must the woman have been an adulteress from the outset, she must also have brought bastards with her into Hosea's home. Both are equally unacceptable. It is quite manifest that the children mentioned in *v.* 2 are those who were born after the marriage.[94]

The woman was immoral and unfaithful to the prophet. The children's names indicated that the adultery took place after the birth of the first child. The name Jezreel does not hint at any matrimonial tragedy. The names given to the second and the third child indicate that the prophet did not avow their legitimacy. The adultery being a fact, the prophet used it as a symbol of the broken covenant between Yahweh and His people.

Now, we have another account of Hosea's marriage, namely that in ch. iii. Here the prophet himself is speaking. This account was presumably narrated by the prophet to his disciples and came to be incorporated in the book alongside the first narrative. In the prophetic books as

---

[94] Adultery being sternly condemned in Israelite custom and law, it is hardly thinkable that the prophet espoused such a woman. The words *'ēšet zᵉnûnîm* cannot be translated 'a woman disposed to fornication' (Ehrlich, Budde, Sellin in his commentary of 1929, etc.), for from that would follow that the children, too, should be thought of as disposed to fornication. The proleptic conception is vindicated by Harper (in *ICC*), Guthe (in *HSAT*), Lindblom (*Hosea*), Weiser (in *ATD*), Wheeler Robinson (*Two Hebrew Prophets*), etc. If the description of the woman is interpreted in this manner, the interesting proposal made by Coppens in the *Nötscher Festschrift*, 1950, pp. 38 ff., loses its foundation, namely that the woman was called a *zōnâh* simply as a member of the apostate people, by Hosea regarded as a *zōnâh*. Similarly Pfeiffer, *Introduction*, p. 569. On the explanation which I have accepted the view presented by Robinson that Gomer had previously abandoned herself to sacral prostitution (*TSK*, cvi, 1934/35, pp. 301 ff., and in *HAT*) becomes unnecessary. It may be added that Nyberg has expressed the opinion that Gomer is called a *zōnâh* as a woman of foreign origin connected with a pagan cult. The woman of ch. iii, says Nyberg, is another wife, an adulterous one whom the prophet married (*UUÅ*, 1941: 7, 2, pp. 30 ff.). In *SBU*, I, cols. 878 and 881, Engnell follows Nyberg. In addition he suggests that Gomer was a temple prostitute. To delete from the text the words 'of whoredom and children of whoredom' (i, 2) as is proposed by Humbert (*RHR*, lxxvii, 1918, pp. 157 ff.), and Batten (*JBL*, xlviii, 1929, pp. 257 ff.: 'a clumsy gloss'), seems to be too drastic.

elsewhere in the revelation literature narratives in the first person and narratives in the third person stand side by side.

The content of the narrative in ch. iii is as follows. The prophet was ordered by God to give his love to a woman who would commit adultery and have a lover.[95] So he bought the woman in question; but as the woman was known to be a wanton, the prophet subjected her to discipline. She was debarred from other men and denied sexual intercourse with her husband. The relation between the prophet and this woman was interpreted by the prophet as a symbol of the relation between Yahweh and His people.

In this narrative, too, the prophet's action in taking the wanton woman into his house is regarded as commanded by Yahweh as are all the significant actions in the life of a prophet. Here, too, the characterization of the woman as an adulteress refers to what happened after the prophet had married her. That she, at any rate, was from the outset a woman of loose character is evident from what is told of the prophet's endeavour to educate her.

Now the question arises how the two narratives of Hosea's marriage are related to each other. We take for granted that both describe events that really occurred in the life of Hosea.[96] There is no convincing foundation for a visionary or purely allegorical interpretation of the narratives. More than thirty years ago the present writer presented the view that the two narratives deal with two different stages of the same matrimonial history of Hosea. What the prophet tells is the first stage, what the disciples tell are the later stages of the same history. Taken together they give us the following picture of the marriage of Hosea.

Hosea fell in love with a woman, Gomer by name, who was known to be of loose character. He bought her to be his wife, according to the custom in ancient Israel. To begin with, he made her undergo a rigid discipline. Then he consummated the marriage and became the father of a child who was given a symbolic name referring to the impending

[95] I read *'ōhebet* to correspond with the active participle *'ōhaḇê* in the following line; cf. Rowley, op. cit., p. 202, note 10. The active participles can in Hebrew represent the present, the past, or the future time (see *Ges.-K.*, 116, 2d). The part. *mēt*, for instance, can signify *mortuus, moriens,* and *moriturus*. Here the future is meant.

[96] Advocates of the visionary explanation are Origen, Maimonides, Kimchi, Hengstenberg, Keil, etc., of the allegorical interpretation in recent times above all Gressmann in *SATA*, II, 1, 1921. Other critics hold that ch. i is historical and ch. iii an allegory: Volz, Marti, Hölscher, Guthe, Pfeiffer, Humbert, Batten, Snaith ('a late inauthentic composition'; *Mercy and Sacrifice. A Study of the Book of Hosea*). For the older literature see further Lindblom, *Hosea*, pp. 2 f. That both ch. i and ch. iii reproduce historical facts seems, however, to be the common opinion among modern critics. Against Gressmann see particularly Schmidt, 'Die Ehe des Hosea', *ZAW*, xlii, 1924, pp. 245 ff., and Budde, 'Der Abschnitt Hosea 1-3 und seine grundlegende religionsgeschichtliche Bedeutung', *TSK*, xcvi-xcvii, 1925, pp. 1 ff.

doom over the royal dynasty. After the birth of the first child Gomer was found to be an adulteress. For this reason the following two children were given their names of ill omen, symbolizing the doom over Israel and the final rejection of the elect people.[97]

What then happened is not told, and will never be known. If this interpretation of the two texts concerning Hosea's matrimonial history is correct, the symbolical meaning of it becomes fully clear. Gomer, first frail, then openly adulterous, is a symbol of Israel, the elect people of God; the prophet's love to his wanton wife symbolizes Yahweh's love to His people. The chastisement which Gomer must undergo symbolizes how Yahweh intends to chastise His people, so that they may repent. The same thought appears, for instance, in ii. 16-17. The names given the last children indicate the radical rejection of the unfaithful people.[98]

In the English Bible the text of iii. 1 runs: 'Go yet [Hebr. '$\delta\underline{d}$], love a woman,' etc. Many scholars maintain that ch. i and ch. iii refer to two different marriages. In the opinion of the present writer the word in question is only an addition by the collector to link together the parallel narratives.[99]

It would not be correct to say that the marriage of Hosea as a whole was a symbolic action. We must not think that the prophet *intentionally* married the wanton woman to present a symbol of the relation between Yahweh and His people. Rather this marriage *revealed* to him Yahweh's paradoxical love to His apostate people and was used by him as a

[97] Consequently I think that the woman of ch. i and that of ch. iii are the same. There are scholars who hold that Hosea married two different women who were both immoral. So Duhm, *Israels Propheten*[2], Tübingen, 1922, p. 98; Nyberg, op. cit.; Fohrer in *TZ*, xi, 1955, pp. 161 ff. On the other hand Steuernagel argued that ch. i and ch. iii contain two independent but parallel accounts of the same occurrence; *Lehrbuch der Einleitung in das Alte Testament*, Tübingen, 1912, pp. 605 ff. It seems that most scholars in recent times think that the woman in ch. iii is identical with Gomer, though their views of the relation between the two narratives vary widely. A somewhat modernizing attempt at a psychological analysis of Hosea's feeling towards Gomer is to be found in Welch, *Kings and Prophets of Israel*[2], London, 1953, p. 151. It is a pleasure to me to note that Lods in *Histoire de la littérature hebraïque et juive*, Paris, 1950, on essential points shares my view of Hosea's marital history. On many points I agree with Rowley, 'The Marriage of Hosea'. Against Rowley, however, I must maintain that ch. i is the sequel to ch. iii. It seems to me more probable that the discipline of the wanton Gomer occurred at the beginning of the story. This I must assert also against Eissfeldt (*Einleitung*[2], pp. 471 ff., with reference to Robinson in *HAT*), with whom in other respects I fully agree.

[98] In the third person narrative the chief stress is laid upon the unfaithfulness of Israel to Yahweh, in the first person narrative again Yahweh's love to His people is emphasized. This fact does not oblige us to think that we have to do with two different marriages (against Weiser). The two ways of looking at the matter are not incompatible, but only represent two different points of view.

[99] So, for instance, Robinson in his commentary and Steuernagel in his above-mentioned work. Others think that 'δd belongs to *wayyōmer yahwêh*, which does not correspond to the position of the word in the sentence.

symbol. But the names given to the children were intentionally symbolic. The prophet meant to convey to his contemporaries that the royal dynasty was doomed to rigorous punishment, that Israel was deprived of Yahweh's mercy, and that the elect people, because of its apostasy, was rejected.

Isaiah performed a symbolic action when he gave his son the peculiar name Shear-yashub, which may be paraphrased: 'There will be a remnant, and it will return' (to Yahweh). The name contains a prediction of the destruction of the nation as a whole, but at the same time of the fact that a small part of the people would be preserved and start a new life in obedience to and trust in Yahweh. At his meeting with Ahaz Isaiah intentionally brought with him his son Shear-yashub, indicating to the king the necessity of turning from his wrong way and putting his trust in Yahweh (vii).[100] The same prophet wrote on a tablet the significant words: Maher-shalal-hash-baz: 'Spoil hastens. Booty hurries', which words he also used as a name for his own son, thus pointing to the fact that in a short time the wealth of Damascus and the spoil of Samaria would be carried away to Assyria (viii).[100a] Another symbolic name was Immanuel ('God is with us') given to the royal child of vii. 14.

During the Assyrian campaign against Ashdod 713-711, Isaiah went naked and barefoot, i.e., without sackcloth (on the prophetic clothing see pp. 65 ff.) and sandals, a sign and symbol indicating that one day the Assyrian king would lead away the Egyptians and Ethiopians barefoot and with buttocks uncovered, as captives to Assyria. This was a warning to Israel not to trust in the alliance with Egypt (xx). [101]

Jeremiah gave Pashhur, the priest, the symbolic name *māḡôr missāḇîḇ* ('terror all around'), thus foretelling the disaster which would befall him, his friends, and his people (xx. 3). He felt himself ordered by Yahweh not to take a wife, nor have sons and daughters, thus proclaiming that parents as well as children would die in Jerusalem (xvi. 1 ff.). He was forbidden to take part in common mourning usages: such a massacre would take place in the city that every kind of mourning custom would be impossible (*vv.* 5 ff.). He was prohibited from entering a house of feasting to eat and drink; for in a short time Yahweh would banish

---

[100] See Additional Note III.

[100a] His wife is here called *nᵉḇî'âh* (*v.* 3), which indicates that she, like many women in ancient Israel, was endowed with prophetic gifts.

[101] It is expressly said (*v.* 2) that the *śaḳ* was a loin-cloth (cf. Jer. xiii). It was woven of goat's hair and formed part of the special dress of the prophet. That Isaiah took off the loin-cloth did not of course mean that he never wore a mantle ('*adderet*). Cf. Dalman, *Arbeit und Sitte*, V, pp. 165, 176, 202. According to Mic. i. 8 Micah also went barefoot and 'naked'. But this was a sign of grief, not a symbolic action in the strict sense.

from Jerusalem 'the sound of mirth and the sound of gladness, the voice of the bridegroom and the voice of the bride' (*vv.* 8 ff.). He brought an earthenware bottle from a potter and took with him some elders and priests and went out to the Potsherd Gate. There he smashed the bottle before the eyes of those who accompanied him and said, 'Thus says the Lord of hosts, "As a potter's vessel is broken and cannot be mended again, so will I break this people and this city" ' (xix). Similar in character is Jeremiah's encounter with the Rechabites (xxxv). Protesting against the agricultural mode of life in Palestine and holding fast to the nomadic customs, the Rechabites did not drink wine. One day Jeremiah brought some members of this clan to the temple in Jerusalem and set before them jars filled with wine, exhorting them to drink. Constant to their principles, they refused to drink. The obedience of the Rechabites to their ancestor's charge was presented by Jeremiah as a model of faithfulness and a rebuke to the unfaithfulness of the Jewish people.

During a visit to Jerusalem of messengers from the neighbouring countries, sent to persuade Zedekiah, the king of Judah, to take part in rebellious plots against Nebuchadnezzar, Jeremiah made a yoke and carried it on his neck. Thus he impressively proclaimed that all these peoples, including Judah, had to bring their necks under the yoke of the king of Babylon so that they might survive (xxvii). Later the false prophet Hananiah took the yoke from Jeremiah's neck and broke it, saying that Yahweh would break the yoke of Nebuchadnezzar from the neck of all these nations (xxviii).

During the siege of Jerusalem, when he was shut up in the guard-court of the palace, Jeremiah bought a field at Anathoth according to the usual procedure, thus prophesying that once more houses, fields, and vineyards should be bought in the land of Judah (xxxii). As usual the action was regarded as depending on a direct command from Yahweh.[102] After his emigration to Egypt Jeremiah took some large stones and buried them at the entrance to the government building in Tahpanhes, thus demonstrating that one day the Babylonian king would come and set his royal throne just above these stones (xliii. 8 ff.).

Symbolic actions played a greater part in Ezekiel's ministry than in

---

[102] I agree with Rudolph and Weiser in thinking that the last words of *v.* 8: 'and I understood that this was Yahweh's word', refer to the immediately preceding request of Hanamel. Not only the presentiment of Hanamel's arrival, but also his proposal itself was regarded by Jeremiah as inspired by Yahweh. Jeremiah understood that the words uttered by Hanamel contained a command from Yahweh which he had to obey. I find this view more probable than that presented by Volz, Welch (*Jeremiah*, pp. 221 f.), and others that the arrival of Hanamel in accordance with the presentiment confirmed that this really was a revelation and a command from Yahweh.

those of the other prophets. He sketched upon a brick the siege of Jerusalem (iv. 1 ff.). For a long time he lay paralysed on his side symbolizing the guilt of Israel and its punishment (vv. 4 ff.).[103] The lack of provisions in Jerusalem during the siege was represented by his eating small quantities of bread, and the life in exile by his eating unclean food (vv. 9 ff.). He shaved off his hair and his beard; the burning, smiting, and scattering of it represented the fate which awaited the inhabitants of Jerusalem (v. 1 ff.). By a series of similar actions he symbolized the advance of the Babylonian army, the distress of the inhabitants of Jerusalem during the siege, the paralysing grief of the Jews in Babylonia at the fall of Jerusalem, the second deportation of the Jews, and the uniting of the two kingdoms of Israel in the age to come.[104]

Finally, a symbolic action is recorded among the revelations of Zechariah. This prophet was commanded to take silver and gold and make a crown and place it upon the head of Joshua, thus pointing to the coming Messiah. Most scholars hold that originally Zerubbabel was meant. Later, in the process of the transmission of this revelation his name was replaced by Joshua. It is, however, at least thinkable that a coronation of Joshua symbolically pointed beyond itself to a future coronation of Zerubbabel as the Messiah.[105] Be that as it may, the action of coronation performed by Zechariah was meant as a prophecy of the future Messianic kingdom of Zerubbabel also called the Branch (vi. 9 ff.).[106]

In the foregoing I have frequently used terms such as 'symbolic', 'symbolize', 'represent', 'indicate', 'point to', 'demonstrate', etc. None of these terms corresponds precisely to the exact significance of the actions in question. It is true that these actions were symbols and pointed beyond themselves to something else. They served to represent to the bystanders an object, an occurrence, a course of events which were of particular importance in connection with the total message of the prophet. They always had such a structure as to evoke in the consciousness of the bystanders the fact which the prophet had in mind. It may be said that the symbolic actions are acted similes. There are even cases in which it is not absolutely evident whether we have to do with a symbolic action or a parable (e.g., the passage about the boiling

---

[103] The original account of this occurrence has been greatly confused by considerable alterations during the process of transmission; see Zimmerli in *BKAT*.

[104] Ezek. xii. 1 ff.; xxi. 23 ff.; xxiv. 1 ff. (perhaps parables not actions); xxiv. 15 ff.; xxxvii. 15 ff.

[105] So Rignell, *Die Nachtgesichte des Sacharja*, pp. 218 ff.

[106] The passage about the stone and the seven eyes (Zech. iii. 8 f.) seems to be based on an action of a symbolic character. What really occurred, has been somewhat obscured in the process of transmission. See the commentaries, and Rignell, pp. 123 ff.

pot in Ezek. xxiv). But it is nearer the truth to say that such an action is a form of the divine word. It is *verbum visibile*, a visible word, and shares in all the qualities which distinguish the divine word.

The characteristics of the divine word have been noted in an earlier section. An important feature was the effective power of this word. As a divine word, the word uttered by a prophet had an effective power. The same is true of the visible word, the so-called symbolic action. Such an action served not only to represent and make evident a particular fact, but also to make this fact a reality. In this respect the prophetic actions were akin to the magical actions which are familiar in the more primitive cultures throughout the world; and the use of such actions by the prophets is no doubt an inheritance from lower stages of cultural development.

But there are significant differences between the symbolic action of an Old Testament prophet and the primitive magical action. The power of the magical action was dependent on the inner power connected with them and their performance in accordance with definite magical laws; the power of the prophetic actions like the power of the prophetic word was derived from Yahweh's will. The prophetic actions were never directed to occasional and merely personal ends, but always served the main end of the activity of the prophets, the fulfilment of Yahweh's plans and purposes concerning Israel, the elect people, and the pagan nations as belonging to the dominion of Him who was the Lord of the heavens and the earth.

This, at all events, was how the prophets themselves looked upon the symbolic actions, though no doubt the common people sometimes regarded them as a sort of sorcery. Such an idea could easily be evoked by the very form of the symbolic actions, which, of course, in some measure suggested common magical performances. The prophets always emphasized that the actions were carried out by Yahweh's command; and they knew very well that their creative effect was guaranteed by Yahweh.

The effect of the prophetic symbolic actions upon the onlookers was consequently not only to present visibly what the prophet had to say, but also to convince them that the events predicted by the prophet would really take place. They were also intended to arouse the emotions of fear or hope, according to circumstances. Thus what was done powerfully reinforced what was said.

All this is true where the records describe actions which were really performed and are not fictitious allegories, or even descriptions of visions. Some scholars have held that Hosea's marriage, for instance, did not in fact take place, but was purely allegorical. As the story has been explained above, there is nothing improbable in it; and we need not hesitate to accept it as fully historical. If the prophetic actions had been of a visionary nature, the narratives of them would certainly have shown traces of being descriptions of ecstatic visions. This is not so; and, moreover, these actions conveyed their meaning only if performed publicly, before the eyes of bystanders.

As to the mental state in which the symbolic actions were performed reference may be made to what has been said above or will be said below about the psychological basis of the prophetic words. In certain cases an ecstatic state of mind may perhaps be assumed; in most cases the actions were deliberately carried out in a normal state of consciousness. We must, however, always reckon with inspiration and a feeling of divine compulsion.[107]

8. The Revelatory State of Mind

As we have already noted, nothing is more characteristic of the prophets than their faculty of receiving revelations from Yahweh. The terms used by the prophets themselves for their revelations, and the forms in which the revelations were expressed have been analysed above (pp. 108 ff., 148). We must now attempt to describe the mental state in which the prophets received their revelations which we may call 'the revelatory state of mind'.

This term is used in the present discussion in preference to the more familiar term ecstasy, which is open to two objections. First, it is used by scholars in varied senses; secondly, the psychological states in which the prophets received their revelations were not always the same, but differed in ways which easily become obscured if they all are labelled as ecstasy.[107a]

Typical of the revelatory state of mind is the feeling of being under an influence external to the self, a divine power, the consciousness of hearing words and seeing visions which do not come from the self, but from the invisible divine world, into which, in the moment of revelation, an entrance has been granted. This feeling of being subject to an external influence is perhaps the most constant element in the revelatory state of mind. This feeling is analogous to the poetic experience of inspiration. The reason for our preferring the expression 'revelatory state' to 'inspiration' is that the former belongs unmistakably to the

[107] Cf. further Fohrer, *Die symbolischen Handlungen der Propheten*, pp. 60 ff.
[107a] The sense in which the present writer uses the term 'ecstasy' of the prophetic experience is indicated above, pp. 4 ff.

field of religion. A revelation is an inward enlightenment, an inner knowledge which is spontaneously referred to God and the divine world. Besides, inspiration does not include, at least in ordinary usage, the typical ecstatic states in which the normal senses are wholly suspended, because consciousness is dominated by one single idea or one single feeling by which the soul is entirely absorbed. The revelatory state of mind includes all degrees of mental exaltation, from ecstasy in the strict sense to states of mind which approximate to the normal consciousness.

The medieval visionaries had a remarkable power of describing the psychic states in which they had their abnormal experiences. Many examples have been quoted in the first chapter of this book. With admirable acuteness and perspicacity they analyse even the most complicated psychic experiences.

The Israelite prophets, too, reflected upon the origin of their revelations and the character of their revelatory states of mind, but, of course, they did not think in psychological categories. Since they consistently regarded their revelations as having come from Yahweh, they used religious terms to describe the extraordinary experiences in which they received them.

The general expressions for the occurrence of a revelation: 'Yahweh said to me', 'Yahweh's word came', 'Yahweh let me see', etc., do not convey much about the prophets' understanding of the revelatory state. But there are some other expressions which give us better information.

Like the early prophets, the later prophets referred their experiences to the effect of 'Yahweh's hand' (*yāḏ*) or 'Yahweh's spirit' (*rûᵃḥ*). Ezekiel in particular often speaks of Yahweh's hand. After the inaugural vision, when he was forced to go to the colony of exiles in Tel-abib, he describes his experience thus: 'Yahweh's hand was strong upon me', or better: 'Yahweh's hand pressed hard upon me' (iii. 14). The description of a later vision of the glory of the Lord is introduced by the expression, 'Yahweh's hand came upon me' (*v.* 22). Once when he was sitting in his house and the elders of Judah were sitting before him, Yahweh's hand fell upon him and he had an ecstatic vision (viii. 1). In xxxiii. 21 f. the same prophet tells us of an ecstatic experience which he had the evening before the arrival of the message of the fall of Jerusalem. He says that Yahweh's hand came upon him. What he saw or heard in this ecstasy is not recorded. According to the text, he had had in the same evening a presentiment of what was to be made known to him on the following day, a presentiment which was the cause of the trance. The ecstatic vision of the dry bones in the valley is regarded as caused by the hand of Yahweh (xxxvii. 1). The same is true of the great temple vision in ch. xl ff. A redactor of the book of Ezekiel introduced the description of the inaugural vision with the same formula: 'Yahweh's hand came upon him' (i. 3).

Isaiah, too, experienced the mysterious hand. When the revelation came to him that Yahweh must be made an ally[107b] and He alone feared, he described his experience in the following words: 'Thus spoke Yahweh to me when the hand grasped me strongly' (viii. 11). When Jeremiah speaks of the hand—'under the pressure of Thy hand I have sat alone' (xv. 17)—he is thinking of the permanent state of being under Yahweh's constraint rather than of occasional fits of ecstasy.

The origin of the idea of Yahweh's hand is a physical sensation of being seized and pressed by an external power connected with the ecstatic experience. It is, of course, impossible to determine to what extent the classical prophets of the Old Testament experienced such physical sensations. Since Ezekiel's extraordinary experiences are, on the whole, described in more detailed and precise terms, we may assume that he really had the sensation of physical pressure. When Isaiah and Jeremiah speak of the hand, the term seems rather to be a general expression for ecstasy or divine constraint.

Closely akin to the idea of Yahweh's hand is the idea of Yahweh's spirit as the cause of the revelatory state of mind. In Hos. ix. 7, 'the prophet' and 'the man of spirit' stand as synonyms. The statement that the prophets were fools and madmen was of course a current popular saying, but the juxtaposition of 'prophet' and 'man of spirit' is Hosea's.[108] In a polemic against the false prophets Micah rebukes them for their covetousness, prophesying that one day they will be deprived of their faculty of having visions and receiving divine oracles. Then the prophet presents himself as a contrast to them: he is filled with power, with the spirit of Yahweh, with justice and strength, to declare to Jacob his rebellion and to Israel his sin (iii. 5 ff.). The spirit obviously stands here as the well-spring of inspiration.[109]

Isaiah cries 'woe' upon those who make plans that do not come from

---

[107b] In viii. 13 I read *takširû* (cf. *BH*) in conformity with the term *ķešer* in the previous verse.

[108] This utterance of Hosea does not contain a criticism of prophets of a vulgar type. Hosea considers himself as belonging to the 'prophets' and the 'men of spirit', who were derided and persecuted by the people. The cause of the hostility towards the prophets was their announcement of doom, which seemed to their opponents to be nonsense. In his own words Hosea refers to the words of these opponents and replies: 'precisely because of your sin the prophets must appear as preachers of the judgement to come.' For the idea of the 'fools' compare Isa. xix. 11.

[109] I cannot find any decisive reason for eliminating 'the spirit of Yahweh' from the text. Sellin, for instance, says that *v.* 8 is overloaded. But if the words in question are retained, we get a good 2+2+2+2 line.

Yahweh and form alliances without the support of Yahweh's spirit (xxx. 1 f.). That 'Yahweh's spirit' is here the same as the prophetic spirit is evident from the following words: 'who set out on the way to Egypt without asking my mouth'. To ask Yahweh's mouth is, as we have seen above, the same as to request an oracle from Yahweh, namely through the prophets.

The prophet who speaks in Isa. lxi. 1, says of himself: 'The spirit of the Lord Yahweh is upon me, for Yahweh has anointed me.' Thus the spirit belongs to the primary equipment of a prophet. In xlviii. 16 a prophet says, 'Now the Lord Yahweh has sent me and His spirit.' Prophet and spirit belong together.[110] The intimate relation between spirit and prophecy is evident again in lix. 21: 'My spirit which is upon you, and My words, which I have put in your mouth, shall not depart from your mouth,' etc. The people as a whole are here thought of as being in possession of the prophetic spirit and the prophetic word, in virtue of the presence of the prophets among them. In the Servant of Yahweh as presented in the first Servant Song in Isa. xlii. 1-4, the present writer sees not a prophet but rather a vassal-king in the service of Yahweh, the King of heaven, entrusted with the mission of making the nations subject to the laws of his Sovereign. Consequently, the spirit mentioned in v. 1 is not the prophetic spirit, but the spirit which belongs to the equipment of an ideal king, of which we have another example in the description of the Messianic king in Isa. xi.[111]

Through His spirit Yahweh sent to His people His torah and His words, and this spirit was working in the succession of the prophets in the earlier history of Israel (Zech. vii. 12). The degenerate prophets of later times also had the spirit, but theirs was an unclean spirit (xiii. 2). According to the familiar prophecy in Joel it shall come to pass in the age to come that Yahweh will pour out His spirit upon all flesh, and all members of the elect people shall prophesy, dream dreams, and see visions (iii. 1 f.).

In the book of Ezekiel the spirit is likewise the power of inspiration and ecstasy. An ordinary revelation is ascribed to the effect of Yahweh's

---

[110] The meaning of v. 16 is not quite clear. Assuming that the text is in order, I suggest the following interpretation: Of the victorious advance of Cyrus Yahweh declares that before it came to pass (cf. xli. 26) He openly announced all this through His prophets. Further, when it took place Yahweh was present in the prophetic word which rightly interpreted the wonderful events. Now this word, inspired by the spirit of Yahweh, was represented by Deutero-Isaiah himself. The last words may of course have been subsequently added by the prophet to the original revelation. Many emendations of the text of the last line have been suggested. Bewer in the *Bertholet Festschrift*, for instance, changes the text, so that it becomes a saying about the sending of Cyrus: 'und jetzt sende ich, Jahwe, meinen Auserwählten' (p. 66).

[111] See further Lindblom, *The Servant Songs*, pp. 14 ff.

spirit. In xi. 5, the prophet says, 'Yahweh's spirit fell upon me, and He said to me,' etc. The same is true of ecstatic visions according to the text of xi. 24 and xxxvii. 1. This prophet prefers the idea of 'the hand' to that of 'the spirit' when describing the revelatory state of mind. The spirit plays, however, a considerable part in other connections when we have to deal with the visionary experiences of this prophet. The spirit is the power which transports the prophet from one place to another. 'A spirit lifted me up and carried me away, and I went and came to the exiles who lived at Tel-abib,' says the prophet in iii. 12 ff. When sitting in his house, surrounded by the elders, he fell into a trance and felt himself transported through the air to Jerusalem. This experience is described in the following words: 'A spirit lifted me up between earth and heaven and brought me in divine visions to Jerusalem' (viii. 3; cf. xi. 1, 24; xliii. 5). The same spiritual force entered the prophet and set him upon his feet after he had fallen upon his face before the divine Majesty, which he saw in the inaugural vision (ii. 2; cf. iii. 24). It would, however, be incorrect to identify the spirit in such connections with Yahweh's spirit in the strict sense. 'Spirit' has here a more general significance and could in certain cases possibly be translated 'a breath of air'.

Thus, according to the opinion of the prophets, the spirit, as well as 'the hand of Yahweh', causes prophetic inspiration and ecstasy, i.e., the revelatory state. It has, however, frequently been pointed out that the part played by the spirit in such connections is not as outstanding as one might expect. Bearing in mind how the spirit was thought of as the effective power in the ecstasies of the early prophets, it is somewhat astonishing that there are relatively few passages where the later prophets speak of the spirit in connection with their extraordinary experiences. Amos never mentions the spirit. The same is true of Jeremiah, in spite of the fact that so large a number of his revelations have been preserved.

The fact that the great prophets make little reference to the spirit in their descriptions of revelatory experiences raises a problem that requires a scientific explanation.[112] One might be tempted to think that

---

[112] Mowinckel discusses this problem thoroughly in *JBL*, liii, 1934, pp. 199 ff. He underestimates the role of the spirit in classical prophecy, and even holds that these prophets consciously rejected the idea of the spirit as the power of inspiration. What the spirit was in earlier prophecy, the 'word' became in classical prophecy. Against Mowinckel, Haldar (following van Imschoot in *RB*, xliv, 1935, pp. 481 ff.) emphasizes that as applied to prophetic inspiration the two terms mean the same; *Associations of Cult Prophets*, pp. 115 ff. In the opinion of the present writer it is not correct to speak of identity, it is more pertinent to say that the spirit was the supernatural power that evoked the revelatory state of mind, while the 'word' referred to the revelation itself, or precisely as Buber puts it in *The Prophetic Faith*, p. 64: 'In the one case one receives the stimulus, in the other the content.'

the later prophets regarded the spirit with some suspicion as a rather primitive idea. Perhaps in the eyes of the classical prophets the *rûaḥ* had something magical and demoniacal about it.[113] But, on the other hand, it is a fact that to the great prophets from Isaiah to Ezekiel, to say nothing of the post-exilic prophets, the spirit of Yahweh was a divine power of the highest ethical significance. Isaiah says, 'The Egyptians are men, and not God, and their horses are flesh, and not spirit' (xxxi. 3); thus to him God and spirit are parallel ideas. To Ezekiel the spirit is the power which in the age to come will bring about the complete religious and ethical renewal of the people: 'I will give you a new heart, and will put within you a new spirit. I will remove the heart of stone out of your flesh, and will give you a heart of flesh. And I will put My spirit within you, and make you follow My statutes and be careful to observe My ordinances' (xxxvi. 26 f.). The reason for the infrequent references to *rûaḥ* in the accounts of the revelatory experiences of the great prophets is that the thought of these prophets was essentially theocentric. In every situation they were in the presence of Yahweh and under His constraint. What they uttered was the word of Yahweh, and what they saw and heard in their visions came from Him. Yahweh had sent them, consequently Yahweh Himself dictated to them the oracles and messages they had to deliver. Accordingly, they had no need of an intermediary power such as the spirit.

In no other prophet is the theocentric feature so marked as in Jeremiah. It is not accidental that he does not claim to be influenced by the spirit. More than other prophets Jeremiah experienced constant and immediate communion with his God. His personal religious life was characterized by an intimate relationship with God in personal prayer and conversation. It was natural, therefore, that he should think of Yahweh as the direct source of his prophetic experiences and of the revelations which came to him.

In addition it may be noted that, unlike their predecessors, the great prophets did not experience ecstasy of a wild and orgiastic type. Their revelatory states were of a more moral and personal character, with the tranquillity of sublime inspiration.[114] In such an experience the content of the revelation was more important than the psychic phenomenon itself. For this reason, too, it was natural to ascribe the experience

---

[113] So Mowinckel in the above-mentioned article, and previously Volz, *Der Geist Gottes*, pp. 62 ff. Koch, *Geist und Messias*, p. 50, explains the fact that certain prophets do not mention the spirit by reference to the use made of this term by the false prophets.
[114] This is rightly emphasized by Mowinckel. Similarly Giesebrecht in *Die Berufsbegabung der alttestamentlichen Propheten*, esp. pp. 138 ff. (an important work in its time).

directly to Yahweh Himself, rather than to a power such as the $rû^{a}ḥ$. It is significant that Ezekiel, whose ecstatic experiences were particularly fantastic, refers to $rû^{a}ḥ$ more frequently than the other great prophets.

Of course the prophets themselves did not speculate about the manner of the spirit's working. Sometimes it is simply said that the spirit was active when a revelation was given to a prophet, sometimes the spirit is regarded as a power coming from outside, but working within the prophet: the prophet is filled with spirit or anointed with spirit. Two features in the conception of the spirit must be kept in mind: first, the spirit does not come from within the human soul; it comes from outside, surprisingly, wonderfully, impressively—'the spirit fell upon' the prophet; secondly, the spirit was never thought of as an independent power as a demon, a jinn, but always as a power emanating or rather sent from Yahweh.

The revelatory state of mind was always regarded as brought about by dynamic influence. The revelatory experiences were mostly emotional and imaginative, not intellectual. They aroused feelings of different kinds. Jeremiah says that the divine revelations put him into a state of joy (xv. 16). Ezekiel says of the scroll which was given him to eat in his inaugural revelation that it was sweet as honey in his mouth (iii. 3), a feeling which has many analogies in the revelation literature. But more often we hear of excitement, agony, fear. When the hand of Yahweh pressed hard upon Ezekiel, i.e., in intense ecstasy, he was filled with 'inner glow' (iii. 14).[114a] The content of a revelation was reflected in the soul of the prophet. Seeing in a vision the advance of ferocious warriors a prophet feels his loins filled with anguish; pangs seize him like those of a woman in travail. He is tortured so that he cannot hear, terror-stricken so that he cannot see (Isa. xxi. 3). Jeremiah bursts out: 'O my soul, my soul! I writhe in anguish! O the agony of my heart! My heart beats wildly within me, I cannot keep silent! For I hear the sound of the trumpet, the alarm of war' (iv. 19). In face of the apostasy of his people and their imminent doom Jeremiah feels himself full of the wrath of Yahweh; he is not able to hold it in (vi. 11). Pressed by the hand of Yahweh and filled with the divine wrath his pain was unceasing, his wound incurable (xv. 18). Habakkuk sees in a vision the arrival of Yahweh to execute judgement on the enemies of Israel. The impression of what he sees and hears is so mighty that he cries out: 'I hear and I tremble inwardly, my lips quiver at the sound. Decay enters my bones, and my steps totter beneath me' (iii. 16).

Such descriptions of the revelatory state of mind are common

[114a] Cf. Zimmerli's explanation in *BKAT*.

wherever ecstatics and visionaries are to be found. They are over-whelmed by something that is stronger and mightier than themselves, and what they experience in the supernormal mental state fills them with extraordinary feelings, which they are unable to resist. It appears that the emotional excitement was reflected in bodily behaviour. For this reason the prophets often made a sensational or even an offensive impression upon the bystanders. Like the primitive prophets they were sometimes derided as fools and madmen (Jer. xxix. 26).

Visionaries often describe their ecstasies and their supernormal states of mind as a kind of sleep. In the first part of this book reference was made to the so-called trance-preachers in modern Finland.[115] When these visionaries preached, they sank into a lethargic state in which they seemed to be asleep, and their revelations came as in the form of dreams. One of these visionaries says expressly that, after the disappearance of a vision, she 'awakened out of her dream'. Teresa says that her prayer sometimes turned into a sleep. Birgitta says that God put her body to sleep; but she emphasizes—and this is noteworthy—that it was not a bodily sleep but a spiritual rest. Many examples of such an identification of ecstasy and sleep occur in the visionary literature. In the light of such descriptions a much debated passage in the book of Jeremiah becomes entirely clear. In xxxi. 15-22, the return of the northern tribes is predicted. This prophecy came in a revelatory experience which filled the prophet with a feeling of wonderful joy. He concludes the revelation with these words: 'Thereupon I awoke and looked up, and my sleep had been pleasant to me.' To the present writer there is no doubt that we are here given a very valuable glimpse into the revelatory experiences of the prophets, the more valuable since such glimpses are rare in the prophetic literature of the Old Testament.[116]

In another passage, Zech. iv. 1, the onset of an ecstatic state is com-pared with an awakening from a sleep. The prophet Zechariah is about to reproduce the vision of the lampstand and the olive trees, a vision which we have explained above as a real ecstatic vision. He introduces the description of what he saw with the following words: 'The angel who was talking with me woke me up like a man who is awakened out

---

[115] See above, pp. 13 ff.

[116] *Vv.* 23-25 are a secondary interpolation, so that *v.* 26 is to be taken as the con-clusion of 15-22. Various explanations of *v.* 26 are mentioned in Rudolph's com-mentary. Rudolph himself thinks that the words are a quotation from a popular song, pointing to the bliss of the age to come. Leslie, *Jeremiah*, p. 327, thinks that *v.* 26 'is a marginal comment of a reader who having read to the end this prophecy of felicity and having lived in it with his very soul comes back from the imaginative world of prophetic hope to face the stern reality of the problems of the postexilic era in which he lives, yet renewed and encouraged like one who awakes from a refreshing sleep'. The psychology of visionary experience makes all such fancies useless.

of his sleep.' Here the normal mental state is regarded as a sleep and the ecstasy as a waking state. There are analogies to this conception in the revelation literature. Birgitta sometimes says that in ecstasy her soul felt as if awakening out of sleep, strengthened and refreshed to see and hear. She asserts that in her trances she was awake, not asleep.

Utterances such as these show that the prophets were aware that their revelatory experiences differed from their normal consciousness. They were also aware of the beginning and the end of such an experience. The description of Ezekiel's great Temple vision in ch. viii-xi of his book ends with a statement that the vision had now come to an end: 'A spirit lifted me up and brought me in the vision back to the exiles in Chaldea. So the vision that I had seen disappeared from me' (xi. 24).

The revelatory states of mind (whether genuine ecstasy, mental exaltation, or inspiration like that of artists and poets) were regarded by the prophets as effected by God. Did they come spontaneously and unexpectedly, or could they be deliberately induced? The ecstasy of the professional prophets of early times was induced. Under the guidance of the teacher the members of the prophetic guilds trained themselves in ecstatic exercises until the desired psychical state was experienced. We never hear of the great prophets engaging in such exercises. There were prophetic schools and prophetic teaching, but their object was knowledge of Yahweh (*da'aṯ yahwêh*) and the preservation of prophetic revelations. Yahweh sent His spirit and His word; and this He did when it pleased Him. Consequently a revelation might not come just when it was needed and expected from a human point of view. We have seen examples of this above. Ambassadors from Edom seeking for an oracle from the renowned prophet in Israel returned to their home-land without one, because the prophet had nothing to reveal to them (Isa. xxi. 11). Once Jeremiah had to wait ten days until the expected revelation came (xlii. 1 ff.).

Thus, 'the wind bloweth where it listeth'. But it is evident that certain conditions predisposed the prophets for receiving revelations. When Isaiah received his inaugural vision he was standing within the Temple precincts, deeply impressed by the holiness of the sanctuary. Prayer was a natural preparation, as can be seen in the Book of Daniel as well as in the revelations of Birgitta. It is evident that Jeremiah's revelations were closely connected with his prayer life.[117] In the Book of Daniel prayer and fasting are mentioned side by side as a preparation for visions.[118] When Habakkuk says, 'I will take my stand upon my watch-tower, and station myself upon the rampart, and watch to see

---

[117] Jer. xxxiii. 3; xxxvii. 3 ff.; xlii. 2 ff.   [118] Dan. ix; x. 3 ff.

what He will say to me,' it is clear that he deliberately prepared himself to receive a revelation (ii. 1; cf. Isa. xxi. 8). But such indications of intentional preparation are rare in classical prophecy. Here, too, the theocentric character of the prophetic religion on its highest level becomes apparent. Yahweh acts when the right moment has come; and prophetic revelation is an action of Yahweh. Music, dancing, and similar methods of inducing the revelatory state are absolutely alien to classical prophecy.

9. THE CALL OF THE PROPHETS

Men and women of the prophetic type commonly point to a moment in their life in which they have been chosen for their special mission. In Israel the certainty of being called by Yahweh was one of the most characteristic features of the prophetic consciousness. This certainly was an impelling force in the lives of the prophets and at the same time a source of confidence and fortitude.

The legitimacy of the true prophet and the authority of his message are established by his call. He knew that he was properly called by Yahweh to carry out his task. The false prophet is declared to be such, and his visions and messages are rejected as valueless, not because he did not have visions and ecstatic experiences, but because he had not been called. To Jeremiah who was constantly in conflict with the false prophets, Yahweh said, 'It is lies which these prophets prophesy in My name. I neither sent them, nor commissioned them, nor spoke to them' (xiv. 14). 'I did not send these prophets, yet they ran; I did not speak to them, yet they prophesied' (xxiii. 21; cf. *v.* 32). In controversy with Hananiah this was the argument which Jeremiah advanced: 'Hear now, Hananiah! Yahweh has not sent you, but you have made this people trust in a lie' (xxviii. 15).

In the Old Testament we have several narratives, or at least short notices, of the call of prophets.

Amos told Amaziah, the chief priest of Bethel, how he became a prophet (vii. 12 ff.). Originally Amos raised cattle and sheep, and cultivated sycamores in the kingdom of Judah.[119] Then he received the

---

[119] Scholars differ about the significance of the terms *bôḳēr* and *nōḳēd* (vii. 14; i. 1). In 2 Kings iii. 4 *nōḳēd* clearly means 'sheep-farmer'. It is true that in Accadian and Ugaritic texts the word sometimes refers to certain cultic functionaries (Engnell, *Studies in Divine Kingship*, p. 87; Haldar, *Associations*, p. 79), but that it *must* so be is unproved. Many scholars change *bôḳēr* (vii. 14) to *nōḳēd*. But no linguistic objection can be made against the common translation of the word *bôḳēr*. Cf. *sōḥēr* from *saḥar*, *'ōrēᵃḥ* from *'ōraḥ*, *gōḏēr* from *gāḏēr*, *šōʿēr* from *šaʿar*, etc. (cf. Nyberg, *Hebreisk Grammatik*, p. 216). It is difficult to explain *bôḳēr* as a scribal error for *nōḳēd*. As to

call, which he briefly describes as follows: 'Yahweh took me off from the flock and said to me, "Go, prophesy to My people Israel."' Here 'Israel' (or 'the house of Isaac', v. 16) means the northern kingdom as distinct from the kingdom of Judah. We hear nothing about the immediate circumstances or the form of this occurrence; perhaps Amos had a vision (Amos was, as we know, a visionary), perhaps he experienced an audition; we do not know. The essential point is that he felt himself called by Yahweh to abandon his herds and go to work as a prophet among the northern tribes. Naturally, Amos attached himself to the sanctuary prophets at Bethel, and there he pronounced his message of the judgement which was impending over the apostate kingdom of Israel. That he really appeared as a prophet in the strict sense is evident from the title used by Amaziah: 'seer', ḥōzêh (at that time 'seer' and 'prophet' were identical), and also from the word 'prophesy' applied to the activity of Amos by Amaziah as well as by Amos himself. Besides it may be noted that Amos mentions the prophets in general with sympathy (ii. 11 f.) and declares his solidarity with them (iii. 7 f.).

A certain difficulty is presented by the words used by Amos in his reply: 'I am no prophet, and I am no member of a prophetic association.'

These words have occasioned much debate among Old Testament scholars. The translation here given implies that Amos declined to be designated as a prophet at the time of his dispute with Amaziah. There are, however, scholars who translate: 'I *was* no prophet or member of a prophetic association,' namely when Yahweh laid his constraint upon me and charged me with a prophet's message.[120] Grammatically both translations are possible. What the true meaning is, must be concluded from the context.

The present writer holds that the reply of Amos has real point in this context only if it expresses what he *is* or *is* not at the present moment, not what he *was* or *was* not before he was called.[121] It then

[120] So Rowley in his article 'Was Amos a Nabi?' in the *Eissfeldt Festschrift*, 1947, pp. 191 ff.; Engnell in *RoB*, viii, 1949, pp. 15 ff.; Würthwein in the important article 'Amos-Studien' in *ZAW*, lxii, 1950, pp. 10 ff.
[121] In this respect I agree with Danell in *SEÅ*, xvi, 1951, pp. 7 ff.

the material objections adduced by Morgenstern, *Amos Studies*, I, pp. 19 f., it may be said that our knowledge of the social and agricultural conditions in ancient Palestine is too uncertain to allow positive conclusions about Amos's mode of life. In *VT*, i, 1951, pp. 293 ff., Bič suggests, on the basis of the terms in question, that Amos was a hepatoscoper. Cogent objections to this are advanced by Murtonen in *VT*, ii, 1952, pp. 170 f. In *Central Ideas in Amos* Kapelrud expresses himself somewhat vaguely. Of the term nōkēd he says that it indicates some connection between Amos and the temple. He may officially have had something to do with the cult, even if his task was only to furnish it with the necessary sheep for the sacrifices; pp. 6 f., 69, 78.

appears, however, as if Amos is contradicting himself: he is a prophet and has a prophet's mission, but at the same time he denies being a prophet. The solution of the problem lies in the fact that 'nabi' is here taken in two senses. Amos was a prophet, but not a prophet in the sense in which Amaziah used the word, referring to the fact that Amos had for the time being attached himself to the sanctuary prophets at Bethel; he was not a 'ben-nabi', i.e., he was not a member of an ordinary association of temple prophets.[122] He says that he professionally raised cattle and sheep, but was not a temple prophet.

What would this declaration mean in this connection? That Amos protested against the title 'seer' (*hōzêh*), which meant the same as 'prophet', is precluded by the fact that he really claimed to be a prophet.[123] Some scholars think that what he protested against was the scornful words uttered to him by the priest: 'Go to Judah, where you can get paid for your prophesying.' The meaning of Amos's reply would then be: It is not for money that I prophesy. I am a prophet by divine constraint, and am compelled by Yahweh to deliver his words.[124] But there is no hint of any scorn in Amaziah's words.

His reaction to the terrible oracles of Amos was one of fear and horror. When he ordered Amos to flee from the dominion of King Jeroboam to his own country it may be that he even hoped to save his life.[125] As for the question of payment it was a normal and legitimate practice for prophets to receive their livelihood from the sanctuaries.

In my view Amos took the words of Amaziah to mean that the priest regarded him as a professional temple prophet. Amaziah in fact treated him as a temple functionary in forbidding him to preach in his sanctuary

---

[122] In itself *ben-nābî'* could of course signify: member of a prophetic non cultic guild, but here the word must be understood in the sense in which the chief priest would naturally have used the term; *nabî'* and *ben-nabî'* are to be regarded as parallel expressions in which the stress lies on the latter term; cf. Baumann in *ZAW*, lxiv, 1952, p. 62.

[123] Morgenstern, op. cit., pp. 30 ff., holds that, in replying that he was not a nabi, Amos simply denies all connection with the nabis of his time. Morgenstern says that it is evident that Amos did not regard himself as a prophet at all. When he uses the term *hinnābê'* here and iii. 8 he does so only because he knows no other word for his mission. Thus, according to Morgenstern, Amos declared that he was a divine messenger of an altogether new type. Against this Rowley rightly points out that it would have been easy for Amos to find other expressions. Moreover, Am. ii. 11 f. tells against the opinion of Morgenstern.

[124] So Rowley, op. cit., p. 198.

[125] On this point I agree with Würthwein (op. cit., pp. 20 f.). I think that in Amos Amaziah saw a genuine prophet. Thus to him Amos was sacrosanct; but the content of his message was intolerable in the temple of Bethel which was a royal sanctuary. Therefore Amos was ordered to leave Bethel at once and flee to another place where he could announce his message (similarly Welch, *Kings and Prophets of Israel*, p. 117). I cannot, however, accept Würthwein's view that the call of Amos implied a vocation to be a nabi of the gregarious type. There would then have been no point in saying to Amaziah that he was *not* a nabi.

and ordering him to go away to another sanctuary and there get his livelihood. What Amos objected to was that Amaziah assumed the right to give him orders and control his prophetic activity. If he had been a member of an ordinary association of cultic prophets, Amaziah would have had the right to exercise authority over him and forbid him to preach or order him to go elsewhere. Since he was not a prophet of this class, he was quite justified in protesting against Amaziah. When the priest said to him, 'O seer, flee away to the land of Judah, and there earn your living [at a sanctuary] by prophesying there, but never again prophesy in Bethel,' Amos quite logically replied that he could not take orders from the priest, because he was not a professional temple prophet, but a prophet who had received a special call from Yahweh. Yahweh alone had power and authority over him; and Yahweh had commanded him to prophesy to the kingdom of Israel. When the priest said, 'You shall not prophesy against Israel' (v. 16), he in fact rebelled against the will of Yahweh.

Accordingly, the narrative of the conflict of Amos with the priest Amaziah presents Amos as a prophet, but as a prophet who did not firmly belong to an ordinary cultic association. He was a free and unattached prophet, who consequently stood directly under Yahweh's command and was thus exempt from taking orders from a chief priest. Professionally he was a cattle-breeder both at the time of his call and also when he stood before Amaziah.

To the question of Amos's attitude to the cultic life of his people we shall return below. Our present concern is with the problem of his prophetic call. The call came to him at his daily work. He was commanded to bring a message from Yahweh to the northern kingdom. There is no hint that at the time of the call he was a member of any prophetic association or guild. But when he was in Bethel he naturally attached himself to the cultic personnel of the royal sanctuary. His sojourn in Bethel may no doubt have influenced his preaching in more than one respect. This is the sum of our knowledge about the call of Amos.

There are scholars who hold that the call of Hosea occurred in immediate connection with his marriage. But the superscription in i. 1 says simply that the marriage took place at the beginning of Hosea's prophetic career. Yet in viii. 1 we have possibly a fragment of an original narrative of the call of Hosea: 'Set the alarm-horn to your mouth. Like an eagle it comes over the house of Yahweh, because they have broken My covenant and rebelled against My torah.' This command together with the following reason for it would be quite appropriate as a description of the prophetic charge given to Hosea at the moment of his call.[126]

We have analysed above (pp. 127 f.) Isaiah's inaugural vision as an ecstatic experience (Isa. vi). It contains a theophany combined with an experience of a call to be a prophet. Three elements are of special significance: (1) the purification of the prophet's lips, (2) the commission, (3) the content of the message to be proclaimed.

(1) It is somewhat curious that on being confronted with the holiness of God Isaiah became aware that he and the whole nation had unclean *lips*. We should have expected that his awe and terror at this manifestation of the *mysterium tremendum* would have been aroused by a sense of *general* sinfulness and uncleanness in himself and the people. I believe that when the vision was subsequently recorded the picture was somewhat obscured by the fusion of two elements: the general act of the forgiveness of Isaiah's sin, and the special act of purifying his lips. This latter motif belongs in a special way to the call. As a bearer of the divine word, as one who brought a message from God, Isaiah must have his lips cleansed and so prepared for this task. The action recalls similar ceremonies for the purification of the mouth in Accadian and Egyptian rituals. In particular it is known that the baru-priests in Mesopotamia, whose task it was to deliver oracles, had to perform various purificatory ceremonies to prepare themselves for this function: washing, putting on clean clothes, anointing with oil, and purifying the lips with cedar wood, meal, and other ritually cleansing substances. Similar usages were known throughout the ancient world.[127]

(2) It is to be observed that Isaiah did not resist the call, but, unlike Jeremiah, obeyed willingly. The different personalities of the prophets are revealed in the manner in which they received their call as well as in their preaching.

(3) As for the message itself, the task of Isaiah was to execute the divine judgement on his people by hardening their heart. Then the people was ω be destroyed politically and materially. Thus the divine word would have a terrible effect. In the Old Testament to harden the heart means to render unresponsive to the divine word. In such a state of mind men stand under judgement and become subject to the divine punishment. The hardening of the heart in this sense is of course a consequence of men's religious and moral conduct. Men who con-

---

[126] The vague and mysterious mode of expression in *v.* 1a is in the ecstatic or oracular style. Cf. for instance Isa. xxi. 1. It is unnecessary to change the text. The meaning is clearly expressed in *v.* 3b: 'The enemy shall pursue him.'

[127] For purification rites see Engnell, *The Call of Isaiah*, pp. 40 f.; Haldar, *Associations*, pp. 1 f., 93 ff., 205; Béguerie, op. cit., pp. 27 ff.

tinuously close their hearts to the divine word ultimately become incapable of response. But in the Old Testament the process is never regarded from the psychological angle, it is always considered as a result of divine action, as furthering God's purpose for Israel and mankind, and must be understood in connection with the theocentric character of Old Testament thought. What the modern man regards as a psychological and religious phenomenon, the Old Testament regards as a divine action.[128]

Thus there is no reason to deny that Isaiah really thought of his prophetic mission in this way. But if we consider his message as a whole, it is clear that the hardening of Israel's heart was not his last word. Two positive elements are prominent in his teaching: he never ceased to exhort his people to repentance, and he was assured that a remnant would be saved from doom and turn to Yahweh.

The first element is to be explained in the same manner as we explain the fact that Amos, in spite of his certainty of the total destruction of the northern kingdom, exhorted the people to seek Yahweh, that they might live. There is here an inner contradiction in the preaching of the great prophets which we must recognize. This contradiction, however illogical it may seem, is born out of the certainty of election, faith in Yahweh's love, and their own love to their people. Isaiah, the first prophet to whom the idea of the remnant was revealed, saw in it the way out of a completely destructive judgement. For him the hardening of the people's heart and their destruction were events leading to the creation of the remnant which would return to God.

Some scholars hold that the idea of the hardening of the people's heart was not present to Isaiah's mind at the time of his call, but was later included in his account of the vision as a *result* of his subsequent experience as a prophet.[129] But Isaiah's preaching, introduced by his call, included from the beginning the thought that the people as a whole were rejected by Yahweh. Moreover, it seems to be quite likely that before Isaiah was called to be a prophet in a special sense, he was so impressed as a religious man by the apostasy and the sins of the people, that at the moment of his call the idea of the hardening of their heart could have formed part of his visionary experience.

But what of the idea of the remnant? Was it, too, an element in the divine message revealed to Isaiah in the inaugural vision?

In my view the reference to a saved remnant is an authentic part of

[128] For the idea of the hardening of the heart see Hesse, *Das Verstockungsproblem im Alten Testament* (for Isa. vi esp. pp. 82 ff.), and Herntrich in his exposition of Isaiah's inaugural vision in *ATD*.

[129] So Hesse, op. cit., p. 84.

the text of Isa. vi. While it may be admitted that *v.* 13 presents some difficulty to the translator, the general sense is clear. The idea of the remnant was in fact part of Isaiah's message throughout his prophetic career. The boy with the symbolic name Shear-yashub must have been born shortly after Isaiah's call. The much debated words at the end of vi. 13, which are missing in the Septuagint, but are (with slight variations) present in the new MS, IQIs[a], are, in my view, authentic.[130] In the Hebrew original used by the Alexandrian translators they had probably dropped off by homoioteleuton.[131] In my view the idea of devastation is dominant in the Massoretic text until the beginning of *v.* 13b. The whole sentence in *v.* 13 may be paraphrased in this way: Even if only a tenth remains in the land of Judah, this will again be burnt down. The *national* destruction will be complete. Yet it will be as when a terebinth or an oak are cut down and only an inconsiderable stump remains of them. Something like this stump will remain in the devastated land of Judah. There will be a little group of individuals left. After the annihilation of the *nation* this group will form a holy race.[132] The conclusion of the vision is indeed paradoxical. The devastation will be total, but a living remainder will spring into existence as by a divine miracle; this remainder will be a holy people, i.e., will stand in the right relationship of trust in and obedience to Yahweh.

What was new in the message which Isaiah received in the inaugural vision was not the rejection and destruction of the people (this was a familiar idea in the teaching of Amos as well as Hosea, and no doubt Isaiah was convinced of it before his call); the new elements were that his preaching would harden the people's heart and thus prepare them for imminent destruction, and, further, the idea of the remnant. These were both original ideas and significant elements in the visionary revelation given to Isaiah at the beginning of his prophetic career.

Thus the antithesis of doom and salvation was constitutive to Isaiah's message from the very beginning. The two elements are absolutely inseparable and fundamental to the preaching of Isaiah from the beginning to the end. It would be strange indeed if the idea of the saved remnant, so basic in Isaiah's preaching, had not been indicated already

---

[130] On this point I agree with Engnell, *The Call of Isaiah*, pp. 47 ff. For the text of IQIs[a] see Brownlee in *VT*, i, 1951, pp. 296 ff. See further Albright in *SVT*, IV, 1957, pp. 254 ff. (with references to suggestions made by other scholars). I do not find that the text in the new MS is more intelligible than that of the Massoretes. Its interpretation varies strongly among those scholars who have given the preference to it.

[131] The scribe's eye may have run on from *maṣṣeḇeṯ bām* to *maṣṣaḥtāh. Metri causa ʾašer* and *bešalleḵeṯ* may be transposed.

[132] For this expression see Ezr. ix. 2.

in the inaugural vision, in which the contents of his prophetic message were defined.

The account of the call of Jeremiah is less detailed than that of the call of Isaiah. Without doubt Jeremiah's experience was also ecstatic and visionary. But the vision itself is simple and restrained, with few descriptive details. Jeremiah seems on the whole to have been less of a visionary than for instance Amos, Isaiah, and, above all, Ezekiel. We hear nothing of a real theophany. The narrative begins with an audition: 'Before I formed you in the womb, I chose you; and before you were born I dedicated you, I appointed you a prophet to the nations.' These words imply the call to the prophetic work. Through the certainty of having been chosen by God before his birth for this extraordinary task, Jeremiah's prophetic consciousness was deepened and strengthened.

The dialogue between Jeremiah and Yahweh which follows indicates Jeremiah's inner resistance to the call and how it was overcome. Jeremiah's hesitation because of his immaturity was removed by a new command, and also by the assurance that he had nothing to fear because Yahweh would help him.

Then follows a concrete feature of a more markedly visionary character without which the ecstatic nature of Jeremiah's call might have been in doubt. Jeremiah had a vision of Yahweh's hand being stretched out to him and touching his mouth; he heard Yahweh saying, 'Behold, I put My words into your mouth; this day I appoint you over the nations and kingdoms, to root up and pull down, to build and to plant.'[133]

The endowment with the divine words is the central feature in Jeremiah's inaugural vision. Ezekiel had a similar but more extraordinary experience. He was given a scroll to eat, covered with writing on both sides. Many men and women of the prophetic type have told of similar experiences.[134]

The putting of the divine words into the mouth of the prophet illustrates the idea of the objective character of the prophetic word. What a prophet speaks does not come from himself but from God. It has nothing to do with human reflection and speculation. Besides, it was to Jeremiah (as well as to Ezekiel) as though the sum-total of his preaching was given him in a single moment, at the time of the call. From the very beginning he had a clear idea of what to proclaim and the certainty of a special equipment for his coming work. Nevertheless, every subsequent revelation was regarded as a new revelation from God.[135]

In xx. 7 Jeremiah looks back to what happened when he was called

---

[133] Concerning the text see *BH*.   [134] See above, pp. 14 ff.
[135] Another case of the same kind is related above, p. 16.

and says that he was enticed and overpowered by Yahweh. Both words express Yahweh's coercive power and Jeremiah's inability to resist. Nothing is more characteristic of the prophets than the feeling of divine constraint. When Jeremiah was called, Yahweh's name was pronounced over him, and so Yahweh took possession of him.

The most detailed inaugural vision in the prophetic literature of the Old Testament is that of Ezekiel. The details of this typically pictorial vision have been analysed above. The core of Ezekiel's vision, as well as of Isaiah's inaugural vision, was the theophany. Yahweh appeared as king sitting on His heavenly throne. The central experience was that of the scroll given Ezekiel to eat, containing the main contents of the prophet's message. The idea of the objectivity of the prophetic word is reflected in this experience which, in addition, clearly shows the strongly sensuous character of the mentality of this prophet. As to the eating of the scroll we know that magical papyri from the Hellenistic age recommend the eating of magical writings so that their contents may be the better remembered.[136] The author of the Apocalypse of John received from an angel a scroll to eat (x. 9). The divine word is thought of as being absorbed by Ezekiel without losing its character as an objective divine word. The same idea is in another passage expressed in this way: 'All My words that I shall speak to you [in future revelations] receive in your heart and hear with your ears' (iii. 10). The eating of the scroll and the endowment with the divine word also gave the prophet the impulse to go and speak to his people.

It is said that the scroll was sweet as honey in his mouth. It is not uncommon for ecstatic inspiration to be accompanied by sensual perceptions such as taste, smell, etc. Jeremiah says that when Yahweh's words came to him he ate them, and they were joy and delight to him (xv. 16). Birgitta exclaims, 'How sweet are the words from Thy mouth!' They are to her the most delicious food, which the soul swallows with the greatest pleasure In the ecstasy Suso experiences a sweet taste, 'wie wenn man ein gut Latwerg aus einer Büchse schüttet und die Büchse dennoch darnach den guten Geschmack behält'. Teresa speaks of 'les véritables douceurs que font goûter les paroles de Dieu'. In the Revelation of John the angel says to the prophet when he gives him the scroll, 'Take it and eat it; it will be bitter in your stomach, but in your mouth it will taste as sweet as honey' (x. 9).[137]

Ezekiel was so overwhelmed by what he saw and heard in his vision

---

[136] See Olsson in *ZNW*, xxxii. 1933, pp. 90 ff.
[137] See further, Lindblom, *Die literarische Gattung*, p. 43, note 2; Seuse, *Deutsche Schriften*, p. 15.

that he fell upon his face (i. 28). 'Numinosum' became to him 'tremendum'. In his commentary St. Jerome makes the striking comment:
Conscientia fragilitatis humanae procidit in faciem. But he was given new
strength. A spirit set him upon his feet, and he heard a divine voice
exhorting him not to fear and not to be dismayed. Yahweh would make
his forehead like adamant, harder than flint (ii. 2; iii. 9).

The narrative of Ezekiel's inaugural vision has been extensively
edited. There are several additions, and the sequence has been somewhat disturbed; but the main features are quite clear: the theophany
which provides the setting for the call, the preparation for prophetic
functions (through the eating of the scroll), the prophet's fear and
trembling, and, finally, his strengthening by Yahweh.

Two of the Servant Songs in Deutero-Isaiah must be classed as
narratives of how a prophet was called, namely xlix. 1-6 and l. 4-9.

In the first of these Songs a prophet (in my view Deutero-Isaiah
himself)[138] describes his call. Like Jeremiah he knows that he was chosen
from his mother's womb. He was appointed to be an instrument in
Yahweh's hand, a sword, an arrow, preserved and guarded for the
moment when it should be used. Just as Isaiah's lips had to be prepared
to speak the divine words, and just as Yahweh put His words in
Jeremiah's mouth, so the Servant of Isa. xlix confesses, 'He made my
mouth like a sharp sword.' The active power of the divine words in the
mouth of this prophet is expressed by the figurative terms 'sword' and
'arrow' just as Jeremiah by means of his words had effective power to
root up and to pull down, to build and to plant. There was a crisis in
the life of the Servant-prophet: he had toiled in vain, he had spent his
strength for naught and vanity. But like Jeremiah he trusted in the
support of Yahweh; his God became his strength.

In ch. l the same prophet says that Yahweh has given him a tongue
like that of disciples, capable of uttering the right words. Yahweh has
also opened his ear (*v.* 5) and so made him able to receive revelations.
Thereafter Yahweh wakens his ear every morning to hear like disciples,
i.e., constantly to receive new revelations.

The experience which this prophet had when he was called, the
preparation of his tongue for the task and the opening of his ear,
corresponds to the putting of the divine words in Jeremiah's mouth.
In this prophetic confession, too, we hear of difficulties which the
prophet had to face. But he knows that Yahweh will help him. For this
reason he has set his face like a flint, and he knows that he will not be
ashamed.[139]

[138] Cf. Lindblom, *The Servant Songs*, pp. 24 ff.   [139] Cf. Lindblom, op. cit., pp. 32 f.

Glimpses into the mystery of the prophetic call are also given in other passages. In Isa. lxi. 1 a prophet confesses, 'The spirit of the Lord Yahweh is upon me, for Yahweh has anointed me. He has sent me to bring good news to the meek', etc. Here the consecration to the future mission is figuratively described as an anointing, like that of a king or a high priest, or occasionally, of a prophet (1 Kings xix. 16). After this occurrence the spirit of Yahweh rests upon the prophet. The call is further regarded as a sending. We have heard above that 'to be sent' was an essential mark of a true prophet. The false prophets were not 'sent'.

Accordingly, the conviction of having been called by Yahweh is an essential element in the prophetic consciousness. The prophet is appointed by Yahweh to perform a high task in His service. This conviction is sometimes deepened so that the prophet knows that he has been chosen from the very beginning of his life. From the moment of his call the prophet is sent by Yahweh, he is Yahweh's messenger and servant; Yahweh's name is pronounced over him, i.e., he is Yahweh's property and belongs to Him in a special way.[140]

This conviction of being called is often based on a particular experience in the life of the prophet, combined with a theophany in the form of an ecstatic vision or audition.

At his call the prophet is commissioned to bring forth Yahweh's word, His message to Israel, sometimes also to foreign nations, or even to the whole universe.

The call implies a consecration and a preparation for the coming prophetic work. The mouth is purified to make it fit to utter the divine word (Isaiah), the divine word is put into the mouth (Jeremiah), a scroll is eaten (Ezekiel), the ear is opened, a tongue is given, the mouth is made as a sharp sword (Deutero-Isaiah), something like an anointing has been performed, the spirit is received (Trito-Isaiah).

Different individuals respond to the call in different ways. One prophet trembles and seeks to evade the task (Jeremiah), another readily submits (Isaiah). But Yahweh is always victorious, the prophet's resistance is overcome. 'Thou didst become too strong for me and didst prevail,' says Jeremiah (xx. 7).

The prophet discovers that hardship and trouble await him. He will meet stubborn resistance and hostility, but he is assured that Yahweh

---

[140] It was generally thought that the pronouncing or writing of a name over or upon a person or a thing implied that the person or the thing in question were made the property of the person named. Of individuals: Isa. xliv. 5; the people Israel: Deut xxviii. 9 f.; Isa. lxiii. 19; 2 Chron. vii. 13 f.; the Temple: 1 Kings viii. 43; Jer. vii. 10 f., 14, etc.; Jerusalem: Jer. xxv. 29, etc.

will aid him and support him. Yahweh makes him 'an iron pillar', 'a bronze wall' (Jeremiah), and his forehead becomes harder than flint (Ezekiel). He will not be put to shame. Yahweh is his strength.

The prophet may begin his work immediately after his call, or there may be a time of waiting during which Yahweh keeps him safe like a sword hidden in the hand, an arrow concealed in the quiver, until the time comes for him to appear before his people. His ear having been opened at the time of his call, he constantly receives new revelations according to what the situation demands. The spirit with which he has been endowed is always working upon him and within him.

The prophets were always conscious of the fact that the call meant a revolution in their lives. To any one of them might be applied what was said to Saul of the ecstatic experience which was to come to him: 'You will be changed into another man.' The chosen one was no longer his own; he belonged to another. He must forsake the ordinary life of men and follow new ways. Amos, the herdsman, said characteristically, 'Yahweh took me away from the herd and said to me, "Go, prophesy to my people Israel" ' (vii. 15).

Jeremiah is a conspicuous example of this radical change. He was not allowed to sit in the company of the merrymakers and to rejoice with them. Under the hand of Yahweh he sat alone (xv. 17). He did not take a wife and have sons and daughters. He did not enter the house of mourning to take part in the common ceremonies of lamentation; nor did he enter the house of feasting to eat and drink (xvi.). He had to live as a solitary, a stranger in the midst of his people, like one who had severed all connections with them. But at the same time the prophet had access to sources of happiness and power unknown to ordinary men. Yahweh's words were a sweet food to him and filled him with joy. The prophet lived on a lofty plane, above the ways of ordinary men.

Here, too, we must allow for differences in individual temperament. The life of Isaiah, for instance, seems to have been more balanced and normal.

So much for the call and its consequences in the external life of the prophets. A few words may be added about the peculiar feeling of coercion which the prophet experienced after he had received the call.

The prophets speak of themselves as servants of Yahweh. Their sole calling is to be messengers of Yahweh. Similarly Birgitta called herself a poor runner carrying the letter of a great Lord. The prophets are Yahweh's instruments, swords in His hand, arrows in His quiver.

All that the prophets did or said, they did and said by Yahweh's command. It was always a word from Yahweh that impelled them. Every sermon given by them, every oracle delivered by them originated in a divine command. So it was with their prophetic acts. By Yahweh's command Amos left his herds, Hosea married Gomer, Isaiah appeared before Ahaz, Jeremiah purchased a field, etc. At his call Jeremiah was commanded: 'Wherever I send you you shall go, and whatever I command you you shall speak' (i. 7).

Amos offered an apologia for his prophetic activity in a passage which recalls the didactic methods of Wisdom. He argues from the effect to the cause or from the cause to the effect, in order to demonstrate the necessity of his prophesying.[141] He was impelled and coerced by Yahweh, and then it was impossible for him not to speak. The chain of statements is concluded by the following rhetorical questions: 'When the lion roars, who does not fear? When the Lord Yahweh speaks, who will not prophesy?' (iii. 3-8). So irresistible, so overwhelming was Yahweh's voice in the soul of Amos that he compared it with the roaring of a lion evoking terror in everyone who hears it.

The sense of compulsion was also present in the revelatory experiences. Ecstasy and inspiration in a more general sense came upon the prophets unsought. Their revelations were given them from above. Expressions such as 'Yahweh's hand seizing or pressing the prophet' or 'the spirit coming upon him' illustrate clearly the feeling of constraint. Ezekiel is an outstanding example of a man who lived under an extraordinary sense of compulsion. The symbolic actions which he carried out were actions behind which stood the overwhelming power of Yahweh.

Jeremiah likens himself, when in a revelatory state of mind, to an intoxicated man: 'I am like a drunken man, like a man overcome by wine because of Yahweh and because of His holy words' (xxiii. 9). More clearly than any other prophet he reveals to us the sense of divine constraint which arose from the conviction of being called. He lays his complaint before Yahweh because, when his predictions remained unfulfilled, he was derided by his fellow-countrymen. He maintains that he has not pressed himself on Yahweh with wicked designs; he has not longed for the day of disaster. Yahweh has coerced him, and what he has spoken has been given him from Yahweh (xvii. 16).[142]

From a psychological point of view the following passage is extremely interesting:

141 See Lindblom in *SVT*, III, 1955, p. 203.
142 Cf. *BH* and Rudolph in his commentary.

Oh Yahweh, Thou hast enticed me, and I let myself be enticed,
Thou didst become too strong for me and didst prevail.
I have become a laughing-stock all day long,
everyone mocks me.
As often as I speak, I must shout,
I must call out, 'Violence and devastation!'
Yes, Yahweh's word has become to me
a reproach and derision all day long.
If I said, 'I will not think of Him,
nor speak any more in His name,'
shut up in my bones it was in my heart as a burning fire.
I was weary of holding it in,
I could not endure it (xx. 7-9).

Jeremiah is in distress. His preaching is scoffed at. His hearers find his denunciation tiresome. Nobody will take his words in earnest. After all his activity in the service of Yahweh he has only reaped ignominy and scorn. Now he protests to Yahweh, reminding Him of the fact that he has not chosen this calling of his own free will; it has been forced upon him by Yahweh Himself. It is very interesting to observe the expressions which Jeremiah uses here. The Hebrew word which I have translated 'entice' means 'deceive', 'seduce', 'bewitch', i.e., persuade without rational arguments, just as a demon or a witch bewiches and lures victims. The very mode of expression contains a suggestion of something 'fascinosum' in the conduct of Yahweh towards the prophet at the time of his call.

Since the call had resulted in experiences which were so discouraging Jeremiah sometimes felt tempted to draw back and give up the prophetic work. But then he was in even worse case. It was as if a burning fire was consuming his inmost being. It was insupportable. Accordingly he must devote himself anew to the service of Yahweh and continue to preach. Trust in Yahweh, the mighty Champion, restored his courage. Since Yahweh was on his side he knew that his persecutors would stumble and not prevail (xx. ii).

In this confession the feeling of living under Yahweh's constraint is particularly evident. But the account of it which is given here raises the question what the character of this feeling really was.

It is natural to seek to understand this feeling of constraint in terms of modern psychological knowledge. The attempt to stifle inspiration and resist the divine impulse often causes the ecstatic actual mental anguish; and sometimes he is even driven to inflict upon himself some form of punishment.[143] On this point we have much to learn from the

[143] Cf. above, pp. 17 f.

psychology of the unconscious. The terms which Jeremiah uses may well suggest such automatic phenomena. When the prophet wanted to keep silence, 'it was in his heart as a burning fire; he could not hold it in and could not endure it'.

On the other hand we must allow for a normal sense of moral obligation. The feeling of being disobedient to Yahweh and failing in the commission which He had given must have caused the prophet pangs of conscience.

I think that it is not necessary to draw a sharp dividing-line between these two kinds of feeling. Purely psychical and ordinary moral elements may well have been combined and it is wise to allow for the presence of both in our analysis of the higher prophetic consciousness.

The divine constraint did not exclude personal freedom. The prophets often appeared as free personalities before Yahweh, for instance when they tried to divert the judgement they had to announce. Jeremiah often made intercession for his people. In such cases the prophet was well aware of the distinction between his own words and those of Yahweh.

Jeremiah took the initiative in praying that Yahweh would end the drought which was devastating the land; but he was forbidden to intercede for the good of the people (xiv). We also find that the prophets tell how they reflected on events, pondered on various problems, and discussed them with Yahweh. Jeremiah mused on the riddle of suffering and complained about his own unhappy fate (xii). He cursed the day on which he was born (xx. 14 ff.) and composed poems in which he confesses his own natural and quite personal sympathy with his people in their affliction. Behind the parable of the farmer in Isa. xxviii. 23 ff., who is not always occupied with the same work, but acts according to the demands of the moment, there lies much personal pondering on the apparently unintelligible vicissitudes in Yahweh's working in history. Sometimes a prophet acts on his own responsibility. Jeremiah once complied with the command of King Zedekiah and by telling a lie kept secret from the officials of the king what had been said in a conversation with the king (xxxviii. 14 ff.). A prophet is able to distinguish between his own thoughts and a word of Yahweh. Jeremiah, when hearing the request of Hanamel to purchase the family inheritance 'recognized' that this was a word of Yahweh (xxxii. 8).[144]

The personal freedom of the prophets is also reflected in their visions. In the vision of the locusts and the vision of fire (Am. vii) there

---

[144] For the problem of the word of Yahweh and the words of the prophets here briefly sketched see further, for instance, Wildberger, *Jahwewort und prophetische Rede bei Jeremia*.

is a discussion between Amos and Yahweh. The same is true in the inaugural visions of Isaiah and Jeremiah, and in Ezekiel's great Temple vision in ch. viii-xi.

Finally, it is to be observed that the revelatory state of mind did not destroy the individuality of the prophets. A prophet's revelations reflect his own personality. There are characteristic differences between Amos and Hosea, between Isaiah and Jeremiah. The divine word passed through the soul of the prophet and was coloured by his personal mode of feeling and thinking. While some would interpret the experiences of the prophets in terms of religion and the supernatural and others in purely psychological terms, it must be recognized that in the life of the prophets constraint and freedom did not exclude each other, but were synthetically combined. But to express the synthesis of freedom and constraint in a formula is impossible.

10. Abnormal Psychological Phenomena. Wonder-working and other Extraordinary Powers

A tendency to ecstasy and visionary experiences is usually accompanied by other extraordinary powers. In all parts of the world where men and women of the prophetic type are to be found, there have been recorded phenomena of a more or less abnormal nature in the physical as well as in the psychical sphere. This is true of the early Hebrew prophets. We must now inquire whether the classical prophets exhibited such phenomena.

The descriptions of the prophets' revelatory experiences often suggest a considerable measure of emotional disturbance. In the account of the ecstatic vision in Isa. xxi the visionary tells us that his loins were filled with anguish and that pangs seized him like those of a woman in travail. He was tortured so that he could not hear, terror-stricken so that he could not see. His mind reeled; shuddering assailed him. In his account of the theophany Habakkuk says that his body trembled, his lips quivered, decay entered his bones, his steps tottered (iii. 16). Of course, the very meaning of the visions must sometimes have filled the visionaries with terror, but also the sense of contact with the supernatural and the experience of the revelatory state of mind must have made a profound impression on the mind and aroused feelings of dismay and awe.

Ezekiel tells us of anguish that he experienced at the time of his inaugural vision. Yahweh's hand was heavy upon him and an inner glow filled him. Then for seven days he was in a state of stupor (iii. 14 f.).

The author of the Book of Daniel, who seems to have been familiar with the phenomena of the prophetic psychology, describes several times experiences which accompanied ecstasy. The visionary was disturbed and distressed; he was terrified and fell upon his face; he lost all his strength; he fell in a swoon with his face to the ground, and he became dumb.[145]

Such phenomena are not often mentioned in connection with the activities of the classical prophets; but it is likely that they had some experience of them. It must be remembered that the chief interest of the collectors of the prophetic revelations was to reproduce and preserve their divine messages, not to describe their psychical experiences. We know that in his inaugural vision Isaiah felt that his lips were touched and that later he experienced that Yahweh's hand was heavy upon him. We know that Jeremiah felt Yahweh's hand touching his lips when the divine words were put into his mouth. Ezekiel felt a sweet taste in his mouth when the scroll was given him to eat. In such cases we are justified in speaking of abnormal psychological phenomena, perhaps of a hallucinatory character.

As mentioned above (pp. 129 f.), there is an example of the phenomenon known to psychologists as 'the secondary personality' or 'split personality' in the vision of the downfall of Babylon recorded in Isa. xxi. The feeling of being lifted up in the air and speedily transported away is mentioned in connection with the visionary experiences of Ezekiel. This feeling depends on the general experience of the temporary suspension of bodily existence in the vision and on the need to be transferred in the vision from one place to another. Such experiences are often mentioned in the visionary literature.

It is not accidental that such phenomena are particularly characteristic of Ezekiel. This prophet was more prone than others to extraordinary experiences of this kind. He had more ecstatic experiences and more visions than other prophets. This fact suggests that other abnormal psychological experiences are also to be found in the life of this prophet. In fact we are told that he had attacks of aphasia (iii. 26; xxiv. 27; xxxiii. 21 f.) and periods of neurotic paralysis (iv. 4 ff.).[146]

An attack of aphasia occurred before the arrival of the message of the fall of Jerusalem. At the coming of the fugitive he regained his

---

[145] Dan. vii. 15; viii. 17 f., 27; x. 8 f., 16 f.

[146] A. Klostermann was the first to study Ezekiel in the light of abnormal psychology; *TSK*, l, 1877, pp. 391 ff. In more recent works a reaction against Klostermann's views is evident. So for instance Herrmann, *Ezechielstudien*, and his commentary on Ezekiel in *KATSl*. On this point the present author agrees with the general views of Bertholet in *HAT*.

ability to speak. The inner tension that Ezekiel experienced while waiting for sure information concerning the definite fate of Jerusalem deprived him of the ability to speak; having ascertained the truth of what had happened to the city, he was liberated from the bond of his tongue and he began to speak again (xxxiii. 21 f.).[147]

In Ezek. iv. 4 ff. we hear of a long period of neurotic paralysis. To Ezekiel himself it was as though Yahweh had placed cords upon him. The last remark (*v.* 8) indicates that the prophet could not do otherwise. The statement that the act was commanded by Yahweh and the symbolic interpretation of it are due to later reflection (cf. also iii. 25).[148]

Visionaries have often had the gift of clairvoyance, telepathy, presentiment, and similar extraordinary powers. Do we find such phenomena among the classical prophets?

The ordinary prophetic predictions of the future do not belong to this category. The contents of these predictions are always related to contemporary historical circumstances and may be explained as the result of a normal faculty of observation combined with an intensified insight into the religious and moral situation of Israel. The main features in the ordinary prophecies of Amos, Isaiah, Jeremiah, etc., are derived directly from history and from the religious and moral consciousness of the prophets. Moreover, they are of a somewhat general character and not very detailed so that normally their fulfilment need not be limited to specific events. Where such prophecies included precise details, they were often not fulfilled. Samaria was not captured by the Assyrians as soon as Isaiah thought (viii. 4). It was the Babylonians, not the Assyrians, who made an end of Judah. Cyrus never became a worshipper of Yahweh as Deutero-Isaiah expected, Babylon was not destroyed in the manner which he foresaw, nor did Zerubbabel become the Messiah as Haggai and Zechariah foretold.[149]

The prophets themselves and their disciples, who preserved and collected their revelations, did not lay much stress upon the details of the predictions. To them the only important thing was on the one

[147] Bewer in *ZAW*, liv, 1936, p. 115, is right in principle in explaining the occurrence described in xxxiii. 21 f. as an attack of aphasia associated with telepathy. In the text the words *wayyiptaḥ 'eṭ pî* imply a sheer contradiction and do not fit into the context. The words are probably inserted by an author who thought that the effect of the 'hand' was a prophetic speech. For the explanation of this passage compare also xxiv. 26 f.

[148] On the history of this event in tradition see above, p. 171.

[149] On this problem see Hempel in *ZST*, vii, 1929/30, pp. 631 ff., and 'Die Mehrdeutigkeit der Geschichte als Problem der prophetischen Theologie', pp. 39 ff.; further, the more detailed discussion in Jenni, *Die politischen Voraussagen der Propheten*. This scholar rightly points out that several predictions became more detailed in tradition than they originally were. The problem in question was noted and discussed already by Giesebrecht, op. cit., pp. 12 and 109 ff.

hand that doom was to come upon the apostate nation, and on the other (this is true at least of most of them) that Yahweh would one day fulfil His purpose for the salvation of the elect people in one way or another. But the question of time, ways, and methods did not trouble them much; sayings which were not fulfilled have not even been removed from the prophecies. The certainty of a coming judgement and the conviction of future salvation were steadfast in spite of all changes of forms and modes of expression, as well as of the vicissitudes of history itself. And Yahweh Himself acted in history not according to mechanical laws, but according to the laws of personal freedom (Isa. xxviii. 23 ff.). Consequently the typical prophetic predictions have nothing to do with second sight.

Jeremiah's prediction of the death of Hananiah (Jer. xxviii. 16 f.) is hardly evidence of clairvoyance; it is rather to be regarded as a death-sentence pronounced upon the false prophet, who had rebelled against Yahweh. The story is a testimony to the effective power of the divine word. The present writer would class this episode with the story of Peter and Ananias and Sapphira in Acts v. The two liars were killed by the divine power of the word of the Apostle.

Jeremiah's foreknowledge that he would be called on by his kinsman Hanamel (xxxii. 6 f.) was a sort of presentiment such as we have all experienced. There are two episodes in the life of Ezekiel which, however, are more like second-sight. Ezekiel knew exactly that on a certain day the Babylonian army would begin to invest Jerusalem. What is more, he was commanded to write down the date for future confirmation (xxiv. 1 f.). He also knew, the day before the arrival of a fugitive from Jerusalem, that the city was captured (xxxiii. 21 f.).[150]

The episode of Pelatiah's death in the Temple of Jerusalem, as Ezekiel was delivering a prophecy of judgement, is sometimes adduced as an example of clairvoyance. But it is to be observed that, apart from the long digressions, the whole of ch. xi belongs to the great Temple vision of ch. viii-xi. Then Pelatiah's death is something that is seen in the ecstatic vision and has nothing to do with clairvoyance. Whether Pelatiah really died is quite unknown to us.

Manifestly the evidence for clairvoyance among the classical prophets is very meagre. Of course there may have been more of it than has been preserved in the prophetic literature. But at all events clairvoyance did not play an important role in the life of the classical prophets.

Isa. xxviii. 9 ff. is often adduced as an example of glossolalia.[151] Here

---

[150] For the passage Ezek. xxiv. 1 f. cf. Fohrer, *Hauptprobleme*, p. 118.
[151] So, for instance, Hölscher, *Die Profeten*, p. 35.

Isaiah quotes a scornful utterance of his enemies who ridiculed his preaching: 'To whom will he teach knowledge; whom will he make to consider revelation? Babes just weaned from the milk, just drawn from the breasts? Because there is ṣaw lāṣāw ṣaw lāṣāw ḳaw lāḳāw ḳaw lāḳāw, a little here, a little there.' The enemies likened the preaching of the prophet to the prattle used in speaking to little children. The derisive description of the prophet's speech referred to the contents of his preaching, not to its form. What the enemies meant was that the message of disaster proclaimed by Isaiah was pure nonsense. They were grown-up people and had understanding enough to comprehend the ways of Yahweh. Isaiah's reply is ironical and biting: one day Yahweh will speak to this people by babbling lips and an alien tongue, when the Assyrian armies with their barbaric language come down upon the land of Israel.[152]

In ancient Israel as elsewhere in the ancient world great importance was attached to dreams. They were regarded as revelations of secret things, especially of future events. To have dreams that came true was also part of the prophetic endowment, as is evident from Num. xii. 6; Deut. xiii. 2; Jer. xxiii. 25 ff., and perhaps xxvii. 9 and xxix. 8. But the classical prophets did not attach value to dreams. In their own revelations they never refer to dreams, and they criticize severely the dreams of the false prophets. They censure these prophets for boasting of their dreams. Dreams can be interesting to tell and to listen to, but they have nothing to do with Yahweh's word. They are empty, erroneous, and powerless, while the divine word is true and mighty. They are like straw compared with the wheat. By their deceitful dreams these prophets make people forget Yahweh, just as their fathers forgot Yahweh's name for the Baal (Jer. xxiii. 25 ff.).

A higher appreciation of dreams appears in the eschatological prophecy in Joel iii. 1 ff. Here it is said that in the age to come the general outpouring of the spirit will make men prophesy, see visions, and dream dreams. On this point Joel holds a unique position in relation to Jeremiah and the other prophets of the classical type.[153]

Of miracle-working we hear nothing in the original collections of the prophetic revelations. Here all is centred on oracle-giving and the preaching of sin, judgement, and salvation. Stories such as that of the turning back of the shadow on the sundial (Isa. xxxviii. 8) and that of the wonderful recovery of Hezekiah (xxxviii. 21; 2 Kings xx. 7) belong

---

[152] Other scholars think of the teaching of a school-master in an infant school: Wellhausen, Procksch, Haeussermann (*Wortempfang und Symbol*, pp. 21 f.).
[153] For the significance of dreams in the Old Testament see Ehrlich, *Der Traum im Alten Testament*.

to the popular legends about the prophets. In later times miracles were regarded as essential in the life of the prophets. In his praise of the fathers Sirach says of Isaiah: 'In his days the sun went back, and he prolonged the life of the king' (Sir. xlviii. 23).

The fact that the divine word in the mouth of the prophets had power to effect wonderful things is quite another matter. When Isaiah (ch. vii) exhorted Ahaz to ask a sign of the Lord, in Sheol or in the heavens, it was Yahweh, not the prophet who was to bring about the wonder. This narrative is not evidence of Isaiah's power to work miracles, but of his daring belief in Yahweh's limitless might, a faith far greater than that of ordinary men.

11. The Prophets in Israelite Society

The prophets whose revelations have been transmitted to us in the prophetic books were only a small minority of the prophets who were active in Israel during the monarchy and the first centuries after the deportation. In the same books mention is often made of contemporary prophets and of those of earlier times. Amos says that before his days prophets had been raised up in Israel by Yahweh (ii. 11). Jeremiah says that Yahweh had sent his servants the prophets, early and late, from the day of the liberation from Egypt even to this day (vii. 25; xi. 7). Both allusions to prophets as true messengers from Yahweh (cf. also Zech. i. 4; vii. 7, 12; viii. 9) and also polemics against prophets who were not sent by Yahweh indicate that for several centuries very many prophets were active in Israel and played an important part in the national life. Prophets were also active among the exiles in Babylonia. The names of individual prophets other than the canonical prophets have been preserved in the historical books as well as in the books of the prophets. In addition to the prophets mentioned in the second chapter of this book we remember figures such as Huldah (2 Kings xxii. 14), Uriah (Jer. xxvi. 20 ff.), Hananiah (xxviii), Ahab and Zedekiah (xxix. 21), etc. It is said that as long as Israel exists, prophecy will never expire (Isa. lix. 21). In the Messianic age the spirit of prophecy will be poured out upon all the members of the elect people (Joel iii. 1 f.). In tradition the term prophet was also applied to other persons who were endowed with special divine gifts: Abraham and the other patriarchs, Moses, Miriam, Deborah.[154]

The importance of the prophets is clear from the fact that they are often mentioned among the leaders of the people. Mention is made of

[154] Gen. xx. 7; Ps. cv. 15; Deut. xviii. 15; xxxiv. 10; Hos. xii. 14; Ex. xv. 20; Judges iv. 4.

the prophets and the priests, or of kings, princes, priests, and prophets.[155] By the glossator in Isa. xxix. 10 the prophets are regarded as the 'eyes' and the 'heads' of the people.

Since the existence of prophets was regarded as a privilege to Israel (Num. xxiii. 23; Deut. xviii. 14 ff.) and a blessing for this time and for the age to come, the disappearance of the prophets was considered as punishment and judgement. Amos says that days are coming when men will wander from sea to sea, and run from north to east, to seek the word of Yahweh (i.e., prophetic oracles), but will not find it (viii. 11 f.). Ezekiel says that when the judgement comes men will in vain ask the prophets to deliver oracles (vii. 26). In times of distress poets lament over the misfortune that no prophets exist (Ps. lxxiv. 9), and that the prophets do not receive visions from Yahweh (Lam. ii. 9).

The authority enjoyed by the prophets among their people depended naturally on the fact that they were regarded as bearers of the divine word. The divine word gave information about obscure matters; the divine word was also an effective power to bring about good fortune or misfortune. As can be seen particularly from the history of Isaiah and Jeremiah, important prophets were often summoned by the kings in critical situations. They could also appear before them on their own initiative, and thus could have a great influence on political life if the kings listened to them. Their main task was, however, to preach wherever people assembled. Because the prophets were regarded as sent by Yahweh and as being in possession of His word, their persons were sacrosanct. It was dangerous to do violence to them, as may be seen, for instance, in the narrative in Jer. xxvi.

Prophets who proclaimed welfare, šālôm, were, of course, popular, not only because people always prefer good news to bad, but above all because it was believed that the preaching of šālôm really created šālôm. According to Isaiah, the people say, 'Speak to us smooth things' (xxx. 10). When Jeremiah announced the capture of Jerusalem, he was accused of undermining the morale of the soldiers and the people by addressing ill-omened words to them. It was said, 'This man is seeking not the welfare (šālôm) of this people, but their ruin' (xxxviii. 4).

While the prophets who preached šālôm were favoured by the people, the prophets who preached judgement were hated and persecuted. The history of the Israelite prophets is a history of martyrdom, the outstanding example being Jeremiah.[156] Hosea encountered hostility

[155] 2 Kings xxiii. 2; Isa. xxviii. 7; Jer. ii. 26; viii. 10; xiv. 18; xxxii. 32; Lam. ii. 9; iv. 13; Hos. iv. 5.
[156] Jer. xi. 18 ff.; xii. 6; xv. 10, 15; xviii. 18; xx; xxvi; xxxii; xxxvi; xxxvii; xxxviii, etc.

(ix. 8); Isaiah was scoffed at (xxviii. 9); the attempt was made to prevent Micah from prophesying (ii. 6); Jeremiah speaks of bloody persecutions of earlier prophets, probably during the reign of Manasseh (ii. 30); a contemporary of Jeremiah, Uriah by name, was killed by the command of King Jehoiakim (Jer. xxvi. 20 ff.); the unknown prophet of the exile was taunted and tortured (Isa. l, 6).[157]

A prophet's task was not only to preach; he was also appointed to be 'an assayer and tester' (Jer. vi. 27, *RSV*). He had to examine his people, distinguishing between that which was good and that which was evil. He had to scrutinize and investigate. On the result of this examination the contents of the prophet's preaching depended. A prophet was also appointed a watchman to his people. He had to look out for what was to happen in accordance with Yahweh's purpose and then warn his compatriots. The prophet who failed in this duty would be held responsible by Yahweh (Ezek. iii. 17 ff.; xxxiii. 7 ff.).

But a prophet's task was also to function as intercessor for the people with Yahweh. In ancient Israelite society intercession with Yahweh was regarded as a function belonging to men who occupied a special position in relation to God. Among the great intercessors of the Old Testament we may note in particular the patriarchs, Moses, Samuel, and kings such as David, Solomon, and Hezekiah. But the prophets were the intercessors par excellence. When Abimelech, the king of Gerar, was afraid of being punished with death because he had taken Abraham's wife Sarah, he was commanded by God not only to restore Abraham's wife to her husband, but also to ask Abraham to pray for him to God, so that his life might be saved: 'for he is a prophet and will intercede for you' (Gen. xx). We have seen above (p. 54) that prayer and intercession were among the functions of the early prophets.[158]

Several of the classical prophets are expressly said to have functioned as intercessors with Yahweh. In the vision of the locusts Amos prayed, 'O Lord Yahweh, forgive; how can Jacob stand? For he is so small.' Then it is said that Yahweh repented of this: 'It shall not be,' said Yahweh (Am. vii. 2 f.). This is repeated in the vision of the fire (*vv*. 4 ff.). Hos. ix. 14 ('Give them, O Yahweh—what canst Thou give? Give them a miscarrying womb and dry breasts') may be interpreted in different ways. It may be taken either as a prayer for merciless judgement, or as a prayer for reduction of the punishment. The latter interpretation is supported by the peculiar formulation of the prayer, which has not a

---

[157] See Lindblom, *The Servant Songs*, pp. 32 ff.
[158] Cf. Johansson, *Parakletoi*; Hesse, *Die Fürbitte im Alten Testament*; de Boer in *OTS*, III, 1943, pp. 53 ff.

threatening but a pitiful and appealing ring, and further by the connection with the immediately preceding words: 'Ephraim must bring out his sons to the slaughterer.' The terrible thought of the sons of Israel being brought to the slaughterer evokes in the prophet the feeling that it were better that no children at all were born.[159]

Isaiah felt for his people the same compassion, which was always a condition for intercession. 'Look away from me,' he says, 'I will weep bitterly; strive not to comfort me for the ruin of the daughter of my people' (xxii. 4). According to the historical narrative in Isa. xxxvii. 4, King Hezekiah requested Isaiah to pray for 'the remnant that is left'.

Among the prophets Jeremiah is the supreme intercessor. In no other prophet do we find so many and so pathetic expressions of compassion for the people: 'My eyes run down with tears night and day, and they may not cease; for the virgin daughter of my people is smitten with a sore wound, with a very grievous blow' (xiv. 17). 'O that my head were water, and my eyes a fountain of tears, that I might weep day and night for the slain of the daughter of my people' (viii. 23). 'For the wound of the daughter of my people I am wounded, I walk in mourning, horror has seized me. Is there no balm in Gilead? Is there no physician there? Why is there no healing for the daughter of my people?' (viii. 21 f.). It is noteworthy that this compassion for the people in its distress is combined with a feeling of solidarity with the people in its sinfulness and guilt. The complaint of distress in xiv. 17-19 passes immediately on to a confession of sin in which the prophet (using the plural pronoun) associates himself with his people: 'We acknowledge, O Yahweh, our wickedness and the guilt of our fathers, that we have sinned against Thee' (v. 20; cf. xiv. 7).[160] Out of such feelings intercessory prayer emerges. A fine example of such intercession is found in ch. xiv in connection with the great drought.

Because the people were unable to repent and the judgement was irrevocable, all intercession by Jeremiah was forbidden by Yahweh: 'Do not pray for the good of this people,' said Yahweh when the drought was at its worst (xiv. 11); and again: 'As for you, do not pray for this people, nor lift up cry or prayer on their behalf, nor intercede with me, for I will not listen to you' (vii. 16; cf. xi. 14). Even if the greatest intercessors such as Moses and Samuel stood before Him, Yahweh would show no favour towards this people (xv. 1).

In spite of his being forbidden to intercede, Jeremiah felt himself

---

[159] This interpretation of the passage is also adopted by Robinson in *HAT* and by Weiser in *ATD*. Sellin, however, thinks that the prophet uses these words to emphasize still more the terrible menace.

[160] See further Jer. iv. 19; ix. 17 ff.; x. 24; xiii. 17.

called to be an intercessor for his people and regarded his intercessory activity as a merit. He says to Yahweh, 'Remember how I have stood before Thee to intercede in their favour, to avert Thy wrath from them' (xviii. 20).

Ezekiel likewise appears as an intercessor with Yahweh for his people. In the great Temple vision (viii-xi) he witnessed a terrible massacre of the apostates in Jerusalem. Then Ezekiel fell upon his face and cried out, saying, 'Ah Lord Yahweh! wilt Thou destroy all that remains of Israel, in the outpouring of Thy fury upon Jerusalem?' (ix. 8). And seeing Pelatiah falling down dead he cried aloud, saying, 'Ah Lord Yahweh! wilt Thou make a complete end of the remnant of Israel?' (xi. 13). From Ezek. xiii. 4 f. it may be concluded that intercession with Yahweh was generally considered as a duty incumbent on the prophets. The false prophets are blamed for not having fulfilled this duty: 'You have not gone up into the breach, neither built a wall for the house of Israel, that they may stand fast in battle on the day of Yahweh.'

As effective intercessors in prayer the prophets were of course held in high regard by their compatriots and occupied an important position in Israelite society. As intercessors with Yahweh the prophets were not only Yahweh's messengers to His people, but representatives of the people before Yahweh. So close was the connection between the prophetic commission and the function of interceding for the people, that Jeremiah regarded even the prophets whom he opposed as intercessors with Yahweh (xxvii. 18). The prophets were specialists in prayer in the same measure as they were specialists in the delivering of divine oracles and the proclaiming of divine revelations. A balanced view of the prophetic commission must take both functions into account.

In recent years the relationship of the prophets to the cult has been keenly discussed.[161] The attitude which the prophets adopted to the cult in itself is a problem which will be discussed in the chapter on the religious ideas of the prophets. Here we are concerned with the relation of the later prophets to the sanctuaries. When dealing with the early prophets we noted that there were various possibilities.[162] There was a special class of 'cultic prophets' in the strict sense, prophets who were more firmly attached to the sanctuaries as members of the ordinary cultic staff, who received their maintenance from the sanctuary, like the priests and other cultic functionaries. The fact that the cultic functionaries normally received their livelihood from the sanctuaries did not of course exclude the possibility of their owning private property in the

[161] See above, pp. 78 ff.   [162] See above, pp. 80 ff.

country. Alongside these cultic associations there existed in ancient times non-cultic prophetic guilds living in communities under the guidance of a 'father'. Finally, there was a third class of prophets, prophets who were not organized in associations or guilds, but worked privately in virtue of their ecstatic endowment and their ability to deliver divine oracles. Naturally prophets of these classes also often went to the sanctuaries and attended the cultic ceremonies. There they met with an attentive audience. There they found a stimulus for their ecstatic enthusiasm. By the presence of the prophets the religious exaltation of the crowd was increased.

From the books of the canonical prophets several passages can be collected which throw light upon the question of prophecy and cultic life so far as the later prophets are concerned.

Hosea says that the prophets were persecuted in the sanctuaries (ix. 8). It was under the influence of the cultic ceremonies that Isaiah received his inaugural vision in the temple of Jerusalem, a fact which surely had significant consequences for his later prophetic life. He speaks in dignified language of the music and the sacral processions combined with the great festivals at the Temple in Jerusalem (xxx. 29). The background of his criticism of the sacrificial ceremonies in the sanctuary of Jerusalem (ch. i) is manifestly his zeal for the holy house of Yahweh. We have to imagine that several of Isaiah's sermons were given in the precincts of the Temple in Jerusalem. Of Jeremiah it is expressly said that he sometimes met the people in the Temple (vii; xxvi). It is a fact that a great number of the prophetic speeches and utterances are strongly influenced by the ritual texts and formulas used at the Israelite sanctuaries, and above all at the Temple in Jerusalem.[163]

Evidence of this kind only proves the positive attitude of the prophets towards the cultic life of their people and the significance of the sanctuaries as meeting-places where they could find an audience.

In considering whether prophets were closely associated with the sanctuaries as ordinary members of the cultic staff we are on sure ground. There is plenty of evidence that this was so. The cultic texts in the form of oracles and liturgies which frequently occur in the Book of Psalms prove that prophets served as ordinary functionaries at the sanctuaries. Priests and prophets are often mentioned in the most

---

[163] It may suffice to recall the identification of 'prophetic liturgies' by Gunkel, Humbert, Balla, Sellin, and others. Among modern biblical scholars Weiser in particular has been anxious to trace ritual influences, especially in his commentary on Jeremiah. The same is done by Haldar in his *Studies in the Book of Nahum* and by Kapelrud in his *Joel Studies*. Haldar, in particular, considerably exaggerates the influence of the cult.

intimate connection with each other. Jeremiah complains for instance that both prophets and priests are ungodly and that even in the house of Yahweh their villainy had been found (xxiii. 11). In the Temple of Jerusalem a particular priest was commissioned to exercise oversight over the prophets, who by their ecstatic behaviour caused disturbance (xxix. 26). Naturally he had to give special heed to the prophets who belonged to the Temple staff. Special lodgings were assigned to the prophets in the sanctuary (xxxv. 4). In Zech. vii. 3 priests and prophets are mentioned together as belonging to the ordinary cultic staff of the restored Temple. In Lam. ii. 20 a poet complains: 'Should priests and prophets be slain in the sanctuary of Yahweh?' In the time of the Chronicler Temple prophets functioned as Temple singers and were incorporated into the Levites (1 Chron. xxv. 1 ff.; cf. 2 Chron. xx. 14 ff.).[164]

Now the question arises whether any of the great prophets were cultic prophets in the strict sense, i.e., were permanently attached to a sanctuary and received their livelihood there. Isaiah seems to have been a prophet of the non-sacral type. He lived a life of his own and was surrounded by a private circle of disciples. There is no evidence that he was attached to the Temple staff.[165] Micah was a man from the country-side, perhaps a small freeholder.[166] Hosea was undoubtedly a farmer.[167] Jeremiah belonged to a priestly family; but it is never stated that he himself was a priest belonging to the Temple staff. The descriptions of his personal life show, on the contrary, that he lived as a private man and worked as an independent prophet.[168] Ezekiel is expressly described as a priest. But he was called to be a prophet in Babylonia, where there was no Jewish temple. Neither Zephaniah nor Haggai seem to have been cult prophets in the strict sense. On the other hand the book of Habakkuk with its liturgical character is more intelligible if we assume that its author really was a Temple prophet. The same is true of the books of Nahum, Joel,

---

[164] See further Johnson, *The Cultic Prophet in Ancient Israel*, pp. 51 ff.

[165] In *MO*, xxv, 1931, pp. 53 ff., Hylander raises the question: Was Isaiah a Nabi? He answers that Isaiah was a 'seer', an 'oracle priest' of the ancient type and that he belonged to the cultic staff in Jerusalem. Hylander calls him a 'Kultdiener'. But the grounds adduced for this view are not very convincing. The author has no clear notion of what a 'Kultdiener' was in ancient Israel. This fault he shares with many scholars who maintain that there was an intimate connection between the prophets and the cult. Acquaintance with and interest in cultic matters are not evidence that a prophet was a 'Kultdiener'. A 'Kultdiener' had fixed duties in the sanctuary and received his livelihood at the sanctuary.

[166] Cf. Lindblom, *Micha literarisch untersucht*, pp. 164 f.

[167] Cf. Lindblom, *Hosea literarisch untersucht*, pp. 143 f.

[168] See also Rudolph and Weiser in their commentaries, and Welch in his book *Jeremiah, his Time and his Work*, p. 34: 'Jeremiah did not belong to the professional priesthood at Jerusalem...He had a wider outlook than the men who were working in association with the court on the question of Judah's religion.'

and Malachi. Zech. vii. 1 ff. makes it clear that Zechariah belonged to the ordinary cultic staff. A deputation came from Babylonia to Jerusalem to ask the priests and the prophets in the house of Yahweh whether the day of the destruction of the Temple in Jerusalem should continue to be observed as a fast day. Zechariah answered on behalf of the priests and prophets that this day and other days of sorrow were to be changed into days of joy, in connection with the coming of the Messianic age (viii. 19).[169]

Amos presents a special problem. The present writer does not agree with those scholars who conclude from the titles *nōkēḏ* and *bôkēr* that Amos was originally a member of a cultic staff.[170] While working as a herdsman in the south of Palestine he received the prophetic call and was commanded by Yahweh to go to the northern kingdom to announce judgement upon Israel. He joined the sanctuary staff at Bethel and worked there for some time. In my opinion this is evident from the episode told of in ch. vii. When Amaziah, the chief priest of Bethel, says to Amos, 'O seer, flee away to the land of Judah, there you may earn your living by working as a prophet', it is indicated that Amos had been maintained at the sanctuary of Bethel, having been temporarily attached to the staff there.

Thus Amos did not belong to the professional prophets from the outset; but for a time he worked as a cultic prophet in Bethel. Of his later life we know nothing.[171]

---

[169] Cf. Elliger's comments in *ATD*.

[170] See further above, pp. 182 ff.

[171] Würthwein in his article mentioned above (p. 183) argues that the call of Amos implied that he became a cultic prophet of the professional type. In this capacity he was a prophet of *šālôm*, not a prophet of judgement. As a cultic prophet he interceded in prayer for his people (so in the first two visions of ch. vii) and announced judgement on foreign peoples, the enemies of Israel (ch. i-ii). It is difficult to assent to this view of the position of Amos. Intercession for the people in the life of the prophets was not only caused by professional and national interests, but also by compassion for the people in its distress, as we have shown when dealing with the prophets (Hosea, Jeremiah, Ezekiel, etc.) as intercessors with Yahweh (see above, pp. 204 ff). In the announcements of judgement upon foreign nations the moral culpability of these peoples in itself is as much emphasized as their hostility against Israel. The formal type of composition in ch. i-ii may depend on the acquaintance of the prophet with cultic formulas without proving that he was a professional cultic prophet. In my opinion, however, it is very probable that this literary type derives its origin from the very ancient tribal poems (cf. *SVT*, I, 1953, pp. 78 ff.; III, 1955, p. 202). For the significance of Amos's answer to Amaziah I refer to my treatment of the call of Amos above (pp. 183 ff). In the article 'The Ritual Background of Amos, i, 2-ii, 16' in *OTS*, VIII, 1950, pp. 85 ff., Bentzen compares the oracles of judgement in the first two chapters with the Egyptian 'execration texts' and maintains that these oracles are imitations of the execrations against foreign nations uttered in the ritual of the New Year festival. Even if this were demonstrated, it would not prove more than a general acquaintance on the part of Amos with the cultic ceremonies at the sanctuaries. In his thesis, *Profetie en Cultus in Israël* Roubos rightly argues that Amos, Hosea, Isaiah, Micah, and Jeremiah were not cultic prophets though in many respects they had a positive attitude towards the cult. He goes too far, however, in denying the existence of any cultic prophets whatsoever in ancient Israel.

Accordingly, there was no *necessary* connection between the prophets and the sanctuaries. There were professional Temple prophets as well as independent prophets. Even of the prophetess Huldah, from whom Hilkiah, the priest, sought an oracle concerning the book of the law which had been found in the Temple, it is expressly said that she dwelt not in the sanctuary, but in the city, in the second quarter of it (2 Kings xxii. 14). She seems indeed to have belonged to the class of the independent prophets. The special prophetic endowment, the gift of ecstasy and the power of receiving revelations and giving oracles, was not limited to special official positions and was not a monopoly of special functionaries; it followed the laws of the spirit that 'bloweth where it listeth'.

12. CONFLICTS WITHIN THE PROPHETIC CIRCLES

Many passages in the books of the classical prophets contain sharp attacks on other prophets.[172] Hosea condemns prophets as well as the priests for having led the people astray (iv. 5). Isaiah says that priests and prophets reel with strong drink; they are dazed with wine; they stagger with strong drink; they reel while having visions; they stumble while giving judgement (xxviii. 7). Micah speaks of prophets who divine for money (iii. 11), prophets who lead the people of Yahweh astray, who preach *šālôm* when they have been supplied with food, but declare war against him who does not put something into their mouths. Therefore night shall come over them so that they shall not have any more visions; they shall be put to shame, because no answer from God is coming to them (iii. 5 ff.). Zephaniah says of the prophets in Jerusalem that they are insolent and treacherous men (iii. 4).

The sharpest and most detailed attacks on certain prophets are to be found in Jeremiah and Ezekiel during the most critical period in the history of the Israelite people. At this time the conflict between the opposed groups within the prophetic circles seems to have been brought to a head.

Jeremiah inveighs against prophets whom he regards simply as liars. What they have to say is falsehood, *šeḳer*.[173] It is characteristic of these prophets that they preach *šālôm*, i.e., they say that all is well; they find

---

[172] A good example of conflict between prophets of earlier times is offered by the narrative in 1 Kings xxii about Micaiah the son of Imlah and the four hundred prophets assembled before the kings of Israel and Judah. The principal difference between Micaiah and the others was that the former announced misfortune while the latter predicted success. This difference was essential in later times also.

[173] Jer. vi. 13; viii. 10; xiv. 14; xxiii. 25; xxvii. 10, 16; xxviii. 15; xxix. 9.

nothing to condemn in the life of the people, and they promise good fortune and prosperity.[174] They have neither been called nor sent by Yahweh.[175] They are not commissioned by Him; they have not been admitted to His council, and are not in possession of His word. This clearly distinguishes them from the true prophets, whose principal privilege it was to have a divine commission, to receive true revelations, and to be bearers of the divine word.[176] All they have to proclaim is empty fancies, deceptive inventions of their own hearts, and valueless dreams. They only use their own tongues; and in addition, lacking real personal inspiration they steal oracles from each other.[177] Besides they are godless, immoral, and criminal personalities.[178] From the prophets of Jerusalem ungodliness has spread through all the land.[179] This they do instead of turning the people from their evil course and their evil doings.[180] The prophets together with the priests plotted against the life of Jeremiah.[181] For all this Jeremiah proclaims merciless judgement on these prophets. They shall be put to shame, they shall be utterly destroyed, they shall be consumed by sword and famine, their bones shall be spread before the sun.[182] Hananiah who rebelled against Yahweh's words spoken by Jeremiah was killed by the prophet's word (ch. xxviii).

To Jeremiah the prophets whom he attacked were really prophets, though not sent by Yahweh. They had many of the characteristics of the true prophets. They had revelations and visions, they performed symbolical actions (xxviii. 10 f.), they imparted regular oracles (xxiii. 31). Moreover, these prophets had this in common with Jeremiah and other prophets that they prophesied 'in Yahweh's name' (xiv. 14; xxix. 9), i.e., they pretended to have been sent by Yahweh and delivered their oracles as true Yahweh oracles (introduced by the formula 'thus says Yahweh'). To Jeremiah this claim was false; for the source of their inspiration was in fact the syncretistic cult, which Jeremiah held to be the worship of the Baal. Therefore Jeremiah says bluntly that these prophets prophesied by the Baal, the false god (ii. 8; v. 31; xxiii. 13).

Ezekiel also had to fight against prophets who in his eyes were false

[174] Jer. vi. 14; viii. 11; xiv. 13; xxiii. 17; xxviii. 2 ff., 11.
[175] Jer. xiv. 14; xxiii. 21; xxviii. 15; xxix. 9.
[176] Jer. v. 13; xiv. 14; xxiii. 16, 18, 22, 30 ff.; xxvii. 18.
[177] Jer. xiv. 14; xxiii. 16, 25 ff.; xxix. 8.
[178] Jer. xxiii. 11, 14.
[179] Jer. xxiii. 15.
[180] Jer. xxiii. 22.
[181] Jer. xxvi. 7 ff.
[182] Jer. vi. 15; viii. 1, 12; xiii. 13 f.; xiv. 15; xxiii. 9 ff.

prophets.[183] They prophesied what was given them by their own mind, not what Yahweh said. Their revelations were not inspired by Yahweh, but false and empty. Thus their oracles were nothing but falsehood, in spite of their claim to speak in the name of Yahweh by using the common Yahwistic oracle formula (xiii. 1 ff.; xxii. 28). By their optimistic preaching of šālôm saying that all was well, they led the people astray (xiii. 10). Ezekiel aptly likened them to men who daub a flimsy wall with whitewash. They disguised the defects in the nation and led the people to think that all was well (xiii. 10 ff.; xxii. 28). In doing this they encouraged the wicked, so that they did not turn from their evil way (xiii. 22). The task of a true prophet was to intercede for the people and to bring them to repentance and righteousness in order to save them from the wrath of Yahweh and secure their existence. This task was neglected by the false prophets. They did not stand in the gap or build a wall for the house of Israel that it might stand fast. They rather resembled jackals uselessly and dismally prowling about among the ruins (xiii. 4 f.). The principal charge against these prophets was that they had not been sent by Yahweh (xiii. 6).

Ezekiel also blames these prophets for taking payment for their oracles (xiii. 19). He adds a new feature to the characterization of this depraved class of prophets. Among them there were women who used primitive means (bands and veils) of exercising magical influence on their clients (xiii. 17 ff.).[184]

These prophets have nothing to expect but judgement and punishment. Yahweh's hand will be against them. In the age to come they will have no place in the council of Yahweh's people, nor be enrolled in the register of the house of Israel, nor be allowed to enter the land of Israel. They will perish in the general destruction that will fall upon Israel and its land (xiii. 8 ff.).

Similar charges against the false prophets are to be found elsewhere. In the book of Lamentations we read: 'Your prophets have divined for you vain things and nonsense; and instead of denouncing your iniquity,

---

[183] 'False prophets' is an expression unknown in the prophetic texts. To the prophets who inveighed against such prophets they were under judgement because their claims were unfounded and their message false. Having this in mind we may safely apply to them the traditional term. We must be on our guard against identifying them with any special class of prophets. Their 'falseness' consisted in their personal attitude, which must be understood from the concrete descriptions found in the prophetic texts, not by more or less general observations. Cf. von Rad in ZAW, li, 1933, pp. 109 ff. Quell, Wahre und falsche Propheten, rightly emphasizes that what distinguishes the false prophet from the true prophet cannot be expressed in a formula. The verdict 'false' can only be given by another prophet, the falseness being ultimately incapable of objective demonstration.

[184] On such usages see Guillaume, op. cit., pp. 261 ff.

to restore your fortune, they have divined for you oracles, vain and misleading' (ii. 14). The judgement came upon Jerusalem, it is said, 'because of the sins of her prophets and the iniquities of her priests' (iv. 13).

The Deuteronomic law also refers to prophets who presume to give oracles in Yahweh's name without being commissioned to deliver them. The law decrees that such a prophet must die (xviii. 20). The same sentence is to be passed on a prophet who delivers oracles in the name of alien gods or seduces people to follow alien gods (xiii. 1 ff.; xviii. 20).

The following are the main criticisms which the great prophets made of those prophets whom they described as liars. First and foremost they led their people astray by their preaching of šālôm, their declaration that all was well in the moral and political life of the nation, and that there was no ground for fear. They did not arouse the people by preaching of sin and judgement, but lulled them into false security. Thus they were liars and traitors. Further, their revelations and visions were subjective inventions of their own minds and empty fancies. Their inspiration was evoked by the syncretistic cult. They stole revelations from each other and delivered oracles for money. Among them were some who had debased themselves by using magical rites. In addition they were accused of wickedness and immorality. They were addicted to drinking; they were reckless and fanatical; they led their people astray to ungodliness.

It was not denied that these persons really were prophets. They had revelations and visions, i.e., ecstatic experiences. They spoke in Yahweh's name, delivered oracles in the customary forms, and performed symbolical actions just like the true prophets; in a word they had all the external characteristics of the prophetic order. But the true prophets denied that they had been called. They were not bearers and announcers of Yahweh's word. The principal characteristic of these prophets was the content of their preaching. They preached šālôm of all kinds, while the other prophets preached of sin and repentance, of punishment and judgement as the necessary way to find salvation.

A simple criterion by which people in general could conclude whether a prophet was really called and sent by Yahweh, or was a prophet without a divine commission, was the fulfilment or non-fulfilment of his prophecies. In his attacks on the false prophets Jeremiah says, 'The prophets who preceded you [Hananiah] and me, from the earliest times, those prophets prophesied against mighty lands and great kingdoms of war, misfortune, and pestilence. Thus when a prophet prophesies of šālôm, that prophet can be proved to be one whom Yahweh has truly sent, only when the word of that prophet is fulfilled' (xxviii. 8 f.). This utterance contains two statements. First, it is the mark of a prophet sent by Yahweh that he announces judgement; secondly, while a prophecy inspired by Yahweh must be fulfilled, a prophecy which is not fulfilled does not come from Yahweh.

Ezekiel says that the fulfilment of that which he foretells will prove that he was a prophet sent by Yahweh (ii. 5; xxxiii. 33; cf. Zech. ii. 13, 15). The same problem is discussed in the Deuteronomic law. The lawgiver imagines that someone asks how to recognize whether an oracle is given by Yahweh or not. The answer he gives is the following: If the oracle that the prophet delivers in the name of Yahweh does not come to pass, that is an oracle which Yahweh did not give, the prophet having spoken presumptuously (xviii. 21 f.).[185] Further, if signs and portents offered by a false prophet *do* come true, his exhortation to follow alien gods shows him nevertheless to be a false prophet. Such a prophet must be put to death (xiii. 1 ff.). Thus various criteria are formulated by which a prophet's character may be judged.

The characterization of the two kinds of prophets was of no essential importance to the true prophets themselves. They knew very well that they were called and that their revelations emanated from Yahweh. As to the other prophets, the true prophets were immediately aware that they had another spirit. It was the common people who needed to be able to distinguish between false and true prophets. The problem with which the medieval visionaries had to wrestle, whether their revelations came from God or from the devil, was unknown to the Israelite prophets. A true prophet did not feel any doubt of his own call or of the message which he had to announce. Certainly they had their own problems, as we can see for instance from the 'confessions' of Jeremiah. But these problems were of a different kind. The divine voice which they heard with the inward ear, their insight into the religious and moral situation of the people, the lessons they learned from the events of history—by all these they were infallibly led. They were not in the service of a religious dogma or a national ideal, they were in contact with the

---

[185] It is said that such a prophet is not to be feared. It would be meaningless to say that they should not fear a prophecy that has not come true. What the law-maker means is that when a prophet's oracle does not come true, this shows that the prophet has not brought forth Yahweh's word. People should not fear such a prophet. Every prophet behind whom Yahweh stands is an object of fear, just as Yahweh Himself is an object of fear. The criterion expressed in Deuteronomy is the same as that expressed in Jer. xxviii. 9 and Ezek. xxxiii. 33. In his valuable study mentioned above, von Rad seems to exaggerate the difference between Deuteronomy and Jeremiah on this point (p. 113).

living God of history. Out of this experience came their prophetic message, the content of which was Yahweh's word and nothing else.[186]

The marks by which one could recognize a true or a false prophet cannot be expressed in a formula. They were not dogmatically fixed. Different features had to be taken into consideration. The preaching of *šālôm* was not always false preaching (e.g., Nahum); some predictions made by the incontestably true prophets did not come true (see above, p. 199). In such cases the moral discernment of a prophet played a decisive part. The general agreement of a prophet's preaching with Yahweh's will, thoughts, and purpose guaranteed the fact that this prophet had been sent by Yahweh and had a true divine message to convey. A prophet who in this way served the living God of Israel would not have been judged as a false prophet either by Isaiah or by Jeremiah and Ezekiel.

The 'false prophets' have often been identified with the cultic prophets attached to the sanctuaries. Such an opinion is without any foundation.[187] Some cultic prophets were filled with a true moral zeal, as can be seen from the cultic prophets whose revelations have been preserved in the Bible. On the other hand there were 'false prophets' among the prophets who were not cultic prophets in the strict sense of the word. Ezekiel inveighs against prophetesses who used magical methods. They were surely not Temple prophetesses. Jeremiah mentions prophets who worked among the exiles in Babylonia, who prophesied falsehood in Yahweh's name, were adulterous, and had committed villainy in Israel (xxix). In the narrative about Hananiah, the prophet from Gibeon, Jeremiah's adversary, there is nothing to suggest that he was a cultic prophet. It is true that the prophets who were condemned by Isaiah, Jeremiah, and others are often mentioned in connection with the priests. From this fact the most that can be inferred is that perhaps the majority of the 'false prophets' were to be found among the cultic prophets. This is quite natural, because one of the main professional tasks of these cultic prophets was to announce *šālôm* in the interest of the royal house and of official policy, to encourage the people, and by the power of their prophetic words influence the course of events in a favourable direction.[188]

---

[186] The last point of view is particularly stressed by von Rad ,op. cit., pp. 119 f. Cf. also Buber in *Die Wandlung*, ii, 1946/47, pp. 277 ff.
[187] Cf. Rowley in *BJRL*, xxix, 1946, p. 8.
[188] Cf. Kraus in *Theologische Existenz heute*, N.F., xxxvi, pp. 41 ff.

13. Concluding Remarks

The relation of the classical prophets to the early or 'primitive' prophets has been keenly debated. In the above discussion we have treated these two groups separately, in order to give as accurate a description of both as possible. Was there any real historical connection between the two groups of prophets, or did the classical prophets form a quite new phenomenon in the religious history of Israel?

First it may be recalled that in Israelite tradition the title *nabi* was applied to both groups. As we have pointed out above (p. 105), it is a mistake to apply the terms *nabi* and *nabiism* only to the primitive prophets as if the canonical prophets were not *nabis*. This usage is not supported by the evidence of the Old Testament. By using the term *nabi* for the later as well as for the earlier prophets the Biblical writers show that the two groups had something essential in common.

A comparison between our description of the early prophets and of the later ones shows immediately that many characteristics are common to both groups: ecstasy of various degrees, sometimes ascribed to the effect of Yahweh's hand or Yahweh's spirit, inspired revelations sometimes in the form of visions and auditions, symbolic actions, oracles and the use of the typical oracle formulas, the consciousness of having admission to Yahweh's council and being bearers of the divine word, the idea of the effective power of the divine word, the sense of divine constraint, the consciousness of having been called and sent by Yahweh, their social and political significance in Israelite society, making them objects of both honour and contempt, their intimate connection with the cult and the sanctuaries, their zeal for Yahweh, the national God, and the cause of their own people.

However, it would be a great mistake if, bearing all these similarities in mind, we denied that there was any difference at all between the earlier and the later prophets. Some significant facts may here be noted.

It is true that ecstasy was characteristic of both the earlier and the later prophets. But there is a difference. In the former orgiastic ecstasy was more prominent. Besides, in the earlier stages of prophecy ecstasy was in some measure an end in itself, being regarded as the climax of all religious experience and, moreover, an experience attained by methodical exercises and deliberate training. This was not the case among the classical prophets. For them ecstasy was only a means of receiving revelations from God. In the books of the great prophets we never hear of training in ecstasy or of artificial methods of producing ecstasy. On the whole ecstasy in the strict sense is less common in the great prophets than what may be called elevated inspiration. The typical visions were no doubt experienced in a state of ecstasy; but most of the prophetic revelations are not visions, but sermons and proclamations uttered in a state of mental exaltation. Extraordinary psycho-physical phenomena such as accompanied fits of ecstasy in the early prophets sometimes appear in the narratives about the later prophets also (notably Ezekiel). But when Jeremiah, for instance, describes his excited feelings when revelations came to him, these feelings are caused by the contents of the revelations more than by the disturbing psychical experience itself.

Other extraordinary gifts such as clairvoyance, wonder-working, and magical actions are practically alien to the great prophets. Dreams do not supply divine revelations. There are traces of the use of external marks (Isa. xx. 2; Zech. xiii. 4 ff.), but they do not seem to have played an important role.

Most of the great prophets lived their own private lives and were not cultic prophets in the strict sense, which does not exclude that some of them could be attached to a sanctuary. They did not live in coenobia or belong to prophetic guilds like the majority of the early prophets, but they sometimes gathered a circle of disciples around themselves, as may be inferred, e.g., from Isa. viii. 17 ff. On the whole it seems that the old non-cultic guilds of prophets had disappeared by the time of the great prophets. In the prophetic texts there is no plain mention of them. They were merged in the associations of the cultic prophets at the sanctuaries. They survived in a new form in the circles of disciples whom the great prophetic personalities assembled round themselves. Some of the great prophets had close relations with the court and the kings; but we never hear of court prophets in the strict sense among them, such as those at the court of David.

However, the distinction between the early prophets and their great successors is in the first place not a matter of psychology, or external behaviour, or position; the essential difference consists in the content of their message. To Amos and his successors the existence of Yahweh's people was at stake. The covenant between Israel and Yahweh was broken or was about to be broken. In sinfulness and unbelief Israel had turned away from her God. Now the task of the prophets was to arouse, rebuke, call to repentance, warn, and threaten with the judgement of Yahweh, and to promise a turn of fortune in a coming age, on condition that there were some who realized the holy will of Yahweh. What stirred Amos and his successors was the desperate religious and moral situation of the people of Israel and the compelling call to work as messengers from God to make the people conscious of the danger to which they were exposed.

There was nothing corresponding to this in the oracles of the early prophets. It is, of course, true that these early prophets, in addition to giving oracles on everyday concerns, were champions of Yahweh against the Baal and his worshippers, and also spoke out against lapses from the old moral standards (e.g., Elijah), condemning severely kings and others who were culpable; but they never called in question the existence of the nation as such, of Israel the elect people. This was exactly what Amos and his successors did. To them Israel as a nation was rejected by Yahweh and must be completely restored anew so that it could survive. For this reason we are justified in saying that a new epoch in Israelite prophecy began with Amos.

The monarchic period was the great period of Israelite prophecy. But prophets of the classical type existed far down into post-exilic times (e.g., Malachi). While Nehemiah was working in Jerusalem there were prophets who, it is true, were adversaries of Nehemiah and tried to obstruct his actions. They were certainly temple prophets.[189] The Chronicler knows of prophets who belonged to the class of Levites and sometimes delivered oracles, but as a rule worked as inspired temple singers.[190] One of the chief tasks of the post-exilic prophets was (as has been pointed out by modern scholars) to represent the divine voice in the temple liturgy.

In the time of the Maccabees prophets were rare or non-existent.[191] In the early Christian church they came into existence again.[192] Everywhere the history of prophecy shows periods of vitality and periods of decline. A rich cultic life is not unfavourable for prophetic phenomena, but the dominance of doctrine and law suppresses the prophetic spirit. The Torah-religion and the learned activity of the scribes during the last pre-Christian centuries did not stimulate vigorous prophetic activity. As true prophecy disappeared, there arose a form of false prophecy. Prophetic charlatans appeared who made themselves despised so that prophecy became utterly disreputable, and this to such a degree that sometimes it was believed that prophets would not exist in the Messianic age, and if anyone had ecstatic experiences he would be anxious to keep them secret.[193] On the other hand the impression made by true prophecy was so vivid that a general endowment with prophetic

---

[189] Neh. vi. 10-14.
[190] 1 Chron. xxv. 1 ff.; 2 Chron. xx. 14 ff.
[191] 1 Macc. xiv. 41.
[192] Cf. for instance Bacht in *Biblica*, xxxii, 1951, pp. 237 ff.
[193] Zech. xiii. 2 ff.

spirit was regarded as an essential element in the blessings of the Messianic age.[194]

I have tried above to describe prophecy in ancient Israel from the psychological and social points of view. I have confined myself to describing the phenomena and have abstained from attempting either a supernatural or a psycho-analytical explanation of them.

The religious man who recognizes in the God of the prophets his own God says that the revelations of the true prophets emanated from God. They are products of true divine inspiration arising from the mysterious contact with the living God which the prophets experienced. But an analysis of the contact of a religious man with his God cannot be carried through by scientific methods. The supernatural mystery of the religious experiences of the prophets is concealed from us and inaccessible to scientific inquiry.

Modern scholars have attempted to explain the religious experiences of the prophets by the methods of modern psychology with its emphasis on the subconscious or, rather, unconscious sphere of the human mind. For the understanding of the prophetic visions and auditions, their spontaneous and sudden occurrence, and their vivid and fanciful contents, the idea of the effective power of the unconscious is of great help. The application of the psychological methods of Freud or Jung to the experiences of the prophets has, however, not yet proved to be very fruitful. Literary documents from so remote a time cannot yield much to the psycho-analyst. Moreover, the application of these methods demands special qualifications which cannot reasonably be expected of a Biblical exegete. For fear lest I should appear as a dilettante entering a domain unfamiliar to me I leave this task to those who are expert in it.[195]

---

[194] Joel iii. 1 f.

[195] For the modern psychological study of the prophets reference may be made to Povah, *The New Psychology and the Hebrew Prophets,* New York, 1925. Hosea in particular has seemed to scholars to call for psychological investigation (von Hauff, *Sexualpsychologisches im Alten Testament,* Bonn, 1924; Sellers, 'Hosea's Motives', *AJSLL,* xli, 1925, pp. 243 ff.; Allwohn, *Die Ehe des Propheten Hosea in psychoanalytischer Beleuchtung (BZAW,* 44), Giessen, 1926). These intricate problems are treated in a commendably sound way in Haeussermann, *Wortempfang und Symbol in der alttestamentlichen Prophetie (BZAW,* 58), Giessen, 1932. Of particular value here are the classification and the analysis of figures, symbols, and visions in the prophetic texts and (sometimes) the interpretation of them in the light of the psychology of the unconscious. The explanations given are often almost truisms and commonplaces, but at times observations about the connection of a symbol with the unconscious, either the individual unconscious or the collective unconscious, contribute to a better understanding. The book also includes useful discussions concerning conscious and unconscious elements in the prophetic words and actions. Klein, *The Psychological Pattern of Old Testament Prophecy,* Evanston, 1956, surveys the most characteristic trends of modern psychology and shows that none of them is serviceable to elucidate the psychology of Old Testament prophecy.

CHAPTER FOUR

THE PROPHETIC LITERATURE

1. INTRODUCTORY

The prophetic books are collections of prophetic revelations, and as with other books of the same kind, it is a long way from the first revelatory experiences of the prophets to the books of the prophets as we now have them. The problem to be solved in this chapter is this: how did it come about that the original personal revelations were put into literary form in books as unusual and varied as the canonical prophetic books.

The term 'collections' which has been used above implies that the prophets were not authors in the modern sense and that it was not they themselves, but others, who may be called collectors, who first put the prophetic material into literary form. The prophets as recipients of divine revelations, their disciples, and those who collected these revelations were the primary actors in the complicated process which finally resulted in the books of the prophets as we now have them.

As we have seen above, reception of divine revelations was the fundamental function of the prophets. Broadly speaking these revelations were of two types: those which referred to the people of Israel, other nations, or particular individuals, and, on the other hand, private revelations which only had reference to the personal life of a prophet. It was quite natural that revelations of the first group should be preserved and later written down; but the recording of the private revelations calls for an explanation. The problem is raised, in particular, by the prophetic confessions such as occur, for instance, in the Book of Jeremiah. Here a momentous fact must be recognized. It is of the very nature of a revelation that it should be made known to others A prophet is never allowed to be a private person; he is always a herald, who has to bring his Lord's message to men. Every revelation is at the same time a message. For this reason the prophet never kept a revelatory experience to himself. Everything that he saw or heard in his revelatory state of mind was regarded by him as a word from God; and a word from God was not his personal property but something imparted to him for the benefit of others. This is true of the visions in which Isaiah, Jeremiah, and Ezekiel received the prophetic call as well as of the personal struggles described in the confessions (e.g., in Jer. xii. 1-6; xv. 15-21; xx. 7-18).

A glance at the prophetic books shows that besides the revelations in the strict sense they contain many passages of a historical character, historical dates and notices, and recitals of episodes in the life of the prophets. Typical examples are the conflict between Amos and the priest of Bethel (Am. vii), the story of the marriage of Hosea (Hos. i, iii), the encounter of Isaiah and Ahaz (Isa. vii), the account of how Isaiah walked about naked (xx), the narratives of the martyrdom of Jeremiah, the conflict between Jeremiah and Hananiah (Jer. xxviii), Jeremiah's purchase of the family inheritance (xxxii), the story of the fidelity of the Rechabites (xxxv), the burning of the scroll (xxxvi), the narratives of Gedaliah and the migration to Egypt (xl ff.), many chronological dates and short notices in Ezekiel, Haggai, and Zechariah. In addition we have the extensive historical conclusions of the books of Isaiah (ch. xxxvi-xxxix) and Jeremiah (ch. lii), the first for the main part, but not exclusively, taken from 2 Kings xviii. 13-xx. 19, the second from 2 Kings xxiv. 18-xxv. 30.

The historical passages in the prophetic books serve different ends. Many of them simply provide the background for the prophetic oracles, indicating what occasioned them, others serve a more direct historical purpose and belong to the literary genre referred to above as 'prophetic legends'. The concluding part of the book of Jeremiah, in which Jeremiah is not even mentioned, was probably added in order to demonstrate how Jeremiah's predictions concerning the disastrous fate of Jerusalem and Judah were fulfilled.

The concluding parts of Isaiah and Jeremiah and many other passages and features in the prophetic books which cannot be assigned to the collectors prove that additions were made by later hands. These books were given their final form at a late period by redactors.

We shall now consider how in the course of time those who originally received the revelations, their disciples, the collectors, and the redactors produced the prophetic books as we now have them, tracing the main outlines of the process and illustrating it by reference to appropriate texts.

2. THE PRIMARY MATERIAL

It is an incontestable fact that the prophets themselves sometimes wrote down oracles which they had received. As we have seen, Isaiah,

Jeremiah, Ezekiel, and Habakkuk are said to have done so.[1] A prophet who was commanded to write did not of course necessarily write with his own hand. Jeremiah was ordered to take a scroll and write on it his prophecies, but, in fact, Baruch wrote at Jeremiah's dictation. Sometimes, however, a prophet himself might write on a tablet or a scroll. At all events, written documents were an integral part of the primary material of the prophetic books. How many of the prophetic revelations were written down in this way it is impossible to say. There may very well have been from the beginning more written material than is indicated in the prophetic texts.

Then we have to allow for revelations which the hearers, and above all the disciples of the prophets, learned and repeated by heart. We have previously argued that in the days of the great prophets the circles of disciples corresponded to the prophetic guilds of earlier times. Within these circles the prophetic revelations were preserved and orally transmitted in their original form. This is above all true of those utterances which were originally metrical in form.

Among the material entrusted to the disciples we may note the prophetic confessions, such as are preserved in the book of Jeremiah, then the visionary experiences (especially the inaugural visions), and, finally, episodes in the lives of the prophets which were particularly worthy of remembrance. Part of this material shows traces of having been communicated by the prophets themselves: it is recorded in the first person. This is the case, for instance, with the visions in the book of Amos, the second narrative of the marriage of Hosea, the inaugural vision of Isaiah, the content of Isa. viii, a good deal of what is narrated in the books of Jeremiah, Ezekiel, and Zechariah. As to the numerous autobiographical narratives it is for the most part impossible to decide with certainty whether they were orally communicated to the disciples or written down by the prophets and handed down to posterity in this form. This problem is particularly acute in the book of Ezekiel. Here the autobiographical style appears throughout. The question is this: is the first person a sign that Ezekiel himself actually wrote, or is it due to the direct dictation to his disciples, or is it only a stylistic form in which the collectors of Ezekiel's revelations have expressed them. To this question we return later on.

The biographical style is often used both in the record of prophetic speeches and in the reproduction of historical episodes. Besides the visions recorded in the first person in the Book of Amos we have in the third person the episode of Amos and the priest Amaziah in Bethel.

[1] See above, pp. 163 f.

Besides the autobiographical story of Hosea's marriage we have the biographical narrative in ch. i. In Isa. vi–ix. 6, the encounter with Ahaz is described in the third person, the rest in the first person, etc.

It would be a great mistake to think that the autobiographical style was later changed into the biographical style or conversely.[2] The two stylistic forms are equally original. They are due to the two different ways in which the disciples originally recorded their material. What can be said is that the autobiographical narratives are more directly related to the communications of the prophets than the biographical narratives, unless there is reason to suspect that the autobiographical style is only a literary form, as it obviously often is in the Book of Ezekiel.

The speeches of the prophets have not always been transmitted to us in their original form; we have many of them only in the form of more or less free reproductions. An illuminating illustration of this is provided by Jeremiah vii and xxvi, which both deal with the so-called temple sermon of Jeremiah. Ch. xxvi contains a very brief abstract of the sermon in direct speech (indirect speech is, as we know, rare in the Hebrew Bible). The same sermon is reproduced again in a more extended, though not quite original, form in ch. vii.

Many of the revelatory speeches in the prophetic books are likewise only more or less free epitomes of the original sermons. This is clearly the case in Jer. xix. 14 f. Having returned from the Potsherd Gate, where he had crushed the earthenware vessel, Jeremiah stood in the court of the temple and said to the people, 'Thus says the Lord of hosts, the God of Israel, "Behold, I am bringing upon this city and upon all its towns all the disaster that I have pronounced against it, because they have stiffened their necks and refused to listen to my words."' This general and colourless speech was of course never delivered in this form. What we have is a very brief epitome of an address uttered publicly in connection with the episode of the broken vessel.

A very interesting summary of prophetic preaching appears in Jer. xi. Jeremiah was ordered to proclaim the words of the covenant, i.e., the covenant of Sinai,[3] to his people; and his message was given him in a

---

[2] Against Budde, *Geschichte der althebräischen Literatur*, p. 76, and *Jesajas Erleben*; Sellin, *Das Zwölfprophetenbuch*, I²⁻³, p. 190; Herntrich in *ATD* (p. 116). In his commentary on Isaiah Duhm changes the third person in ch. vii into the first person. Such textual emendations are of course quite illegitimate. They are due to a wrong idea of the way in which the prophetic revelations were transmitted, and ultimately arise from the conception of the prophetic books as literary products created by the prophets themselves.

[3] So rightly Rudolph and Weiser in their commentaries in *HAT* and *ATD*. 'The words of the covenant' were formulated in the temple ritual and ultimately based upon the Decalogue and similar documents. For Jeremiah's relation to Deuteronomy see also the somewhat divergent view presented by Rowley in *SOTP*, pp. 157 ff.

revelation. Three things are notable in this passage: it is not an epitome of a single sermon, but of a series of sermons to be delivered to the inhabitants of Jerusalem and the population of Judah. Further, it is in the form of a revelation communicated to the prophet before the sermons were delivered. Finally, the summary is given in two forms, *vv.* 3-5 and *vv.* 6-8. We have here, in fact, doublets (to this phenomenon we return later on).[4]

Amongst the revelations of Ezekiel, too, there are many passages which are free reproductions. xii. 22 f. is a good example of a brief epitome of this kind. The prophet is summoned to refute the statement of the people that the prophetic visions come to nothing. He is to say to them, 'The days are at hand when every vision will be fulfilled.'[5] A similar short summary is contained in the parallel text xii. 27 f. The extensive discourses of this prophet are also for the most part more like free reproductions than original speeches, whether they were composed by the prophet himself or by his disciples.

Such free reproductions are also to be found in the earlier prophets. Am. vi. 8-10, which describes the annihilation of the inhabitants of Samaria by a gruesome plague, does not give the impression of an original oracle by Amos. It is a free reproduction of something that Amos said. The same is true of Am. vi. 14 and vii. 11. There are also passages in the book of Isaiah in which we have reminiscences of utterances of the prophets rather than his words in their original form (e.g., x. 24-27). xx. 3-6 contains a summary of discourses given by Isaiah as an interpretation of the symbolic action described in *v.* 2. The narrative in the third person ('as my servant Isaiah has gone', etc.) shows manifestly that someone other than Isaiah is speaking.

Such summaries and abstracts are for the most part in prose. Critics have often maintained that the prose portions of the prophetic utterances are not authentic simply because they are prose. This is a mistake. The authenticity or otherwise of a prophetic saying is proved by its content, not by its form. If a saying is in accordance with a given prophet's general mode of thought, we are not justified in rejecting it, even if it is in prose. The prose form may of course be original; but usually it is a sign that an original prophetic utterance has been paraphrased.

---

[4] *Vv.* 1-5 and 6-8 are doublets, put together by the collector of the Jeremianic revelations, and belong with equal right to the text (against Volz: 'Eine der Fassungen muss an den Rand gesetz werden.' It is difficult to say what is the meaning of this statement). The first passage must have been formulated by someone who was intimately familiar with the Deuteronomic mode of expression. In *v.* 2 the text is not correct. I think that *šim'û* is influenced by *šim'û* in *v.* 6b and is to be replaced by *ḳᵉrâ* or something similar.

[5] At the end of *v.* 23 a word seems to have dropped out.

Since the primary material of the prophetic books, the utterances of the prophets and the historical narratives, may have been transmitted by different disciples of the prophets, it follows that different versions could be preserved of one and the same utterance or one and the same episode. This is the reason for the existence of doublets in the prophetic books.

A well-known example is the double account of the matrimonial history of Hosea. As we have tried to show, i. 2-9 is a parallel to iii. 1-3. The marriage is the same, though the latter narrative tells us only of the first stage of the marriage. In ch. iii we have a narrative by the prophet himself; in ch. i a disciple gives us an account of the same event though from another point of view. Thus we are justified in regarding the two narratives as doublets.[6]

The oracle of the mountain of the Lord's house in Isa. ii appears also in Mic. iv. How this has come about we shall see later on. Here we are concerned to note that this oracle has been preserved in these two contexts in slightly varying forms. Apart from minor differences such as the alternation of the words *gôyîm* and *'ammîm*, the conclusion in Micah is not the same as in Isaiah. In such instances there is, of course, no justification for textual emendation. The differences are due to a divergence in oral tradition.

Isa. v. 8-25 and ix. 7-x. 4 raise a special problem. In the former passage the ejaculation 'woe' appears six times; in the latter the following refrain occurs four times: 'For all this his anger is not turned back, and his hand is stretched out still.' The first poem may be called 'the woe-song', the second 'the refrain-song'. Neither of the two songs looks like an original poem composed by a poetic genius of the stature of Isaiah. There are in both many irregularities and obscurities. Both songs have obviously been modified to some degree in oral transmission. There are rhythmical anomalies; there are gaps and additions; there are reminiscences from other Isaianic revelations, and so on.

What is most striking in the two songs is that, though essentially different and independent, they have characteristic elements in common, a fact which calls for explanation. In the woe-song we unexpectedly meet the burden of the refrain-song (v. 25b); in the refrain-song, equally unexpectedly, a cry of woe appears (x. 1 ff.). The whole of v. 25 would fit more appropriately into the refrain-song. It is to be observed that the tenses indicate punishments in the past as in the refrain-song. On the other hand the woe in x. 1 ff. is constructed in the same manner as the woes of ch. v, for which reason critics usually

[6] See further above, pp. 165 ff.

say that it 'belongs' to that series. Because of the insertion of the woe at the end of the refrain-song the final refrain (in x. 4b) is quite disconnected. It presupposes events of the past, as in ch. ix, not events of the future.

What is the relation between the two songs, and how are the similarities in passages otherwise so different to be explained? Many suggestions have been made by critics. The commentaries speak of marginal glosses, redactional additions and deletions, and transpositions of larger or smaller passages. Theories of literary transposition are particularly common. But it seems quite impossible to arrive at a satisfactory solution of the problem on lines such as these.

In my view the only practicable way to overcome the difficulties is to take serious account of oral transmission. The prophet Isaiah left behind, amongst his numerous revelations, two very characteristic poems, one consisting of a series of woes, the other of a series of descriptions of punishments all ending with one and the same refrain. The two poems were repeated and transmitted in the circles of disciples. In transmission both songs underwent certain changes. *Inter alia* some elements from one song were blended with the substance of the other song. In this way these two songs reached their present structure in which in part they are doublets. The originals are lost for ever. What we possess is the poems in the forms they acquired in the process of oral transmission.[7]

Another instance of a doublet is the oracle against Edom ascribed to the prophet Obadiah, which is partly incorporated in the prophecy against Edom in Jer. xlix. 7 ff. The Edom oracle in the present Book of Jeremiah consists of authentic elements of an original Jeremianic poem on Edom, of words taken from Obadiah's Edom oracle and, in addition, of single words taken from elsewhere.[8] All these elements were put together in oral tradition, and in this form the oracle was taken over by the collector of the Jeremianic revelations and incorporated in the series of oracles against foreign nations. The fact that elements from different poems and narratives are often conflated in oral tradition

---

[7] In his book, *Zum hebräischen Traditionswesen*, Birkeland deals thoroughly with these songs. He emphasizes rightly that they were originally orally transmitted. His surmise that the two songs were also at one time connected in a literary document (p. 31) is not probable. This complicates the solution of the problem. It is simpler to assume that the collector of the Isaianic revelations took up the two songs just in the form in which they were available to him and placed them there where they now stand. In the mouth of Isaiah the songs certainly have had a more original and better shape. We know them only in the form given them by tradition. Transpositions of a literary nature are not acceptable.

[8] Cf. Eissfeldt, *Einleitung²*, p. 440.

is well known. Like attracts like. This law is familiar to everyone who has studied oral tradition. Accordingly, in these texts we ought not to speak of the 'literary' dependence of one text on the other, or of textual emendations or transpositions of substantial passages. We know the oracle on Edom in Jeremiah only as it was formed in oral tradition, and there is no hope of reaching the form in which Jeremiah uttered it.[9]

A fine example of doublets is offered by Jer. vii and xxvi, two passages which we have dealt with above from another angle. Two different persons have recorded the same event, and then the two accounts were brought together when the Jeremianic revelations were collected.

Jer. xxi. 8-10 and xxxviii. 2 f. are also doublets. The original identity of the two utterances is manifest. The common theme is this: Jerusalem will be conquered by the king of Babylonia; everyone who stays in the city will die by violence in some way; but he who surrenders to the Babylonians will escape. Apart from minor differences in the wording, the introductory words in xxi. 8 ff. ('behold, I set before you the way of life and the way of death') have no equivalent in xxxviii. 2 f. Because of these words the two versions, preserved by two different traditionists, have both been recorded in the Book of Jeremiah.[10]

The oracles on the return of the dispersed Israelites in Jer. xvi. 14 f. and xxiii. 7 f. are doublets of one and the same oracle with slight variations. They have been placed where they now stand by the collector of the Jeremianic revelations. In the first setting the oracle forms an antithesis to the preceding prophecy of doom. In the second setting it completes the oracle of the coming Messiah.[11]

[9] Pfeiffer holds that the oracles on Edom in Jeremiah and Obadiah are free reproductions of an earlier poem (*Introduction*[2], p. 507). An original oracle against Edom has been preserved in two recensions, both of them 'considerably rewritten and textually not intact' (p. 585). At all events the original Jeremianic poem on Edom is lost for ever. Nor can it be reconstructed by the excision of the Obadianic elements, for original Jeremianic words may have been suppressed in oral transmission. The Edom oracle in Obadiah looks like an original homogeneous composition. In this respect I agree with Engnell in *SBU* (*vv.* 19-21 seem to be redactional). The homogeneity of Obadiah is vindicated also by Bič (in *SVT*, I, 1953, pp. 11 ff.), who advances the original suggestion that Obadiah is an 'historical cult drama' from ancient times.

[10] The words in xxxviii. 2 are of course not 'a marginal gloss' from xxi. 9 (so Rudolph). They are as much part of this version of the oracle as of the version which appears in xxi. 8 ff. On the other hand Rudolph is right in regarding xxi. 11 f. and xxii. 1-5 as parallel texts deriving from different quarters. Rudolph, however, speaks of literary 'sources', while I prefer to speak of different traditionists.

[11] It is not correct to say that the saying is an 'insertion' or an 'addition' in xvi. 14-15. It has always formed part of the text. Its position in both contexts is due to the collector who took it from oral tradition. *lākēn* (xvi. 14 and xxiii. 7) is the usual connective particle used by the collector to link one saying to another. There is no reason for interpreting it as a causal adverb in the strict sense.

Jer. xxix. 16-19, which is inappropriately incorporated in Jeremiah's letter to the exiles, is obviously a parallel to ch. xxiv. This chapter contains a description of the symbolic vision of the two baskets of good figs and bad figs, and the interpretation of it. The speaker in Jer. xxix. 16-19 has dropped or has forgotten the vision itself and uses the bad figs simply as an illustration of the fateful situation of those who remained in Palestine. The two passages resemble each other not only in content but also, to some extent, in vocabulary. They obviously derive from different persons, who reproduced the same saying in variant forms. The collector of Jeremiah's revelations used the variant about the bad figs as a complement to the passage in Jeremiah's letter dealing with the happy future of the exiles.[12]

At the beginning of the book of Ezekiel we find a characteristic doublet in the dating of Ezekiel's inaugural vision. In *v.* 1 the prophet himself is speaking in the first person, in *vv.* 2 f. another person speaks in the third person of the same occurrence. There is a difference in the dating, but not a contradiction. The 'other person' dates the prophet's call in the fifth year of the exile of King Joiachin; the prophet himself says that he was called in the thirtieth year, viz. of his life. In my view there is no sufficient ground for assuming two different calls, one in the prophet's homeland, the other in Babylonia. The great vision described in ch. i-iii is (if we except the interpretative parts) clearly comprehensible as a unity; consequently the two dates in i. 1-3 must refer to the same event. It is as natural that the prophet should mention his own age to fix the date, as that the other person should date the occurrence in terms of King Joiachin's exile. There is no ground at all for changing the text. I think that the problem of the introductory verses is very simply solved by the above assumption that they contain doublets. The alternation of the first and the third person recalls Hos. i and iii. The difference in the dating caused a collector to place both notices side by side. He did not feel free to drop either of them. To the dated description of the vision, originally dictated, or perhaps written down, by the prophet himself, he added the second date taken from his own memory or from the memory of another disciple. It can reasonably be objected that the notice of the age of Ezekiel does not suffice to date the vision. Yet, what is more plausible than the surmise that the prophet's own dating originally included a reference to the year of the

---

[12] It is difficult to understand why 'a reader of a late time' would have composed such an expansion, which in reality spoils the tenor of the letter. It would be much more natural that a collector should so use an element which he had received from tradition and for which he had to find a setting, joining it to the letter which was probably known to him only from oral repetition.

exile of King Joiachin but was suppressed by the collector when he inserted the other dating? Likewise the collector in his third person notice left out the fourth month, because it was already mentioned in the first person narrative. In the present text composed presumably by a collector we are supplied with two dates which conveniently complete each other.[13]

That the inaugural vision is connected with an account of the mission given to the prophet and the message he had to proclaim, is quite natural. This was also true of the visions in which Isaiah and Jeremiah received their call. The mission of Ezekiel is contained in ii. 3-7. It is communicated in the vision in the form of a divine speech. Ezekiel is commanded to proclaim Yahweh's words to his people. They will be impudent and stubborn and even deaf to the prophet's preaching. Yet, Ezekiel must not fear, even if thistles and thorns and scorpions are round about him. Whatever the circumstances, he must persist in speaking that which God gives him to speak.

As a part of the visionary experience, this speech may be called an 'audition'. However, it is obvious that we have here not a literal rendering of what the prophet really heard, but a free reproduction of what at the moment of his call was given him to do. Hence the rather general and far from concise form of the speech.

Now in iii. 4-11 we have a passage which closely resembles this revelatory speech in ch. ii. Here, too, the prophet is commanded to go and proclaim Yahweh's words to his people. Yet, unlike what the pagan nations would do, Israel will not listen to him, because she has a hard forehead and a stubborn heart. The prophet must not fear them. Yahweh will make his face and forehead as hard as theirs, Yahweh will make his forehead like adamant, harder than flint. All the words which Yahweh will speak to him he must receive in his heart and attend to. He must persist in preaching whether they hear or decline to hear. The similarities are evident. New elements in iii. 4-11 are the comparison between Israel and the Gentiles and the promise that Yahweh will give the prophet a hard face and make his forehead hard like flint. Nevertheless, I think that this passage is a doublet of the speech in ii. 3-7. If the first speech was perhaps related by the prophet himself, the second was recorded by a disciple. A collector retained both and placed them, one after the first scene of the vision, the second after the second scene of the same vision. That the second passage also belongs to this context is proved by the words: 'All the words that I am speaking to you, receive in your heart and hear with your ears' (v. 10),

[13] See Additional Note IV.

a passage which obviously refers to the vision of the hand with the
scroll in ii. 8-iii. 3.[14]

In two passages in the Book of Ezekiel the prophet is appointed a
watchman (*ṣōpêh*) to his people: iii. 16-21 and xxxiii. 1-9. The task of
the prophet as a watchman was to warn the wicked among his compatriots lest they die because of their wicked conduct. The two passages
have in common not only the main ideas but also, to a great extent, the
actual phraseology. The essential differences are that in iii. 16 ff. there
is a passage concerning the warning of the righteous man, to which
nothing corresponds in xxxiii. 1 ff., and further that in ch. iii, the figure
of the watchman calling is linked to the vocation of the prophet, while
in ch. xxxiii it is joined to a parable of the watchman who blows the
trumpet to warn his people when attacked by enemies.

The two passages are obviously doublets formulated by different
persons in the oral transmission of Ezekiel's revelations, with similarities
and dissimilarities such as are typical of such doublets.

Those critics are certainly right who hold that the oracle about
Ezekiel's mission as a watchman was originally (when he uttered it)
associated with the parable as an element in its interpretation, and that
its setting in the narrative of the call is secondary. It was no doubt
natural for a collector to think that the task of a watchman was given
Ezekiel from the beginning as an element in his general prophetic
calling.[15] Further, there is good reason to suppose that the prophet
became conscious of his mission as a watchman at a later stage of his
prophetic career rather than at its beginning, when general judgement
and punishment were the chief themes of his preaching.

Individual retribution is dealt with in two discourses which look like
doublets: xviii. 1-32 and xxxiii. 10-20. They have a series of ideas in
common: if a wicked man turns from his sins, he shall live; if a righteous
man turns from his righteousness, he shall die; people say, 'The way
of the Lord is not equal'; Yahweh will judge everyone according to his
ways; Israel is summoned to turn from her evil ways; Yahweh has no
pleasure in the death of the wicked. In ch. xviii there is a passage which

---

[14] In ii. 3-7 Ezekiel was sent to 'the children of Israel', in iii. 11 the prophet is
commanded to preach Yahweh's words to the *gôlâh*. This divergence does not preclude
the possibility of doublets, particularly if the doublets were originally oral doublets,
which for the most part is the case in the prophetic literature. Moreover, in the second
speech it is also said that the prophet is sent to the house of Israel (*v.* 4). As regards
the use of the name Israel in Ezekiel (esp. ch. i-xxiv) Danell has shown that this name
has no uniform sense there. It often means the exiled community; but the population
left in Judah and Jerusalem goes by this name, too. Besides, Israel appears occasionally
in the sense Northern Israel. Finally, there are contexts in which it must mean the
whole people; *Studies in the Name Israel in the Old Testament*, p. 254.

[15] Cf. for instance Hölscher, *Die Profeten*, p. 407.

has no equivalent in ch. xxxiii: the law of individual retribution applied to three generations (*vv.* 5-18). In addition, the discourse in ch. xviii is associated with the proverb: 'The fathers have eaten sour grapes,' etc., that in ch. xxxiii with the saying: 'Our transgressions and our sins lie upon us, and under them we waste away; how then can we live?'

It is more than probable that these two discourses have a common origin in one and the same utterance of Ezekiel. They were transmitted in somewhat varying form. I think that Ezekiel's discourse concerning retribution was originally connected with the current proverb about the sour grapes. Its position immediately after the parable of the watchman (xxxiii. 1-9) is due to a collector who wanted to use the discourse about retribution as an explanation of this parable.

In the prophecy against the mountains of Israel in ch. vi. 3-7 there are so many reiterations of the same expressions that it is difficult to believe that the passage originally formed a unit. In *vv.* 3 f. we hear of destruction of the high places, desolation of the altars, breaking down of the incense altars, and slain people everywhere in the land. Exactly the same motifs recur in *vv.* 6 f. I do not believe that this phenomenon can be explained only on the hypothesis of redactional amplification or on the assumption of a late 'imitator' as the commentators say. All becomes intelligible if we regard the two passages as doublets arising from two different versions of an original sermon delivered by Ezekiel, linked together by a collector.

The same is true of the sermon about the end which is to come upon the land in vii. 2-4 and vii. 5-9.

The inaugural vision of Yahweh's throne returns unexpectedly in ch. x, in connection with the great temple vision in ch. viii-xi. The similarities are so striking that there can be no question of two quite independent visions. The best solution of the problem seems to be that the collector had at his disposal two different descriptions of the same vision. He placed the better of them (probably from his own material) in his narrative of Ezekiel's call. The other was placed within the later temple vision, where the glory of the Lord played a predominant role.[16]

An oracle on the fulfilment of the prophecies was transmitted in two forms: xii. 21-25 and xii. 26-28. According to one traditionist the oracle was caused by the popular saying: 'The days grow long, and every vision

[16] Baumann (in *ZAW*, lxvii, 1955, pp. 56 ff.) thinks that the vision described in ch. i originally preceded the great vision of the bones in the valley in ch. xxxvii. This author finds the inaugural vision in ii. 3-iii. 9. If account is taken of the structure and psychology of ecstatic visions, it must be admitted that the vision in ch. xxxvii is a whole, complete in itself, and does not require a detailed theophany as an introduction. The vision in ch. i is, as Fohrer and Zimmerli have shown, appropriate as a preparation for what is recorded in ii. 8 ff.

comes to nothing.' According to another it was an answer to the current dictum: 'The vision which he sees is for many days hence; he is prophesying of times far off.' Which of the two accounts is original, it is impossible to say; both were current, and the collector has placed them side by side.

The same is true of the oracle against Ammon in ch. xxv. *Vv.* 6 f. are only a variant of 3-5. Two parallel traditions have here been combined by the collector. The assumption of two short 'sketches' made by the prophet himself seems less natural.

Ezekiel left a number of revelations about Tyre, which now are to be found in ch. xxvi-xxviii of his book. xxvi. 3-6 and xxvi. 7-14 contain two different oracles of judgement upon Tyre. In the first the destruction of Tyre comes about by the attack of 'many nations'; in the second it is accomplished by Nebuchadnezzar's army. Each oracle has characteristics of its own; but, at the same time, the oracles have some specific elements in common: the demolition of the walls and the breaking down of the towers; Tyre reduced to a bare rock and a place for spreading nets; her daughters on the mainland slain by the sword. The two revelations now look like doublets, but because of the characteristic divergences it is wiser to assume that from the beginning they were independent poems, but that in the course of oral transmission they borrowed individual elements from each other. Thus their relationship would resemble that of the woe-song and the refrain-song of Isa. v. 8-25 and ix. 7-x. 4.

There are examples of the oral transmission of an oracle in three forms, e.g., in xxx. 20-26. The chief motif here is the breaking of Pharaoh's arms. In one version, *v.* 21, the arms are already broken; in another, *vv.* 22-24, Yahweh will in the future strengthen the arms of the king of Babylon, while he will break the arms of Pharaoh and scatter the Egyptians among the nations. The third version, *vv.* 25 f., is a parallel to the foregoing, but contains some characteristics of its own. Because of the divergences in the three versions the collector preserved them and placed them side by side.

The oracle against Edom in xxxv gives the impression of being composed of at least two different versions of the same utterance, as is shown by the treatment of the passage in the standard commentaries.

The extended prophecy concerning Gog's attack on the land of Israel in the last time (xxxviii-xxxix) is very instructive. At first sight it appears that here at least two versions have been combined and conflated by the collector of Ezekiel's revelations. The march of the armies of Gog against the land of Israel at the beginning of ch. xxxix is incompatible with the description of the annihilation of the enemies at the end of the previous chapter. A critical scholar cannot but make an attempt to disentangle the one version from the other at least in rough outline. In general agreement with the analysis made by Bertholet I think that one version ran as follows. Yahweh takes the initiative. He Himself leads Gog and all his army by force towards the land of Israel. There they will all be defeated. The fallen warriors will be food for the ravenous birds and the wild beasts. According to the other version Gog himself will plan the mischievous scheme. He will assault the peaceable people and the open land of Israel. But on the day when Gog invades the land of Israel there will be an earthquake in the land and all kinds of calamities will occur. The warriors of Gog will be seized by panic. The weapons will provide sufficient firewood for seven years, and for seven months the people of Israel will be engaged in burying the dead bodies.

In my view we must understand the relation between these two narratives as follows. Arising out of, e.g., Jeremiah's prophecy of the enemy from the north (see Ezek. xxxviii. 17), there came to Ezekiel a revelation of Gog (Gyges?) and his army making an assault on Israel and her land. By a divine wonder the dreadful enemies would be annihilated, and thus Yahweh's glory would be manifested among the Gentiles, and Israel would know that Yahweh was her God. After the utter destruction of this last enemy Israel would live in safety for ever.[17]

Of this prophetic revelation two of Ezekiel's disciples have given two different accounts. I think that the first account corresponds closely, though not in every detail, to the original. In the second account another traditionist has remoulded the original revelation after his own taste or after the taste of a later time. The details are now still more miraculous and frightful. This observation is significant, for it proves that those who transmitted the prophetic revelations did not always endeavour to reproduce the original sayings mechanically; they sometimes re-modelled them freely in accordance with other ways of thinking. They were not only transmitters; they were also themselves something like prophetic personalities.[18]

I have treated the book of Ezekiel in the same way as other prophetic books, since I regard it as a collection of prophetic revelations analogous to the collections of the revelations of Isaiah, Jeremiah, etc. We return to the vexed problem of the composition of Ezekiel below. Only when

[17] The end of ch. xxxix comprising vv. 23-29 is an independent revelation and has of course nothing to do with what precedes.

[18] That the transmitters were also sometimes charismatically inspired prophets is rightly emphasized by Mowinckel in *Prophecy and Tradition*, pp. 67 f.

the discussion is complete will it become manifest whether my general view on the book of Ezekiel is probable or not.

The later prophets may be discussed briefly. In Deutero-Isaiah the most striking parallels are the satires on the idol-worshippers in xl. 19 f.; xli. 6 f.; xliv. 9-20; xlvi. 6 f. These are parallels but not 'doublets', because each has its own characteristic content. They all belong to a special literary genre which emerged during the exile, which may be termed idol satire. Another specimen of the same genre in the prophets is Jer. x. 3-9. Isa. xliv. 9-20 seems to be a relatively complete example; the other passages are fragments of larger units.

They were all inserted in their present contexts by the collector of the Deutero-Isaianic revelations; and in these contexts they serve a definite purpose. The small fragment, xli. 6 f., is intended to show how the idolaters encourage themselves in the dreadful situation created by the appearance of Cyrus. The others serve to demonstrate the uniqueness of Yahweh, the God of Israel.

The four passages in question illustrate how a collector has done his work with the available material, freely and not mechanically. The objections made against the Deutero-Isaianic origin of this material are, in my opinion, not quite conclusive.

That the two utterances Hag. i. 4-6 and i. 9-11 somehow belong together is obvious. Both describe the situation in the land of Judah immediately before the beginning of the rebuilding of the temple in Jerusalem. Bad harvests had led to famine. The cause of the miserable conditions was that Yahweh's house was still in ruins, while people were anxious to erect their own houses. Once the temple was founded, the situation would be altered.

Certain scholars make the two passages into one coherent speech by means of textual changes and transpositions. In my view it is a better solution of the problem to regard the two sayings as two different summaries of speeches given by Haggai during the time before the restoration of the temple. The collector of the oracles of Haggai brought them together, one introducing, the other following the exhortation in *v.* 8 to erect the temple.[19]

In Zechariah the oracle about Yahweh's jealousy for Zion appears twice, i. 14 and viii. 2. The short oracle, originally connected with the vision of the horses in ch. i, was also used by the collector as a suitable

---

[19] Eissfeldt thinks that two different collections of Haggai's words may have been combined, one being the memoirs of Haggai, the others a 'looser' collection of his words (*Einleitung*², p. 526). In the light of the general literary nature of the prophetic books the assumption of two different traditionists seems to be a much simpler solution of the problem.

introduction to the series of oracles of divine bliss in the age to come in ch. viii. The formulation of the oracle varies a little.

The enumeration of doublets made above is of course not complete. The material adduced may be regarded only as a series of typical examples. How the collectors worked in detail will be shown later.

As a result of the above investigations the following can be established concerning the primary material underlying the prophetic books.

First we have to allow for writings deriving from the prophets themselves, whether written by them or by the hand of another. A famous example of the latter group is the two scrolls written by Baruch, the *sōpēr* or scribe of Jeremiah.

Most of the revelations of the prophets were, however, orally transmitted by the disciples of the prophets. They learned them by heart, and thus they were handed down from generation to generation. But many of them must have been written down; so the oral and the scribal transmission ran parallel with each other. Revelations learnt by heart were in the first place those which were expressed in rhythmical form.[20]

It was not only sermons in the strict sense that were imparted by the prophets to their disciples, but also events and experiences in their lives, such as visions and, above all, the prophetic 'confessions', i.e., communications about the inner lives of the prophetic personalities. They were imparted either in the first person (corresponding more directly to the prophets' own words) or, more freely, in the third person. Both forms are equally original. It is not allowable to say that one form is 'secondary' in relation to the other. Among the primary material we must also notice narratives of happenings in the lives of the prophets which may be classed with the old genre of prophetic legends. They are particularly frequent in the book of Jeremiah.

A considerable part of the content of the prophetic books, the books of Jeremiah and Ezekiel in particular, consists of free reproductions or abstracts of prophetic sermons derived from what the disciples remembered. These summaries are, naturally, in prose and differ in characteristic ways from the revelations which are preserved to us in their original poetic form. They are sometimes lengthy, sometimes considerably abridged, but for the most part without the striking and impressive tone that characterizes the original creations of the prophets.

---

[20] The importance of oral tradition is particularly emphasized by Nyberg in *Studien zum Hoseabuche*. In *Prophecy and Tradition* (*passim*) Mowinckel makes wise observations on the existence of oral and written tradition at the same time. On this point there seems nowadays to be a general consensus among competent scholars.

The presence of doublets in the prophetic books is a natural consequence of the manner in which the prophetic revelations were transmitted. One disciple transmitted a speech or an occurrence in one way,
another in a somewhat different way. The collector did not suppress
one or other of them, particularly when the divergences were significant,
but brought them together in one way or another. Sometimes he put
them side by side, sometimes he placed them in quite different contexts,
sometimes he combined and conflated them in a speech or narrative
composed by himself on the basis of the traditions he had at his disposal.
Such combinations of different elements have often deranged the sequence of the text and the thought. It is quite unjustifiable to 'correct'
such passages by textual operations of any sort. The only legitimate way
to treat such passages is to regard them as textual units, but, at the
same time, as traditional compositions, as are, for instance, the traditions of the Pentateuch and those of the Gospels.

This view of the transmission of the prophetic revelations and
experiences on the one hand and the work of the collectors on the other
also has significant consequences for the higher critic.

If I am right in believing that the work of the collector consisted in
bringing together traditional material, written or oral, and arranging it
as he thought best, and if he sometimes had at his disposal doublets for
which he also had to find a place, it is only to be expected that the order
of the different units sometimes seems to be unsatisfactory. This fact
has, of course, always been noticed by the commentators. Assuming
that the prophetic books were composed on more or less literary
principles, they have frequently maintained that a particular unit
'belongs' to another context and that for some reason it has been
'misplaced'. Then we often notice that passages are transposed in the
commentaries in order to produce a better 'order', a more logical
'coherence'. Such changes must be regarded as pointless. The problem
is not how to arrange the units in a better order but how to explain
every single passage and its present position in the text. Though
additions may later have been made to the text, the original order of the
units within the prophetic books remained unchanged after the collector
had finished his work. We may recognize, however, that occasionally
individual lines, or groups of lines, have been transposed through the
carelessness of copyists, and that glosses from the margin have entered
the text.

A special problem is raised by the section of the book of Jeremiah
which contains the oracles on the foreign nations (xlvi-li). In the Massoretic text this section is placed at the end of the book (before the

redactional conclusion, which was added later), while in the Septuagint it follows the words in xxv. 13: 'And I will bring upon that land [Babylonia] all my words which I have pronounced against it, all that is written in this book.' Moreover, in the Septuagint the passage about the wine cup of wrath (xxv. 15 ff.) follows the oracles against foreign nations.

Which was the original order? The present writer holds that the order in the Massoretic text is original. The Septuagint represents a secondary arrangement. We must bear in mind that the order of the Jeremianic revelations, as of other prophetic collections, is due to a collector who followed certain principles and made his arrangement accordingly. In particular the collectors were anxious to begin and end their collections in an impressive way. It is not likely that the collector of the Jeremianic revelations concluded his work with the episode of the complaint of Baruch and the consolation offered to him by Jeremiah in the year 605. The oracles of judgement on the nations were an appropriate conclusion. The arrangement in the Septuagint can easily be explained as an endeavour to attain uniformity with the books of Isaiah and Ezekiel. xxv. 13, with its prophecy of judgement on Babylonia and the reference to 'this book', was a not inappropriate point of connection for the series of oracles against foreign nations. In the Septuagint the placing of the vision of the wine cup of wrath after the oracles against foreign nations shows how arbitrary is the Septuagint's arrangement of the different sections. To this complicated problem we shall return in our discussion of the methods of the collectors.[21]

Another problem connected with the collection of the Jeremianic revelations is worth noticing. Many of the utterances, in particular the summaries of the speeches, have analogies with Deuteronomy and writings with a Deuteronomic stamp. Examples of common ideas and phraseology are: Egypt, the iron furnace; the land flowing with milk and honey; the land given to the fathers for all time; the oath sworn to the fathers; the words of the covenant; cursed be the man who, etc.; do not oppress the resident alien, the orphan, and the widow; walk after other gods; the way of life and the way of death; Yahweh shows kindness to thousands; He acts with signs and wonders, with a strong hand and

---

[21] There is no agreement among scholars concerning the original place of the oracles against the nations. The order in the Septuagint is defended by Volz, Pfeiffer, Rudolph, Weiser, Eissfeldt. The Massoretic text has found a skilful advocate in Mowinckel. On good grounds this scholar argues that the section xlvi-li originally followed xlv; *Zur Komposition des Buches Jeremia*, pp. 14 f. In speaking of the Septuagint we must take into account the possibility that the Greek translators had before them a Hebrew text in an Egyptian recension, which might in certain respects have diverged from the Hebrew prototype (cf. Albright in *BASOR*, 140, 1955, pp. 27 ff.).

an outstretched arm, with anger, fury, and great wrath; Yahweh's delight in doing good. The 'pulpit style' and the monotony of such passages have often been noted.

How is this phenomenon to be explained? Scholars have spoken of different literary sources in the Book of Jeremiah. One of these sources has been called 'the Deuteronomistic source', because the 'redactor' of this source is thought to have belonged to the so-called 'Deuteronomistic school'.[22] On the general view outlined above the passages in question never formed an independent literary source (indeed, it is difficult to realize the object of such an independent recension of a part of Jeremiah). The difference between the more markedly Deuteronomistic passages and others is due to the individuality of whoever transmitted the former. He was familiar with the ideas and phraseology that are characteristic of Deuteronomy. It is not necessary to argue that he deliberately sought to follow the Deuteronomic model; according to recent investigations, Deuteronomy itself reflects liturgical instruction and preaching at the sanctuary.[23] Thus it is better to say that whoever gave shape to the 'Deuteronomistic revelations' in the Book of Jeremiah had been strongly influenced by the cultic tradition of the temple at Jerusalem, and accordingly he has given us some of Jeremiah's utterances in a form diverging somewhat from the original revelations.[24]

In the Book of Jeremiah there are also traces of influence from the thought and terminology of the Wisdom school. Good examples of such influence are found in xvii. 5-8, 9 f., 11, where the tree planted by waters as a symbol of the righteous man, the deceitful heart and the Lord's searching the heart and trying the reins, and, finally, the proverb about the partridge suggest the teaching in the Wisdom schools. The same is true of the characteristic Wisdom phrase 'receive correction' (lāḳaḥ mûsār), which appears frequently in the Book of Jeremiah. In this case it is not justifiable to maintain that there was a single traditionist who belonged to the Wisdom circles. The fact that reminiscences of Wisdom are spread over the whole book suggests that Jeremiah himself as well as his disciples had special connections with the Wisdom school.[25]

---

[22] See Additional Note V.

[23] See above all the works by von Rad, *Das formgeschichtliche Problem des Hexateuchs*, and *Deuteronomium-Studien*.

[24] Cf. Weiser in his commentary, p. 482, note 1. It is, of course, not excluded that Jeremiah himself occasionally made use of 'Deuteronomistic' phrases and the 'Deuteronomistic' style.

[25] See further Lindblom in *SVT*, III, 1955, pp. 192 ff.

3. THE WORK AND METHODS OF THE COLLECTORS

Every prophet had a circle of disciples who transmitted the utterances of their master, various communications made by him, and, in addition, what they themselves remembered of the lives of the prophets. Generally speaking, the task of the *collectors* was to bring this material together in larger or smaller collections which then became the groundwork of the prophetic books. We must now consider how these collectors proceeded and what was the result of their work.

In this connection we must recognize that what we call prophetic books cannot have been identical with the earliest collections. The narrative of Baruch's writing down Jeremiah's revelations from dictation is very instructive in this respect. It shows that, before the composition of the present Book of Jeremiah, there existed a considerable collection of Jeremianic revelations, which was preceded by a still earlier collection burned by King Jehoiakim. What is true of the Book of Jeremiah may *mutatis mutandis*, possibly, though not necessarily, also have been true of other prophetic books.[26]

The position can be established only by an examination of the individual prophetic books.

Amos. The oracles against the peoples in i. 3-ii. 16 seem at first sight to form a collection of individual sayings originally independent of each other. But, apart from some minor additions, this section was surely a unity from the very beginning. We have here a specimen of the literary genre which the present writer has called 'the tribal poem', here enlarged to comprise peoples and nations. Typical examples of the tribal poem in the Old Testament are 'the Blessing of Jacob' (Gen. xlix)

---

[26] Birkeland in his book *Zum hebräischen Traditionswesen* strongly emphasizes the importance of oral tradition in the growth of the prophetic books. The individual prophetic sayings were at an early stage combined into what Birkeland calls 'Traditionskomplexe'. These 'Traditionskomplexe', which were handed down orally, were of fundamental importance in the development of the prophetic books (similarly Mowinckel in *Prophecy and Tradition*, p. 60). Birkeland's main object in his book is to determine the shape and contents of these 'Traditionskomplexe'. He tries to show how individual sayings or narratives were collected in smaller complexes, which were later combined to give larger complexes. The connective links were catch-words and common ideas. Bearers of tradition were early disciples of the prophets. Different groups of disciples produced parallel complexes, often influencing each other. The complexes, at the beginning orally transmitted, were later, though at a relatively early time, written down. The following investigation shows several points of contact with the theses of Birkeland. The main difference between me and the Norwegian scholar is that I hold that the complexes (collections as I call them) being the result of the activity of *collectors* of the prophetic revelations in a proper sense, as a rule (although perhaps not exclusively) were created in connection with the writing down. The simplicity of my view is an argument in its favour. Birkeland's 'Traditionskomplexe' have often a very complicated history. It goes without saying that my 'collections' in numerous cases diverge from Birkeland's complexes.

and 'the Blessing of Moses' (Deut. xxxiii). The song of Deborah in Judges v was probably modelled on a tribal poem. The same is true of the benedictions of Shem and Japhet and the curse of Canaan in Gen. ix. 25-27, and the lays of Balaam in Num. xxiii-xxiv. I am convinced that Amos himself composed this series of oracles about the nations, forming them into a coherent poem.[27] The reiterated formula 'for three transgressions and for four' originates in my view in the teaching of the Wisdom schools. There much stress was laid upon didactic and pedagogic devices of different kinds.[28]

It is reasonable to suppose that the revelations introduced by 'hear', iii. 1-v. 6, once formed a special collection; but this cannot be proved. A 'hear'-oracle is also to be found in viii. 4 ff., and the series of 'hear'-oracles is in several places interrupted by oracles which are not introduced by 'hear'. Nor did the 'woe'-speeches in v. 7-vi. 14 necessarily constitute a separate collection.[29] In this section there are many individual oracles which have no connection at all with the original 'woe'-speeches. Against the assumption that the visions originally formed a collection is the fact that the last vision in ix. 1 is separated from the series of visions that ends in viii. 1 f. It is difficult to see why originally coherent groups of revelations should later have been divided up.[30]

There are no cogent reasons for assuming earlier collections in the Book of Amos. Apart from the last redactional additions, the book as a whole is the result of the collecting work of one of the disciples of Amos, probably completed after the end of the master's prophetic career. Very appropriately he placed the series of oracles against the nations at the beginning of the book. Then he brought together a number of utterances and oracles in no discernible order. The three visions in vii. 1-9 are, of course, brought together because of their content. The episode of Amos and the priest Amaziah in Bethel was linked with the vision of the

---

[27] See Lindblom in *SVT*, I, 1953, pp. 78 ff. Bentzen in *OTS*, VIII, 1950, pp. 85 ff., refers to the Egyptian 'Ächtungstexte'.

[28] See Lindblom in *SVT*, III, 1955, pp. 192 ff. (esp. pp. 202 f.).

[29] For v. 7 see *BH*.

[30] I cannot share Weiser's opinion that at one time all the visions formed a literary unit composed by Amos himself. On the whole Weiser's literary view of the book of Amos is difficult to approve. There are no grounds for assuming that the present arrangement of the Book of Amos is not original. No doubt it is the work of the collector who arranged the various items according to his own judgement. Maag, *Text, Wortschatz und Begriffswelt des Buches Amos*, pp. 46 f., likewise contests Weiser's view of the literary unity of the visions, particularly pointing to the different introduction to the last vision in ix. 1. The position which I have outlined above also makes it impossible for me to share the very original view of Morgenstern, expounded in his stimulating book *Amos Studies*, that the prophet Amos delivered, not a series of addresses or prophetic utterances, but one single, closely integrated address, delivered at the Northern national sanctuary at Bethel on the great, solemn New Year's Day. Nor can I approve the textual transpositions which Morgenstern suggests.

plumb-line because of the end of this vision: 'I will rise against the house of Jeroboam with the sword.' This motif appears again in Amaziah's report to the king: 'Thus has Amos said, "By the sword shall Jeroboam die."' After the fourth vision, the vision of the summer fruit, the point of which is this word: 'The end has come upon my people Israel, I will never again forgive them' (viii. 2), a series of oracles about the inevitable and utter annihilation of the people follows in a continued crescendo, culminating in the vision of the overthrow of the temple in Bethel and the significant word: 'Not a single one of them will get away, not a single one of them will escape.' What follows is a variation of the same theme, issuing in this terrible word, with which the authentic revelations of Amos end: 'I will destroy it [the sinful kingdom] from the face of the earth' (ix. 8a).

It would be too much to expect the collector to have produced an entirely logical order. In many cases the reasons for his combining of different oracles are not discernible, but, as we have seen above, it is sometimes possible to detect them. It will appear below that the same holds good of all the prophetic books. There is always a tendency to link together passages which have some point of similarity. That is all we can say. In many cases there are no obvious principles at all and never have been.

In the Book of Amos it is relatively easy to separate one oracle from the other. The individual utterances often begin with the usual oracle formula 'thus says Yahweh'. We also find characteristic introductory expressions such as 'hear this word', 'hear this', 'woe!', 'Yahweh has sworn', 'behold, Yahweh is commanding', 'it shall come to pass', 'behold, days are coming'. Sometimes short sayings are linked to each other without any connecting words; sometimes the collector has inserted a *kî* or a *lāḵēn*, obviously without causal meaning, only to mark the connection.[31]

Was this collection of the revelations of Amos orally transmitted from the beginning, or was it originally written down? It is of course not out of the question that prophetic revelations of a cognate content or form were already combined in oral tradition; but in this case it seems more likely that the collection had a written form from the very beginning, and, accordingly, that the collector of the orally transmitted revelations was also a scribe. An oral complex would have looked different. It would have been arranged more obviously on mnemonic principles. The way in which the Book of Amos is composed tells decidedly in favour of the assumption that the collector, who was, of course, a

[31] For the neutral significance of *lāḵēn* see Pedersen, *Israel*, I-II, p. 116.

disciple of Amos, was a scribe, who at a relatively early time assembled what he could find of the revelations of his master, and wrote them down at once, in order to preserve them for posterity. *When* this occurred, is impossible to say, probably after the prophet's death.[32] What we know of oriental usage makes it quite likely that what had been committed to writing was subsequently learnt by heart and transmitted orally by the disciples.[33]

To the editing of the Book of Amos we shall return later. At the present it may suffice to say that, in my view, at least the following passages did not belong to the original collection: most of the introductory words in i. 1; further i. 2; the so-called doxologies in iv. 13, v. 8-9, and ix. 5-6; the conclusion of the book dealing with the Messianic age ix. 8b-15; and, probably, the oracle on Judah in ii. 4-5.

That the editor of the book changed the order of the original collection cannot be proved. The theory that considerable transpositions have taken place is without any foundation. Apart from some minor additions, the Book of Amos has always had its present arrangement. What looks like disorder, or even confusion, is to be attributed to the collector.

Hosea. In the Book of Hosea, too, scholars have sought to find subordinate collections. In particular a collection of the first order has been seen in the section i-iii. It is true that this section is dominated by the idea of the adultery of the prophet's wife and, analogously, the adultery of Israel; but adultery is a theme that frequently recurs later in the book.

No good grounds have been advanced for regarding i-iii as an independent collection. The view that the prophet himself composed this section and made it public in the form of a 'fly-sheet' is quite unconvincing. That the first person style should have been changed into the third person style is a quite arbitrary assumption. There is nothing to suggest that the man who collected the revelations of Hosea contained in iv-xiv was not also the collector of the various units in i-iii, who placed them as an introduction at the head of the whole collection.

He had at his disposal two accounts of the marriage of Hosea, one in the third person, the other in the first person. As we have seen above, both types of transmission are original and must be accepted. How the

---

[32] Watts in *ET*, lxvi, 1954-55, pp. 109 ff., gives a vivid picture of the transmission of the revelations of Amos: they were remembered, repeated and finally reduced to writing by some of the prophetic circles in Bethel; then they were brought to Judah, perhaps by refugee prophets or priests. All this is of course possible but by no means demonstrated.

[33] Cf. above all Widengren, *Literary and Psychological Aspects of the Hebrew Prophets.*

two accounts stand to each other, we have discussed above.[34] In my view the most plausible solution of the problem is that the prophet's own narrative deals with the first stage of his matrimonial history, while the third person narrator was mostly interested in what happened at a later stage. His account may be regarded as a complement to that of the prophet. It is very likely that the latter once contained more details which the collector left out because of the other narrative. The collector who belonged to a later age and perhaps had no personal memory of Hosea's life, did not understand the relationship between the two narratives which he had received. He believed that there was a second marriage in Hosea's life (either with the same Gomer or with another wife); and so he linked the two narratives together by the connective word 'ôḏ, 'once more'.

The symbolic names which are given in the first account to the second and the third child (lô' ruḥāmâh and lô' 'ammî: 'She-who-is-unpitied' and 'Not-my-people') express the idea of Israel's rejection. Very appropriately the collector, though without any connective word, linked with this passage the sermon about the adultery of Israel and her rejection (ii. 1-3 belongs to the later redaction of the book[35]), comprising vv. 4-15 of ch. ii.[36]

Remarkably enough a revelation follows (ii. 16 f.) which predicts a bright future for Israel. It is, however, a future made possible by prior chastisement and education. The idea is the same as in iii. 3-5. The connective lāḵēn is used to introduce the passage. Here the collector shows a significant interest in linking a prophecy of hope to a prophecy of judgement, an instance of principle of which there are many examples in the collections of the prophetic revelations. ii. 18-25 belongs to the later redaction.

iv. 1-11, introduced by 'hear', the formula of address, and iv. 12-19 are put together because of resemblances in their content. In iv. 10 it is said: 'They have forsaken Yahweh to practise harlotry,'[37] and in v. 12: 'A harlotrous spirit has led them astray, and in harlotry they have apostatized from their God.' The ideas of apostasy and harlotry connect these two revelations with the story of Hosea's marriage in i-iii.

---

[34] See above, pp. 165 ff.
[35] It contains ideas characteristic of the exilic and post-exilic time. Israel will one day in the future 'go up' (as once she went from Egypt) to the holy land, min hā'āreṣ probably meaning: from the whole earth, wherever they had been dispersed (cf. Jer. iii. 18; Ezek. xxxvii. 21 f.). The redactor here shows himself to be a prophetic personality, effectively completing the words of Hosea, taking up ideas of a later time, but using Hoseanic terms.
[36] For the following cf. my book Hosea literarisch untersucht.
[37] Cf. BH.

v. 1-14 is in form ('hear' *v.* 1) and substance (the priests *v.* 1, adultery *vv.* 4 and 7) closely cognate with the preceding discourses. v. 8-14 is dominated by the idea of judgement upon Ephraim just as was the preceding speech.[38] v. 15-vi. 3 has several ideas in common with the foregoing: Yahweh's 'going forth' (v. 14 and v. 15), 'tearing' (v. 14 and vi. 1), 'healing' (v. 13 and vi. 1).

vi. 4-vii. 16 was regarded by the collector as Yahweh's answer to the preceding penitent speech of the people. viii. 2 (part of the following unit) refers to the crying of the people to God, as vii. 14. The catchword 'devour' (viii. 7 and viii. 8) links viii. 8-10 to viii. 1-7. The phrase: 'He will remember their guilt and punish their sins' (viii. 13 and ix. 9) connects ix. 1-9 with viii. 11-14.

As a conclusion to the collection of the revelations of Hosea a series of sayings follows from ix. 10 onwards which give a retrospect of the history of Israel from Egypt until the time of the prophet. There has been a continued religious and moral regress. At the end of xiii and the first verse of xiv the whole culminates impressively in a prediction of inevitable annihilation. This series is only interrupted in xi. 8 f. by a word of hope in accordance with the collectors' habit of placing here and there a prophecy of blessing after a prophecy of judgement.[39] xiv. 2 ff. is redactional.

This is a brief survey of the composition of the Book of Hosea. The collector did not arbitrarily bring together the various revelations; in general he followed certain principles. For the most part he tried to connect with each other passages of cognate content or those which had some ideas or expressions in common. Sometimes his arrangement was made on purely formal grounds.

The collector was not Hosea himself, but a disciple of his. Only some person other than the prophet would have brought together doublets such as the two stories of the marriage of Hosea. Further, in the Book of Hosea there are no traces of a chronological order (apart from the account of the prophet's marriage, which belonged to the beginning of Hosea's prophetic career). To arrange the different passages on the principles mentioned above was only natural to a man of a later generation. The prophet himself or a disciple of the first generation would surely have arranged the revelations differently.

There are no positive grounds for assuming that earlier and shorter

---

[38] For the historical background of this passage, which I regard as a unit, see Alt, *Kleine Schriften zur Geschichte des Volkes Israel*, II, pp. 163 ff. The words about Judah are here original, motivated as they are by the historical situation.

[39] xi. 10-11 presupposes the exile and is an insertion by the redactor of the Book of Hosea.

written collections existed before the present book. There is also in the book nothing which precludes the assumption that individual revelations and episodes were orally transmitted from the beginning and were written down only when they had been collected. Perhaps some of the Hoseanic revelations had already been combined in oral tradition. The use of catch-words tells in favour of this surmise. Catch-words were originally a mnemonic device and they could continue to serve as such after the material had been written, when written and oral tradition existed side by side.

Isaiah. The collection of the Isaianic revelations is to be found in chapters i-xxxv of the present Book of Isaiah. The history of this collection differs considerably from that of the Books of Amos and Hosea. All critical scholars agree in regarding xxiv-xxvii as relatively late, certainly as post-exilic. Thus there must have existed a collection of Isaianic oracles comprising i-xxiii, to which xxiv-xxvii was joined not earlier than the fifth century B.C. Curiously enough, to this section another group of prophetic sayings has been added, which, apart from several late poems, contains a good deal of authentic Isaianic material (xxviii-xxxv). The problem of the larger sections xl-lv and lvi-lxvi of the present Book of Isaiah can best be dealt with below when we consider the formation of the Book of Isaiah. Our present concern is the process by which i-xxxv came into existence.

The first question to be answered is: did smaller, independent collections of Isaianic revelations exist before the present collection came into existence?

Most scholars agree that there was once an independent collection which began with vi. A narrative of the call of a prophet is, of course, more fitted to introduce a collection than to appear unexpectedly in the middle of one. The question is how much of what now follows belonged to this collection. In my view there was a 'collection of the first order' comprising vi. 1-ix. 6.

The collector of this section was particularly interested in Isaianic oracles related to the varied events during the Syro-Ephraimitic war. The chief themes of these oracles are the collapse of the kingdoms of Syria and North Israel, the birth of Immanuel, and the future devastation of the kingdom of Judah by the armies of Assyria. The collector obviously lived some time after the events. The order of the different oracles is rather confused. For this reason the section in question has always presented problems to Biblical scholars.

The placing of the narrative of the call of Isaiah at the head of the collection needs no explanation. If this collection was the first one, it was quite natural to let it begin with the call. Moreover, the destruction of the land of Judah, which plays so great a part in what follows, was already predicted in the story of the call. This story, told as it is in the first person, had been communicated by the prophet himself to his disciples. Of the following oracles, introduced with short historical notices, sometimes given in the first person, sometimes in the third person, several are direct communications from the prophet, others are free reproductions of oracles handed down in tradition.

The first saying of Isaiah recorded by the collector begins with a free reproduction in prose of an address to King Ahaz, containing an exhortation not to fear the two hostile kings of Ephraim and Syria.[40] It culminates in an utterance in typical oracle style: 'It shall not stand, and it shall not come to pass,' etc. To this oracle is linked the dialogue concerning the famous sign, connected with what precedes by the phrase: 'And Yahweh [or possibly Isaiah] continued speaking.' It is impossible to repeat here all the different opinions concerning the sign, the *'almâh*, and the person of Immanuel.[41] The views of the present writer on these problems may be briefly expressed as follows.[41a] The Hebrew word *'ôṭ* has a double meaning: sign in the usual sense of the word and miracle or wonder as a token of Yahweh's omnipotence. In *v.* 11 the word is taken in the first sense, in *v.* 14 in the second. Such a play on words is not uncommon in the prophetic style. Not only Immanuel himself, but all that will happen in connection with his birth, is the *'ôṭ* foretold by Isaiah.[42] The point of what Isaiah said is that with the birth of Immanuel a new prosperous and blessed age will dawn, including the destruction of the two hostile kingdoms (the text in *v.* 16b being original, whereas the words of the king of Assyria at the end of

[40] In this connection I should like to draw attention to the very interesting article by Albright on Tabeel in Isa. vii. 6 in *BASOR*, 140, 1955, pp. 34 f.: Tab'el a land, not a person; the man in question a prince of Judah, whose maternal home was in the land of Tab'el in northern Palestine or southeastern Syria.—The warning of Isaiah in *v.* 4 Kraeling rightly refers in particular to Ahaz's planned surrender to the Assyrian king (2 Kings xvi. 7); *JBL*, l, 1931, pp. 277 ff.

[41] A survey of studies of the Immanuel passage is given by Stamm in *RTPh.*, N.S., xxxii, 1944, pp. 97 ff., and *VT*, iv, 1954, pp. 20 ff. See also Hammershaimb in *St.Th.*, iii, 1949, pp. 124 ff., and Coppens in *ALBO*, ser. II, fasc. 35, 1952. For earlier works see von Bulmerincq in *ACUT: B*, XXXVII, 1.

[41a] For details see Lindblom, *A Study on the Immanuel Section in Isaiah.*

[42] For the different significations of the word *'ôṭ* see the Inaugural Dissertation by Keller, *Das Wort OTH als 'Offenbarungszeichen Gottes'*. I cannot share Keller's view of the Immanuel prophecy in Isaiah, but the examples cited by him make it clear that the word *'ôṭ* in the Old Testament means a 'sign' in the strict sense, pointing to another event in life or history, but also a wonderful divine action which reveals the almighty God. After Ahaz had declined 'the sign' offered him by Isaiah, the prophet gave up *the sign* and foretold him a *wonder*, manifesting God's superiority to all human calculations. Of course, a *wonder* is always at the same time a *sign* as being a testimony to God's power.

v. 17 are an erroneous gloss). For the rest, my opinion is that the child is a royal child, the hoped-for first-born son of King Ahaz and the queen (Hezekiah?).[43] Recent investigations have shown that the expressions used by Isaiah must be conceived of as traditional formulas familiar to Isaiah, though certain points are still rather obscure.[44] When it is said in *v.* 17 that Yahweh will bring upon you, and upon your people, and upon your father's house such days as have not been since Ephraim parted from Judah, this clause must continue the thought of the preceding statement, with which it is asyndetically associated. A time of prosperity will come such as has not been seen during the long period from the partition of the Davidic kingdom until now.[45]

Then follow, unexpectedly, four short oracles on the devastation of the land of Judah: 18 f.; 20; 21 f.; 23-25.[46] They are introduced by the connecting phrase: 'And it shall come to pass in that day,' or the like. Their position here is to be attributed to the collector. They have nothing to do with the scene depicted in *vv.* 3-17. When did Isaiah utter these oracles? I think that it was after it had become clear to him that Ahaz and his people did not trust in Yahweh, the God of Israel, i.e., after the events recorded in 2 Kings xvi. 7 ff., when Ahaz, forsaking the mighty God of Israel, had begun to seek the assistance of the

---

[43] As to the meaning of the word *'almâh* I agree with Köhler's explanation in *Lexicon* and *ZAW*, lxvii, 1955, p. 50: young woman until the birth of her first child. For the chronology of this period, esp. the reigns of Ahaz and Hezekiah, see Ricciotti in *The History of Israel*, I, pp. 370 f.

[44] For the most recent publications concerning the cultic problems connected with this section see Stamm in *VT*, iv. See further Mowinckel, *He that Cometh*, pp. 110 ff. On the essential points I agree with Mowinckel. The cultic stamp of the whole section vi. 1-ix. 6 is stressed by Vischer in *Th.St.*, 45, 1955. Vischer here assembles a series of allusions to the cultic texts belonging to the Zion Festival (according to Kraus's hypothesis which Vischer adopts). For the expression 'the young woman shall bear a son' reference is often made to a similar phrase in the Ugaritic text Nikkal and the Kathirat: 'Lo! a lass shall bear a son' (Driver, *Canaanite Myths and Legends*, p. 125). The relationship between this exclamation and Isa. vii. 14 has, however, not yet been clearly demonstrated by any scholar who has dealt with this question. The phrase, to which there are several analogies in other Ugaritic texts, could equally well belong to everyday language; cf. Gen. xvi. 11; Judges xiii. 3; 2 Kings iv. 16; Job iii. 3; Jer. xx. 15; Ruth iv. 17. See also Granqvist, *Birth and Childhood among the Arabs*, pp. 38, 76 ff.—Junker in an article in *SVT*, IV, 1957, pp. 181 ff. (reprinted in *Trierer theologische Zeitschrift*, lxvi, 1957, pp. 193 ff.), emphasizes that the basis of Isaiah's belief in a blessed future was the promise of an eternal kingdom given to David (2 Sam. vii. 16), for which reason the prophet sought to persuade the king not to surrender to the Assyrian king. Thus this scholar maintains the Messianic interpretation of Immanuel in a traditional sense. But Immanuel could equally well be a son of Ahaz, though partly described in Messianic terms.

[45] On this as on several other essential points I agree with the views of Hammershaimb in his article mentioned above.

[46] The oracle in *vv.* 21 f. contains a mixture of prophecy of judgement and prophecy of bliss. An original oracle on the future devastation of the land has been transformed in late tradition to express the idea of 'the remnant' and its conditions after the catastrophe.

Assyrian king. Probably the collector put these oracles here because he understood the statement that Yahweh will bring upon Judah such days as have not come since Ephraim parted from Judah, as a prediction of misfortune (as did the glossator at the end of *v.* 17).[47]

The episode of 'Maher-shalal-hash-baz' viii. 1-4, related in the first person, is not connected with what precedes it, but belongs in substance to the episode of Immanuel. In viii. 5 ff. we are confronted again with the idea of the Assyrian assault (cf. vii. 18-25). The oracle is also communicated in the first person and is linked to the preceding passage by the phrase: 'And Yahweh continued speaking.' The failure to trust in the God of Israel is here conveyed by the expression that the people of Judah has spurned the waters of Shiloah.[48] The oracle on the miscarriage of the assault of the peoples in *vv.* 9 f. probably expresses Isaiah's conviction that the northern kingdoms will perish.[48a] The term 'Immanuel' in *vv.* 8 and 10 connects the two oracles with each other.

In the next passage (joined to the foregoing by the connective *kî*) Isaiah tells of an ecstatic experience in which an oracle was given him, the content of which was an exhortation to him and his disciples not to fear the alliance of the northern kingdoms, but only to keep to Yahweh.[49] The oracle is from the beginning of the Syro-Ephraimitic war. In substance it is closely akin to the address to Ahaz about the necessity of faith in ch. vii.

Without any connecting word at all an utterance follows in which Isaiah in the form of a 'prophetic confession' gives an account of his conduct at a time of darkness and severe distress. He withdraws from the public and retreats to the narrow circle of his disciples for their instruction and guidance, himself in stillness waiting for Yahweh. This utterance issues in a gloomy prophecy of a future catastrophe. The passage ends with *v.* 22. I think that it is from the dark and frightening days after the surrender of Ahaz to the Assyrian king, when it was clear

---

[47] I think that all the four oracles deal with the devastation of Judah. If these oracles are definitely separated from the foregoing, there is no reason for thinking here of the devastation of North Israel by the armies of Assyria (against Hammershaimb).

[48] In viii. 6 *mᵉśôś* does not give any acceptable sense. With Procksch and Kissane I read *ûmāsôś*, but think, unlike them, that it introduces the apodosis to the preceding causal clause. The inf. abs. stands instead of a finite verb. I translate: 'Because this people spurns the waters of Shiloah, that flow gently, it shall surely dissolve [observe the word-play with *mā'as*, 6a] together with Rezin and the son of Remalyahu.' Isaiah says that the people of Judah will share the fate of the enemies in the northern kingdoms and be consumed by the Assyrians.

[48a] On this point I agree with the explanation by Bentzen in his commentary on Isaiah.

[49] For the text in viii. 11-15 see, *inter alia*, the interesting suggestions by Driver in *JTS*, New Series, vi, 1955, pp. 82 ff.

to Isaiah that the end of his people, Judah and North Israel alike, was near.[50]

viii. 23 is a connecting link betweeen the preceding prophecy and the poem in ix. 1-6. It derives from the collector, who thought wrongly that the following poem was a prophecy of the restoration of the northern districts of Israel, which had been conquered and devastated by Tiglath-pileser III in the year 733 (cf. 2 Kings xv. 29). The poem itself, however, is concerned with other matters, namely the birth of Immanuel and the beginning of a time of good fortune for Judah under the government of this wonder-king.[51]

This poem ends the first collection of Isaianic oracles, one of the features of which is the absence of a strict chronological order. Connective words are often lacking, but now and then they are inserted. Of special interest is the collector's attempt to provide a historical situation for the poem in ix. 1 ff. We may also note the alternation of the first person and the third person style, which the collector has preserved.

The rubric in ii. 1 indicates the beginning of another collection. It ends in v. 30. Originally the first unit in this collection was ii. 6-9, the prophecy about the mountain of Yahweh's house being an insertion by the redactor of the book.[52] The second passage, ii. 10-21, is linked to the foregoing by the motif of the humiliating of the proud men. To the series of oracles of judgement in iii a prophecy of the holy remnant is

---

[50] For the expression 'the house of Jacob' (v. 17) see Danell, *Studies in the Name of Israel*, p. 183. For the context in vv. 16-22 see above, pp. 161 f.

[51] Alt in *Kleine Schriften*, II, pp. 206 ff., explains v. 23 in another way. His 'territorial-geschichtliche' comments on the passage are of special importance. As regards poem itself, I think (against Alt) that the prophet composed it immediately after the birth of the royal child (vii. 17). As the tenses show (particularly in v. 5) the poem refers to something that has already happened, not to a happening in the future. See further my article about the eschatology of the prophets in *St.Th.*, vi, 1952, pp. 79 ff. (esp. p. 103), and Ringgren in *ZAW*, lxiv, 1952, pp. 120 ff. (esp. pp. 132 f.). The joyful proclamation of the birth of a male child was usual in the ancient Orient, as it still is. Cf. Jer. xx. 15; Job iii. 3, and several instances in the Ugaritic texts. See also Granqvist, *Birth and Childhood*, pp. 76 ff. Margaret Crook, *JBL*, lxviii, 1949, pp. 213 ff., rightly suggests that this poem has something to do with a royal ritual. For the rest it is difficult to accept her hypotheses.

[52] It may not be objected that *kî* (v. 6) cannot introduce a new section, for this *kî* was inserted by the redactor to connect ii. 6 ff. with the foregoing oracle.—As regards the prophecy about the mountain of Yahweh the following ought to be said. The fact that this prophecy with slight variations also occurs among the revelations of Micah makes it very probable that it is an anonymous oracle which two redactors incorporated in the books of Isaiah and Micah. It is a fact that such unattached oracles were always in circulation. The idea of the conversion of the Gentiles here clearly expressed makes it evident that the oracle is by a prophet who had been influenced by Deutero-Isaiah (see below, pp. 400 ff.). Wildberger in *VT*, vii, 1957, pp. 62 ff., tries to vindicate the probable Isaianic origin of the oracle by pointing to certain similarities in form and substance between the oracle and the cultic 'Zion hymns' which must have been familiar to Isaiah. But he underestimates the importance of the presence in the oracle of the Deutero-Isaianic idea of the whole-hearted conversion of the Gentiles.

joined in iv.[53] The collection ends with some predictions of judgement in v. The section xiii-xxiii includes an independent collection of 'massa'-oracles against various nations. This series of 'massa'-oracles is here and there interrupted by passages of varied character, some of which are Isaianic, others of later origin. The authentic sayings have been extensively modified.

There are no certain traces of other collections of the first order in the earliest form of the Book of Isaiah. A second collector had the above collections at his disposal, probably in written form; he inserted in them and added to them many other original sayings, transmitted to him orally or, in some cases, in the form of written documents (cf. the notice in xxx. 8). He often linked them together because of similar ideas and terms.

Very impressively he placed at the opening of his collection a revelation (i. 2-9) beginning with the significant words: 'Hear, O heavens, and give ear, O earth, for Yahweh speaks.' With this saying he associated another (i. 10-17, deriving from a quite different time) because of the common terms Sodom and Gomorrah (*vv.* 9 f.), followed by a series of sayings of cognate content. Catch-words and similar ideas served to make oral recitation easy. After the section vi-ix. 6, from the time of the Syro-Ephraimitic war, he placed appropriately the refrain poem ix. 7-x. 4 (partly a doublet to v. 8-25),[54] referring mainly to the northern kingdom,[55] to which another 'woe' (against Assyria) is joined, x. 5 ff. xi-xii derive from a later time and are inserted by the redactor of the book (see below). The same holds good of xxiv-xxvii, xxxvi-xxxix, and some parts of xxviii-xxxv. To the work of the redactor of the Isaianic book in its different stages we shall return later on.

Micah. The Book of Micah is a very interesting specimen of how a prophetic book came into existence.

After a short superscription[56] the collector placed at the head of the collection an oracle, the beginning of which made it an appropriate introduction to the whole collection: 'Hear, O peoples, all of you!' whereupon follows an impressive description of a theophany. To the oracle of judgement upon Samaria there is linked an oracle against

---

[53] There is no good reason for denying the essential authenticity of iv. 2-6. What seems not original is due to later remoulding. The placing of the prophecy is in accordance with the usual tendency to place prophecies of happiness after prophecies of judgement.

[54] For this poem and the doublet in v see above, pp. 225 f.

[55] Cf. Danell, op. cit., pp. 172 f.

[56] The superscriptions to the prophetic books have for the most part been enlarged by the redactors. The original superscription to Micah was probably: 'Yahweh's word which came to Micah, the Morashtite', or similar.

Jerusalem (i. 8 ff.). Doubtless the collector thought it fitting that the two capitals should be mentioned side by side.[57]

The woe-speech, ii. 1-5, gives the reasons for the judgement,[58] as does the following utterance, ii. 6-11. The description of social oppression in the country is common to both (vv. 2 and 8).[59] iii. 1-4 also deals with social wrongs, for which high officials are denounced. In iii. 5-8 the false prophets are included in the denunciation. The last speech in iii. comprising vv. 9-12, refers to both officials and prophets.

The next authentic revelation from Micah is iv. 9-10a (to *ûḇā'ṯ*) +14 (iv. 1-8 being redactional). Thus, in the original collection, iv. 9-10a+14 was immediately connected with iii. 12. The passage iv. 9-10a+14 belongs to a time when Jerusalem was besieged. The fatal hour for Jerusalem has come. In iii. 12 the catastrophe is predicted: 'Zion shall be ploughed like a field, and Jerusalem shall become a ruin, and the temple mountain a wooded hill.'[60]

Of the authentic Micah corpus three revelations still remain: vi. 1-8, vi. 9-16, and vii. 1-4. It is impossible to discover a logical connection between vi. 1-8 and the passage ending with iv. 14, which originally preceded it. Such a connection is lacking also between the three last revelations. The last three units of the Micah corpus give an impression of having been brought together fortuitously. But at least it may be said that the last woe-speech with its consistently pessimistic view of the moral situation in Judah and its closing prediction of future judgement is an appropriate conclusion to the whole collection.

Consequently the original Micah corpus consisted of two parts. The first part comprised the authentic passages of i-iv; the second part consisted of vi. 1-vii. 4. Because of the inner continuity of the first part, the lack of coherence in the second part, and the lack of connection between the two, we must assume that the collection of the revelations of Micah took place in two stages. First the revelations contained in the first part were collected and written down; then the three revelations of the second part were added as *revelationes extravagantes*.

---

[57] For the idea of world judgement in i. 2 see Lindblom, *Micha literarisch untersucht*, pp. 21 ff. For my views on other points in the Book of Micah reference may be made to this work.

[58] On this passage see Alt in the *Mowinckel Festschrift*, pp. 13 ff.

[59] The exilic or post-exilic passage ii. 12 f., like other passages of the same kind, is dealt with below in connection with the analysis of the redactional work.

[60] In my opinion iv. 11-13, like iv. 9 ff., refers to the siege of Jerusalem in 701. But the content of iv. 11-13 shows that it does not come from Micah. It was composed by a nationalistic prophet. There were always at work in Jerusalem, particularly amongst the cultic prophets at the temple, prophets of national wellbeing, and it was to these circles that he belonged. It is interesting to observe that the collector of Micah's revelations on occasion incorporated with them a passage of such alien origin. See further *Micha literarisch untersucht*, pp. 91 ff.

In the book of Micah there is no chronological order; individual revelations are connected because they contain similar ideas. Sometimes there is no clear connection at all.

Zephaniah. A series of short oracles of judgement introduces the collection of the revelations of Zephaniah, comprising *vv.* 2-13 of the first chapter of the present book. Some scholars are of the opinion that the idea of world judgement is secondary in Zephaniah. But if Isaiah could speak of a world judgement, ii. 10 ff. (which few Biblical scholars are disposed to doubt), there are no reasons for eliminating this idea from the thought-world of his disciple.[61] The series may be divided in the following way: 2 f.; 4-6; 7-9; 10 f.; 12 f. The first oracle (on world judgement) is placed at the head of the whole collection as an impressive introduction. It gives at once an appropriate background for the following oracles of judgement on the inhabitants of Jerusalem: the worshippers of pagan gods, the high-born courtiers who indulged in foreign customs, the covetous tradesmen, the prosperous, self-confident, and unsuspecting citizens. The oracles are closely akin to each other in content. Formulas referring to 'Yahweh's day' are used to connect them.

The exhortation in ii. 1 ff. is well motivated by the repeated description of Yahweh's day in i. 14 ff.[62]

The series of oracles against foreign nations, introduced by a connective *kî* (ii. 4-15), is a prophetic composition modelled on earlier compositions. It seems that at one time it ended an independent collection of Zephaniah oracles. What follows consists of a conglomeration of utterances of varying content. There is first a woe-speech addressed to the leaders of Judah, iii. 1-5, a parallel to the oracles in ch. i. Then comes another oracle of doom, *vv.* 6-8. As a conclusion to the original corpus there follow some oracles on the age to come, of which one at least is authentic, *vv.* 11-13 (notice the Isaianic idea of 'the remnant of Israel').

Accordingly, in the collection of the revelations of Zephaniah we have to allow for two stages. The first is represented by i-ii, to which another collector probably added some *revelationes extravagantes,*

---

[61] See Gerleman, *Zephanja textkritisch und literarisch untersucht.* Cf. also my article in *St.Th.*, vi, 1952, p. 92. Elliger in *ATD* suggests that in *vv.* 2-3 a redactor has enlarged an original saying of Zephaniah in an eschatological direction. In my book, *Profetismen i Israel,* I expressed the opinion (referring to Cossmann, *Die Entwicklung des Gerichtsgedankens bei den alttestamentlichen Propheten*) that the universal judgement in Zephaniah was a fanciful poetical overture to the judgement upon Judah and Jerusalem rather than a real eschatological prediction (p. 487).

[62] Exegetically this passage is very obscure. See Gerleman, op. cit., and Elliger in *ATD.*

unknown to the first collector. A few unauthentic words have been added by the redactor of the book.

Nahum. The corpus of authentic revelations in Nahum is the section i. 12-iii. 19, which may be analysed into seven oracles or prophetic poems of varying types: i. 12 f.; i. 14; ii. 1; ii. 2-14; iii. 1-7; iii. 8-17; iii. 18 f. These were brought together by a collector on grounds partly of chronology and partly of content. The first three utterances are oracles on the ruin of the Assyrian empire, probably deriving from the time after the death of Assurbanipal (626 B.C.), an event to which ii. 1b also manifestly alludes: 'Never again will the wicked pass through you.'[63] The following four poems are dominated by the same theme. They depict the ruin of Nineveh expected in the immediate future. They were composed shortly before 612.

The poem with which the book opens presents many literary and textual problems. It looks like a hymn of a liturgical character with rather conventional phraseology. It describes the power of Yahweh, the dreadful avenger and the merciful helper. The hymn ends with an allusion to Nineveh and its evil king.

It is not probable that this hymn was composed by Nahum. The best solution of the literary problem is that it was added to the collection of Nahum's revelations to adapt it to cultic usage.

If I am right in my analysis, the Book of Nahum is based on a homogeneous collection of the revelations of this prophet, who presumably belonged to the cultic staff of the temple in Jerusalem.[64] A redactor who added the introductory poem made the collection more suitable for liturgical purposes.

Habakkuk. The main literary problem of the Book of Habakkuk is: did the different units of which it is composed exist as independent units, or were they originally combined with each other?

The first unit, i. 2-4, is clearly in the form of a psalm of lamentation. In the psalm itself the usual motif of confidence, or the oracle of consolation, is missing; but it appears in i. 5 ff. On that account it must be assumed that the two units were combined from the very beginning. i. 12-17 contains a complaint about the iniquity of a foreign conqueror and is entirely incomprehensible as an independent composition. Clearly it must be closely connected with the previous description of a

---

[63] So Elliger, op. cit. This scholar rightly rejects the conception of the Book of Nahum as a liturgy used at the New Year Festival in 612 (Humbert, Sellin). 'Es liegt vielmehr echte Prophetie vor' (see 'Einleitung'). Similarly Eissfeldt, *Einleitung.*

[64] So rightly Haldar, *Studies in the Book of Nahum*, p. 6. Haldar, nevertheless, greatly exaggerates the extent of cultic influence upon the style and the diction of the book. This scholar also rejects the view that the book is a liturgy.

hostile nation. The same is true of ii. 4-20 with its introduction ii. 1-3
As to the psalm in iii one can be doubtful. But in *v.* 16b the hostile
nation described earlier is mentioned again. Thus it becomes evident
that this passage, too, is organically connected with the other parts of
the book.[65]

The line of thought in the Book of Habakkuk is as follows: A lamentation over the wrongdoing, strife, and violence, within the prophet's
own people (i. 2-4)[66] is answered by a divine declaration that a nation is
about to arise which Yahweh has appointed to chastise the corrupt
Jewish people (i. 5-11). But this nation is ruthless and tyrannous, and
mercilessly slays innocent peoples (i. 13). In face of its unbridled reck-
lessness and cruelty the prophet prays that his own people may be saved
and that the foreign conqueror may be crushed because of his arrogance
(i. 12-17). The passages which follow contain predictions of the ruin of
the dreadful enemy. The whole is rounded off by a thanksgiving hymn
in mythological-cultic style (iii).

Undeniably there is a logical sequence in the Book of Habakkuk, and
a clear coherence between the different units can easily be discovered.
It is not surprising that several scholars have seen in this book a liturgy
which was actually performed on a specific occasion in the temple at
Jerusalem.[67] There is, indeed, much to be said for this view. If it is
adopted, the Book of Habakkuk belongs to the same literary category as
Isa. xxiv-xxvii, a liturgical composition (a 'cantata', as I have called it),
used on a certain occasion in Jerusalem.

Consequently the Book of Habakkuk is not the work of a secondary
collector of prophetic revelations, but a composition by the prophet
himself, who was certainly a cultic prophet at the temple of Jerusalem.

As to the problem of the reckless conqueror I believe that the prophet

[65] This of course does not necessarily mean that Habakkuk himself was the original
author of the psalm. It looks rather like a cultic document which the prophet may
have borrowed and incorporated in his liturgy, adapting it to the actual situation. For
the psalm as a cultic document see Irwin in *JNES*, i, 1942, pp. 10 ff. Albright in
SOTP, pp. 1 ff., shows that the psalm contains very old material. See also Mowinckel
in *TZ*, ix, 1953, pp. 1 ff., who defends the unity of the psalm.

[66] The expressions used in this passage can of course refer to political matters, but
they are equally applicable to social corruption within the Jewish people; cf. Schmidt
in *ZAW*, lxii, 1950, pp. 52 ff., who understands the psalm as a lamentation of an
innocent person. In my view *v.* 12 means that Yahweh has raised up the foreign
power for the chastisement of His own people because of its sinfulness. In many
passages in Jeremiah, a contemporary of Habakkuk, the moral corruption of the
Jewish people at that time is described in similar terms: v. 1 ff.; v. 25 ff.; vi. 13 ff.;
vii. 3 ff.; ix. 1 ff., etc.

[67] Balla, Sellin, Humbert, Mowinckel, Engnell. Nielsen in *St.Th.* vi, 1952, pp. 54 ff.,
argues cogently that the book is a liturgical composition intended for cultic usage or
an imitation of one. He analyses carefully both the cultic elements and the concrete
historical allusions.

composed his work at the time of the Chaldean menace during the period following 612. He saw in the Chaldeans a nation appointed to chastise his own people; but he prays for his people, hoping that through faithful adherence to Yahweh they will save their life (ii. 4).[68]

Jeremiah. We are better informed about the origin of the Book of Jeremiah than about any other prophetic book. We know that a scribe, Baruch by name, by Jeremiah's command and at his dictation wrote out a collection of the prophet's revelations deriving from the time between 626 and 605 (xxxvi). This scroll was burnt and cannot, of course, be taken into consideration in an analysis of the Book of Jeremiah. Of the second scroll, produced after the destruction of the first, it is said that at Jeremiah's dictation Baruch wrote on it all the words of the first scroll and, in addition, many similar words.

It is reasonable to suppose that this scroll was preserved within the frame of the Book of Jeremiah; but, unfortunately, it has proved impossible to recover it from the present structure of the book. The fact is that the second scroll of Baruch *in its original form* has been lost. That its contents were used in part or in whole in the composition of the book is evident; but it is equally clear that it has been split up, so that we have to seek its various parts in different contexts. Attempts have been made, and may be made, to determine which passages belonged to the two scrolls of Baruch, but little agreement has been attained or can be attained on this point. Thus the analysis of the Book of Jeremiah must essentially follow the same lines as the analysis of other prophetic books.

Our main interest here must be to make clear how the collector worked and what he did with the material he had at his disposal: on the one hand the scroll written by Baruch, on the other material derived from elsewhere.

In ii-vi he has brought together, or preserved relatively intact, a series of sayings the theme of which is the apostasy of Israel against the background of its election and Yahweh's love to His people as shown in its history, and, as a consequence of this apostasy, the impending judgement. These revelations derive from the earliest period of Jeremiah's prophetic career, and nothing forbids us to assume that this is a fragment of the Baruch scroll in more or less unaltered form (passages such as iii. 14-18 and v. 18 f. are probably later insertions). The section has a

---

[68] The details in the description of the foreign nation should not be pressed. Such descriptions for the most part conform to a traditional pattern. Manifestly there are also many mythological traits; cf. Staerk in *ZAW*, li, 1933, pp. 1 ff.

special superscription and is followed by a section on a different theme with a superscription of its own.

Another literary complex is the section xxx. 1-xxxi. 26. It contains a series of oracles concerning the age to come. It was written down by Jeremiah by Yahweh's special command and used by the collector in its original form.[69]

Finally, a third collection contains the oracles on the pagan nations xlvi-xlix (later enlarged by various additions). The superscription clearly indicates an independent literary unit: 'What came as Yahweh's words to Jeremiah, the prophet, concerning the nations.'

Most of the remaining revelations contained in the Book of Jeremiah were derived from oral tradition, if they were not at the collector's disposal in the form of written documents, *inter alia* parts of the Baruch scroll. But it is usually impossible to decide whether a revelation was orally transmitted or in writing.

Some scholars are of the opinion that there was a written 'source' whose author belonged to the 'Deuteronomistic school' and in which the superscriptions differed from those in the Jeremianic book ('The word that came to Jeremiah from Yahweh'). As has been said above, the present author cannot agree with these scholars.[70] Not all the passages in question have a 'Deuteronomistic' stamp. They are fairly varied in their content; and there are some doublets. The 'typical' superscription is not regularly used. The passages belonging to the supposed 'Deuteronomistic source' must be dealt with as separate individual revelations. The undeniably 'Deuteronomistic' stamp may be explained on the assumption that the transmitter of these utterances was influenced more than others by the style of the cultic sermons delivered by the cult prophets in the temple at Jerusalem. This influence is reflected in the way in which he has reproduced the sayings of his master.

At the head of the corpus of the revelations of Jeremiah the collector appropriately placed the narratives of the call and the visions of the twig of an almond tree and the cauldron which are connected with the call. These narratives are based on Jeremiah's own communications as preserved in tradition. The position of the first primary collection, ii-vi, immediately after the narrative of the call is due to the fact that its content belonged to the early part of Jeremiah's career.

The temple sermon, vii. 1-15, with its main theme, apostasy and judgement, continues the line of thought of the previous collection.

---

[69] The notice in xxxi. 26 refers to the end of the inspired state of mind in which the preceding revelation was composed by Jeremiah (see above, p. 180). It marks the end of the section in question.

[70] For the problem of written sources in Jeremiah see above, p. 238.

Chronological considerations are entirely disregarded, this temple sermon having been delivered at the beginning of the reign of King Jehoiakim (cf. xxvi. 1). It was transmitted by the man who, as mentioned above, had been influenced by the (Deuteronomistically coloured) cultic style and diction. The temple sermon is followed by a series of Yahweh words, all presenting variations on the same theme: illegitimate cult and terrible punishment.

A new section opens at viii. 4 and extends to x. 25. It begins: 'You shall say to them.' The different sayings deal with apostasy from various points of view. There is a prediction of dire judgement followed by a moving series of laments. Most of the sayings are words of Jeremiah in almost their original form. There are also some passages which look like free reproductions. The satire on idolatry, x. 2-16, has been interpolated by the redactor of the book.

xi. 1-17. Israel has broken the Sinai covenant and worshipped the Baal. The doublets 1-5 and 6-8 are to be noted. The second passage is less Deuteronomistic than the first and comes from a different traditionist. *Vv.* 15-17 come nearer to the original words of Jeremiah.

xi. 18-xii. 6: The martyrdom of Jeremiah as a consequence of his message of denunciation. Personal problems evoked by his sufferings. This section is based on direct communications by Jeremiah.[71]

xii. 7-13: Yahweh's complaint about His chosen people, a parallel to the previous complaint of Jeremiah (14-17 inserted by the redactor).

xiii. To Yahweh's complaint of the devastation of the land of Judah are linked some oracles on the deportation of the people. The connection between the units is rather loose. In the narrative of the loin-cloth Jeremiah himself is the speaker.—xiv. 1-xv. 4: a composition by the collector dealing with the great drought, partly based on Jeremiah's own words.—xv. 5-9: a description of a catastrophe associated with the above because of similarity of subject. Notice the connective particle *ki* in *v.* 5.—xv. 10-21: personal problems, connected with the prohibition of praying in the previous passage.[71a]—xvi. 1-13: further personal experiences. 10-13 has a clear cultic-didactic stamp and must be ascribed to the transmitter of vii. 1-15; xi. 1-5, etc. The insertion of

---

[71] Transpositions proposed by commentators in this passage are not advisable. For instance, it was natural for the traditionist to take the words in xii. 4 as an element in the description of the wickedness of the impious previously mentioned. Literary transpositions of different passages in the prophetic literature are on the whole precarious if we accept the view of the growth of the prophetic books outlined above. Inconsistencies in tradition are not to be eliminated by textual operations.

[71a] 13 f. is manifestly a doublet of xvii. 3 f. Was it placed here by the collector because of the mention of iron and bronze in *v.* 12? If so the obscure passage was already in his time misunderstood.

14 f. (=xxiii. 7 f.) and 19-21 is due to the redactor of the book.—
xvii. 1-4 continues the picture of Judah's sinfulness and punishment.—
xvii. 12 f.: the high place of the sanctuary in Jerusalem opposite to
the sacred hills in the land of Judah (xvii. 2 f.). This quite natural
connection, with other evidence, shows that *vv.* 5-11 with their wisdom
sentences are secondary.—xvii. 14-18: further personal problems
which Jeremiah had to face in the fulfilment of his prophetic calling.
People doubted the fulfilment of Yahweh's words, i.e., the predictions
of the destruction of the nation. Thus Yahweh had become a terror to
the prophet.—xvii. 19-27. The sanctity of the sabbath must be respected;
if not Jerusalem will be burnt to the ground. The utterance ends
with a prediction of judgement like that of xvii. 18. The passage
on the sabbath is to be ascribed to the traditionist who had been
influenced by the cultic diction.—xviii. 1-12. In Jeremiah's account of
his visit to the potter the content of *vv.* 11 f. resembles that of xvii. 27.
The poem about Israel's unnatural apostasy (xviii. 13-17) links up with
the idea of Israel's refusal to repent (*v.* 12). Notice the connective
particle *lākēn*.—xviii. 18-23 tells of the consequences of the previous
utterance. In the account of the broken vessel (xix) two different
occurrences have been conflated in oral tradition: the symbolic action
with the earthenware vessel and the speech about Topheth. Here, once
more, we recognize the hand of the traditionist who was responsible for
vii. 3-15. This passage serves as an introduction to the following martyr
history of Jeremiah with its numerous episodes, its oracles addressed for
the most part to kings, and its 'confessions' concerning the prophet's
personal problems. The false prophets are classed with the corrupt
national leaders (xxiii. 9-32). The vision of the two baskets of figs in
xxiv is loosely joined to the oracles of judgement which it follows. The
speech about the figs deals with judgement, as does the following
passage (xxv. 1-11).

The series of episodes from Jeremiah's life story, which is for the
most part a martyr history, continues in the section xxvi-xlv. To these
personal episodes belong also the letters sent to the exiles (xxix. 1-23
and xxix. 24-32). Both letters are only free reproductions based on what
was remembered of the original letters. There are no convincing
grounds for the assumption that copies of the originals were preserved
and thus were at the disposal of the collector of Jeremiah's revelations.
Possibly Baruch, the scribe, communicated the contents. *Vv.* 16-19,
which contain a doublet of the narrative about the two baskets of figs
in xxiv, did not originally belong to the letter, it was placed here by the
collector to complete the words about the exiles with an oracle about

those who stayed in the homeland. The reason for the placing of the oracles about the Messianic restoration of Israel (xxx-xxxi) between the letters to the exiles and the story of the purchase of the family inheritance in xxxii is of course that all these sections are related to the promise of the age to come.[72] The oracle addressed to Zedekiah (xxxiv. 1-7) and the episode of the fidelity of the Rechabites (xxxv) were perhaps placed here following the Messianic revelations because of the promises given to the king on the one hand and to the Rechabite group on the other. The episode of the broken pledge to the slaves (xxxiv. 8-22) served the collector as an appropriate background for the narrative of the law-abiding Rechabites.

The following chapters xxxvi-xlv, introduced by the narrative of the burning of the scroll by King Jehoiakim, contain chronologically arranged episodes from the last years of Jeremiah's prophetic career.

The oracles against the pagan nations present a special problem of a complicated nature, to which reference has been made above (pp. 236 ff.), and to which we now revert to illustrate in greater detail the methods of the collector. It may be assumed that these oracles once formed an independent collection written on a scroll with its own superscription (xlvi. 1). This scroll is possibly referred to in xxv. 13, where it is said that Yahweh will bring upon the land of the Chaldeans all His words which are written in 'this book'. Possibly these words once stood at the end of the same book, perhaps in a more original form. That an oracle of judgement addressed to the Chaldeans might once have belonged to the series of oracles against the pagan nations is quite likely. Jeremiah thought that the exiles would be released after seventy years. A release of the captives could not, of course, occur without the downfall of the Babylonian empire. That Jeremiah really had the downfall of Babylon in view is proved by the story of the scroll thrown into the Euphrates (li. 59-64).[73]

The original collection of oracles against the nations has manifestly been to some extent disintegrated by the collector. He placed the prophecy that Babylon would fall in seventy years' time after xxv. 11, because of the reference to seventy years of exile. As to the vision of the cup of wrath and its interpretation in xxv. 15-38, I agree with those scholars who think that this passage (apart from later additions) once

---

[72] The series of oracles in the present ch. xxxiii is a composition produced in exilic and post-exilic Jeremianic circles. It is partly based on some authentic words of the prophet as handed down in tradition. For the details and the chronological problems see the commentaries.

[73] In *ZAW*, liii, 1935, pp. 209 ff., and liv, 1936, pp. 240 ff., Bardtke gives a thorough investigation of the prophecies against foreign peoples in Jeremiah, and maintains that Jeremiah had composed an oracle against Babylon which was later suppressed.

formed an introduction to the book against the nations. The collector placed it here as an appropriate sequel to xxv. 14 and also as an episode in the life of Jeremiah.

There is no generally accepted view about the original position of the collection of oracles against the nations. It seems to me very improbable that our collector would have interrupted the narrative of historical events which he had begun in xix and finished in xlv by inserting so lengthy a section on so different a theme. By placing the oracles against the nations at the end of his collection he preserved the logical arrangement of his material and, moreover, gave it its due effect.

The Book of Jeremiah must be treated in the same manner as the earlier prophetic books. It must be regarded as a collection of the Jeremianic revelations. Once again the literary problem is: How did the collector work? Then the question arises: What was the contribution of the final redactor of *the book*? To the latter question we return below.

The material that the collector had at his disposal consisted partly of some collections of the first order. Above all the scroll of Baruch, of which we probably have a coherent part in the section ii. 1–vi. 30, and then individual passages scattered about in the book, many of which can no longer be identified with certainty. Then comes the Messianic section in xxx–xxxi. 26. Finally the collector adopted and used the oracles against pagan nations which had already been put together to form a coherent series.

Most of his material, however, was derived from oral tradition. Possibly some individual passages were written on leaves. Of the letters sent to the exiles in xxix we probably have only free reproductions. Coherent written 'sources' of larger extent did not exist apart from those mentioned above. Instead of the 'Deuteronomistic source' which some scholars presuppose, we have to assume a traditionist influenced by the cult preaching in the temple at Jerusalem.

The collector generally arranged his material from the point of view of its content. For this reason he also disintegrated the Baruch scroll. At the beginning of the collection and in the historical narrative of the last period of Jeremiah's life (based at least in part upon information derived from Baruch) he followed a chronological order. Sometimes the connection of the different passages is very loose. Connective particles typical of the collectors (for instance *lākēn*) are to be found, but not frequently. The autobiographical and the biographical styles alternate. Very often we may detect communications made by Jeremiah himself. But often we have only free reproductions, in which it is not possible to distinguish between Jeremiah's own words and the words of the traditionists.

Ezekiel. The Book of Ezekiel is one of the most keenly debated parts of the Old Testament. It is impossible here to take up in detail the different problems connected with it. I can only state here summarily my own conclusions, with which many would no doubt disagree. On such complicated problems, differences of opinion are bound to exist.[74]

I am convinced that Ezekiel, like other prophets, spoke in public. This is evident from many passages in his book. From the very moment of his call the prophet knew that it was his vocation to speak to his people Yahweh's words, using the traditional oracle formula 'thus says Yahweh', whether they would listen or not (ii. 4, 7). After having eaten the scroll given him by the divine hand he had to go and speak to the house of Israel (iii. 1). Frequently the prophet is expressly commanded to speak words which came to him in the form of typical revelations. In this respect there is no essential difference between Ezekiel and other Israelite prophets. If, on occasion, the prophet wrote down revelations which he had received, that did not distinguish him from other prophets. He probably wrote more than Amos and even Isaiah, but the difference is only in degree.

The problem of the place where Ezekiel lived and worked as a prophet is a vexed one. Three possibilities come into consideration: in Babylonia, in Palestine, and in both countries. The most weighty reason for the thesis that the prophet worked exclusively or partly in Palestine is that many of his speeches seem to have been addressed to the inhabitants of Jerusalem and Judaea rather than to the exiles in Babylonia. The same is true of many of his symbolic actions. The conclusions drawn from this are, however, generally insecurely based. They depend on an inadequate conception of the nature of a revelatory speech. What

---

[74] For the different theories presented by Hölscher, Torrey, Berry, Smith, Messel, Herntrich, Herrmann, Harford, Allen, Irwin, Oesterley-Robinson, Bertholet, H. W. Robinson, Pfeiffer, and many others, and, in addition, for the view of other critical scholars who approximate to the traditional standpoint, see Fohrer, *Die Hauptprobleme des Buches Ezechiel* (cf. also Irwin in *VT*, iii, 1953, pp. 54 ff.). On essential points I agree with Fohrer's defence of Ezekiel's Babylonian ministry. I can also endorse the statement by Eissfeldt in the new edition of his *Einleitung* (p. 451): 'Was Zeit und Ort der Wirksamkeit des Propheten angeht, muss die Bemerkung genügen, dass wirklich durchschlagende Gründe gegen die Zuverlässigkeit der namentlich in der Datierung vieler Abschnitte des Buches zum Ausdruck kommenden Überlieferung, Hesekiel sei 593 im Exil zum Propheten berufen worden und habe dort als solcher bis 573 oder noch etwas länger gewirkt, nicht bestehen und dass alle an ihre Stelle gesetzten Hypothesen mit viel grösseren Schwierigkeiten belastet sind als sie.' Many strong arguments for the traditional view of the scene of Ezekiel's ministry are presented by Weir in *VT*, ii, 1952, pp. 97 ff.

is a revelatory speech? It is a speech based on a revelation given to the prophet in a mental state of high inspiration, or even ecstasy. From a religious point of view it can be said that what is given to the prophet comes from God; the psychologist says that it emerges from the prophet's own unconscious. At all events it comes in a compelling manner; it drives the prophet on to proclaim what he has received. The content of a revelatory speech was not necessarily addressed to those who were actually listening to the prophet when it was uttered. Usually, of course, it was addressed to the prophet's immediate audience, warning, censuring, exhorting, or encouraging them, according to the need of the moment. But the oracles against foreign nations, for instance, of which there are many, prove that what a prophet said might apply directly to those who were not present to hear it. The woe-speech against Samaria in Isa. xxviii was delivered by Isaiah in Jerusalem and not in Samaria. In the medieval visionary literature there are many examples of speeches addressed to personalities and peoples who lived at a distance.

The prophet could do nothing but proclaim the message which he had received. Thus he was to a great extent independent of his audience; and it does not follow that, because Ezekiel's words and actions applied to the inhabitants of Jerusalem rather than to the exiles in Babylonia, they must have been uttered in Palestine. It should also be noticed that the prophecies about Jerusalem and the Jews in Palestine were often also applicable to the exiles.

We must, moreover, allow for the possibility that some of Ezekiel's revelations were sent to Jerusalem and Judaea as messages from the exiled prophet. We know that there was a fairly lively intercourse between the *gôlâh* and the homeland. Jeremiah wrote letters to the exiles, and from the prophet Shemaiah letters came to Jerusalem (Jer. xxix). There are in the Book of Ezekiel some revelations which are more easily understood if they are taken as messages sent to the Jews in the homeland. I think in the first place of a passage such as xx. 1-32, a discourse containing a retrospect of Israel's history from Egypt to 'the present day', leading up to the declaration that Yahweh would not be inquired of by such a defiled and idolatrous people.[74a] It is reasonable to suppose that a deputation may have come from Jerusalem to seek an oracle from the well-known prophet. It is said that some elders of Israel came to inquire of Yahweh and sat down before the prophet. The occurrence was regarded as very important; the date of the arrival of the elders is precisely stated. A similar situation is described in viii. 1,

---

[74a] Note especially the mention of human sacrifices and idols in *v.* 31.

but there it is said that on a certain day some elders of Judah were sitting before Ezekiel. Presumably these elders belonged to the *gôlâh*. The extended allegory in xvi, which has much in common with the historical review in xx, could very well be a message sent to Jerusalem. The same is true of the discourses in xxii and xxiii. In all these passages the messages are not in their original form but in more or less free reproductions. Some other passages seem to belong to this group of messages sent to Jerusalem.

Most modern scholars are agreed as to the general literary character of the Book of Ezekiel. It is not a homogeneous work written by one hand. There are many traces of literary development of a complicated nature. For this reason numerous theories have been advanced about the 'authorship' and the composition of the book. On the one hand the material is clearly arranged. First we have a series of prophecies concerning the judgement on Jerusalem and the people of Israel. Then follows a section containing oracles on pagan nations. A third section contains predictions of the expected restoration ending with an extended sketch of the new temple and the cultic life in the restored community. On the other hand there are many inconsistencies in the book. It abounds in doublets and expansions of various kinds. There is a curious alternation of fine poetry and long prose discourses. There are, in short, many signs that the book has passed through many stages and many hands before it reached its present form.[75]

My own conclusion from the evidence is that the literary history of the Book of Ezekiel is substantially analogous to that of other prophetic books in the Old Testament. The only difference is that in this book the distance from the original sayings of the prophet is for the most part greater than in other prophetic books.

The difficulties connected with the literary growth of the Book of Ezekiel can be met only if we take into account the partly oral, partly scribal transmission of Ezekiel's revelations and narratives of episodes in his prophetic life. The process of transmission must have been a protracted one, so that many variants arose, as the numerous and divergent doublets indicate.

The collector played a decisive part in the composition of the book. He had abundant and varied material at his disposal. His task was to shape it into a tolerably coherent whole; and clearly he was reluctant to discard any item of importance. His mode of procedure can best be illustrated by examples.

Collections of the first order, such as we have observed in Isaiah and

[75] See Additional Note VI.

Jeremiah, are not to be found in the Book of Ezekiel. There are no superscriptions or conclusions indicating the beginning and the end of such collections. The dates which introduce several passages belong to the revelations which follow them, to which cognate sayings often have been added by the collector. The complexes which have been built up because of similarity in content are a result of the activity of the main collector. There are no traces of oral or scribal collections before him.[76] This is true also of the three long sections we have mentioned above. None of them ever existed as an independent whole. The same is in particular true of the prophecies about foreign nations in xxv-xxxii. They are not brought together under a common superscription and cannot be assigned to the same period or the same historical situation. Every individual passage once existed as an independent unit; and it is much more likely that they were combined by the main collector than in earlier oral or scribal tradition. What holds them together is only similarity of content, a feature which clearly affected the work of all the collectors of the prophetic books.

The sketch of the organization of the Jewish community with the temple as its centre in the age to come (xl-xlviii) is a tolerably coherent unit in the form of an ecstatic vision, in which, however, many disparate and even secondary elements are discernible. As we have seen above, this sketch originated in a real vision, but additions were later made, based on subsequent reflection. There are no good grounds for denying that *the main* substance may be attributed to Ezekiel. If I am right in holding that reflection continued what vision had begun, more can be so attributed than many scholars think. It is highly probable that the original revelation was immediately written down by the prophet himself or by a scribe (cf. xliii. 11). Accordingly xl-xlviii is not a 'collection' in the proper sense, but was used as a written document by the collector of Ezekiel's revelations and incorporated into his work as a fitting conclusion of it.[76a]

The following comments may be made on the collector's methods. The logical arrangement of the three main sections has already been noted. Clearly chronological considerations led to the placing of the

---

[76] I am at one with Birkeland (*Zum hebräischen Traditionswesen*) in recognizing the importance of oral tradition. Likewise I assume complexes, consisting of cognate material, but, unlike Birkeland, I ascribe most of them not to oral tradition but to the collector, who assembled them and wrote them down. Birkeland is right in maintaining that the complexes in a way go back to authentic utterances of the prophet, but that we cannot always distinguish between what is genuine and what is not. Like Birkeland, I hold that the final redaction took place at a relatively late time.

[76a] As to the traditio-historical problems of this section see Gese, *Der Verfassungsentwurf des Ezechiel*.

inaugural vision at the beginning. But first and foremost the collector was influenced by similarity of content. Thus the oracles and dirges concerning foreign peoples (xxv-xxxii), composed by Ezekiel according to an old tradition, were brought together although they belonged to different dates. The order in which they are arranged is a geographical one. They begin with the eastern and southern neighbours: Ammon, Moab, and Edom. Then the collector passes on to the Philistines in the west, and to Tyre and Sidon in the north. Finally comes the more distant land of Egypt.

iv-v contains a series of symbolic actions presenting the catastrophe which was to come upon Jerusalem, its people, and its king. Then follows an extended series of predictions of judgement because of the radical sinfulness of Israel.

The individual units in this section are often linked together by common ideas, sometimes also by significant catch-words. Often there is no clear connection. Connecting particles such as *lākēn* and *kî* are very common. Introductory phrases such as 'thus says Yahweh', 'Yahweh's word came to me', 'and you, son of man, prophesy', frequently mark the opening of a new saying. Many units are introduced by chronological details which are for the most part based upon reliable tradition.

As we have previously pointed out, doublets occur more frequently in the Book of Ezekiel than in other prophetic books. The existence of doublets reflects the varied forms in which the prophet's sayings and the narratives of his life were transmitted. The collector gathered up what was available and placed the different traditions according to the principles noted above.

Of a particular interest are passages in which the doublets are not put in different places but conflated. As we have seen, the introduction to the book is a good example of this. The much debated dates come from two different traditionists, one of whom, using the third person style, dated the inaugural vision in the fifth year of King Jehoiachin's exile, the other, using the first person style, added the year of the prophet's life. The collector was anxious to make use of both notices. Hence arose the somewhat curious dating at the beginning of the book.

The collector was still less successful in combining the two accounts of the cauldron in xxiv. One of them originally spoke of the boiling in the cauldron of bones and flesh, till all was spoiled. In the other Jerusalem was likened to a rusty cauldron that was overheated, so that it entirely melted down together with its rust. Originally two independent but parallel motifs were presented by the prophet. Then the motifs were put together by the collector into one symbolic action (or perhaps parable). The result was the confused account which appears in the present text.[77]

It is generally agreed that most of the sayings and sermons in the Book of Ezekiel are more like free reproductions and have been more extensively expanded than those of other prophets.[78] In explanation of this it has been suggested that the prophet himself rewrote his sayings, perhaps more than once, and even 'edited' his own work in different forms. To me it is very difficult indeed to imagine a prophet in ancient Israel working in this way like a modern writer. It seems far more probable that the literary character of the Book of Ezekiel is the work partly of those disciples of his who transmitted the revelations of their master, partly of the man who collected them and made of them a unified work, partly, in a measure, to the final redactor of the present book and interpolators of glosses at different periods.

The book has the formal appearance of having the prophet himself as its author. As a rule the prophet speaks, using the first person style. The individual oracles and sermons are presented as revelations given by Yahweh to the prophet; and the prophet reproduces them with phrases such as 'Yahweh's word came to me'. Of course this first person style may in certain cases be original; in particular this is the case where the text is based upon the prophet's own communications, such as descriptions of visions and other intimate and personal experiences. But in most cases the first person style is only formal and must be ascribed to the collector who sought to give the impression that his material was based upon the prophet's own communications. In this he was not entirely wrong; for it is in the nature of traditions of this kind that they ultimately go back to those who originally received the divine revelations. The original core around which the more discursive

[77] It is of course impossible to decide with absolute certainty the origin and character of this passage. Fohrer is of the opinion that the obscurity is due to textual corruption. He thinks that only one symbolic action in two parts is dealt with, the performance of which is obscured by the inserted interpretation (*Die Hauptprobleme*, pp. 35 f.). To me it seems more likely that the spoiling of the contents of the cauldron and the destruction of the cauldron itself are two different motifs, which were originally separate. Considering the way in which the collectors worked, I have suggested above that two traditions have been conflated; but it is of course possible that the combination had already been made in oral tradition. Whether the present account is based on two real symbolic actions (so, e.g., Steinmann in *LD*, 13) or two parables (notice the term *māšāl* in v. 3), it is difficult to say. There is also a third possibility: two allegorical visionary experiences, analogous to, e.g., that of the loin-cloth (Jer. xiii) and some of the night visions of Zechariah.

[78] A fine example of how a traditionist could remould a revelation is the detailed description of the tragic end of King Zedekiah in xii. 12 f. The real historical events were obviously in his mind when he reproduced the saying of the prophet about the deportation of the inhabitants of Jerusalem.

and reflective sayings are grouped can often be discerned. While the Book of Ezekiel may be said to bear more traces than other prophetic books of the activity of traditionists, we may nevertheless recognize that by their work they have given us a reliable account of Ezekiel's religious thought in its principal features.[79]

Deutero-Isaiah. Though the revelations presented in Isaiah xl-lv belong to a variety of literary genres, they are so similar in their general character that the process by which they were assembled is not difficult to discern. Significant ideas and various catch-words link them together. Introductory phrases seldom occur. But the oracle formula, 'thus says Yahweh', and the formula of appeal, 'hear', are both used. The occurrence of such formulas often makes it easy to define the individual units. *Gattungsforschung* is a valuable tool in the treatment of these chapters.[79a] As in other prophetic books, passages in which the subject matter is similar are linked together; but there are no collections of the first order.[80]

Subject matter suggests a division into two groups. One is dominated by the thought of the triumph and deliverance of Israel, vengeance on its enemies, its return, and its future glory. These may be called 'the triumphal revelations'. They culminate in the Cyrus oracles. In many of them the hope of deliverance is connected with actual historical events, above all with the person of Cyrus and his victories, whether the name of Cyrus is mentioned or not.[81] The other group deals with Israel's missionary task in relation to the Gentiles and culminates in the Ebed-Yahweh Songs.[82] The main themes of these revelations are the conversion of the Gentiles, Israel as an instrument of their salvation, and the preparation of Israel for the fulfilment of this task. These may be termed 'the missionary revelations'. These two groups probably

[79] My view of the Book of Ezekiel as presented above is in general agreement with that of Hempel briefly expressed in *Die althebräische Literatur*, p. 170 (cf. Bentzen in *Introduction*², II, p. 126). Hempel thinks that the sayings of Ezekiel circulated orally amongst the exiles and were then collected and completed by different hands. He speaks rightly of parallel reproductions of the same utterance which were piously preserved by the redactor. I would emphasize the early existence of written notes and documents and the significance of one main collector, who gathered together and wrote down material passed on to him by different bearers of tradition. A middle course is taken by Howie, *The Date and Composition of Ezekiel*: a dictation by Ezekiel comprising the first part of the book was written down. Then one or more disciples, starting from the written document, made a collection gathering other material from memory and records (p. 101).

[79a] See above all Begrich, *Studien zu Deuterojesaja*, and v. Waldow, *Anlass und Hintergrund der Verkündigung des Deuterojesaja*.

[80] For the following cf. the investigations in my book *The Servant Songs in Deutero-Isaiah*, the main contentions of which I still hold to be sound.

[81] For details see Lindblom, op. cit., esp. p. 65.

[82] The expression 'missionary' must not be misunderstood. 'Mission' means here that Israel is charged with the mission to enable the Gentiles to share in the eschatological salvation. The modern idea of mission is of course out of the question.

belong to different stages in Deutero-Isaiah's prophetic ministry. It seems that the watershed in his prophetic career was Cyrus's peaceful occupation and clement treatment of Babylon. That event certainly put an end to the prophet's expectation that Babylon would be totally destroyed and that the exiles would return in triumph to the homeland after vengeance had been wreaked on their enemies. None of these things really happened. The triumphal tone of the prophet must have died away, and thus the conditions were created for 'the missionary revelations' with their new ideas, their new view of Israel's historical situation and its mission in the world.[83]

However, these two groups of revelations, clearly distinguishable with regard to time and content, never existed as independent collections. Nor were they assembled together by the collector; they were spread throughout the whole book. Oracles from the one group were placed beside those from the other for reasons which are usually easy to recognize.

Since both 'the missionary revelations' and 'the triumphal revelations' are to be found in all parts of the book, the usual division of Deutero-Isaiah into two main sections, xl-xlviii and xlix-lv, must be abandoned. It is true that Cyrus is not expressly mentioned in xlix-lv, but the expected sequel of the Persian victory is several times alluded to also in the latter part.

The main literary problem in Deutero-Isaiah is connected with the Ebed-Yahweh Songs. If these Songs (xlii. 1-4; xlix. 1-6; l. 4-9; and liii. 2-12),[84] as many scholars hold, deal with an individual personality, conceived of as a 'Torah-teacher' or a saviour of his people in one sense or another, it would be impossible to explain why these Songs are placed where they now stand. The surmise that these Songs are a later insertion does not help much.[85] Nevertheless the question remains why

---

[83] See Additional Note VII.

[84] The usual delimitation of the fourth Song is lii. 13-liii. 12. For my delimitation see The Servant Songs, pp. 42 ff.

[85] Duhm was the first to argue that the Servant Songs had been inserted into the book of Deutero-Isaiah by a later hand. According to him their hero was a bright figure of the first, dark century of the post-exilic community. The theory that the Servant Songs are late interpolations has also been advanced more recently. In ZAW, lxvii, 1955, pp. 67 ff., Press argues that the Servant Songs were inserted into the book to correct the prophet's message. It is easier, says Press, to assume that a later hand has rectified the prophecies of Deutero-Isaiah than that he himself had contradicted his own former teaching. Press thinks that the Servant was a historic personality and also an eschatological figure. Mowinckel in He that Cometh, pp. 187 ff., thinks that the Servant Songs come from the circle of Deutero-Isaiah's disciples at a later time, and are best understood as a subsequent development, and, in part, modifications of the master's thought and message. Mowinckel emphasizes that the Songs must be explained as independent poems unrelated to the passages which precede and follow them. He holds that the Servant is an eschatological figure, but is linked

they occupy their present position. The matter assumes a different aspect if we admit that at least *the collector* of the Deutero-Isaianic revelations thought that the Ebed of the Songs referred to Israel in some sense. If this is true, it can easily be shown that these Songs have been appropriately placed among other poems concerning the people of Israel, the servant of Yahweh, its contemporary situation, and its prosperous future.[86]

It is of great importance to observe that the Servant Songs proper are closely connected with some passages which follow up the ideas expressed in the Songs. Thus xlii. 5-9 is closely connected with xlii. 1-4, xlix. 7 with xlix. 1-6, and l. 10-11 with l. 4-9. In the same way lii. 13-liii. 1 cannot be separated from liii. 2-12. If the Servant Songs proper are taken together with the passages which are closely akin to the Songs (together they may be called the Servant Oracles), the connection with the context becomes still more obvious.

What connects xlii. 1-9 with the preceding section is the thought that the pagan gods cannot foretell the important events of history, whereas Yahweh is able to declare new things before they spring forth. In addition there is a significant antithesis between the figure of Cyrus in xli. 25 and the figure of the Servant in xlii. 1 ff. The Song of praise in xlii. 10-12 is a very appropriate sequel to the declaration about the sublime task entrusted to Israel. The connection of the second Servant Oracle with what precedes is likewise quite clear. The common idea is the redemption and glorification of Israel as celebrated by the whole world. The theme of both *vv.* 1-7 and 8-21 is the antithesis of despondency and promise. In l. 2 f. the prophet speaks of Yahweh's power to save. This motif returns in l. 7 ff.: Yahweh helps me; near is my Vindicator. This

---

[86] In *The Servant Songs*, taking it for granted that xlix. 1-6 was a prophetic confession which originally dealt with an individual, I translated *v.* 3 in this way: 'And He said to me, "You, my servant, you are [i.e., symbolize] Israel, and through you I shall be glorified."' In accordance with my general view of the significance of tradition in the prophetic literature I now prefer to say that the word 'Israel' was not originally in the text at this point. It was inserted by a transmitter who, influenced by the words about Israel in *v.* 7, referred the Song to the people of Israel in some sense. Thus the problem of the word is not strictly a textual problem, but a traditio-historical one. If this is correct, we have plain evidence that the Servant Songs were early interpreted as bearing upon the people of Israel. Cf. the text of the Septuagint in xlii, 1.

---

with a definite person known to the prophetic author. Mowinckel underestimates the difficulty that on his view of the Servant and the Songs the placing of the Songs is quite inexplicable. It is true that the prophetic sayings must be treated as units; but it is equally true that the collectors generally combined them according to certain principles. The collector who placed the Songs where they now stand did not act at random; he realized what he was doing. If we assume that the Songs deal with Israel in one sense or another, their position in the collection is seen to be entirely appropriate. Who the Servant really was, or what he signified, in the thought of the first author is quite another thing. To this question we shall return in the last chapter of this book.

thought combines the third Servant Oracle with the foregoing. The connection of this oracle with the following passage is also quite clear. In li. 1 the prophet addresses 'those who pursue righteousness'; this expression is similar to the phrase 'whoever among you fears Yahweh' in l. 10. As to the fourth Servant Oracle it is noteworthy that the idea of the exaltation and glorification of the Servant and the revealing of Yahweh's arm upon him corresponds to the thought of the triumphal progress of the exiled Jews and the baring of God's holy arm in the sight of all nations, lii. 7-12.[87] The subsequent passage, liv. 1-10, manifestly embodies many ideas which allude to the foregoing Servant Oracle.

On the whole the collector of the revelations of the anonymous prophet of the exile followed the same principles and methods as the collectors of other prophetic books. How much of his material was available in written and how much in oral form, it is impossible to decide.

The rhetorical style which is characteristic of the Deutero-Isaianic revelations indicates that they were originally orally recited before an audience. Doubtless their *Sitz im Leben* was public days of national lamentation, gatherings in the synagogues, and private circles. A close study of the literary categories supports this view. Possibly the sayings were sometimes written down and circulated as fly-sheets among the exiles.[87a] There is nothing to suggest that the prophet himself put the book together. It gives the impression of being the work of a disciple, who was also a collector of the revelations of his master. In this respect the literary history of the Book of Deutero-Isaiah resembles that of other prophetic books.

Trito-Isaiah. In the post-exilic community numerous prophetic oracles and other sayings were current, deriving from different times and different prophetic personalities. A number of them were incorporated in books of well-known prophets. One particular group was collected and written down on a special scroll; and thus the anonymous book, now called Trito-Isaiah, came into existence.

The collection (which perhaps also contained individual sayings of an earlier date) was intended for reciting at cultic assemblies in the post-exilic community. There is much to suggest that the individual passages of which the collection consists were originally delivered orally

---

[87] For liii. 1 see *The Servant Songs*, pp. 39 f.

[87a] I am in full agreement with the opinion of v. Waldow that Deutero-Isaiah like other prophets was a speaker, not a writer. This scholar suggests the public days of lamentation as an appropriate *Sitz im Leben* for the Deutero-Isaianic utterances, especially for the oracles of bliss. On these solemn occasions Deutero-Isaiah functioned, says v. Waldow, as a sort of cult prophet. Curiously enough he takes no notice of the synagogues and the sabbath assemblies, which in all probability were in vogue in the exile.

in a cultic setting. The characteristic prophetic formulas 'thus says Yahweh' and 'utterance of Yahweh' are used. Once the speaker confesses that the spirit of Yahweh is upon him, that he has been anointed by Yahweh and sent by Him to announce good news (lxi. 1). He is conscious of having heard the divine command to speak aloud in public: 'Cry aloud, hold not back, lift up your voice like a trumpet' (lviii. 1). An oracle is communicated in which it is said that the prophetic spirit will never depart from the Jewish people (lix. 21).[88] In spite of all such points of contact with genuine prophecy, the impression remains that what we have here is imitation rather than revelation, reflection rather than vision.

Some of the sayings are in the form of typical cultic sermons containing historical surveys of past history, moral admonitions, and instruction in cultic affairs. There are also confessions of sin, psalms of lamentation and thanksgiving, such as may be ascribed to cult prophets.[88a] The whole section lxiii. 7-lxv. 25 has been explained as a typical liturgical composition. The prophetic character is evident from eschatological promises, announcements of judgement, and rebukes of different classes in the community. But these utterances are not the voice of genuine prophecy but that of epigoni. The reminiscences of older prophets are many; but there is a loss of power. Terms taken from earlier scriptures are sometimes given a different shade of meaning.

In this book the collector's method is the same as in other prophetic books. What links the different units together is similarity of subject matter and phraseology. Notice for instance the eschatological complex lx-lxii; the lamentations in lxiii. 7-lxiv. 11; the rebukes in lvi. 9-lvii. 13; the antithesis of righteousness and unrighteousness, judgement and salvation in lxv. 1-16 and lxvi. 1-4. Connecting words and particles are frequent: w^e (also in an adversative sense), $l\bar{a}\underline{k}\bar{e}n$, $k\hat{i}$, w^e'$\bar{a}mar$ (lvii. 14).

As an introduction to the whole collection the collector appropriately used a sermon containing some of the main ideas of the book and beginning thus: 'Thus says Yahweh, "Observe what is right and do righteousness, for my salvation is near at hand and my righteousness ready to be revealed." '

[88] The expression 'your seed and your seed's seed' as bearers of the prophetic gift indicates that the oracle refers to the people, not to an individual. But the nation itself is not considered as Yahweh's spokesman, 'like the inspired prophets' (so Kissane); the *berith*, the solemn assurance, implies that prophets endowed with Yahweh's spirit and words will never be lacking in Israel. The oracle is eschatological and is an appropriate sequel to the eschatological prophecy in the preceding verses.
[88a] Morgenstern in *HUCA*, xxiii, 1950-51, pp. 185 ff., sees in Isa. lxiii. 7-14 an original unit, a psalm of the same character as Ps. cvi, composed about 460 B.C. on the occasion of a tragedy which had befallen the Jewish people in the post-exilic period (see further *HUCA*, xxvii, 1956, pp. 101 ff.).

Because of the strongly varying content and level of the different passages it is not very probable that all the utterances contained in this book come from one single personality. Of course, some groups of sayings may plausibly be attributed to one and the same prophet. More than that cannot be said with certainty.[89]

Haggai. This book contains six oracles by the prophet Haggai. The first oracle is an exhortation to build a new temple dated on the first day of the sixth month of the second year of Darius, i. 1-11. The second oracle, 'I am with you', in i. 13 looks like a brief summary of a longer address. The third oracle is intended to encourage the people by a promise that the future splendour of the new temple will be greater than that of its predecessor. It is dated on the twenty-first day of the seventh month (of the second year of Darius), ii. 1-9. The fourth oracle, from the twenty-fourth day of the ninth month of the same year, is a warning against accepting from those who are unclean help in the building of the temple, ii. 10-14. The fifth oracle contains a promise of Messianic blessing. It was uttered at a time when stone had been laid upon stone in the new temple (ii. 15), i.e., when the building had begun and was in progress, ii. 15-19. The sixth oracle is dated on the same day as the fourth one. It is addressed to Zerubbabel and contains a solemn appointment of him to assume the office of a Messianic prince in the restored community, ii. 20-23.

Although elsewhere in the book there is no mention of events without an accompanying oracle, in i. 14 the statement that Zerubbabel and Joshua began work on Yahweh's house stands alone. In addition, the date in i. 15a is somewhat detached.[90] I agree with those scholars who hold that the oracle ii. 15-19 was originally connected with this episode and this date. After the beginning of the restoration of the temple an assurance of the future blessing was appropriate. Presumably it was later placed by another hand where it now stands because the Messianic blessing promised in ii. 19b seemed to be in keeping with the Messianic prospects in ii. 20-23.

---

[89] From the above it will be evident that I do not share the view that Trito-Isaiah is essentially a unity, which has been energetically presented by Elliger in various works. There are indeed many points of contact between Trito-Isaiah and Deutero-Isaiah in both substance and style (see for instance Odeberg, *Trito-Isaiah. A Literary and Linguistic Analysis*); but this can be explained on the assumption that the authors of the oracles and also the collector were strongly influenced by Deutero-Isaiah. Janssen has shown that the religious situation presupposed in Trito-Isaiah accords well with the conditions prevalent in Judaea in the exilic and post-exilic time (*Juda in der Exilszeit*, pp. 65 ff.).

[90] The date in i. 15a seems originally to have belonged to ii. 15 ff., whereas the date in i. 15b should be connected with the speech which follows (cf. further Elliger in *ATD*).

Consequently the notice in ii. 18, where this oracle is dated on the twenty-fourth day of the ninth month, must be regarded as a gloss based on the assumption that this oracle formed a unity with ii. 10-14.

The Book of Haggai is not likely to have been composed by the prophet himself. He would hardly have placed the fifth oracle there where it now stands; nor would he have used the third person style. The book consists of a collection of oracles by this prophet brought together by a man who remembered them and wanted to preserve them for posterity. The doublets in ch. i (4-6 and 9-11, two different summaries of speeches given by Haggai) show that he made use of other traditions, too. This original collector was anxious to preserve precise dates and arrange the oracles in chronological order. In the work of the original collector a later hand made the re-arrangement mentioned above.

Zechariah. The core of this book is the series of 'visions' received by Zechariah and supposed to have been seen during the course of one night.[91] They are recorded in the first person style and were written either by the prophet himself or at his dictation. About this core are grouped oracles of various kinds and of varying dates (one of them, in vi. 9-15, is connected with a symbolic action: the coronation of Joshua or probably of Zerubbabel[91a]) some in the first person style, others in the third person style. Others again are simply introduced by the usual oracle formula. All the evidence suggests that this book consists of a collection of Zechariah's revelations, brought together by a collector and centring in the series of night visions. The introductory address is a general exhortation to repentance. The symbolic action which follows the visions is an impressive conclusion to the whole series of future prospects. The inquiry about fasting in vii. 1 ff. is dated in the fourth year of Darius, which is somewhat later than the night visions. This inquiry leads on to a discourse about wrong fasting in vii. 4-14. Finally, there is a series of short oracles about the age to come. Of these oracles the saying about fasting in the fourth, fifth, seventh, and tenth month, viii. 19, was originally the answer given to the inquirers in vii. 1-3. It is placed here because of its similarity in subject to the concluding series of oracles. It was replaced by the discourse about wrong fasting. Of the doublets ('I am highly zealous for Zion', etc.), i. 14 and viii. 2, one originally belonged to the first vision, the other was appropriately included in the concluding series of oracles on the age to come because of its eschatological tendency.

[91] For the psychological nature of these visions see above, pp. 143 ff.
[91a] iii. 8 f. may also refer to a similar symbolic action; see Elliger in *ATD*.

The various insertions in the descriptions of the visions (i. 16; i. 17; ii. 10-13; ii. 14-17; iii. 8-10; iv. 6-7; iv. 8-10) present a special problem. On general grounds I hold that they owe their position in the book to the collector of Zechariah's revelations. He had sundry oracles by the prophet for which he had to find an appropriate place in the collection. Some of them he placed at the beginning or at the end; others he inserted within the series of night visions using them as additions to and commentaries on the visionary oracles. In all probability they are all authentic words of Zechariah, arranged by the collector for the most part on the principle of association of ideas.[92] It is on this principle that most of the book is arranged, though chronological considerations have also played a part.

Malachi. Here, too, the hand of a collector is evident. Whether from memory or oral tradition, or perhaps even from written sources, he has brought together the utterances of a cult prophet in the form of sermons, didactic sayings, and oracles, sometimes recorded verbatim, sometimes paraphrased. In ii. 10-16 similarity of subject has led him to conflate two speeches, one protesting against marriages with pagan women, the other protesting against divorce.

The order of the different units is in accordance with the usual practice of the collectors. At the opening of the book there is a declaration of Yahweh's love to His chosen people culminating in the noble saying: 'Great is Yahweh over the region of Israel' (i. 2-5). But Yahweh is not honoured as a loving father by the priests (i. 6-ii. 9) or by the people in general (ii. 10-16). Judgement is at hand (ii. 17-iii. 5); as an introduction the collector refers to the wrong statement that the evildoers will not be punished: he says 'the God of justice' is about to appear. To the statement at the end of this passage of the reason for judgement there is linked another description of the sinfulness in the people, leading up to an exhortation to repentance (iii. 6-12). The collection ends with a description of the last judgement (iii. 19-21), preceded by a declaration that on that day the difference between those who fear God and the sinners will be revealed (iii. 13-18).

Some scholars have suggested that some passages have been 'trans-

---

92 Rignell, *Die Nachtgesichte des Sacharja*, explains most of these insertions as authentic words uttered by the prophet on other occasions. He claims that Zechariah placed them in their new contexts in order to 'actualize' them, as he expresses it, in connection with the visions. I agree with Rignell in thinking that the words in question come from the prophet himself and that their connection with the visions is not fortuitous but intentional. However, it seems to me more likely that they were placed where they now stand by the collector of Zechariah's revelations (not even by a late redactor, as often has been maintained), to whom the arrangement of the different elements in the book must, on the whole, be attributed.

posed' from their 'original contexts'. But this is based on a misunder-
standing of the growth of the prophetic literature. As we have seen
above, the collector, in arranging his material, worked fairly consistently
on lines of his own, which are not necessarily those which to us seem
most logical. It is not easy to see how the supposed transpositions in the
prophetic literature could have taken place. The several units originally
existed independently, and the collectors brought them together into
one whole according to their own mind.

Deutero-Zechariah (Zech. ix-xiv). Although these chapters contain
various ideas which are typical of apocalyptic literature, they are,
neither in whole nor in part, an apocalypse, i.e., a book containing a
system of secret doctrines concerning the cosmos, history, and the age
to come, but a prophetic book although with a prevailingly eschatological content.[93] Accordingly the literary methods applied to other
prophetic books are also appropriate here.

Clearly it is not a coherent and homogeneous literary work, but a
collection of prophetic sayings. The collector had at his disposal 'a
collection of the first order': xii. 1-xiii. 6. This section has a superscription of its own: 'Oracle. Yahweh's word concerning Israel. Utterance of Yahweh.' It contains a series of originally independent oracles
concerning the annihilation of the enemies of Israel, the glorifying of
Jerusalem, and the cleansing of the inhabitants of Jerusalem and of the
land of Judah.

This section is preceded by a string of sayings, six in number, all
dealing with the coming age: the ruin of the neighbouring kingdoms,
ix. 1-8 (probably from the time when Alexander the Great advanced
against Tyre); the appearance of the Messianic king, ix. 9 f.; the return
of the dispersed Israelites and Israel's victory over its enemies, ix. 11-17;
blessing from Yahweh filling the land, x. 1 f.; the triumph of the
dispersed Jews over their enemies and their glorious return, x. 3-12;
the miserable ruin of the pagan kingdoms, xi. 1-3. These sayings are
taken together by the collector because of similarity of content. They
are followed by the much debated passage about the shepherd and the
sheep to be slaughtered. It is important to understand this curious
picture correctly. A prophet is here describing what he claims to have
seen in a vision. But the vision is not to be regarded as a real, ecstatic
vision, but as a 'literary vision' created by the inspired fancy of the
prophet and with a strongly allegorical character. It may be classed
with the majority of the night visions of Zechariah.[94] xiii. 7-9 ('Up,

---

[93] For the difference between eschatology and apocalyptic see below, p. 422.
[94] See further the analysis given above, pp. 146 f.

sword, against my shepherd') also belongs to the vision, but was given its present setting by the collector because of its affinity with the subject matter of the previous section. In particular the passage xiii. 9, about the purification of the people and its devotion to Yahweh may be compared with the words about conversion and cleansing in xii. 10-xiii. 6.[95]

The whole collection ends with a not entirely homogeneous composition, depicting various scenes of the eschatological drama (ch. xiv). This composition consists of material which the collector brought together because of similarity of substance.

The collector's contribution to the growth of the book of Deutero-Zechariah may be described in the following way. His interest was to preserve and combine a number of prophetic sayings which were in circulation. The primary material available to him was as follows: first the allegorical vision of an entirely unknown prophet (xi. 4-16+xiii. 7-9); then a collection of the first order, containing a series of small oracles (xii. 1-xiii. 6); and finally a number of individual prophetic oracles which he divided up into two groups, one at the beginning of his collection, the other at the end. The introductory group was linked to a particular historical occurrence (Alexander's assault on Tyre), regarded as a prelude to the age to come; the latter group, containing oracles referring to Yahweh's day in more supra-historical and supra-natural terms, was well fitted to end the corpus. The origin of the oracles in these groups is entirely obscure. Probably they were derived from several different prophets. To one of these we may attribute xii. 1-xiii. 6; to another the allegorical vision in which the leading ideas and the picture of the situation of the Jews present a marked contrast with the other passages.[96]

The Book of *Joel* has a character of its own. It is a mixture of liturgical elements and other prophetic sayings, for the most part with an eschatological content. It begins with a description (partly in the form of a lament) of a catastrophe in the land caused by locusts and severe drought. So terrible was the devastation, that the prophet feared that Yahweh's day, the judgement on Yahweh's people, was near at hand. The lamentation issues in an exhortation by the prophet to the priests to proclaim a day of fasting. He puts a prayer of lamentation in the mouth of the congregation to be assembled (ch. i).

The calamity increases, and the prophet renews his demand to the

---

95 The form of xi. 17 differs markedly from its context. It was interpolated here by a later hand as a substitute for xiii. 7-9.
96 A somewhat different analysis of Deutero-Zechariah is given by Jepsen in *ZAW*, lvii, 1939, pp. 242 ff. While I agree with his view of the shepherd passage as an allegory with an eschatological purport, I find the details of his analysis unconvincing.

priests to order a sacred fast, to call a holy assembly. Now he sees in the locusts forerunners of still more gruesome locusts, appearing in a supernatural form and introducing Yahweh's day of judgement. To the exhortation to fast because of the calamity in nature he now adds an exhortation to repentance, followed by another prayer for the day of fasting (ii. 1-17).

Then we hear an oracle, an answer from Yahweh to the prayer of the congregation, ii. 19 f.+ii. 25-27, formulated by the prophet, containing the assurance that the catastrophe will be averted. Between the two halves of the oracle come vv. 21-24, in which the prophet exhorts the people to rejoice and to praise Yahweh for his wonderful work.

This part of the Book of Joel centres in the locust and drought plague and once existed as an independent complex. What follows in the rest of the book is a series of purely eschatological prophecies which have no direct connection with the foregoing, but were joined to it probably because they derived from the same prophet.

In the opinion of the present author Joel was a cultic prophet in Jerusalem to whom we owe the sayings of this book with the probable exceptions of the utterance about Tyre, Sidon, and Philistia in iv. 4-8. He lived at a time when the Jews were scattered among the nations (iv. 2). Someone who wanted to preserve the sayings of Joel for posterity collected them and brought them together into a whole. From him derive the superscription of the book and the notice in ii. 18 f. ('Then Yahweh became solicitous for His land and had pity upon His people; and Yahweh answered and said to His people'), introducing the oracle following in vv. 19 ff. Finally the collector divided the oracle from Yahweh into two halves, inserting the exhortation to praise Yahweh. The reason for this operation was the catch-word 'do great things' in vv. 20 and 21, a feature with many analogies in the prophetic books.

The prayers in i. 15-20 and ii. 17, the oracle in ii. 19 f.+25-27, and the exhortation to praise, ii. 21-24, are all liturgical in character. The other passages are prophetic sayings of the usual kind.

Thus the Book of Joel may be appropriately described as a blend of liturgical texts and other prophetic sayings, probably all the work of a single prophet, which have been gathered together by a collector.[97]

In consequence of what has been said above the Book of Joel differs considerably from Habakkuk and the so-called Isaiah Apocalypse (Isa.

---

[97] Thus I cannot agree that the Book of Joel is a liturgy (cf. Engnell in *SBU*), or even that it is 'built up in the way of a liturgy' (Kapelrud, *Joel Studies*, p. 9). In *VT*, vii, 1957, pp. 149 ff., Treves has made a noteworthy attempt to date the Book of Joel in the time of Ptolemy, the son of Lagos, who ruled Egypt from 323 to 285 B.C.

xxiv-xxvii). Both these books are genuine liturgical compositions by
prophetic personalities and were employed on specific cultic occasions;
they are not collections of independent prophetic utterances, or complexes of prophetic utterances, like other prophetic books dealt with
above. The Book of Obadiah also (at least *vv.* 1-18) is seemingly a
homogeneous composition, whether it is a liturgical text or not.

The results of the preceding survey may be summarized in the
following way.

The prophetic books of the Old Testament must in the first place be
understood as collections of prophetic revelations. Thus the collectors
played an essential part in the production of these books. The material
they had at their disposal was varied in character. The fundamental
elements were oracles, other sayings, and larger prophetic compositions
and, in addition, short narratives about episodes in the life of the
prophets. For the most part this material was orally transmitted, but
sometimes had been recorded in writing either by the prophets themselves or by their disciples. In many cases the utterances were not
preserved in their original form, but in the form of free summaries or
abstracts. Sometimes they were brought together at an early stage in
primary collections or 'collections of the first order', which are recognizable by their homogeneous nature, particular superscriptions, etc.

The task of the chief collector was to bring all this material together
into larger units or compositions, which constitute the essential content
of our prophetic books. The principles adopted in this task may still be
discerned. Similarity of subject matter played a dominating part.
Antithetical ideas (e.g., righteousness and unrighteousness, judgement
and salvation) led to passages being linked together. Passages with the
same formal structure often form a series: 'woe'-speeches, 'hear'-
sermons, etc. Sometimes individual catch-words were the operative
factor. Connecting particles and expressions were amply used. The
collectors often adopted a chronological and historical arrangement.
They were anxious to begin and end their collections in an impressive
way. Sometimes a logical arrangement of the whole is evident.

The same material was often handed down by more than one transmitter. Thus doublets were available. If the doublets were identical,
the collector contented himself with one of them; if they were more
significant variants he made use of both and placed them side by side or
at different points in the collection. Sometimes doublets were conflated
with the result that incongruent elements have been handed down in a
given passage. Occasionally a collector has added a note of his own.
There are also superscriptions, introductions, and historical notices

which are most naturally to be ascribed to the collectors. Several examples occur of the disintegration of original units and even of subjective interpretations of sayings and events for which the collectors must have been responsible.

The collectors belonged, of course, to the circles of disciples and adherents of the prophets. As a rule they did their work after the death of the prophet whose teaching they recorded; how long it is impossible to say. Generally the collectors recorded the material in writing, but smaller collections may from the beginning have circulated in oral form. The main intention of the collectors was to preserve the divine words for posterity and to adapt them for practical use. The individual passages were linked together in such a way as to facilitate memorization and oral recitation, which must have continued even after the material had been written down.

It need hardly be said that the structure of the original collections must have been modified by later additions and glosses. To recover the original and 'authentic' words of the prophets is often a hopeless enterprise both because of the nature of tradition and history of the text. Redactional or occasional transpositions of passages in the books, such as are frequently suggested in the commentaries, are not likely to have often occurred. Defective arrangement is as a rule to be assigned to the collectors. Textual amendments, when justifiable, help us first and foremost to a better conception of the collectors' text.

Nevertheless, the tradition represented by the collectors is on the whole essentially reliable as a record of the ideas of the prophets. First and foremost we are on solid ground when we have sayings in rhythmical form. In the free reproductions we must be satisfied with the authenticity of the general lines of thought.

4. THE BOOKS

Our present prophetic books are not identical with the original collections. These collections have undergone changes and transformations of different kinds. There are countless examples of additions, enlargements and comments, which show that the text was not regarded as in any way sacrosanct, but was subjected to alterations in accordance with the taste and the needs of later times. In short, the text was not finally fixed for centuries, but remained fluid.

Besides the work of revisers who continually tried to improve the text, we have to take into account a variety of changes which were made in order to give a collection the character of a complete whole, to put it into what we may call book form. These changes are the work of 'the redactors'. There are many indications that they worked during the exile and the post-exilic period; accordingly they had as models some of the historical books which were finished during the same epoch.

The collectors were in the habit of putting headings at the opening of their collections indicating the name of the prophet whose revelations they recorded. The headings were as a rule very short: 'Vision of Isaiah, the son of Amoz', 'Words of Jeremiah, the son of Hilkiah', 'Yahweh's word which came to Hosea, the son of Beeri', or the like. The redactors have made those headings more detailed, adding further details, mainly historical and chronological. Thus we are informed that Amos was one of the sheep-breeders of Tekoa, that Jeremiah belonged to the priests who were at Anathoth in the land of Benjamin, and that Zephaniah had a noble pedigree, whether or not Hezekiah was the king.[98]

Above all the redactors have given us information concerning the periods at which the different prophets were active. Of Isaiah we hear that he worked as a prophet in the days of Uzziah, Jotham, Ahaz, and Hezekiah, kings of Judah. The statement that he received his revelations concerning Judah and Jerusalem during these reigns is true of the general substance of the book and does not of course imply that Isaiah's prophecies against foreign peoples were not uttered at that time. The redactors were no formalists. But it can be said with certainty that whoever formulated the heading did not have xxiv-xxvii, xl-lv, and lvi-lxvi in mind. Those sections were combined with the book of Isaiah, the son of Amoz, a long time after the completion of that book.

As to the dating of Amos and Hosea it is noticeable that, although these prophets worked in North Israel, the kings of Judah are mentioned before Jeroboam, the North-Israelite king, and that in Hosea only the renowned Jeroboam, not his successors, is mentioned. This is evidence of the fact that these books were edited in Judaean circles. For different reasons the same must also be assumed for the other prophetic books.

The redactors were also responsible for adding to the Isaianic and Jeremianic collections the extended historical conclusions (Isa. xxxvi-xxxix; Jer. lii), both for the most part taken from 2 Kings.

[98] It is uncertain whether 'of Tekoa' belongs to 'Amos' or to 'the sheep-breeders'. Weiser, Maag and many other scholars join it with the name of the prophet. While the name does not necessarily need any further determination, the contrary is the case with the sheep-breeders. I think that the original superscription, 'The words of Amos', derives from the collector who was a disciple of Amos. To him and his contemporaries this simple heading was sufficient. What follows is to be ascribed to the later redactor of the book.

Although promises of bliss and salvation occur in the pre-exilic collections, their general tenor is condemnation, judgement, punishment. When in the national catastrophe of 586[98a] the predictions of judgement were fulfilled, it became necessary to make the prophetic collections available for use among the Jews who were living in exile, and this need continued after the return. For this reason the redactors added to the original collections passages which referred to the new conditions. Such passages often had a marked revelatory stamp and apparently originated with anonymous prophets of later times. Such redactional additions are recognizable by references to the end of the national independence, the downfall of the Davidic dynasty, the destruction of Jerusalem and the Temple, and the dispersion of the Jews all over the earth. They promise a new realm, a new king, the rebuilding of the ruins, the return of the diaspora, in other words the complete restoration of all that had been lost in the catastrophe. Instances of such redactional additions are Am. ix. 8b-15, where all the ideas just mentioned are expressed;[99] further Isa. xi, where the downfall of the Davidic dynasty is presupposed (v. 1) and a new and wonderful kingdom is predicted.[100] To these redactional additions referring to the exile also belong passages such as Hos. ii. 1-3; xi. 10 f,; Mic. ii. 12 f.; iv. 6-8; v. 1-14; vii. 7-20; Zeph. iii. 9-20 and several others.

To the prophets who worked during the Assyrian period the Assyrian

---

[98a] For this date cf. Vogt in *SVT*, IV, 1957, p. 95.

[99] It is astonishing that there are scholars who still believe that this passage is an authentic saying of Amos. It must of course be seen in connection with other passages of the same type in the pre-exilic prophets. After the prediction of the total annihilation of the people of Israel in ix. 1-8a the passage introduced by *'epes kî* bears a clear stamp of an addition. For a correct interpretation of *vv.* 8b-10 it is necessary to make clear what the figure of the sieve means. Dalman, *Arbeit und Sitte*, III, pp. 141 f., expresses the opinion that the reference is to a fine corn-sieve, in which the grains of corn are left behind together with very small pebbles. The simile means that in the exile there will be a separation. All insolent sinners who believe that they will escape the eschatological judgement will be killed by the sword. The other members of the nation (even the less valuable) will be preserved with the greatest accuracy, so that not a single one will perish. Maag, op. cit., pp. 246 ff., defends the authenticity of the saying, referring *inter alia* to the theory of a pre-prophetic popular eschatology. If such a theory is not adopted, the chief argument for the authenticity loses its conclusive power. Kapelrud has recently denied the authenticity of the conclusion of Amos on good grounds; *Central Ideas in Amos*, pp. 53 ff.

[100] In *v.* 1 *geza'* means the stump of a tree which is left after the tree has been cut down. In Job xiv. 8 f. it is said of a hewn tree: if its root becomes old in the ground, and its stump dries in the soil, it can nevertheless put forth shoots. In Isa. xl. 24 the word is employed of a cutting used as a sapling. The primary sense is the same (*gāza'* meaning 'cut off'). The significance of the expression 'the stump of Jesse' is identical with that of 'the fallen hut of David' in Am. ix. 11. Against the opinion that the prophecy in Isa. xi belongs to the cycle of Immanuel prophecies in vii. 1-ix. 6 is the fact that it has not been included in this collection. Its position, together with ch. xii, between the anti-Assyrian oracle at the end of ch. x and the anti-Chaldean oracle in ch. xiii suggests strongly that it is a redactional addition.

empire was the primary instrument of Yahweh's castigation of His people. Prophecies referring to Babylon and Babylonia cannot be earlier than the rise of the Chaldean empire after 626 or rather 612.[100a] If in the Book of Isaiah there are some oracles against Babylon, they cannot be authentic; they have been added by the redactor of the Book of Isaiah in order to make it relevant even after the Assyrian empire had vanished. Accordingly, we must regard as redactional passages such as Isa. xiii: a picture of the conquest of Babylon by the Medes; xiv. 4-21: a satire on the king of Babylon; xxi. 1-10: a vision of the assault of the Elamites and the Medes on Babylon. For various reasons the long prophecy against Babylon in Jer. l-li cannot be an authentic prophecy of Jeremiah; it must be regarded as a redactional addition. The idea that Babylon must be crushed as a punishment for its outrage upon Israel is entirely alien to Jeremiah, who saw in Babylon an instrument of well-deserved punishment on Israel. It is true that Jeremiah expected the exile to end and the Babylonian empire to collapse, (see, e.g., xxiv. 6; xxv. 11 ff.; xxvii. 7; xxix. 10; li. 59-64); but the downfall of Babylon was never regarded by him as the vengeance of Yahweh for its evil deeds against Israel. It is probable that amongst Jeremiah's prophecies against foreign nations there was an oracle on Babylon. This oracle was judged by the redactor of the Book of Jeremiah to be too moderate, and accordingly he replaced it by a series of oracles taken from the mass of anti-Babylonian prophecies which were produced during the exile, before the conquest of Babylon by the Persians.

According to my opinion the idea of the conversion of the Gentiles did not emerge before Deutero-Isaiah. It was an invaluable fruit of the experience of exile. After Deutero-Isaiah's proclamation of the surrender of the pagan nations to the God of Israel this thought continued to be a vital element in the faith of the Jewish people. It was expressed in numerous oracles of the exilic and post-exilic period. Parallel with this thought was the apparently contrary idea of Israel's vengeance upon the Gentiles because of their cruelty to the people of the Lord. That foreign nations were enemies of Yahweh and would be punished by Him was an old idea; but after the national catastrophe, when Israel became a victim of the merciless violence of the Babylonians, the hostility against foreign peoples extended to the pagan world as a whole, and fierce hopes were cherished that the entire Gentile world would be destroyed.

To the redactors of the pre-exilic prophetic books it was necessary

---

[100a] According to Vogt, op. cit., p. 69, Nabopolassar ascended the throne in 626. In 612 occurred the conquest and destruction of Nineveh by Nabopolassar and Cyaxares.

that these important ideas should find expression in these books, which were recited in the cultic assemblies; and for this reason many prophecies of this kind were added to the original collections. As examples of the former type we may adduce, e.g., the following passages: Isa. xvii. 7 f.: men (mankind) will look to their Maker, and their eyes will turn to the Holy One of Israel; xviii. 7: the Ethiopians will bring tribute to Yahweh; xix. 18-25: Yahweh will reveal Himself to the Egyptians, and the Egyptians will acknowledge Yahweh; xxiii. 17 f.: Tyre will dedicate her commercial gain to Yahweh; ii. 2-5 (= Mic. iv. 1-4): the Gentiles will go up to Yahweh's mountain to be instructed in His way; Jer. xii. 14-17: one day the Gentiles will learn the ways of Israel and to swear by Yahweh's name. The following are examples of the latter type: Isa. xi. 12-16: the foreign peoples will be brought under the power of Israel; xiv. 1 f.: they will be slaves in the land of Israel; Mic. v. 6-8: the remnant of Israel will be in the midst of the peoples like a lion amongst flocks of sheep;[101] Am. ix. 11 f.: one day Israel will possess the remnant of Edom and other nations which once have belonged to the dominion of Israel, the people of Yahweh.[102] All such passages are certainly exilic or post-exilic.

In the books of the pre-exilic prophets there are many other passages which contain seemingly post-exilic ideas, though not so striking as those mentioned above. It is the task of the critic to decide whether such passages belong to the original collections or were inserted by the redactors of the books. In such cases great care is needed because many ideas formerly regarded as exclusively post-exilic have proved (particularly in the light of the cultic traditions) to be sound pre-exilic conceptions. Also several motifs generally considered as apocalyptic and therefore of late origin must, in view of the highly fanciful and often mythologically coloured character of Hebrew poetry, be judged to be pre-exilic.[103] About the conclusion of the book of Hosea (xiv. 2-9), for instance, opinions are divided and must be so, because the general tone sounds exilic or post-exilic, while there are no concrete ideas which absolutely compel us to assume so late an origin. The present writer is most disposed to believe that the passage in question is a prophecy

---

[101] The previous passage is, in my view, also a redactional addition. I do not believe that in *vv.* 4 f. Assyria is to be equated with Syria of the Seleucids, and that consequently this is a Hellenistic addition. I hold that here as in vii. 12; Hos. xi. 11; Zech. x. 10, 'Assyria' is an oracular designation for Babylonia. The pre-exilic prophetic books were completed during the exilic and the early post-exilic periods. Glosses and minor textual changes and amendments may of course date from much later times. But this does not affect the dating of the main work of the redactors of the books.

[102] For the meaning of the expression 'Yahweh's name called over' see Galling in *TLZ*, lxxxi, 1956, cols. 65 ff.

[103] These problems I have discussed at length in *St.Th.*, vi, 1952, pp. 79 ff.

composed after the catastrophe and added by the redactor of the book to the original collection as a suitable conclusion.[104]

Isa. xxix. 17-24 is certainly a redactional addition.[105] The same is true of xxxii. 1-8, 15-20, and the section xxxiv-xxxv.[106] Chapter xxxv is closely akin to the Deutero-Isaianic prophecies, but it is, of course, not necessary to ascribe it directly to the great anonymous prophet of the exile. We must assume that this prophet, like others, had a group of disciples who imitated his style and reproduced his ideas. The redactors of the prophetic books, not always being themselves prophets, sometimes gathered their material from prophecies circulating in different quarters in their time.

The redactors intended to make the collections of the prophetic revelations more suitable for cultic use. Accordingly it is not surprising that secondary cultic passages are to be found embedded in the prophetic texts. The introductory word at the beginning of the Book of Amos is undoubtedly a quotation from a cultic text. The same is true of the so-called doxologies Am. iv. 13; v. 8 f.; ix. 5 f.[106a] Psalms such as Isa. xii and Nah. i. 2 ff. belong to the same category.

The final redaction of the books took place within the Jewish community. Thus it was natural that passages referring only to Israel should be completed by words referring to Judah (e.g., the oracle of judgement against Judah in Am. ii. 4 f. and the promise of salvation for Judah in Hos. i. 7). Many so-called Judaean interpolations are more appropriately characterized as secondary glosses than as redactional additions, although they serve the same end (see below).

The conclusion of the Book of Hosea ('Whoever is wise, may consider this, and whoever is discerning may understand it', etc.) indicates that the final redactor of this book belonged to the Wisdom circles (if the verse was not added by a copyist). The penultimate word in Malachi ('Remember the law of Moses', etc.) proves that this book was 'edited' by a Torah teacher. The concluding word about the sending of Elijah looks like a final addition by an apocalyptist.

Since the redactional additions and the late secondary enlargements

104 See further Lindblom, *Hosea*, pp. 109 f. For *v.* 10 see below.

105 Note the ideas of the transformation of nature and other Deutero-Isaianic conceptions, e.g., the reference to Abraham.

106 The 'prophetic liturgy' Isa. xxxiii is difficult to date. There is much to be said for the assumption that it refers to the advance of Alexander the Great towards Phoenicia and Palestine after 333 B.C. Thus it would have the same historical background as Zech. ix. 1 ff. If this is the case, this passage would be one of the latest additions to the book of Isaiah. For the relation between Isa. xxxiv-xxxv and Deutero-Isaiah see Pope in *JBL*, lxxi, 1952, pp. 235 ff.

106a Watts in *JNES*, xv, 1956, pp. 33 ff., thinks that the doxologies together originally formed a hymn celebrating Yahweh's perfect domination over creation.

and glosses for the most part serve the same end, it is often impossible to distinguish between them. In general it can be said that extended additions, more independent of the context, in particular those placed at the end of the books, derive from the redactors, while smaller additions often dovetailed into the original text, are from the hands of glossators of different kinds.

Every prophetic book had a literary history of its own, though the redactional work was similar in character.

The Book of Amos existed in the form of a collection of the revelations of Amos until the exile. The redactional addition at the end proves that the book obtained its present shape after the national catastrophe and before the return in the time of Cyrus, i.e., during the first half of the sixth century, and probably in Babylonia. The Davidic dynasty has ceased to reign; the nation is crushed, the cities are ruined, and the population deported. The situation is the same as that of Deutero-Isaiah before 539.

What is true of Amos is true of Hosea. Israel is dispersed, but the return to the homeland is expected (ii. 1 f., 25; xi. 10 ff.). Israel and Judah will reunite under one king. A national and religious restoration will take place (ii. 1 ff., 18 ff.). Egypt and Assyria are mentioned as places of the diaspora (xi. 11). Some scholars think that Assyria here is a name for Syria and that the prophecy is from the Hellenistic period. It is more probable that the redactor, who had in mind v. 5 ('he shall return to the land of Egypt, and Assyria shall be his king'), thought in reality of the exile to Egypt and Babylonia in the Chaldean period.

The Book of Micah as a redactional work must also be assigned to the exilic time. The return of the exiles and the rebuilding of the walls are expected (ii. 12 f.; iv. 6 ff.; vii. 11). A new king of the Davidic dynasty will appear (v. 1 ff.). Assyria and the land of Nimrod here mentioned as the main enemy of Israel, are, of course, oracular names for Babylonia.[107]

The very comprehensive Book of Isaiah has had a more complicated history. There are many indications that an Isaianic book in a redactional sense first came into existence in Babylonia during the exilic period. The many anti-Babylonian prophecies presuppose that the downfall of Babylon was longed-for and expected, but had not yet occurred. The

---

[107] Gunkel discovered in Mic. vii. 7-20 a liturgy, *ZS*, ii, 1924, pp. 145 ff. Reicke in *SEÅ*, xii, 1947, pp. 279 ff., tries to show that ch. vii as a whole is a ritual text corresponding to a liturgy performed at an ancient oriental New Year festival. As for Mic. v. 1 ff. Alt in the *Mowinckel Festschrift* (p. 22, n. 9) tries to preserve for Micah v. 1, 3a, 4a, 5b. I think it is sounder to take v. 1-5 as a whole and regard it as a redactional addition from the exilic period.

mention of the Medes as the conquerors of Babylon (xiii. 17; xxi. 2) points to a time shortly after 550. The hope of the return of the exiles and passages closely akin to Deutero-Isaiah support this dating. The historical appendix, taken from 2 Kings, does not tell against it, for this book was at all events compiled before the middle of the sixth century.[107a]

The collection of the prophecies of Deutero-Isaiah was joined to the Proto-Isaianic book during the last third of the sixth century. In the view of the present author the 'missionary revelations' including the Servant Songs were received by the anonymous prophet just after the occurrences of the year 539. Soon afterward all the sayings of this prophet were collected by one of his disciples, and later a subsequent redactor wrote the collection on a scroll containing the proto-Isaianic book as an appendix to it. The reason for it was not the surmise that the two works derived from the same prophet, but the impression that they were akin in subject matter. At that time interest in questions concerning authorship and similar historical subjects was non-existent. Both the collectors and the redactors were guided only by practical points of view. For reading at cultic assemblies it was convenient to have these two books written on the same scroll, dominated as they were by similar ideas and even dealing with the same historical facts, the downfall of Babylon and the coming of the 'Messianic' age. It must be kept in mind that, when the Deutero-Isaianic book was appended to Proto-Isaiah, the latter already contained the secondary anti-Babylonian and even Messianic passages which were incorporated in the original collection of the revelations of Isaiah ben Amoz.

This combination of Proto-Isaiah and Deutero-Isaiah could, accordingly, be described as a 'second edition' of Isaiah. A third 'edition' came into existence when the so-called Isaiah-Apocalypse (Isa. xxiv-xxvii) was inserted among the Proto-Isaianic revelations, in connection with the prophecies against foreign peoples. If I am right in thinking that this 'Apocalypse' is in fact a 'Cantata' performed in the temple of Jerusalem on the occasion of the conquest of Babylon by Xerxes in 485, it cannot have been combined with the Isaianic book before this date.

The reason for the incorporation of the Cantata in the book of Isaiah was that the author of this work had closely imitated the style and mode of expression of the Isaianic book. The author appeared in fact as a true disciple of Isaiah.[108] If, as I hold, the devastated city is Babylon, it was very suitable to incorporate the Cantata in the book of Isaiah, which

---

[107a] See Eissfeldt, *Einleitung*, p. 343.
[108] See my book, *Die Jesaja-Apokalypse*, pp. 111 ff., and Mulder, *Die Teologie van die Jesaja-Apokalipse*, pp. 67 ff.

also included Deutero-Isaiah, in which the downfall of Babylon played so great a part. Also, the glorious age to come was an idea common to Isaiah in the wider sense and the Cantata.

The concluding part of the Book of Isaiah, the so-called Trito-Isaiah, was incorporated in the book last of all. The affinity between this section and the foregoing has often been pointed out. It is impossible to decide when the Trito-Isaianic collection was appended to the Isaianic book unless the date of the different parts of Trito-Isaiah has first been established; and this may never be achieved. At all events it took place at a relatively late period.

Using modern terms it may be said that the present Book of Isaiah is a result of redactional work in four stages; it was 'published' in four 'editions', as four different books were combined with each other.

It is also possible to distinguish in the Book of Zephaniah between the prophet's original revelations, to be dated some time before King Josiah's reform, and the later work of redaction. The end of the book (iii. 14 ff.) promising, in Deutero-Isaianic terms, the return of the exiles, proves that it was completed during the exile.

The material in the Book of Jeremiah was probably collected in Egypt. When Jeremiah and Baruch emigrated to Egypt, they presumably brought with them the scroll written by Baruch. In Egypt Jeremiah uttered some other oracles which were incorporated with his Palestinian revelations. Among those who went to Egypt there must have been other disciples of Jeremiah who, like Baruch, remembered and transmitted their master's sayings. One of them collected the available material, and so the main Jeremianic corpus came into existence.[109] The historical conclusion, taken from 2 Kings, and the extended prophecy against Babylon in l-li do not derive from the collector, but from the redactor or the redactors of the book. Since the prophecy against Babylon presupposes the rise of the Persian power, but the downfall of Babylon is still expected, the redactor must have completed his work between 550 and 539. Probably the prophecy against Babylon was composed in Palestine.[110] Together with the historical supplement, the prophecy xxxiii. 14-26,[111] and some other passages it was added to the Jeremianic corpus in post-exilic times in Palestine. It is, however, possible that the redactional work proceeded in stages.

[109] I do not believe that the collector (or redactor) was Baruch (so, e.g., Volz). If Baruch had compiled the book, it might have been expected that his own scroll had been preserved in its original shape. This is, as we have seen above, not the case.
[110] So Weiser in *ATD*, p. 435.
[111] From the omission of this passage in the Septuagint nothing can be concluded concerning the date of its composition. The omission was probably caused by the fact that the passage has striking parallels elsewhere in Jeremiah.

Concerning the Book of Ezekiel little need be added to what was said above. In this book the activity of an individual redactor is less evident than in other books. Here the collector was also in essence a redactor. Joel and Haggai were given their final form as books by the collectors; and Habakkuk is a homogeneous liturgy. The literary redaction of the Book of Zechariah offers a more interesting problem.

I have tried above (pp. 273 ff.) to analyse the two main parts of the Book of Zechariah as two independent collections of prophetic revelations from quite different times. Now we have to find an answer to the question why a very late post-exilic collection has been combined with a collection from the end of the sixth century. The reason was the fact that they had many subjects in common. Most of the ideas of Proto-Zechariah recur in Deutero-Zechariah. The dispersed will return to the homeland (x. 6, 8). People and land will be cleansed of sin and uncleanness (xiii. 1 ff.). Jerusalem will be a holy city (xiv. 20 f.). Yahweh is present in the midst of His people (ix. 8). The restored land will be populous (x. 8 ff.). Israel will really be Yahweh's people (xiii. 9). The enemies will be crushed (xii. 2 ff.; xiv. 1 ff.). The remainder of the pagan nations will go up to Jerusalem to worship the God of Israel (xiv. 16 ff.). Finally the vision of the shepherd in xi and xiii has a certain similarity to the visions in Proto-Zechariah.

The redactional compilation of *the books* was not the last stage in the transmission of the prophetic texts. Once written on scrolls containing one prophetic work or more, the books underwent textual changes of different kinds. Modern critical commentaries frequently speak of additions, interpolations, expansions, glosses, etc., made for various reasons. In many cases the commentaries are wrong in considering such passages as *textual* alterations because many, perhaps most, of what they call textual alterations were not changes in the written text of the books, but are to be ascribed to the transmitters of the oral tradition on one hand and the activity of the collectors and the redactors of the books on the other. The bearers of the oral transmission, the collectors, and the redactors of the books have all in various ways contributed to give the prophetic sayings and actions the shape they now have, differing in many respects from the original. But there are also textual alterations in the strict sense. The work on the content of the prophetic books continued for centuries in the form of glosses or notes of different kinds, which were as a rule originally written in the margins of the scrolls or between the lines,[112] and later incorporated by the copyists in the text itself. Larger glosses seem to have been composed and inserted by the

[112] See, for instance, additions made by a second hand in IQIs[a].

copyists themselves. Glosses are often difficult to distinguish from contributions of the kinds just described (in many cases they serve the same end); but we can often easily recognize them by their intention, their position in the text, and the brevity which in most cases is characteristic of them.

The glossarists continued the tendency of both collectors and redactors to turn the edge of one-sided and radical prophecies of doom. When we find in a description of a disastrous assault upon Judah by an enemy from afar the unexpected remark that Yahweh *will not make a full end*, Jer. v. 18, this is a marginal note by one who knew that a remnant was saved. A similar gloss is to be found in Jer. xliv. 14, where it is said that none of the Jews who have gone to Egypt will escape *except some fugitives*. In Jer. iv. 27 and v. 10 the negations *lô'* and *'al* are to be ascribed to glossarists or copyists who wanted to mitigate the dire oracles of total destruction.

In Isa. x. 12 a gloss on the punishment of the Assyrian king has been wrongly transferred from the margin into the king's arrogant speech. A gloss on the conversion of mankind, in accordance with the taste of a later time, has been inserted for instance in Isa. xxxi. 7 (cf. xvii. 7 f.). Similarly, the prayer in Jer. x. 25, that Yahweh's wrath may be poured out upon the Gentiles, because of their having devoured and consumed Jacob, is to be judged as a late gloss.

In Mic. i. 2 the idea of world judgement must be ascribed to a glossarist, misled by the appeal to all the nations and the description of the theophany in the following verses.

Late 'Judaean interpolations', of the nature of glosses, referring to Judah in passages dealing with North Israel, are to be found, e.g., in Hos. iv. 15; v. 5; vi. 11; viii. 14.[113] The words 'and David, their king', in iii. 5, regarding the expected conversion of Israel from a Judaean point of view, belong to the same category of post-exilic glosses.

When in Mic. iv. 10 the inhabitants of Jerusalem during the siege of the city by Sennacherib are told of exile to Babylon and rescue from there, this is of course impossible in this context. Here we manifestly have to do with an ill-considered post-exilic gloss.

A liturgical gloss is to be found in Hos. xii. 6: 'Yahweh, the God of hosts, Yahweh is His name.'[114] In Isa. xxv. 10 ff. an oracle against Moab has been unexpectedly inserted. A late glossarist wanted to complete

[113] The mention of Judah in v. 8 ff. is due to particular historical facts and belongs to the original text. See above, p. 244. For the Judaean interpolations see Welch in *AOF*, iv, 1927, pp. 66 ff. This scholar thinks of a slightly earlier time: some years before the exile.

[114] The liturgical additions in the Book of Amos are not glosses in the strict sense, but come from the redactor of the book, who intended to adopt the book for liturgical use by inserting a series of liturgical formulas at various points.

the eschatological prophecy. Such complements of various kinds, commentaries on and expansions of the text, are very common. The passage on corrupt worship in Isa. i. 10 ff. seems to have been expanded. The same is true of the curious passage on the adornment of the daughters of Zion in Isa. iii. 16 ff.; the description of the judgement upon Egypt in xix. 5 ff.; the enumeration of the doomed peoples in Jer. xxv. 19 ff.; the polemics against the idol-worshippers in Isa. xl. 19 f.; xli. 6 f.; xlvi. 6 f.; Jer. x. 3 ff.; the description of the splendour of the Tyrian king in Ezek. xxviii. 13; the description of the new temple in Ezek. xl ff., etc.

Historical or interpretative additions are to be found for instance in Isa. vii. 4 f. (see *BH* and the commentaries!), vii. 17, 20 ('the king of Assyria'), Mic. vi. 5 ('king of Moab', 'from Shittim to Gilgal'). In Zech. xi. 8 a glossator has introduced into the allegory of the shepherd a concrete detail taken from the history of his time.[115] Interpretations of figurative expressions are inserted, e.g., in Isa. ix. 14; xxv. 4; xxix. 10; xl. 7; Ezek. xxiii. 4, 9. A quasi-etymological explanation of the word *bāmâh* is given by a glossarist in Ezek. xx. 29.

Learned notes to be ascribed to glossarists occur in Zech. iv. 12 (concerning the two olive branches in the vision of the lamp-stand) and xiv. 4 f. and 10 (about the transformation of the land in the age to come).

A prophecy *ex eventu* of great interest has been inserted by a glossarist in Isa. vii. 8: 'And within sixty-five years Ephraim shall be broken in pieces so as to be no longer a people' (written after other hostile actions against North Israel during the reign of Esarhaddon and Assurbanipal).[116]

A sententious phrase formulated by a Wisdom teacher has been inserted in Isa. iii. 10 f. Pious reflections interrupting the sequence occur in Isa. ii. 22; xlviii. 22; Mic. vi. 9; Hab. ii. 13; Mal. ii. 7, etc.

Some glosses are quotations or reminiscences from other scriptural passages: Jer. x. 25 (from Ps. lxxix. 6 f.); Mic. ii. 1 (partly from Ps. iv. 5; v. 6; xxxvi. 5); Hab. ii. 14 (from Isa. xi. 9).

One of the longest glosses is to be found in Jer. xxiii. 34-40, the expansion concerning Yahweh's *maśśâ'*. It has rightly been remarked that this is a specimen of Talmudic learning, which has nothing at all to do with the prophecies of Jeremiah.[117]

To some degree the glosses serve the same end as do the additions made by the collectors and the redactors of the books; and accordingly, as has been pointed out above, it is not always possible to decide

---

[115] So rightly Elliger in *ATD*.
[116] Cf. Ezr. iv. 2 and 10. See Kittel, *Geschichte des Volkes Israel*, II[7], p. 400, n. 1; Ricciotti, *History of Israel*, I, pp. 391, 393.
[117] So Rudolph in *HAT*.

whether an interpolation was made by a glossarist or by another. In particular, the process by which Ezekiel's oracles were handed down makes it very difficult, and at times impossible, to distinguish between free paraphrases of the prophet's words and later interpolations.

In general, however, the glosses consist of relatively small passages, easily distinguishable from the context. This is above all the case when they have been inserted into the text from the margin. The 'Talmudic' passage in Jer. xxiii. 34-40 is exceptionally long. The most comprehensive addition, written between the lines in the complete Isaiah scroll from the Qumran cave (IQIs^a), consists of thirty words.

The importance of a strict definition of what a gloss is must be carefully considered. A gloss is a late secondary addition to the *written text* made by readers or copyists. Additions made by the transmitters in the oral tradition or by the redactors of the books ought not to be called glosses.

It need hardly be said that the examples given above are only a selection from the numerous glosses that are to be found in the prophetic books.

CHAPTER FIVE

THE RELIGION OF THE PROPHETS

1. INTRODUCTORY

In this chapter we shall examine the religious ideas of the prophets. We shall be primarily concerned with the ideas proclaimed by the prophets in their public preaching. Of the individual religious experiences of the different prophets there is less to say. (Some points of special interest relating to these experiences will be discussed below.) The importance of the prophets in the religious history of mankind arises from their inspired messages, not their personal confessions.

The religious ideas of the prophets could be comprehensively presented in a coherent dogmatic system. Alternatively the teaching of each individual prophet might be described. In the first case the differences and nuances in the religious thinking of the prophets would be missed; in the latter the essential unity would be obscured.

Here a third method will be adopted. Israelite prophetism had a history. We can distinguish between different periods and different groups of prophets characterized by different historical circumstances. The prophets were not philosophers or theorizing theologians detached from the vicissitudes of history. They were involved in the historical process and concerned with the course of events, not as passive bystanders, but with passionate interest drawing instruction from them and proclaiming what they had seen as divine messages to their people. At the same time the prophets shared the internal life of the nation. They were critical observers of the national and social, the religious and moral state of their people, and felt themselves called to intervene, censuring, warning, judging, encouraging. Accordingly their preaching mirrors the actual conditions of successive ages.

We have, then, to distinguish between different groups of prophets, each group working in a particular historical situation and therefore sharing in a measure a common field of thought. The main groups are the pre-exilic, the exilic, and the post-exilic prophets. The pre-exilic period is characterized by the fact that the people lived under the monarchy in highly developed social conditions, adopted for the most part from the superior Canaanite culture, with all the advantages and disadvantages of a settled culture in the ancient Orient, and worshipping the national God often in grossly syncretistic forms. Exhortation to repentance, rebuke, and judgement are the most prominent traits in the preaching of the prophets of this period, though promises of salvation and blessing (on condition that the people turned to Yahweh) are also present. During the exile the state was crushed and the people shattered. The cultic life in its inherited forms had come to an end. The prevailing mood was one of despair. In this situation the prophets had a new mission. Consolation and encouragement were the dominant elements in their preaching. After the return to the homeland a new community had to be built up, with the Temple of Jerusalem as its centre and under the political government of a foreign ruler. Now the prophets' task was to build up the community, stimulating their compatriots to establish a new Temple cult, to purify the religious and moral life, and to hold fast the hope of a new age when all the divine promises would be fulfilled.

The religious thought-world of the prophets was considerably modified by these vicissitudes in the historical life of ancient Israel. In analysing it we have to take into consideration both these general modifications and also the personalities of the individual prophets. Of course, such an analysis cannot be carried through apart from the literary criticism of the prophetic books. It may be true that from a traditio-historical point of view what has been transmitted to us in the prophetic books is in a large measure not the prophetic sayings in their original form, but sayings in a form given them by disciples and collectors. But this does not mean that no critical analysis is possible. On the contrary, the literary character of the prophetic books makes such an analysis necessary. If we really seek historical data in the prophetic texts, we must inquire what is authentic and what is secondary. It may be that the answer often remains uncertain, but in many instances critical analysis leads to sure results. No critical scholar assigns to Isaiah, the son of Amoz, utterances which refer to the Babylonian empire or the return of the exiled Jews. Difficulties are of course raised by passages which consist of authentic utterances which have been tendentiously revised by later hands or have been slightly modified for use in the cult; but such difficulties should not deter us from trying to carry out the critical task, which remains the same whether we attribute prior importance to oral transmission or apply to the prophetic texts the methods of literary criticism. These two approaches to the prophetic texts by no means exclude each other.

To the group of pre-exilic prophets we assign Amos, Hosea, Isaiah, Micah, Nahum, Zephaniah, Jeremiah, and individual passages of unknown origin inserted in the books named after these prophets. Habakkuk raises a special problem. This prophet has been assigned to different periods, from the Assyrian age until the time of Alexander the Great. The present writer shares the view that the book is a liturgy composed in the face of the Babylonian menace, and is to be dated at the end of the seventh century B.C. From a methodological point of view it is wrong to expect every detail in the description of the enemy to be exactly applicable to the Babylonians, since the description is poetical and mythological in character and follows a conventional and traditional pattern. On this dating Habakkuk was a contemporary of Jeremiah.[1]

From the exilic period come Ezekiel and Deutero-Isaiah, and also several passages inserted in other books. From the post-exilic period come the other canonical prophets: Joel,[2] Obadiah, Haggai, Zechariah, Malachi, and, in addition, the numerous passages in the other books which presuppose the conditions prevailing after the return of the *gôlâh*. Daniel and Jonah are omitted from this inquiry, since the one is an apocalyptic work and the other a prophetic legend.

2. The Personal Religion of the Prophets

By the personal religion of the prophets we do not mean primarily their ecstatic or revelatory experiences, or the moral and religious messages which they had to convey from Yahweh to their people, but rather the experiences which they had as individual religious personalities, though admittedly these experiences cannot be entirely separated either from their prophetic calling or from their preaching about God and His will.

Of the personal religion of the individual prophets in this sense we know comparatively little. Their personal religious experiences were kept in the background because their message was primary. Their main task was not to witness to what they themselves experienced in their relation to Yahweh, but to proclaim to their people the words Yahweh had given them in their hours of inspiration.

So far as the earliest prophets are concerned, if we seek for direct references to their personal devotional life, only occasional details are to be found in their books. Out of compassion for his people, Amos, as we have seen above, prayed for its salvation when the catastrophe was imminent. The same is true of Isaiah, and later of Ezekiel, and above all of Jeremiah. In the intercession of these prophets for their people it is difficult to separate what they did as pious men from what they did in virtue of their prophetic mission. When Isaiah, in his inaugural vision, face to face with Yahweh's holy majesty, felt that he was unclean

---

[1] See above, pp. 253 ff.   [2] See above, pp. 276 ff.

and dwelt among an unclean people, he showed that he was conscious of his own sinfulness and his participation in the iniquity of his people. When, having heard the proclamation of the terrible doom, he asks, 'How long, Yahweh?' not only does he show familiarity with the phraseology of the liturgical psalms of lament, but also gives us a glimpse into his own inner encounter with his God. That he did not only require from his people quietness and confidence in Yahweh, the almighty God, and fear of the Holy One,[3] but also himself lived in the same quietness, confidence, and even fear, is evident from viii. 11-18: in an ecstatic revelation the prophet was warned not to adopt the outlook of the people and summoned, together with his disciples, to fear Yahweh alone and trust in Him, waiting steadfastly for Him and setting his hope on Him. The same attitude is expressed in Mic. vii. 7 (for our present purpose the question of authorship is irrelevant): 'I will look confidently to Yahweh, I will wait for the God of my salvation; my God will hear me.' The God of Israel was also the personal God of the prophets.[4]

As we have seen above, prayer became a personal problem for Jeremiah. The general corruption being irreparable and the doom inevitable, prayer was against the purposes of Yahweh and hence contrary to His will. The prophet felt himself forbidden to continue praying on behalf of his people.

Internal and external conflicts made life a torment and his calling a heavy and almost unbearable burden to Jeremiah. In the face of those who insidiously sought his life he felt like an innocent lamb that is led to the slaughter. In some of his utterances he wishes, like Job, that he had never been born and calls down curses on the day of his birth: 'Woe is me, my mother! that you bore me as a man of strife and a man of contention to the whole land' (xv. 10). 'Cursed be the day on which I was born! The day on which my mother bore me, let it not be blessed' (xx. 14).

The distress caused by his prophetic calling brought him into conflict with his God, too. Sometimes he felt tempted to cease prophesying and speaking in Yahweh's name. Then it was in his heart like a burning fire shut up in his bones; he could not endure it (xx. 9). These words mirror the psychical suffering caused by the attempt to suppress the inspiration and keep back the revelations, and at the same time the moral self-reproaches for being disobedient to God. This implied an inner conflict which had also reference to Jeremiah's personal religion.

People scoffed at him because his predictions were not fulfilled. This caused another conflict in Jeremiah's devotional life. He upbraids

[3] Isa. vii. 9; xxviii. 16; xxx. 15.   [4] 'My God' also Isa. vii. 13; Hos. ix. 17.

Yahweh for having put him in this precarious position. He had not forced himself upon Yahweh, imploring Him to make him a prophet, in order to bring trouble upon his people. Now it was Yahweh's obligation to help him out of this situation. In phrases which echo the language of the laments he prays: 'Heal me, O Yahweh, that I may be healed; save me that I may be saved.' By adding: 'Thou art my praise,' he expresses immediately the certainty that in these straits too he will be rescued (xvii. 14 ff.).

Jeremiah went still further. Like Job in his sufferings he bursts into accusations that God had deceived him. He says that Yahweh is to him like a wadi, a treacherous brook, the waters of which dry up in the summer (xv. 18). At his call Yahweh had promised to stand at his side as his supporter and helper. Yahweh had not fulfilled these promises. Consequently Yahweh appeared to him as a traitor. But in such situations he felt judged on his conscience. He had been rebellious against God, the Almighty. Self-reproach took the form of a revelation. He heard Yahweh saying, 'If you return, I will let you stand in My presence [as My servant] again. And if you bring forth what is precious, without anything base, you shall be My mouthpiece' (v. 19). Jeremiah had been on the point of losing his prophetic mission. Only by being converted he could continue working in the service of Yahweh. Only patient and submissive men can be so used by God.

In hours of despondency he implores Yahweh to inflict harsh punishment on his adversaries and to let him see vengeance done on them (xi. 20). He prays: 'Think of me, and visit me; avenge me on my persecutors ... Know that for Thy sake I have suffered rebuke' (xv. 15). 'Let those be put to shame who persecute me, but let me not be put to shame. Let them be confounded, but let me not be confounded' (xvii. 18). Upon those who had 'dug a pit for his life', and for whose benefit he had interceded with Yahweh he calls down the most terrible calamities: 'Give up their children to famine, and hand them over to the sword. Let their wives become childless and widows, and their men be slain by pestilence', etc. (xviii. 20 ff.).

It testifies to the depth of Jeremiah's faith that, in spite of all he had to suffer, he held fast his confidence in Yahweh and the certainty that Yahweh would in the end let him triumph: 'Yahweh is with me as a dread warrior; therefore my persecutors will stumble and will not prevail,' etc. (xx. 11).

In considering such appeals to Yahweh to punish the enemies we have to keep in mind that Jeremiah was fighting not only for his own cause but for God's cause. Yahweh's righteousness was at stake. The problem was the same as in Job. Jeremiah's triumph over his enemies was also a triumph of Yahweh's justice. Moreover it may be observed that in such passages Jeremiah also speaks as a prophet. The attacks of his adversaries were attacks against the bearer of Yahweh's word. Rebellion against him was rebellion against Yahweh Himself. It belonged to the self-consciousness of the prophets that as messengers from God and men of God they were sacrosanct and inviolable. He who assailed them assailed Yahweh Himself.

The adversities he had to suffer led Jeremiah to take up the problem of retribution in all its bitterness. Seeing his enemies prosper and succeed, while he himself was haunted by misfortune and suffering, he ventured to indict Yahweh. His supreme desire was to obey Yahweh and stand in His service..He had not forced himself upon Yahweh, but only submitted to His command. To receive the divine revelations had been to him like sweet food. Yet he must suffer more than anyone else. He must live as a solitary without family and friends, a disaster more bitter to an ancient Israelite, with his strong social consciousness, than to modern individualistic men. Then the question arose: Why does this happen? Why do the adversaries enjoy šālôm, while all things are going ill with him? And this problem was not a problem which had reference only to Jeremiah, it grew unto a general problem concerning mankind: 'Why does the way of the wicked prosper? Why do all the faithless live in comfort? Thou plantest them, and they take root; they grow, and they bring forth fruit' (xii. 1 f.). Such experiences impelled him to doubt the righteousness of God; but no objective answer to such questions was given. The problem must be solved in a personal way. Jeremiah must learn that men must live without understanding every difficulty. Much more intricate problems awaited him: 'If you have raced with men on foot, and they have wearied you, how will you compete with horses? And if in a safe land you fall down, how will you do in the jungle of Jordan?' (v. 5).[5] The prophet probably thinks here of the catastrophe which awaited the elect people as a whole, and himself in connection with this calamity, in comparison with which his present personal difficulties were not very momentous.

The personal religious life of Jeremiah is more accessible to us than that of any of the other prophets; but although they were more reticent about themselves we are not justified in concluding that they did not in fact have similar experiences. It would be wrong to suppose that the prophetic books contain all that the prophets said. It would also be

[5] Thus RSV, partly in accordance with Driver's suggestion in SOTP (p. 59), BH and most commentators read lô' ṭibṭaḥ.

wrong to think that every prophet should have transmitted his personal experiences to posterity in the form of 'confessions'. We must not think of a one-sidedly evolutionary process of religious development to the later stages of which individual religion belonged. Individual religion undoubtedly existed in Israelite religion at every period, even though literary references to it are comparatively rare.[6] Why should not Hosea, for instance, an intensely living personality as he was, have had experiences like those of Jeremiah? Accordingly it is not correct to say that Jeremiah was the first representative of individual religion in ancient Israel. It is true that we have a more intimate knowledge of Jeremiah than we have of other prophets, but this fact does not prove that he was quite unique. His individual disposition may have contributed to his frankness in recording his personal conflicts and victories. In addition, Jeremiah was a man of poetic gifts. Such personalities have always a propensity for giving literary expression to their feelings and other personal experiences.[7]

The personal religion of the prophets was of course an indispensable condition of their prophetic calling. They were strong religious personalities before they became prophets. 'Before they became prophets they were of the stuff from which prophets could be made.'[7a] Their personal faith in the living God supplied them with a knowledge of God without which they could not have been messengers of God to their people. They lived in personal communion with God before they proclaimed His essence and will to men. The personal communion of the prophets with their God in its deepest aspects is not accessible to scientific analysis. But it may be said that the God of the prophets was essentially the same as the God of Israel, and what they knew of Him was mediated to them by history and tradition. The God of the prophets was no other than the God of the Mosaic tradition as preserved in the old popular narratives, the ancient laws, and the time-honoured cultic formulas. The personal religion of the prophets manifested itself in personal surrender in faith and life to Yahweh, in pure knowledge of Him, in the conformity of their will with His will, their sharing in His love and wrath (see for instance Jer. vi. 11), their profound and terrifying insight

---

[6] Cf. above all Sellin, *Beiträge zur israelitischen und jüdischen Religionsgeschichte*, I
[7] In *Prophet und Gott*, Hertzberg offers many fine observations, but exaggerates the uniqueness of Jeremiah in the religious history of Israel. Skinner (*Prophecy and Religion*, p. 203) rightly observes: 'We find here a certain expansion or sublimation of the prophetic consciousness into the larger relationship which is properly called religion . . . That transformation, for all we can tell, may have taken place more than once in the history of prophecy, but the solitary record of it is the Confessions of Jeremiah.'
[7a] Scott, *The Relevance of the Prophets*, p. 151.

into the religious and moral depravity of their people.[8] Being endowed with prophetic gifts they were overwhelmed by what they had seen and experienced so that they could not resist the call to preach it to their people. When the influx of important ideas and powerful emotions disturbed the balance of normal mental life, they experienced ecstasy in various degrees.

The significance of the personal religion of the prophets cannot be sufficiently emphasized, but it would be wrong to deny the great importance of the extraordinary experiences which we have called 'revelatory experiences'. In fact, as we have tried to show above, these experiences played a great part in the life of the Israelite prophets as in all men and women of the prophetic type. It must be strongly emphasized that such abnormal experiences do not reduce the value of the religious experiences and ideas in the strict sense. Ecstasy and similar experiences only influence the form in which revelation is received and perhaps the intensity of the feelings which accompany it. They are not the ultimate sources of divine revelation. They do not create quite new religious and moral ideas; nor do they increase or reduce their inherent value.[9]

3. THE RELIGION OF THE PROPHETS AND MYSTICISM

Before leaving the personal religion of the Israelite prophets, it is necessary to say some words about another question which is of importance for its characterization, viz. the relation of the religion of the prophets to what is called 'mystical religion' or 'mysticism'. It is the more necessary to examine this problem, since the prophets have been labelled as mystics in scientific as well as in more popular expositions,[10] while on the other side, there are authors who have denied any connection between the religion of the Israelite prophets and mysticism. Thus Professor G. Scholem says outright, 'It would be absurd to call Moses, the man of God, a mystic, or to apply this term to the prophets, on the strength of their immediate religious experience.'[11] Such different

[8] The personal religion of the prophets is treated in full detail in Seierstad, *Die Offenbarungserlebnisse der Propheten Amos, Jesaja und Jeremia*. Likewise, in a very illuminating way, in Mowinckel, *Die Erkenntnis Gottes bei den alttestamentlichen Propheten*. See also Knight, *The Hebrew Prophetic Consciousness*.

[9] I would strongly maintain this in opposition to Seierstad, who from interest in the personal religion of the prophets reduces their supernormal experiences to a minimum.

[10] In Söderblom, *The Nature of Revelation*, Jeremiah, for instance, is classed as a mystic, p. 95. See further the more popular book, Tyciak, *Prophetie und Mystik*.

[11] Scholem, *Major Trends in Jewish Mysticism*², pp. 6 f.; cf. Hempel, *Gott und Mensch*², p. 104. Heiler sharply distinguishes between mystical and prophetic religion. He says, 'The contrast between this prophetic vital feeling and the mystical is as sharp as possible'; *Prayer*, p. 144.

opinions arise from different presuppositions about the nature of either mysticism or the religion of the Israelite prophets.

In numerous publications I have compared the prophets in ancient Israel with the medieval and other mystics.[12] In doing so my interest has always been to use *the visionary experiences* of the mystics to throw light upon the revelatory experiences of the prophets. In addition I was convinced that a study of medieval *revelation literature* would help towards a better understanding of the character of the prophetic books in the Old Testament, their origin, growth, and composition. I was never of the opinion that the personal religion of the prophets was of the same nature as that of the mystics and that prophetic religion should be designated as religious mysticism. Since I have sometimes been misunderstood on this point, it would be useful here to discuss briefly the religion of the Old Testament prophets in its relation to mysticism. Moreover the question is one of general interest for psychology and the history of religion.

Though the term 'mysticism' is often used in the study of religion, considerable confusion is caused by the fact that different scholars use it in different senses. A good impression of the range of meanings in which the term is employed may be gained from the list of 'definitions of mysticism and mystical theology' which Dr. Inge has compiled as an appendix to his well-known Bampton lectures on this theme.[13] When mysticism is said to be belief in something irrational in our existence, every form of religion is naturally to be described as mysticism. But no competent student of religion can be content with such a general notion. Mysticism is not the same as religion; mysticism is a special sort of religious life. Much better is the definition suggested by Rufus Jones and endorsed by Scholem, according to which mysticism is the type of religion which puts the emphasis on an immediate awareness of relation with God, on a direct and intimate consciousness of the Divine Presence.[14] Evelyn Underhill means the same thing when she sees in mysticism the establishment of immediate communication between the spirit of man and God.[15] This definition becomes still better if it is amplified by a definition formulated by J. B. Pratt: mysticism is the sense of the presence of a being or reality through other means than the ordinary perceptive processes or the reason.[16]

[12] See, above all, *Die literarische Gattung der prophetischen Literatur* and, further, 'Einige Grundfragen der alttestamentlichen Wissenschaft' in the *Bertholet Festschrift*, pp. 325 ff.
[13] Inge, *Christian Mysticism*, pp. 335 ff.
[14] Scholem, op. cit., p. 4.
[15] Evelyn Underhill, *Mysticism*[12], p. 4 and *passim*.
[16] Pratt, *The Religious Consciousness*, p. 337.

It is obvious that what the best experts have in mind when they use the term 'mysticism' is the introversive side of the devotional life. Certainly all true religion includes an element of introversion, something that refers to the inner life, something mysterious and ineffable (intense religious feeling tends always to be tinged with mysticism); but if the devotional life is dominated by the internal experiences, and the objective, exterior elements are forced into the background, the term 'mysticism' is justly used.

Adopting the substance of these latter definitions and using terms borrowed from modern psychology, the present writer would speak of mysticism as *introspective religion* in contrast to what might be called *extrospective religion*. These two types of religious attitude are in particular to be distinguished within the higher religions, especially the Biblical religions.[17]

In introspective religion God encounters man in his innermost being. In extrospective religion man finds God in the exterior life. The character of introspective religion is admirably expressed by the saying of Hugo of St. Victor: 'The way to ascend to God is to descend into oneself.'[18] In both types we are entitled to speak of a divine revelation; but in the former knowledge of God is obtained by seeking Him in the depths of man's own personality, by an act of introspection and introversive contemplation, in the latter God reveals Himself through His deeds in creation and in history, through the sacred book, the godlike personality, or other objective facts. In introspective religion the communication of man with God takes place in the depths of the soul, where God is seen and made known, and manifests itself in the movements of the emotional life, as love and enjoyment (*fruitio Dei*); in extrospective religion the attitude of man towards his God is characterized by surrender in faith and obedience.

In history we seldom meet with absolutely pure forms of religion. Most men live by two religions or more. Thus introspective and extrospective religion are often mingled together. In using the term 'mysticism' or 'introspective religion' we think of forms of religion in which introspection and introversion, immanent communion with God and emotional experience of revelation are the essential features of the religious life.

[17] This distinction was made by the present writer for the first time in an article, 'Profetforskningens metod' in the *Söderblom Festschrift*, 1926, pp. 314 ff. Instead of the word 'circumspective' there used (pp. 324 ff.) I now prefer the psychological term 'extrospective'. Simultaneously Andrae in his book *Mystikens psykologi* designated religious mysticism as 'religious introversion' (p. 77). Some years earlier Heiler had characterized mysticism in a similar way; *Prayer*, p. 144.

[18] Inge, op. cit., p. 141.

The well-known distinction 'mysticism of personality' and 'mysticism of infinity' made by N. Söderblom presupposes that all religion which claims to grant a certain immediate experience of the divine, which, in a word, includes something original and inexplicable, is mysticism. 'The difference', says Söderblom, 'lies in the role which personal life plays.' There is a way to knowledge of the divine Being which is a way of negation (via negationis), leading to a reception of the divine in self-sacrifice and the extinction of the mystic's own personality. There is another way to God, a way of affirmation (via positionis), which leads to a richer and stronger personal life. But to both these ways Söderblom applies the term 'mysticism'. In accordance with these definitions the Brahmans of India, the Neoplatonists, the Areopagite, and Meister Eckhart are mystics, but also Jeremiah, the Apostle Paul, Augustine, Luther, Pascal, John Bunyan, Kierkegaard.[19] That Söderblom, surprisingly indeed, designates the religious attitude of both these groups as mysticism, arises from the fact that he finds in both the original and the inexplicable element which to Söderblom constitutes the mystical experience and the mystical life.

However, the difference between these two groups of religious personalities (for instance between Meister Eckhart and Luther) is so great, that, in my opinion, it is better not to use the same term for both. I prefer to designate the religion of the former group as mysticism or introspective religion and that of the latter group as extrospective religion or the religion of faith. Of Luther, for instance, nothing was more characteristic than his clinging to the objective revelation given in the Word of God and the person of Jesus Christ as a historical fact. Nothing was more alien to him than subjectivity in every form.

But introspective religion or mysticism is not entirely homogeneous. There are two types of introspective mysticism. One type is represented by what Söderblom calls 'the mysticism of infinity', but which the present writer prefers to call mysticism of unity or impersonal mysticism, because its goal is complete oneness with the divine conceived of as a more or less impersonal substance. It is characteristic of the other type that the personality is preserved, both the personality of the divine and the personality of the religious man. Many Christian mystics have not claimed to attain identity or complete fusion with God, so that the human personality should be absorbed by and melt away into God, and so that an interpenetration of substances should take place. The divine remains to them personality, and they themselves remain personalities, though (as mystics) they seek for the divine in the interior domain of

<hr />

[19] Söderblom, op. cit., pp. 74 ff.

personality. The polarity between *tu* and *ego* is maintained, and there is no desire for identity or amalgamation.

An example of such *personal mysticism* is the bridal mysticism, e.g., of Birgitta of Sweden, in which Jesus Christ is the object of the devotional love. St. Birgitta says that her soul is filled with Christ. Christ is within her and dwells in her heart. The heavens and the earth cannot hold Him; yet He will reside in the little lump of flesh which is her heart. In her heart she has communion with the Bridegroom in love, but there is no talk of complete unity or identity.

Another fine example of personal mysticism is Julian of Norwich.[20] This saint speaks frequently of God or Christ (these two are practically identical both to Julian and to her Scandinavian counterpart) as dwelling or sitting in her soul; and 'her own substance is a creature in God'. In the interior of her soul she has communication with God, and she experiences the touch of God in her soul. The devoted soul is knit and united to God. Nevertheless, there is no talk of the annihilation or dissolution of personality. God is God, and man is man. The antithesis of *tu* and *ego* is always preserved. The oneness consists in inward prayer and worship, peace, love, holiness, and unity of willing. But the soul which participates in God is never lost in God; on the contrary the soul which enters into communion with God finds there at last its very self.

This form of mysticism, represented by personalities such as Birgitta of Sweden and Julian of Norwich, can be appropriately described as 'personal mysticism'. This 'personal mysticism', however, is not the same as Söderblom's 'mysticism of personality', which is a term of much wider compass. The examples adduced by Söderblom indicate that it is to be applied in the first place to personalities whose religious attitude (according to the terminology used by the present writer) is not mysticism at all, but extrospective religion, or the religion of faith, though it is of an intimate, intense, original, creative character.

Personal mysticism is very common among the Christian mystics of the Middle Ages, but it is often connected with the mysticism of unity. St. Bernard of Clairvaux is a good example of a devotional life which includes both sorts of mysticism. He often speaks of Christ as the Beloved in terms taken from the Song of Songs, maintaining the contrast between *tu* and *ego*; but he also says of the blessedness of internal communion: *Sic efficitur deificatio*. The soul becomes like iron made glowing by fire, like the air penetrated by the beams of the sun. This is the mysticism of unity.

[20] See above, pp. 36 ff.

Jewish mysticism is, as a rule, personal mysticism, although there are Jewish mystics who speak of God in terms belonging to the mysticism of unity and also claim to have experienced *unio mystica* in its radical form. Scholem, the eminent expert in this field, says, however, that, even leaving aside the distinction between earlier and later documents of Jewish mysticism, it is only in extremely rare cases that union with God means that the human personality abandons itself to the rapture of complete immersion in the stream of divine being. The Jewish mystics almost invariably retain a sense of the distance between the Creator and His creatures. M. Buber says of Hasidic mysticism: 'Mysticism here allows the soul of the individual, who separates himself from society, to feel the presence of God in burning intimacy, but even in the ecstasy the situation remains as it was, even the relationship of the most intimate reciprocity remains a relationship; unshaken in the relation to a being, which cannot be identified with our being. Even the ecstasy is unable to turn inwards to such an extent as to be able to find complete satisfaction and fulfilment in inwardness . . . Never, in the eyes of the soul, has this God become to such an extent its God, the God of the soul, that He would cease to be the God of Sinai.'[21] Consequently, in the terminology of the present writer Jewish mysticism should for the most part be designated as personal mysticism.

The essential religious experience of Christian mysticism is immediate contact with the divine in the depths of the soul, whether the divine is conceived of as the Infinite or, more personally, as *dulcis hospes animae*. Consequently objective revelation has no necessary or primary importance for the mystic. The external revelation supplies him with symbols for delineating experiences of the devotional life; it offers patterns and models for the inner life and, as an object of meditation, it stimulates inner experiences. History becomes, as the mystics say, an object of *meditatio* and *representatio*. It furnishes *exempla* and *probamenta*. The mystic has to revere and to follow these examples of history: *mysteria venerari, exempla sectari*; he has to imitate in his interior life, the significant events of the holy history of the Bible. Thus this history becomes an *iter quo ostendatur*. The historical person of Jesus Christ becomes an example and a prototype; He becomes a teacher, a *magister* of the mystic life. The word of God in the Bible becomes a *stimulus* to mystic experiences, but no real revelation, containing a unique and paradoxical message of salvation from God to men. For the mystic the soteriological history loses its importance as 'the

[21] Scholem, op. cit., pp. 122 f.; Buber, *Hasidism*, p. 199.

power of God unto salvation to every one that believeth'. The history of revelation develops in the soul of the mystic. Bethlehem of Judah becomes the Bethlehem of the soul, the Saviour's birth becomes the birth of Christ in the inner man. Henri Bremond rightly says that the mystic knowledge is an immediate apprehension of the divine, containing all theology, the entire Creed, intuitionally apprehended, essentially without the aid of objective documents.[22]

The antithesis of seeing and belief, vision and faith, is well known to the mystics themselves. Aegidius, a disciple of Francis of Assisi, said, 'I know a man who saw God so distinctly, that he lost his faith.' And Catherine of Genoa said with reference to her deepest religious experience, 'Faith seems to be lost, hope expired, because I possess in certainty what I otherwise believed and hoped.'[23]

The emancipation from the soteriological history often leads to a more general and abstract idea of God. This characteristic often appears in mystics of all religions. Friedrich Heiler rightly says, 'Weil das mystische Erlebnis immer dasselbe ist, ist der mystische Heilsweg zu Gott immer der gleiche, darum ist auch die Sprache und Bildwelt der Mystik allenthalben dieselbe.' We may appropriately speak of an *ecclesia spritualis* of all mystics, who always understand each other, using as they do approximately the same terminology. Mysticism, particularly in its impersonal form, tends always and everywhere to empty the divine of its concrete content. God becomes ultimately something *incomprehensibile* and *ineffabile*. The essence of God is conceived of as a *complexio oppositorum* or as a total of superlative attributes. But the highest expression of the real essence of God becomes silence. St. Augustine went so far as to say: *Melius scitur Deus nesciendo.* When symbols are used they are mostly taken from nature, not from personal life: fire, sun, light, life, fervour, water, sea, darkness, abyss, wild, waste, etc.[24] In 'personal mysticism' more personal expressions are of course used, particularly those derived from the erotic life.

It is quite natural that mysticism should always tend towards pantheism, just as pantheism is often the origin and the basis of mysticism. God tends, particularly in the mysticism of unity, to be a neuter instead of a living personality. Thus the highest experience of a mystic of this sort is the fusion of man with this *unum incommutabile* and *summa*

---

[22] Bremond, *Histoire littéraire du sentiment religieux en France*, II, pp. 585 ff. Other examples in Inge, op. cit., pp. 99 ff., and Underhill, op. cit., pp. 95 ff. Cf. also Merkel, *Die Mystik im Kulturleben der Völker*, pp. 19 f.

[23] Buber, *Ekstatische Konfessionen*, pp. 59 and 151.

[24] Heiler in *Numen*, i, 1954, pp. 161 ff. Saint-Martin says, 'All mystics speak the same language, for they come from the same country'; Underhill, op. cit., p. 80.

plenitudo, is *to be God*. A Persian mystic says, 'Who comes into the true essence, becomes absorbed in God, is God.'[25]

The idea of the revelation of God and communion with God in the depths of man's being presupposes the conception that there are faculties in the human soul capable of receiving the divine and of making mystical communication with the divine possible. There is a sphere or a point within the soul, a 'point of juncture', where God takes His abode, where God 'touches' the soul, approaching it in quite other ways than the psychologically normal ones. The experience of God is to the mystics a *miraculum*; and the spiritual faculties engaged are of a supernatural and supra-rational nature. The mystics speak of an 'inner sight', of *oculus mentis, ratio superior, summus et intimus mentis sinus, apex mentis, acies mentis*, 'Seelengrund', 'bottom' of the soul, *scintilla*, etc. These are all different names for the organ by which our personality holds communion with God and receives knowledge of God. This extraordinary equipment of the soul has some affinity with the divine essence itself; and without this affinity it would be impossible to men to attain an immanent union with God. Eckhart says, 'The eye with which I see God is the same as that with which He sees me.' The famous word of Goethe is here applicable: 'Wär' nicht das Auge sonnenhaft, die Sonne könnt' es nie erblicken.'[26]

In the foregoing we have tried to distinguish between and characterize two essential types of religion: *extrospective religion*, or religion of faith, and *introspective religion*, or religion of immediate contact with the divine in the depths of the soul. Now the question arises: to which of the two types do the Israelite prophets belong? I think here of the great classical or canonical prophets. In answering this question we must allow for the fact that the religion proclaimed by the prophets in their preaching corresponded to their personal faith. The orgiastic religion of the primitive prophets has been sufficiently described in the second chapter of this book. It is more akin to the religion of spiritual possession than to mysticism in a strict sense or to the religion of faith.

A series of characteristic features in the religion of the prophets gives the answer to the above question.[27]

For the prophets the sources of divine revelation are the events of the

---

[25] Buber, op. cit., p. 14.

[26] This motif has been carefully examined by the present writer in an article 'Det solliknande ögat', *STK*, iii, 1927, pp. 230 ff. The same motif occurs in Persian mysticism: 'Gott mit Gottes Auge betrachtend, sah ich Gott durch Gott'; Buber, op. cit., p. 15.

[27] For the problems here discussed see also Lindblom in *ZAW*, lvii, 1939, pp. 65 ff., and, substantially following the same lines, Knight, *The Hebrew Prophetic Consciousness*, pp. 30 ff.

external world, behind which stands Yahweh's omnipotent will. The things that happen in the world are Yahweh's actions, the manifestations of His purposes and designs. Natural occurrences are His actions, but much more so are the events of world history, and, above all, the wonderful events in the history of the people of Israel. The prophets stand there as watchmen and observers of the historical scene; they trace there the deeds of Yahweh and bear witness of them to other people. One of the great pioneers of modern Old Testament research says of the prophets, 'Sie erscheinen als Sturmboten, wenn ein geschichtliches Gewitter aufzieht; sie heissen Wächter, weil sie von hoher Zinne schauen und melden, wenn etwas Verdächtiges am Horizont sich sehen lässt.'[27a]

The prophets never refer to a God who dwells in the depths of the human soul. The prophets never pretend to draw knowledge of Yahweh from inner, subjective sources; nor do they assume such an immanent mysterious revelation within other men. They never direct men to what they might possibly discover of God in the depth of their own souls. They direct them out into the same wide field of history in which they have taken their own stand, and endeavour to open the eyes of men to what they themselves have discovered.

We never find in the prophets any suggestion of secret faculties in human nature by means of which men could realize an immediate contact with God. Nor do they claim to be themselves in possession of a special level in the soul, a 'Seelengrund', where they can grasp and appropriate the divine essence. Yahweh reveals Himself not *within* men, but *to* men. Men have only to see and hear what happens around them. Very characteristic are the words of Isaiah about his compatriots: 'Their feasts are lyre and harp, timbrel and flute and wine, *but the doing of Yahweh they regard not, and the work of His hands they see not*' (Isa. v. 12).

In the prophets we never find anything that we could call a pantheistic tendency. The prophetic idea of God is throughout personalistic. Characteristic of the prophets is the antithesis of *tu* and *ego*, *ego* and *tu*. The prophets never say, as do mystics in all parts of the world: 'Thou art I, I am Thou'. Consequently we find in their religion dualism, not oneness; distance, not immediacy; the maintenance of the human personality, not its absorption in the divine Being.

God is to the prophets never completely ineffable. They always speak of Yahweh as One of whom men can have knowledge. They seek the loftiest words and metaphors to express the essence of Yahweh in His sublime being and in His action. But their figurative language is always

[27a] Wellhausen, *Israelitische und jüdische Geschichte*[5], p. 115.

concrete and clear. It is true that, according to the prophets, Yahweh's ways sometimes seem to be obscure and difficult to understand. In such dark situations the prophets reassure themselves with the certainty that Yahweh's thoughts are not the thoughts of men, and that the ways of men are not Yahweh's ways. As the heavens are higher than the earth, so are Yahweh's ways higher than the ways of men, and Yahweh's thoughts than the thoughts of men (Isa. lv. 8 f.) Yahweh's counsel is wonderful, His wisdom is great (xxviii. 29). His deeds in the history of the elect people are marvellous, but sometimes strange or seemingly alien (xxix. 14; xxviii. 21). But this is not the ineffability of the divine of which the mystics speak. Here the question is of occasional problems concerning Yahweh's working in history, which have no reference to the essential nature of God. The prophets never follow the *via negationis* when they speak of Yahweh. They never feel it necessary to keep silence before Yahweh as something *incomprehensibile et ineffabile* in itself. The silence before Yahweh which they demand (Hab. ii. 20; Zeph. i. 7) is silence in the presence of the *numinosum fascinosum et tremendum* of the divine majesty and the divine actions in the world, not silence before something which cannot be expressed in words. When Deutero-Isaiah says that Yahweh is a God who 'keeps Himself hidden' (Isa. xlv.15), he is thinking of the unexpected and surprising in the eschatological working of Yahweh. The God of the prophets is a God who is well known, a God about whom one can speak. This He is, because He is a God of history, who rules according to personal laws and whose character displays personal features.

The subject of the prophetic religion is in the first place the people as a community. It can easily be shown that the national religion proclaimed by the prophets also includes individual religion; but the religion of the people is unmistakably prominent in the preaching of the prophets.[28] However, the God of the individual is no other than the God of the people and preserves throughout the features of the national God. Here is a marked difference from mysticism. The religion of the mystics cannot be conceived in forms other than those of individual religion. Only individual men can realize communion with God, the introspective *unio mystica*. The *ecclesia spiritualis* of the mystics is not comparable with the people of Israel in the prophetic religion. The former is the sum total of men who share similar personal religious experiences; the latter is a historically conditioned community with a political and social structure and a common faith and cult.

Mystical religion is essentially aristocratic. It is a religion for elect

---

[28] See further, *inter alios*, Hempel, *Das Ethos des Alten Testaments*, pp. 32 f.

souls. It presupposes a high spiritual standard. The great masses have no possibility of attaining the spiritual refinement which mystic religion demands. This is true of personal mysticism and the mysticism of unity as well. Origen justified an esoteric mystery-religion for educated men and a mythical religion for the vulgar, in appealing to the example of the Persians and Indians.[29] The Israelite prophets address their message to all people. The knowledge of Yahweh which they proclaim and call for is not a knowledge for a few; their words, which are Yahweh's own words, are meant to be accepted and realized by everybody.

Being a God of history, revealing Himself in the course of events, Yahweh is a God of extramanence, not a God of immanence. Thus the religious relation of man to God is, to the prophets, faith and obedience. The essence of the prophetic religion is surrender of the whole personality to Yahweh, not emotional movements in the soul. Consequently religious training plays no part in the religious life of the prophets. Mysticism is in large measure a religion of effort; the religion of the prophets is a religion of the overpowering might of God.

Mysticism is, in accordance with its essence, tolerant. The mystics come from 'the same country' and recognize each other as belonging to the same fraternity. They show sympathetic appreciation of other forms of religion. There is in their opinion only one God, and He reveals Himself to everyone who is genuinely devout. The prophets of Yahweh were fundamentally intolerant. To them the supreme sin was to halt between two opinions. To go after other gods was 'whoring'. To the prophets an essential feature in the essence of Yahweh was His zeal, ķin'âh, which reacted against all rivals in the assembly of the gods.

Accordingly, the essential characteristics of mysticism are missing in the religion of the prophets. The prophetic religion represents a quite other type. What gives the religion of the prophets its distinctive mark is the conception of God as a God of history, who reveals Himself not in the internal feelings of the human mind, but in the course of external events.

But what of ecstasy and the extraordinary experiences in the lives of the prophets? When Yahweh's word comes to the prophet and Yahweh speaks to him, when the prophet has visions and auditions, stands in the council of Yahweh and listens to His designs, is not this mysticism, and are not such personal experiences to be considered as mystic experiences?

First it is to be observed that the prophets never present their own extraordinary experiences as models to be imitated by other men. What they demand of others is fear of Yahweh, confidence in Him, and

[29] Inge, op. cit., p. 101.

obedience to His commands, but not experiences of a supernatural nature. This fact in itself shows that ecstasy in different forms was not regarded by the prophets as *religion*, it was not constitutive of the relation of men to God, but a gift peculiar to the prophets as prophets and an element in their special prophetic endowment.

Nor was ecstasy essential to the personal religion of the prophets. So far as the early prophets are concerned, one might reasonably say that ecstasy was an essential element in their religion. The personal religion of the great prophets was, on the contrary, fundamentally independent of their ecstatic experiences. There is no suggestion that in ecstasy they arrived at the highest level of religion, which had to be attained by effort and training, and by climbing the mystical ladder, *scala perfectionis*, with its different stages. The visionary experiences of the prophets were connected with their prophetic calling, not with their personal religion as such.

Ecstasy (or high-tensioned inspiration in various degrees) in the life of the prophets was not a source of their fundamental knowledge of Yahweh; it was a peculiar mental state in which they received revelations of various kinds by visions or auditions. Knowledge of Yahweh (*da'aṯ yahwêh*) was given them from history and tradition. Ecstasy set in when the religious ideas and feelings overwhelmed them so mightily that the everyday mental balance was lost.

Even when it is said that Yahweh speaks to the prophets or that Yahweh's word is in them, even when Yahweh is speaking in the first person through their mouths, this has nothing to do with the *unio mystica* of the mystics. The prophets speak as the mouthpieces of Yahweh, they preach what Yahweh has, so to speak, dictated to them (then Yahweh quite naturally speaks through their mouths in the first person). They do not speak like those who have the divinity dwelling within the soul and are unified with God in a mysterious union; they speak as the messengers of God, reproducing the words of Him who has sent them.[30]

It is very characteristic of the prophets that they speak of 'the hand', 'the spirit', 'the word of Yahweh' as causes of their revelatory experiences. This, too, warns us against speaking of *unio mystica* with God in the Old Testament prophets.

Accordingly, ecstasy is an accessory and accidental phenomenon in the religious life of the great prophets, belonging to their special prophetic calling. It is a fact that ecstasy can be connected with every kind of religion; it can even appear outside the boundaries of religion.

[30] Cf. Wildberger, *Jahwewort und prophetische Rede bei Jeremia*.

From ecstasy in itself no conclusion can be drawn concerning the nature of a religious attitude.[31] The core of religion is to the prophets surrender to Yahweh, the God of the holy tradition, the God of nature and history. The deepest source of their knowledge of God was history, above all the history of the chosen people. The essence of the religion of the prophets was not subjective religious introspection and *unio mystica*, but faith in and obedience to an objectively revealed personal Power and Will.

4. The Religious Preaching of the Pre-exilic Prophets

A. *General Structure*

In attempting to describe the religion of the Israelite prophets we must guard against a false systematization of the prophetic teaching. Israelite thought was never systematic; and the great religious personalities of the Old Testament were never concerned to sum up their ideas into a coherent whole. The task of the prophets was to deliver a message, not to present a theological or philosophical system. This message must be our starting-point in describing the religious ideas of the prophets. The central message was always the same; its application changed from time to time with changing historical circumstances.

What was this central message of the prophets? The answer given by the Old Testament is this: the mighty acts of Yahweh in judging and saving His chosen people.

This message, as will be shown in detail below, was not a new one, founded on an original discovery made by the prophets. That Yahweh was the God of Israel and Israel the people of Yahweh, was an idea inherited from the days of the Exodus from Egypt. That Yahweh was also a God who both inflicted punishment and was active as a Saviour, was an ancient truth impressed on the mind of the Israelite people by tradition and cult. What the prophets did was to bring home this truth in every concrete situation, calling sinners to repentance in the face of impending doom and encouraging those who turned to Yahweh with promises of future blessing.

In the light of the fundamental idea of the special relationship between Yahweh and His people, the new discovery of the pre-exilic prophets (with whom we are at present concerned) was that Israel had fallen away from Yahweh, her God, had been rejected as a nation and would

---

[31] See above, pp. 4 f., 106 f., and further Zaehner, *Mysticism Sacred and Profane. An Inquiry into some Varieties of Praeternatural Experience.*

be punished. This is the presupposition for a right understanding of these prophets. To begin with anything else (monotheistic doctrine, moral admonitions, or even 'messianic' promises) is to miss the way to a real understanding of pre-exilic prophecy.

It is not difficult to find in the pre-exilic prophets incisive expressions of the idea of rejection. Amos says in Yahweh's name, 'The end has come upon My people Israel; I will never again forgive them' (viii. 2). Hosea was commanded by Yahweh to give one of his sons the name Lo-'ammi, Not-my-people, to symbolize that Israel was no longer Yahweh's people (i. 9). In his inaugural vision Isaiah was commanded to make the mind of his people obdurate, lest it should repent and be restored. Micah knew that Jerusalem, the capital, would become a ruin and the people be destroyed (iii. 12; iv. 9 f.). Zephaniah declared that Judah would be judged in the general world-judgement. Jeremiah says that Yahweh has rejected and cast off His people, which has become 'the generation of His wrath' (vii. 29).

Such words had never before been heard in Israel. The new message was amazing and shocking. The descriptions, often drastic, of how the judgement would come about made it still more terrifying. To this we return below.

The idea of rejection presupposed that Israel was Yahweh's people, His chosen people. Of the pagan nations it could be said that they were doomed, not that they were rejected. Thus the message of the prophets was based upon the fundamental idea in the religious faith of Israel, the idea of election. This idea appears in many forms as a constant element in all prophetic preaching. It was taken up from the Mosaic tradition as an unquestioned article of faith. But to the prophets, in contrast to the common opinion, this idea did not signify that Yahweh's choice of Israel to be His people was a natural necessity, the basis of a relationship that could not be broken. By a free and sovereign decision (so the prophets taught) Yahweh had chosen Israel from all the nations of the earth to become His own people. The prophets saw in this decision an act of Yahweh's unfathomable love to His people. But love could be turned into wrath. This was precisely what had happened in the contemporary situation.

A consequence of the fact that Yahweh had chosen Israel to be His people was that Yahweh made certain claims on them. Israel ought to live in accordance with their position as Yahweh's people. Israel should be a holy people fulfilling Yahweh's holy will, expressed in what the prophets call *mišpāṭ* and *ṣeḏāḳâh*, justice and righteousness. Yahweh's claim on His people was first that they should remain faithful to their

God, and secondly that they should obey Yahweh's moral commands as expressed in law and tradition.

But they deserted their God and trampled His commands under foot. Now Yahweh's love turned into wrath. Yahweh's wrath required the judgement and the rejection of the people. This was the historical turning-point with which the prophets were confronted.

Nevertheless the people were Yahweh's people, the chosen people, the object of Yahweh's love. What would become of the election and of Yahweh's plan for Israel and for mankind if the rejection became total and final. A tension ensued between Yahweh's love and Yahweh's wrath. In prophecy we find different attitudes towards this fundamental problem. These attitudes will be examined in detail below.

Election was an act in history and manifested in history. Accordingly, history is necessarily of central significance in the religion of the prophets. Through historical events they became certain of the reality of election, through history, i.e., Yahweh's acts in history, they came to know Yahweh's love and Yahweh's wrath. To the prophets divine revelation was revelation in history. In history Yahweh revealed Himself to everyone who could understand the language of history. This was precisely what the prophets could do.

The view of history as divine revelation, the certainty of the election of Israel as an act of divine love, the knowledge of Yahweh's will and commands, the realization of the fact that the people had failed in faith and obedience and, accordingly, were subject to doom and rejection, the possibility that Yahweh's love would nevertheless find a way to gain its final end, these are the chief elements in the religion of the pre-exilic prophets.

Before proceeding to analyse the individual ideas, we must try to answer two general questions connected with the religion of the prophets. The first concerns the origin of their religious views in general; the second has reference to a special problem: the relationship of doom and promise, adversity and bliss, destruction and salvation, in their preaching.

Considering all that was new and startling in the prophetic preaching, one might be tempted to conclude that the prophets were founders of a new religion, giving their people a new conception of God, a new ethic, a new idea of the divine revelation. Nothing could be more erroneous. The prophets themselves never regarded it as their personal mission to give their people a new religion. They assumed that their words could be immediately understood and accepted; and it seemed to them wholly enigmatic and paradoxical that the people were deaf to their preaching.

To the people's question what they should offer to Yahweh to find favour with Him the prophet Micah answered with manifest reference to the Mosaic tradition: 'You have been told, O man, what is good; and what does Yahweh require of you but to do justice and to love faithfulness, and to walk humbly with your God?' (vi. 8). Jeremiah expected at least the great ones among his people to know the way of Yahweh, the requirements of their God (v. 5). He exhorted the people to ask for the ancient paths, where the good way is (vi. 16). But he came to realize that the people did not listen to Yahweh's words because they had stiffened their necks. He was convinced that whatever he said, they would not listen; he might call, they would not answer. Therefore the prophet should say to them, 'This is the people that would not listen to the voice of Yahweh, their God' (vii. 26 ff.). He found that, paradoxically enough, their ears were uncircumcised, so that they *could* not listen (vi. 10).

Isaiah saw a people so hard-hearted, so stubborn, that his preaching would be fruitless. So he was shown in his inaugural vision that his mission was to make the people obdurate, so that the inevitable judgement might come speedily (vi). Ezekiel had to discover that he was to the people like a singer of love songs, with a beautiful voice. They listened, but did not understand and would not obey (xxxiii. 32). The hostility which the prophets encountered baffled them. They saw in the unresponsiveness of the people something irrational, something mysterious. The people *ought* to have understood and assented to their preaching; but they *could* not because their hearts were hardened. The content of the prophetic preaching was comprehensible; but the attitude of the people was incomprehensible. In this respect the situation of the Old Testament prophets was the same as that of Jesus Christ according to the Gospels.

The ideas of the prophets concerning God, the election of Israel, the divine revelation, and the moral demands of Yahweh were not new; they were old ideas, but applied by the prophets in a new way. They were all founded on the Mosaic inheritance expressed in the historical traditions, the cult in its noblest forms, and legal usage. The religion of Israel was founded as a new religion in connection with the Exodus from Egypt, when Yahweh of Sinai became the God of Israel, and His essence and will were revealed to the Hebrew tribes by Moses. Only when the achievement of Moses is rightly appraised can the development of Israelite religion be understood. Not least this is true of the religion of the prophets. It has been rightly said of them: 'They claimed to bear a torch kindled by Moses from the flames of Sinai, and passed from hand to hand by the prophetic leaders and makers-of-history throughout generations.'[31a]

Moses taught his people that Yahweh, and He alone, was their God. Yahweh Himself had chosen this people to be His own people; and this became manifest through the deliverance from Egypt, i.e., through a historical event. Thus Yahweh had entered the historical sphere and appeared as a God of history. The noblest moral ideas, developed in the nomadic culture, were identified by Moses with the will of Yahweh and regarded as Yahweh's inviolable demands. As the God of election Yahweh was conceived of not as a blind natural force, but as a personality working according to personal laws. The essential content of the Mosaic religion was of a personal character. The chief categories of religion now became faith, love, gratitude, obedience. Nevertheless, it would be a great mistake to overlook the physical features in Yahweh. Yahweh always retained, even in the thought of the prophets, an element of natural power, of 'the demonic';[32] but the essential element in His nature was the personal quality.

This was the basis of the preaching of the prophets. The revolutionary element in it was their denunciation of their compatriots for having forgotten the God of their fathers, for worshipping Yahweh only in name, and for having trampled His holy demands under foot. Yahweh being a holy God and a punisher of sin was now about to reject His people and destroy them, so that they should no longer be a people. The only way to be saved was in faith and obedience to turn to Yahweh again. Through repentance and conversion alone could life and blessing be attained.

What the prophets had to say to their people was in accordance with true Yahwism, but opposed to the popular way of thinking. What was new in their message was given them as a revelation from their God. It came to them in their inner life, in their personal communion with God. Here is the point where scientific examination can go no further.[33]

Even a superficial study of the books of the pre-exilic prophets reveals the tendency to combine prophecies of doom with prophecies of good fortune and bliss. A literary analysis shows that many of the latter

[31a] Scott, *The Relevance of the Prophets,* p. 51.
[32] Cf. Volz, *Das Dämonische in Jahwe.*
[33] In contrast to an exaggerated emphasis on the importance of the prophets as 'religious personalities' Duhm in his book *Israels Propheten* emphasized that the prophets did not come with new doctrines, they really represented the true Mosaic tradition. This point of view was taken to extremes by Cramer in *Amos. Versuch einer theologischen Interpretation.* Cramer goes much too far. He objects to any psychological approach to the Israelite prophets. The visions of Amos, for instance, are only, says Cramer, stylistic methods of presenting his ideas. Cramer has committed a serious blunder in not having studied the Israelite prophets in their religio-historical context.

x

are not original, but were added to the authentic sayings by the redactors of the prophetic books. This has been discussed in detail in the fourth chapter of this book. But apart from such secondary additions the alternating pattern of doom and blessing is to be found. It belonged apparently to the original preaching of the pre-exilic prophets. Even in Amos, the most radical of the prophets of judgement, there are words about a happy future. As has been shown above, I find it impossible to regard the conclusion of the book of Amos as an authentic saying by this prophet; but no objection need be made against the authenticity of the words of v. 4, 6, 14: if the people decide to seek Yahweh and to do His will, they will live, and Yahweh will be gracious to them.[34] Still more conspicuous is the combination of doom and promise in Hosea, Isaiah, and Jeremiah. What grounds are there for this apparently fixed scheme of future misfortune and future happiness?

More than fifty years ago the German scholar H. Gressmann gave an answer which has played an important role in Old Testament research, viz., that the prophets were dependent on a pre-prophetic eschatology, which was a living element in the people's faith, but had come from abroad.[35] The prophets adopted fragments of this supposed eschatological system, but moulded them in accordance with their characteristic religious ideas. Gressmann started with the idea of 'Yahweh's day' in Amos (v. 18 ff.) as the basis of his entire hypothesis. In the pre-prophetic popular eschatology this idea was, according to Gressmann, a fixed point, round which all the other ideas circled. The eschatological ideas formed two groups, called by Gressmann 'Unheilseschatologie' and 'Heilseschatologie'. These were indissolubly connected both in the popular eschatology and also in the prophetic preaching. It was a consequence of this view that Gressmann defended as authentic many so-called Messianic passages in the earlier prophets which were regarded by the representatives of the literary criticism of his time as post-exilic.

The weakness of Gressmann's standpoint is first and foremost that neither Gressmann nor any one else has succeeded in demonstrating the probable existence of any such pre-prophetic eschatological system

---

[34] In Am. v. 4 f. there seems to be a contradiction between the hope of life and the word of doom uttered over Bethel and Gilgal. But this word is not a prediction of the destruction of the Israelite kingdom, but an exposure of and imprecation on the radical corruption of the two sanctuaries. This passage provides no support for the opinion that Amos, like Isaiah, was familiar with the idea of a 'remnant' which would be saved. The whole people is addressed.

[35] Gressmann, *Der Ursprung der israelitisch-jüdischen Eschatologie*. In *Der Messias* Gressmann thinks particularly of the Amorites as having mediated to Israel the 'court style', which was significant for the Messianic king of the Old Testament.

in the ancient world.[36] Further, Gressmann seems to support his hypothesis by arguing in a circle. From the sayings of the prophets he deduces
the existence of a pre-prophetic eschatology, and by the hypothesis of
a pre-prophetic eschatology he explains the prophetic teaching. Finally,
much of what the German scholar calls eschatology is not eschatology
at all. A theophany has in itself nothing to do with eschatology. The
oracular style, frequently used by the prophets, gives their utterances
an irrational character, in some measure reminiscent of eschatological
sayings. Purely historical events are often clothed in a mythological
garb; prophecies are frequently given the form of fantastic visions;
poetical language with bizarre figures and symbols far removed from
reality (in accordance with oriental taste) is commonly used. All of this
has points in common with eschatology but is not itself eschatology.

It is curious to observe that though most critical scholars of the present
generation reject Gressmann's general view in theory, yet, consciously
or unconsciously, they accept his opinion that there was in fact in the
pre-prophetic period an idea of a new age in an eschatological sense.
The ground of this opinion is first and foremost the mention of 'Yahweh's day' in the book of Amos.

It is of fundamental importance to make clear what this expression
means here. It meets us in a coherent revelation that begins with a woe-
cry in v. 18 and ends with the oracle formula 'says Yahweh' (*v.* 27).[37]
The prophet combats the false opinion of his audience that Yahweh's
day will be light, i.e., a joyful and happy day. He says that this day
will be a day of disaster. What Yahweh's day here is becomes clear
from the context, where the prophet continues: 'I hate, I despise your
feasts, and I take no pleasure in your festal assemblies,' etc. (*vv.* 21 ff.).
'Yahweh's day' is consequently the designation of a cultic festival
for the worship of Yahweh, exactly as 'the days of the Baals' in Hos.
ii. 15 denote cultic festivals for the worship of the Baals. We may also

---

[36] Cf. Mowinckel, *He that Cometh*, p. 127, with references to the literature. Černý,
The Day of Yahweh and some Relevant Problems, likewise denies the existence of an
eschatological system before the canonical prophets. Of the day of Yahweh he says,
however, that it was a popular expectation older than these prophets; it was 'a day
decreed by Yahweh, in which He Himself will newly shape the fate of His nation', p. 103.
[37] It would be entirely out of accord with the methods of the collector of the sayings
of Amos if *vv.* 21-27 should be separated from *vv.* 18-20, so that we had to do with two
different revelations instead of one. Had the collector regarded the passages in question
as two independent utterances, he would without doubt have marked the end of the
former or the beginning of the latter by an oracle formula or another word or expression
such as he used to separate different sayings from each other. Most scholars have
overlooked this fact; and consequently the false interpretation of the expression
'Yahweh's day' has become common in exegetical works. Sellin in *Das Zwölfprophetenbuch* and, above all, Mowinckel in several works, last in *He that Cometh* (p. 132),
have shown the right way.

compare Hos. ix. 5, where the New Year festival is called *yôm ḥaḡ yahwêh*, the day of the feast of Yahweh. In Accadian texts *ûm ili* means a cultic festival day.[38]

Now the prophet says that the people eagerly longed for this festival as a day of rejoicing, while it would in fact be a day when judgement would come upon Israel. The prophet thought, no doubt, of the festival par excellence, the great New Year festival. At this festival Yahweh's triumph over His enemies in nature and history was celebrated with joy and exultation. By its ceremonies fertility, prosperity, victory and good fortune in every respect were guaranteed. On the same day debauchery and profligacy in connection with the cultic performances went to extremes. Precisely on that day, Amos says, the divine judgement will come upon the people.

According to the Hebrew way of thinking the New Year festival was conceived of as *one* day, quite regardless of the several days in which this day, so to speak, was manifested. So 'on Yahweh's day' corresponds to what we should express by saying: 'at a New Year festival'. At a New Year festival, usually a feast of joy and exultation, judgement would come upon the people. That the judgement would come precisely at a New Year festival, the prophet had been assured through a divine revelation received in the vision described in ch. ix, in which he saw the temple in Bethel collapse, burying the cultic assembly in its ruins, a terrible introduction to the total annihilation of the people.[39]

Accordingly, from the mention of Yahweh's day in Amos no conclusions may be drawn about a pre-prophetic eschatology in ancient Israel. When in ch. ii of his book Isaiah speaks of Yahweh's day, this expression is not a fixed term. Isaiah generally says that 'Yahweh has a day', i.e., has determined a time which will bring about the destruction of all that is proud and lofty on earth. After Isaiah the expression increasingly became a real *terminus technicus* with an eschatological sense, as can be seen, for instance, in his disciple Zephaniah.

---

[38] Landsberger, *Der kultische Kalender der Babylonier und Assyrer*, p. 12; Černý, op. cit., pp. 14 f.

[39] On this point I agree to a great extent with Mowinckel in *Jesaja-Disiplene*, p. 94, and *He that Cometh*, p. 132. Sellin in his commentary mentioned above shows a close dependance on Gressmann in saying that the expectation of 'Yahweh's day' as a day of bliss was current among the contemporaries of Amos, but, he goes on, this 'da,' was thought of as occurring on the day of Yahweh's enthronement, i.e., the New Year festival (p. 232). In his *Amos Studies* Morgenstern likewise combines the eschatological day of Yahweh with the New Year's day; 'The roots', says Morgenstern (p. 408), 'of the concept of the Day of Yahweh were not new in any sense. They were embedded in the observance of the day of the fall equinox as the New Year's Day.' Especially to the two last mentioned scholars Yahweh's day is one thing and the New Year's day another, though in some way combined with each other. In my view Yahweh's day in Amos is the same as the New Year festival.

Modern scholars who reject Gressmann's view have expressed the opinion that the pattern of disaster and happiness in the prophets was taken direct from the cult.

In several works Mowinckel has strongly emphasized the significance of the cultic mythology of the New Year festival for eschatology as a whole and for the pattern of disaster and happiness in particular, especially in the later prophets. Ivan Engnell thinks that this pattern was from the very beginning a fixed ideology in the prophets, originating in the dramatic strife between darkness and light, life and death, expressed in myth and action in the syncretistic cult.[40]

Modern studies of the ancient Israelite cult lend support to the view that the antithesis of life and death played a dominating role in it. But the question is whether this antithesis influenced the thought of the prophets to the extent held by some modern scholars. We must first note that Amos, for instance, entirely rejects the contemporary cult in its Canaanite forms. He says in Yahweh's name, 'I hate, I despise your feasts, and I take no pleasure in your festal assemblies.' Is it likely that he would have taken from this hated syncretistic cult an essential motif such as the necessary combination of life and death and made a dogmatic ideology of it? Above all, in this cult the antithesis of life and death was an unconditional one. It was intimately bound up with the idea of the dying and rising god or the withering and renewing of vegetation. In prophetic teaching death is Yahweh's punishment for apostasy and sin, and life is His recompense for righteousness and repentance, both deeply rooted in the ethical nature of Yahweh.

Mowinckel does not think of the dying and rising god. He lays stress upon the fact that at the enthronement festival the cultic assembly really experienced the 'turn of fortune', the transition from affliction to salvation. Each New Year the people passed over from an age of affliction to an age of happiness. Each New Year Yahweh's victory over chaos in nature and history was celebrated and experienced.[41]

It may be true that this pattern of affliction and salvation was intimately connected with the cultic performances and hymns of the New Year festival; but is it certain that this cultic pattern influenced the prophetic ideology of doom and salvation as much as Mowinckel believes? I cannot agree that it did.

It seems to be a weakness in Mowinckel's theory that on this point he distinguishes between the earlier prophets and their 'disciples', holding that the former were not influenced by the cultic pattern,

---

[40] See *SEÅ*, xii, 1947, pp. 110 ff., and the article 'Profeter, profetism' in *SBU*.
[41] See above all *Psalmenstudien*, II, pp. 77 ff.

whereas the latter were dependent on it. If the New Year festival with its ceremonies and liturgies was celebrated already in the early monarchical period, which is more than probable, it is difficult to understand why Amos, Hosea, Isaiah, etc., should not also have derived the parallel prophecies of affliction and bliss from the cult, like the later prophets, whom Mowinckel calls their 'disciples'. But first and foremost it must not be overlooked that in the prophetic books the juxtaposition of judgement and salvation, death and life, is of two different kinds. On the one hand hope of life and certainty of judgement are deeply rooted in the fundamental religious views of the prophets concerning God and man, in particular concerning Yahweh, the God of election, in His relation to His chosen people, which makes an assumption of cultic influence quite unnecessary; on the other hand the combination of words of doom and words of bliss are very often of a formal, literary nature.

What gave rise to pre-exilic prophecy in its typical form? It was horror at the apostasy of Israel. The prophets saw that their people had lost their way and gone astray, away from their God and His will. The greatest part of their preaching consists in pictures of the sinfulness of the people. The standard by which they assessed the religious and moral state of the people was, as we have seen above, the genuine Mosaic tradition inherited from the past and expressed in historical traditions, legal usage, and the Yahwistic cult. The bad condition of the people seemed to them the worse inasmuch as they were the elect people, chosen by Yahweh to be a holy people wholeheartedly dedicated to His worship. Apostasy was faithlessness to His election. Having failed to fulfil the obligations of election, the people was subject to Yahweh's judgement. The God who had chosen them was a righteous God, who rigorously punished apostasy and faithlessness. The idea of the avenging righteousness of Yahweh was axiomatic in the faith of the prophets, having in ancient times been a vital element in the noblest traditions of Israel. Such being the historical and spiritual situation, the main feature of the preaching of the pre-exilic prophets was necessarily the castigation of sin and threats of punishment. 'Death' in the utterances of these prophets always meant punishment and doom, not an inevitable fate, as was the case in the Canaanite cult.

But there was a way of escape from destruction and annihilation, namely righteousness and repentance. On this condition life was attainable. Accordingly promises of bliss and happiness found a place in the preaching of the prophets. Yahweh was not only a punitive God, but also a gracious God, faithful to His own promises and merciful towards those who were faithful to Him and obeyed His commands. The idea of Yahweh's mercy was as much a part of the religious tradition of Israel as was the idea of the punitive God.

There was in the preaching of the pre-exilic prophets a constant tension between election and rejection, avenging righteousness and mercy, judgement and salvation. How the prophets resolved this tension is one of the most interesting features of their message.

Accordingly, the opinion of the present writer is that the pattern of death and life, distress and salvation, typical of the prophets, did not derive from the cult; its origin is to be found in the basic religious ideas of Israel, inherited from the past and, of course, it may be emphasized, reflected also in the Yahwistic cult.

On the other hand the literary combination of judgement and bliss calls for an explanation. In the previous chapter it was demonstrated that in numerous cases the combination of words of punishment and words of happiness must be assigned to the redactors of the prophetic books. The redactional work was carried out in the exilic and post-exilic periods. Consequently the question arises what circumstance in these periods might have led to the juxtaposition in the prophetic books of prophecies of doom and promises of future happiness. The answer is the reading of Scripture in cultic assemblies. Although cultic acts of the traditional kind, such as sacrificial rites, were impossible during the Babylonian Exile, the reading in the synagogues, or similar places of meeting, of the authoritative Scriptures, not least the collections of the prophetic revelations, served as a substitute. Now that the earlier prophecies of doom had come true, they no longer had a value in themselves, but combined with the promises of salvation and bliss they could permanently serve for the edification of the oppressed people and initiate them into the counsels and thoughts of the living God.

Though the ancient cult did not bring about the juxtaposition of doom and salvation in the preaching of the prophets, as modern scholars believe, yet its significance for prophecy was considerable. Not only are the prophetic utterances rich in cultic formulas, expressions, and allusions (to say nothing of the direct 'prophetic liturgies'), but a good deal of the *material* relating to the prospects of the future is taken from the cult. A noteworthy example is provided by the prophecies of Deutero-Isaiah about the deliverance and return of the exiled Jews at the time of the fall of Babylon. As has often been shown, the ritual of the New Year festival served as a pattern for these prophecies. As to the content of the prophetic predictions of doom and blessing we must also take into account individual ideas drawn from popular Israelite belief (e.g., ideas about the end of the world[42]) and also the physical conditions of Palestine, the nature of oriental poetry, oriental and Hebrew mythology, primitive conceptions of the demonic nature of Yahweh and His unlimited miraculous power. This must all be considered; but for the basic principles we have to assume a different origin.

B. *Yahweh, the God of Israel, and His Demands upon His People*

It is not my intention here to present a detailed analysis of prophetic teaching such as would repeat much of what has been said many times before in the Theologies of the Old Testament and special works on the prophets, but rather to take up the most important items, discussing them and presenting my own views on the points discussed.

Nothing is more characteristic of the preaching of the prophets than its theocentric nature. Everywhere God is present in it; everywhere His voice is heard; everywhere we are reminded of His action in nature and history.

We have emphasized above (pp. 299 ff.) the difference between the God of the mystics and the God of the prophets. To the mystics, God is more or less *divinity*, approaching men in the depths of their personality and made known to them in the experiences of the inner life. The prophetic idea of God is throughout *personalistic*. God is active will, and what is known of God is given first and foremost by His objective revelation in history.[43]

Half a century ago the great Swedish theologian Einar Billing laid great stress upon the fundamental difference between Greek thought and the teaching of the Israelite prophets. He saw this fundamental difference in the different attitudes towards history. With the Greek philosopher, who sought for a sum of universal truths and eternal ideas, he contrasted the Israelite prophet, who stood in the midst of history and whose task it was to discern what was happening in history and interpret it as divine revelation. 'Ah! the roaring of many peoples, that roar like the roaring of seas, and the surging of nations, that surge like the surging of mighty waters' (Isa. xvii. 12); such, says Billing, was the milieu in which the prophets lived and prophecy came into existence. In the great events of world-history the prophet heard Yahweh's voice. Likewise he traced Yahweh's activity in the history of His own people. The Swedish theologian expresses the contrast pointedly: 'What the discovery of the value of general concepts as real knowledge was to the

---

[42] See for instance Isa. li. 6 and liv. 10.
[43] The personality of the Israelite God is strongly emphasized in Graham, *The Prophets and Israel's Culture*. See also Eichrodt, *Das Gottesbild des Alten Testaments*.

Greeks, the march across the Red Sea was to the Israelites.' Characteristic of the Greek philosophers was intellectualism, the theoretical approach, whereas the Israelite prophets were dominated by the idea of the divine activity. Further the ethical ideal in Greek thought was the free development of the individual, whereas the ethical ideal of the prophets was obedience to the divine commands. Knowledge meant to the Greeks theoretical understanding; to the prophets 'knowledge of Yahweh' meant cognizance of the will of the God of Israel and practical surrender to this will.[44]

It may also be said that, while Greek thought was harmonious and static, Israelite thought was dynamic,[45] or, as I should prefer to say, 'dramatic'. What distinguished the prophetic way of thinking was its dramatic character.

History was to the prophets the field of divine action. As Wellhausen put it, 'The element in which the prophets live is the storm of the world's history'.[45a] In the events of history they saw God at work. History was to them revelation. They fixed their eyes upon the great moments of history, interpreted them to their people as true manifestations of the essence and will of Yahweh, and drew from them conclusions which might also be applied to less significant historical occurrences. For the right understanding and interpreting of history a special competence was needed. This competence was given the prophets in their personal communion with God. Revelation in Israelite prophecy came about 'through a complex of personality and event'. There were always 'personal and impersonal factors woven together'.[46]

The first of the canonical prophets, Amos, expressly refers to history in instructing his hearers about Yahweh. He reminds them that Yahweh brought up the people from Egypt, led them through the wilderness and destroyed the Amorites. But the horizon of Amos is not limited to

[44] So above all in Billing's main theological work, *De etiska tankarna i urkristendomen*, published in Uppsala 1907. A second edition, including some other essays, was published in Stockholm 1936. See esp. the first edition, pp. 73 ff.

[45] So Boman, *Hebrew Thought Compared with Greek*, p. 27. The same problem is penetratingly discussed by the German philosopher Hessen in his work *Platonismus und Prophetismus*. This scholar emphasizes the volitional character of the Israelite idea of God. God was experienced by the prophets as an active God working in history. The notion of God is not static, but dynamic (p. 68). God is not in a state of quiescence but active power (p. 76). The Greek man experienced the world essentially as nature, the prophet as history (p. 91).

[45a] *Prolegomena to the History of Israel*, p. 398.

[46] Rowley, *The Faith of Israel*, pp. 34, 40 ff., 48 etc. Pidoux, *Le Dieu qui vient*, likewise emphasizes the Old Testament idea of God in history. He rightly says, 'Dans la Bible l'histoire se présente sous l'aspect d'un drame immense, qui va des origines à la fin du monde' (p. 12). This scholar explains eschatology from the Israelite conception of God, pp. 49 ff. Here I miss a thorough analysis of the importance of the idea of election as an essential basis of Old Testament eschatology.

the history of Israel. He also points to the fact that Yahweh brought up the Philistines from Caphtor and the Syrians from Kir. Hosea refers over and over again to the deliverance from Egypt. Isaiah knows that world-history lies in Yahweh's hands. At pleasure He raises or calls up on the stage of history foreign peoples, Assyrians, Egyptians, Syrians, Philistines, to use them as His instruments. Micah, beginning with the deliverance from Egypt, presents a series of events in the history of Israel, so that the people might 'understand the saving deeds of Yahweh'. Jeremiah reproaches his people for having forgotten that Yahweh brought them up from Egypt, guided them through the desert, led them to a blessed land. He also knew that the foreign peoples, who menaced Israel, were raised up by Yahweh to carry out His plans for the elect people.[47] History as the scene of Yahweh's powerful deeds, both the history of Israel and world-history, was always of vital moment to these prophets. One could say that what Golgotha and the cross are to the Christian Church, the deliverance from Egypt was to Israel and her prophets.[48]

The prophetic idea of Yahweh's activity in history was not quite unparalleled in the ancient world. We find similar ideas in Egyptian, Accadian, and Hittite texts. Divinities are frequently implored or praised for intervention in the history of the peoples.

In a hymn of victory of Thut-mose III on a stele in the temple of Karnak, Amon-Re says, 'I establish thee in my dwelling place ... I give thee valor and victory over all foreign countries; I set the glory of thee and the fear of thee in all lands ... I bind the barbarians of Nubia ... as living captives ... Thou treadest all foreign countries ... There is none who can thrust himself into the vicinity of thy majesty, while I am thy guide ... I cause thy victories to circulate in all lands . . I have come, that I may cause thee to trample down those who are in Asia, thou smitest the heads of the Asiatics of Retenu,' etc.[49] In the prologue of the Code of Hammurabi we read: 'When Marduk commissioned me to guide the people aright, to direct the land, I established law and justice in the language of the land.'[50] In a list of the deeds of Hammurabi it is recorded: 'Through the great power of Marduk he overthrew the army of Turukku, Kakmu and of the country Subartu. . . . With the mighty power which Anu (and) Enlil have given him, he

[47] Am. ii. 9 f.; iii. 1; ix. 7; Hos. ii. 17; xi. 1; xiii. 4; Isa. vii. 18; ix. 10 f.; x. 5 f., 26; Mic. vi. 3 ff.; Jer. ii. 6 f.; xxxi. 32, etc.
[48] For a discussion from principal viewpoints of the question of history in the Israelite religion see *inter alios* Hempel, *Altes Testament und Geschichte*; Weiser, *Glaube und Geschichte im Alten Testament*; North, *The Old Testament Interpretation of History*.
[49] *ANET*, p. 374.   [50] *ANET*, p. 165.

defeated all his enemies as far as the country of Subartu.'[51] In an oracle given to Esarhaddon we read: 'I am Ishtar of Arbela . . . I have fixed your throne under the wide heavens . . . For you, with my own hands, your foes shall I crush.'[52] In a Hittite prayer Telepinus is implored that he may stand with the king, the queen, and the princes, and grant them a man's valiant (and) victorious weapon, and set the countries of the enemy beneath their feet.[53] On the Moabite stone King Mesha confesses that Chemosh had saved him from all the kings and caused him to triumph over all his adversaries.[54]

What distinguishes the prophetic view of history from that of other oriental peoples is not the thought that Yahweh works in historical events, but rather that the prophets regarded the history of Israel as a *coherent* history directed by *moral principles* and in accordance with a *fixed plan*. At the beginning of that history stood the fact of election, manifested in the deliverance from Egypt. The events which followed were the consequences of this historical fact; and the final goal of this historical sequence was the full realization of the idea of election. Other ancient peoples had nothing corresponding to this view of history. Among them the king was sometimes regarded as chosen by the deity (as the land was sometimes regarded as privileged by the gods); among them, too, it was believed that the gods intervened at certain significant points in history; but nothing like the prophetic idea of the history of Israel as the realization of a fixed divine plan from its beginning to its end is to be found elsewhere in the ancient world.

In the light of the historical election Israel discovered its own history as a real history; but Israel also had an idea of history as such, the history of mankind, which was a framework to the history of the elect people. Among other peoples of the ancient Near East we find many lists of sovereigns and eponyms, annals, genealogies, chronicles, enumerations of battles, victories, treaties, and heroic deeds, recorded for the glorifying of kings and heroes, but not history-writing in the strict sense.

Among the Greeks Herodotus describes many fascinating scenes from history, which, however, for the most part lack any close and coherent sequence—they form a 'dramatic series of pictures', as a great Swedish historian (Harald Hjärne) says. Thucydides was indeed a forerunner of modern history-writing, but he did not understand how to write a coherent national history or a world-history, and, moreover, he was much later than the great Hebrew historical works.[55]

[51] *ANET*, p. 270. [52] *ANET*, p. 450. [53] *ANET*, p. 397.
[54] *ANET*, p. 320.
[55] For history-writing in the ancient world see *The Idea of History in the Ancient Near East*, ed. by Dentan.

The conclusion is inevitable: Israel was the pioneer of history-writing, and became so by virtue of its religion. Through the work and influence of prophets and prophetic personalities the art of history-writing was given to this people.

The greatest gift given by history to the people of Israel was the consciousness of being chosen by Yahweh to be His people in a special sense. As we just suggested, in some old oriental documents a king declares that he has been chosen by a god or a goddess, that he is the favourite of the deity and an object of his special grace. There are also traces of the thought that there exists some sort of relationship between the peoples or the lands and the gods.[56] But nowhere do we find anything that corresponds to the Israelite idea of election.

This idea implied to the prophets that Yahweh, in sovereign love, had chosen Israel out of all the peoples of the earth to be His own people, an object of His special care and education, destined to realize His divine will and make His name glorified in the world. There is no doubt that this idea was central in the religion of ancient Israel and in the thought of the prophets as well.[57]

In the books of the pre-exilic prophets many different terms are used to present this idea. In slightly various ways they give expression to the fundamental thought that Israel stands in a special relationship to Yahweh, in which Yahweh's love, Israel's devotion and obedience, and, finally, the great goal are the chief elements.[58]

Amos uses the word *yāḏaʿ*, which in this connection signifies 'care for', 'be interested, concerned in'. He represents Yahweh as saying, 'You alone I have cared for among all the clans of the earth' (iii. 2).[59] When in vi. 1 he calls Israel 'the first of the nations', he is, of course, speaking ironically; but nevertheless his words would have been

[56] Cf. Smith, 'The Chosen People', *AJSLL*, xlv, 1928-29, pp. 73 ff.; Rowley, *The Biblical Doctrine of Election*, pp. 16 ff.; Vriezen, *Die Erwählung Israels nach dem Alten Testament*, p. 84.

[57] It is difficult to agree with Köhler in his statement that the idea of Yahweh having chosen Israel does not play so outstanding a role in the Old Testament as has been held by Biblical scholars; *Old Testament Theology*, p. 82. It is true that the term 'choose' is not as common as one might suppose; but the very fact that Yahweh had assigned to Israel a unique position among the other peoples of the world as beloved by Him and destined for a high goal is fundamental to Israel's religion. So rightly Rowley, op. cit., pp. 15 f., and Vriezen, p. 80.

[58] Cf. Vriezen, op. cit., pp. 36 ff. Vriezen rightly emphasizes that the idea may very well be present even though the precise term 'choose' is missing (p. 90).

[59] So rightly Köhler in his *Lexicon*. The word manifestly has this meaning, e.g., in Isa. i. 3. I do not believe that Vriezen's statement 'erkennen=Gemeinschaft haben mit' (pp. 37 and 89) is quite to the point. Cf. *An Outline of Old Testament Theology*, pp. 128 ff. Pidoux, *L'homme dans l'Ancien Testament*, p. 43, says pertinently, 'Le verbe hébreu signifiant connaître ne désigne pas la connaissance intellectuelle pure, mais il introduit une nuance de sympathie entre le sujet connaissant et l'objet connu.'

unintelligible if he had not himself been conscious of the fact that Israel held a unique position among the peoples of the earth.

The very term *bāḥar*, choose, so common in Deuteronomy and Deutero-Isaiah, is not used by Amos and other pre-exilic prophets.[60] But one of the most simple and common expressions of the idea of election, from Amos down to the latest prophets, is that Israel is Yahweh's people. As a chieftain or a king has his tribe or his people, which he calls his own, so Yahweh has a people, viz., Israel. According to the oriental mode of thinking, the king's people is his possession. Behind this expression, consequently, lies the idea that Israel is Yahweh's property, but also that Yahweh is King over Israel, though the pre-exilic prophets seldom say expressly that Yahweh is King. To this phenomenon we return later on.

The idea that Israel is Yahweh's possession is also expressed by the phrase that Yahweh's name has been called over (*šēm yahwêh niḳrā' 'al*) the people.[61] When a name was mentioned over or written on an object, this object was declared to be the property of him whose name it was.[62] Israel is also called Yahweh's *naḥ^alâh*, 'share heritage'.[63] This was the term for the portions of the land of Canaan assigned to the different tribes. From the cultic sphere are taken 'consecrated gift' (*ḳōḏeš*) and 'first fruits of harvest'.[64] Israel is Yahweh's flock, Yahweh being thought of as a shepherd.[65] Allegorically Israel is likened to a loin-cloth, closely bound around the hips.[66] Israel is a plantation which Yahweh has founded. We read in Isaiah: 'The vineyard of the Lord of hosts is the house of Israel, and the men of Judah are His pleasant planting.'[67] Israel is a choice vine, planted by Yahweh, Yahweh's olive tree, His fertile field.[68]

Israel is Yahweh's son; the Israelites, as belonging to the elect people, are His children, and Yahweh is Israel's Father. Isaiah says in Yahweh's name, 'Sons have I reared and brought up, but they have rebelled against Me.'[69] The relationship between Yahweh and His son is never regarded as a physical one (physical birth from the gods was a common

---

[60] Passages such as Isa. xiv. 1; Jer. xxxiii. 24 are secondary.
[61] So Jer. xiv. 9 in the prayer on the occasion of the drought: 'Yet Thou, O Yahweh, art in the midst of us, and Thy name is called over us; leave us not.' Other passages: Deut. xxviii. 10; 2 Chron. vii. 14; Isa. xliii. 7; lxiii. 19; Sir. xxxvi. 17 (Hebr.); xlvii.18 (Hebr.); Bar. ii. 15; 2 Macc. viii. 15.
[62] Individual devotees of Yahweh: Isa. xliv. 5; the Temple: 1 Kings viii. 43; 2 Chron. vi. 33; Jer. vii. 10, 14; xxxii. 34; xxxiv. 15; the Ark: 2 Sam. vi. 2; Jerusalem: Jer. xxv. 29; Dan. ix. 18; foreign peoples: Am. ix. 12; a prophet: Jer. xv. 16. For the meaning of the phrase see further Galling in *TLZ*, lxxxi, 1956, cols. 65 ff.
[63] Jer. xii. 7 f.   [64] Jer. ii. 3.   [65] Jer. xiii. 17; xxiii. 1 f.
[66] Jer. xiii.   [67] Isa. v. 7.   [68] Jer. ii. 21; xi. 16; xii. 10.
[69] Isa. i. 2; cf. *v.* 4; xxx. 1, 9.

idea in the ancient Orient), but is more appropriately described as adoption.[70] Hosea says that from the time of the sojourn in Egypt Yahweh has called Israel His son.[71] Through the deliverance from Egypt Israel was chosen, and through the election Israel became Yahweh's son. The relation between Yahweh and Israel was established in history. Like grapes in the wilderness Yahweh *found* Israel. Then Yahweh took care of Israel, as good parents look after their children. 'I taught Ephraim to walk. I took them up in My arms,' Yahweh says in the Book of Hosea.[72] Jeremiah says that Yahweh gave Israel a privileged rank among all His children and gave them a pleasant land, the most beautiful heritage among all the nations. What He thereafter yearned for was to hear from their mouth the name 'Father'. Of North Israel Yahweh says, 'I have become to Israel a Father, and Ephraim is My first-born.'[73]

The most intimate expression of the relation of election is the marriage motif. Since it first appears in Hosea, it may seem natural to think that Hosea was the first to use this symbolism; but this can hardly be so. It is true that his own marriage played a great role in his understanding of the relation between Yahweh and His people. But he would surely not have taken his tragic marriage as a type of religious relationship if the idea of religion as a marriage had previously been unknown to him. It is a well-known fact that the ancient Semites, particularly at the stage of tribal culture, took many of their religious symbols from the family and kinship. It is not necessary to think primarily of Canaanite influence. The symbol in question lay close at hand.[74]

As a consequence of this marriage symbolism Yahweh's love for Israel was often described in erotic terms. This is the case not only in Hosea; Jeremiah similarly says in Yahweh's name, 'I remember the devotion of your youth, your bridal love, how you followed Me through the desert, through a land unsown' (ii. 2). So it was in the 'honeymoon period'.[74a] But all was changed. Israel became unfaithful, and then was

[70] Cf. Robertson Smith, *Kinship and Marriage in Early Arabia*, pp. 52 ff.; Bräunlich in *Islamica*, vi, 1934, *passim*; Gerleman in *STK*, xxii, 1946, pp. 242 ff.

[71] xi. 1. I read *lôw bᵉnî*; cf. Lindblom, *Hosea*, pp. 100 f., n. 2. The verb *ḳārâ'* means 'cry', 'call'. in *v.* 1 as well as in *v.* 2. The basic sense of the word is the same in both cases (*pace* Sellin).

[72] Hos. ix. 10; xi. 3.

[73] Jer. iii. 19; xxxi. 9.

[74] Fahlgren, *ṣᵉdāḳā, nahestehende und entgegengesetzte Begriffe im Alten Testament*, pp. 39 ff. This explanation seems to me to be more probable than that the idea of a marriage between Yahweh and His people is a transformation of the idea of the covenant (so Ziegler, *Die Liebe Gottes bei den Propheten*, pp. 73 f.).

[74a] Hyatt, *Prophetic Religion*, p. 88.

rejected: 'I have given the beloved of My soul into the hands of her enemies' (xii. 7). Later, in Ezekiel, this symbolism takes extreme forms.

An important expression of the relation between Yahweh and His people is *berît*, the covenant. Covenants of various kinds played an immense role in ancient Israel as in the Semitic world in general.[75] In Israel the idea of a covenant between Yahweh and His people was a dominating one, 'a formula for the ideology of history'.[76] According to popular Israelite belief, the covenant between Yahweh and Israel was founded on various acts of alliance, the most important being that of Sinai. Here Yahweh took the initiative. The establishment of the covenant was an act of His love. Thus the idea of covenant could be parallel to the idea of election.

In pre-exilic prophecy the idea of covenant is pushed into the background. Inherited as it was from the past, perhaps from the Mosaic age, it was, of course, familiar to the prophets through historical tradition and cult; but of Jeremiah's predecessors only Hosea mentions the covenant, and that in only two passages: vi. 7 and viii. 1, where he reproaches his people for having transgressed the covenant. However, the idea is not central in his teaching, where, as we have seen, the dominant idea is that of a marriage between Yahweh and His people. Not until Jeremiah does the idea of the covenant become prominent. He reminds the people of the covenant established at Sinai. To him it was a guarantee for Yahweh's mercy to His people (xiv. 21); at the same time it imposed exacting religious and moral obligations on the people (xi. 6 ff.). Now Israel had broken it (xi. 10). The old covenant was an imperfect one. Therefore Yahweh was about to establish a new and better covenant with Israel in the age to come (xxxi. 31 ff.). That the idea of covenant filled a relatively large place in Jeremiah's preaching was doubtless the result of influence from the ideology of the Josianic reform and Deuteronomy.

The relative paucity of references to the covenant in the pre-exilic prophets is presumably to be ascribed to the fact that the juridical character of this idea led the people to make claims on their God as of right and to cherish ambitious dreams of a supposedly inevitable glorious future. It was a prime task of the pre-exilic prophets to combat such false illusions. To them the essential was not the claim of the people on Yahweh, but Yahweh's claim on Israel in virtue of election.

---

[75] Pedersen, *Der Eid bei den Semiten*, and *Israel, Its Life and Culture*, I–II, pp. 263 ff. ('community with all the privileges and duties implied in it', p. 285); Quell in *TWBNT*, II, pp. 106 ff.; Eichrodt, *Theologie des Alten Testaments*, I[5], pp. 9 ff.
[76] Weiser, *Glaube und Geschichte im Alten Testament*, p. 59.

To this thought the covenant in their view did not give appropriate expression.[77]

The election of Israel was demonstrated by the deliverance from Egypt. But this wonderful event was not isolated, it was followed by a series of occurrences, consequences of the great basic event.

The march across the Red Sea and the annihilation of the Egyptians in its waves were closely connected with the Exodus. Then followed the successful march through the wilderness, the land of horrors. The crossing of the Jordan is also mentioned, as is the episode of Balak and Balaam. The conquest of the promised land played a central role. The appearance of great personalities such as Moses, Aaron, Miriam, prophets and nazirites also belonged to the same wonderful history.[78]

As the elect of Yahweh, Israel was an object of His fostering care during its entire history. Even national calamities were regarded as means by which Yahweh would lead His chosen people towards its great goal. The tragedy was that Israel would not draw instruction from such events. It did not listen to the warnings. 'In vain did I smite your children, they took no correction,' says Yahweh (Jer. ii. 30);[79] and further: 'I set watchmen over them, saying, "Give heed to the sound of the trumpet." But they said, "We will not give heed"' (vi. 17).

The entire history of Israel was a chain of events continuing the basic act of election. The prophets were given the ability to understand this history and the task of interpreting it to their people. But the people were deaf to their words. Isaiah complains: 'Their feasts are lyre and harp, timbrel and flute and wine, but the doing of Yahweh they regard not, and the work of His hands they see not!' (v. 12). In Micah the Lord exhorts the people to remember His acts in history, that they may 'understand the righteous [i.e., merciful and saving] acts of Yahweh' (vi. 5).

The prophets were not the first to discover the divine election and guidance in the life of the people. These ideas were known already in the pre-prophetic historical sources of the Pentateuch and in the oldest cultic hymns and prayers. In ancient Israel there were two views of election. According to one of them the fact of election was connected with the history of the patriarchs, according to the other the certainty

---

[77] Similarly Eichrodt, op. cit., pp. 19 f.: 'Ein Pochen auf statutarische Ordnungen, auf feste Gewohnheiten und Bräuche, auf genau angeordnete Leistungen an die Gottheit trat ihnen entgegen und ein ebenso selbstverständliches Rechnen auf Jahves Gegenleistung . . . Darin lag die Schwäche dieser Idee, dass sie durch ihren juristischen Charakter das religiöse Leben gefährden und selbst zum Nährboden der Schmarotzerpflanze einer *Do ut des*=Religion werden konnte.'

[78] See, for instance, the classical passages Am. ii. 9 ff.; Mic. vi. 4 f.; Jer. ii. 6 f.

[79] The children are, of course, the members of the people of Israel. Alteration of the text is unnecessary.

of election was founded on the deliverance from Egypt.[80] It is note-worthy that the pre-exilic prophets adopted only the latter tradition and neglected the patriarchal tradition. The chief reason for this fact was that the patriarchal tradition with all its national aspirations and glorious promises was the basis of the ambitious dreams of the people, which the prophets of judgement sought to dispel. The deliverance from Egypt manifested Yahweh's free and personal love to Israel; but this love was no sure guarantee of national greatness and glory. If the people appeared to be unworthy of this love because of their ingratitude, the love changed into wrath; and doom, not glory, was at hand. The reason for the rejection of the patriarchal traditions was analogous to the reason for the reluctance to use the idea of covenant.[81]

In many passages the prophets combat a popular conception of election, which impiled a dangerous misinterpretation of this sublime idea. Again and again the prophets met with the objection to their warn-ings and threats: 'Yahweh is with us, Yahweh is in our midst; all is well.' Micah, for instance, quotes this utterance: 'Is not Yahweh in our midst? No misfortune can befall us' (iii. 11).[82] Against such popular fancies the prophets never tired of emphasizing that election and doom were not necessarily mutually exclusive. Amos even says that election made the guilt of the people still worse (iii. 2).

The prophetic view of election can be summarized in the following way. Election was a manifestation of Yahweh's power. Before the chosen people other peoples must be overthrown, even the mighty Egyptians. This happened through the mighty hand of Yahweh. In election Yahweh's specific love to Israel was demonstrated. Without any merit Israel became a privileged nation among all other nations of the world. This was wonderful evidence of an incomprehensible love. In return this love demanded love and gratitude from the people. Yahweh's love became an important motivation for the ethical admonitions of the

---

[80] See Galling, *Die Erwählungstraditionen Israels*.

[81] In Hos. xii the prophet Hosea recalls the history of the ancestor Jacob. However, the original wording of this revelation has been considerably obscured by redactional additions. In my book, *Hosea literarisch untersucht*, I have attempted to separate the secondary elements from the original text (pp. 102 ff.). I am still convinced of the essential correctness of the analysis there made. Jacob is rebuked for having sup-planted his brother in the womb; in his manhood he strove with God; he fled to the land of Aram and did service for a wife. In virtue of the unity of an ancestor with his descendants, Israel shared in the deceitfulness and rebelliousness of the patriarch. The favourable features are all to be assigned to the redactor, of whose work there are also other signs (e.g., the doxology in *v.* 6 and the exhortation to repentance in *v.* 7). —In Jer. ix. 3 there is another allusion to the treacherous conduct of the same patriarch: Every brother beguiles the other, *'āḳôḇ yaʿḳōḇ*. Such passages prove that the pre-exilic prophets consciously dissociated themselves from the old Yahwistic traditions with their glorification of the patriarchs.

[82] Cf. Am. v. 14; Hos. viii. 2; Isa. xxviii. 15; Mic. ii. 6 f.; Jer. v. 12, etc.

prophets. Yahweh's love made the apostasy of the people the more heinous. On the other hand, in times of distress Yahweh's love could serve to evoke courage and confidence. Finally, election implied Yahweh's demand that Israel should own Him alone as God. Israel had Yahweh and no other god to thank for having been chosen and delivered from Egypt. In Hosea Yahweh says, 'I am Yahweh, your God, from the land of Egypt; and you know no God but Me, and there is no saviour except Me' (xiii. 4).

These thoughts were not new; but in the preaching of the prophets they were actualized in a new way and at the same time cleansed from popular corruption, above all from the illusion that election was a self-evident guarantee of a happy future, and from a false view of the national religious and moral situation.

The prophets held that Yahweh's power was unlimited. Yahweh says in a revelation to Jeremiah, 'Behold, I am Yahweh, the God of all flesh; is anything too hard for Me?' (xxxii. 27). The omnipotence of Yahweh implies that history and nature are at His disposal. The peoples of the earth, as well as the resources of nature, serve Him as means whereby His purposes may be achieved.

The universal power of Yahweh was to the pre-exilic prophets an axiom. They seldom refer, like Deutero-Isaiah, to the fact that Yahweh has created heaven and earth. The doxologies in Amos are redactional insertions.[83] There are practically no parallels to the sayings in Jeremiah: 'Thou hast made all these things' (xiv. 22); and, Yahweh 'has given the sun for light by day and fixed moon and stars for light by night' (xxxi. 35), where influence from cultic hymns is evident.[84]

The conception which the pre-exilic prophets held of Yahweh, the Ruler of heaven and earth, the Sovereign of mankind, whose glory fills the whole earth, who is everywhere and from whom there is no escape, whose words in the mouth of the prophets are valid for heaven and earth and for all nations of the world, and who one day will judge not only His own people but also other peoples and the whole created world —this conception of Yahweh looks like monotheism, but is not monotheism in a theoretical or abstract sense.[85] The pre-exilic prophets never

---

[83] See above, p. 284.   [84] Cf. Weiser in his commentary.
[85] See passages such as Am. iv. 7 ff.; ix. 2 ff., 7; Isa. i. 2; ii. 11 ff.; vi. 3; vii. 11, 18 ff.; Mic. i. 2; Zeph. i, 3, etc.; Jer. i. 5, 10; xv. 2 f.; xvi. 4; xxi. 6; xxiii. 23 f.; Hab. iii. 3. In *Essays presented to Leo Baeck* (1954), pp. 106 ff., Morgenstern discusses the universalism of Amos. He speaks rightly of universalism not in an absolute, but in a practical sense. Though Yahweh was Israel's God, He controlled the world and all nations in it. Amos did not deny the existence of other gods, but in his thought Yahweh was the only God in all the world who merited consideration. The transferring of ix. 7 immediately before iii. 2 suggested by Morgenstern is, on my explanation of ix. 7, needless (see below, p. 334).

say that there are no other gods at all in the world. When he calls the pagan gods 'vanities' (*hᵃbālīm*) Jeremiah is simply describing them as weak and powerless. Deutero-Isaiah was the first theoretically to deny the existence of the pagan gods. The pre-exilic prophets were not concerned with the problem of existence. What was important to them was that Yahweh was the mightiest ruler in the world, and that in the end nothing could resist Him. If we use the term monotheism, it is appropriate to speak of the *dynamic monotheism* of the pre-exilic prophets.

All intense religions have a tendency to extend the power of the divinities over their special regions to include heaven and earth. This tendency is reinforced by the practice of applying to the deity lofty epithets in the hymns and prayers of the cult. Thus many of the Accadian special gods appear as universal gods, as rulers of heaven and earth, e.g., Shamash, Marduk, Sin, Ninlil, and others. They fix the destinies of heaven and earth; they are rulers of the universe, kings of the earth, judges of the lands, makers of mankind; heaven and earth and all mankind are in their possession.[86] There is, however, a difference between the universalism of such texts and the universalism of the prophetic texts of the Old Testament. There we have a universalism which never breaks the bounds of polytheism; here we have a universalism which develops into monotheism in the strict sense. In the former case the universalistic epithets are in the first place tributes of homage to a god to whom the worshipper wishes to pay special honour; in the latter the universalism is conceived of as reality. From polytheism there is no way to monotheism. Real monotheism implies a protest against polytheism and is everywhere closely associated with the work of a personal reformer.[87] The universalistic view of Yahweh in the form of a dynamic monotheism in the pre-exilic prophets and the absolute monotheism of Deutero-Isaiah and later prophets were ultimately based upon the henotheistic faith of Israel founded by Moses. The monotheistic tendency was also favoured by the fact that Yahweh was increasingly freed from local limitations. Amos knows that Yahweh is everywhere. It is not possible to escape from His hand either in Sheol or in heaven, either on the top of Carmel or at the bottom of the sea (ix. 2 f.). Isaiah in his inaugural vision sees Yahweh sitting on His heavenly throne; only the train of His robe fills the temple. The whole earth is full of His glory (vi). When Yahweh draws near to judge He

---

[86] Examples are to be found in the Accadian hymns collected in *ANET*, pp. 383 ff.; Jastrow, *Die Religion Babyloniens und Assyriens*, I, pp. 393 ff.; Cumming, *The Assyrian and Hebrew Hymns of Praise*, pp. 53 ff.

[87] Cf. Pettazzoni, *Essays on the History of Religions*, pp. 1 ff.

comes from far (xxx. 27). In Jeremiah Yahweh says, 'Am I a God near at hand, and not a God afar off? Can a man hide himself in secret places, so that I could not see him? Do not I fill the heavens and the earth?' (xxiii. 23 f.).[88]

If He must be located somewhere, heaven is thought of as Yahweh's abode. Yahweh dwells in the height and descends to appear on the earth.[89] When it is said that Yahweh comes from Sinai, this is an archaic-poetic expression.[90] It is also said that Yahweh dwells on Zion or that the Temple is Yahweh's house. Such phrases depend on the fact that Jerusalem with its Temple was the principal seat of the Yahweh cult and the place of His appearance in a visionary or cultic sense.

The land of Israel is Yahweh's land. Sometimes it is even called Yahweh's house; but this only means that this land was chosen by Yahweh as an abode for the elect people, whose King Yahweh was, and a place where the Yahweh cult was celebrated. The Canaanite Baal was bound to the soil in a quite different sense.[91]

Nor was Yahweh bound to the people of Israel. Yahweh freely chose Israel from the mass of the peoples of the world to be His people, but His existence was by no means bound to this people. If Israel were to be rejected, Yahweh would continue to exist as the ruler of history. Amos was convinced that Israel must perish. Because of their apostasy they had become to Yahweh like the Ethiopians. But if Yahweh wanted to choose another people as His own, there were other nations at His disposal, such as the Philistines and the Syrians, whose history was likewise directed by Yahweh (ix. 7).[92] The universalism in the essence of Yahweh manifests itself not the least in the universality of His ethical demands.

It is true that Yahweh's ethical demands primarily coincided with

[88] This remarkable word must be understood in its connection with the polemics against the false prophets. The God of these prophets was a God who revealed Himself by low, earthly means, dreams, etc. The God of Jeremiah, the true prophet, was a God of heaven and earth. Exalted over all that was earthly and trivial, He used sublime agencies to make Himself manifest. His divine word, like fire, and like a hammer which breaks the rock in pieces, was working in the true prophets, while the false prophets had not access to the heavenly council of Yahweh, were not bearers of the divine word, and used vulgar methods.

[89] Isa. xviii. 4; xxx. 27; xxxi. 4; Mic. i. 3; vi. 6.

[90] Hab. iii. 3.

[91] Hos. viii. 1; ix. 3, 15; Isa. xiv. 25; Jer. ii. 7; xii. 7.

[92] For this explanation of the remarkable word in Am. ix. 7 I am indebted to Mowinckel, who has vindicated it in several books, most recently in *He that Cometh*, p. 132. The resemblance to the Ethiopians is the heathen character of the apostate Israel. The Philistines and Syrians are mentioned as possible successors of Israel in the position of a people of Yahweh. They were, like Israel, objects of Yahweh's care. Thus this utterance of Amos is analogous to the saying of John the Baptist in Matt. iii. 9: 'Do not presume to say to yourselves, "We have Abraham as our father", for I tell you, God is able from these stones to raise up children to Abraham.'

the religious and moral norms which, during the history of Israel from the tribal stage onwards, were crystallized in Israelite custom and tradition. But the most essential among them were not nationally and geographically limited but of universal applicability. So it was with charity, justice, humanity, honesty, humility, etc. Such qualities could be required from any man, irrespective of the nation to which he belonged. Thus to the prophets Yahweh's ethical will was valid for all mankind. Amos holds that Yahweh sees to it that His ethical laws are observed beyond the boundaries of Israel and that He also punishes foreign peoples who flout His demands of faithfulness, pity, and mercy (ch. i-ii).[93]

Yahweh requires of all men that humility which is the reverse of *hybris*. Isaiah knows that one day the pride of men will be humbled and that all that is proud and high, lofty and tall, will be brought low (ii. 10 ff.). Because of their pride and arrogance judgement is proclaimed by the prophets on Assyria, Babylonia, and other peoples. The fact that Yahweh's ethical demands are valid for mankind, and that these demands are flouted by the peoples of the earth, is one of the roots from which grew the idea of Yahweh's world judgement.

Yahweh's distance from, and His sublimity over, all terrestrial, mundane, temporal regions and things is expressed by the term *ḳōḏeš*, holiness. Yahweh's holiness is the same as His divinity considered as *mysterium fascinosum et tremendum*. When Yahweh swears by His holiness (Am. iv. 2) He swears by His divinity, by Himself as God. That is the most sacred oath. The expression 'the Holy One of Israel', frequently used by Isaiah, means the same as 'the God of Israel' in all His sublimity. The predilection of Isaiah for this designation results from his personal impression of Yahweh's exaltation, His heavenly majesty, particularly as experienced in the inaugural vision. In the remarkable and rather anthropomorphic passage, Hos. xi. 8-9, the ideas of divinity, non-human being, and holiness are paralleled. The prophet

---

[93] I think it would misrepresent the view of Amos if one maintained that Damascus, Gaza, Edom, etc., were to be punished only because they were enemies of Israel. In the first place they are condemned because of their wickedness and cruelty as such, because of the fact that they have offended against the holy will of Yahweh, which is valid for all peoples. So rightly Kapelrud, *Central Ideas in Amos*, pp. 17 ff. There is of course no *theory* behind this ethical universalism in Amos, a theory of Noachite commandments, of a general moral consciousness in mankind or the like. The ethical universalism of Amos was a consequence of his dynamic monotheism. If Yahweh was ruler of the world His holy will was valid for all mankind. As to the origin of this universalism in Amos, Kapelrud thinks that Amos took over the universalism which was characteristic of the ancient supreme god, El 'Elyon (p. 46). Is such an explanation necessary? There was a tendency to universalism in Israelite faith before Amos; and his personal experience of Yahweh might have developed this tendency in an extraordinary measure. Cf. North, *The Old Testament Interpretation of History*, pp. 63 ff.

refers to these qualities in Yahweh in order to emphasize that Yahweh's acts towards His people are determined not by fierce anger as an incidental emotion, but by the fundamental character of His divine being, i.e., His love for the elect people.

It is of importance to observe that, in the prophets, the holiness of Yahweh particularly implies distance from human uncleanness and sin and violent reaction against it. Confronted by Yahweh's holy majesty in the inaugural vision, Isaiah feared for his life, first because he had seen the heavenly King, and then because he was unclean.[94] Amos says that the sexual rites profane Yahweh's holy name (ii. 7). For a similar reason it can be said that Yahweh's exaltation reveals itself in righteousness and that His holiness exhibits itself in justice, Yahweh being here thought of as a righteous Judge (Isa. v. 16).[95]

As regards Yahweh's relation to Israel, the prophets first and foremost emphasize Yahweh's love. The Hebrew words for Yahweh's love, the verb 'āhab and the noun 'ahªbâh, are the same as are used for love between man and woman, parents and children. Things can also be objects of love when strongly liked and coveted by men.[96] Love implies an affection, but an affection that impels to action. Yahweh's love was the foundation of His choice of Israel to be His own people. The pre-exilic prophets never speak of any reason for the choice of this particular people. Yahweh's love for Israel was irrational and paradoxical, spontaneous and unmotivated. Yahweh 'found' Israel with the same joyful surprise as one finds grapes in the wilderness and the first figs on the fig tree (Hos. ix. 10). Yahweh's love was not motivated by any merit on the part of the people: 'When Israel was a child, I came to love him,' Hosea says in Yahweh's name (xi. 1). Hosea's love for Gomer must have helped him to understand what love is.

Of the nearly related notions rahªmîm and hesed the first means 'compassion', 'mercy', presupposing the suffering, distress, or weakness of the other party, the latter means 'faithfulness', 'solidarity', 'loyalty', evinced in acts of devotion and friendship, and is conditioned by the fact that there are two parties connected with each other by ties of family, tribe, nationality, alliance, covenant, etc. Yahweh is merciful to Israel when they are in distress, and faithful to them because of His

---

[94] Cf. my analysis of the inaugural vision of Isaiah, pp. 186 ff.

[95] Ringgren, *The Prophetical Conception of Holiness*, emphasizes that holiness in the Old Testament is primarily a quality in Yahweh. Holiness means Yahweh's divinity in general, further His elevation over all that is human and earthly, finally His power to carry out the divine will. He correctly says that Yahweh's holiness was first and foremost experienced in the cult.

[96] See, e.g., Hos. ii. 7 ff.; iii. 1; iv. 18; viii. 9; ix. 1; x. 11. Cf. Ziegler, *Die Liebe Gottes*, pp. 13 ff.

covenant with the chosen people. Very characteristically Jeremiah says in Yahweh's name, 'With an everlasting love I love you, therefore I maintain faithfulness towards you' (xxxi. 3).[97] Yahweh's love manifested in His covenant with the elect people is the condition of His faithfulness to it.[98]

Yahweh's love is exclusively love to Israel, the elect people. The pre-exilic prophets never say that Yahweh loves other peoples, or that mankind is an object of His love. All those passages in the pre-exilic prophetic books in which pagan peoples are spoken of as objects of Yahweh's sympathy and affectionate care are exilic or post-exilic. But Yahweh's actions in the history of Israel are dictated by His love. Behind election lies Yahweh's love. The same is true of His punitive educative work as well as of His gracious gifts in the continued course of history and of the restoration in the age to come. The blessed future is ultimately a creation of Yahweh's paradoxical love and nothing else.

In the thought of the pre-exilic prophets Yahweh's wrath ('ap, 'ebrâh, ḥēmâh, za'am) was the antithesis of His love. The calamities in the history of Israel were frequently understood as moments in the education of the people, dictated by Yahweh's love, but often they were regarded as evidence of a spontaneous reaction of the holy God against unholiness and sin. The ravages of the Babylonians in the land of Judah in 597 are described by Jeremiah in terms which indicate that he regarded them as manifestations of Yahweh's wrath: 'Who will have pity on you, O Jerusalem? Who will bemoan you? Who will go out of his way to ask about your welfare? You have cast Me off, says Yahweh, in drawing back. So I stretched out My hand against you to destroy you, being weary of relenting' (xv. 5 f.). Here wrath triumphs over mercy and love. The people have brought afflictions upon themselves through neglecting their God (ii. 17). Yahweh has rejected His people, who had become 'the generation of His wrath' (vii. 29). In the catastrophe of the year 586 Jeremiah saw an outpouring of Yahweh's anger and fury (xlii. 18). In Isaiah Yahweh calls Assyria 'the rod of My anger'; and Israel is the people of His wrath (x. 5 f.). Hosea says that Yahweh's wrath burns against the Baal worshippers in Samaria (viii. 5).

In the pre-exilic prophets the wrath of Yahweh is described in many different ways. Especially in the predictions of the final destruction of the people, wrath is predominant. The prophecies of judgement in

[97] For the right understanding of the tenses see Nyberg, *Hebreisk grammatik*, pp. 263 ff., esp. § 86 j and m.
[98] On this idea see further Johnson in the *Mowinckel Festschrift*, pp. 100 ff., and earlier Glueck, *Das Wort ḥesed*; Ziegler, op. cit., pp. 22 ff.; Lofthouse in *ZAW*, li, 1933, pp. 29 ff.

Amos are dominated by the idea: *fiat justitia, pereat mundus*. Of Israel Yahweh says, 'The end has come upon My people Israel. I will never again forgive them' (viii. 2). Yahweh's eye is set upon them for evil and not for good (ix. 4). Similar expressions are to be found in almost all the pre-exilic prophets. The time when the judgement will come is expressly called 'the day of the wrath of Yahweh' (Zeph. ii. 2).

While Yahweh's love was valid only for Israel, the elect people, His wrath could be kindled against the pagan peoples also. The oracles of Amos against foreign nations deal in reality with Yahweh's wrath because of their evil deeds. To Isaiah Assyria was an object of Yahweh's anger. The same is true of Nineveh in the prophecy of Nahum, of the sinful inhabitants of the earth in Zephaniah, and the pagan nations in Habakkuk: 'In fury Thou settest foot upon the earth, Thou tramplest the nations in anger' (iii. 12).

The idea of Yahweh's wrath had its origin in Israel's own experience. In the course of history Yahweh had frequently shown how He mercilessly overthrew His enemies, all who opposed Him and resisted His purposes. The historical traditions of Israel offered many concrete examples of this. The prophets often refer expressly to these traditions when they speak of the wrath of Yahweh by which their own contemporaries were confronted.

Thus in the pre-exilic prophets the real antithesis of Yahweh's love is Yahweh's wrath. The idea of 'righteousness', *ṣedāḳāh*, is in these prophets not often used as an attribute of Yahweh. The reason for this is that, as we have seen, they avoid the idea of *berît*. Yahweh's *ṣedāḳāh* belongs to the group of concepts that are closely connected with the covenant. *ṣedāḳāh* does, however, occur in the sense of 'salvation' in Isa. i. 27 (if this passage is authentic),[99] in Jer. xxiii. 6, where the Messianic king is called 'Yahweh is our salvation' (*ṣidḳēnû*), and, in the plural form *ṣedāḳât* in the sense of acts of salvation, in Mic. vi. 5. Sometimes *ṣedāḳāh* in the sense 'justice' is ascribed to Yahweh in His capacity as Judge: Isa. v. 16; Zeph. iii. 5; Jer. xi. 20; xx. 12.[100]

---

[99] Most modern scholars think that this verse is exilic or post-exilic: Buhl, Procksch, Mowinckel in *GTMMM*, Bentzen, etc. However this may be, the words *mišpaṭ* and *ṣedāḳāh* must be taken in the sense they have in Deutero-Isaiah, as having reference to the saving righteousness of Yahweh. So also Herntrich in *ATD*, who, however, regards the verse as authentic.

[100] In Jer. ix. 23 the sense of the words 'justice' and 'righteousness' is somewhat doubtful. Are they synonymous with *ḥesed*, or do they introduce another idea: the judging righteousness of Yahweh? The former explanation is maintained by Fahlgren, Mowinckel in *GTMMM*, Weiser ('kurze Umschreibung des Heils'), and Ziegler, the latter by Volz and Rudolph. If the word is Jeremianic, it seems to be more in accordance with the style of this prophet if two different qualities are here assigned to Yahweh, the Judge of the world: on the one hand the mercy of the divine Judge, on the other His inexorable retributive justice.

Yahweh's passionate ardour, *kin'âh*, is not often mentioned in the pre-exilic prophets, this conception being typical of a later time. However, in Isa. ix. 6 Yahweh's ardour designates the extremity of His love to and care for His people; in Zeph. i. 18 and iii. 8 it is the culmination of His wrath. Even though the word is rare in the pre-exilic prophets, the passionate attitude of Yahweh, manifested in His acts and demands, is always a reality to the prophets. The 'pathos' of Yahweh has rightly been described as a typical prophetic idea.[100a]

What is the relation between Yahweh's love and Yahweh's wrath in the preaching of the pre-exilic prophets? According to the view of history represented by these prophets two parallel lines ran through the history of the Israelite people, one determined by love, the other determined by wrath. There was a course of events which served to demonstrate how Yahweh worked for His people's good and for the fulfilment of their election. There was another course of historical occurrences, of which the sole aim was the victory of Yahweh's punitive will and the satisfaction of His wrath. There is no real organic connection between the two. They represent two different sides in Yahweh, both equally proper to His divine character.

In all the pre-exilic prophets there is a tension between Yahweh's love and Yahweh's wrath. In Hosea, in particular, this tension is exceptionally evident because of the marriage symbolism. In Hosea's matrimonial history love and resentment alternated with each other. To him Yahweh's love and Yahweh's wrath are powers struggling with each other within Yahweh. Yahweh's wrath demanded that the apostate people should be abandoned to destruction like Admah and Zeboim. But Yahweh's love required the salvation of the people. Here love prevailed over wrath. Yahweh *could* not destroy His own people.[101]

In Jeremiah there are two passages where, once more, love and wrath are in conflict with each other. In one of them wrath prevails; Yahweh

---

[100a] The Polish scholar Heschel, who holds that theophany and inspiration ('Eingebung') rather than ecstasy are characteristic of the prophetic experiences (his conception of ecstasy being rather biased), strongly emphasizes the 'pathos' of the God of the prophets. God not only acts and demands, God is emotionally involved in the happenings of history. 'Nicht das Vorherwissen eines zukünftigen Geschehens', says Heschel, 'sondern das Wissen um das gegenwärtige Pathos ist der geistige Besitz der Propheten'; *Die Prophetie*, pp. 143 f. This emphasis on the divine pathos is of course fully justified, particularly as a reaction against a one-sided intellectualist view.

[101] Hos. xi. 8 f. Some scholars think that this saying predicts merciless doom: Nyberg, *Studien zum Hoseabuche*, p. 90; Robinson in *HAT*; Mowinckel in *GTMMM*. In *Hosea literarisch untersucht*, p. 65, I offered the interpretation of the verses which is assumed above and find no reason to alter my view. The same explanation is more recently presented by Weiser in *ATD*. I now, however, give up the hypothesis that xi. 8 f. was originally connected with ii. 16 f.; *lāķēn* in ii. 16 is only a connecting particle, inserted by the collector of the revelations of Hosea.

says, 'You have cast Me off in drawing back. So I stretched out My hand against you to destroy you, being weary of relenting' (xv. 6). In the other passage love triumphs over wrath. Because Ephraim, in spite of his apostasy, really is Yahweh's dear son, His darling child, Yahweh, as often as He speaks harshly about him, *must* think of him with compassion. He *must* have pity upon him (xxxi. 20).[102]

The prophets knew of no synthesis between love and wrath in the nature of Yahweh. Every moment they lived in fear of Yahweh's wrath and trust in His love. This absence of 'certainty of belief' is typical of Israelite religion as a whole. What Yahweh was about to do, was not to be determined in advance. His thoughts were not identical with the thoughts of men. There was no security in Yahweh's presence. Man had no right to make demands upon Him. In the relation to Yahweh there was always a *perhaps*.[103] Amos exhorted his people to hate evil and love good. *Perhaps*, he says, Yahweh will be gracious to the descendants of Joseph (v. 15).[104]

The election of Israel was not motivated by any ethical quality or moral achievement on the part of the people. It had its ground exclusively in Yahweh's paradoxical love. But to the prophets it was an axiom that because of election Yahweh made religious and moral demands upon His people.

First and foremost Yahweh demands to be the only God for Israel, the only object of their worship. In Hosea Yahweh says, 'I am Yahweh, your God, from the land of Egypt; and you know no God but Me, and there is no saviour except Me' (xiii. 4).

The prophetic preaching contains many expressions for the right relation to Yahweh. The pre-exilic prophets speak frequently of knowing Yahweh (*yāḏaʿ yahwêh*), which is not only to have a correct knowledge of Yahweh's nature and His cultic and moral demands, but also, according to Hebrew linguistic usage, to hold to, be devoted to Yahweh, and to obey His commands.[105] Hosea denounces the priests for having neglected to impart to the people knowledge of Yahweh's *tôrâh* (iv. 4 ff.).

---

102 *dibber bᵉ* in the sense 'speak inimically against (about)', 'scold at' Num. xii. 1, 8; xxi. 7; Job xix. 18; Ps. l. 20; lxxviii. 19; *zāḵar* in the sense 'care kindly for' Gen. viii. 1; xix. 29; xxx. 22; Judges xvi. 28; 1 Sam. i. 11; Ps. viii. 5.
103 The same uncertainty about Yahweh's action appears also in Zeph. ii. 3; Joel ii. 14; and Jonah iii. 9.
104 *šᵉʾērît yôsēp* sometimes rendered 'the remnant [so *AV, RV, RSV*] of Joseph' (North Israel), is not to be taken in an eschatological sense, nor does it refer to those who will possibly be saved from a catastrophe; it simply refers to the descendants of the patriarch Joseph (cf. 2 Sam. xiv. 7; Isa. xiv. 22). The term is used to mark the relative feebleness and poverty of the offspring of the great patriarch as an object of Yahweh's mercy and compassion; cf. 'he is so small', vii. 2, 5.
105 Cf. Mowinckel, *Die Erkenntnis Gottes bei den alttestamentlichen Propheten*, pp. 5 ff.

But religious knowledge is also practical, moral (iv. 1), and whole-hearted devotion to Yahweh, synonymous with faithfulness to Yahweh (v. 4; vi. 3, 6).[105a] Jeremiah uses the same terminology. He complains that the people do not know the way of Yahweh, the rights of their God. Here he is thinking both of theoretical insight into and practical obedience to Yahweh's commands (v. 4 f.). He says that migrating birds know, i.e., keep the times of their coming and leaving, but Israel does not regard (*yāḏaʻ*) the ordinances of Yahweh (viii. 7). Knowledge of Yahweh consists in doing justice and righteousness and defending the cause of the poor and needy (xxii. 15 f.). In the age to come everyone will know Yahweh, i.e., have a complete insight into Yahweh's nature and will, resulting in right worship and obedience (xxxi. 33 f.). In the light of such passages the introductory words of the book of Isaiah are to be understood in the following way: The ox and the ass are interested in and hold to their owner and their master's crib, but Israel is indifferent to its God, having forsaken Yahweh and in disobedience spurned the Holy One of Israel (i. 3 f.).

The expression 'seek Yahweh' (*biḳḳēš*, *dāraš*) originated in cultic terminology. Men sought the deity at the sanctuary, particularly in order to receive oracles. The pre-exilic prophets use the term for the right worship of Yahweh in a general sense. Amos says, 'Seek Yahweh, that you may live' (v. 6). 'Seek Yahweh' is to hold to Yahweh in order to have His help (Hos. vii. 10). Related expressions are 'look to', 'think of', 'remember', etc. The contrast is 'forsake', 'reject', 'spurn', 'forget' Yahweh.

If the relation to Yahweh is thought of as a covenant, a marriage, kinship, the chief demand of Yahweh is faithfulness or loyalty (*ḥeseḏ*), including obedience to Yahweh's commands. The reverse is 'faithless-ness', 'fornication', 'treachery'. Occasionally, in bridal symbolism, there is mention of Israel's love (*'aháḇâh*) to her God (Jer. ii. 2).

Yahweh in His glorious majesty demands humility on men's part. What the Greeks called *hybris* was also familiar to the Israelite prophets. They call it 'haughtiness' (*gaḇhûṭ*). Yahweh hates all that is proud, exalted, high, and lofty in the human world. One day it will be humbled and brought low by Him (Isa. ii. 10 ff.). The pagan nations also draw down upon themselves Yahweh's judgement because of their arrogance. So do the Assyrians in Isaiah, Nineveh in Nahum, and the Babylonians in Habakkuk. In Micah it is said that Yahweh requires nothing from His people but to do justice, to love faithfulness, and to walk humbly with

---

[105a] For religious knowledge in Hosea see McKenzie in *JBL*, lxxiv, 1955, pp. 22 ff., where the relation between *daʻaṭ yahwêh* and *daʻaṭ 'elōhîm* is also discussed.

their God (vi. 8).[105b] Zephaniah says: 'Seek righteousness, seek humility, perhaps you may be hidden on the day of the wrath of Yahweh' (ii. 3).

Before Yahweh in His power and His wrath men ought to be in fear (*yir'âh, paḥaḏ*). Yahweh should be the fear of His worshippers; Him alone and no other they should fear (Isa. viii. 13). Isaiah blames his people that they worship Yahweh with their lips, but do not have the right fear of Him (xxix. 13). Israel does not fear Yahweh, say Hosea (x. 3) and Jeremiah (ii. 19).

The profoundest expression for Israel's relation to Yahweh in the pre-exilic prophets is belief, trust, confidence in Yahweh (*he'emîn, bāṭaḥ*). Isaiah is the first to have presented belief and confidence in Yahweh as a central religious demand. In his teaching this notion has a very concrete significance. In every critical situation in the political life of the people he ventured to make resolute confidence in Yahweh the only sure way of deliverance. At the outbreak of the Syro-Ephraimitic war he uttered the famous word: 'If you do not have confidence [in Yahweh], you will surely not stand steadfast' (vii. 9). This implied a condemnation of all human expedients. There seems to be something paradoxical, something utopian about this saying, uttered in a critically dangerous political situation; but it is entirely credible in the mouth of a great prophet. Later, when Judah was menaced by the armies of Sennacherib, Isaiah repeated the same appeal: 'In returning and rest you shall be saved, in quietness and confidence shall be your strength' (xxx. 15). Neither alliance with the Egyptians, nor the strengthening of their own defensive forces could help. In confidence in Yahweh and nothing else lay salvation. The true meaning of words such as these is not that quietness and confidence in itself would help, but that confidence would create the condition on which alone Yahweh could intervene as a helping power in the distress of the people. The people had, indeed, confidence of a kind in Yahweh; but it was associated with belief in the efficacy of cultic performances and temporal expedients without the necessary observance of the spiritual commands of Yahweh. What Isaiah sought was quietness combined with true devotion.

The people rejected Isaiah's admonitions and went to meet their ruin. But within the people there was a group who listened and obeyed, the circle of Isaiah's disciples. They understood and embodied the true Yahweh religion, a religious attitude cleansed from all those false outgrowths which marred the popular religion. This pure and unadulterated religion is what Isaiah describes in metaphorical language in the well-known saying of the cornerstone (xxviii. 16 f.). The prophet here

---

[105b] For this passage see Anderson in *SJT*, iv, 1951, pp. 191 ff.

presents Yahweh as a builder erecting a house. The house has a foundation-stone and walls raised by means of measuring-line and plummet.
The text itself gives the true interpretation. The foundation-stone
means confidence in Yahweh, the walls mean justice and righteousness.
These are the marks of the true Yahweh religion. Those who understood and practised this religion would be saved from ruin, while the
'scoffers', those who made lies their refuge, would perish.[106]

The same teaching is found in Zephaniah. He reproaches the population of Jerusalem for not having trusted in Yahweh and not having
drawn near to their God (iii. 2). Similarly Habakkuk is told in a vision
that while the tyrant (the Babylonians) shall perish because of his
wickedness and *hybris*, the righteous (i.e., Judah, who is innocent in
comparison with the Babylonians; cf. i. 13) shall live (i.e., be saved) by
adhering steadfastly to Yahweh and trusting in His help (ii. 4).[107]

Any study of the teaching of the pre-exilic prophets about God must
include some account of Yahweh's moral demands.

At first glance we observe that the ethics of these prophets refer
mainly to social life. The ethical admonitions are rather monotonous.
There are frequent exhortations to mercy and charity to the poor and
in general to the needy and defenceless. Orphans and widows, helpless
and oppressed people, strangers and people without legal rights play a
great part in the exhortations and diatribes of the prophets. To take up
their cause, to protect them, defend them, to prevent violence and
outrage, and to maintain judicial impartiality and fairness are major
elements in the prophetic ethical ideal, as are honesty in commercial
life, veracity and faithfulness, respect for the life and property of other
men. Marriage and family life must be held sacred. The ideal Israelite
is simple, modest, and chaste. He does not build luxurious palaces. He
is content with his inheritance from his forefathers and free from greed
of gain and the desire to accumulate wealth and lands. The social ideal
of the pre-exilic prophets was the simple life of farmers, shepherds, and
craftsmen, not business life and the luxury and extravagance of the rich.[108]

---

[106] On this remarkable passage see further Lindblom in the *Mowinckel Festschrift*,
pp. 123 ff.—For the original meaning of the notions 'belief', 'trust', etc., in the Old
Testament see the semantic investigation by van Dorssen in *De derivata van de stam
'mn in het Hebreeuwsch van het Oude Testament*. See also the examination of the
relevant ideas in Vriezen, *Geloven en Vertrouwen*, with interesting comments on the
views of Buber.

[107] There appears to be a contradiction between i, 2 ff., where, in my view, the moral
decay of Judah is described, and the statement in ii. 4b. But if *ṣaddîk* is taken in the
same sense as in i. 13, the 'righteousness' of Judah is seen in relation to the reckless
brutality of the Babylonians. See further above, pp. 253 ff.

[108] Am. ii. 6 ff.; iv. 1; v. 7, 10 ff., 15; vi. 4, 8; viii. 4 ff.; Hos. iv. 2, 18; vi. 9 f.; x. 4;
Isa. i. 17, 23; iii. 16 ff.; v. 8 ff., 22 f.; x. 2; xxix. 21; Mic. ii. 2, 8 f.; iii. 1 ff.; vi. 10 ff.;
vii. 2 ff.; Zeph. i. 13; Jer. vii. 5 f.; xxi. 12; xxii. 3, 13 ff., 16 f., etc.

This teaching is characterized by the principle of solidarity. Behind the demand for charity and justice towards the poor and defenceless lies the idea of the *people*, the people as an organic whole, united by election and the covenant. As members of the same chosen people all Israelites were members of a sacrosanct organism and must be treated accordingly. The general expression of this solidarity is *ḥeseḏ*, which, as a moral quality, is brotherliness in attitude and action. When wealthy magnates oppressed the poor and defenceless, the sacred unity was broken. Amos sternly censured those who, at the cultic festivals, stretched themselves out upon divans, eating lambs from the flocks, singing and drinking, but were not concerned about 'the ruin of Joseph' (i.e., national disaster; vi. 6). Micah was deeply concerned about national solidarity. He rebuked the upper classes for treating the common people (the true people of Yahweh) harshly, plucking off the garments of peaceful men and expelling women from their homes (ii. 8 f.). They 'eat the flesh of My people', says Yahweh (iii. 3). It is not only the heartlessness in itself that fills Micah with indignation, but above all that such treatment should be meted out to men and women who also belonged to the people of Yahweh.[109]

Another feature in the ethical ideal of the pre-exilic prophets is hostility to a more developed, refined culture, typical of an advanced settled stage of civilization. There is a conspicuous reactionary tendency in the preaching of these prophets. For them the best times were times long past. The days of the 'childhood' of Israel were sometimes regarded as the happiest days in the history of the people (Hos. ii. 17; xi. 1; Jer. ii. 2; iii. 4). Hosea holds that progress in culture was regress in religion and morals (x. 1). Jeremiah recalls the happy time when the people followed Yahweh through the desert and gave Him her bridal love (ii. 2). The French Old Testament scholar, A. Causse, speaks with good reason of 'la nostalgie des temps primitifs' in Israel.[110] The prophets shared this 'nostalgie'. But we must be careful not to lay too much stress on the wilderness period as the ideal time. It was not the nomadic culture but the simple agricultural life that the prophets regarded as the ideal. Hosea says that Yahweh is going to allure Israel and bring her into the wilderness to speak to her heart (ii. 16 f.). But this second sojourn in the wilderness is thought of by him as a period of education, which is followed by a blessed life in the sown land. This utterance of Hosea is manifestly modelled on the narratives about the first Exodus.[111]

---

[109] See further Lindblom *Micha literarisch untersucht*, pp. 172 ff. and 176 f.
[110] See *RHPh.*, ii, 1922, p. 152.
[111] On the much discussed question of Hosea's attitude to the monarchy see Alt in *Kleine Schriften*, II, pp. 116 ff., esp. pp. 125 f.

It is characteristic that the blessed age to come is never thought of as a time when the people will wander in the wilderness with tents and flocks; in that age the people will be in possession of fields to plough, vineyards to cultivate, and cattle to rear. The interest of the prophets in the past had of course nothing to do with reactionary conservatism or with dreamy romanticism, it was rooted in the experience that the cultural development in the milieu of the highly developed civilization of Canaan was accompanied by the corruption of the Yahwistic religion and morals, and that the ultimate cause of Israel's apostasy was the influence of the Canaanite Baal cult.

The ethical ideals of the prophets were not invented by them, but were taken from life and tradition and had been impressed on the mind of the people by the moral instruction given at the sanctuaries in connection with the cult.[112] The ideal of social solidarity was apparently ultimately an inheritance from the tribal culture of nomadic and semi-nomadic times.[113] Since the legislation of several peoples of the ancient Near East has become known, many parallels have been established between the laws of those peoples and the laws of the Old Testament.[114] There are also analogies to the ideal of humanity in social relationships. Suffice it to recall the epilogue of Hammurabi's law, where the kingly legislator says that he has been commissioned to protect the weak against the strong and defend the cause of the widows and orphans.[115] It is, however, wrong to suppose that Israel and its prophets *borrowed* such principles from neighbouring peoples. The Hebrews themselves brought them from the tribal stage, which was much nearer to them than it was to Canaanites, Assyrians, Babylonians, etc., and for this reason influenced them to a still higher degree than these other peoples. A sectarian group such as the Rechabites shows how tenaciously the nomadic tradition with its characteristic usages could survive at a higher level of culture. The Rechabites only represent the extreme of a tendency which during the entire monarchical period manifested itself in the noblest of Israel's religious leaders. The prophets embodied the good old customs in their admonitory preaching and gave them divine sanction.

---

[112] See above all Alt, op. cit., I, pp. 322 ff.

[113] For this problem see *inter alios* Nyström, *Beduinentum und Jahwismus.*

[114] See *inter alios* Ring, *Israels Rechtsleben im Lichte der neuentdeckten assyrischen und hethitischen Gesetzesurkunden*; Puukko, *Die altassyrischen und hethitischen Gesetze und das Alte Testament*; Jirku, *Altorientalischer Kommentar zum Alten Testament*, pp. 90 ff.; Fuchs, *Die alttestamentliche Arbeitergesetzgebung im Vergleich zum Codex Hammurapi, zum altassyrischen und hethitischen Recht*; Neufeld, *Notes on Hittite Laws.*

[115] *ANET*, pp. 177 ff. Other examples in Dürr, *Ursprung und Ausbau der israelitisch-jüdischen Heilandserwartung*, pp. 77 ff.; Engnell, *Studies in Divine Kingship*, pp. 37 ff. See also the Ugaritic Aqhat-text, Driver, *Canaanite Myths*, p. 53. For the basis of the ethical teaching of the prophets see Porteous in *SOTP*, pp. 143 ff.

Prophetic ethics are theonomic ethics. Ethics divorced from religion would be an absurdity to the Old Testament prophets. Behind all that they apprehended as right and good they set Yahweh as Authority and Guardian. The ideal of humanity in the classical or modern sense was quite alien to them. The theocentric feature, so characteristic of their view of history, recurs also in their view of morality. Every offence against moral demands was at the same time an offence against Yahweh's holy will. In the prophetic preaching we do not find any rational motivation of moral demands. The Old Testament prophets were neither theologians nor philosophers. They accepted the best elements in the moral tradition of their people and regarded them as Yahweh's commands. The ethical ideal was to the prophets Yahweh's demand on His people by virtue of election. Therefore a description of the ethical ideal of the prophets has its right place in connection with their general view of God.

The content of the ethical ideas of the prophets was taken from tradition in its best forms. What was new was the earnestness with which they presented them as inviolable divine commands and, further, the discovery that these commands were flouted and that, for this reason, Yahweh's people stood under Yahweh's judgement.

C. *The Prophetic View of the Moral and Religious State of their People*

The settlement of the Hebrew tribes in Canaan led to far-reaching changes in their cultural and social conditions. This process has been studied and described by many authors: the sociologist M. Weber, the historian E. Meyer, Biblical scholars such as A. Causse, A. Lods, J. Morgenstern, and many others.

The main features of the tribal organization survived for a long time after the settlement, but were gradually replaced by the new social forms, created by the village, city, and state culture. The chief bond of society was no longer blood relationship but the fact of living together in settled communities. The descendants of nomads and semi-nomads became farmers and craftsmen. Trade in different forms began to flourish. Commercial intercourse with neighbouring nations opened the door for foreign influences. In time the monarchical system eliminated the social peculiarities of tribal culture and gave rise to a large staff of public functionaries (the king's servants, as they are called), several lists of whom are found in the Old Testament. These officials, civil and military, inevitably became keen rivals of the old heads of tribes and families and, finally, made their authority ineffective. To maintain the power of the king there was created a military organization, including both a standing army and a royal bodyguard; a royal court was set up; and there was a well organized system of taxation.

With the break-up of tribal organization and the dissolution of collective solidarity the individual and individual interests were more in evidence. The right to hold private property and to amass possessions was both recognized and practised. Thus the foundation was laid of a fatal class distinction between the rich and the poor, between those who were able to enjoy luxury and plenty and those who had to toil for the barest necessities. The poor and defenceless were often oppressed and fleeced by the wealthy. The judges were bribed to pronounce unjust judgements in favour of those who had power and influence.

The new social conditions were combated by the lawgivers, by anti-cultural groups (e.g., the Rechabites), and, above all, by the prophets. The prophets regarded the new state of things as apostasy from Yahweh and revolt against His will. An essential part of their preaching consists in denunciation of the new customs, which were at variance with their ethical ideals, the divine demands they were commissioned to defend and contend for.

Criticism of the conditions prevalent in society appears everywhere in the preaching of the pre-exilic prophets. Amos rebukes (ii. 6) the wealthy for selling the innocent for money and the needy for a pair of sandals (even today the Arabs say 'sandal string' to denote a ridiculously low price).[116] He blames the judges for turning justice to wormwood, the sellers for falsifying measures and scales, the magnates for oppressing the poor and for abandoning themselves to luxuriance and extravagance, building splendid palaces after foreign models and gorging themselves with dainty meat and drink.[117] Hosea goes still farther. Israel is a nation of rascals and murderers. There is no fidelity in the land. It is filled with cursing, lying, murder, drunkenness, theft, adultery. One crime follows upon another. In particular Hosea condemns the political revolutions and the regicides. He blames the priests for having neglected their duty to give sound instruction in the Torah. For Hosea the entire history of Israel from the first ancestor down to his own time was filled with sin and apostasy; and development in culture meant development in moral corruption.[118]

Micah's criticism is levelled chiefly against the leaders of the people:

[116] Jacob, *Altarabische Parallelen zum Alten Testament*, p. 17. With Sellin, Hammers-haimb, *Amos*, pp. 43 f., and others I believe that *ṣaddîḳ* here is the innocent party in a lawsuit and that, consequently, the passage deals with the evil custom of bribing judges to condemn poor and defenceless people in the interest of the wealthy; cf. Isa. i. 23; v. 23.

[117] Am. ii. 8; iii. 9 f.; iv. 1; v. 7, 10 f.; vi. 4; viii. 4 ff.

[118] Hos. iv. 1 f., 6; viii, 1 ff., 4 f.; x. 4, 9, 13; xi. 1 f.; xiii. 6.

royal officials, judges, prophets, and priests, and, above all, the wealthy, who oppressed and plundered the poor and defenceless. Later his view becomes still more pessimistic. The godly, he says, have perished from the land; there is none righteous among men. It has been as in the gleanings of a vintage, when there is not a cluster to eat.[119]

Isaiah saw the situation in the same light. In particular he castigates foreign customs and usages that had entered the land.[120] In this Zephaniah follows him closely,[121] as does Jeremiah. Jeremiah represents sinfulness as universal, affecting every section of the people; it is an inheritance from the past. 'Such has been your way from youth,' Yahweh says (Jer. xxii. 21). The corruption is radical and irreparable: 'Though you washed yourself with lye and used much soap, your guilt would stand filthy in my sight' (ii. 22). The people are incapable of repentance and amendment. For them it is as impossible to do good as for the Ethiopian to change his skin or the leopard his spots (xiii. 23). For this reason Jeremiah was forbidden by Yahweh to intercede for his people.

In my view the lamentation at the beginning of the Book of Habakkuk refers to the moral situation in Judah. The prophet complains of wrong-doing, destruction and violence, strife and contention. The law is paralysed. The wicked circumvent the innocent.[122]

It would be a mistake to treat in isolation such descriptions of national moral corruption which appear everywhere in the books of the pre-exilic prophets. In the view of these prophets moral depravation was a consequence of religious apostasy. If the people had kept to Yahweh, they would have understood what Yahweh's will was and would have obeyed His ethical commands. It is often said by the prophets that their people had despised *mišpāṭ*, the Hebrew word for the sum of all the obligations which were incumbent upon the people by virtue of the covenant. *mišpāṭ* includes moral demands *and* religious obligations, obedience to ethical precepts as well as the right attitude to Yahweh. The two belong together and are not strictly distinguished in Hebrew thought, ethical requirements being regarded as ultimately prescribed by Yahweh, and fear of Yahweh and love to Him providing the impulse to act in accordance with His will.

Israel's apostasy from Yahweh is a theme which constantly recurs in the preaching of the pre-exilic prophets. Various expressions are used to describe it. Amos refers to the consciousness of power and the self-confidence which dominated the ruling classes after the national

[119] Mic. ii. 1 f., 8 f.; iii. 1 ff., 5, 9 ff.; vi. 10 ff.; vii. 1 ff.
[120] Isa. i. 21 ff.; ii. 6 f.; iii. 14 f., 16 ff.; v. 8 ff.; x. 1 f.; xxviii. **3, 7** f.
[121] Zeph. 1. 8 f., 12; iii. 3 f.
[122] See above, pp. 253 ff.

successes during the reign of Jeroboam II (vi. 1, 13). This self-confidence led the people to set Yahweh aside. Amos also condemns the assurance with which they nevertheless believed that Yahweh was with them (v. 14) and that they had nothing to fear in the future (v. 18 ff.). The cultic worship was worthless, and even detestable, being a false substitute for the one thing needful: mišpāṭ. To a more detailed examination of the special problem of the attitude of Amos and other pre-exilic prophets towards idolatry and the cult, we return below.

Hosea says that Israel has lost the right knowledge of Yahweh. She has broken the covenant (viii. 1). It is characteristic of this prophet that he describes apostasy as adultery. Israel has forsaken Yahweh and given herself to the Baal. Israel has surrendered herself to faithlessness and fornication. The worship of Yahweh has turned into idolatry, the prophetic label for the syncretistic cult. Superstitious usages, sacral prostitution, and the worship of idols mar the religious life of the people. Alliances with foreign peoples are a special manifestation of apostasy. Such attempts to enlist the aid of foreign powers are regarded by Hosea as deceit and treachery (vii. 11; viii. 9; xii. 2).

Micah likewise condemns the worship of idols as rebellion against Yahweh (i. 5 ff.). Yahweh's lawsuit against His people in ch. vi presupposes that Israel has forgotten Yahweh's beneficent deeds in the history of the people and in pride has turned its back upon Him. In their blindness the people have quite misunderstood Yahweh's attitude to them, believing that they had Yahweh with them in spite of the fact that they themselves had in fact forsaken Him (ii. 6 f.; iii. 11).

The criticism of the religious situation in Israel which we have found in these prophets recurs in detail in Isaiah. Pride and lack of faith in Yahweh are the most characteristic features in his picture of the apostate people. Isaiah emphasizes that the apostasy is unnatural. An ox is interested in his owner and holds to him, but Judah is unconcerned about its own God (i. 3). The holy city has become a harlot (i. 21). The noble vineyard has yielded wild grapes (v. 2). The people are obdurate, and the damage is irreparable. Zephaniah's criticism is similar to that of his master, Isaiah.

Jeremiah says that Judah has dealt treacherously with its God. It has forsaken Him and has no fear of Him. It is faithless to Him as a woman is faithless to her lover. The people have forgotten their Lord and exchanged their God for idols and for that which is useless. They have forsaken the fountain of living water and hewn for themselves cisterns, broken cisterns that can hold no water. Yahweh has become to Judah like a wilderness, like a land of thick darkness; they say that they will not come to Him. All this is unnatural. Israel has acted worse than the pagan nations, worse than the brute animals. This apostasy from Yahweh is the worse since Yahweh's love, manifested in the history of Israel, always has been boundless. The apostasy is radical; repentance has become impossible.[123]

Such is the picture that the pre-exilic prophets give of the spiritual situation of their people. Nahum alone has nothing to say about the religious and moral apostasy of Israel. His interest is exclusively concentrated upon the destruction of Nineveh. Of course, there are glimpses of light. The prophets knew that, if the people determined to turn to Yahweh, He would show mercy and grace. Amos exhorts his people to seek Yahweh that they may live (v. 4, 6, 14).[124] Hosea puts upon the lips of the people a prayer of repentance (vi. 1 ff.). Micah points to Yahweh's merciful deeds in the history of Israel; perhaps the people will learn to understand them (vi. 3 ff.). In the preaching of Isaiah, too, we find exhortations to repentance. 'Remove the evil of your doings from before My eyes; cease to do evil, learn to do good. Seek justice', etc. (i. 16 ff.). Jeremiah knows that Yahweh is full of kindness and that He will not keep up His anger for ever, if only there is in Israel an acknowledgement of guilt (iii. 12 f.). He, too, appeals for repentance: 'Return, apostate children, I will heal your apostasy' (iii. 22). He even formulates a confession of sin to be used by the people. Yahweh's answer is: 'If you return, O Israel, you may come back to Me; if you do away with your abominations, you do not need to waver from Me' (iii. 22 ff.; iv. 1 ff., 14; vi. 8). The Hebrew term for 'repentance' is šûb, the original meaning of which is 'turn', 'turn back'.[125]

Such exhortations to repentance only prove that in spite of their

---

[123] Jer. ii. 1 ff.; iii. 1 ff.; v. 7 ff.; viii. 7; xiii. 23; xxii. 21.

[124] There is apparently a contradiction between these passages and Amos's general view concerning the future of Israel: the people has been rejected by Yahweh because of its apostasy and, consequently, is subject to His punitive judgement. This problem is discussed in ZAW, lxviii, 1956, pp. 1 ff., by Hesse. This author is right in maintaining that the words in question indicate that though Amos was convinced that the people were under divine condemnation he still believed that Yahweh was a merciful God who had once chosen Israel. A revelation from Yahweh gave the prophet the assurance that Yahweh's gracious purpose still stood and would be realized if the people repented. But I cannot agree with Hesse's view that the solution of the problem lies in the idea of a remnant, which is, in fact, absent from the teaching of Amos. še'ērît yôsēp in v. 15 cannot refer to a future group within the people which would be saved (so important an idea would have been expressed in other and plainer terms), but is a designation for North Israel as a whole, as we have attempted to demonstrate above (p. 340, n. 104). The paradoxical juxtaposition of promise and condemnation is characteristic of all the prophets and must not be eliminated from their preaching. It is to be explained by the inner tension between their belief in election and their certainty of imminent judgement.

[125] For the meaning of the term šûb in the prophets see Wolff in ZTK, xlviii, 1951, pp. 129 ff. šûb, Wolff says, is Israel's 'Rückkehr' in the sense of 'Wiederherstellung eines ursprünglichen Status'. The term belongs to the preaching of judgement and then to the preaching of the blessed age to come.

pessimistic view the prophets at times did not entirely give up the hope of a change in the attitude of their people, just as they held fast at one and the same time to their belief in both the love and the wrath of Yahweh. This attitude was typical of the prophets. But the hope was extinguished, and the final result was that the people rejected the admonitions of the prophets. They called and warned in vain; the people turned a deaf ear to their preaching and ultimately became incapable of repentance and conversion. It is true that Isaiah and other prophets following him believed that a small group of the people would be saved from the future catastrophe and be converted to Yahweh (an important idea which we shall discuss in detail in connection with the eschatological ideas of the prophets); and it is also true that Isaiah saw in his own disciples a sound kernel, the origin of a renewed people, in whom the thought of election would be realized. Nevertheless it remains true that in the view of the majority of the pre-exilic prophets the people as such, the nation as a whole, was incapable of repentance and for that reason rejected by Yahweh.

Before passing to the pre-exilic prophets' teaching about the future we must discuss a special problem concerning the spiritual situation of the people, namely the problem of the cult. As we know, the cultic performances played an essential part in the religious life of Israel. It is well known, too, that criticism of the cult was a central element in the denunciations of the pre-exilic prophets. There is, however, little agreement amongst Biblical scholars as to the fundamental attitude of these prophets towards the cult. For this reason it is worth while to examine this question briefly.

To clarify the position some preliminary observations must be made. First it is necessary to make clear what cult is. Cult is a system of religious performances regulated by tradition or law, carried out in the first instance by the religious congregation, but also by individuals as members of the congregation. Secondly, cult is never homogeneous; there are many different elements in the cult, which can be judged of in different ways. Thirdly, it would be erroneous to say that there is a fundamental contrast between prophetic religion and the cult. In Israel, for instance, the post-exilic prophets had a decidedly positive attitude towards the cult. Fourthly, it would be wrong to judge even the pre-exilic prophets alike. We must allow for differences in their attitude to the cult. Many expositions of the relation of the prophets to the cult are defective because they take no account of such distinctions.[125a]

[125a] I agree on essential points, though not in all details, with Hentschke, *Die Stellung der vorexilischen Schriftpropheten zum Kultus.*

All Biblical scholars are agreed that what the pre-exilic prophets criticized was, in the first place, the cult as it was practised in their own day. It is a well-known fact that after the settlement in Canaan the religion of the Hebrew tribes underwent important changes. That a cult of some sort existed during the nomadic period is self-evident, even if we know little about it. After the settlement in Canaan the 'Mosaic cult', if we may use the term, assumed a syncretistic character, adopting many elements from the cult of the Canaanites. This was the case first and foremost in North Israel. It is unnecessary here to describe the characteristic features of Canaanite religion, which centred in the worship of the vegetation deities and in rites the object of which was to further fertility and growth, the renewal of life of every kind. We have ample evidence about the cultic performances on the *bāmôt*, the sacred hills, the sacrifices of the produce of herds and fields, sacramental meals, sexual rites, etc., practices which are frequently mentioned in the anti-cultic polemics of the prophets who worked in the Northern Kingdom.

The attitude of Amos to the cult is evident from several utterances in his book, above all v. 18-27. This passage must be treated as a whole. To separate *vv.* 21-27 from what precedes, as is often suggested in commentaries, is to disregard the custom of the collector of the revelations of Amos, who distinctly marks the end of one revelation and the beginning of another. The criticism of the religious festivals in *vv.* 21 ff. is the appropriate sequel to the word about Yahweh's day in *v.* 18. Thus, as we have seen above, Yahweh's day must itself be a term for a cultic festival day; and it is natural to think of the most important of all feasts of the Hebrew calendar, namely the New Year festival, Yahweh's day *par préférence*. What Amos says is this: The people always long for this festival, looking forward eagerly to its joyful rites by which life is to be renewed; but they will find that one day this festival will be a day of judgement and death instead of happiness and life; it will be the beginning of the total ruin of the people of Israel.

In connection with his prediction of the grim festival day, Amos quite naturally pronounces judgement upon the cultic feasts as a whole with all their varied ritual acts. To Yahweh they were offensive. Instead of such cultic achievements He required a total change of the moral life: let justice and righteousness (i.e., obedience to Yahweh's will) be a dominating power in the nation. The ethical sense of 'justice and righteousness' (*mišpāṭ* and *ṣeḏāḳâh*) becomes evident if we compare passages such as v. 7, 15 and vi. 12, where the ethical content is manifest. It may seem remarkable that the pronouncement of judgement which continues in *v.* 25 and terminates in *v.* 27 with the prediction of exile beyond Damascus is interrupted by the admonitions in *vv.* 23 f.: 'Take away from Me the noise of your songs,' etc., and: 'Let justice roll on like water,' etc. This inconsistency is not to be removed by textual and literary means. It reflects the fluctuation in the prophet's mind between hope and despair, belief in the possibility of repentance and conviction that doom is certain. The preacher of doom could in the same breath appeal for repentance. The significant 'perhaps' of v. 15 stamps the preaching of Amos until, at last, he comes to regard the doom as radical and inevitable.[126]

Now the question arises: why does Amos criticize the cultic ceremonies as severely as he does here and in other parts of his book? In ii. 7 f. the cult is condemned because it was mingled with directly immoral elements (sacral prostitution, pledged garments, and the wine of fined persons used in the sanctuaries). In viii. 14 the worship of foreign deities and idols is condemned.[127] In iv. 4 f. and v. 4 f. the extravagant cult at the different sanctuaries is condemned because it was alien to Yahweh and apostasy from Him. In v. 21 ff., finally, the cult is repudiated because it was a false homage to Yahweh, who above all required of His worshippers justice and righteousness. Thus it is difficult to deny that Amos rejected not only the immoral rites but the entire sanctuary cult, as it was celebrated in his time. That this is the case is confirmed by the question in v. 25: 'Did you bring to Me sacrifices and offerings for forty years in the wilderness, O house of Israel?' From the non-existence of sacrifices (regarded as essential elements of the cult) during Israel's sojourn in the wilderness Amos concludes that the entire cult, as it was celebrated at the sanctuaries, was alien to the genuine Yahweh religion and detested by Yahweh. Whether from a historical point of view Amos was right in denying the existence of sacrifices in the wilderness or not is of no significance. What is important is that this was his conviction.

---

[126] The meaning of *v.* 24 is keenly discussed by Biblical scholars. The explanation presented above coincides with that of Marti, Nowack, Robinson, Sellin (1929), Cripps, Fahlgren (pp. 93, 134), Hammershaimb and many others. Weiser is of the opinion that 'justice and righteousness' here refer to the judgement that will come upon Israel; and Hyatt in *ZAW*, lxviii, 1956, pp. 17 ff., maintains the Deutero-Isaianic significance of *mišpāṭ* and *ṣᵉdāḳāh*, suggesting that *v.* 24 refers to the salvation and redemption which come from God. The usual explanation is supported by the parallels in the book of Amos. The verb form *wᵉyiggal* is a quite normal jussive. The *wāw* has, as often in Hebrew, an adversative force. To say that the morality required by Yahweh should roll along like water and an everflowing river means that the moral change must be a radical one if it is to lead to the saving of the people.

[127] Originally the text alluded to a cult of Ashima in Samaria and of Dod in Beer-sheba. The god of Dan is probably the golden bull worshipped at Dan. See for instance the careful discussion of the text in Cripps's commentary on Amos, esp. Additional Notes, pp. 316 ff.

Did Amos conceive of a better cult, a cult more compatible with the essence of the true Yahweh religion? This we do not know. No saying of his on this subject has been transmitted. And why should he speak of a better cult? The ruin of the people was imminent. In a cultic reform he had no interest. The only way to escape was a moral revival, mighty as a swelling stream. But of such a moral revolution in the life of his people, there was, finally, no hope.

Hosea inveighs against the bull idols, in which he saw images of the Baal (ii. 10; viii. 4 ff.). He says that Yahweh will bring to an end all the cultic festivals; He will punish Israel for the 'Baal feasts' with all their ceremonies (ii. 13 ff.). During the period of chastisement to which Hosea for a time looked forward, Israel will be deprived of every possibility of performing the cultic rites (iii. 4). The sacrifices are simply described as sin (iv. 8). The cult on the sacred hills with its sacrifices and sexual rites brings about the ruin of the people (iv. 13 f.). What Yahweh requires is faithfulness and the knowledge of God, not burnt offerings (vi. 6; cf. viii. 13). Here the entire sacrificial cult at the *bāmôt* is condemned. This word is a clear parallel to Am. v. 21 ff. With scorn Hosea speaks of the cessation of the cultic feasts and performances on the day when Israel will be deported to foreign countries (ix. 3 ff.) and of the total devastation of the temple at Bethel (x. 5 ff.). The more culture, the more cult, says Hosea, referring to the development of the syncretistic cult in Canaan. But one day Yahweh Himself will break the altars and destroy the sacred pillars (x. 1 f.). The syncretistic cult is to Hosea simply worship of the Baal; it is regarded as sin and apostasy (xi. 2; xiii. 2).

The attitude of Hosea to the cult is similar to that of Amos. Like Amos, Hosea speaks exclusively of the contemporary syncretistic cult, which was to him sin and apostasy from Yahweh, being, as he says, in fact the worship of the Canaanite Baal. In particular, Hosea condemns the bull idols. It is also characteristic of him that he regards cultic development as parallel to cultural development. Like Amos, Hosea ultimately condemns the entire syncretistic cult. What Yahweh required was not such a cult, but wholehearted devotion in faith and obedience, which Hosea calls the knowledge of God. Hosea nowhere speaks of a cult which is well pleasing to Yahweh. For him one thing was urgently needful: a right personal relation to Yahweh. For a short time he hoped for national repentance and conversion; but later he abandoned this hope. The total ruin of the nation was in the end as certain to him as it was to Amos. Accordingly, we cannot expect to find in him any idea of a reformed cult.

Like Amos and Hosea, Micah denounces the syncretistic cult of the northern kingdom (i. 6 f.). He also foretells the total destruction of the Temple in Jerusalem. Jerusalem shall become a ruin, and the Temple mountain a wooded hill (iii. 12). That means of course the definite end of the cult in Jerusalem. In the famous lawsuit between Yahweh and His people in ch. vi, Yahweh declares that every conceivable sacrifice is worthless in the eyes of Yahweh as a means of expiation. Only one thing is really good, only one thing is required by Yahweh: that men do justice (*mišpāṭ*), love faithfulness (*ḥeseḏ*), and walk humbly with their God. This passage is a close parallel to Am. v. 24 and Hos. vi. 6. The complicated way in which Micah's revelations have been transmitted makes it impossible to say with certainty whether he had an idea of a blessed future awaiting his people. His idea of the true people of Yahweh, in contrast to the people as a whole, indicated in passages such as ii. 8 f.; iii. 3, could provide the basis of an eschatological message. But it seems that Micah did not draw the consequences of this idea. Perhaps the true people of Yahweh was in the end included in the *massa perditionis* described in vii. 1 ff. Be that as it may, there is no hint of a reformed cult in the book of Micah. What is certain is that for him the contemporary cult had no value in Yahweh's eyes.

The attitude of Isaiah towards the cult is more complicated. In ch. i, *vv.* 11 ff., he says that Yahweh entirely condemns animal sacrifice. He has had enough of burnt-offerings; the blood of sacrificial animals displeases Him. He wants no more offerings. He detests the smoke of sacrifices. Here animal sacrifice as such is rejected by Yahweh. But the prophet goes further. The cultic feasts are also intolerable to Yahweh; He hates them; they are a burden to Him which He is weary of bearing. Why the feasts are rejected is not expressly said; the context suggests that at the great feasts the number of animal sacrifices was greatly increased. It is remarkable that Isaiah also repudiates cultic prayer. The reason is that the congregation which offered the prayers was defiled by blood-guilt. Therefore Yahweh did not listen to their prayers. According to the ceremonial rules the offerings had to be *ritually* pure in order to be well pleasing to God; but the prophets held that all cultic acts were displeasing to Yahweh which were performed by *ethically* polluted hands and hearts. The criticism of the cultic performances ends with an exhortation to cease to do evil and instead to do good, to seek righteousness, in particular in the social field.[128]

---

[128] Obviously the utterance of i, 11 ff. has not been preserved to us in its original form. There are several additions intended to develop the main theme in greater detail to expound its meaning for a later generation. The uneven rhythm is in itself one indication of this. I believe that *minḥâh* in *v.* 13 in the original text meant sacrifices in

This passage seemingly shows that the attitude of Isaiah towards the cult of his own day, particularly in the Temple in Jerusalem, was as radical as that of Amos and Hosea. The reason for his condemnation of the cult was on one hand that the slaughter of animals for sacrifice was unworthy of the sublimity of Yahweh, and on the other hand that the worship was offered by morally polluted people. In other passages Isaiah condemns the syncretistic cult: the sacred trees (i. 29), idols (ii. 8, 20), rites borrowed from the vegetation cult (xvii. 10 f.), etc.

But there are in the sermons of Isaiah words which reflect a positive attitude towards the official cult. The inaugural vision of Isaiah took place in the Temple of Jerusalem, where he saw Yahweh, the Holy One, sitting on His throne. The account in ch. vi shows no traces of hostility to the Temple cult. The Trisagion of the seraphim was presumably taken directly from one of the ritual hymns. Isaiah's unclean lips were cleansed by a red-hot stone taken from the incense-altar. Isaiah speaks with sympathy of the ritual singing at the great cultic feasts and of the processions accompanied by music (xxx. 29). To him the Temple is Yahweh's dwelling-place. It is to see Yahweh's face that the cultic congregation assembles; and it is His courts that they trample (i. 12). Isaiah knows that a blessed future awaits his people. A remnant will be saved from the general destruction of the Jewish nation. This remnant will be a holy people, in whom the idea of election will be realized. In the age to come this holy people will dwell on Mount Zion, the Temple hill, where they will practise the true Yahweh religion (xxviii. 16 f.). Zion, as Yahweh's cultic dwelling-place and the seat of the new people, will withstand all the tempests of history; Yahweh has founded it (xiv. 32). In the age to come Mount Zion will be wonderfully protected by Yahweh, and cultic assemblies will continue to celebrate holy ceremonies (iv. 5 f.).[129]

This represents an attitude to the cult different from that adopted by the prophets mentioned above. Isaiah condemns the animal sacrifices and all the cultic ceremonies performed by morally unclean men. He denounces, of course, the syncretistic cult, too. But he accepts a cult with singing, praying, music, and festival processions performed by a holy people. His view of the age to come includes a purified cult of this kind.

[129] In my view Isa. iv. 2-6 is substantially an authentic Isaianic revelation which has been somewhat modified in the course of transmission.

general and *kᵉṭōreṭ* smoke from the burnt offerings. Probably *šāw'* and *hî'* in *v.* 13 are secondary additions; so is *'āwen waᶜaṣārâh* at the end of the verse; the words 'I cannot endure' belong to what precedes. *'attûḏîm* in *v.* 11b is an added detail in the description of the different sacrifices.

Zephaniah condemns the syncretistic cult and the worshippers of foreign deities (i. 4 f.). We cannot say with certainty what his cultic ideal was, but it is clear that to him the Temple and the Temple cult were in themselves holy (iii. 4), though profaned by the priests, and Mount Zion was 'the holy mountain' of Yahweh (iii. 11). Nahum, who seems to have been a cultic prophet in the strict sense, belonging to the cultic staff in the Temple of Jerusalem, adopts a positive attitude towards the official cult in Jerusalem. On some occasion when good news had been received (probably that of the death of the Assyrian king Assurbanipal in 626[130]), he uttered the exhortation, 'Celebrate your feasts, O Judah, fulfil your vows' (ii. 1).

The picture that Jeremiah gives us of the cultic situation in his time is really astonishing. It is remarkable that even after Josiah's reform syncretism and foreign cults flourished to such an extent in Jerusalem and the land of Judah. The reform must only have been a brief interlude, to which Jeremiah paid surprisingly little attention. He soon realized that the reform did not alter the essential spiritual situation of the people in Yahweh's eyes. In fact, the cultic interest of Deuteronomy and the stress laid on the Temple in Jerusalem led the people astray. What Yahweh required was something else; repentance, moral reform, the abolition of all the cultic usages which were alien to the true Yahweh religion, in short, what had been proclaimed of old by the traditions of Yahwism.[131]

What Jeremiah condemns in the cult is, in the first place, the syncretism, the corruption of the true Yahweh worship by Canaanite elements. Jeremiah calls this syncretistic cult worship of the Baal. In language reminiscent of Hosea's denunciations he speaks of adultery and fornication. He deplores the worship of many gods and the erection

---

[130] So Elliger in *ATD*.

[131] I am in full agreement with Puukko and more recent commentators such as Volz, Nötscher, Rudolph, and Weiser (cf. also Leslie, *Jeremiah*) in denying that the expression 'the words of this covenant' in ch. xi refers to the contents of Deuteronomy. It is far more likely that what the prophet has in mind is the Sinai covenant, the provisions of which were known through the cultic ritual texts, particularly the Decalogue. In *The Prophetic Faith* Buber says, 'Over against the "lying words" of false confidence the prophet sets the decalogue' (p. 172). Granted that Jeremiah regarded the 'words' of the Sinai covenant as authentic words from Yahweh, his utterance concerning sacrifices in vii. 21 ff. is fully comprehensible, as is his criticism of the written laws in viii. 8. For the literary problems of ch. xi see above, pp. 223 f. Probably Jeremiah received the command in question in a revelation in direct connection with a particular cultic occasion. This would account for the expression 'this covenant'. In *SOTP*, pp. 157 ff., Rowley defends the older opinion concerning Jeremiah's attitude towards Deuteronomy. Although I cannot accept the whole of his argument, I agree with him in maintaining that Josiah's lawbook was Deuteronomy, that Jeremiah had some knowledge of its content and style, and that he subsequently perceived its spiritual failure and therefore condemned its insufficiency.

of many altars, criticizing the cult of foreign gods such as the Accadian Ishtar ('the queen of heaven'), and other celestial deities, idols set up in the temple in Jerusalem, the sacrifice of children in the Valley of Hinnom, etc. According to him this corrupt cult in its official or more popular forms was detestable in Yahweh's eyes, because it meant apostasy from the God of election, the only God of Israel, whose unity was menaced by the many deities worshipped by the people and by the many sanctuaries, because this cult included grossly immoral elements and, finally, served as a substitute for sound ethical conduct.[132] Since the priests were naturally deeply involved in this reprehensible cult, they are often strongly condemned in Jeremiah's sermons.

Jeremiah's criticism of the cult is directed not only against syncretistic and pagan usages, but also against normal Israelite sacrificial practice. In vi. 20 Yahweh says, 'What care I for the frankincense that comes from Sheba, or the sweet cane from a distant land? Your burnt offerings are not acceptable to Me, and your sacrifices bring Me no pleasure.' Burnt offering and cereal offering cannot gain deliverance for the people (xiv. 12). In the famous passage vii. 21 ff. the prophet goes still further. Sarcastically Yahweh exhorts the people to add their burnt offerings to their sacrifices and then eat the flesh. Yahweh does not want flesh, either from the 'ōlôṯ, which were entirely devoted to God, or from the zᵉḇāḥîm, of which God received only a part. Since Yahweh does not need it, the people might as well consume it all.

The reason given for this rejection of the sacrificial cult is remarkable. When Yahweh brought the fathers out of Egypt, He gave no command concerning burnt offerings and sacrifices. What He required was only obedience to His ethical commands, which they neglected, stiffening their necks and doing evil more than their fathers.

This is not the place to discuss the problem of the 'Mosaic' legislation. The fact remains that Jeremiah believed that in the time of Moses commands about animal sacrifices were unknown. (There is, of course, no need to deny that a simple sacrificial system was in fact practised in the nomadic period.) Jeremiah saw in the Decalogue the authentic Mosaic legislation, and there nothing was said about offerings. No doubt he found also in other cultic texts referring to the covenant at Sinai further support for his view that the Mosaic legislation included no directions about sacrifice. In the Book of the Covenant (Ex. xx. 22-xxiii. 33), in Deuteronomy, and elsewhere he certainly saw human ideas which did not express the genuine will of Yahweh (cf. viii. 8). However, it would be too much to say that in vii. 21 ff. Jeremiah rejects all

[132] Jer. ii. 20 ff., 26 ff.; iii. 8 f.; vii. 18, 31; viii. 2; xi. 13; xxiii. 11; xliv.

cultic practice. In this passage he speaks only of animal sacrifices. That he really accepted more spiritual forms of cult will appear in the following.

There are many passages in the Book of Jeremiah which reflect a positive attitude towards the cult.

First it is to be observed that Jeremiah, like Isaiah, had a great reverence for the Temple. Frequently Jeremiah calls the Temple in Jerusalem 'Yahweh's house'. Yahweh's name is 'called over' it, i.e., it is, according to Hebrew linguistic usage, regarded as Yahweh's property. He who enters the Temple stands before the face of Yahweh (vii. 10 f., 30; xxxiv. 15). Jeremiah accepts the idea of Yahweh's spiritual dwelling in the Temple. Jerusalem with the Temple in its midst is called the throne of Yahweh's glory (xiv. 21; cf. xvii. 12). With the greatest indignation he says of the Temple, Yahweh's holy property, that it has been regarded as a robber's cave, a den and a shelter for felons (vii. 11).

Nevertheless, Jeremiah rebukes the false estimation of the Temple which was common in the time after Josiah's reform. In the famous Temple sermon in ch. vii he combats false confidence in the Temple, the mistaken conviction that the Temple would be an unconditional guarantee of the welfare of the people. He predicts that because of the wickedness of the people Yahweh will do to the Temple, in which they trust, as He did to Shiloh, to wit, entirely destroy it. Jeremiah's standpoint is this: the Temple is in itself holy and Yahweh's house, but because of the wickedness of the people and the false use made of it by the people it will be destroyed.

The Book of Jeremiah contains many passages which express directly a high appreciation of outward expressions of worship, some in sections referring to the age to come. Some of them are certainly not authentic; others are highly uncertain. It is generally admitted that the revelations of Jeremiah have been handed down very freely. There are many secondary additions and also many indications that original sayings of Jeremiah have been modified in such a way as to alter not only their form but their sense. In the certainly authentic passage xxxi. 6 it is said that in the Messianic age people from the Northern Kingdom will go on pilgrimage to Zion, 'to Yahweh, their God'. Here, in fact, the reference is to a cult without Temple and sacrifices. The Temple was doomed to destruction, and in the descriptions of the restoration in the age to come there is no reference to a new Temple (cf. xxx. 18).

Accordingly, Jeremiah condemned the contemporary cult in its syncretistic and pagan forms, regarding it as apostasy from Yahweh. But he also condemned the legitimate offerings, in particular the animal sacrifices. The Temple was, to be sure, Yahweh's house, but it was badly misused by the people. Because of this misuse and the general wickedness of the people, the Temple would be destroyed. In the age to come Jeremiah expected a spiritual form of cult without Temple building and offerings.

The above examination of the attitude of the pre-exilic prophets towards the cult shows that we must beware of generalizing too freely on this subject. These prophets condemned the contemporary cult because of its syncretistic character, because the people who practised it defiled it by their sinfulness, and because it was regarded as a guarantee of salvation and a substitute for ethical reform. Ideas of a reformed and purified cult are rare and rather vague. In view of the catastrophe which was about to befall the nation the pre-exilic prophets had little interest in sketching a cultic programme for the future. But it seems that sometimes they envisaged a more spiritualized cult, a cult without animal offerings.[132a]

D. *Judgement and Salvation*: *Eschatology*

If eschatology is a doctrine of the end of the world and the history of mankind, there is no eschatology at all in the Old Testament prophets. In a study of prophetic teaching it is inappropriate to start from the strict sense of *eschaton* or from ideas belonging to Jewish and Christian Apocalyptic and Christian dogmatics. If we wish to apply the term 'eschatology' to the teaching of the prophets, we must use it in a sense adapted to the general character of their thought; otherwise we may seriously misunderstand and misrepresent them.[133]

Our starting point must be the idea of the two ages rather than that of the end of all things. As we know, the terminological distinction between 'this age' and 'the age to come' first appears in Jewish Apocalyptic, in the rabbinical literature, and in the New Testament, but the fact itself is to be found in the prophets, and in the expressions 'the days are coming' (particularly common in Jeremiah), 'on that day' (*bayyôm hahû*', e.g., Isa. vii. 18 ff.), 'at the end of the days' (*be'ahᵃrît hayyāmîm*,

---

[132a] For the whole problem of the estimation of the pre-exilic prophets of the cult cf., *inter alios*, Rowley in *JSS*, i, 1956, pp. 338 ff., and further the doctoral dissertation by Roubos, *Profetie en Cultus in Israël*.
[133] For this view of the eschatology of the prophets see further Lindblom in *St.Th.*, vi, 1952, pp. 79 ff., and Vriezen in *SVT*, I, pp. 199 ff. Cf. also Jacob, *Theology of the Old Testament*, pp. 317 ff., who particularly emphasizes the idea of the arrival of Yahweh as an element in the eschatological hope. Frost in *VT*, ii, 1952, pp. 70 ff. starting from the linguistic meaning of *eschaton*, takes eschatology in a narrower sense. Eschatology, he says, is characterized by 'finality'.

e.g., Isa. ii. 2), etc., we have at least a beginning of the later terminology.[134]

Merely to recognize the existence of the idea of the two ages does not take us very far, however. We must attempt to determine what the idea meant to the prophets and what grounds there are for attributing to them the expectation of the age to come in the special sense.

It is generally agreed that there are many references in the prophecy of every period to a coming transformation of prevailing conditions so great that a new order may be said to have come into existence. But this new order does not presuppose 'the end' in the strict sense, the passing away of this world and the creation of another. It is appropriate to speak of a new order when changes of so far-reaching a character have taken place that a new epoch may be said to have dawned. Predictions of such a new age (an age when the normal course of historical and natural events is disturbed by abnormal changes) may be called eschatological in a sense which is typical of the Old Testament prophets. Of course, it is not always possible to distinguish clearly between what is eschatological and not eschatological in the Old Testament, since 'normal' historical events can be described in such exalted terms that they appear to have an eschatological character; but generally it is practicable to make the distinction here proposed.

Thus all events that refer to the age to come are to be designated as eschatological, even when they form part of the historical process. Though some scholars have tried to enumerate the distinctive marks of the prophetic eschatology, no such attempt has fully succeeded. Adjectives such as 'suprahistorical', 'supernatural', 'transcendent', and others of the same kind are not very illuminating, because, in Old Testament thought, what we call the normal historical process is the setting of supernatural actions. Nor is the idea of a *restitutio in integrum* (so important in itself), or that of sensational catastrophes in nature and history helpful as distinguishing marks of eschatology. Such features do sometimes appear in eschatological passages, but only sometimes; and therefore they cannot be regarded as distinguishing marks of eschatology in general.

The distinction between 'this age' and 'the age to come', however, is an essential element in all eschatology and also a characteristic feature of the preaching of the Israelite prophets. Passages which describe the

---

[134] As to the second expression Munch in his treatise *The Expression bajjôm hahū* has shown that it is to be understood as a general temporal adverb. When it is used in an eschatological context, it can become an eschatological term. The same seems to be the case with the third formula. In itself it generally designates a distant future (see for instance Gen. xlix. 1; Num. xxiv. 14; Deut. iv. 30; xxxi. 29). In eschatological contexts it acquires an eschatological meaning (e.g., Isa. ii. 2).

new age may be said to express a *positive* eschatology; those which speak only of the end express a *negative* eschatology. Where the predictions refer to Israel we have a *national eschatology*; but if the eschatological perspective is widened to include the world and all mankind, we may appropriately speak of a *universal eschatology*. When the age to come is thought of as an age of happiness and bliss, we have an eschatology of salvation or 'Heilseschatologie', as the Germans say. By contrast there is also the eschatology of misfortune or 'Unheilseschatologie'. The term eschatology is often applied to beliefs about life after death. For many reasons such an individual eschatology falls outside the scope of the present inquiry. Finally we may note that many ideas which appear in eschatological passages are not eschatological in themselves; they become eschatological by being integral parts of an eschatological view. The important idea of 'the remnant', for instance, becomes eschatological as an element in predictions of a new age. When the term is simply applied to the survivors of some devastation it has, of course, no eschatological content. In the debate on Old Testament eschatology, much has been made of the catastrophes in the descriptions of doom. Earthquake, pestilence, fire, etc., are, of course, often regarded as elements in the future judgement, but they are frequently presented as purely natural events, readily understandable in the milieu of the Old Testament.

Even though eschatology is taken in this wider sense, the eschatological sayings, particularly in the earlier books, are not quite so numerous as has often been maintained. The eschatological interpretation of the prophetic texts has been greatly exaggerated. This is true above all of the writings of H. Gressmann, and also of many others who, though rejecting his main thesis concerning the origin of Israelite eschatology, follow him in other respects.

The prophets were primarily men with a message for their own time, denouncing the sins of their people and summoning them to repentance. Many predictions which have been interpreted as eschatological obviously deal with events which the prophets expected to happen within the normal course of history. The common, but in my opinion erroneous, interpretation of many prophetic utterances as eschatological sayings depends on a number of peculiarities in the prophetic sermon, which suggest an eschatological content, but which are characteristic of the general prophetic style and mode of thought. It may be useful to recapitulate here what was said above when the general structure of the religious preaching of the pre-exilic prophets was described.

We may note, for instance, the oracular style with its elements of obscurity and mysteriousness. Again, Yahweh's interventions in history are often described as theophanies. But not all theophanies are eschatological. Accounts of purely historical events often include mythological features. The prophets like to think and speak in mythological categories, even when describing events which belong to the normal process of nature and history. It is particularly tempting to give an eschatological interpretation to descriptions of ecstatic visions. On the whole, in interpreting the prophetic texts we need to make allowance for the prophets' use of exalted and poetic language, the visionary or revelatory character of their utterances, their highly-strung temperament, and, last but not least, their use of symbols, metaphors, and ambiguous diction. Because of these features the prophetic sayings often seem to refer to another sphere of existence or an entirely new order; but this need not indicate an eschatological content. It was an essential part of the prophetic thought and experience to be acutely aware of the divine presence, the divine realm, and the divine power in history and nature. This is reflected in the prophetic utterances; but it does not always imply eschatology. An examination of the teaching of the individual prophets about the future of Israel and mankind will show that there are great differences between them.

The authentic revelations of Amos show no traces of a positive eschatology, least of all of a happy future for Israel.[135] It is true that there are gleams of light and exhortations to repentance ('seek Yahweh, seek the good that you may live'). Even a prophet who proclaimed inexorable judgement had to take account of Israel's election and to allow for the possibility that Israel would turn to Yahweh and be graciously received by Him. The solicitude of Amos for his people appears also in the visions in which he interceded in order to avert their annihilation. His affectionate compassion is evident when he pleads for Jacob 'because he is so small' and when he calls the northern tribes 'the remnant of Joseph', and rebukes the wealthy and self-confident sybarites in Zion and Samaria because they do not feel for the ruin of Joseph. There is in the revelations of Amos no hint of a remnant that will be saved. The destruction of the people is decisive, as complete as the destruction of a sheep or a goat of which a pair of shank bones or a piece of an ear are retrieved by a shepherd from the mouth of a lion (iii. 12).[136] The final

---

[135] For the literary problems of the Book of Amos and the books of the later prophets see the preceding chapter.

[136] The ironical tone of this word is unmistakable. Amos says that any possible deliverance will be of the same kind as the deliverance of a sheep or a goat devoured by a lion. Weiser says correctly, 'Mit beissender Ironie redet auch Amos von der "Rettung" des Volkes, die aber alles andere sein wird als Rettung ... Er nimmt das Wort Rettung

message of Amos is expressed in words such as these: 'Fallen, no more to rise, is the virgin Israel, prostrate in her land with none to raise her up' (v. 2), and: 'The eyes of the Lord Yahweh are upon this sinful kingdom; I will destroy it from the face of the earth' (ix. 8).

If the utter destruction of the Israelite nation may be called an eschatological idea, we find in Amos only a negative eschatology. What Amos may have thought of the future of the southern kingdom, we do not know. There are no authentic revelations in his book concerning the fate of Jerusalem and Judah.[137]

In his descriptions of impending judgement Amos is not bound to a dogmatic scheme. Sometimes he speaks of a terrible plague spreading death among the people (v. 16 f.; vi. 9 f.). In other passages he thinks of an earthquake (ii. 13; ix. 1).[138] In one of the visions he sees locusts which consume the vegetation in the field; in another he sees fire or heat devouring the land. Sometimes the destruction comes through attacks by foreign enemies. The land will be laid waste, the king killed, and the population carried into exile. In one passage the mythological idea of the dragon of the sea is used to describe the annihilation (ix. 3).

All these motifs lay ready to hand for a prophet living in an oriental milieu in ancient times. Catastrophes in nature and attacks by political enemies were everyday occurrences in ancient Palestine. Mythological ideas common to the entire Near East were also current in Hebrew folklore and were also sometimes used by poets and prophets. There is no need to explain such references by the hypothesis of a more or less systematic pre-prophetic eschatology.

In Hosea the hope of a new age in an eschatological sense plays a greater part than in Amos. During a certain phase of his prophetic career he was assured that after a period of chastisement and trial, bringing about national repentance and conversion, a new age would follow, rich in happiness and blessing of every kind. Such hopes reflect the influence on Hosea's teaching of the earlier phase of his domestic tragedy, the period of the discipline and probation of Gomer, the frail

---

[137] In my view the messages of judgement in Amos refer solely to the Northern Kingdom, which he calls Israel. Unlike Danell (*Studies in the Name of Israel*, pp. 110 ff.). I cannot accept the authenticity of ii. 4 f. and ix. 11 ff. The incidental reference to Zion in vi. 1 is of no consequence for the problem in question. The brook of the Arabah in vi. 14 must signify the southern boundary of the territory of Jeroboam II. For the geographical situation see Cripps, *Commentary on Amos*, pp. 216 f. and 305 f.
[138] As to the simile in ii. 13, Dalman, the best expert in such matters, thinks of a cart for transporting sheaves to the threshing-floor; *Arbeit und Sitte*, III, pp. 52 and 58.

---

auf und wendet es an auf eine Situation, in der von Rettung überhaupt nicht mehr die Rede sein kann.' This passage has nothing to do with the Isaianic idea of the remnant. Ex. xxii. 12 f. is often cited to explain the comparison.

woman. To this phase we may assign the saying in iii. 5, that Israel will return and seek Yahweh, their God, and with trembling approach Yahweh and His goodness in future days. From the same period comes the saying in ii. 16 f., that Yahweh is going to allure Israel out into the wilderness, where He will speak appealingly to her, whereupon a new time of happiness and bliss will begin.

But these hopes were confined to a brief period of Hosea's life. The light went out, and after the flagrant adultery of Gomer the prophet became convinced that conversion was impossible and that the annihilation of the Northern Kingdom was inevitable. A devastating drought will reduce the land to a wilderness. Hostile peoples will conquer the land, the king will be swept away, and the people carried into exile.[139] The names given to the two last children, 'Not-pitied', 'Not-my-people', refer to the final form of Hosea's prophetic message.

According to the analysis of the Book of Micah made in the previous chapter, the so-called Messianic prophecies in this book are all redactional. Like Amos, however, Micah could not entirely give up the thought that his people might repent, as appears from the account in ch. vi of Yahweh's lawsuit with His people. It seems also that Micah, at least to begin with, entertained hopes of the lower classes in the people, whom he called Yahweh's true people. But by and by it became clear to him that the religious and moral decay was general and radical. Judgement and destruction alone remained. Samaria would be destroyed by a terrible earthquake. Jerusalem with its temple would be laid in ruins. The land would be conquered by enemies and the population deported into a foreign country. Thus the end had come upon Israel. It had no future to hope for.[140]

Amos, Hosea, and Micah were all exclusively occupied with the future of Israel. The world and mankind fell outside the range of their vision. Amos, it is true, proclaimed doom on some of Israel's neighbours, but that did not mean a general world judgement. The first to proclaim a universal judgement and thus to present a universal eschatology was Isaiah.

The main elements of Isaiah's teaching about universal judgement are to be found in ch. ii of his book. ii. 10-21 must be treated as an independent revelation with its own line of thought. Here Isaiah speaks not only of Israel but of mankind. The scene of Yahweh's action is the whole earth, not the land of Israel (vv. 19 and 21). What provokes the fury of Yahweh and His merciless judgement is the pride of men, which

---

[139] Hos. ii. 4-15; v. 7; vii. 16; viii. 8 ff.; ix. 2 ff.; x. 5 ff.; xi. 5 f.; xiii. 3; xiv. 1.
[140] Mic. i. 6 f., 10 ff., 16; ii. 4; iii. 12; iv. 9 f.

is depicted by metaphors taken from nature (the cedars of Lebanon, the oaks of Bashan, etc.) and from the self-sufficiency of human culture (high towers, fortified walls, etc.). Pagan idolatry is also mentioned as an affront to the divine majesty of Yahweh and as a cause of His anger. In this passage the universal character of Isaiah's eschatology is based on his faith in the sublimity of Yahweh as a God of the world and his conviction that all that flouts this divine majesty, men's *hybris* and the worship of other gods, is subject to inexorable and final judgement.

In iii. 13 it is said that Yahweh is about to judge the peoples. In the light of ii. 10 ff. the peoples (*'ammîm*) must be mankind, not the tribes of Israel.[141] The punishment of the elders and princes of Judah is here regarded as an individual feature in a general world judgement. In xiv. 24-27 the Assyrians, the oppressors of Yahweh's people, will be crushed in His land. But a similar fate will also befall the other peoples of the world: 'This is the purpose that is formed against all the earth; this is the hand that is stretched out against all the nations.' Clearly Isaiah holds that not only the Assyrians but all the nations of the world have defied Yahweh and therefore must one day be judged by Him.

The message to the Ethiopians in xviii. 1 ff. has a reference to all nations. All the inhabitants of the world are exhorted to pay attention when a signal is raised on the mountains and listen when a trumpet is blown. I hold that the allusion here is clearly to a universal judgement, an event concerning which the prophet has received a special revelation (*v.* 4). What follows is a parable depicting how, when His time has come, Yahweh will inflict sudden and inexorable judgement.[142] The world judgement is finally proclaimed in xxviii. 22. In a special revelation Isaiah has heard of a decisive sentence of doom on the whole world.

As Isaiah was the first among the prophets to present a universal eschatology,[143] he was also the first to describe a blessed future for Israel after the national disaster which he foretold. From the time of his call he was convinced that both Israel and Judah would be destroyed because of their apostasy. In the inaugural vision it was revealed to him that his mission was to harden the people lest they repent and be healed. So the land would be entirely laid waste (ch. vi). In iii a period of anarchy, of total dissolution of the social *šālôm* (harmony), is foretold as a form of Yahweh's punishment of the apostate people. Popular ideas may lie

[141] Duhm: 'Die israelitischen Stämme'. The Septuagint has 'His people', which is a mistaken attempt to correct the Hebrew. No textual change is necessary. Herntrich in *ATD* gives here the right explanation.
[142] For a detailed exegesis of this passage see Lindblom in *St.Th.*, vi, 1952, pp. 79 ff.
[143] This statement does of course not exclude the possibility that the idea of a universal judgement may have been proclaimed before Isaiah in some ritual texts used in the cult.

behind such descriptions of the judgement. First and foremost Isaiah saw in the empires of his time, above all the Assyrians, instruments used by Yahweh in executing the inevitable judgement. The land would be laid waste by invaders and the population deported (v. 13, 17; vii. 18 ff.). Sometimes Isaiah uses popular mythological motifs to illustrate the extreme character of the judgement (v. 14). This belief in the national ruin of Israel had been held by earlier prophets. But Isaiah's teaching contains a quite new idea, an idea of immense significance for later thought, namely the idea of the remnant: the nation as such would be destroyed, but a small minority would survive the catastrophe. These survivors, the remnant, would turn to Yahweh; they would be a holy people, in them the election would be fulfilled. I believe that in the inaugural vision this idea was already hinted at in oracular style. It was plainly proclaimed in the symbolical name of the prophet's son, Shear-jashub: there will be a remnant (after the catastrophe), and this remnant will turn to Yahweh.[144] The remnant was an object of faith, a future reality, an element in the Isaianic conception of the new age. It was accordingly here an eschatological idea. Of the members of the remnant it is said that they will no longer lean upon their tormentor (the Assyrian empire); they will lean in truth upon Yahweh, the Holy One of Israel (x. 20).[145] In the age to come Yahweh will be a beautiful crown and a glorious diadem to the remnant (xxviii. 5), which owes its existence to the zeal of Yahweh for His people (xxxvii. 32). Although it belonged to the future, it had already begun to take shape in the little flock of men and women who surrounded the prophet as his adherents, who responded to his words, and realized his idea of faith in Yahweh as the essential element in the true Yahweh religion. These followers of the prophet were regarded as signs and portents, pointing forward

---

[144] For the text of Isa. vi. 13 see above, pp. 187 f. The name of Isaiah's son, Shear-jashub, shows that from the time of his call he cherished the conviction that a remnant would be saved from the catastrophe. It also seems clear that 'remnant' should be understood as referring primarily to those who have escaped from some kind of catastrophe, such as an invasion; see Müller, *Die Vorstellung vom Rest im Alten Testament*; de Vaux in *RB*, xlii, 1933, pp. 526 ff.; Heaton in *JTS*, New Series, iii, 1952, pp. 27 ff. From a linguistic point of view the meaning of the name is open to dispute. Blank in *JBL*, lxvii, 1948, pp. 211 ff., concludes from the position of the first element that it is to be translated: 'no more than a remnant will turn', the name being one of ill omen. Köhler in *VT*, iii, 1953, pp. 84 f., maintains that *yāšûḇ* is 'ein nackter Relativsatz' and translates: 'der Rest, der umkehrt'. This seems to be somewhat obscure. Perhaps the expression could be translated: 'a remnant, it will turn [to Yahweh]', i.e., there will be a remnant, and this remnant will turn. The brevity of the expression arises from the cryptic nature of the name.

[145] *Vv.* 22 f. are obviously secondary, forming a sort of commentary on the preceding statement. Here the thought is that *only* a remnant will be saved, presupposing a pessimistic view of the future of Israel. To Isaiah the idea of the remnant serves to evoke hope and, at the same time, summon to repentance. Further, the diction of these verses is clearly dependent on xxviii. 22.

to the eschatological remnant and the blessed future (viii. 16-18); they are called 'the afflicted' or 'the poor' (people without external resources) among the people (xiv. 32), they exercise true faith and confidence in Yahweh and realize the idea of justice and righteousness (xxviii. 16).[146]

How Isaiah imagined the new age is manifest from other passages. He thought of a new social and political community cleansed from all iniquity and apostasy. This community would be given judges and counsellors like those of the early age of Israel's history; then the new community would be called the righteous and faithful city (i. 24-26).

The somewhat obscure passage iv. 2-6 contains some authentically Isaianic thoughts embedded in elements which belong to a later tradition. In the age to come, what the land itself produces will be pride and glory for the restored people, the survivors of Israel (here Israel means Judah). The new people will be a holy people, cleansed from all iniquity. Yahweh Himself will be present in Zion and serve as a refuge and a shelter to the new people. This hope is based on the genuine Isaianic idea of the remnant which will survive the catastrophe and inherit a new age of bliss.

Did Isaiah speak of a Messiah in a proper sense, an ideal king of the restored kingdom in the age to come? In the previous chapter a literary analysis was made of the Book of Isaiah, and the conclusion was drawn that a number of the so-called Messianic passages are exilic or post-exilic. This is true of Isa. xi. 1-9; xi. 10; xvi. 5; xxxii. 1-8. As has been shown, these passages all presuppose the conditions which were prevalent after the end of the monarchic period, and bear traces of ideas which were characteristic of a later time. Accordingly, they do not provide evidence for the hope of a Messianic king in the teaching of Isaiah.

The sayings from the time of the outbreak of the Syro-Ephraimitic war raise a special problem. As I have already argued, the oracle of Immanuel refers to the birth of a royal child, a successor to the throne of Ahaz.[147] With the birth of this child Isaiah associated the most exalted hopes. It would introduce a new epoch, when the hostile allies would be crushed and blessings of every kind would abound in the land of Judah. I also hold that the poem in ix. 1-6 refers to the same Immanuel-child. Immanuel had now been born, and the prophet expresses all the hopes

---

[146] As I have argued in the *Mowinckel Festschrift*, pp. 123 ff., the corner-stone symbolizes confidence in Yahweh, the walls symbolize the moral elements: justice and righteousness. The true Yahweh religion is considered as a building which Yahweh is about to erect in Jerusalem. The bearers of this true Yahweh religion are the adherents of the prophet, the core of the future remnant. The passage is differently interpreted by Dreyfus in *RSPT*, xxxix, 1955, pp. 361 ff.: the corner-stone is the Messiah, the building the community of the believers, the remnant.

[147] See above, pp. 246 f.

which he associated with the royal child. A period of happiness and joy would follow. The enemies would be crushed by Yahweh, and a period of peace would ensue. In exalted language based on oriental court and cult style Isaiah describes the coming reign of the newborn prince.

The prophecies of bliss uttered when Judah was menaced by her hostile neighbours in the north are not eschatological in the strict sense. They do not refer to the age to come, i.e., the age which would follow the final ruin of the nation. But their oracular style and half mythological character give them an eschatological flavour which has often led commentators to identify both Immanuel and the royal child in ch. ix with the Messiah, a figure who, in fact, is alien to Isaiah, as to all the prophets of the eighth century.

Isaiah's primary thought was the destruction of the nation. It dominated his preaching from beginning to end. But there was a way to salvation, namely whole-hearted devotion to Yahweh. Therefore Isaiah never ceased to appeal for repentance: 'Wash yourselves; make yourselves clean; remove the evil of your doings from before My eyes; cease to do evil, learn to do good; seek justice, correct oppression; defend the fatherless, plead for the widow . . . If you are willing and obedient, you shall eat the good of the land' (i. 16 ff.).[148] 'In returning and rest you shall be saved, in quietness and in trust shall be your strength' (xxx. 15). Such admonitions were heard during the entire career of Isaiah. But they fell on deaf ears, and the words of judgement prevailed. The hopeful prophecies during the years of the Syro-Ephraimitic war were confined to a brief episode. Soon the announcement of doom became predominant again and with it the message about the remnant and its future. The Isaianic idea of the remnant prepared the way for a positive eschatological message which was of great importance in later prophecy.

The main lines of Isaiah's thoughts were continued by Zephaniah. He, too, announced a universal judgement. Men and animals will be swept away, men because they are wicked, the animals because they cause sin and apostasy (i. 2 f.).[149] The great day of Yahweh (here an

---

[148] In my view, Isaiah's generally gloomy view about the sinfulness of the people makes it very difficult to regard i. 18 as a promise of full forgiveness. I hold that this verse is the beginning of a new saying; and I paraphrase thus: If your sins are as detestable as they in fact are, how can you, as you believe, come to be regarded by Yahweh as quite blameless and righteous (because of your cultic performances)? For the construction see Brockelmann, *Hebräische Syntax*, 54a.

[149] So correctly Gerleman, *Zephanja*, pp. 3 ff.: 'Die Tiere müssen umkommen—denn sie haben Fall und Verführung bewirkt. Ebenso die Menschen—und zwar die Gottlosen unter ihnen.' I now differ from Gerleman in thinking that the words are essentially authentic. The idea of a world judgement is quite appropriate in a disciple of Isaiah. Perhaps the saying has been somewhat modified in transmission.

eschatological term), described as a day of sacrifice, is near. It is a day
of wrath and a day of distress and anguish, a day of ruin and destruction.
An end will be made of all sinners (i. 7 ff., 14 ff.). The universal doom
is sometimes extended to all mankind and the whole earth. This cannot
be taken literally. Zephaniah cannot mean that the whole earth will be
totally destroyed, since he expressly speaks of a continuation of history
on this earth. There is here an element of poetic exaggeration. On this
view there is no need to delete the expressions in question as secondary.
The same is true of iii. 8: on the day of judgement Yahweh will gather
the nations to pour out upon them His indignation, for in the fire of
His jealous wrath the earth will be consumed.

The announcement of a world judgement in Zephaniah is secondary
to the prediction of judgement upon apostate Judah, for which it serves
as a background. In the catastrophe which will befall mankind the
sinners in Jerusalem will perish. But (and this is an important element
in Zephaniah's message about the future) the destruction will not come
upon the whole population: a remnant will be saved, consisting of
individuals who have faith in Yahweh and are obedient to His will.
They will form a new community in Judah not harassed by enemies and
enjoying an uninterrupted peace: 'I will leave in the midst of you a
people humble and lowly. They shall seek refuge in the name of
Yahweh, those who remain in Israel; they shall do no wrong and utter
no lies, nor shall there be found in their mouth a deceitful tongue. For
they shall pasture and lie down, and none shall make them afraid'
(iii. 12 f.).[150]

The books of Nahum and Habakkuk deal with the foreseen downfall
of the Assyrian and Babylonian empires. In the view of these prophets
those events will of course be of immense significance to the Jewish
people, they will bring relief and peace, but a new age in an eschatological
sense is not described in these books. The ethical viewpoint is in these
prophets pushed into the background.

Jeremiah is familiar with the thought that Yahweh is the ruler of the
world and has the destinies of the pagan nations in His hands. The
prophetic mission assigned to Jeremiah refers not only to his own
people but also to the pagan nations (i. 10). The predictions of judgement upon a number of foreign peoples in chs. xxv and xlvi-li accord

---

[150] I think that the exhortation in ii. 3 presupposes that there was already a small
group of true believers in the land (*pace* Elliger in *ATD*). Why should not a good
kernel exist in Zephaniah's time as well as in the time of Isaiah? As regards the
beginning of ch. ii, I believe that Gerleman is right in holding that *vv.* 1 f. contain an
uncanny word of doom. He translates: 'Häuft euch wie Stroh, ja werdet wie Stroh,
o ungeratenes Volk!', etc.

well with Jeremiah's prophetic mission. But it may be questioned whether Jeremiah's threats against foreign peoples refer to all the nations of the earth, to mankind as such, so that a universal judgement is meant. As the prophecies against foreign peoples now stand, that is what they describe. In the vision of the cup in ch. xxv all the kingdoms of the world shall drink (v. 26). In the words connected with the vision it is said that Yahweh's sword will be summoned against all the inhabitants of the earth (v. 29; cf. vv. 30 ff.). However, it is evident that this section has been considerably edited in the course of transmission. It can easily be proved that the sayings which deal with universal judgement belong to the secondary enlargements in the book of Jeremiah.[151] Of course Jeremiah, like Isaiah, *could* have spoken of a judgement on sinners everywhere, on all the proud and wicked inhabitants of the earth; but it is highly probable that he in fact referred only to those nations of whom he had particular knowledge. In the authentic Jeremianic revelations there is no idea of a world destruction and no universal eschatology.[152]

Jeremiah was convinced that Israel was doomed. This conviction dominated his preaching and aroused in him the feelings of grief which were so typical of him. In his revelations natural catastrophes such as plague and famine recede into the background. As a rule the destruction which he predicts is caused by invaders. From the beginning of his ministry Jeremiah knew that the invaders would come from the north. This was made clear to him by the early vision of the cauldron in the field on which the high wind blew from the north (i. 13 ff.).[153] Did the prophet think of the Scythians, who were at that time spreading terror in the Near East? I think that 'the enemy from the north' is to be taken in a wider sense.[154] In my opinion reports had reached the prophet of political upheavals in the northern countries, where different peoples (Assyrians, Babylonians, Medes, Scythians, etc.) were struggling for supremacy. From those regions Yahweh would take his instruments for the destruction of Judah. After the downfall of the Assyrian empire in 612 and the emergence of the Babylonian kingdom, Jeremiah was convinced that it was the appointed instrument of doom. Judah would cease to exist. The population would be deported to Babylonia, and the land devastated.

---

[151] Cf. Rudolph in *HAT*.
[152] Most Biblical scholars hold that iv. 23 ff. describes a world judgement. What Jeremiah describes is an ecstatic vision presenting allegorically Judah's impending doom. Cf. above, pp. 126 f.
[153] For the interpretation of this symbolic vision see above pp. 139 f.
[154] Cf. Lauha, *Zaphon. Der Norden und die Nordvölker im Alten Testament*.

It is interesting to observe that although Jeremiah announced a terrible doom upon Judah, he continued to appeal to his fellow country-men to repent and amend their ways. Before the menace of advancing armies he cries, 'Woe to us, for we are ruined', yet at the same time he makes the appeal, 'O Jerusalem, wash your heart from wickedness, that you may be saved' (iv. 13 f.). Descriptions of impending and seemingly inevitable devastation end with appeals to return from apostasy: 'Be warned, O Jerusalem, lest I be alienated from you; lest I make you a desolation, an uninhabited land' (vi. 8). The prophet was forbidden to intercede for his people; he was assured that it was as impossible for the people to repent as it was for an Ethiopian to change his skin or the leopard to change his spots (xiii. 23); but, notwithstanding, he could not cease urging his people to turn to Yahweh. He even put confessions of sin in the mouth of the apostate people (iii. 22 ff.; xiv. 7 ff.). This is true of every period of his ministry. Of this there can be no question, in spite of the fact that the exhortations to repentance have perhaps been somewhat expanded in the passages of his book which have been influenced by Deuteronomic ideas. Here we find the same paradoxical phenomenon as in the earlier prophets. The prophets never forgot that Israel was a people chosen by Yahweh and beloved by Him. They themselves were filled with love and compassion for her. It followed therefore that their teaching contained both predictions of doom and exhortations to repentance. Justice and mercy, wrath and love were all present in Yahweh's nature; and this was also reflected in the attitude of His prophets towards the people, and, consequently, in their preaching.

To Jeremiah the end of the nation did not mean the complete annihil-ation of Judah. Jeremiah continued Isaiah's teaching that a minority of the people would inherit a happy future. He did not apply to them the term 'remnant' (in Jeremiah's usage this word denotes survivors in a general sense);[155] but we can easily recognize the Isaianic remnant in those who were deported to Babylonia. They are symbolized by the good figs in the vision of the two fig baskets in ch. xxiv. They are called good not because they were innocent in a religious and moral sense, but because they were regarded by Yahweh as fitted to be in His hands a new creation, a new people, in whom the election would be fulfilled. It is, I think, reasonable to suppose that the distress which they experienced in exile prepared them in some measure to be the object of this creative act of Yahweh. But the dominating point of view is in Jeremiah the

---

[155] Jer. vi. 9; viii. 3; xv. 9; xxiv. 8; xxxi. 7; xlii. 15, 19; xliv. 7, 12, 14, 28. xxiii. 3 sounds post-exilic and is probably not Jeremianic; cf. Volz and Rudolph.

power of Yahweh's love. Of the group in question it is said that one day (according to xxix. 10, seventy years, perhaps two generations, must first pass by)[156] they will come back to their native land. There they will form a new ideal community. The fact that few if any of those who were deported in 597 ever came back, is irrelevant, for the ancient Hebrews generally thought in collective and not in individual categories.

Jeremiah emphasized above all the spiritual renewal of the future Israel, which would be re-created by Yahweh as a holy people. In the vision of the figs Yahweh says that after the exiles have returned He will give them a heart to know that He is Yahweh; and they will be Yahweh's people and Yahweh will be their God. This is a striking formulation of the fulfilment of election. The complete conversion to Yahweh, which this implies, is conceived of as a wonderful act of Yahweh, whose power is limitless. In xxxii. 27 Yahweh says, 'Behold, I am Yahweh, the God of all flesh; is anything too hard for Me?' In the prophecy of the new covenant in xxxi. 31 ff., which is addressed to all Israel, Yahweh's creative love is the dominating idea. Yahweh will make a new covenant with His people, a counterpart of the covenant of Sinai, different from it in that the divine law now will be put within men and written upon their hearts. So the people will be a holy people, and all their earlier transgressions will be forgiven.

After the return of the exiles new conditions will come into existence in the land. The population will greatly increase; material prosperity, peace, and security will prevail. Jeremiah appears to cherish, for the future, the idea of a spiritual cult, without sacrifices and similar rites.[157]

To complete this account of Jeremiah's hopes for the future two further ideas must be considered.

First the idea of the return to Palestine of the northern tribes. This idea is expressed in the significant chapters xxx-xxxi. Manifestly this section has been considerably enlarged in the process of transmission; at all events it contains a series of sayings which deal with the future of the northern tribes. They are referred to as Israel, Jacob, Ephraim. As in an audition the prophet hears a voice from Ramah, lamentation and bitter weeping. It is Rachel, the mother of the central northern tribes, who is weeping for her children, because they are not. The expected restoration will take place upon the mountains of Samaria. The chief features in the description are the following: the dispersed tribes will be gathered again to their own land; Yahweh will make an end of the

---

[156] Cf. xxv. 11 f. and xxvii. 7. Perhaps the doctrine of world ages is implied; cf. Rudolph.

[157] Jer. xxiv. 6; xxx. 19 f.; xxxi. 36; xxxii. 42 ff., etc. Cf. above, pp. 359 f.

nations which have oppressed them; for all time to come the restored Israel will live in prosperity and in security without being troubled by hostile attacks; the capital will be rebuilt and an ideal community established; the good old times will return. Pilgrimages will be made to Zion to worship Yahweh; the purpose of election will be fulfilled.[158]

The second idea to be noticed is that of the ideal ruler in the age to come. He is mentioned in two passages. The first is concerned with the return of the northern tribes (xxx. 21). After being established on the mountains of Samaria the new Israelite community will be governed by a ruler, *mōšēl*, of whom it is said that he will be one of themselves. His chief function will be to represent his people before Yahweh, since, unlike ordinary men, he will have the right of access to Yahweh. The sacral character of this ruler, who is not called 'king', is manifest. It seems that he is regarded as the first ruler after the foundation of the new community.[159] His relationship to the Messianic king in Jerusalem is obscure.

In the prophecy concerning the re-establishment of Judah a similar figure is mentioned (xxiii. 5 f.). Here the ruler is expressly called a 'king'. He will be a right (legitimate) member ('branch', 'scion', *ṣemaḥ*) of the Davidic dynasty. He will show insight, deal wisely, and have success.[160] He will execute justice and righteousness in the land. In his reign Judah will enjoy peace. His name will be: 'Yahweh is our salvation' (i.e., saviour and bestower of every kind of bliss). This name alludes to the name of the last king of Judah, Zedekiah. Thus the idea of the expected new king, the ideal ruler in the age to come, i.e., the idea of the Messiah in the strict sense, arose at the time of the overthrow of the pre-exilic monarchy.[161]

To sum up, then, the following may be noted as the main eschatological elements in the teaching of the pre-exilic prophets.

Amos, Hosea, and Micah predicted a complete and final ruin.[162] Isaiah's teaching about the remnant opened the way to a happy future for his people. His line of thought was continued by Zephaniah and

---

[158] For the explanation of Jer. xxx-xxxi see above all the commentaries by Volz and Rudolph.

[159] There is no need to suppose that the prophecy about the coming *mōšēl* is not authentic. Granted that the prophecy refers to North Israel, as I hold, it comes from a time after the end of the monarchy in the Northern Kingdom. Because that land was subject to foreign kings the hope of an indigenous king was quite natural (*pace* Mowinckel, *He that Cometh*, p. 20). xxx. 8-9 sounds like a post-exilic addition. See further Volz and Rudolph.

[160] Cf. Nyberg's analysis in *SEÅ*, vii, 1942, pp. 41 ff., of the meaning of *hiśkîl*.

[161] Jer. xxxiii. 15 f. is, of course, a doublet of this prophecy.

[162] Whether Amos and Hosea had any idea of a better future for Judah is quite obscure. Their authentic utterances give no hint of it.

Jeremiah. To the remnant were linked all the hopes of a happy future including the return of the dispersed exiles, the establishment of a new community, peace, and prosperity of every kind, the return of the good old conditions, and, above all, religious and moral renewal, i.e., the fulfilment of the election of Israel. In Jeremiah we meet for the first time with the idea of the Messianic king in the strict sense. He also was the first to express the idea of the return of the northern tribes. The idea of a world judgement was proclaimed by Isaiah and after him by Zephaniah. The eschatology of the other pre-exilic prophets refers apparently only to Israel.

5. PROPHECY DURING THE EXILE

The political catastrophe which made an end of the Judaean kingdom for centuries and dispersed the Jewish people also had far-reaching consequences for the religious life of the people. Through the destruction of Jerusalem and the ruin of the temple, the cult in the homeland became to a great extent paralysed, and for the deported Jews the worship of their God according to the old forms became impossible.

The terrible disaster also influenced the internal aspect of religion. We must now consider how those significant changes were reflected in the teaching of the great prophets who lived in the exile, and in that of their disciples who imitated them.

Our sources are the revelations of Ezekiel and Deutero-Isaiah, and also secondary passages of exilic date in the books of the pre-exilic prophets. To avoid tiresome repetition we shall restrict ourselves to the more salient differences from the pre-exilic prophets.

To strengthen the faith of the despondent people in Yahweh as the God of election, new details in the history of Israel were pointed out. Deutero-Isaiah repeatedly recalls the wonderful crossing of the Red Sea and the destruction of the Egyptian army. He points to the testimonies of Yahweh's love to David. So urgent was the need to find as many guarantees as possible for the future salvation of Israel, that a new significance was attached to the patriarchs, whom the pre-exilic prophets passed over in silence (for Hosea's mention of Jacob in ch. xii see above, p. 331), because it was to the patriarchs that the popular ideas of a splendid future were linked. Abraham is often mentioned. He, Yahweh's friend, as he is called, is the ancestor of Israel, from whom Yahweh's love has gone over to his descendants. The people were encouraged by the story of Abraham and Sarah. When Abraham was but one, Yahweh called him and blessed him and made him many.

Long ago Abraham had been redeemed by Yahweh. So the deported Jews would one day be liberated by their God. During this period Israel began to be called 'the seed of Abraham, Isaac, and Jacob', and, further, descendants of Jacob and David. Indeed the people was itself called Abraham, in accordance with the common Hebrew conception that the ancestor lives in his descendants and the descendants live in their ancestor. By virtue of this idea that the genealogical organism forms a living unity, what is true of Abraham is true of the people which descended from him. Yahweh's faithfulness to Israel is motivated by His oath to the fathers. Further, as once Yahweh swore that the waters of Noah should no more go over the earth, so He now swears that He will no more be angry with His own people.[163]

Contemporary history was also used to demonstrate Yahweh's power. In the appearance of Cyrus and his brilliant victories Deutero-Isaiah saw Yahweh's mighty deeds. Yahweh had roused him from the east. He gave up nations before him, so that he trampled kings under foot. 'Who has performed and done this?' Yahweh asks; and the answer runs: 'I, Yahweh, who am the first, and with the last I am He.'[164]

All these references to history, which are so numerous in the literature of this period, serve to present new grounds for the faith. In particular the early history of Israel acquired a new significance as the prototype of the history foretold by the prophets. The deliverance from Egypt became a prototype of the deliverance from Babylonia, the crossing of the Red Sea a prototype of the march from the land of captivity to the homeland, the old covenant a prototype of a new covenant, the old election of a new election, etc. Israel's historical traditions, carefully preserved and eagerly studied during the exile, now placed a rich material at the disposal of the spiritual leaders of the people. The typological way of contemplating history yielded guarantees of the realization of the religious and national expectations.

Furthermore the creation of the world now acquired a new importance as a support for the faith. Deutero-Isaiah repeatedly refers to

[163] Isa. xxix. 22 (sec.); xli. 8; xliii. 16 f.; li. 2, 9 f.; liv. 9; lv. 3; Jer. xxxiii. 26 (sec.); Ezek. xx. 5 f.; Mic. vii. 20 (sec.). The interest of Deutero-Isaiah in the traditions of the Pentateuch is noteworthy; cf. Rignell, *A Study of Isaiah, passim*.
[164] Isa. xli. 2-4. The conqueror here referred to is of course Cyrus; cf. the parallel passages xli. 25; xliv. 28; xlv. 1 ff., 13; xlvi. 11; xlviii. 14 ff. I cannot share Kissane's view that xli. 2-4 and 25-26 refer to Abraham. These passages belong to independent revelations (xli. 1-5a and xli. 21-29) and must be interpreted without respect to the other parts of this chapter. The description of the military success of the hero in *vv.* 2-3 and 25 are not (in spite of Gen. xiv) applicable to Abraham. The passages in question must be understood in connection with the other Cyrus poems in Deutero-Isaiah, which make clear their reference to the Persian king. Rignell holds that the text deals with Cyrus, but that the narrative about Abraham in Gen. xiv is alluded to; op. cit., p. 23.

Yahweh's wonderful deeds in connection with the creation of the world. Yahweh has stretched out the heavens and laid the foundations of the earth. He brings out the host of heaven; He gives breath to the people upon the earth. Yahweh and no other has done and does all this, so great is His power. Thus the despondent people must trust in His power to overcome the oppressors and release the oppressed. Creation is also a testimony to the wisdom of Yahweh. He will surely find means of bringing His purposes to fulfilment. As Creator of the world, Yahweh shows His superiority to the idols. He alone has made all things. The idols are powerless and ineffective.[165]

The regularity of the natural order is also cited as a support for faith. Jeremiah had pointed to the laws (*ḥukkîm*) of nature to strengthen the faith of his people (xxxi. 35 ff.). This idea of the regularity of nature acquired increased importance in the exilic and post-exilic periods.[166]

During this period the idea of God became definitely universalistic and monotheistic. The exile brought Israel into closer contact with other lands and other nations, and consequently her mental horizon was widened in various ways. When the people went into exile the worship of Yahweh took place in a wider geographical setting. Surrounded by pagan religion with its polytheism and idolatry they learned to understand Yahweh's unique power and sublimity better than before. It was this contact with the larger world outside the boundaries of Palestine that also helped to stimulate the idea of the conversion of the Gentiles to Yahweh and of world mission as a task given to Israel by Yahweh.

Now Yahweh is expressly called 'the God of the whole world'. He dwells on high, sitting above the circle of the earth. He is 'king of the nations', 'the everlasting king'. The currency of the idea of Yahweh's universal kingship during this period is noteworthy. When Yahweh is about to redeem Israel the whole universe shouts for joy.[167]

Monotheism, which had earlier been of more practical nature (we have used the term 'dynamic monotheism') now became an object of reflection and reasoning, and developed towards absolute monotheism. Deutero-Isaiah led the way. In his sermons we often meet with

---

[165] Isa. xl. 12, 22; xli. 4; xlii. 5; xliv. 24, 27; xlv. 7, 18; xlviii. 13; l. 2; li. 13, 15 liv. 5; Jer. x. 10 ff.; li. 15 ff.(sec.).

[166] In the non-Jeremianic passages Jer. xxxiii. 19 ff. and 23 ff. the idea of natural law is expressed by the phrases 'Yahweh's covenant with the day and the night' and 'the ordinances (*ḥukkôt*) of heaven and earth'. It is, of course, difficult to decide if these passages are exilic or post-exilic. In *De etiska tankarna i urkristendomen*[2] (pp. 253 ff.) Billing ingeniously displays the significance of the Old Testament views of the regularity of nature.

[167] Isa. xl. 22 ff.; xlii. 10 ff.; xliv. 23; liv. 5; Jer. x. 6 f., 10 (sec.).

sayings such as these: I am the first and the last; besides Me there is no God; before Me no God was formed, nor shall there be any after Me; besides Me there is no saviour; I am God, and there is no other.[168]

This monotheistic thought was displayed in vehement polemics against idols and idolaters. A literary genre was created which we may call idol satire. Here, too, Deutero-Isaiah was a forerunner. He ridicules the idols as material artifacts, the product of human labour, and derides their impotence and ineffectiveness. The idolaters are all blinded and without understanding.[169] Against the background of the vain idols Yahweh is described not only as the only God, but also as 'the living God', i.e., a God who works and acts in nature as well as in history and human life.[170]

The 'metaphysical' qualities in Yahweh are, on the whole, more prominent than before. His majesty, sublimity, and holiness are strongly emphasized. Ezekiel's visions of the divine throne are good examples of this. Deutero-Isaiah frequently emphasizes that Yahweh knows beforehand what will happen in the future. What He has revealed to His prophets always comes to pass. Yahweh's power of foretelling and fulfilling, Yahweh as the God of true prophecy, is opposed to pagan astrology, soothsaying, and divination. The pagan diviners are themselves duped and dupe others. In this respect, too, Yahweh is opposed to the idols. They know nothing and are incapable of foreseeing or foretelling anything. According to Deutero-Isaiah, the remarkable events of his time, the appearance of Cyrus and his amazing achievements and everything that would happen in the blessed age expected had been hidden from all the wise of this world. But to Yahweh and his prophets it had been known and foretold long in advance. Thus at this period Yahweh's power as the God of prophecy, like the tokens of His power in nature and history, was invoked to support faith in His power to deliver His people.[171]

Belief in Israel's election was intensified. An impressive variety of imagery was used to express the relationship between Yahweh and His people. The idea of Yahweh's kingship became more prominent. The reluctance of the pre-exilic prophets to use the term 'king' for Yahweh was a thing of the past. Several texts from this period describe

---

[168] Isa. xli. 4; xliii. 10 f.; xliv. 6, 8; xlv. 5 f., 14, 18, 22; xlvi. 9; xlviii. 12; cf. Jer. x. 6 f. (sec.).

[169] Isa. xl. 19 f.; xli. 7, 23 f., 29; xlii. 17; xliv. 9 ff; xlv. 20; xlvi. 1 f.; Jer. x. 1 ff. (sec.); li. 17 f. (sec.).

[170] Jer. x. 10 (sec.); Hos. ii. 1 (sec.).

[171] Isa. xli. 22 ff.; xlii. 9; xliii. 9; xliv. 7; xlv. 21; xlvii. 13; xlviii. 14.

Yahweh as the King of Jacob, the King of Israel. The election of the people was often regarded as an act of creation. In a sublime passage in Deutero-Isaiah Yahweh says, 'I am Yahweh, your Holy One, the Creator of Israel, your King.' Yahweh has made Israel and formed her from the womb. Yahweh, Israel's Maker, is also her Helper and Deliverer.[172] The election of Israel is regarded as a parallel to the creation of the world and, as it were, a continuation of God's creative work.

The servant symbolism, which was alien, or almost alien, to the pre-exilic prophets is characteristic of Deutero-Isaiah. Israel, this prophet says, is the servant of Yahweh as having a mission to perform at the command of their Master. Israel is the messenger of Yahweh to the world. It is also said of Israel that they are Yahweh's witnesses in the world. Israel is called to testify to Yahweh's wonderful activity in the history of His people and to the unity and sovereignty of Yahweh.[173]

In pre-exilic prophecy Yahweh was seldom called Father of Israel, and Israel the son of Yahweh. In the exilic period this symbolism becomes more common. Deutero-Isaiah says in Yahweh's name, 'I will say to the north, "Give up!" and to the south, "Do not withhold; bring My sons from afar and My daughters from the end of the earth"' (Isa. xliii. 6). As a tender father Yahweh has borne Israel from their birth, carried them from the womb. Even to their old age and to grey hairs He will bear them (xlvi. 3 f.). In the exilic passages Hos. ii. 1 and xi. 10 the dispersed Israelites are called Yahweh's sons, whom Yahweh will one day return to their homes.

Deutero-Isaiah likes to call Yahweh the *gō'ēl* of Israel. This term is taken from Hebrew family law. The *gō'ēl* is the member of the family who has the responsibility of vindicating the cause of the family in various ways. He has to take over the property after his next of kin when it is in danger of passing out of the family, or to recover it when it has already been lost. By Levirate marriage he must maintain the name of a male relative who has died without leaving a son to succeed him. He ransoms a member of the family who has been sold as a slave; and he acts as an avenger of blood when a relative has been killed. So the *gō'ēl* is the protector, the upholder, and the restorer of the family. When it is said that Yahweh is the *gō'ēl* of Israel, this means that He is the protector of His own people, that He vindicates the right of His

---

[172] Isa. xliii. 15; cf. xli. 21; xliv. 2; lii. 7.
[173] Isa. xli. 8 f; xlii. 19; xliii. 10; xliv. 1 f., 21, etc.; cf. Jer. xxx. 10; xlvi. 27 f. For details see Lindhagen, *The Servant Motif in the Old Testament*, pp. 192 ff. Concerning the servant motif in the Ebed Yahweh Songs see pp. 400 f.

people, in particular by redeeming them from their oppressors. Thus *gō'ēl* becomes practically identical with *môšîaʿ*, 'helper', 'saviour'.[174]

In this period there is an increased emphasis on Yahweh's love as the ground of election and of His will to help His people and to bear with their sins. When Deutero-Isaiah says that Yahweh blots out the transgressions of His people not because of their sacrifices and the like, but 'for His own sake', this is a reference to Yahweh's paradoxical, sovereign love (Isa. xliii. 22 ff.).[175] Yahweh is ready to give the richest and most prominent among the nations as ransom for Israel (xliii. 3 f.). It is expressly stated that the reason is that Israel is precious in Yahweh's eyes, and honoured, and that Yahweh loves (*'āhab*) her. In a secondary passage in Hosea (xiv. 5) it is said that Yahweh will of His own love and free will heal the faithlessness of His people. Ezekiel emphasizes that Yahweh will restore Israel, but *not* because of its fidelity to the covenant (xvi. 61 f.). This thought was of great importance at a time when the people were oppressed by despondency and sense of guilt.

The unchangeable nature of Yahweh is increasingly emphasized. He is always the same, faithful, everlasting, reliable, and steadfast, as a firm rock. His word stands for ever. The singular Deutero-Isaianic phrase *'anî hû'* expresses the thought that Yahweh always and in all situations is Yahweh, i.e., the only, living, and active God, who acts in accordance with His essential nature as the unequalled, mighty, and merciful God.[176]

A quite new theme, not found in earlier prophecy, is Yahweh's solicitude for His glory. After Israel had broken her isolation and now appeared upon the stage of world history, it was under the scrutiny of the pagan nations, the more so since Israel claimed to be the elect people and the object of God's particular care. The destruction of Israel's national existence, her deportation and dispersion among the nations seemed to show that Yahweh's purpose had proved unsuccessful. Consequently Yahweh, the God of Israel, must defend Himself against the scorn of the pagan nations. For the sake of His name He must show

---

[174] Isa. xli. 14; xliii. 14; xliv. 24; xlvii. 4; xlviii. 17; xlix. 7, 26; liv. 5, 8. For the notion *gō'ēl* see Procksch in *TWBNT*, IV, p. 331. Pedersen, *Israel*, I-II, pp. 390 f., emphasizes that the task of the *gō'ēl* is to be the upholder of the family, its restorer. Johnson in *SVT*, I, 1953, pp. 67 ff., thinks that the basic idea is that of protection. It is the function of the *gō'ēl* to protect the life or vitality of both the individual and the kin-group and thus preserve their standing in society by keeping intact their essential unity or integrity.

[175] The interpretation of xliii. 22 ff. is much debated. In my opinion the language used excludes any reference to sacrificial practice during the monarchy. The sacrificial cult is not criticized here; it is only (with a touch of irony) stated as a fact that no offerings at all have been made. All that the people have succeeded in doing is to sin and sin again. Yahweh's love and nothing else is the ground of His merciful action. See further my *Servant Songs*, pp. 59 f.

[176] Isa. xl. 8, 28; xli. 4; xliii. 10, 13; xliv. 8; xlvi. 4; xlviii. 12; xlix. 15 f.; liv. 6, 10, etc.

forbearance; in the interest of His own glory He could not forsake His people. Yahweh must also show His superiority to the pagan gods, so that their ineffectiveness might be manifested to the whole world. 'How should My name be profaned? My glory I will not give to another', says Yahweh in Deutero-Isaiah (xlviii. 11). And further: 'My glory I give to no other, nor My praise to graven images' (xlii. 8). Ezekiel says that all the gracious deeds of Yahweh in the history of Israel were done for the sake of His name, that it might not be profaned in the sight of the nations among whom they dwelt (xx). The wonderful acts now expected, the deliverance of the people from exile and the restoration to the homeland, would also be performed not according to the conduct of the people, but only for the sake of Yahweh's name and to manifest His holiness (i.e., His divine majesty) in the sight of the nations. By means of the glorious restoration Yahweh would make Israel understand that He really was Yahweh; and all the Gentiles would acknowledge Him as the only God worthy of the name. All flesh would see the glory of Yahweh. All nations of the earth would sing Yahweh's praise when He delivered His people. The nations would know that there was no other god besides Yahweh. Kings would see and arise; princes would prostrate themselves because of the Holy One of Israel. This is the aim of Yahweh's election of Israel, that they should understand that Yahweh is the only God and that they should declare His praise. Sometimes this solicitude for the glory of Yahweh is called His 'zeal' or 'jealousy' for His holy name.[177]

Yahweh's covenant with Israel was seldom mentioned by the pre-exilic prophets; they preferred the idea of election. In this period it became more prominent. Ezekiel reminds the people of the old covenant and rebukes them for breaking it (xvi. 59). Sometimes the covenant is invoked, together with election, as a guarantee of salvation. In Ezekiel Yahweh says that He will remember His covenant with Israel in the days of her youth (xvi. 60). Jeremiah spoke of a new covenant better than the old one. This thought reappears in exilic prophecy. In Deutero-Isaiah Yahweh says that He is about to establish with Israel a new covenant which will never be removed. It will be a covenant of šālôm, a covenant that will bring with it welfare, harmony, and prosperity in

---

[177] See further Isa. xl. 5; xli. 20; xlii. 10 ff.; xliii. 10; xlv. 3, 6; xlviii. 9 ff.; xlix. 7, 23, 26; lii. 5 f., 15; Ezek. xxxvi. 16 ff.; xxxvii. 28; xxxix. 25. 'Know that I am Yahweh' is a favourite expression in Ezekiel. It stands in sermons of doom as well as in sermons dealing with the blessed future. It refers to Israel, but also to foreign nations. The significance of the phrase is that through His deeds in history Yahweh will be recognized as Yahweh in His essential nature, as He who acts in unequalled, sovereign power, wrath and love. See the thorough examination of the origin and the significance of the phrase in question in Zimmerli, *Erkenntnis Gottes nach dem Buche Ezechiel.*

every sphere (liv. 10). Ezekiel says that Yahweh will establish an everlasting covenant of *šālôm* (xvi. 60; xxxvii. 26). Deutero-Isaiah foresees
a new covenant for his people in which Yahweh will confer upon Israel
the favour shown to David. David was a witness to the peoples, a
leader and commander of the nations. Israel will, one day, gather about
her unknown nations who have recognized the power of Yahweh (lv. 3
ff.). This thought refers to the spiritual empire of Israel, for which in
xlii. 6, another term is used: *berît 'am*, the confederation of peoples
with Israel as its centre, linked together by a common adoration of
Yahweh, the God Israel.[178]

Closely connected with the covenant is the idea of Yahweh's *ṣedeḳ*,
ṣedāḳâh, which in modern versions is generally rendered 'righteousness'.
This idea plays a prominent role in the exilic and post-exilic periods
and refers precisely to Yahweh's attitude to the covenant which is
established by Him with His people. Yahweh's *ṣedāḳâh* is His faithfulness to the covenant and the obligation that He has imposed upon
Himself by virtue of the covenant. Because of the covenant Yahweh was
closely bound to His people and zealous to defend its cause and to give
it a blessed future. Deutero-Isaiah speaks repeatedly of Yahweh's
ṣedāḳâh, Yahweh's faithfulness. Time and again he makes use of this
idea to encourage the exiles. For both him and them it was a guarantee
of the re-establishment of the people. Yahweh's faithfulness would be
manifested in the deliverance of the exiled Jews from Babylonia and
their release from the hand of their oppressors. Nothing grander could
be said of Yahweh than that He was *ṣaddîḳ* in this sense. In His faithfulness Yahweh manifested His glory. There is in Deutero-Isaiah no
difference between Yahweh's *ṣedāḳâh*, 'righteousness', and His mercy
and favour; *ṣedāḳâh* often becomes practically equivalent to help,
salvation, deliverance. Yahweh says in Deutero-Isaiah, 'I bring near
My *ṣedāḳâh*, it is not far off, and My salvation will not tarry' (Isa.
xlvi. 13).[179]

Conscious as he was of the depth and extent of Israel's sinfulness
Deutero-Isaiah nevertheless encouraged his people with the assurance
that they had completed the compulsory service which they had been
obliged to undergo as penance for their guilt. Now their guilt was
blotted out and full expiation was made; moreover they had received
from Yahweh double for all their sins. The consequence was that there
was a hope of deliverance and restoration (Isa. xl. 2). The idea of per-

---

178 See further Lindblom, *The Servant Songs*, pp. 21 and 55, and recently Vriezen,
An Outline of Old Testament Theology, p. 362.
179 See further Fahlgren, *ṣedāḳā*.

sonal retribution occupied a similar place in the thought of Ezekiel. He emphasizes that one generation will not suffer because of the sins of an earlier one. By repentance and righteousness it is possible to move Yahweh to avert punishment and give His blessing (xviii; xxxiii). We shall return below to this break with the traditional doctrine of retribution in Ezekiel.

In pre-exilic prophecy love and wrath were the dominant features in Yahweh's nature. In the exilic period, because of the change of the historical situation, wrath is spoken of as something belonging to a bygone epoch. The message of hope implies that wrath has ceased, and love, faithfulness to the covenant, or solicitude for Yahweh's own glory prevail. Yahweh, it is said, was angry with His people and gave them into the power of the Babylonians (Isa. xlii. 25; xlvii. 6). Now the time has come to remove wrath from the people and deal with them in mercy. Yahweh says, 'In overflowing wrath for a moment I hid My face from you, but with everlasting faithfulness I will have pity upon you' (liv. 8). 'Behold, I take from your hand the cup of staggering, the bowl of My wrath. You shall drink it no more, and I will put it into the hand of your tormentors' (li. 22 f.).[180]

As for Yahweh's demands upon His people, the ideals of the pre-exilic prophets reappear in the religious and ethical preaching of this period. The foremost duty of the people is to realize their election, i.e., to live in accordance with their calling to be Yahweh's people and fulfil the mission given to Israel in the world. The people must lean upon Yahweh, sanctify His name, and hearken to His commandments. Together with the social virtues inculcated by the earlier prophets the right worship of Yahweh as the only God is strongly emphasized by the prophets of this period. Idolatry of every kind is vigorously denounced. Nothing is so bitterly censured as Israel's proneness to worship foreign gods and practise pagan ceremonies. Ezekiel's sternest condemnation is directed against the pagan symbols and rites in Judah and Jerusalem.[181]

The most striking feature in exilic prophecy in this connection is the positive and plainly expressed interest in the cult. The description given in Ezek. xl-xlviii of the cult which will be instituted in the new community of the age to come is symptomatic. The profanation of the temple in Jerusalem was to Ezekiel the most atrocious of abominations. In the temple Yahweh's glory dwells, requiring purity and sanctity. An anonymous oracle of this period foretells that the mountain of Yahweh's

[180] Cf. Isa. xii. 1: 'Thou wast angry with me, Thy anger turned away, and Thou didst comfort me.' The date of this psalm is of course uncertain, but it may have been composed and sung among the exiles in Babylonia to express their hope of deliverance.
[181] Ezek. v. 11; vi. 3 f., 13; viii. 5 ff.; xx. 39; xxii. 3 f., 9; Mic. v. 12 ff. (sec.), etc.

house will one day be the centre of the world; to it and to Yahweh's house all nations will flow. According to both Ezekiel and Deutero-Isaiah, one of the blessings of the age to come would be the rebuilding of Yahweh's sanctuary and its establishment in the midst of the people for evermore. There correct sacrifices would be offered. The rules of holiness and sanctity would be scrupulously observed.[182]

Ezekiel also emphasizes the importance of correct observance of the sabbath. He rebukes the priests for their neglect of it. The sabbath is one of Yahweh's greatest gifts to Israel. One of the worst of Israel's past transgressions was the profanation of holy days.[183]

Furthermore, Ezekiel points to the privilege of the ritual and moral statutes and ordinances given by Yahweh to His people, so that men should live by their observance. He maintained that the ruin of the people was caused by their rebellion against Yahweh in not walking in His statutes and not observing His ordinances strictly.[184]

There is, of course, a considerable difference between Ezekiel and Deutero-Isaiah in their attitude towards cultic matters. Ezekiel's priestly interest is evident in several ways. His prophetic teaching is, manifestly, both materially and formally dependent on the sacral law with which as a priest he was familiar.[185] His religious ideal is to a great extent determined by his priestly and cultic interest, and it was the combination in his teaching of prophetic and priestly ideals which appropriately provided the norm for post-exilic religion.

The emphasis on cult and law was of vital importance for the preservation of Israel's national and religious independence at a time when it was attacked by paganism on every hand. During the exile and after the restoration the national identity of the Jews was at stake. Cult and Torah became the most effective means of defending the independence of Yahweh's people among the nations and of enabling them to realize their unique calling in the world.

[182] See the anonymous oracle in Isa. ii. 2 f. and Mic. iv. 1 f.; cf. Jer. xxxiii. 11, 18 (sec.); Ezek. viii; xx. 40 f.; xxii. 8, 26; xxxvii. 26 ff.; Isa. xliv. 28; lii. 11.

[183] Ezek. xx. 12 ff.; xxii. 8, 26; xxiii. 38.

[184] See esp. Ezek. xx. 11 ff. The expression '*ḥuḳḳôṭ* and *mišpāṭîm*' indicates that the reference is in the first place not to the customary moral tradition, but to the emphatically formulated prescriptions regarded as sacral, divine commandments, corresponding to what Alt calls 'das apodiktisch formulierte Recht'; *Kleine Schriften*, I, pp. 278 ff. In *v.* 25 Ezekiel says that some of these statutes were given to Israel by Yahweh to fill them with horror and awe before Yahweh's divine majesty. In this way Ezekiel explains the existence of such statutes as that of the offering by fire of the first-born (cf. Ex. xxii. 28), statutes not wholesome and not furthering life, i.e., incapable of saving men from destruction and death, while the good statutes were given to guarantee life and welfare (cf. Lindblom, *Das ewige Leben*, pp. 10 ff., esp. p. 13, note 2). This is Ezekiel's dogmatic theory, which has, of course, nothing to do with historical facts.

[185] This is demonstrated in a very interesting way by Zimmerli in *ZAW*, lxvi, 1954, pp. 1 ff.

In order to understand aright what the exilic prophets had to say about the spiritual condition of their people it is essential to note to whom they were speaking. The oracles of both Ezekiel and Deutero-Isaiah were not always directed to the same audience.

Sometimes they think of Israel, or Judah, as units, condemning their history from beginning to end. Ezekiel says that he is sent to the children of Israel, to rebels who have rebelled against Yahweh, they and their fathers having revolted against Yahweh up to the prophet's own time (ii. 3).[186] He knows that he is called to denounce not only the sins of his contemporaries, but also the abominations committed by their fathers. Relentlessly he exposes their rebelliousness and treachery from the deliverance from Egypt to his own day (xx). Addressing Jerusalem as representing the nation, Ezekiel says that even their origin was polluted: 'Your father was an Amorite, and your mother a Hittite.' The whole subsequent history of Judah was sullied by harlotry. Judah was even worse than Samaria and Sodom and more corrupt than they in all its ways. Now judgement would be executed upon it (xvi).[187]

In Ezek. xx we are told that on a certain day some elders of Israel came to Ezekiel seeking an oracle. The prophet refused, referring not only to Israel's past apostasy, but also to her present offences. 'Thus says the Lord Yahweh,' the oracle runs, "Will you defile yourselves after the manner of your fathers by running in harlotry after their detestable things? When you offer your gifts and make your sons pass through fire, you defile yourselves with all your idols to this very day. And should I be inquired of by you, O house of Israel?" ' It is difficult to think that child sacrifices were practised among the exiles in Babylonia. In my opinion it is most probable that the deputation of elders came from Jerusalem to receive an oracle from the renowned prophet.[188] However that may be, what the prophet censures in this chapter is the religious corruption of the entire Israelite people from Egypt to his own day.

Deutero-Isaiah uses milder words, but he, too, often rebukes the whole people. It is characteristic of him that he regards the exiles as representatives of the whole people. Turning to them, he addresses Israel as a unit, saying in Yahweh's name, 'Let us argue together; set forth your case, that you may be proved right. Your first father sinned,

[186] The words *'el gôyîm* are probably a marginal gloss indicating that Ezekiel's mission was also to the pagan nations; cf. Zimmerli, *Ezechiel*, pp. 9 and 72.
[187] Against the background of the total worthlessness and wretchedness of the people its election by Yahweh appeared the more incomprehensible and paradoxical. Israel's deplorable plight is vividly presented in the description in Ezek. xvi of the blood-stained and outcast foundling. Cf. Zimmerli in *ZTK*, xlviii, 1951, pp. 249 ff.
[188] See above, pp. 262 f.

and your mediators transgressed against me. Therefore I profaned the sacred princes,[189] I delivered Jacob to the ban and Israel to reviling' (xliii. 26 ff.).[190]

Most of the sermons of the exilic prophets are naturally addressed to the exiles. Many passages indicate that spiritual conditions in the Jewish colonies were by no means perfect. It would be a great mistake to conclude from Isaiah's prophecies about the remnant, or Jeremiah's vision of the good figs, that those Jews who were deported to Babylonia were the moral elite of the Jewish people. The Babylonians did not select them for religious and moral reasons. As for the Isaianic idea of the remnant, its implication was simply that a part of the people would be saved from the general ruin and then turn to Yahweh; in Jeremiah's vision the deported Jews were symbolized by good figs as being material in Yahweh's hands for the creation of a new people.

Ezekiel knows that he is surrounded by briers, thorns, and scorpions; the *gôlâh* is called 'a rebellion house' (ii. 6 ff.). They are people who have eyes to see, but see not, who have ears to hear, but hear not (xii. 2). They despise the serious admonitions of the prophet (xxxiii. 30 ff.). The *gôlâh* is likened to a flock in which there are fat sheep and lean sheep; the former oppress the latter (xxxiv. 17 ff.). Ezekiel is made a watchman to warn the wicked from his wicked way (iii. 17 ff.). Many false prophets and prophetesses are also active in Babylonia (xiii; see esp. *v.* 9 and cf. the letter of Jeremiah to the exiles in Jer. xxix). Idolatry exists even among the leaders of the *gôlâh* (xiv). The exiles are hopeless and despondent. They say, 'Our bones are dried up, and our hope is lost; we are clean cut off' (xxxvii. 11). Ezekiel has to exhort the exiles to repent and turn from all their transgressions, that they may not die (xviii. 30 ff.).

In Deutero-Isaiah, too, there are many passages which show that the prophet has a low estimate of the *gôlâh*. They are blind and deaf, insensitive to Yahweh's words and to the meaning of contemporary events (xlii. 18 ff.). They have burdened Yahweh with their sins and wearied Him with their iniquities (xliii. 24). They are afraid and despondent and have forgotten that their God is an almighty God (li. 12 f.). There are among the exiles those who persecute and torment the prophet (l. 5 ff.), and likewise some who are enemies of those who fear Yahweh, of whom it is said that they kindle a fire, but that they will all together perish in the fire they have kindled (*v.* 11). The prophetic

---

[189] The sacred princes are the kings as anointed and therefore endowed with a sacral character.
[190] Cf. Isa. xlii. 24 f.; xlviii. 1 ff.

'woe' is uttered against those who strive with their Maker about the means used for their deliverance (xlv. 9 f.). The prophet's hearers are directly called 'transgressors' (xlvi. 8). As apostates, as wicked and unrighteous men, they must be exhorted to turn to Yahweh (xliv. 22; lv. 7). It is evident that the *gôlâh* was divided into two groups, one consisting of people who had alienated themselves from the true faith by unbelief and even by indulgence in pagan cults, and the other consisting of adherents of the true prophets, who listened to their words and contended for righteousness, truth, and faithfulness to the genuine Israelite traditions even in a pagan land. Deutero-Isaiah refers to this cleavage in the *gôlâh* when he contrasts with the apostates those of whom he says, 'Who among you fears Yahweh and obeys the voice of His servant?' (l. 10). He thinks here of the group of believers among the *gôlâh*, who continue steadfast in the fear of Yahweh. They live, it is true, in distress and oppression; they are persecuted by malignant enemies; but the prophet exhorts them to trust in Yahweh and rely upon their God. The same group is addressed in li. 7, where they are described as those who know righteousness (*ṣeḏeḳ*: the right attitude to Yahweh, the God of the covenant, and His holy will) and bear Yahweh's Torah in their hearts. They must not fear the insults of men or be frightened by their revilings.

According to the analysis given above, all idealized conceptions of the moral quality of the Babylonian *gôlâh* must be abandoned. Since this was the spiritual situation among the exiles, the prophets who worked in the exile naturally felt obliged to bring into existence a kernel of true Yahweh believers, who would form the beginnings of a new Israel, heirs of the promises, who were prepared to meet the age to come. In this work it became necessary to seek out individuals and influence them. Whereas in the earlier period the community was the main object of the preaching and working of the prophets, the individual now came to the fore in religious teaching.

This individualistic trend is particularly evident in Ezekiel and can best be studied in his sayings about individual repentance. Ezekiel is conscious of having been called to serve as a 'watchman', being responsible for the life of every single member of the *gôlâh*. He is sent to give them warning from Yahweh. If he does not warn the wicked man to turn from his way, the wicked man's blood will be required at his hand.[191]

The individual is distinguished from the community so that the righteous may not perish when catastrophe befalls the great mass of

[191] Ezek. iii. 16 ff.; xviii; xxxiii.

the guilty. If in an impious land there were only three righteous men: Noah, Daniel, and Job, they would deliver but their own lives by their righteousness. They would deliver neither sons nor daughters; they alone would be delivered when the whole land was laid waste (xiv. 12 ff.).

The individual is separated from the preceding and the following generations. Children shall not pay the penalty of the sins of their parents, and parents shall not suffer because of the transgressions of their children. Everyone shall bear the consequences of his own conduct. Ezekiel expressly inveighs against the current law of collective retribution formulated in the proverb: 'The fathers have eaten sour grapes, and the children's teeth are set on edge' (xviii. 2).

Personal repentance now becomes of vital importance. A wicked man can turn from his wickedness and so escape the consequences of his past life. Likewise a righteous man who turns to wickedness has no advantage of his righteousness. What a man is now is decisive.

A consequence of the idea of religious individualism, developed during the exilic and post-exilic periods, was the conception of a mechanical retribution, the necessary connection between sin and suffering on one hand and righteousness and welfare on the other. This unrealistic conception had, as we know, tragic consequences for the religious life of later Judaism.

There had, of course, been a preparation in earlier times for the emergence of religious individualism. In every period of the history of Israel's religion the individual mattered. In the Old Testament we meet a long series of men and women who were true religious personalities. When apostasy of one kind or another flourished the individual always had to decide for or against the genuine Yahweh religion. The Isaianic idea of the remnant implied a trend towards religious individualism. This remnant was composed of individuals in whom were fulfilled the ideals proclaimed by the prophets. The prophetic appeal for faith, humility, and the surrender of the heart required an individual response. What has been called the emergence of religious individualism in the later period involved a more positive and reflective attitude to the religious status of the individual and a greater emphasis on the inward aspect of the religious life. This development was accelerated by the political disintegration of the nation and the consciousness that Yahweh had rejected the people as a corporate unit. As the thought of the people as a unit receded into the background, greater prominence was given to the thought of the individual and of a community of pious individuals in whom the election would be fulfilled in the eschatological crisis. The final stage of this development was the Christian idea of the new Israel consisting of all those individual men and women who believe in Jesus Christ.[192]

The task of the pre-exilic prophets was in the first place to proclaim the rejection of the elect people as a whole and the ruin of the nation as a punishment for its apostasy. When the catastrophe had occurred the prophets came to regard themselves as heralds of a new blessed age. In this they were the heirs of the Isaianic idea of the remnant and Jeremiah's teaching about the new covenant.[193]

Before the second fall of Jerusalem in 586 Ezekiel repeated in extreme terms the message of doom which the pre-exilic prophets had proclaimed. After the total destruction of the city and another large-scale deportation of the population to Babylonia he set himself to prepare his people for the age to come. The return of the exiles and the establishment of a new people and a new state in the homeland became naturally now the chief themes of the exilic prophets. This future prospect appears in Ezekiel in the famous vision of the bones in the valley (xxxvii). Deutero-Isaiah describes the march of the exiles from Babylonia to Palestine as a new Exodus in terms taken from the rituals of the New Year festival.[194] The great event is described as a theophany accompanied by miraculous events. When the Gentiles witness these things they will be filled with amazement and praise the mighty God of Israel.

As we have seen, Jeremiah had expressed the thought that the dispersed northern tribes would also come back. By the symbolic action of the two sticks Ezekiel gave expression to the thought that Israel and Judah would be gathered from the diaspora and make one nation in Palestine: 'One king shall be king over them all; and they shall no longer be two nations and no longer divided into two kingdoms' (xxxvii. 15 ff.). The same idea is expressed in the late passage Hos. ii. 2: 'The people of Judah and the people of Israel shall be gathered together, and they shall appoint for themselves one head'; likewise in the insertion Jer. iii. 18: 'In those days the house of Judah shall join the house of

[192] This individualistic view did not, of course, imply the suppression of the old Hebrew group conception. The group conception still remained dominant, notwithstanding the extreme consequences as to moral and religious responsibility which Ezekiel draws from his individualistic teaching; so Wheeler Robinson in *BZAW*, LXVI, 1936, p. 54. On Ezekiel's doctrine of individual retribution Zimmerli in his above-mentioned article, p. 22, rightly draws attention to the influence upon Ezekiel of ancient sacral law and practice in ancient Israel.

[193] The significance of Jeremiah for Ezekiel's message is demonstrated by Miller in *Das Verhältnis Jeremias und Hezekiels*. He points to similarities in the views of the two prophets on the past history of Israel, in their condemnation of idolatry, their teaching about doom as inevitable, the remnant, individual retribution, eschatology, etc. Ezekiel, says Miller, consciously continued in the *gôlâh* Jeremiah's activities in Jerusalem.

[194] So for instance Gyllenberg in *SEÅ*, v, 1940, pp. 83 ff.

Israel, and together they shall come from the land of the north to the land that I gave your fathers for a heritage.'[195]

The restored people will form a holy community, a society of righteous and pious men, among whom there will be no ungodly or wicked persons. All idolatry and all uncleanness will be abolished. This ideal was of course also maintained by some pre-exilic prophets, but now greater importance began to be ascribed in the prophetic teaching to the cult and cultic purity. In the extended sketch of the new community given by Ezekiel in the form of a vision (xl-xlviii) interest in the cult and in ritual holiness is very evident. In another passage Yahweh says that on His holy mountain He will accept all sacred offerings, the cultic gifts of the people (xx. 40 f.). Deutero-Isaiah calls Jerusalem the holy city into which there shall no more come uncircumcised and unclean people (lii. 1). In an addition to Jeremiah's great prophecy on the return of the northern tribes, Jerusalem and Judah are called a habitation of righteousness, a holy mountain (xxxi. 23). The forgiveness of all the people's transgressions is an essential part of the process of sanctification. Ezekiel says in Yahweh's name that when He forgives them all that they have done they will be so overcome with shame that they will never open their mouth again (xvi. 63). Again, Yahweh says, 'I will cleanse them from all the guilt of their sin against Me, and I will forgive all the guilt of their sin and rebellion against Me' (Jer. xxxiii. 8, sec.).[196] And further: 'In those days iniquity shall be sought in Israel, and there shall be none, and sin in Judah, and none shall be found; for I will pardon those whom I leave as a remnant' (Jer. l. 20, sec.).

It is said that Yahweh will have His dwelling-place in the midst of the new people. He will be Judge, Ruler, and King of the people. He will protect them and ward off every attack, fighting for His people as a warrior who gives victory. The external manifestation of Yahweh's presence is the Temple. As we have seen above, the exilic prophets accord to the Temple of Jerusalem an importance unknown to the pre-exilic prophets. Ezekiel devotes the utmost care to his description of the new Temple in the age to come, where Yahweh will dwell in the midst of the people. In the exilic oracle in Isa. ii. 2 ff. and Mic. iv. 1 ff. it is said that the mountain of the house of Yahweh will be the centre of the world, to which all nations will flow, to be instructed in Yahweh's Torah. It is said that Mount Zion will be the place of the name of the Lord of hosts.[197]

[195] For the secondary character of this passage see Rudolph's Commentary. Cf. also Jer. l, 4.
[196] Cf. Rudolph.
[197] Isa. xviii. 7 (sec.); Mic. iv. 7 (sec.); Zeph. iii. 15, 17 (sec.); Ezek. xxxvii. 27 f., etc.

In Ezekiel's words about the interior transformation of the people we find the culmination of the teaching on spiritual renewal. Yahweh says, 'I will sprinkle clean water upon you, and you shall be clean from all your uncleanness; and from all your idols I will cleanse you. A new heart I will give you, and a new spirit I will put within you. And I will take out of your body the heart of stone and give you a heart of flesh. And I will put My spirit within you, and cause you to walk in My statutes and be careful to observe My ordinances' (xxxvi. 25 ff.). Some significant ideas may be observed here. In accordance with his priestly ideal, Ezekiel begins with the well-known cultic motif of sprinkling with clean water. Then he passes on to the genuine prophetic ideal of an interior transformation presented in very striking metaphors. Further the moral change is described as a fruit of the spirit of Yahweh poured into the souls of men. The result is that the people are made capable of unswerving obedience to all the commandments of the Torah. All this is thought of as Yahweh's wonderful work based upon His solicitude for His own name, not as a consequence of human efforts. Obviously this ideal is closely akin to and perhaps influenced by the ideal of the new covenant in Jeremiah. What is new in Ezekiel is the thought that the great change will be caused by the spirit of Yahweh.[198] Summarizing, Deutero-Isaiah says, 'All your sons will be disciples of Yahweh' (Isa. liv. 13).

In effect this is a complete fulfilment of what is implied in the formula of election: 'You shall be My people, and I will be your God,' words which the exilic prophets often repeat.[199]

According to ancient Hebrew thought, moral perfection is always accompanied by šālôm in the material as well as the spiritual sense. As might be expected in this period, prophecies of the future include vivid descriptions of every kind of welfare and bliss: ruined cities rebuilt, renewed fertility, abundant produce from fields and orchards, an increased population, peace and security; in a word, all that was included in the earthly ideal of ancient Israel. Ezekiel foretells that the population will be multiplied, the cities inhabited, and the waste places rebuilt. It is characteristic of Ezekiel's priestly outlook that he describes how one day the population will be like flocks of sheep and goats thronging together in Jerusalem at the festivals (xxxvi. 37 f.). Deutero-Isaiah

[198] In the exilic and post-exilic periods the thought of the spirit of Yahweh as a renewing power acquired greater importance than it had formerly. Here it is thought of as the instrument of a new religious and ethical creation. In Isa. xliv. 3 the spirit brings about physical renewal and is a parallel to the divine bᵉrākāh; cf. Isa. xxxii. 15; Ezek. xxxvii, and the following section.
[199] Ezek. xi. 20; xiv. 11; xxxvi. 28; xxxvii. 23, 27, etc.

gives us in the most brilliant colours a picture of the rebuilt Jerusalem (Isa. liv. 11 f.). Many exilic additions to the earlier prophetic collections contain descriptions of material abundance and wellbeing, e.g., Hos. ii. 1: the number of Israel will be like the sand of the sea; ii. 20 ff.: in the age to come Yahweh will make a covenant with the beasts and abolish all instruments of war, creating complete safety and tranquillity in the land; xiv. 6 ff.: Israel will blossom as the lily and flourish like Lebanon; Am. ix. 13: the ploughman will overtake the reaper, and the treader of grapes him who sows seed; Isa. xi. 6 ff.: peace will rule in nature, the wolf will dwell with the lamb, the conditions of the garden of Eden will return; Isa. ii. 4 (Mic. iv. 3): universal peace will be established and all the nations of the earth will live in peace and concord.[200]

The new age is regarded as a restoration of the blessings of the good old days, a full renewal, after the destruction of the nation, of the relation between Yahweh and His people. Yahweh will again have pity upon Israel, it is said; He will once more choose Israel. The old covenant will be replaced by a new, an everlasting covenant. The former kingdom will be re-established. The deliverance from Babylonia is described as a new Exodus. A new Paradise will be created on the earth. The expression 'once more' (or 'again') is typical of the descriptions of the new age, during this period. As for the expression 'choose once more', it must be explained in the light of the conception of election found in the exilic prophets. Even after the ruin of the people as a nation, they were still convinced that as a divine decree election still stood secure. Thus the expression must refer to election as an act, not as a decision. The restoration of the destroyed people is considered as a parallel to the events in the earliest period of Israel's history by which election was first manifested. Everything that was expected for the age to come is summed up in the common term *šûb šebût*: 'turn the fortune', used of Yahweh's gracious re-establishment of His chosen people. We have already noted some of these ideas in the sayings of Jeremiah; but during this period they became generally current.[201]

The idea that the great eschatological transformation will include the cosmos is characteristic of both exilic or post-exilic prophecy and apocalyptic. Probably the saying in Isa. xxx. 26 belongs to an exilic

---

[200] See further exilic passages and additions such as Isa. xxx. 23 ff.; xxxii. 15 ff.; xxxv. 1 f.; xlix. 18 ff.; liv. 1 ff.; Ezek. xxxiv. 14 ff., 25 ff.; Hos. ii. 23 f.; Mic. v. 6; vii. 11.
[201] Isa. xliii. 18 f.; lv. 3; Ezek. xvi. 59 f.; xxxiv. 25; xxxvii. 26; xxxix. 25, and the secondary passages Isa. xi. 6 f.; xiv. 1; Jer. xvi. 14 f.; Hos. vi. 11; Am. ix. 14; Mic. iv. 4, 8; Zeph. iii. 20. For the expression 'choose once more' see further Vriezen, *Die Erwählung Israels nach dem Alten Testament*, pp. 74 and 98 f. For the phrase *šûb šebût* see above all Dietrich, *Schûb schebût. Die endzeitliche Wiederherstellung bei den Propheten*.

addition. Here it is said that the light of the moon will be as the light of the sun, and the light of the sun will be sevenfold, at the time when Yahweh binds up the hurt of His people and heals its wounds. In the prophecy against Babylon in Isa. xiii, where the conquest and ruin of that city is described against the background of a general world judgement, it is said that the stars of the heavens will not give their light; the sun will be dark at its rising, and the moon will not shed its light (v. 10). It is difficult to say to what extent such pictures are to be taken literally. Perhaps they must be understood, at least partially, as poetical descriptions intended to present the eschatological hope in a more impressive and convincing manner. That some popular eschatological fancies are reflected in such descriptions seems to me to be evident. This may be assumed, of course, without adopting the theory of a pre-prophetic eschatological *system*.

Two questions still require an answer: the question of the 'Messianic' kingdom and that of the fate of the Gentiles in the age to come.

In the face of the downfall of the Judaean kingdom and the end of the Davidic dynasty, Jeremiah foretold that one day in the future Yahweh would raise up another member of the Davidic family, who would reign as king, executing justice and righteousness in the land, and establishing safety and peace. Alluding to the name of the last Judaean king, *Ṣidḳiyyāhû*, he said that the name by which he would be called would be 'Yahweh is our salvation' (xxiii. 5 f.). After the great catastrophe prophetic voices were heard which proclaimed the hope that in the coming restoration another monarchy and a new kingdom would be established. In xxxiv. 23 f. Ezekiel says that after the return of the exiles Yahweh will set up over them a 'shepherd', i.e., a king, to rule over the two parts of the Israelite people (cf. xxxvii. 16 ff.). This king is called 'Yahweh's servant David', which does not mean that he will be a *David redivivus* in the strict sense, but that he will be a member of the Davidic dynasty. He is called David in accordance with the ordinary Hebrew conception that the ancestor lives on in his descendants.[202] The designation must of course be conceived of as a collective one. History does not end with the first phase of the restoration, but will continue for ever, as is frequently emphasized in descriptions of the age to come (cf., e.g., xxxvii. 25 ff.). The king is here not called *meleḵ*, but *nāśî*, a favourite term of Ezekiel, the priest. It seems that both titles are used without discrimination. In the parallel passage

---

[202] See further Ezek. xxxvii. 24 f.; Jer. xxx. 9; Hos. iii. 5. Schmidt in *Der Mythus vom wiederkehrenden König im Alten Testament*, Gressmann in *Der Messias* (pp. 255, 274), and others maintain that a *David redivivus* in person is thought of. On this point I am in agreement with Mowinckel in *He that Cometh*, pp. 161 ff.

xxxvii. 21 f., it is said that all Israelites will be gathered from all quarters of the world and brought to their own land. There they will form *one* nation, and *one* king (*melek*) will rule over them. And further: 'My servant David shall be king [*melek*] over them, and they shall all have one shepherd' (*v.* 24).

In the great vision of the new Temple in xl ff. the prerogatives and the duties of the *nāśî'* are described in detail, particularly with regard to the cult: how he is to enter and withdraw from the sanctuary, and where he is to take his stand; his personal portion of the land and the tributes that are to be given him by the people; his responsibility for the sacrificial service in the Temple, where he is required to make some offerings and to offer prayer.[202a]

The king of the age to come and his kingdom are finally referred to in the allegory in xvii. 22 ff. Yahweh will take a sprig from the top of the cedar (i.e., Judah) and plant it on the mountain of Israel. It will become a huge tree, on the branches of which the birds will nest. All other trees of the field will recognize the power of Yahweh, who has planted this cedar. The sprig signifies the king of the new age, who is identical with the new David and the *nāśî'* mentioned above. Here it is added that the pagan nations will stand in amazement at what Yahweh has done with His people Israel in establishing the wonderful Messianic kingdom.

The ideal king of the age to come is mentioned in several passages deriving from prophetic personalities of the exilic age, which have been included in the earlier prophetic books.

In the exilic conclusion of the Book of Amos it is said that in the coming age Yahweh will restore the fallen booth of David, i.e., re-establish the Judaean kingdom in ideal forms. There is here no explicit reference to a new king; but the re-established Davidic kingdom must of course have a king. It is said that it will be as in the days of old. Hos. ii. 2: Israel and Judah will appoint for themselves one head, i.e., a common king; iii. 5: after having been chastised, the children of Israel will seek David, their king, i.e., they will all yield to the ideal king of the Davidic dynasty, who will reign in the new age;[203] Isa. xi. 1-9: after the overthrow of the Davidic dynasty another descendant of the old royal family will arise, establishing the ideal kingdom of the age to come, himself endowed with all the qualities characteristic of an ideal king in ancient Israel;[204] xvi. 5: in love and faithfulness Yahweh will

---

[202a] For the figure of the *nāśî'* see Noth, *Das System der zwölf Stämme Israels*, pp. 151 ff., and Gese, op. cit., pp. 85 ff. and 110 ff.
[203] For this perhaps post-exilic interpolation see above, p. 289.
[204] See above, p. 281.

establish a throne in Jerusalem, upon which will sit a king who will judge with justice and be swift to do righteousness;[205] xxxii. 1 f.: a king will reign in righteousness, surrounded by princes, all of whom will protect the people and further their prosperity; Mic. v. i-5: another member of the ancient royal family will appear, originating from the insignificant Bethlehem, the city of David, and will be ruler in Israel, fulfilling in his person the mysterious Isaianic oracle on Immanuel (Isa. vii. 14), which had been carefully preserved in tradition. He will tend and protect his people and deliver them from all their enemies. His power will be experienced and recognized all over the world.

Remarkably enough the figure of the ideal king in this sense is entirely missing from the sermons of Deutero-Isaiah and in prophecies directly influenced by him. There is, however, in this prophet a substitute for the idea of the ideal king, namely the idea of Yahweh, the King of Israel, who comes to His people in the theophany of the age to come. As we have seen above, Deutero-Isaiah, unlike the pre-exilic prophets, favours the idea of the kingship of Yahweh. As King of Israel Yahweh defeats the enemies of His people and delivers them from the Babylonian oppressors. He leads the exiles through the desert back to their own land to establish there a kingdom where the promises will all be fulfilled. When the exiles return to Zion Yahweh Himself comes with might. His reward is with Him and His recompense before Him, i.e., He comes together with His liberated people (Isa. xl. 10).[206] Yahweh Himself will go before the returning exiles, and He will be their rearguard (lii. 12). He leads them in a way they do not know (xlii. 16). As the King of Israel Yahweh sends men to Babylon to overthrow it (xliii. 14 f.). After the return to the homeland Yahweh will pour His blessing upon the people and make them a great and mighty people (xliv. 1 ff.). Yahweh will restore the waste places and transform the whole land (li. 3). In all that Yahweh does with His people His kingdom becomes manifest. He returns to Zion as a triumphant and victorious King (lii. 7 ff.). As a ruler of the new people Yahweh will protect them and defend them against all hostile attacks (liv. 14 ff.). Similar ideas appear in secondary passages influenced by Deutero-Isaiah. In the new community they will exult in the Holy One of Israel, seeing all that He has done with them (Isa. xxix. 17 ff.). Yahweh Himself comes with vengeance; He comes to save the exiles (xxxv. 4). Yahweh Himself will be in the midst of the re-established kingdom as a warrior who gives

---

[205] V. 5 looks like an interpolation. It is rhythmically very irregular and interrupts the sequence of thought.
[206] Cf. Rignell, A Study of Isaiah ch. 40-55, p. 14.

victory (Zeph. iii. 17). Yahweh leads the march of the returning exiles: 'Their King will pass before them, Yahweh at their head' (Mic. ii. 13). Of the re-established people it is said, 'Yahweh will be King over them in Mount Zion from this time and for evermore'; so will come 'the former dominion, the kingdom of the daughter of Jerusalem' (iv. 7 f.). As a good king Yahweh will 'shepherd His people with His staff, the flock of His inheritance' (vii. 14).

In such a future prospect there is no room for an earthly king of the type described above. The consistently theocentric view of Deutero-Isaiah is the reason for his silence about a human king, a scion of David who would establish an ideal kingdom in the age to come.

In the above survey the term 'Messiah' has been avoided, because it does not occur in the texts quoted. As we know, it belongs to a much later time.[207] But the ideal king of the age to come is, of course, essentially the same as he who was later called 'the Messiah' or 'the Messiah of the Lord'. The thought of the ideal king which we have considered above is, like that of the Messiah, an eschatological idea, in so far as all the ideas typical of the age to come are eschatological. The eschatological character of the expected king is not inconsistent with descriptions of him as an earthly king. He is thought of as a member of the Davidic family and is expected to be ruler in a kingdom established in the land of Israel; but at the same time he is described as endowed with divine or at least supernormal qualities in accordance with the new order of things.

Like the heroes of early times and the prophets, the ideal king will be endowed with the spirit of Yahweh. This divine endowment manifests itself in wisdom, good counsels, power, personal righteousness, and fear of the Lord. He will be a just king and judge, defending the cause of the poor and lowly. His words will be powerful and effective. He will smite the earth with the rod of his mouth; and with the breath of his lips he will slay the wicked. He will create a state of perfect peace on the earth. His power will extend to the ends of the earth. The Gentiles will stand in amazement at his actions, his might and glory. He will be a powerful protector of his people and defend it against hostile assaults of every kind. He will further prosperity and welfare in the land. He will perform the duties of a sacral king, functioning as ruler and priest in one person.

There are manifest variations in the picture of the ideal king. Sometimes more emphasis is laid on his spiritual endowment and the spiritual character of his activity; sometimes he is more like an ordinary king; sometimes (as in Ezekiel) his sacral position and sacral functions are

---

[207] See Mowinckel, *He that Cometh*, pp. 3 ff., 291 f.

more accentuated; but always he is described as a being whose qualities and capacity surpass normal human standards.

It is easy to trace the origins of the main features of this ideal king. His connection with the historical monarchy in ancient Israel is manifest. He is a member of the Davidic family and will reign in the land of Israel. In the age to come he will be a counterpart to the historical kings of the past. Secondly, we recognize in the figure of the eschatological king the traditional Hebraic ethical ideal of a good king, resembling that found among all the ancient peoples of the Near East. Thirdly, the picture of the ideal king is strongly influenced by the ideology of sacral kingship, varying forms of which appear throughout the ancient world. Fourthly, there are traits which can be explained as deriving from the ancient oriental royal or court style.[207a]

Finally a brief word must be added about the relation in the new kingdom between the ideal king and Yahweh. As we have seen, Deutero-Isaiah so strongly emphasized the kingship of Yahweh in the age to come, that there was no place for an earthly king. When the ideal king is conceived of as the real ruler in the new kingdom, this does not of course imply that Yahweh is dethroned as 'the King of Jacob'. We must surely assume that Yahweh was thought of as the heavenly King, while 'the ideal king' was regarded as His vicegerent on the earth or, perhaps, as His vassal-king, serving Him and performing His commission. Thus the eschatological restoration can be declared to be a work of Yahweh and at the same time a work of the ideal king.[208]

We now pass to the problem of the fate of the Gentiles in the age to come.

The pre-exilic prophets regarded the Gentiles as objects of Yahweh's judgement. Sometimes (e.g., Amos and Jeremiah) they had in view only the neighbouring nations, sometimes (e.g., Isaiah, Zephaniah) they said that Yahweh's doom would come upon the proud and wicked all the world over. In our period reference is often made to Yahweh's judgement on the pagan nations; and naturally particular prominence is

---

[207a] Since it is not my purpose here to analyse the origin of the idea of the Messianic king, it is unnecessary to enumerate all the literature relevant to this important problem. It must suffice to refer to the detailed exposition in Mowinckel's above-mentioned book (esp. pp. 21-95). The idea of a general oriental 'court style' has been expounded by Gressmann in *Der Ursprung der israelitisch-jüdischen Eschatologie* and *Der Messias*; further by Dürr in *Ursprung und Ausbau der israelitisch-jüdischen Heilandserwartung*. For the influence of the ideology of divine kingship on the figure of the Messianic king see Ringgren, *The Messiah in the Old Testament* (a work with which I find myself in only partial agreement), with rich documentation.

[208] For this problem see Wolff in *ZAW*, liv, 1936, pp. 168 ff. This scholar solves the problem by the thought of the Messiah 'als Erscheinungsform des alttestamentlichen Gottes'. This expression, as applied to the historical figure of the Messiah, sounds in my ears somewhat unrealistic.

given to the Babylonians, the oppressors *par excellence* of Israel at this time. Deutero-Isaiah frequently describes how one day vengeance will be taken upon the Babylonians for all that they have done to Yahweh's people. Israel's enemies will all perish and be as nothing. They will be utterly crushed by Israel, or, as is frequently said, by Yahweh Himself. Babylon and the Babylonian dominion are to be overthrown, and all resistance will be ruthlessly suppressed. The enemies will become Israel's slaves. Yahweh Himself will go forth as a warrior, fighting for His people.[209] These ideas occur in those revelations of Deutero-Isaiah which we have called 'the triumphal revelations' because they deal with the triumph of Israel over all her adversaries. In these 'triumphal revelations' Cyrus, the Persian king, plays an outstanding part as the chosen instrument in Yahweh's hand, by which Yahweh will perform His purposes for Israel. He was foretold in the prophecies, and his actions imply the fulfilment of the promises.[210]

Also Ezekiel is convinced that a terrible judgement awaits all the enemies of Israel and of Yahweh. Like some of the pre-exilic prophets, Ezekiel has a series of prophecies against foreign peoples, who in different ways have incurred guilt. In an oracle on the restoration of Israel Yahweh says that He will execute judgement upon all the nations who have treated Israel with contempt (xxviii. 26; cf. xxxvi). The nations mentioned by Ezekiel are all neighbours of Israel or at least are on its historical and geographical horizon.

The most famous prophecy in Ezekiel against the Gentiles is the oracles against Gog in xxxviii-xxxix. In an earlier chapter we have dealt with this section from a literary point of view. Here it suffices to note that Gog hardly means the pagan nations as a whole, but refers to the enemy from the north in Jeremiah. Jeremiah's predictions about this enemy, which he regarded as in fact fulfilled in the Babylonian assaults, were to Ezekiel still impending, and were taken up in his eschatological view. These things would come to pass in the final restoration of the Israelite state in the age to come.[211]

---

[209] Isa. xli. 11 f., 14 ff.; xlii. 13 f.; xliii. 14; xlv. 14 ff.; xlvi. 1 f.; xlvii. 1 ff.; xlviii. 14; xlix. 22 ff.; li. 22 f.

[210] On 'the triumphal revelations' see above, pp. 267 f.

[211] It is a common opinion among Biblical scholars that Gog 'represents' the world power, all the peoples of the earth who are regarded as hostile to Yahweh. This is an abstract theory without support in the text. Presumably Ezekiel thought of Gog as ruler over a specific region. Gressmann (*Der Ursprung der israelitisch-jüdischen Eschatologie*, pp. 174 ff.) thought that the idea of the attack of Gog is only an instance of a pre-prophetic, mythological, and eschatological concept, applied by the prophets to different concrete historical situations. Gressmann is right in his view that the description of Gog and his attack on the holy people on the navel of the earth has a strongly mythological colouring. But this is due to the prophetic way of thinking in mythological categories. We have to take seriously the words in xxxviii. 17, where Gog is said to

The historical situation at this period helps to explain the fact that greater prominence is given to the judgement on Israel's enemies and oppressors than to a general world judgement. But the description in Isa. xiii of the downfall of Babylon against the background of the general doom of sinful mankind shows that the idea of a world judgement existed in the exilic period. We should probably also assign to that period the saying in Mic. vii. 13: 'The earth will be desolate because of its inhabitants, for the fruit of their doings.'

Similar prophecies about the future judgement on the pagan nations are to be found in several exilic additions to the pre-exilic collections of prophetic utterances. Isa. xiv. 2: the enemies will be slaves of the Israelites, and the captors will themselves be captives; xiv. 4 ff.: the terrible fall of the Babylonian king is foretold; xxxv. 4: Yahweh comes with vengeance upon the enemies of Israel; Mic. v. 7: the remnant of Jacob will be among the nations like a lion among the beasts of the forest, among the flocks of sheep, which mercilessly treads them down and tears them in pieces; Zeph. iii. 19: in the age to come Yahweh will make an end of all the oppressors of Israel.

Yahweh's vengeance upon His adversaries and Israel's triumph over her enemies were only one side of the teaching of the exilic prophets about the future of the Gentiles. The other side was their belief in the conversion of the Gentiles to the God of Israel.

The exilic prophets frequently speak of the effect upon the Gentiles of the wonderful deeds of Yahweh in restoring His people. Deutero-Isaiah says (Isa. xl. 5) that the deliverance and return of the exiles will be a manifestation of Yahweh's glory, 'and all flesh shall see it together'. The Gentiles will stand amazed at Yahweh's mighty deeds. In all that befalls Israel, the people of Yahweh becomes a witness to the Gentiles of Yahweh and His omnipotence. This theme recurs in many varied forms in Deutero-Isaiah. In the allegory of the cedar tree Ezekiel says that even the foreign nations will recognize the mighty deeds of Yahweh, the mightiest of gods (xvii. 24). In an exilic passage in Micah (vii. 16 ff.) it is said that the Gentiles will be witnesses of the new Exodus. They will be ashamed of all their might. They will lay their hands on their mouths. They will lick the dust like the serpent and come trembling out of their strongholds in dread of the God of Israel. All this has

---

have been spoken of by former prophets. Because the enemies are thought of as coming from the north, it is natural to suppose that Ezekiel was in the first place recalling the prophecies of Jeremiah about 'the enemy from the north'. In the conception of the enemy from the north there is a fusion of mythological and historical elements; see further above, pp. 232 f., and Gerleman's interesting article in *SEÅ*, xii, 1947, pp. 148 ff.

nothing to do with a real conversion, with a turning of the heathen to
the genuine Yahweh religion. What is meant is that the Gentiles will
be dismayed by the manifestation of the power of Yahweh and seized
by fear of this mighty God. Similarly Deutero-Isaiah says: 'Kings shall
see and arise; princes, and they shall prostrate themselves' (xlix. 7);
and: 'Kings shall shut their mouths' in amazement at what befalls the
servant of Yahweh: 'for what has not been told them they will see, and
what they have not heard they will have to consider' (lii. 15).

The conversion of the Gentiles is quite another thing. Now the idea
is that the Gentiles really become worshippers of Yahweh, sharing in
Israel's faith, taking over the true Yahweh religion. The idea is that the
Gentiles will no more be enemies of Israel, hated and opposed by her,
but adherents of the same religion and together with Israel members
of one and the same religious community.

The idea of the conversion of the Gentiles was the most important
of those which emerged during the exilic period. Its originator was
Deutero-Isaiah. There are scholars who maintain that he was a consistent nationalist, regarding the pagan nations only as objects of doom
or as witnesses of Yahweh's wonderful actions towards Israel, paying
homage to Yahweh with their mouths, not surrendering to Him with
their hearts. I cannot share this opinion. The relevant passages must,
in my judgement, be interpreted in a very different way.[212]

I believe that the conversion of the Gentiles is a basic idea in the
Deutero-Isaianic oracles on the servant of Yahweh, comprising the
Servant Songs proper together with those passages connected with them
which further develop their contents, with a plain reference to Israel,
viz. the faithful group in the gôlâh.[213] In the first servant oracle (xlii. 1-9)
it is said that the task of the servant as Yahweh's agent in the world is
to bring forth and vindicate to the nations the statutes and ordinances
of Yahweh, including, of course, demands for obedience to and belief
in Him. That is what is called in the sequel the Torah, of which it is
said that the coasts wait eagerly for it, that is to say, that the Gentiles
are prepared to receive the true Yahweh religion. Together with Israel
the converted Gentiles will form a spiritual unity. That is what, in my
opinion, is meant by berît 'am, a confederation of peoples (v. 6). Thus
Israel will mediate welfare and salvation ('ôr) to the pagan nations.
Blind eyes will be opened and prisoners released. These metaphorical
expressions describe the fundamental religious change in the pagan
world. In the second Servant Song (xlix. 1-6) this thought is expressed

[212] See Additional Note VII.
[213] For a more detailed discussion of what follows see my book *The Servant Songs in
Deutero-Isaiah*, also the literary analysis given above, pp. 267 ff., and Additional Note VIII.

by the declaration that the prophet is called to be a light to the nations, so that Yahweh's salvation may reach to the end of the earth, which symbolically refers to the mission of the faithful group among the exiles to the pagan world. The fourth song takes a step further. Here it is said that the suffering of the faithful Israel in exile, symbolized by the figure of the leprous man, is intended to be vicarious suffering. Israel takes upon itself the penalty which the Gentiles had to pay for their unbelief and rebelliousness. So Yahweh's wonderful plans for mankind will be realized. The mission of Israel to the world, accomplished by witnessing to the true Yahweh belief and by vicarious suffering, is the culmination of the message given by Yahweh to His people. This message and its fulfilment are 'the new things' which Yahweh now declares.

There are some other sayings by Deutero-Isaiah, the contents of which correspond closely to the leading ideas of those Ebed-Yahweh oracles: xlv. 22 f.: all the ends of the earth are summoned to turn to Yahweh, the only God, that they may be saved; every knee will bow, every tongue will swear to Yahweh; li. 4 f.: Yahweh's Torah will be known and established in the world for the welfare of the pagan nations, Yahweh's salvation is at hand, His arms will govern and judge the nations, the far coasts are waiting for Him; lv. 1 ff.: as King David was a witness to and a leader of the peoples, Israel will call upon nations she does not know and, together with the Gentiles, form a spiritual empire, another expression of the idea of the $b^e rît$ 'am.

In Isa. xliv. 3 ff. I find a further allusion to the conversion of the Gentiles and a picture of the new Israel consisting of true Israelites and converted Gentiles together. In v. 5 two categories are mentioned: those who expressly confess that they belong to Yahweh, and those who give themselves the name Israel. The former are the true, the faithful Israelites, who will participate in the new holy community of the age to come; the latter are proselytes from the pagan nations who have adopted the true Yahweh religion.[214]

Thus there are in Deutero-Isaiah many passages which, correctly understood, show that he looked forward to a day when other nations would come home to the one true God. In his revelations 'not only the geographical horizon but the horizon of faith has been enlarged'. Here is the true prophetic gospel.[215]

It is, in the opinion of the present author, difficult to imagine that

---

[214] Thus I dissociate myself from those commentators who in v. 5 think either of Jews or of proselytes; the passage refers to both categories. The text must, however, be emended; see BH and, in addition, instead of $ûb^eš\bar{e}m$ read $w^ez\hat{e}h\ b^ešēm$, which greatly improves the metre.

[215] So rightly Anderson, The Prophetic Gospel, p. 15.

the prophet proclaimed at the same time conversion or salvation of the Gentiles and their subjugation or annihilation. It would on the other hand be a quite arbitrary procedure to attribute the different groups of revelations to different prophetic personalities. The difficulty can, it seems to me, be better removed if the historical situation in which Deutero-Isaiah lived is taken into consideration. Before the occupation of Babylon by Cyrus, the prophet was convinced that Babylon would be destroyed, the exiles triumphantly released and a terrible vengeance taken upon the enemies of Israel. As we know, none of these things happened. Cyrus spared the city and showed its inhabitants clemency. He paid homage to Marduk, the principal god of Babylon, and made Babylon one of the many capitals of the Persian king. The company of Jews that followed Sheshbazzar, the appointed governor of Judah, was inconsiderable. The great hopes set upon the victorious Persian king thus came to nothing.

With the occupation of Babylon the exalted tone that sounded in the series of Deutero-Isaianic sayings which we have called 'the triumphal revelations' must have died away. The triumph of Israel having been reduced to dust, the prophet must look for new revelations from his God to explain the altered situation and show new ways in which God's purposes for Israel would be accomplished. Now the prophet came to understand that Israel had a still higher aim than triumph and national splendour. Israel had been given a missionary task, the task of being an instrument in Yahweh's hand for the conversion and salvation of the Gentiles. That task would be performed through witnessing to Yahweh and His Torah in the world on the one hand, and through suffering for the benefit of the sinners on the other. These thoughts dominate 'the missionary revelations' of Deutero-Isaiah, culminating in the Ebed-Yahweh oracles.

The idea of the conversion of the Gentiles and their incorporation in the restored Israel occurs in several passages in other prophetic books which for different reasons must be regarded as deriving from the exilic period and influenced by the teaching of Deutero-Isaiah. It is, of course, sometimes impossible to be certain whether they are from the time of the Babylonian exile or perhaps from the period immediately after the return. The following examples may be cited: Isa. ii. 2 ff. (Mic. iv. 1 ff.): the nations will flow to Jerusalem to be instructed in the true Yahweh religion; xi 10: the nations will seek the Messiah of the age to come; xvii. 7 f.: men will turn from idolatry to their Maker, the Holy One of Israel; Zeph. ii. 11: all the idols will be famished and the Gentiles will worship Yahweh alone; Hab. ii. 14: the earth will be filled with the knowledge of the glory of Yahweh as the waters cover the sea; Jer. iii. 17: in the age to come all nations will gather to Jerusalem to worship Yahweh's name and no longer follow their own evil hearts; xii. 16: the Gentiles will take over the true Yahweh religion and learn to swear by Yahweh's name; thus they will be united with Israel; xvi. 19 ff.: the Gentiles will understand the uselessness of idols and idolatry and become worshippers of Yahweh, the only true God.

In some of these passages Deutero-Isaianic influence is manifest. Thus they lend support to our view of the missionary teaching of the great anonymous prophet of the exile. It must, I think, be admitted that Deutero-Isaiah originated the idea of the conversion of the pagan nations and that it lived on among the Jews after his time, alongside the idea of the judgement upon the Gentiles.[216] A connecting link between the two apparently disparate thoughts is sometimes expressed in this way: those among the Gentiles who obey the message of the living God and are converted to Yahweh will be saved. The refractory will receive severe punishment at Yahweh's hand (Jer. xii. 16 f.; Mic. v. 14).

The following tendencies and ideas were characteristic of exilic prophecy: the attempt to find in history and nature new grounds of support for the faith (references to the ancestors of Israel and to creation); fully developed monotheism and universalism; the use of new symbols for the relation between Israel and her God (particularly the *gō'ēl* motif and the servant symbolism); an emphasis on Yahweh's glory and His *ṣedāḳāh* as motives for salvation; a marked attention to cult, ritual holiness, and law; the individualization of religion; the dominance of the future hope including, above all, the ideas of the complete restoration of Israel, cosmic miracles, the appearance of the ideal king of the age to come, and, finally, the conversion and salvation of the Gentiles through the mediation of Israel.

6. POST-EXILIC PROPHECY

The character of post-exilic prophecy was to a great extent determined by the historical circumstances in which the prophets of this period lived and worked. A part of the Babylonian *gôlâh* had returned to the homeland; but there were still dispersed throughout the world Jews whose ingathering was eagerly awaited.

---

[216] It is true that Ezekiel taught that the restoration of Israel and the revelation of Yahweh's glory in connection with the wonders of the age to come would have as their consequence the acknowledgement of Yahweh's majestic name by the nations. This is, however, not a religious conversion comparable to that foretold by Deutero-Isaiah. Ezekiel never says that the Gentiles will one day join with Israel in a common, purified, true Yahweh religion. Cf. Miller, op. cit., p. 183.

The chief task of those who had come back, and in the first place of the prophets, was to build up a new community in the old land, corresponding to the national ideals and the promises of the earlier prophets.

In doing this they had to contend with many difficulties: poverty, bad harvests, opposition from adversaries, invasion by foreigners, internal corruption, apostasy and idolatry, despondency and despair among their own people.

To a great extent the prophets of this period lived on the ideas of the earlier prophets, and in particular those of the exilic prophets. Their special characteristics are seen less in original ideas of their own than in certain marked tendencies and in the ways in which they modified the ideas they borrowed.

The sphere of Yahweh's manifestations in history was extended even more than in the previous period. Malachi connects the election of Israel with Yahweh's favouring of Jacob at the cost of Esau, in spite of the fact that they were brothers. He says in Yahweh's name, 'I loved Jacob, but I hated Esau' (i. 2 f.). This choice of Jacob, and in him the people of Israel, was motivated by nothing else than Yahweh's sovereign love. So Malachi could point to a new and solid support for Israel's consciousness of being Yahweh's elect people and of having a right to hope for Yahweh's aid and salvation. In Trito-Isaiah a prophet reminds the people of the fact that the land of Israel was the heritage of Jacob, their father, which Israel might possess and enjoy if they carefully observed the sabbath (Isa. lviii. 13 f.). The significance for post-exilic prophecy of the past history of Israel from its first beginning is impressively reflected in the liturgical composition in Isa. lxiii. 7 ff.

Yahweh is Israel's Father and Maker. Therefore Yahweh is implored not to be exceedingly angry or to remember iniquity for ever (Isa. lxiv. 7 f.; cf. lxiii. 16). On the other hand, in the fact that Israel had a common Father and a common God, who had made them, Malachi sees something that pledged them to strict matrimonial faithfulness (ii. 10 ff.).

The covenant, *berît*, is often mentioned in this period. The term is used in several senses. In Trito-Isaiah there is mention of a new covenant, an everlasting covenant, which Yahweh will make with Israel in the age to come (lxi. 8). This idea is obviously taken over from Jeremiah. The covenant made at Sinai between Yahweh and Israel is alluded to in Deutero-Zechariah when it is said that the restoration of Israel will be carried out because of the blood of the covenant, poured out by Israel in connection with the sacrificial service in the Temple. This sacrificial blood is called 'blood of covenant' as required by

Yahweh in virtue of the old covenant (ix. 11).[217] The term is used in the same sense in Mal. ii. 10, referring to the matrimonial regulations in the law, whereas in *v.* 14 'covenant' seems to mean the special marriage contract. In Isa. lvi. 4 'covenant' simply means the law, the Torah with all its statutes and ordinances. It is said that the eunuchs who keep the sabbaths and hold fast Yahweh's covenant will be blessed by Yahweh. In the curious allegory of the shepherd in Deutero-Zechariah we hear of a staff in the hand of the shepherd that is called 'Grace'. The breaking of this staff signified that the covenant which Yahweh had made with all the peoples was annulled (xi. 7, 10). The covenant with the peoples probably means that during a certain period the peoples were prohibited by Yahweh from attacking the Jewish people.[218] Malachi speaks of the covenant which Yahweh had made with Levi, the ancestor of the priests, a covenant which the priests of his time had corrupted (ii. 4 ff.). The idea of a covenant with Levi is in conformity with passages such as Deut. xviii and xxxiii. 8 ff. Another reference to a covenant made by Yahweh with the Levitical priests occurs in the secondary passage Jer. xxxiii. 17 ff. There we also hear of a covenant with David, containing the promise that David shall never lack a man to sit on the throne of the house of Israel. In the so-called Isaiah Apocalypse we read of a covenant which applies to all mankind, i.e., the general moral order which from earliest times was valid for all peoples and not only for Israel (Isa. xxiv. 5).[219] Some difficulty is raised by the expression *mal'ak berît*, the messenger or angel of the covenant, mentioned in Mal. iii. 1, of whom it is said that Israel delights in him. I share the opinion that there is an allusion here to the covenant between Yahweh and Israel and that the angel of the covenant is identical with the guardian angel of the people of Israel who is mentioned in later documents.[220] Thus in this period the idea of covenant is split up into a variety of senses.

As we have seen above, Deutero-Isaiah frequently used the term

---

[217] The covenant made at Sinai is probably referred to in the somewhat uncertain text of Hag. ii. 5.

[218] Elliger thinks that the original reference was to Yahweh's covenant with the people of Israel. This is not probable. The words in xiii. 8 ff. would not have been formulated in this way if the prophet (who in my view is the speaker in both xi. 4 ff. and xiii. 7 ff.) had imagined that Yahweh's covenant with Israel had been broken. I believe that Sellin and Horst have given the right explanation.

[219] For the explanation of this passage see my book *Die Jesaja-Apokalypse*, pp. 15 f. On the rabbinic doctrine of six commandments for all mankind given to Adam, and the seven commandments given after the flood to Noah for all his descendants, see Moore, *Judaism*, I, pp. 274 f. I hold that Isa. xxiv. 5 expresses a similar idea, using the term 'covenant' for this universal moral law.

[220] Elliger in *ATD*. However, it seems unnecessary to assume that the words about 'the angel of covenant' are a later interpolation.

'servant' to express the relation of Israel to Yahweh. Israel was Yahweh's servant, having been chosen to perform a charge given her by her God. So far as I see, this term has entirely disappeared in our period. In Trito-Isaiah, where we meet so many Deutero-Isaianic ideas, Israel is never called Yahweh's servant, though there are several references to the *servants* of Yahweh in the plural. Foreigners who have joined themselves to Yahweh are called Yahweh's servants (Isa. lvi. 6). The whole of the people of Israel, Israel as a nation, will not be entirely destroyed for Yahweh's servants' sake. These servants of Yahweh are also called Yahweh's chosen and are identical with the faithful group within the people (lxv. 8 f.). They will enjoy the blessings of the age to come, while the idolaters and apostates will perish (*vv.* 13 ff.). Then it will be known that Yahweh's hand is with His servants (lxvi. 14).

This change in the use of the term 'servant' is significant. In the post-exilic period the division of the Jewish people into two different groups, the faithful and the apostates, became even more marked than before. Israel as a people could no longer be called Yahweh's servant; the individual members of the people who were faithful to Yahweh were regarded as Yahweh's servants. The individualization of the Yahweh religion had been taken a step further.

Yahwistic monotheism and the idea of Yahweh as the God of the universe are expressed in new ways in the prophetic literature of the post-exilic period. In Zech. iv. 10 it is said that Yahweh's eyes rove through the whole earth. Different interpretations have been offered of the passage Mal. i. 11: ' "From the rising of the sun to its setting My name is great among the nations, and in every place incense is offered to My name, and a pure offering; for My name is great among the nations," says the Lord of hosts.' I adhere to the view that the reference here is to the monotheistic tendency of pagan religion during the Persian period. Worship of the only God, of the most high God, of the God of heaven, was widespread. This tendency was observed by the Jewish prophet; and he identified the worship of this God with the worship of Yahweh, the God of Israel, regarded as the God of the universe.[221]

The prophetic personality who speaks in Isa. lxvi. 1 f. draws an important conclusion from the idea of Yahweh as the God of the universe. He declares in Yahweh's name, 'Heaven is My throne and the earth is My footstool; what is the house which you will build for

---

[221] Chary, *Les prophètes et le culte à partir de l'exil*, pp. 179 ff., is correct in his view that there is no reference here to syncretism of any kind; but his opinion that the saying refers to the future is precarious.

Me, and what is the place of My rest? All these things My hand has made, and so all these things have come into existence.'[222] The only natural interpretation of these words is that we have here a protest against the rebuilding of the Temple in Jerusalem after the return from the Babylonian exile. Thus we can conclude that there were in the new Jewish community two groups, one which insisted that a Temple should be built, and another which maintained that Yahweh did not need any Temple, because the whole universe was His dwelling-place. Representatives of the former group were the prophets Haggai and Zechariah, the other group had a spokesman in the prophet from whom the saying in Isa. lxvi. 1 derives. The existence of a group of Jews who disapproved of the building of a Temple is evident from the book of Haggai. There the opposition comes from people who for different reasons wanted to postpone the work; here the resistance is founded on religious considerations. The opposition to the building of a Temple did not necessarily imply that all common worship was rejected. It is reasonable to suppose that the Synagogue as an institution and synagogal worship had existed in Palestine since the late monarchic period, or at all events since the Babylonian exile. It is more than probable that the prophet who speaks in Isa. lxvi. 1 f. had Synagogues and synagogal worship in mind when he remonstrated against the rebuilding of the Temple with all the cultic apparatus it would bring in its train.[223]

The problem is not that such a remonstrance should have been uttered in the Jewish community, but rather that it should have been preserved in the prophetic scriptures. This fact can be explained only by a reference to the idea of the authority of the divine word. Our passage in Isa. lxvi. 1 f. is given the form of a solemn divine oracle uttered by a true prophet. As such it was sacrosanct and had an eternal significance. The preservation of an oracle was more important than its coherence with other prophetic sayings.

This negative attitude towards the Temple and its cult was, however, by no means typical of the post-exilic prophets. On the contrary, they held that the Temple with its cult and ceremonial institutions in general were ordained by Yahweh; and accordingly they showed a special interest in them. It is true that the prophets of this period also set before their hearers the ethical demands of Yahweh in accordance with ancient tradition: care for the hungry and poor, for widows, orphans

---

[222] It seems unnecessary to adopt the reading implied by the Septuagint: 'so all these things are mine'. The Hebrew words are only another expression of the creation of the world.

[223] See the important article by Morgenstern, 'The Origin of the Synagogue' in *Studi Orientalistici in onore di Giorgio Levi Della Vida*, II, pp. 192 ff.

and hirelings, impartiality in judgement, kindness, mercy, justice, faithfulness, truth, the fear of God and the like.[224] But more often we find them appealing for a correct performance of the ritual usages prescribed in the ceremonial laws.[225]

We know that after the return the prophets Haggai and Zechariah urged their compatriots to set about erecting a new Temple. In Trito-Isaiah a prophetic voice calls the Temple Yahweh's house of prayer and a prayer house for all peoples (Isa. lvi. 7). The priests are regarded as entrusted with a sublime task. They stand in the service of God (Joel i. 13; ii. 17). In a post-exilic passage in the Book of Jeremiah (xxxiii. 17 ff.) it is said that Yahweh has a covenant with the Levitical priests, who stand in His service. This covenant is as steadfast as the laws of nature: if day and night should fail to come at their appointed time, then also Yahweh's covenant with the Levitical priests will not stand. An ample supply of priests is regarded as a peculiar blessing: as the host of heaven cannot be numbered and the sands of the sea cannot be measured, so Yahweh will multiply the Levitical priests. Because of the exalted position and the great responsibility of the priests, judgement upon them is the more severe if they abuse their position. Malachi rebukes the priests for despising Yahweh's name by offering defective sacrifices and imparting false teaching. Therefore Yahweh will bring shame upon them and cruelly punish them. Nevertheless, this prophet has a high regard for the priestly office as such. It is founded on a covenant with Levi, a covenant guaranteeing him life and šālôm and requiring from him the fear of Yahweh; yet the descendants of Levi have corrupted this covenant. At the last judgement the priests will first be purified and refined till they present right offerings to the Lord.[226]

The laity, too, are reminded of the importance of the sacrificial cult and of correct offerings. A curse is pronounced upon the cheat who has in his flock unblemished animals and yet sacrifices to the Lord what is blemished (Mal. i. 14). But Yahweh hates not only ritually defective offerings but also those brought by men who are defiled by flagrant sins. This was a familiar thought in the pre-exilic prophets. Malachi says that Yahweh cannot accept the offerings of men who had callously divorced their wives (ii. 13 ff.). In Trito-Isaiah there is a threat of severe punishment on men who offer sacrifice to Yahweh, but at the same time secretly observe pagan rites (lxvi. 3 ff.).

---

[224] Isa. xxvi. 2 ff.; lvi. 1 f.; lviii. 6 f.; lix. 3 ff., 13 ff.; lxvi. 2; Joel ii. 13; Zech. vii. 8 ff.; Mal. iii. 5, 20.
[225] For the following cf. Chary, op. cit. This scholar stresses rightly the immense influence of Ezekiel on the cultic theories of the post-exilic prophets.
[226] Mal. i. 6 ff.; ii. 1 ff., 4 ff.; iii. 3.

The offerings of righteous men, presented in accordance with the requirements of the law, are agreeable to Yahweh. Proselytes who have become true worshippers of Yahweh, who keep the sabbath and observe the Torah, are welcome to share in the joyful cult in Jerusalem: their offerings will be accepted on Yahweh's altar (Isa. lvi. 6 f.). Joel regarded it as a terrible disaster that, because of the ravages of the locusts, there were insufficient supplies for the regular offerings (i. 9 ff.). The sacrificial service rightly performed in Jerusalem is regarded as a guarantee that the dispersed Jews will be brought back to the homeland (Zech. ix. 11). One element in the future hope is that there will never be any lack of Levitical priests to present upon the altar burnt offerings, cereal offerings, and sacrifices (Jer. xxxiii. 18).

Other ritual duties are also mentioned. Malachi (iii. 7 ff.) reproaches the people for being negligent in bringing the prescribed contributions to Levites and priests. Thus they robbed God of what belonged to Him and turned away from Him. The characteristic prophetic emphasis is evident here.

The sabbath must be carefully kept. Sometimes observance of the sabbath is mentioned as one of the most important religious duties. 'Blessed is the man', it is said, 'who keeps the sabbath, not profaning it, and keeps his hand from doing any evil' (Isa. lvi. 2), and further: 'To the eunuchs who keep My sabbaths, who choose the things that please Me and hold fast My covenant, I will give in My house and within My walls a monument and a name' (vv. 4 f.). Of the proselytes it is said: 'Everyone who keeps the sabbath, and does not profane it, and holds fast My covenant—these I will bring to My holy mountain and make them joyful in My house of prayer' (vv. 6 f.). The whole people is exhorted: 'If you turn back your foot from the sabbath, from pursuing your own business on My holy day . . . then you shall take delight in Yahweh, and I will make you ride upon the heights of the earth' (lviii. 13 f.).

Passages such as these indicate a development towards the teaching of later Judaism with its emphasis on the sabbath as one of the most conspicuous characteristics of the true Jewish faith.

At a time of the utmost distress Joel proclaims a general fast. But as a true prophet he emphasizes that the fast must be combined with a return to Yahweh with the whole heart (ii. 12 f.). In Trito-Isaiah (Isa. lviii) a post-exilic prophet criticizes the people's fasts. The people ask why they should fast when Yahweh seems to be indifferent. The prophet replies that their fasting is ineffective because in the day of the fast they pursue their own business, oppress the workers, quarrel and fight. Fasting, the prophet says, is not only to bow down one's head like a rush and to spread sackcloth and ashes under oneself. The fast that Yahweh will regard is to let all the oppressed go free and show charity to the poor and defenceless. I do not believe that this prophet's attitude to fasting differs greatly from that of Joel. What he condemns is not fasting in itself (he is no anti-ritualist), but fasting without obedience to the moral commandments of Yahweh. He calls right moral conduct 'true fasting' as something that ought to accompany ritual fasting.

Thus we may conclude that, when the post-exilic prophets speak of ritual usages as indispensable, they always emphasize that they are worthless unless combined with obedience to Yahweh's ethical demands. They differ from the pre-exilic prophets in laying more stress on the ordinances of the ceremonial law; but they are like them in regarding faith in Yahweh and righteousness in social life as indispensable if ritual acts are to be acceptable to Yahweh. Like ritual uncleanness, moral impurity mars cultic acts.

The great interest of the post-exilic prophets in the cult includes an increasing interest in the ceremonial law, written or unwritten, and the ordinances of the law as a whole. In Mal. iii. 22 a written law seems to be meant, but this passage belongs to the late redactional additions to the book of Malachi. If, as has been suggested, the Trito-Isaianic passage Isa. lix. 21 (where it is said that Yahweh's spirit given to Israel and Yahweh's words put in the mouth of the people will never depart from the mouth of the people) refers to the inspired Torah, we would here have interesting evidence of the estimation of the law during this period.[227] But this interpretation of the passage is improbable (cf. above, p. 271).

The ideal of the post-exilic prophets was a perfect community, realizing true faith in Yahweh and unswerving obedience to His commands. But these prophets recognized that their contemporaries fell far short of the ideal. After the return and the establishment of the new community the people were divided into two groups: the true Yahweh believers on the one hand and those who were not recognized as genuine members of the ideal community on the other. The former are called Yahweh's chosen and Yahweh's servants (Isa. lxv. 8 f.). They call upon Yahweh's name; they constitute the remnant which will be saved when judgement comes upon all of those who have turned away from Yahweh (Joel iii. 5). They fear Yahweh's name, and for them the sun of salvation will rise with healing in his wings (Mal. iii. 20). In them election will be fulfilled. Yahweh will say of them, 'They are My people,' and they will answer, 'Yahweh is my God' (Zech. xiii. 8 f.).

[227] So van Imschoot, *Théologie de l'Ancien Testament*, I, p. 187.

The latter group consisted in the first place of people who had adopted pagan cult and beliefs. There are interesting descriptions of such pagan rites and usages in Isa. lvii. 5 ff.; lxv. 3 ff.; lxvi. 3.[228] When Deutero-Zechariah says that Yahweh will cut off the names of the idols from the land (Zech. xiii. 2), this presupposes that idolatry existed in Judah in the post-exilic period, too. Ancient customs such as the use of teraphim, divination, and the cruder kinds of prophecy are attacked by the prophets (Zech. x. 2; xiii. 2 ff.). The group also included those who wantonly violated the ethical commands of Yahweh which had been inculcated by the earlier prophets (see, for instance, Isa. lviii. 3 ff.; lix. 3 ff.; Mal. iii. 5).

The future hope includes the conviction that wicked and apostate Jews will be destroyed. Only pure and righteous men may be members of the community of the age to come. Of the apostates it is said that 'their worm shall not die, their fire shall not be quenched, and they shall be an abhorrence to all flesh' (Isa. lxvi. 24), a reference to the rotting corpses and the funeral pyres in the Valley of Hinnom.

Whereas the pre-exilic prophets had spoken of a judgement to come on the whole nation, it was now thought of as affecting the evil elements in the nation. Their punishment is imagined as a summary catastrophe which will come upon them suddenly. It is described symbolically in the allegorical visions of the flying scroll and the ephah with the woman in Zech. v, and in many other passages. In Zech. xiii. 2 it is said that in the age to come Yahweh will cut off from the land all idolaters and all prophets who have an unclean spirit.

The ideas of such a cleavage within the people and of the summary catastrophe upon the wicked affect the interpretation of a number of post-exilic psalms and other passages from the same period.[229]

After the destruction of the wicked (who are, of course, not a religious party but simply the apostates), those who remain will form a purified community in which the ideal of the elect people will be fulfilled. Since it belongs to the age to come, it is an eschatological community. Many descriptions are given of its excellences: 'Your people shall all be righteous; they shall possess the land for ever, the shoot of My planting, the work of My hands, that I may be glorified' (Isa. lx. 21). 'No evil, no harm will be done in all My holy mountain,' i.e., the land of Israel (lxv. 25). 'In Mount Zion there shall be those who have escaped; and it shall be holy' (Ob. 17).

The purity of the eschatological community will be brought about

---

[228] See Chary, op. cit., pp. 100 ff.
[229] See further Lindblom in *Horae Soederblomianae*, I, 1, pp. 21 ff.

not only by the removal of the unclean members, but also by the purification of those who remain from sin and uncleanness. When in the vision of Zechariah in ch. iii the high priest Joshua is divested of his filthy garments, this symbolizes the purification of the community. It is said that 'on that day there shall be a fountain opened for the house of David and the inhabitants of Jerusalem to cleanse them from sin and uncleanness' (Zech. xiii. 1). The same thought appears in the obscure passage about the people's penitence after having slain an innocent man (xii. 10 ff.), in whom, as I believe, the figure of the suffering servant of the Lord in Isa. liii is reflected.[230] In a single day, it is said, Yahweh will remove the guilt of the land (iii. 9).

All the descriptions of the re-established Israel as cleansed from all evil elements and purified from guilt and sin are strongly theocentric. Yahweh, and Yahweh alone, brings it about. The new community is the shoot of His planting, the work of His hands. He opens the fountain of lustration; He pours out the spirit of repentance; He removes the guilt of the land. The rise of a new Israel is always thought of as a work of Yahweh's wonderful power and His paradoxical love for His elect people.

It is typical of this period that the idea of the purity of the new community has a strongly ritual aspect. It appears in the idea of the fountain, the waters of which will be used for cleansing from sin and uncleanness. Even the bells of the horses will be holy. On them there will be inscribed: 'Holy to Yahweh.' The Temple vessels used for menial service will be as holy as those used for the sprinkling of blood on the altar. Moreover, every vessel in Jerusalem and Judah will be sacred to Yahweh, so that all who sacrifice may come and take of them and boil the flesh of the sacrifice in them (Zech. xiv. 20 f.). In accordance with the ritual ideal, the purified people will be called priests of Yahweh and ministers of God (Isa. lxi. 6).

The holiness will be centred in Jerusalem and the Temple. It is said that Jerusalem will be a holy place where Yahweh will take abode (Joel iv. 17). Yahweh's mountain will be called the holy mountain (Zech. viii. 3). Yahweh will be a wall of fire round about Jerusalem; and His glory will shine within her (ii. 9). Yahweh will reign as a king on Mount Zion; and before His elders He will manifest His glory (Isa.

---

[230] See further Elliger in *ATD*. If the leprous man in Isa. liii is the model of 'him whom they have pierced' in Zech. xii. 10, the former has undergone certain modifications. Instead of a man afflicted by disease we now hear of a murdered man. This does not, of course, rule out the probability that the latter depends on the former, the description of the figure in Isa. liii being very vague and admitting different interpretations. Another example of the use by a later prophet of an earlier mysterious prophecy is Mic. v. 2, which undoubtedly refers to Isa. vii. 14.

xxiv. 23). Of the dispersed Jews it is said that in the age to come they will come and worship Yahweh on the holy mountain at Jerusalem (Isa. xxvii. 13). The proselytes will come to Yahweh's holy mountain and rejoice in Yahweh's house of prayer (lvi. 7). Jerusalem will be called the city of Yahweh, the Zion of the Holy One of Israel (lx. 14).[230a]

In this period there is a greater emphasis than ever before on the spirit of Yahweh. In the remarkable review of Israel's history in Isa. lxiii. 7 ff. the spirit is conceived of as a representative or manifestation of Yahweh on earth. The spirit guided the people through the wilderness and gave them rest in the promised land. By their rebellious acts the people grieved this spirit. The spirit is also thought of as the divine power working in Moses, the great hero of the Exodus (v. 11). This may be appropriately described as an 'extension of Yahweh's personality'.[231]

In particular, great importance is attached to the spirit of Yahweh in the descriptions of the age to come. Ezekiel had seen the spirit as the power which would renew the moral life of the people. In the late passage Isa. xxxii. 15 the spirit is conceived as the power by which nature would be transformed. As the spirit guided the people in the Exodus from Egypt (cf. Isa. lxiii), so according to Haggai (ii. 5) the spirit will abide in the midst of the new community. Zechariah says that the spirit will help Zerubbabel to overcome all difficulties and hindrances and carry through the building of the new Temple (iv. 6). In the vision of the four chariots the spirit brings about the return of the dispersed Jews from Babylonia to their own land to establish a new community (vi. 8).[231a] In Zech. xii. 10 the spirit is regarded as moving men to remorse and repentance. Joel, finally, foresees a general outpouring of the spirit in the age to come. To him the spirit is a spirit of prophecy: 'Your sons and your daughters shall prophesy, your old men shall dream dreams, and your young men shall see visions. Even upon the menservants and maidservants in those days I will pour out my spirit' (iii. 1 ff.).

To understand the increased importance of the spirit in the religious thought of the post-exilic period it is necessary to realize the double tendency in the conception of God which was characteristic of the prophetic preaching at this time. On the one hand there is a tendency to minimize the distance between men and God. As we have seen above, it is often said that in the age to come Yahweh will dwell in Zion, in the

---

[230a] On the sacral significance of Jerusalem as the resting place of the ark see Noth in *OTS*, VIII, 1950, pp. 28 ff.
[231] Cf. Johnson, *The One and the Many*, esp. pp. 17 ff.
[231a] For this interpretation see, for instance, Elliger in *ATD*; cf. Bewer, *The Prophets*, p. 580.

midst of His people. On the other hand the distance between heaven and earth is increased. Yahweh becomes a God 'afar off'. There is, accordingly, a need for intermediaries between God and men. The spirit of Yahweh is such an intermediary. Probably we are right in assuming that post-exilic prophecy was influenced by popular ideas on this point as on others which we have to consider below.

Nature and the cosmic order are included in the transformation which is expected in the age to come. Marvellous fertility and productivity in fields and orchards are predicted. The cattle will graze in spacious pastures. On every mountain there will be streams brimming with water (Isa. xxx. 23 ff.). There will be unprecedented prosperity. Instead of bronze Yahweh will bring gold, instead of iron He will bring silver, instead of wood, bronze, and instead of stones, iron (lx. 17). The threshing floors will be full of grain, and the vats will overflow with wine and oil (Joel ii. 24).

The population of Jerusalem and the land of Israel will be immense. The least one will become a clan and the smallest one a mighty nation (Isa. lx. 22). Jerusalem will be inhabited like unwalled villages in the open land, because of the multitude of men and cattle in it (Zech. ii. 8). The population of the land will be as numerous as of old (x. 8). Death will lose its power in human life. Infant mortality, so familiar in the ancient as in the modern Orient, will be no more. There will be no more any who do not survive to old age (Isa. lxv. 20). Old men and old women will again sit in the streets of Jerusalem, each with staff in hand for very age. The streets of the city will be full of boys and girls playing there (Zech. viii. 4 f.). In Isa. xxv. 8 it is said that Yahweh for ever will 'swallow up' death. I do not believe that the sense is that there will be no death at all in the age to come. The expression must, in my opinion, be explained in the light of the passages just mentioned: nobody will die before he has reached a very great age. In this manner the power of death is really broken. Thus there will no longer be any reason for weeping and wailing.[232]

A further step is taken in Isa. xxvi. 19. Here a divine oracle, answering a national lamentation, declares that the dead will rise and live again. The dead are Israelites who, by a wonderful act of Yahweh, will come to life and repopulate the land of Israel, which is at present so sparsely

---

[232] As regards the covering that is cast over all peoples and the veil that is spread over all nations (Isa. xxv. 7) I believe that they are thought of as tokens of mourning; cf. Lindblom, *Die Jesaja-Apokalypse*, pp. 37 ff. (see, for instance, 2 Sam. xv. 30; xix. 5; Jer. xiv. 3 f.; Esth. vi. 12). On this point I agree with Duhm, Bentzen, Mowinckel in *GTMMM*, Bewer, op. cit., p. 66, Martin-Achard (*De la mort à la résurrection*, p. 104), etc. Other scholars hold that the removal of the veil symbolizes the revelation of Yahweh to the Gentiles (Procksch, Kissane).

inhabited.[233] This passage is unique in the prophetic literature (Daniel must be classed as apocalyptic).

The middle of the sixth century was for the Jewish people a time of ardent expectation. The political upheavals in Persia and Media awoke hopes of the downfall of Babylon, the city of oppression. This expectation sometimes took an eschatological form. The assault on Babylon was, as we have seen, regarded as an incident in a general world catastrophe, heralding the age to come. Descriptions of those events lapsed into fantasy. Popular ideas about the destruction of the world and other cosmic changes were borrowed, partly to give added vividness to the descriptions, partly as essential elements in the prophecies. A typical example is the prophecy on the overthrow of Babylon in Isa. xiii. During our period there were further developments in the interest in an eschatological transformation of the cosmos. In the liturgical Cantata, Isa. xxiv-xxvii, the changes in the cosmic order are strongly emphasized. The windows of heaven are opened and the foundations of the earth tremble. The earth is broken and rent asunder. It staggers like a drunken man and sways like a field-watcher's hut (Isa. xxiv. 18 ff.). The moon will be confounded and the sun ashamed (v. 23). All the host of heaven will rot away and the sky roll up like a scroll. The stars will fall down like leaves falling from the vine or from the fig tree (xxxiv. 4). The earth will quake, the heavens tremble. The sun and the moon will be darkened and the stars withdraw their shining (Joel ii. 10). Sometimes the cosmic changes are depicted as favourable to the holy community of the age to come. Cold and frost will be no more. There will be no alternation of day and night, but a continuous day (Zech. xiv. 6 f.). In such pictures it is of course impossible to distinguish exactly between literal sense and poetic fantasy.

There will also be great geographical changes. The Mount of Olives will be split in two, so that there will be a valley from east to west. Living waters will flow out from Jerusalem, half of them to the eastern sea and half of them to the western sea, continuing in summer as in winter. The whole land will be turned into a plain from Geba to Rimmon in the Negeb (Zech. xiv).[233a]

A constant element in the eschatological drama is the judgement upon the Gentiles and upon all who have rebelled against Yahweh. In

---

[233] See *Die Jesaja-Apokalypse*, pp. 47 ff., 63 ff. Sutcliffe, *The Old Testament and the Future Life*, pp. 128 ff., disputes that this is a reference to a real resurrection. He thinks of a national restoration. He overlooks, however, the connection in form and content between the oracle in v. 19 and what precedes. Martin-Achard thinks rightly of a real resurrection, op. cit., pp. 106 ff.

[233a] For the text see Elliger.

the first place it would come upon Israel's pagan neighbours, who had been their enemies: Moab, Edom, the Philistines, etc., then all the peoples who had scattered them, and, finally, the whole of pagan mankind. Ezekiel's prophecy about the massacre of the armies of Gog in Israel's own land (which probably reflects the defeat of the Assyrians before the walls of Jerusalem as described by Isaiah) is recalled by the idea that Yahweh will gather all the pagan nations in the land of Judah and enter into judgement with them (Joel iv. 2 ff.). Jerusalem will be made a cup of reeling to all the peoples and a heavy stone for all the nations; all who lift it will hurt themselves (Zech. xii. 2 f.). Yahweh will smite all the peoples that wage war against Jerusalem. Their flesh will rot while they are still on their feet; their eyes shall rot in their sockets, and their tongues in their mouths. A popular, half mythological motif is that a panic from Yahweh will fall upon them, so that they begin to fight with each other (xiv. 12 f.).[234] Of this day of judgement upon all pagan nations it is said that it is near at hand (Ob. 15). Leviathan and the dragon in the sea in Isa. xxvii. 1 are probably symbols of the totality of the pagan peoples whom Yahweh will punish. The figures used are taken from Canaanite mythology and are now familiar from the Ugaritic texts. Judgement upon heathen mankind is a constant feature in Isa. xxiv-xxvii and is connected with the downfall of Babylon. In xxiv. 21 f. it is said that the kings of the earth together with 'the host of heaven' will be fettered as prisoners in the Abyss. The kings of the earth are, of course, the monarchs of the kingdoms of the world (cf. Hag. ii. 22). 'The host of heaven' means the celestial powers, the angels or spirits connected with the stars. Accordingly, the world judgement will also include the transcendental beings. That is pure mythology.[235]

From Deutero-Isaiah and other exilic prophets are derived the ideas that the pagan neighbours will be subjugated by the Jews (Isa. xi. 14 ff., sec.); that the captors will bring the exiled Israelites back to the homeland (Isa. lxvi. 20); that treasures from the whole earth will be carried to the land of Israel (Isa. lx. 5 ff.; lxi. 6; Hag. ii. 7); that the oppressors will be slaves of those whom they have oppressed (Isa. lx. 10, 14; lxi. 5; Joel iv. 8; Zech. ii. 13), and that the Jews will take bloody vengeance on their enemies (Ob. 18; Zech. ix. 13 ff.).

[234] I think Elliger is right in regarding Zech. xi. 1-3 as an independent passage referring to the world judgement. The various territories are mentioned to symbolize the pride and the rapacity of the pagan kingdoms (cf. Isa. ii. 10 ff.). Other passages dealing with the same motif are Zech. xii. 6, 9; xiv. 1-3. In xiv. 17-19 we meet with the original idea that the judgement will come upon those among the survivors of the pagan nations who do not go up to Jerusalem to worship Yahweh and celebrate the feast of Tabernacles.
[235] See further Die Jesaja-Apokalypse, pp. 27 f., and Bentzen, Jesaja, I, pp. 206 ff.

Hope of judgement upon the pagan world and of vengeance on Israel's enemies is only one side of the attitude of the post-exilic prophets towards foreign nations. The other is the possibility of their conversion to Yahweh, the God of Israel.

We have pointed out above that the idea of conversion of the Gentiles to the true Yahweh religion was derived from Deutero-Isaiah, to whom this idea was revealed in the period after the occupation of Babylon by the Persians, when the hope was lost of a catastrophic overthrow of the abhorred city and of a triumphal return of the exiled Jews to the homeland. This idea lived on during the post-exilic period and was often proclaimed by the prophets of this period.

Pagan nations will join themselves to Yahweh and become His people, i.e., share the status and the privileges of Israel (Zech. ii. 15). They will seek Yahweh in Jerusalem and entreat His favour (viii. 20 ff.). It is in the light of such sayings that we must understand Isa. xxv. 6: the Gentiles will take part in a sumptuous festal banquet arranged by Yahweh of hosts on the occasion of His enthronement as King of the world. Zech. xiv. 16 expresses the curious idea that after the judgement upon the Gentiles some of them will remain and will make the annual pilgrimage to Jerusalem to worship Yahweh as King and to celebrate the feast of Tabernacles. Sometimes, however, wholehearted conversion is replaced by a more general homage paid to Yahweh. In the age to come the Ethiopians will bring tribute to the God of Israel (Isa. xviii. 7). Sometimes there is only the hope that the Gentiles will see and recognize the glory of Yahweh (Isa. lxvi. 18 f.), a thought which, as we have seen, often appears in the prophecies of Deutero-Isaiah. Sometimes individual nations are specifically referred to, for instance the Egyptians and Syrians. Sublimely it is said in a late interpolation that Egypt and Syria will be blessed by Yahweh as His own peoples together with Israel, His heritage (Isa. xix. 19 ff.). Elsewhere it is said that individual Gentiles will be converted and become proselytes. This idea appears in Isa. lvi. 3 ff. The proselyte who has joined himself to Yahweh is incorporated in the people of Yahweh. If he keeps the sabbath and holds fast the covenant, he is entitled to share in the Temple cult in Jerusalem. The proselytes are so highly esteemed that some of them will be taken as priests and Levites (lxvi. 21).

The holy community was recruited from Jews who returned from Babylonia to the homeland under the guidance of Sheshbazzar and their descendants, from converted heathen, and from Israelites who were dispersed throughout the world. In addition to those already gathered, Yahweh will bring together more and more of the dispersed members of His people. In prophetic imaginative visions they are seen coming from afar. They come flying like clouds, like doves to a dovecote. They will be brought to Jerusalem from all the nations as an offering to Yahweh, upon horses, in chariots, in litters. From Babylonia and Egypt they will come and worship Yahweh on the holy mountain of Jerusalem. Yahweh will release them from the east and from the west and bring them to Jerusalem to be incorporated into His people. He will bring them back because He has compassion on them. They will be as though He had not rejected them. In terms such as these the prophets of our period describe the return of the dispersed members of the elect people.[236]

Similar passages prove that in the post-exilic period the Jewish diaspora was widely scattered throughout the ancient world. Even the northern tribes are included in this hope of a return, the ideal being that in the age to come Ephraim and Judah will be united into one state.[237]

What of the ideal king of the age to come, who played so great a part in the previous period? We know that the prophet Haggai linked the hope of the ideal king to a particular historical person, Zerubbabel, a member of the royal family, a descendant of David. *Ca.* 520 B.C. this Zerubbabel functioned in Jerusalem as a sort of commissioner appointed by the Persian government. To him Haggai addressed his oracle about the urgent need to erect a new Temple; and in obedience to the prophet he started the work. Haggai, who believed that the new age would come after the Temple had been built, regarded Zerubbabel as the man whom Yahweh had destined to be ruler in the coming ideal kingdom. One of his oracles runs: 'On that day, says the Lord of hosts, I will take you, O Zerubbabel, the son of Shealtiel, my servant, and make you like a seal; for I have chosen you' (ii. 23). The seal is one of the most precious objects among a man's possessions (Gen. xxxviii. 18; Cant. viii. 6; Jer. xxii. 24). Yahweh speaks here as the King of heaven. The royal seal attests decisions which are authoritatively promulgated (cf. Esth. iii. 10; viii. 2, 10). Thus the seal is a sign and symbol of the royal power. Yahweh's choice of Zerubbabel meant that he was destined to carry out a commission from Yahweh. Both expressions refer to the Messianic mission of Zerubbabel: his mission to be, in the age to come, the vassal king of Yahweh on the earth.

Zechariah, Haggai's contemporary, also saw in Zerubbabel the man who was destined by Yahweh to be ruler in the ideal kingdom. According

---

[236] Isa. xxvii. 12 f.; lvi. 8; lx. 4 ff.; lxii. 10; lxvi. 20; Joel iv. 7; Zech. vi. 1 ff.; viii. 7 f.; ix. 11 f.; x. 6.
[237] See particularly Isa. xi. 10 ff.; Jer. xxxiii. 23 ff.; Ob. 17 ff.; Zech. ix. 13; x. 6 ff.

to what is probably the original text of Zech. vi. 9 ff., the prophet expresses Zerubbabel's future Messianic status by a description of a coronation.[238] In an oracular utterance he designates him as *ṣemaḥ*, the Branch, manifestly alluding to Jeremiah's oracle: 'I will raise up for David a righteous Branch' (xxiii. 5). He will have a great success; he will complete the building of the Temple and rule in regal splendour. This symbolic action involving Zerubbabel corresponds to a similar action performed for the priest Joshua, namely the presenting to him of the stone with seven eyes (iii. 9). Alongside the Messianic ruler Joshua will function as high priest. These two leaders of the holy community of the age to come are symbolized by the two olive trees in the vision of the lampstand in ch. iv.

The Temple was erected and the cult re-established; but of the fortunes of Zerubbabel we hear nothing more. The first attempt to connect the Messianic hopes with a historical individual seems to have come to nothing. The ideal king of the age to come is mentioned again by a prophet of our period in Deutero-Zechariah. A herald's message is brought to Zion, an exhortation to rejoice because of the advent of the ideal king (Zech. ix. 9 ff.). Attention must be paid to every element in the description of him. He is *ṣaddîk* and *nôšā'*, i.e., successful and victorious; he is *'ānî*, i.e., humble and meek; he rides on an ass; he will entirely pacify Israel; he speaks peace to the nations; his dominion will extend to the ends of the earth. The prophet here employs a number of conventional features to differentiate the king from ordinary earthly rulers. The statement that his dominion will include the whole earth is a conventional feature taken from oriental court style. But it is in peaceful activities that his triumphs will be displayed. Instead of making war upon the peoples, he will speak peaceably to them. Having a wholly peaceful mission to perform he is personally modest and humble, not fierce and boastful. In token of his peaceful task and his meek nature, he rides upon an ass, not upon a charger. Riding on an ass is an archaic feature.[239] But here it is not simply a sign of noble birth and position, but an expression of the king's peaceful and humble nature. This picture of the ideal king has nothing in common with the suffering servant of Yahweh in Isa. liii. Here the prophet is describing the Messianic king in deliberate contrast to the martial rulers of his own age, particularly

---

[238] That the coronation refers to the Messianic kingship of Zerubbabel holds good even on the interpretation suggested by Rignell, that the act was symbolic and that Joshua was crowned with reference to Zerubbabel; see above, p. 171.

[239] In ancient times princes rode on asses: Judges v. 10; x. 4; xii. 14, etc. See further, Köhler, *Kleine Lichter*, pp. 52 ff., and Noth, *Gesammelte Studien zum Alten Testament*, pp. 142 ff.

Alexander the Great, to whom the preceding saying probably refers, exactly as the figure of the servant of Yahweh in Isa. xlii. 1 ff. is presented as a contrast to Cyrus.

The advent of the Messianic king does not, of course, mean the end of history. He is followed on the throne by a series of successors, all of whom will be endowed with supernatural qualities. The house of David, it is said, will be like God, like Yahweh's angel (Zech. xii. 8; cf. Jer. xxxiii. 17 ff.).

The prophets of our period do not often refer to the ideal king of the age to come. In Trito-Isaiah there is no mention of him at all. In the previous period he played a much greater role. The reason for this is, it seems to me, that under the pressure of the Persian supremacy it would have been imprudent to make public the expectations of a coming king. Also the failure of the attempt to make Zerubbabel king in the new community surely contributed to a muting of the Messianic expectations in their monarchic form.

We have noted above the increasingly fantastic forms in which the general hope of a radically new age was expressed. All the events of the new age were summed up in what was called 'Yahweh's day', a designation of the age to come together with everything that would happen during that age (the use of the word 'day' in this sense is characteristically Hebraic). 'The day of Yahweh', or simply 'that day' or 'the day', became a regular *terminus technicus* for the coming age. The origin of this term was discussed above (pp. 317 f.). It is often said that the day is at hand. It comes with terror and destruction for all the enemies of Yahweh but with blessing for all those who submit to His sceptre.

It is said that on that day new heavens and a new earth will come into existence. Isa. lxv. 17: 'Behold, I will create new heavens and a new earth; and the former things shall not be remembered or come into mind.' The new heavens and the new earth which Yahweh will make will remain before Him for ever, lxvi. 22. Such utterances do not mean that this universe will entirely pass away and a totally new universe be created; they simply give forceful expression to the thought that all the conditions of the present age will be altered and that 'etwas ganz anderes', a quite new order, will come into existence. There will be continuity; but at the same time everything will be changed in a way which is often described as a restoration of old conditions, a turning of fortune, a *restitutio in integrum*. There will be a new covenant, Israel will be chosen once more, Paradise and the good old times will come again.[240]

[240] Isa. lxi. 8; lxv. 25; Joel iv. 1; Zech. i. 17; ii. 16; x. 8.

Yahweh's day will come surprisingly and suddenly, as a divine wonder. There are few references to any preparation for it. In Mal. iii. 1 it is said that Yahweh will send a messenger, probably the guardian angel of the people of Israel, to prepare the way before Him, announcing His coming and summoning men to repentance and conversion.[241] The mention of a return of Elijah to carry out a preparatory work before the great and terrible day of Yahweh comes (iii. 23 f.) seems to be a learned interpolation.[242] But Joel speaks of various portents which will herald the coming of the day of Yahweh: there will be blood and fire and columns of smoke; the sun will be turned to darkness, and the moon to blood (iii. 3 f.). Here popular, half mythological elements are included. Such ideas of what will occur before the coming of the great day are rare in the prophetic literature, but appear frequently in apocalyptic.

The following features may be noted as particularly characteristic of prophecy during the Persian period. The scope of the history of the divine revelation is widened, so that the early ancestors of Israel play an even greater part than in the preceding period. Nationalistic tendencies are more marked, e.g., hostility towards foreign nations and attempts to preserve national individuality. The individualization of religion is further developed: the pious and faithful members of the people, for instance, are called 'servants of Yahweh', whereas 'Yahweh's servant' was formerly a designation of Israel as a community. As in the earlier period, there are many references to the conversion of the pagan nations, and also to the proselytization of individuals. Much more stress is laid on the cult, the temple, sacrifice, fasting, the sabbath, etc., than before. Holiness and ceremonial purity are constantly demanded in the prophetic sermons. Perfect holiness (including ritual holiness) belongs to the eschatological ideal for the new community. There is a strong emphasis on the transcendence of Yahweh, the Only God, and on His universal kingdom; and the spirit of Yahweh plays a greater part than before as an intermediary between God and men. On the other hand the ideal king of the age to come has somewhat retired into the background. The cosmos, the natural order, and material blessings all loom larger in the eschatological hope than hitherto. Many popular ideas are here adopted. Eschatology is often enriched by the addition of fanciful mythological details. It must, however, be recognized that in spite of new elements in their teaching the post-exilic prophets may not unfairly be described as epigoni.

[241] Cf. above, p. 405. I think that the *mal'āk* whom Yahweh is about to send and *mal'ak habberît* are identical, both referring to the guardian angel of Israel.
[242] On the late idea of the return of Elijah see Volz, *Die Eschatologie der jüdischen Gemeinde*, pp. 195 ff.

The mere presence of mythological elements does not necessarily mean that any given eschatological saying in the prophetic literature must be classed as apocalyptic. Mythological colouring appears in Hebrew poetry and prophecy of every period. The difference between eschatology and apocalyptic does not lie in the character of the individual ideas employed, but is seen rather in the entire literary character of the two genres. All prophetic sayings which really refer to the age to come, to the new order, may be called eschatological, because their content is eschatological in a prophetic sense. In the apocalyptic writings of later Judaism, a sustained attempt is made to give a coherent and systematic form to eschatological ideas taken over from the prophets and from popular belief, presenting them as *divine secrets* and *mysterious doctrines* concerning history, the cosmos, and the age to come, revealed, as a rule, to personalities of the past, with special authority, and codified in scriptures generally intended to be read by the groups of the initiated.[243] It is of a great importance carefully to distinguish between prophetic eschatology and apocalyptic. The confusion between them which frequently occurs even in learned works arises from the erroneous conception that individual ideas are determinative. What is determinative is general tendency, psychological background, and literary character. In using the term 'apocalyptic ideas' we mean that there are certain ideas which are particularly favoured by the apocalyptists and characteristic of apocalyptic literature, whereas they are missing or uncommon in prophecy proper.

The only book in the Old Testament that may be called an apocalypse is the Book of Daniel, particularly the second part of it. For that reason the Book of Daniel has been excluded from this examination of prophecy proper.

---

[243] See Lindblom in *St.Th.*, vi, 1953, pp. 113 f. Cf. Ringgren's brief but lucid article 'Jüdische Apokalyptik' in *RGG*³, I, cols. 464 ff. See also Rowley, *The Relevance of Apocalyptic*, a very judicious work. Frost, *Old Testament Apocalyptic*, uses the term 'apocalyptic' in a wider sense, in my opinion much too wide. There is in this book no clear distinction between prophetic eschatology and Jewish apocalyptic.

ADDITIONAL NOTES

NOTE I (p. 106, n. 1)

It follows from what is said on pp. 105 ff. that my general view of the psychology of the classical prophets is with certain modifications the same as that maintained by scholars such as Duhm, Gunkel, Hölscher, T. H. Robinson, Mowinckel, and many others. On the opposite side we find, for instance, the Norwegian scholar Ivar Seierstad, who in his book *Die Offenbarungserlebnisse der Propheten Amos, Jesaja und Jeremia* seeks to minimize the supernormal experiences of the prophets in order to emphasize the personal character of prophetic religion. J. Ridderbos, *Profetie en Ekstase*, adopts a similar standpoint. Ridderbos is of the opinion that vocation and what he calls 'inspiration' constitute the essence of prophecy. In prophets other than Ezekiel he acknowledges only 'visionary ecstasy'. But Isaiah says that Yahweh's hand grasped him strongly even when a vision in the strict sense is not mentioned (viii. 11). Why could not other prophets have experiences such as those which Ezekiel had? It is a common mistake to draw unwarranted conclusions from the incomplete evidence of our literary sources. Furthermore, the evidence of modern psychology tells against the view that persons who have ecstatic predispositions can experience ecstasy only in special situations such as visions in the strict sense. Among English-speaking scholars who have opposed the views represented by Hölscher, Robinson, etc., we may mention Buttenwieser (*The Prophets of Israel*) who maintains that 'the inspiration of the great literary prophets has nothing in common with the ecstasy of the prophets of the older type'. Micklem (*Prophecy and Eschatology*) holds that the ecstatic element in prophecy has been exaggerated. He admits that the classical prophets had ecstatic visions (which he wrongly calls 'hallucinations'), but he thinks that this was an infrequent experience. Smith (*The Prophets and Their Times*) holds that 'they were mystics rather than ecstatics.' On the other side Skinner (*Prophecy and Religion*) refers to the 'sub-conscious self' and reminds us of the fact that under strong emotion religious ideas and convictions do sometimes give rise to visual or audible representations which cannot easily be distinguished from sense impressions. He says that there is ample evidence in Christian biography that this is compatible with perfect sanity of mind and balance of judgement. It is along these lines that he understands the experiences of the prophets (p. 12). Paterson (*The Goodly Fellowship of the Prophets*) draws attention to the unparalleled elements in the classical prophets, but emphasizes that 'the boisterous sons of the prophets' are the ancestors of the later classical prophecy (p. 2). On the entire problem see Rowley, 'The Nature of Old Testament Prophecy', *HTR*, xxxviii, 1945, pp. 1 ff. (fully documented); reprinted in *The Servant of the Lord and Other Essays on the Old Testament*. See also Eissfeldt in *OTMS*, pp. 134 ff.—The present writer prefers to avoid the word 'hallucination' as well as the somewhat antiquated term 'sub-conscious'. What characterizes the classical prophets is *inspiration, the extreme form of which is ecstasy*. The great majority of the prophetic revelations are based on experiences of exalted inspiration; but the prophets had more genuinely ecstatic experiences than, e.g., Micklem admits. Although the 'divine action' upon the inner life of the prophets cannot be analysed, there is no ground for denying that God can influence man by way of His 'unconscious self' as well as through his normal consciousness.

NOTE II (p. 160, n. 81).

Of the many scholars who have contributed to this discussion, mention may be made of T. H. Robinson, Nyberg, Birkeland, Engnell, Mowinckel, Widengren, and van der Ploeg. A general survey of the course of the debate is to be found in the article 'The Prophetic Literature' written by Eissfeldt in *OTMS*. There the titles of the relevant books and articles before 1951 are referred to. The first, or, at any rate, one of the first, to state the problem was Gunkel in his 'Einleitungen' in vol. II, 2 of *Die Schriften des Alten Testaments in Auswahl*. Then followed many books and articles by Robinson. Gunkel held that many prophetic oracles were circulated in the form of 'fly-sheets', while Robinson emphasized the oral transmission of the prophetic sayings from generation to generation. Nyberg (*Studien zum Hoseabuche*) went considerably further. He laid a rather one-sided stress on oral transmission and held that only an insignificant number of written documents were handed down from the pre-exilic period. A similar position was adopted by Nielsen (*Oral Tradition*). Birkeland (*Zum hebräischen Traditionswesen*) is often associated with Nyberg's views, but a careful study of his book shows that he emphasizes the parallelism between oral and written transmission (for which he cites Islamic evidence). He holds that the writing down of the oral traditions occurred relatively early. Similar positions are adopted by Mowinckel, Widengren, van der Ploeg (*RB*, liv, 1947, pp. 5 ff.), Ringgren (*St.Th.*, iii, 1949, pp. 34 ff.), and myself (*Bertholet Festschrift*, 1950, pp. 332 ff.). Engnell strongly advocates the application of a traditio-historical method to the prophetic literature, but distinguishes between the liturgical type and the diwan-type, the former having been recorded in writing from the beginning, the latter having been derived from oral transmission. On the Old Testament literature as a whole he maintains the somewhat hazardous opinion of Nyberg that most of our O.T. literature was not committed to writing until the exilic or post-exilic period (*SEÅ*, xii, 1947, pp. 110 ff.; *The Call of Isaiah*, pp. 54 ff.). In this connection mention must be made of the introduction to Morgenstern's *Amos Studies* with its brilliant picture of the process of poetical transmission among modern bedouin.

NOTE III (p. 169, n. 100)

The name is ambiguous, as is frequently the case with cryptic names. People could read different meanings into the name. The question is what the prophet himself meant. From the grammatical construction of the phrase šᵉ'ār yāšûb no positive conclusions can be drawn precisely because of the oracular formulation. Köhler (*VT*, iii, 1953, pp. 84 f.) takes the verbal form as 'einen nackten Relativsatz' (without *'ᵃšer*) and translates: 'der Rest, der umkehrt'. But other explanations are more plausible. In my view both terms are equally significant: there will be a remnant, and this remnant will return. What does this mean? Blank (*JBL*, lxvii, 1948, pp. 211 ff.) suggests that the phrase simply means that only a remnant will come back alive (from some unspecified campaign). Heaton (*JTS*, New Ser., iii, 1952, pp. 27 ff.) agrees substantially with Blank. He says that both elements in the name are ambiguous, but holds that the remnant refers to what was left after some process of physical destruction. Müller (*Die Vorstellung vom Rest im Alten Testament*) thinks of a remnant which will be rescued from a general destruction and then will be converted to faith in Yahweh (pp. 54 ff.). In my view three ideas are involved in the phrase: there will be a destruction, a remnant will be rescued, this remnant will turn to Yahweh (and share in the age to come). Consequently the name contains firstly an announcement of doom, secondly a promise, thirdly an appeal for conversion. I think that this explanation is in agreement with the general view of the national, political, and religious situation which Isaiah had held ever since his prophetic call.

NOTE IV (p. 229, n. 13)

The chronological notices in Ezek. i. 1 ff. contain one of the most discussed problems in the book. Bertholet (in *HAT*) holds that we have to take into account two different stages in Ezekiel's prophetic career. He exercised a prophetic ministry both in Palestine and in Babylonia. Bertholet tries, further, to show that the vision in i-iii consists of two different visionary experiences, one inaugurating Ezekiel's ministry in Palestine, the other his work in Babylonia. Bertholet regards this as the key to the solution of the chronological problem. The fifth year of the exile of King Joiachin (*v.* 2) is the date of the vision in ii. 8-iii. 3, which occurred in Palestine, the thirtieth year is the date of the vision in i. 4 ff., which the prophet saw in Babylonia. Bertholet changes the thirtieth year to the thirteenth year (=585). Bertholet's views were adopted by Steinmann (*Le prophète Ézéchiel*) and before him by Auvray in the *Jerusalem Bible*. His idea of the two visionary experiences is convincingly refuted by Fohrer in *Die Hauptprobleme des Buches Ezechiel*, p. 214, and then by Zimmerli in *BKAT*. The theory that Ezekiel exercised a prophetic ministry in Palestine arises in part from an inadequate recognition of the nature of revelatory experiences. Thus another explanation of the thirtieth year must be found. Fohrer deletes the words as a late insertion (cf. his comment in *HAT*). Zimmerli regards the problem as insoluble, but is inclined to attribute the date to the learned chronological calculations of a later time. Irwin (*The Problem of Ezekiel*, pp. 266 ff.) holds that the thirtieth year is the only authentic date in the book (*v.* 2 being a worthless gloss), and that it refers to Ezekiel's age, while Howie (*The Date and Composition of Ezekiel*), referring to Albright and others, argues that the thirtieth year (of the exile of Joiachin) was the time when Ezekiel first dictated the book to a disciple. Then there must be a lacuna between the two chronological notices, and the text must be rearranged (pp. 40 f. and 91 f.). It may be added that Eissfeldt (*Einleitung*) allows for the possibility that the thirtieth year refers to the age of Ezekiel (p. 445), and that Pfeiffer and Bentzen regard the thirtieth year as a problem for which no satisfactory solution has been offered.

NOTE V (p. 238, n. 22)

The discoverer of 'the Deuteronomistic source' in Jeremiah was Mowinckel (*Zur Komposition des Buches Jeremia*). He assigned about fifteen passages to this source. Most of these, but not all, have a common superscription: 'The word that came to Jeremiah from Yahweh.' They are written in monotonous prose; they reproduce speeches and sermons which abound in characteristic expressions and ideas recalling those typical of Deuteronomy. This source contains several passages which have parallels in the other parts of Jeremiah. Rudolph, who endorses Mowinckel's discovery of 'the Deuteronomistic source', reduces the number of passages to ten in all: vii. 1-viii. 3; xi. 1-14 (17); xvi. 1-13 (18); xvii. 19-27; xviii. 1-12; xxi. 1-10; xxii. 1-5; xxv. 1-14; xxxiv. 8-22; xxxv. This selection of texts does not quite coincide with that of Mowinckel. Rudolph also regards the monotonous mode of expression, the superscriptions, and the Deuteronomistic style as sufficient grounds for the ascription of these passages to a special Deuteronomistic source. He emphasizes that they are not independent compositions, but based on Jeremianic sayings. The reason for my rejection of 'the Deuteronomistic source' is that the entire theory of written 'sources' or 'recensions' presupposes a conception of the growth of the prophetic books which I cannot share. If the prophetic sayings were as a rule orally transmitted and reproduced, it is better to ascribe to one or some of the transmitters the peculiarities which Mowinckel and Rudolph have found in their 'Deuteronomistic source'. It may be noted that in *Prophecy and Tradition* Mowinckel has modified his earlier view. Now he says that no separate literary source existed. There was a circle of tradition within which certain of Jeremiah's sayings were transmitted and transformed according to the Deuteronomistic ideas and stylistic forms (p. 62). With this revision of his theory I am in essential agreement. Eissfeldt also maintains the Jeremianic origin of the Deuterono-mistically coloured passages, but allows for secondary enlargements (*Einleitung*, p. 428). Pfeiffer thinks that Baruch was the originator of the speeches in question. In his view Baruch prepared an edition of the Book of Jeremiah, combining the prophet's book with his own, and revising or rewriting entirely many of his master's speeches in his own Deuteronomistic style (*Introduction*, p. 505). In my opinion the role of Baruch was that of a collector and a scribe rather than of a reviser. This is also the opinion of Fohrer in *TZ*, v, 1949, pp. 401 ff. Fohrer rightly rejects the theory of a Deuteronomistic source, but, in view of the many doublets, it is in my opinion, better to assume a Deuterono-mistically influenced traditionist than a marked 'Deuteronomistic trend' in Jeremiah himself. Even if there is no definite evidence that Jeremiah had disciples like those of Isaiah, he must at all events have had hearers and ad-herents who could hand on his words. Finally, reference may be made to the theory advanced by Miller in his treatise *Das Verhältnis Jeremias und Hesekiels sprachlich und theologisch untersucht*. Miller observes that it is characteristic of the prose sermons of Jeremiah that they show similarities to, but also differences from, the Deuteronomic literature. This fact is to be explained in this way: Jeremiah himself derived the structure and in part the terminology of his sermons from the cultic teaching in the Temple of Jerusalem, on which Deuter-onomy itself is modelled. This may sometimes have been the case. But generally it is better to assign the Deuteronomistic stamp to the traditionist or traditionists of the Jeremianic revelations. On this problem see also Hyatt in *JNES*, i, 1942, pp. 156 ff. Hyatt's view is that the Book of Jeremiah, as we now have it, received expansion and redaction at the hands of 'Deuteronomic' editors, whose purpose in part was to claim for Deuteronomy the sanction of the great prophet. The same problem is discussed in a very sound way by Bright in *JBL*, lxx, 1951, pp. 15 ff.

NOTE VI (p. 263, n. 75)

As a background to what I have to say in the sequel it may be appropriate to recall some modern theories concerning the composition of the Book of Ezekiel and its authorship. Two parallel recensions of the book, one deriving from the prophet himself and written in the first person style, were combined by a redactor (Kraetzschmar). After the death of Ezekiel his book (written by himself) circulated in several varying 'editions' and were later combined by the Jewish scribes into one authoritative text (Budde). The book consists of numerous individual passages and collections, produced by Ezekiel himself during his prophetic career, and subsequently combined into one whole (Herrmann). In the first place the poetical passages, relatively few in number, were composed by Ezekiel; but the bulk of the book, which is in the form of prose and in its general character displays affinities with the late Torah-literature, derives from much later hands (Hölscher). Prophecies delivered by Ezekiel in Jerusalem were edited by a redactor living in exile and given a Babylonian setting (Herntrich). The book contains prophecies delivered partly in Judah and partly in Babylonia. Its primary material consisted of loose leaves left behind by Ezekiel himself. Later hands brought this material together. The doublets are in many cases the result of the prophet's revisions of his own drafts. Numerous passages are additions or parallels appended by redactional hands (Bertholet). Ezekiel, working partly in Judah and partly in Babylonia, collected and wrote down his prophecies in three volumes. Our present book has been edited and arranged by redactors who were active in the period 560-444 (Pfeiffer). Various secondary collections of Ezekiel's relatively few prophecies (from both Jerusalem and Babylonia) were used by a later editor. Many generations of pious Jews made additions and composed commentaries and comments on comments; and by this process the book as we have it was produced, so that it is a child of Judaism (Irwin). Ezekiel himself wrote down his speeches and actions. They were never orally transmitted. The doublets are to be explained by the fact that the prophet returned more than once to the same theme. He also made additions. Other hands composed individual collections and then the entire book (Fohrer). From the first person style and from investigations of the literary types and some stylistic peculiarities it is concluded that Ezekiel himself collected and wrote down his sayings in a book. Later more material was added, which had originally formed no part of the original book (von Rabenau). Two works were composed by Ezekiel himself in the first person style. In addition he left behind a number of sermons and poems which were combined by another hand with the memoirs. Secondary passages and expansions were added later (Eissfeldt). A critical discussion of the problems connected with the Book of Ezekiel and a copious list of works relating to these problems are to be found in Rowley, 'The Book of Ezekiel in Modern Study', BJRL, xxxvi, 1, 1953, pp. 146 ff.

NOTE VII (p. 400, n. 212)

In 'The Servant of the Lord in Deutero-Isaiah' (SOTP, pp. 187 ff.) Snaith denies the existence of a universalistic missionary tendency in Deutero-Isaiah. He says that this prophet is essentially nationalistic in outlook, and that he is responsible for the narrow and exclusive attitude of the post-exilic age. The whole prophecy is concerned with the restoration and exaltation of Israel, the servant of the Lord, and any place which the heathen have in the new order is entirely and debasingly subservient. de Boer, *Second-Isaiah's Message* (*OTS*, XI) follows the same lines. He maintains that the texts do not allow us to assume that Yahweh's servant had a world-wide missionary task. Foreign nations, this eminent scholar says, are mentioned only as peoples to be conquered, into whose hands the cup of wrath will be put; or as the instrument of Yahweh's deliverance of His people; or, as it is rhetorically expressed, to be witnesses of Yahweh's glory, which will be shown only in the elect people, raised up from death to life (p. 90). In Second-Isaiah's message all is relative to one event, the experience of the exiles. The Gentiles are impressed by Yahweh's wonderful deeds, but there is no mention of a conversion of the pagan peoples to Yahweh. de Boer is quite right in strongly emphasizing the significance which the deliverance of the Jews has for the Gentiles in the teaching of Deutero-Isaiah. He says, summarizing: 'Everyone who sees the redemption of the Judaean people, even great nations, kings and princes, will be astonished and will respect it as a wonderful salvation' (p. 92). But is that really sufficient? Both scholars mentioned above arrive at their results by a somewhat original but sometimes hazardous exegesis of the relevant passages. xlii. 1 ff., for instance, is taken to mean no more than that the Gentiles will discern Yahweh's justice and judgement as manifested in the redemption of the exiles. What the coastlands wait for is Yahweh's mighty act for His own people. In xlv. 22-25, v. 22 refers to all the scattered Israelites throughout the pagan world, v. 23 to the humble subservience of the Gentiles (Snaith). It seems to me that the exegetical interpretations given by Snaith and de Boer are often forced and unconvincing, so that I am not ready to give up my own position in this respect. The universal mission of Israel does not of course consist in a 'swarming off in the whole world' to bring a missionary message from one point to all the ends of the earth (de Boer, p. 100). The conversion of the pagan nations is conceived of as a divine wonder of an eschatological nature, and Israel is involved only as an instrument in Yahweh's hand by witnessing and suffering. In my view all the relevant passages taken together point in the direction of a wonderful change in the pagan world, consisting in real conversion to the God of Israel. Is not the conversion of the pagan nations a familiar idea in prophecy after Deutero-Isaiah? Snaith as well as de Boer says that the universalistic interpretations presented by myself and many other scholars, though with considerable variations, are due to the prejudice that there is missionary universalism in Deutero-Isaiah. It would be equally correct to say that their own interpretation depends on their idea that the prophet was a consistent nationalist. de Boer says that if the interpretation which ascribes a world-wide missionary task to the servant is right, we must recognize the presence of a *corpus alienum* in Deutero-Isaiah. This remark lacks cogency if I am right in maintaining that the nationalistic outlook belongs to the earlier period of the prophet's career, the universalistic view to the time after 539.

NOTE VIII (p. 400, n. 213)

The debate about the identity of the servant in the Servant Songs has for the most part been concerned with the question whether the servant is an individual or a community, or, possibly, both. This discussion can be traced back to the earliest times. See above all North, *The Suffering Servant in Deutero-Isaiah*, 1948, and then the more recent studies: Rowley, *The Servant of the Lord*,

1952 (pp. 3-57); Cazelles, 'Les poèmes du Serviteur' in *RSc.R.*, xliii, 1955 (pp. 5-25); Mowinckel, *He that Cometh*, 1956, (pp. 187-257); de Leeuw, *De Ebed Jahweh-profetieen*, 1956; Zimmerli and Jeremias, *The Servant of God*, 1957. Reference should also be made to Eissfeldt's *Einleitung*[2] (pp. 402-13). Apart from the purely individualistic interpretations with their many ingenious attempts to explain the different elements in the figure, many attempts have been made in recent years to combine the individual and the collective interpretation. The servant has been identified with Israel (in various senses) and at the same time with the ancestor of the people, with the prophet himself, with an unknown historical personality, and with the Messianic king or some other future representative of the people. Some of these theories seem to be vague, far-fetched, and unrealistic. A distinction is not always made between the figures which might have served as models for the *picture* of the servant and *the servant himself* as a historical reality. In my opinion the most attractive solution on this line is given by Wheeler Robinson in his important study 'The Hebrew Conception of Corporate Personality', mentioned above. According to Robinson the figure of the servant varies in the different songs. But the reconciliation of the individualistic view and the collective view lies in the idea of corporate personality, according to which the individual comprises and represents the group, and the group lives in the individual member. 'In the light of this conception', says Robinson, 'the Servant can be both the prophet himself as representative of the nation, and the nation whose proper mission is actually being fulfilled only by the prophet and that group of followers who may share his views' (p. 59).

In my opinion, however, the problem may be solved in another way. I regard as a fact that the figures described in the Songs are conceived as individuals and, further, that they are different in different Songs. To begin with the latter point, it is clear to me that the figure in the second Song and that in the third Song are the prophet himself. Why else should the hero of these Songs speak in the first person? To this question a satisfactory answer has never been given by scholars who deny that the prophet is speaking. If the prophet is the speaker, we have here only one example among hundreds in the prophetic literature of the appearance of a prophet in an autobiographical speech. The first and the fourth Song are creations of the imagination, 'revelatory fancies', as it were. In the fourth Song the hero is a leprous and pious man who bears his suffering for the benefit of others, in the first Song he mostly resembles a vassal-king or vicegerent, who extends the rule of his royal Lord among the nations of the world. What does the prophet mean to convey by these figures? The purely individualistic interpretation is in my opinion bound up with insoluble difficulties, which have often been demonstrated. Very popular is the view that the figures in question are simply 'personifications' of Israel in one sense or another. I prefer to say that the figures described are *symbols* for the faithful Israel in exile, and that what is related of them is allegorically applied to the situation and task of Israel in this sense. In symbols and in allegorical speech there is no question of any absolute identity of figure and reality. Symbols and allegorical or parabolical speeches have a certain independence in relation to that which they symbolize and represent. Only certain leading features are to be taken into consideration. Finally it is characteristic of allegories that the reality symbolized often breaks through the figurative speech. The narrator forgets, as it were, his part. There are several instances of this in the Servant Songs. That the prophet should have taken his own person and his personal experiences as symbols and as an allegory of Israel and her life, is by no means unique. Hosea took his private matrimonial history as a symbol of the relation of Israel to her God. Against my attempt to explain the Servant Songs it has been objected that the allegorical character of the pictures ought to have been better expressed. It is, however, to be remembered that we have the Songs only in the form given them in tradition. Originally the allegorical character might very well have been more accentuated.

LIST OF ABBREVIATIONS

AAA   *Acta Academiae Aboensis*
AASF   *Annales Academiae Scientiarum Fennicae*
AB   *The Complete Bible. An American Translation*
Act.Or.   *Acta Orientalia*
ACUT   *Acta et Commentationes Universitatis Tartuensis (Dorpatensis)*
AfO   *Archiv für Orientforschung*
AJSLL   *American Journal of Semitic Languages and Literatures*
ALBO   *Analecta Lovaniensia biblica et orientalia*
Alt Festschrift. Geschichte und Altes Testament (BHT, 16), Tübingen, 1953
ANET   *Ancient Near Eastern Texts Relating to the Old Testament*[2], edited
     by J. B. Pritchard, Princeton, 1955
ANVAO   *Avhandlinger utgitt av Det Norske Videnskaps-Akademi i Oslo*
AOF   *Altorientalische Forschungen*
AOr.   *Archiv Orientální*
ATA   *Alttestamentliche Abhandlungen*
ATANT   *Abhandlungen zur Theologie des Alten und Neuen Testaments*
ATD   *Das Alte Testament Deutsch*
AV   *The Holy Bible. Authorized Version*
BASOR   *Bulletin of the American Schools of Oriental Research*
Bertholet Festschrift. Festschrift Alfred Bertholet zum 80. Geburtstag gewidmet,
     Tübingen, 1950
BET   *Beiträge zur evangelischen Theologie*
BFCh.Th.   *Beiträge zur Förderung christlicher Theologie*
BH   *Biblia Hebraica*[3], edited by R. Kittel, Stuttgart, 1937
BHT   *Beiträge zur historischen Theologie*
BJRL   *Bulletin of the John Rylands Library*
BKAT   *Biblischer Kommentar. Altes Testament* (Neukirchen)
BSAW   *Berichte über die Verhandlungen der sächsischen Akademie der*
     Wissenschaften zu Leipzig
Buhl Festschrift. Studier tilegnede Professor, Dr. phil. og theol. Frants Buhl i
     Anledning af hans 75 Aars Födselsdag den 6 September 1925, København,
     1925
BWANT   *Beiträge zur Wissenschaft vom Alten und Neuen Testament*
BWAT   *Beiträge zur Wissenschaft vom Alten Testament*
BZAW   *Beihefte zur Zeitschrift für die alttestamentliche Wissenschaft*
EI   *Enzyklopaedie des Islam*
Eissfeldt Festschrift 1947. Festschrift Otto Eissfeldt zum 60. Geburtstage 1.
     September 1947 dargebracht, Halle (Saale), 1947
Eissfeldt Festschrift 1957. Von Ugarit nach Qumran. Beiträge zur Alttestament-
     lichen und Altorientalischen Forschung, Berlin, 1958.
ET   *Expository Times*
FFC   *Folklore Fellows Communications*, publ. by the Finnish Academy of
     Science
FRLANT   *Forschungen zur Religion und Literatur des Alten und Neuen Testa-*
     ments

Ges.-Kautzsch. Gesenius, W., and Kautzsch, E., Hebräische Grammatik[27], Leipzig, 1902

GTMMM Det Gamle Testament, oversatt av S. Michelet, S. Mowinckel og N. Messel, Oslo, 1929 ff.

HAT   Handbuch zum Alten Testament

HAW   Handbuch der Altertumswissenschaft, begründet von I. v. Müller

HKAT   Handkommentar zum Alten Testament

HS   Horae Soederblomianae, Travaux publiés par la Société Nathan Söderblom

HSAT   Die Heilige Schrift des Alten Testaments, edited by E. Kautzsch, 4th edition by A. Bertholet, I-II, Tübingen, 1922-23

HTR   The Harvard Theological Review

HUCA   Hebrew Union College Annual

ICC   The International Critical Commentary

JBL   Journal of Biblical Literature

Jerusalem Bible. La sainte Bible, traduite en français sous la direction de l'École biblique de Jérusalem, Paris, 1949 ff.

JNES   Journal of Near Eastern Studies

JSS   Journal of Semitic Studies

JTS   The Journal of Theological Studies

KATSl.   Kommentar zum Alten Testament, edited by E. Sellin

KHKAT   Kurzer Handkommentar zum Alten Testament

Kittel Festschrift. Alttestamentliche Studien Rudolf Kittel zum 60. Geburtstag dargebracht (BWAT, 13), Leipzig, 1913

LD   Lectio divina, Paris, 1946 ff.

LSS   Leipziger Semitische Studien

LUÅ   Lunds universitets årsskrift

LVT   Köhler, L., Baumgartner, W., Lexicon in Veteris Testamenti libros, Leiden, 1953

MGWJ   Monatshefte zur Geschichte und Wissenschaft des Judentums

MO   Le monde oriental

Mowinckel Festschrift. Interpretationes ad Vetus Testamentum pertinentes Sigmundo Mowinckel septuagenario missae, Oslo, 1955

MVAG   Mitteilungen der Vorderasiatisch-aegyptischen Gesellschaft

Ne.TT   Nederlands Theologisch Tijdschrift

NGWG   Nachrichten der Gesellschaft der Wissenschaften zu Göttingen

Nötscher Festschrift. Alttestamentliche Studien Friedrich Nötscher zum Geburtstage 19. Juli 1950 gewidmet (Bonner biblische Beiträge, 1), Bonn, 1950

OTMS   The Old Testament and Modern Study. A Generation of Discovery and Research, edited by H. H. Rowley, Oxford, 1951

OTS   Oudtestamentische Studiën

RB   Revue biblique

RGG   Die Religion in Geschichte und Gegenwart[3], Tübingen, 1957 ff.

RHPh.   Revue d'histoire et de philosophie religieuses

RHR   Revue de l'histoire des religions

RoB   Religion och Bibel. Nathan Söderblom-sällskapets årsbok

RSc.R   Recherches de science religieuse

RSPT   Revue des sciences philosophiques et théologiques

RSV   The Holy Bible. Revised Standard Version

RTPh.	*Revue de théologie et de philosophie*
SATA	*Die Schriften des Alten Testaments in Auswahl*
SBBA	*Sitzungsberichte der Deutschen Akademie der Wissenschaften zu Berlin*
SBT	*Studies in Biblical Theology*
SBU	*Svenskt bibliskt uppslagsverk*
SEÅ	*Svensk exegetisk årsbok*
SHR	*Studies in the History of Religion*
SJT	*Scottish Journal of Theology*
SKGG	*Schriften der Königsberger Gelehrten Gesellschaft*
SM	*Scripta minora Reg. Societatis humaniorum litterarum Lundensis*
SNVAO	*Skrifter utgitt av Det Norske Videnskaps-Akademi i Oslo*
Söderblom	*Festschrift. Till Ärkebiskop Söderbloms sextioårsdag 15. 1. 1926, Stockholm, 1926*
SOFSO	*Societas orientalis fennica. Studia orientalia*
SOTP	*Studies in Old Testament Prophecy presented to Professor T. H. Robinson, 1946, Edinburgh, 1950*
SSR	*Scandinavian Scientific Review*
STK	*Svensk teologisk kvartalskrift*
St.Th.	*Studia theologica cura ordinum theologorum Scandinavicorum edita*
SVSK	*Skrifter udgivne af Videnskabsselskabet i Kristiania*
SVT	*Supplements to Vetus Testamentum*
TEH	*Theologische Existenz heute*
Th.St.	*Theologische Studien* (Zürich)
TLZ	*Theologische Literaturzeitung*
TSK	*Theologische Studien und Kritiken*
TWBNT	*Theologisches Wörterbuch zum Neuen Testament*
TZ	*Theologische Zeitschrift*
UUÅ	*Uppsala universitets årsskrift*
VT	*Vetus Testamentum*
WO	*Die Welt des Orients*
ZAW	*Zeitschrift für die alttestamentliche Wissenschaft*
ZDMG	*Zeitschrift der Deutschen Morgenländischen Gesellschaft*
ZNW	*Zeitschrift für die neutestamentliche Wissenschaft*
ZRP	*Zeitschrift für Religionspsychologie*
ZS	*Zeitschrift für Semitistik*
ZST	*Zeitschrift für systematische Theologie*
ZTK	*Zeitschrift für Theologie und Kirche*

BIBLIOGRAPHY

ACHELIS, T., *Die Ekstase in ihrer kulturellen Bedeutung*, Berlin, 1902.
AKIANDER, M., *Historiska upplysningar om religiösa rörelserna i Finland i äldre och senare tider*, I-VII, Helsingfors, 1857-63.
ALBRIGHT, W. F., *From the Stone Age to Christianity*[2], Baltimore, 1946.
'New Light on Early Recensions of the Hebrew Bible', *BASOR*, 140, 1955, pp. 27 ff.
'The High Place in Ancient Palestine', *SVT*, IV, Leiden, 1957, pp. 242 ff.
'The Psalm of Habakkuk', *SOTP*, pp. 1 ff.
'The Son of Tabeel (Isaiah 7, 6)', *BASOR*, 140, 1955, pp. 34 f.
ALLEGRO, J. M., 'The Meaning of the Phrase šeṭūm hā'ayin in Num. xxiv. 3, 15', *VT*, iii, 1953, pp. 78 f.
ALLWOHN, A., *Die Ehe des Propheten Hosea in psychoanalytischer Beleuchtung* (*BZAW*, 44), Giessen, 1926.
ALPHANDÉRY, P., 'Prophètes et ministère prophétique dans le moyen-âge latin', *RHPh.*, xii, 1932, pp. 334 ff.
ALT, A., 'Das Gottesurteil auf dem Karmel', *Kleine Schriften*, II, pp. 135 ff.
'Das Königtum in den Reichen Israel und Juda', *Kleine Schriften*, II, pp. 116 ff.
'Der Stadtstaat Samaria', *Kleine Schriften*, III, pp. 258 ff.
'Die Ursprünge des israelitischen Rechts', *Kleine Schriften*, I, pp. 278 ff.
'Hosea 5, 8-6, 6. Ein Krieg und seine Folgen in prophetischer Beleuchtung', *Kleine Schriften*, II, pp. 163 ff.
'Jesaja 8, 23-9, 6. Befreiungsnacht und Krönungstag', *Kleine Schriften*, II, pp. 206 ff.
Kleine Schriften zur Geschichte des Volkes Israel, I-III, München, 1953-59.
'Micha 2, 1-5', *Mowinckel Festschrift*, pp. 13 ff; *Kleine Schriften*, III, pp. 373 ff.
AMANDRY, P., *La mantique apollinienne à Delphes*, Paris, 1950.
ANDERSON, G. W., 'A Study of Micah 6, 1-8', *SJT*, iv, 1951, pp. 191 ff.
The Prophetic Gospel. Studies in the Servant Songs, London, 1952.
ANDRAE, T., *Mohammed. The Man and his Faith*. Transl. by T. Menzel, London, 1936.
Mystikens psykologi, Stockholm, 1926.
ARBMAN, E., 'Shamanen, extatisk andebesvärjare och visionär', in: Å. Hultkrantz, *Primitiv religion och magi*, Stockholm, 1955, pp. 49 ff.
BACHT, H. 'Wahres und falsches Prophetentum', *Biblica*, xxxii, 1951, pp. 237 ff.
BALLA, E., art. 'Habakkuk', *RGG*[2], II, 1928, cols. 1556 f.
BARDTKE, H., 'Jeremia der Fremdvölkerprophet', *ZAW*, liii, 1935, pp. 209 ff.; liv, 1936, pp. 240 ff.
BATTEN, L. W., 'Hosea's Message and Marriage', *JBL*, xlviii, 1929, pp. 257 ff.
BAUMANN, E., 'Der linnene Schurz Jer. 13, 1-11', *ZAW*, lxv, 1953, pp. 77 ff.
'Die Hauptvisionen Hesekiels', *ZAW*, lxvii, 1955, pp. 56 ff.
BAUMGARTNER, W., *Die Klagegedichte des Jeremia* (*BZAW*, 32), Giessen, 1917.
BEGRICH, J., *Studien zu Deuterojesaja* (*BWANT*, 4. Folge, 25), Stuttgart, 1938.

BÉGUERIE, P., 'La vocation d'Isaïe', *Études sur les prophètes d'Israël* (*LD*, 14), pp. 11 ff., Paris, 1954.

BENTZEN, A., *Introduction to the Old Testament*[2], I-II, Copenhagen, 1952.

Jesaja, I, *Jes. 1-39*, København, 1944.

'The Ritual Background of Amos i, 2-ii, 16', *OTS*, VIII, 1950, pp. 85 ff.

'Zur Erläuterung von Jesaja 5, 1-7', *AfO*, iv, 1927, pp. 209 ff.

BERTHOLET, A., *Hesekiel* (*HAT*), Tübingen, 1936.

BEWER, J. A., 'Das Datum in Hes. 33, 21', *ZAW*, liv, 1936, pp. 114 ff.

'Textkritische Bemerkungen zum Alten Testament', *Bertholet Festschrift*, pp. 65 ff.

The Prophets, New York and London, 1957.

BIČ, M., 'Zur Problematik des Buches Obadja', *SVT*, I, Leiden, 1953, pp. 11 ff.

BIETENHARD, H., art. ὄνομα in *TWBNT*, V.

BILLING, E., *De etiska tankarna i urkristendomen*, Uppsala, 1907; 2nd ed., Stockholm, 1936.

BIRGITTA, *Revelationes caelestes s. Birgittae suecae*, Monachii, 1680.

Revelationes extravagantes; see Hollman.

BIRKELAND, H., *Zum hebräischen Traditionswesen. Die Komposition der prophetischen Bücher des Alten Testaments* (*ANVAO*, II, 1938), Oslo, 1938.

BLANK, S. E., 'The Current Misinterpretation of Isaiah's *she'ar yashub*', *JBL*, lxvii, 1948, pp. 211 ff.

DE BOER, P. A. H., *De Voorbede in het Oude Testament* (*OTS*, III), Leiden, 1943.

Second-Isaiah's Message (*OTS*, XI), Leiden, 1956.

BÖHL, F. M. T. DE LIAGRE, 'Profetisme en plaatsvervangend lijden in Assyrië en Israël', *Ne.TT*, iv, 1949-50, pp. 81 ff., 161 ff.

BOMAN, T., *Das hebräische Denken im Vergleich mit dem griechischen*, Göttingen, 1952. [Eng. Trans.: *Hebrew Thought Compared with Greek*, London, 1960].

BRÄUNLICH, E., 'Beiträge zur Gesellschaftsordnung der arabischen Beduinenstämme', *Islamica*, vi, 1934, pp. 68 ff., 182 ff.

BREMOND, H., *Histoire littéraire du sentiment religieux en France*, I-XI, Paris, 1916-36.

BRIGHT, J., 'The Date of the Prose Sermons of Jeremiah', *JBL*, lxx, 1951, pp. 15 ff.

BRILIOTH, Y., *Den senare medeltiden* (Holmquist, H., and Pleijel, H., *Svenska kyrkans historia*, II), Stockholm, 1941.

BROCKELMANN, C., *Hebräische Syntax*, Neukirchen, 1956.

BROWN, J. P., *The Darvishes or Oriental Spiritualism*, ed. by H. A. Rose, London, 1927.

BROWNLEE, W. H., 'The Text of Isaiah vi, 13 in the Light of DISa', *VT*, i, 1951, pp. 296 ff.

BUBER, M., *Ekstatische Konfessionen*, Jena, 1909.

'Falsche Propheten', *Die Wandlung*, ii, 1946-47, pp. 277 ff.

Hasidism, New York, 1948.

The Prophetic Faith. Transl. from the Hebrew by C. Witton-Davies, New York, 1949.

BUDDE, K., 'Der Abschnitt Hosea 1-3 und seine grundlegende religionsgeschichtliche Bedeutung', *TSK*, xcvi-xcvii, 1925, pp. 1 ff.

Geschichte der althebräischen Litteratur, Leipzig, 1909.

Jesajas Erleben: Eine gemeinverständliche Auslegung der Denkschrift des Propheten (Kap. 6, 1-9, 6), Gotha, 1928.

BUHL, F., *Jesaja oversat og fortolket*[2], Köbenhavn, 1912.

VON BULMERINCQ, A., *Die Immanuelsweissagung (Jes.* 7) *im Lichte der neueren Forschung (ACUT*, B, 37), Tartu, 1935.

BUTTENWIESER, M., *The Prophets of Israel*, London, 1914.

CANAAN, T., *Aberglaube und Volksmedizin im Lande der Bibel*, Hamburg, 1914.

CAUSSE, A., *Du groupe ethnique à la communauté religieuse. Le problème sociologique de la religion d'Israël*, Paris, 1937.

CAZELLES, H., 'Les poèmes du Serviteur. Leur place, leur structure, leur théologie', *RSc.R*, xliii, 1955, pp. 5 ff.

ČERNÝ, L., *The Day of Yahweh and some Relevant Problems*, Prague, 1948.

CHARY, T., *Les prophètes et le culte à partir de l'exil*, Paris, 1955.

COPPENS, J., 'L'histoire matrimonial d'Osée. Un nouvel essai d'interprétation', *Nötscher Festschrift*, Bonn, 1950, pp. 38 ff.

La prophétie de la 'Almah (ALBO, ser. II, 35), Gembloux, 1952.

COSSMANN, W., *Die Entwicklung des Gerichtsgedankens bei den alttestamentlichen Propheten (BZAW*, 29), Giessen, 1915.

CRAMER, K., *Amos. Versuch einer theologischen Interpretation (BWANT*, 3. Folge, 15), Stuttgart, 1930.

CRIPPS, R. S., *A Critical and Exegetical Commentary on the Book of Amos*, London, 1955.

CROOK, M. B., 'A Suggested Occasion for Isaiah 9, 2-7 and 11, 1-9', *JBL*, lxviii, 1949, pp. 213 ff.

CUMMING, C. G., *The Assyrian and Hebrew Hymns of Praise*, New York, 1934.

DALMAN, G., *Arbeit und Sitte in Palästina*, I-VII, Gütersloh, 1928-42.

DANELL, G. A., *Studies in the Name Israel in the Old Testament*, Uppsala, 1946. 'Var Amos verkligen en nabi?', *SEÅ*, xvi, 1951, pp. 7 ff.

DELACROIX, H., *Études d'histoire et de psychologie du mysticisme*, Paris, 1908.

DENTAN R. C. (editor), *The Idea of History in the Ancient Near East (American Oriental Series*, 38), New Haven and London, 1955.

DHORME, É., *Recueil Édouard Dhorme. Études bibliques et orientales*, Paris, 1951.

DIETRICH, E. L., *Schûb schebût. Die endzeitliche Wiederherstellung bei den Propheten (BZAW*, 40), Giessen, 1925.

DONNER, K., *Bei den Samojeden in Sibirien.* Aus dem Schwedischen übersetzt und herausgegeben von W. H. v.d. Mülbe, Stuttgart, 1926.

VAN DORSSEN, J. C. C., *De derivata van de stam 'mn in het Hebreeuwsch van het Oude Testament*, Amsterdam, 1951.

DREYFUS, F., 'La doctrine du reste d'Israël chez le prophète Isaïe', *RSPT*, xxxix, 1955, pp. 361 ff.

DRIVER, G. R., 'Two misunderstood Passages of the Old Testament', *JTS*, New Series, vi, 1955, pp. 82 ff.

Canaanite Myths and Legends, Edinburgh, 1956.

'Difficult Words in the Hebrew Prophets', *SOTP*, pp. 52 ff.

DUCHESNE-GUILLEMIN, J., *The Hymns of Zarathustra, being a Translation of the Gâthâs together with Introduction and Commentary.* Transl. from the French by Mrs. M. Henning, London, 1952.

Zoroastre. Étude critique avec une traduction commentée des Gâthâ, Paris, 1948.

DUHM, B., *Das Buch Jeremia erklärt* (*KHKAT*), Tübingen and Leipzig, 1901.
Das Buch Jesaia übersetzt und erklärt[3] (*HKAT*), Göttingen, 1914.
Israels Propheten[2], Tübingen, 1922.
DÜRR, L., *Die Wertung des göttlichen Wortes im Alten Testament und im antiken Orient* (*MVAG*, 42, 1), Leipzig, 1938.
Ursprung und Ausbau der israelitisch-jüdischen Heilandserwartung, Berlin, 1925.
EHRLICH, E. L., *Der Traum im Alten Testament* (*BZAW*, 73), Berlin, 1953.
EICHRODT, W., *Das Gottesbild des Alten Testaments*, Stuttgart, 1956.
Theologie des Alten Testaments, I-III, Leipzig, 1933-1939 (Vol. I[5], 1957).
EISLER, R., 'Das Qainzeichen und die Qeniter', *MO*, xxiii, 1929, pp. 48 ff.
EISSFELDT, O., *Der Gott Karmel* (*SBBA*, Kl. für Sprachen, Literatur und Kunst. Jahrg. 1953, 1), Berlin, 1953.
'Die Komposition der Bileam-Erzählung', *ZAW*, lvii, 1939, pp. 212 ff.
Einleitung in das Alte Testament[2], Tübingen, 1956.
'Silo und Jerusalem', *SVT*, IV, Leiden, 1957, pp. 138 ff.
'The Prophetic Literature', *OTMS*, pp. 115 ff.
ELIADE, M., *Le chamanisme et les techniques archaïques de l'extase*, Paris, 1951.
ELLIGER, K., *Das Buch der zwölf kleinen Propheten*, II (*ATD*), Göttingen, 1950.
ENGNELL, I., articles in *SBU*.
'Profetia och tradition. Några synpunkter på ett gammaltestamentligt centralproblem', *SEÅ*, xii, 1947, pp. 110 ff.
'Profetismens ursprung och uppkomst. Ett gammaltestamentligt grundproblem,' *RoB*, viii, 1949, pp. 1 ff.
Studies in Divine Kingship in the Ancient Near East, Uppsala, 1943.
The Call of Isaiah. An Exegetical and Comparative Study (*UUÅ*, 1949: 4), Uppsala, 1949.
FAHLGREN, K. H., *ṣᵉdāḳā, nahestehende und entgegengesetzte Begriffe im Alten Testament*, Uppsala, 1932.
FASCHER, E., ΠΡΟΦΗΤΗΣ. *Eine sprach- und religionsgeschichtliche Untersuchung*, Giessen, 1927.
FOGELKLOU, E., *Birgitta*[2], Stockholm, 1955.
FOHRER, G., *Die Hauptprobleme des Buches Ezechiel* (*BZAW*, 72), Berlin, 1952.
Die symbolischen Handlungen der Propheten (*ATANT*, 25), Zürich, 1953.
Elia (*ATANT*, 31), Zürich, 1957.
Ezechiel (*HAT*), Tübingen, 1955.
'Jeremias Tempelwort, 7, 1-15', *TZ*, v, 1949, pp. 401 ff.
'Umkehr und Erlösung beim Propheten Hosea', *TZ*, xi, 1955, pp. 161 ff.
FROST, S. B., 'Eschatology and Myth' *VT*, ii, 1952, pp. 70 ff.
Old Testament Apocalyptic. Its Origin and Growth, London, 1952.
FUCHS, K., *Die alttestamentliche Arbeitergesetzgebung im Vergleich zum Cod. Hammurapi, zum altassyrischen und hethitischen Recht*, Heidelberg, 1935.
GALLING, K., *Biblisches Reallexikon*, Tübingen, 1937.
'Der Gott Karmel und die Ächtung der fremden Götter', *BHT*, 16 (*Alt Festschrift*), Tübingen, 1953, pp. 105 ff.
'Die Ausrufung des Namens als Rechtsakt in Israel', *TLZ*, lxxxi, 1956, cols. 65 ff.
Die Erwählungstraditionen Israels (*BZAW*, 48), Giessen, 1928.
'Die Exilswende in der Sicht des Propheten Sacharja', *VT*, ii, 1952, pp. 18 ff.

GERLEMAN, G., 'Hesekielsbokens Gog', *SEÅ*, xii, 1947, pp. 148 ff.
'Till den gammaltestamentliga utkorelsetankens symbolik', *STK*, xxii, 1946, pp. 242 ff.
Zephanja textkritisch und literarisch untersucht, Lund, 1942.
GESE, H., *Der Verfassungsentwurf des Ezechiel* (*BHT*, 25), Tübingen, 1957.
GESENIUS, W., and KAUTZSCH, E., *Hebräische Grammatik*[27], Leipzig, 1902.
GIESEBRECHT, F., *Die Berufsbegabung der alttestamentlichen Propheten*, Göttingen, 1897.
GLUECK, N., *Das Wort ḥesed im alttestamentlichen Sprachgebrauche* (*BZAW*, 47), Giessen, 1927.
GOLDZIHER, I., *Abhandlungen zur arabischen Philologie*, I, Leiden, 1896.
GÖTZE, A., *Kleinasien* in: *Kulturgeschichte des Alten Orients* (*HAW*, III, 1:3.3, 1), München, 1957, pp. 146 ff.
GRAHAM, W. C., *The Prophets and Israel's Culture*, Chicago, 1934.
GRANQVIST, H., *Birth and Childhood among the Arabs. Studies in a Muhammedan Village in Palestine*, Helsingfors, 1947.
GRESSMANN, H., *Der Messias* (*FRLANT*, 43), Göttingen, 1929.
Die älteste Geschichtsschreibung und Prophetie Israels (*SATA*, II, 1[2]), Göttingen, 1921.
Der Ursprung der israelitisch-jüdischen Eschatologie (*FRLANT*, 6), Göttingen, 1905.
GRETHER, O., *Name und Wort Gottes im Alten Testament* (*BZAW*, 64), Giessen, 1934.
GUILLAUME, A., *Prophecy and Divination among the Hebrews and other Semites*, London, 1938.
GUNKEL, H., 'Der Micha-Schluss. Zur Einführung in die literaturgeschichtliche Arbeit am Alten Testament', *ZS*, ii, 2, 1924, pp. 145 ff.
'Einleitungen', in *SATA*[2], II, 2, pp. IX ff.
'Jesaja 33, eine prophetische Liturgie', *ZAW*, xlii, 1924, pp. 177 ff.
GUTHE, H., 'Der Prophet Hosea' in *HSAT*[4], II, Tübingen, 1923.
GYLLENBERG, R., 'Till julevangeliets exeges', *SEÅ*, v, 1940, pp. 83 ff.
HALDAR, A., *Associations of Cult Prophets among the Ancient Semites*, Uppsala, 1945.
Studies in the Book of Nahum (*UUÅ*, 1946:7), Uppsala, 1947.
HAMMERSHAIMB, E., *Amos*, København, 1946.
'The Immanuel Sign', *St.Th.*, iii, 1949, pp. 124 ff.
HÄNEL, J., *Das Erkennen Gottes bei den Schriftpropheten* (*BWAT*, Neue Folge, 4), Stuttgart, 1923.
HARPER, W. R., *Amos and Hosea* (*ICC*), Edinburgh, 1905.
HARVA, see HOLMBERG-HARVA.
HAUER, J. W., *Die Religionen*, Stuttgart, 1923.
VON HAUFF, W., *Sexualpsychologisches im Alten Testament*, Bonn, 1924.
HAEUSSERMANN, F., *Wortempfang und Symbol in der alttestamentlichen Prophetie. Eine Untersuchung zur Psychologie des prophetischen Erlebnisses* (*BZAW*, 58), Giessen, 1932.
HEATON, E. W., 'The Root š'r and the Doctrine of the Remnant', *JTS*, New Ser., iii, 1952, pp. 27 ff.

HEILER, F., *Prayer. A Study in the History and Psychology of Religion*. Eng. Trans. by S. McComb and J. E. Park, London, 1932.
'Der Gottesbegriff der Mystik', *Numen*, i, 1954, pp. 161 ff.
HEITMÜLLER, W., '*Im Namen Jesu*' (*FRLANT*, I, 2), Göttingen, 1903.
HEMPEL, J., *Altes Testament und Geschichte*, Gütersloh, 1930.
Das Ethos des Alten Testaments, Berlin, 1938.
Die althebräische Literatur und ihr hellenistisch-jüdisches Nachleben, Wildpark-Potsdam, 1930.
Die Mehrdeutigkeit der Geschichte als Problem der prophetischen Theologie (*NGWG*, NF, *Fachgruppe* V, i, 1, 1936).
'Glaube, Mythos und Geschichte im Alten Testament', *ZAW*, lxv, 1953, pp. 109 ff.
Gott und Mensch im Alten Testament[2], Stuttgart, 1936.
'Vom irrenden Glauben', *ZST*, vii, 1929-30, pp. 631 ff.
HENTSCHKE, R., *Die Stellung der vorexilischen Schriftpropheten zum Kultus* (*BZAW*, 75), Berlin, 1957.
HERNTRICH, V., *Der Prophet Jesaja. Kap. 1-12* (*ATD*), Göttingen, 1950.
Ezechielprobleme (*BZAW*, 61), Giessen, 1932.
HERRMANN, J., *Ezechielstudien* (*BWAT*, 2), Leipzig, 1908.
Ezechiel übersetzt und erklärt (*KATSl.*), Leipzig, 1924.
HERRMANN, S., 'Die Königsnovelle in Ägypten und in Israel', *Wissenschaftliche Zeitschrift der Karl Marx-Universität Leipzig, Gesellschafts- und sprachwiss. Reihe*, 3 Jahrg. 1953/54, 1, pp. 51 ff.
HERTZBERG, H. W., *Prophet und Gott* (*BFCh.Th*, 28, 3), Gütersloh, 1933.
HESCHEL, A., *Die Prophetie*, Krakow, 1936.
HESSE, F., 'Am. 5, 4-6. 14 f.', *ZAW*, lxviii, 1956, pp. 1 ff.
Die Fürbitte im Alten Testament, Hamburg, 1951.
Das Verstockungsproblem im Alten Testament (*BZAW*, 74), Berlin, 1955.
HESSEN, J., *Platonismus und Prophetismus. Die antike und die biblische Geisteswelt in strukturvergleichender Betrachtung*, München, 1939.
HOLLMANN, L. *Den Heliga Birgittas reuelaciones extrauagantes* (*Samlingar utgivna av Svenska Fornskriftsällskapet*. Ser. 2, Latinska skrifter. Band V), Uppsala, 1956.
HOLMBERG-HARVA, U., *Die religiösen Vorstellungen der altaischen Völker* (*FFC*, 125), Helsinki, 1938.
Die religiösen Vorstellungen der Mordwinen (*FFC*, 142), Helsinki, 1952.
HÖLSCHER, G., *Die Profeten. Untersuchungen zur Religionsgeschichte Israels*, Leipzig, 1914.
Hesekiel, der Dichter und das Buch (*BZAW*, 39), Giessen, 1924.
HORST, F., *Die zwölf kleinen Propheten. Nahum bis Maleachi* (*HAT*), Tübingen, 1938.
HOSCHANDER, J., *The Priests and Prophets*, New York, 1938.
HOWIE, C. G., *The Date and Composition of Ezekiel* (*JBL, Monograph Series*, 4), Philadelphia, 1950
HUMBERT, P., 'Essai d'analyse de Nahoum 1, 2-2, 3', *ZAW*, xliv, 1926, pp. 266 ff.
'Les trois premiers chapitres d'Osée, *RHR*, lxxvii, 1918, pp. 157 ff.
HYATT, J. P., 'Jeremiah and Deuteronomy', *JNES*, i, 1942, pp. 156 ff.
Prophetic Religion, New York and Nashville, 1947.
'The Translation and Meaning of Am. 5, 23-24', *ZAW*, lxviii, 1956, pp. 17 ff.

Hylander, I., 'War Jesaja ein Nabi?', *MO*, xxv, 1931, pp. 53 ff.

van Imschoot, P., 'L'esprit de Jahvé, source de vie dans l'Ancien Testament', *RB*, xliv, 1935, pp. 481 ff.
Théologie de l'Ancien Testament, Tournai, I-II, 1954-56.

Inge, W. R., *Christian Mysticism*, London, 1899.

Irwin, W. A., 'Ezekiel Research since 1943', *VT*, iii, 1953, pp. 54 ff.
The Problem of Ezekiel, Chicago, 1943.
'The Psalm of Habakkuk', *JNES*, i, 1942, pp. 10 ff.

Jacob, E., *Théologie de l'Ancien Testament*, Neuchâtel and Paris, 1955. [Eng. Trans. *Theology of the Old Testament*, London, 1958.]

Jacob, G., *Altarabische Parallelen zum Alten Testament*, Berlin, 1897.
Beiträge zur Kenntnis des Derwisch-Ordens der Bektaschis (Türkische Bibliothek, 9), Berlin, 1908.

Jacobi, W., *Die Ekstase der alttestamentlichen Propheten (Grenzfragen des Nerven- und Seelenlebens, 108)*, München, 1920.

Janssen, E., *Juda in der Exilszeit. Ein Beitrag zur Frage der Entstehung des Judentums (FRLANT, Neue Folge, 51)*, Göttingen, 1956.

Jastrow, M., *Die Religion Babyloniens und Assyriens*, I, Giessen, 1905.

Jenni, E., *Die politischen Voraussagen der Propheten (ATANT, 29)*, Zürich, 1956.

Jepsen, A., 'Kleine Beiträge zum Zwölfprophetenbuch', II, *ZAW*, lvii, 1939, pp. 242 ff III, *ZAW*, lxi, 1945-48, pp. 95 ff.
Nabi. Soziologische Studien zur alttestamentlichen Literatur und Religionsgeschichte, München, 1934.

Jeremias, J., see Zimmerli.

Jirku, A., *Altorientalischer Kommentar zum Alten Testament*, Leipzig, 1923.

Johansson, N., *Parakletoi. Vorstellungen von Fürsprechern für die Menschen vor Gott in der alttestamentlichen Religion, im Spätjudentum und Urchristentum*, Lund, 1940.

Johnson, A. R., 'Hesed and Hāsîd', *Mowinckel Festschrift*, pp. 100 ff.
The Cultic Prophet in Ancient Israel, Cardiff, 1944.
The One and the Many in the Israelite Conception of God, Cardiff, 1942.
'The Primary Meaning of g'l', *SVT*, I, Leiden, 1953, pp. 67 ff.

Jones, D., 'The Traditio of the Oracles of Isaiah of Jerusalem', *ZAW*, lxvii, 1955, pp. 226 ff.

Jørgensen, J. J., *Saint Bridget of Sweden*. Transl. by I. Lund, London, 1954.

Julian of Norwich, *Revelations of Divine Love*[13], edited by G. Warrack, London, 1952.

Junker, H., *Prophet und Seher in Israel. Eine Untersuchung über die ältesten Erscheinungen des israelitischen Prophetentums, insbesondere der Prophetenvereine*, Trier, 1927.
'Ursprung und Grundzüge des Messiasbildes bei Isajas', *SVT*, IV, Leiden, 1957, pp. 181 ff.

Kandinsky, V., *Kritische und klinische Betrachtungen im Gebiete der Sinnestäuschungen*, Berlin, 1885.

Kapelrud, A. S., *Central Ideas in Amos (SNVAO, II, 1956, 4)*, Oslo, 1956.
'Cult and Prophetic Words', *St.Th.*, iv, 1951-52, pp. 5 ff.
Joel Studies, Uppsala, 1948.

KELLER, C. A., *Das Wort OTH als 'Offenbarungszeichen Gottes'. Eine philologisch-theologische Begriffsuntersuchung zum Alten Testament*, Basel, 1946.

KISSANE, E. J., *The Book of Isaiah*, I-II, Dublin, 1941-43.

KITTEL, R., *Geschichte des Volkes Israel*, II⁷, Gotha, 1925.

KLEIN, W. C., *The Psychological Pattern of Old Testament Prophecy*, Evanston, 1956.

KLOSTERMANN, A., 'Ezechiel. Ein Beitrag zu besserer Würdigung seiner Person und seiner Schrift', *TSK*, l., 1877, 3, pp. 391 ff.

KNIGHT, H., *The Hebrew Prophetic Consciousness*, London, 1947.

KOCH, R., *Geist und Messias. Beitrag zur biblischen Theologie des Alten Testaments*, Wien, 1950.

KÖHLER, L., *Deuterojesaja (Jesaja 40-55) stilkritisch untersucht* (*BZAW*, 37), Giessen, 1923.

Kleine Lichter. Fünfzig Bibelstellen erklärt, Zürich, 1945.

Old Testament Theology. Transl. by A. S. Todd, London, 1957.

'Syntactica', II, *VT*, iii, 1953, pp. 84 f.

'Zum Verständnis von Jes. 7, 14', *ZAW*, lxvii, 1955, pp. 48 ff.

KÖHLER, L., BAUMGARTNER, W., *Lexicon in Veteris Testamenti libros*, Leiden, 1953.

KRAELING, E. G., 'The Immanuel Prophecy', *JBL*, l, 1931, pp. 277 ff.

KRAETZSCHMAR, R., *Das Buch Ezechiel* (*HKAT*), Göttingen, 1900.

KRAUS, H.-J., *Die Königsherrschaft Gottes im Alten Testament. Untersuchungen zu den Liedern von Jahwes Thronbesteigung* (*BHT*, 13), Tübingen, 1951.

Gottesdienst in Israel. Studien zur Geschichte des Laubhüttenfestes (*BET*, 19), München, 1954.

Prophetie und Politik (*TEH*, N.F., 36), München, 1952.

KUHL, C., *Israels Propheten*, Bern, 1956. [Eng. Trans.: *The Prophets of Israel*, Edinburgh, 1960.]

LANDSBERGER, B., *Der kultische Kalender der Babylonier und Assyrier* (*LSS*, 6), Leipzig, 1943.

LAUHA, A., *Zaphon. Der Norden und die Nordvölker im Alten Testament* (*AASF*, B. XLIX, 2), Helsinki, 1943.

DE LEEUW, V., *De Ebed Jahweh-profetieen. Historisch-kritisch onderzoek naar hun ontstaan en hun betekenis*, Assen, 1956.

LESLIE, E. A., *Jeremiah. Chronologically arranged, translated and interpreted*, New York and Nashville, 1954.

LEUBA, J. H., *The Psychology of Religious Mysticism*, London, 1925.

LINDBLOM, J., *A Study on the Immanuel Section in Isaiah*, Isa. vii, 1-ix, 6 (*SM*, 1957-1958: 4), Lund, 1958.

Das ewige Leben. Eine Studie über die Entstehung der religiösen Lebensidee im Neuen Testament, Uppsala, 1914.

'Der Eckstein in Jes. 28, 16', *Mowinckel Festschrift*, pp. 123 ff.

'Der Kessel in Jer. 1, 13 f.', *ZAW*, lxviii, 1956, pp. 223 f.

'Det offentliga talet i det gamla Israel', *Buhl Festschrift*, pp. 112 ff.

'Det solliknande ögat. En religionshistorisk skiss till ett litterärt motiv', *STK*, iii, 1927, pp. 230 ff.

'Die "Eschatologie" des 49. Psalms', *HS*, I, 1, Stockholm, 1944, pp. 21 ff.

'Die Gesichte der Propheten', *Studia theologica*, I, Riga, 1935, pp. 7 ff.

Die Jesaja-Apokalypse. Jes. 24-27 (*LUÅ*. N.F.I, 34, 3), Lund and Leipzig, 1938.

Die literarische Gattung der prophetischen Literatur. Eine literargeschichtliche Untersuchung zum Alten Testament (*UUÅ*, 1924, Teologi. 1), Uppsala, 1924.
'Die Religion der Propheten und die Mystik', *ZAW*, lvii, 1939, pp. 65 ff.
'Ecstasy in Scandinavian Christianity', *ET*, lvii, 1946, pp. 236 ff.
'Einige Grundfragen der alttestamentlichen Wissenschaft', *Bertholet Festschrift*, pp. 325 ff.
Genom öknen till Sinai, Stockholm, 1930.
'Gibt es eine Eschatologie bei den alttestamentlichen Propheten?', *St.Th.*, vi, 1952, pp. 79 ff.
'Historieskrivningen i Israel och dess ställning inom forntidens hävdateckning', *STK*, xi, 1935, pp. 211 ff.
Hosea literarisch untersucht (*AAA*, Hum., V), Åbo, 1927.
Micha literarisch untersucht (*AAA*, Hum., VI: 2), Åbo, 1929.
'Profetforskningens metod. Tillika ett bidrag till frågan om profetisk och mystisk fromhet', *Söderblom Festschrift*, Stockholm, 1926, pp. 314 ff.
Profetismen i Israel, Stockholm, 1934.
'The Political Background of the Shiloh Oracle', *SVT*, I, Leiden, 1953, pp. 78 ff.
The Servant Songs in Deutero-Isaiah. A New Attempt to Solve an Old Problem (*LUÅ*, N.F.I., 47, 5), Lund, 1951.
'Wisdom in the Old Testament Prophets', *SVT*, III, Leiden, 1955, pp. 192 ff.
'Zur Frage des kanaanäischen Ursprungs des altisraelitischen Prophetismus', *Eissfeldt Festschrift* 1957.
LINDHAGEN, C., *The Servant Motif in the Old Testament. A Preliminary Study to the 'Ebed Yahweh Problem in Deutero-Isaiah*, Uppsala, 1950.
LODS, A., *Histoire de la littérature hébraïque et juive depuis les origines jusqu'à la ruine de l'état juif*, Paris, 1950.
Israël des origines au milieu du VIIIᵉ siècle, Paris, 1932. [Eng. Trans. *Israel from its Beginnings to the Middle of the Eighth Century*, London, 1932.]
Les prophètes d'Israël et les débuts du judaisme, Paris, 1935. [Eng. Trans. *The Prophets and the Rise of Judaism*, London, 1937.]
'Une tablette inédite de Mari, intéressante pour l'histoire ancienne du prophétisme sémitique, *SOTP*, pp. 103 ff.
LOFTHOUSE, W. F., 'Ḥen and Ḥesed in the Old Testament', *ZAW*, li, 1933, pp. 29 ff.
MAAG, V., *Text, Wortschatz und Begriffswelt des Buches Amos*, Leiden, 1951.
MACDONALD, D. B., art. 'Derwish' in EI.
MARTIN-ACHARD, R., *De la mort à la résurrection d'après l'Ancien Testament*, Neûchatel and Paris, 1956. [Eng. Trans. *From Death to Life. A Study of the Development of the Doctrine of the Resurrection in the Old Testament*, Edinburgh, 1960.]
McKENZIE, J. L., 'Knowledge of God in Hosea', *JBL*, lxxiv, 1955, pp. 22 ff.
MEEK, J. T., *Hebrew Origins*, New York, 1936. 2nd. ed. 1950. 3rd. ed. 1960.
MERKEL, R. F., *Die Mystik im Kulturleben der Völker*, Hamburg, 1940.
MEYER, E., *Die Israeliten und ihre Nachbarstämme*, Halle, a.S., 1906.
MICKLEM, N., *Prophecy and Eschatology*, London, 1926.
MILLER, J. W., *Das Verhältnis Jeremias und Hesekiels sprachlich und theologisch untersucht mit besonderer Berücksichtigung der Prosareden Jeremias*, Assen, 1955.

MOORE, G. F., *Judaism in the first Centuries of the Christian Era, the Age of the Tannaim*, I-III, Cambridge, Mass., 1927-30.

MORGENSTERN, J., *Amos Studies*, I-III, Cincinnati, 1941.

'Isaiah 63, 7-14', *HUCA*, xxiii, 1950-51, pp. 185 ff.

'Jerusalem—485 B.C.', *HUCA*, xxvii, 1956, pp. 101 ff.

'The Origin of the Synagogue', *Studi Orientalistici in onore di Giorgio Levi Della Vida*, Vol. II, Roma, 1956, pp. 192 ff.

'The Universalism of Amos', *Essays Presented to Leo Baeck on the Occasion of his Eightieth Birthday*, London, 1954, pp. 106 ff.

MOWINCKEL, S., 'Der Ursprung der Bil'āmsage', *ZAW*, xlviii, 1930, pp. 233 ff.

Die Erkenntnis Gottes bei den alttestamentlichen Propheten, Oslo, 1941.

'Ecstatic Experience and Rational Elaboration in Old Testament Prophecy', *Act. Or.*, xiii, 1935, pp. 264 ff.

He that Cometh. Transl. by G. W. Anderson, Oxford, 1956.

Jesaja-Disiplene. Profetien fra Jesaja til Jeremia, Oslo, 1926.

Offersang og Sangoffer, Oslo, 1951. [Eng. Trans. *The Psalms in Israel's Worship*. Trans. by D. ap-Thomas, Oxford, 1962.]

Profeten Jesaja. En Bibelstudiebok, Oslo, 1925.

Prophecy and Tradition. The Prophetic Books in the Light of the Study of the Growth and History of the Tradition (*ANVAO*, II, 1946, 3), Oslo, 1946.

Psalmenstudien, II. *Das Thronbesteigungsfest Jahwäs und der Ursprung der Eschatologie* (*SNVAO*, II, 1921, 6), Kristiania, 1922.

Psalmenstudien, III, *Kultprophetie und prophetische Psalmen* (*SNVAO*, II, 1922, 1), Kristiania, 1923.

'The Spirit and the Word in the Pre-exilic Reforming Prophets', *JBL*, liii, 1934, pp. 199 ff.

'Zum Psalm des Habakuk', *TZ*, ix, 1953, pp. 1 ff.

Zur Komposition des Buches Jeremia (*SVSK*, Hist.-fil. Kl., 5), Kristiania, 1914. See also *GTMMM*.

MULDER, E. S., *Die Teologie van die Jesaja-Apokalipse. Jesaja 24-27*, Groningen and Djakarta, 1954.

MÜLLER, V., *En Syrie avec les bédouins*, Paris, 1931.

MÜLLER, W. E., *Die Vorstellung vom Rest im Alten Testament*, Leipzig, 1939.

MUNCH, P. A., *The Expression bajjôm hahū, is it an Eschatological Terminus technicus?* (*ANVAO*, II, 1936, 2), Oslo, 1936.

MURRAY, G., *The Oresteia, translated into English Rhythmic Verse*, London, 1946.

MURTONEN, A., 'The Prophet Amos — a Hepatoscoper?', *VT*, II, 1952, pp. 170 ff.

MUSIL, A., *The Manners and Customs of the Rwala Bedouins* (*American Geographical Society, Oriental Explanations and Studies*, 6), New York, 1928.

NEHER, A., *Amos. Contribution à l'étude du prophétisme*, Paris, 1950.

L'essence du prophétisme, Paris, 1955.

NEUFELD, E., *Notes on Hittite Laws* (*A.Or.*, xviii, 4), Prague, 1950, pp. 116 ff.

NIELSEN, E., *Oral Tradition. A Modern Problem in Old Testament Introduction* (*SBT*, 11), London, 1954.

'The Righteous and the Wicked in Habaqquk', *St.Th.*, vi, 1952, pp. 54 ff.

NILSSON, M. P., *Geschichte der Griechischen Religion*, I²-II (*HAW*, V, 2), München, 1955, 1950.

NORTH, C. R., *The Old Testament Interpretation of History*, London, 1946.
    The Suffering Servant in Deutero-Isaiah. An Historical and Critical Study,
    London, 1948.
NOTH, M., *Amt und Berufung im Alten Testament*, Bonn, 1958.
    Das System der zwölf Stämme Israels (*BWANT*, 4. Folge, I), Stuttgart,
    1930.
    Gesammelte Studien zum Alten Testament, München, 1957.
    Geschichte Israels, Göttingen, 1950.
    'History and the Word of God in the Old Testament', *BJRL*, xxxii, 1949-50,
    pp. 194 ff.
    'Jerusalem und die israelitische Tradition', *OTS*, VIII, 1950, pp. 28 ff.
    Überlieferungsgeschichte des Pentateuch, Stuttgart, 1948.
    Überlieferungsgeschichtliche Studien, I (*SKGG*, 18. Jahrg. Geisteswiss. Kl. 2),
    Halle (Saale), 1943.
NOWACK, W., *Die kleinen Propheten übersetzt und erklärt*[2] (*HKAT*), Göttingen,
    1903.
NYBERG, H. S., 'Deuteronomium 33, 2-3', *ZDMG*, xcii, 1938, pp. 320 ff.
    Die Religionen des alten Iran. Deutsch von H. H. Schaeder (*MVAG*, 43),
    Leipzig, 1938.
    Hebreisk grammatik, Uppsala, 1952.
    Hoseaboken. Ny översättning med anmärkningar (*UUÅ*, 1941:7, 2), Uppsala,
    1941.
    'Smärtornas man. En studie till Jes. 52, 13-53, 12', *SEÅ*, vii, 1942, pp. 5 ff.
    *Studien zum Hoseabuche. Zugleich ein Beitrag zur Klärung des Problems der
    alttestamentlichen Textkritk* (*UUÅ*, 1935: 6), Uppsala, 1935.
NYSTRÖM, S., *Beduinentum und Jahwismus. Eine soziologisch-religionsgeschicht-
    liche Untersuchung zum Alten Testament*, Lund, 1946.
ODEBERG, H., *Trito-Isaiah (Isaiah 56-66). A Literary and Linguistic Analysis*
    (*UUÅ*, 1931, Teologi, I), Uppsala, 1931.
OLSSON, B., 'Die verschlungene Buchrolle', *ZNW*, xxxii, 1933, pp. 90 f.
ÖSTBORN, G., *Tōrā in the Old Testament. A Semantic Study*, Lund, 1945.
OESTERLEY, W. O. E., *The Sacred Dance. A Study in Comparative Folklore*,
    Cambridge, 1923.
OESTERREICH, T., *Die Besessenheit*, Langensalza, 1921.
OTTO, R., *Aufsätze das Numinose betreffend*, Gotha, 1929.
OTTO, W., *Priester und Tempel im hellenistischen Ägypten*, I-II, Leipzig and
    Berlin, 1905-08.
PATERSON, J., *The Goodly Fellowship of the Prophets. Studies, Historical,
    Religious and Expository, in the Hebrew Prophets*, New York, 1948.
PEDERSEN, J., *Der Eid bei den Semiten in seinem Verhältnis zu verwandten Er-
    scheinungen sowie die Stellung des Eides im Islam* (*Studien zur Geschichte und
    Kultur des islamischen Orients*, 3), Strassburg, 1914.
    Israel. Its Life and Culture, I-II, London and Copenhagen, 1926. III-IV,
    ibid., 1940. 2nd ed. 1959.
    'The Rôle played by Inspired Persons among the Israelites and the Arabs',
    SOTP, pp. 127 ff.
PETTAZZONI, R., *Essays on the History of Religions*. Author. Trans. by H. J.
    Rose (*SHR*, I), Leiden, 1954.

PFEIFFER, R. H., *Introduction to the Old Testament*[2], New York and London, 1952.

PHILO, *Opera*, ed. L. Cohn and P. Wendland, Berlin, 1896 ff.

PIDOUX, G., *Le Dieu qui vient. Espérance d'Israël* (*Cahiers théologiques*, 17), Neuchâtel and Paris, 1947.

L'homme dans l'Ancien Testament (*Cahiers théologiques*, 32), Neuchâtel and Paris, 1953.

VAN DER PLOEG, J., 'Le rôle de la tradition orale dans la transmission du texte de l'Ancien Testament', *RB*, liv, 1947, pp. 5 ff.

PLÖGER, O., 'Priester und Prophet', *ZAW*, lxiii, 1951, pp. 157 ff.

POPE, M., 'Isaiah 34 in Relation to Isaiah 35, 40-66', *JBL*, lxxi, 1952, pp. 235 ff.

PORTEOUS, N. W., 'Prophecy', *Record and Revelation. Essays on the Old Testament by Members of the Society for Old Testament Study*, ed. by H. W. Robinson, Oxford, 1938, pp. 216 ff.

'The Basis of the Ethical Teaching of the Prophets', *SOTP*, pp. 143 ff.

POVAH, J. W., *The New Psychology and the Hebrew Prophets*, New York, 1925.

The Old Testament and Modern Problems in Psychology, New York, 1926.

PRATT, J. B., *The Religious Consciousness*, New York, 1946.

PRESS, R., 'Der Gottesknecht im Alten Testament', *ZAW*, lxvii, 1955, pp. 67 ff.

PROCKSCH, O., *Jesaia I* (*KATSl.*), Leipzig, 1930.

Art. Λύτρον in *TWBNT*, IV.

PUUKKO, A. F., *Die altassyrischen und hethitischen Gesetze und das Alte Testament*, *SOFSO*, I, 1925, pp. 125 ff.

'Ekstatische Propheten mit besonderer Berücksichtigung der finnisch-ugrischen Parallelen', *ZAW*, liii, 1935, pp. 23 ff.

'Jeremias Stellung zum Deuteronomium', *Kittel Festschrift*, pp. 126 ff.

QUELL, G., art. Διαθήκη in *TWBNT*, II.

Wahre und falsche Propheten (*BFCh.Th.*, 46, 1), Gütersloh, 1952.

VON RABENAU, K., 'Die Entstehung des Buches Ezechiel in formgeschichtlicher Sicht', *Wissenschaftliche Zeitschrift der Martin-Luther-Universität Halle-Wittenberg*, Ges.-Sprachw. Jahrg. v, 4, 1956, pp. 659 ff.

VON RAD, G., *Das formgeschichtliche Problem des Hexateuchs* (*BWANT*, 4. Folge, 26), Stuttgart, 1938.

Deuteronomium-Studien (*FRLANT*, neue Folge, 40), Göttingen, 1948.

'Die falschen Propheten', *ZAW*, li, 1933, pp. 109 ff.

RADLOFF, W., *Aus Sibirien*, Leipzig, 1884.

REDPATH, H., *God's Ambassadress. St. Bridget of Sweden*, Milwaukee, 1947.

REICKE, B., 'Mik. 7 såsom "messiansk" text med särskild hänsyn till Matt. 10:35 f. och Luk. 12:53', *SEÅ*, xii, 1947, pp. 279 ff.

RENDTORFF, R., 'Zum Gebrauch der Formel *ne'um jahwe* im Jeremiabuch', *ZAW*, lxvi, 1954, pp. 27 ff.

REPO, E., *Der Begriff 'Rhema' im Biblisch-Griechischen*, I-II, Helsinki, 1951-54.

RIBOT, T., *Essai sur l'imagination créatrice*[7], Paris, 1926.

RICCIOTTI, G., *The History of Israel*. Transl. by C. Della Penta and R. T. A. Murphy, Milwaukee, 1955.

RIDDERBOS, J., *Profetie en ekstase*, Aalten, 1940.

RIDDERBOS, N. H., *Israëls profetie en 'profetie' buiten Israël* (*Exegetica*, II, 1), Den Haag, 1955.

RIGNELL, L. G., *A Study of Isaiah ch.* 40-55 (*LUÅ*. N.F. I, 52, 5), Lund, 1956.
Die Nachtgesichte des Sacharja. Eine exegetische Studie, Lund, 1950.
RING, E., *Israels Rechtsleben im Lichte der neuentdeckten assyrischen und hethitischen Gesetzesurkunden*, Stockholm and Leipzig, 1926.
RINGGREN, H., art. 'Jüdische Apokalyptik' in *RGG*³, I, 1957, cols. 464 ff.
'König und Messias', *ZAW*, lxiv, 1952, pp. 120 ff.
'Oral and Written Transmission in the Old Testament', *St.Th.*, iii, 1949, pp. 34 ff.
The Messiah in the Old Testament (*SBT*, 18), London, 1956.
The Prophetical Conception of Holiness (*UUÅ*, 1948: 12), Uppsala, 1948.
'Vredens kalk', *SEÅ*, xvii, 1952, pp. 19 ff.
Word and Wisdom. Studies in the Hypostatization of Divine Qualities and Functions in the Ancient Near East, Lund, 1947.
ROBINSON, H. W., 'The Hebrew Conception of Corporate Personality', *BZAW*, LXVI, Berlin, 1936, pp. 49 ff.
Two Hebrew Prophets. Studies in Hosea and Ezekiel, London, 1948.
ROBINSON, T. H., *Die Zwölf kleinen Propheten. Hosea bis Micha* (*HAT*), Tübingen, 1936.
'Die Ehe des Hosea', *TSK*, cvi, 1934-35, pp. 301 ff.
Prophecy and the Prophets in Ancient Israel, London, 1948.
ROHDE, E., *Psyche. Seelenkult und Unsterblichkeitsglaube der Griechen*, I-II³, Tübingen and Leipzig, 1903.
ROST, L., 'Bemerkungen zu Sacharja 4', *ZAW*, lxiii, 1951, pp. 216 ff.
Die Überlieferung von der Thronnachfolge Davids (*BWANT*, 3. Folge, 6), Stuttgart, 1926.
ROUBOS, K. *Profetie en Cultus in Israël*, Wageningen, 1956.
ROWLEY, H. H., *The Biblical Doctrine of Election*, London, 1950.
'The Book of Ezekiel in Modern Study', *BJRL*, xxxvi, 1, 1953, pp. 146 ff.
The Faith of Israel. Aspects of Old Testament Thought, London, 1956.
'The Marriage of Hosea', *BJRL*, xxxix, 1, 1956, pp. 200 ff.
'The Nature of Old Testament Prophecy in the Light of Recent Study', *HTR*, xxxviii, 1945, pp. 1 ff.
'The Prophet Jeremiah and the Book of Deuteronomy', *SOTP*, pp. 157 ff.
The Relevance of Apocalyptic. A Study of Jewish and Christian Apocalypses from Daniel to the Revelation, London, 1944.
'Ritual and the Hebrew Prophets', *JSS*, i, 1956, pp. 338 ff.
The Servant of the Lord and other Essays on the Old Testament, London, 1952.
'The Unity of the Old Testament', *BJRL*, xxix, 2, 1946, pp. 3 ff.
'Was Amos a Nabi?' *Eissfeldt Festschrift* 1947, pp. 191 ff.
The Zadokite Fragments and the Dead Sea Scrolls, Oxford, 1952.
RUDOLPH, W., *Jeremia* (*HAT*), Tübingen, 1947.
SARLIN, K., *En profetissa i våra dagar*, Kuopio, 1921.
SCHMID, TONI, *Birgitta och hennes uppenbarelser*, Lund, 1940.
SCHMIDT, H., *Der Mythus vom wiederkehrenden König im Alten Testament*, Giessen, 1925.
'Die Ehe des Hosea', *ZAW*, xlii, 1924, pp. 245 ff.
'Ein Psalm im Buche Habakuk', *ZAW*, lxii, 1950, pp. 52 ff.
SCHNEIDER, C., *Die Erlebnisechtheit der Apokalypse des Johannes*, Leipzig, 1930.
SCHOLEM, G., *Major Trends in Jewish Mysticism*², New York, 1946.

Scott, R. B. Y., 'Isaiah xxi. 1-10; the Inside of a Prophet's Mind', *VT*, ii, 1952, pp. 278 ff.
The Relevance of the Prophets, New York, 1947.
Seierstad, I. P., *Die Offenbarungserlebnisse der Propheten Amos, Jesaja und Jeremia* (*SNVAO*, II, 1946, 2), Oslo, 1946.
Sellers, O. R., 'Hosea's Motives', *AJSLL*, xli, 1925, pp. 243 ff.
Sellin, E., *Beiträge zur israelitischen und jüdischen Religionsgeschichte*, I, Leipzig, 1896.
Das Zwölfprophetenbuch übersetzt und erklärt²,³, I-II (*KATSl.*), Leipzig, 1929-30.
Einleitung in das Alte Testament⁵, Leipzig, 1929.
Seuse, H., *Deutsche Schriften. Vollständige Ausgabe auf Grund der Handschriften.* Eingeleitet übertragen und erläutert von N. Heller, Regensburg, 1926.
Sister, M., 'Die Typen der prophetischen Visionen in der Bibel', *MGWJ*, lxxviii, 1934, pp. 399 ff.
Skinner, J., *Prophecy and Religion. Studies in the Life of Jeremiah*, Cambridge, 1948.
Smith, J. M. P., 'The Chosen People', *AJSLL*, xlv, 1928-29, pp. 73 ff.
The Prophets and their Times, 2nd. ed. rev. by W. A. Irwin, Chicago, 1941.
Smith, W. R., *Kinship and Marriage in Early Arabia*, London, 1903.
Snaith, N. H., *Mercy and Sacrifice. A Study of the Book of Hosea*, London, 1953.
'The Servant of the Lord in Deutero-Isaiah', *SOTP*, pp. 87 ff.
von Soden, W., 'Verkündung des Gotteswillens durch prophetisches Wort in den altbabylonischen Briefen aus Mari', *WO*, 1950, pp. 397 ff.
Söderblom, N., *The Nature of Revelation*, London, 1933.
Stadling, J., *Through Siberia*, ed. by F. H. H. Guillemard, Westminster, 1901.
Shamanismen i norra Asien, Stockholm, 1912.
Stamm, J. J., 'Die Immanuel-Weissagung. Ein Gespräch mit E. Hammershaimb', *VT*, iv, 1954, pp. 20 ff.
'La prophétie d'Emmanuel', *RTPh.*, N.S., xxxii, 1944, pp. 97 ff.
Staerk, W., 'Zu Habakuk 1, 5-11. Geschichte oder Mythos?', *ZAW*, li, 1933, pp. 1 ff.
Steinmann, J., *Le prophète Ézéchiel et les débuts de l'exil* (*LD*, 13), Paris, 1953.
Steuernagel, C., *Lehrbuch der Einleitung in das Alte Testament*, Tübingen, 1912.
Strömbäck, D., *Sejd. Textstudier i nordisk religionshistoria*, Stockholm, 1935.
Suso, see Seuse.
Sutcliffe, E. F., *The Old Testament and the Future Life*, London, 1946.
Treves, M., 'The Date of Joel', *VT*, vii, 1957, pp. 149 ff.
Tushingham, A. D., 'A Reconsideration of Hosea, Chapters 1-3', *JNES*, xii, 1953, pp. 150 ff.
Tyciak, J., *Prophetie und Mystik. Eine Deutung des Propheten Isaias*, Düsseldorf, 1953.
Underhill, E., *Mysticism. A Study in the Nature and Development of Man's Spiritual Consciousness¹²*, London, 1930.
de Vaux, R., 'Le "Reste d'Israël" d'après les prophètes', *RB*, xlii, 1933, pp. 526 ff.
Vischer, W., *Die Immanuel-Botschaft im Rahmen des königlichen Zionsfestes* (*Th.St.*, 45), Zürich, 1955.

VOGT, E., 'Die neubabylonische Chronik über die Schlacht bei Karkemisch und die Einnahme von Jerusalem', *SVT*, IV, Leiden, 1957, pp. 67 ff.

VOIPIO, A., 'Observations on Somnambulic Preaching', *SSR*, ii, 2, 1923, pp. 93 ff.

Sleeping Preachers. A Study in Ecstatic Religiosity (*AASF*, B: 75, 1), Helsinki, 1951.

VOLZ, P., *Das Dämonische in Jahwe*, Tübingen, 1924.

Der Geist Gottes und die verwandten Erscheinungen im Alten Testament und im anschliessenden Judentum, Tübingen, 1910.

Der Prophet Jeremia[2] (*KATSl.*), Leipzig, 1928.

Die Eschatologie der jüdischen Gemeinde im neutestamentlichen Zeitalter[2] Tübingen, 1934.

VRIEZEN, T. C., *An Outline of Old Testament Theology*, Oxford, 1958.

Die Erwählung Israels nach dem Alten Testament (*ATANT*, 24), Zürich, 1953.

Geloven en Vertrouwen, Nijkerk, 1957.

'Prophecy and Eschatology', *SVT*, I, Leiden, 1953, pp. 199 ff.

VON WALDOW, H.-E., *Anlass und Hintergrund der Verkündigung des Deuterojesaja*, Bonn, 1953.

WALZ, R., 'Die rassenpsychologische Deutung prophetischer Berufungserlebnisse', *ZAW*, lix, 1942-43, pp. 111 ff.

WASILJEW, J., *Übersicht über die heidnischen Gebräuche, Aberglauben und Religion der Wotjaken in den Gouvernements Wjatka und Kasan* (*Mémoires de la société finno-ougrienne*, 18), Helsingfors, 1902.

WATERMAN, L., 'Hosea, Chapters 1-3 in Retrospect and Prospect', *JNES*, xiv, 1955, pp. 100 ff.

WATTS, J. D. W., 'An old Hymn preserved in the Book of Amos', *JNES*, xv, 1956, pp. 33 ff.

'The Origin of the Book of Amos', *ET*, lxvi, 1954-55, pp. 109 ff.

WEBER, M., *Gesammelte Aufsätze zur Religionssoziologie*, 3. *Das antike Judentum*, Tübingen, 1921.

WEIDEL, K., 'Zur Psychologie der Ekstase', *ZRP*, ii, 1908, pp. 190 ff.

WEIR, C. J. M., 'Aspects of the Book of Ezekiel', *VT*, ii, 1952, pp. 97 ff.

WEISER, A., *Das Buch der zwölf kleinen Propheten*, II (*ATD*), Göttingen, 1949.

Das Buch des Propheten Jeremia (*ATD*), Göttingen, 1952-1955.

Glaube und Geschichte im Alten Testament (*BWANT*, 4. Folge, 4), Stuttgart, 1931.

WELCH, A. C., *Jeremiah. His Time and his Work*, Oxford, 1951.

Kings and Prophets of Israel, ed. by N. W. Porteous, London, 1952.

Prophet and Priest in Old Israel, Oxford, 1953.

'The Editing of the Book of Hosea', *AOF*, iv, 1927, pp. 66 ff.

WELLHAUSEN, J., *Israelitische und jüdische Geschichte*[5], Berlin, 1904.

Prolegomena zur Geschichte Israels[6], Berlin, 1905.

Reste arabischen Heidentums[2], Berlin and Leipzig, 1927.

WESTERMARCK, E., *Ritual and Belief in Morocco*, I-II, London, 1926.

WESTMAN, K. B., *Birgitta-Studier*, Uppsala, 1911.

WIDENGREN, G., *Literary and Psychological Aspects of the Hebrew Prophets* (*UUÅ*, 1948: 10), Uppsala, 1948.

Sakrales Königtum im Alten Testament und im Judentum, Stuttgart, 1955.

WILDBERGER, H., 'Die Völkerwallfahrt zum Zion, Jes. ii, 1-5', *VT*, vii, 1957, pp. 62 ff.

Jahwewort und prophetische Rede bei Jeremia, Zürich, 1942.

WILLIAMS, W. G., 'Jeremiah's Vision of the Almond Rod', *A Stubborn Faith. Papers on Old Testament and Related Subjects Presented to Honor W. A. Irwin*, ed. by E. C. Hobbs, Dallas, 1956, pp. 91 ff.

WOLFF, H. W., 'Das Thema "Umkehr" in der alttestamentlichen Prophetie', *ZTK*, xlviii, 1951, pp. 129 ff.

Dodekapropheton. Hosea (BKAT), Neukirchen, 1956 ff.

'Herrschaft Jahwes und Messiasgestalt im Alten Testament', *ZAW*, liv 1936, pp. 168 ff.

WORDSWORTH, J., *The National Church of Sweden*, London, 1911.

WÜRTHWEIN, E., 'Amos-Studien', *ZAW*, lxii, 1950, pp. 10 ff.

YSANDER, T., *Studien zum B'eštschen Ḥasidismus in seiner religionsgeschichtlichen Sonderart (UUÅ, 1933, Teologi 2)*, Uppsala, 1933.

ZAEHNER, R. C., *Mysticism Sacred and Profane. An Inquiry into some Varieties of Praeternatural Experience*, Oxford, 1957.

ZIEGLER, J., *Die Liebe Gottes bei den Propheten. Ein Beitrag zur alttestamentlichen Theologie (ATA, XI, 3)*, Münster i. W., 1930.

ZIMMERLI, W., 'Das Gotteswort des Ezechiel', *ZTK*, xlviii, 1951, pp. 249 ff.

Der Prophet im Alten Testament und im Islam, Basel and Zürich, 1943.

'Die Eigenart der prophetischen Rede des Ezechiel', *ZAW*, lxvi, 1954, pp. 1 ff.

Erkenntnis Gottes nach dem Buche Ezechiel. Eine theologische Studie (ATANT, 27), Zürich, 1954.

Ezechiel (BKAT), Neukirchen, 1955 ff.

ZIMMERLI, W., and JEREMIAS, J., *The Servant of God*, London, 1957.

ZORELL, F., *Lexicon Hebraicum et Aramaicum Veteris Testamenti*, Roma, 1940 ff.

Addenda

Works bearing on prophecy outside Israel:

LANCZKOWSKI, G., 'Ägyptischer Prophetismus im Lichte des alttestamentlichen', *ZAW*, lxx, 1958, pp. 31 ff.

NOTH, M., 'Remarks on the Sixth Volume of Mari Texts', *JSS*, i, 1956, pp. 322 ff.

SCHMIDT, W., *Der Ursprung der Gottesidee*. XI: *Die asiatischen Hirtenvölker*. XII: *Synthese der Religionen der asiatischen und der afrikanischen Hirtenvölker*, Münster in Westfalen, 1954 and 1955.

On the Old Testament prophets in general:

ANDERSON, B. W. and HARRELSON, W. (ed. by), *Israel's Prophetic Heritage. Essays in honor of James Muilenburg*, New York and London, 1962.

DHEILLY, J., *The Prophets (Faith and Fact Books, 66)*, London, 1960.

ENGNELL, I, Articles in *SBU*, second edition, I-II, 1962 and 1963.

HAMMERSHAIMB, E., 'On the Ethics of the Old Testament Prophets', *SVT*, VII, 1960, pp. 75 ff.

HEATON, E. W., *The Old Testament Prophets*, Harmondsworth, 1961.

HEMPEL, J., *Worte der Profeten*, Berlin, 1949.

JENNI, E., *Die alttestamentliche Prophetie* (*Theologische Studien*, Heft 67), Zürich, 1962.

OSSWALD, E., *Falsche Prophetie im Alten Testament* (*Sammlung gemeinverständlicher Vorträge und Schriften aus dem Gebiet der Theologie und Religionsgeschichte*, 237), Tübingen, 1962.

von RAD, G., *Theologie des Alten Testaments. II. Die Theologie der prophetischen Überlieferungen Israels*, München, 1960.

WHITLEY, C. F., *The Prophetic Achievement*, Leiden, 1963.

On the early prophets:

AHLSTRÖM, G., 'Profeten Natan och tempelbygget', *SEÅ*, xxv, 1960, pp. 5 ff.

DAVIES, L. J. D. L., *The Origin and Development of Early Hebrew Prophecy in special Relation to the Development of Yahwism in Israel*. Diss. Bonn, 1959.

ROBERTSON, E., 'The Rôle of the Early Hebrew Prophet', *BJRL*, xlii, 1959/60, pp. 412 ff.

ROWLEY, H. H., 'Elijah on Mount Carmel', *BJRL*, xliii, 1960, pp. 190 ff.

On Isaiah:

BLANK, S. H., *Prophetic Faith in Isaiah*, New York, 1958.

COPPENS, J., 'L'interprétation d'Is. vii, 14 à la lumière des études les plus récentes' (*Lex tua veritas* (*Junker Festschrift*), Trier, 1961, pp. 31 ff.

EICHRODT, W., *Der Heilige in Israel. Jes. 1-12* (*Die Botschaft des Alten Testaments* 17, I). Stuttgart, 1960.

FOHRER, G., *Das Buch Jesaja*. I-II. (*Zürcher Bibelkommentar*), Zürich, 1960 and 1962.

KAISER, O., *Der Prophet Jesaja* (ATD), Göttingen, 1960 ff.

MAUCHLINE, J., *Isaiah 1-39. Introduction and Commentary* (*Torch Bible Commentaries*), London, 1962.

RIGNELL, L. G., 'Das Immanuelszeichen', *St. Th.*, xi, 1957, pp. 99 ff.

SCOTT, R. B. Y., Isa. i-xxxix in *The Interpreter's Bible*, Vol. V, New York and Nashville, 1956.

STAMM, J. J., 'Die Immanuelsweissagung und die Eschatologie des Jesaja', *TZ*, xvi, 1960, pp. 439 ff.

VAWTER, B., *The Conscience of Israel: Pre-exilic Prophets and Prophecy*, London, 1961 (1962).

WOLFF, H. W., 'Immanuel—das Zeichen, dem widersprochen wird' (*Biblische Studien*, 23), Neukirchen, 1959; revised edition *Frieden ohne Ende*, Jesaja 7, 1-17 und 9, 1-6 ausgelegt (*Biblische Studien*, 35), Neukirchen, 1962.

On Deutero-Isaiah:

KAISER, O., *Der Königliche Knecht. Eine traditionsgeschichtlich-exegetische Studie über die Ebed-Jahwe-Lieder bei Deutero-jesaja* (*FRLANT*, Neue Folge, 52), Göttingen, 1959.

MUILENBURG, J., Isa. xl-lxvi in *The Interpreter's Bible*, Vol. V, New York and Nashville, 1956.

STEINMANN, J., *Le livre de la consolation d'Israël et les prophètes du retour de l'exile* (*LD*, 28), Paris, 1960.

WHITLEY, C. F., *The Exilic Age*, London, 1957.

On Trito-Isaiah:

KESSLER, W., 'Studie zur religiösen Situation im ersten nachexilischen Jahrhundert und zur Auslegung von Jesaja 56-66', *Wissenschaftliche Zeitschrift*, Gesellsch. und Sprachwiss. Reihe, 6, Halle-Wittenberg, 1956/57, pp. 41 ff.

On Jeremiah:

BLANK, S. H., *Jeremiah: Man and Prophet*, Cincinnati, 1961.

HYATT, J. P., *Jeremiah, Prophet of Courage and Hope*, New York and Nashville, 1958.

NEHER, A., *Jérémie*, Paris, 1960.

ROWLEY, H. H., 'The Early Prophecies of Jeremiah in their Setting', *BJRL*, xlv, 1962, pp. 198 ff.

On Ezekiel:

EICHRODT, W., *Der Prophet Hesekiel* (*ATD*), Göttingen, 1959 ff.

TOURNAY, R., 'À propos des babylonismes d'Ézéchiel, *RB*, lxviii, 1961, pp. 388 ff.

ZIMMERLI, W., *Ezechiel* (*BKAT*) Neukirchen, 1955 ff.

On the Book of the Twelve:

BEYERLIN, W., *Die Kulttraditionen Israels in der Verkündigung des Propheten Micha* (*FRLANT*, Neue Folge, 54), Göttingen, 1959.

COHEN, S., 'Amos was a Navi', *HUCA*, xxxii (*Morgenstern Festschrift*), Cincinnati, 1961, pp. 175 ff.

DELCOR, M., 'Hinweise auf das samaritanische Schisma im Alten Testament', *ZAW*, lxxiv, 1962, pp. 281 ff.

HAMMERSHAIMB, E., 'Einige Hauptgedanken in der Schrift des Propheten Micha', *St. Th.*, xv, 1961, pp. 11 ff.

JONES, D. R., *Haggai, Zechariah and Malachi. Introduction and Commentary* (Torch Bible Commentaries), London, 1962.

KAPELRUD, A. S., 'Eschatology in the Book of Micah', *VT*, xi, 1961, pp. 392 ff.

LAMARCHE, P., *Zacharie IX-XIV*. Structure littéraire et Messianisme (*Études Bibliques*), Paris, 1961.

ÖSTBORN, G., *Yahweh and Baal. Studies in the Book of Hosea and related Documents* (*LUÅ*, N.F., 1, 51:6), Lund, 1956.

REHM, M., 'Die Hirtenallegorie Zach. 11, 4-14', *Biblische Zeitschrift*, Neue Folge, iv, 1960, pp. 186 ff.

REVENTLOW, H. Graf, *Das Amt des Propheten bei Amos* (*FRLANT*, Neue Folge, 80), Göttingen, 1962.

STEINMANN, J., *Le prophétisme biblique des origines à Osée* (*LD*, 23), Paris, 1959.

VUILLEUMIER, R., *La tradition cultuelle d'Israël dans la prophétie d'Amos et d'Osée* (*Cahiers théologiques*, 45), Neuchâtel and Paris, 1960.

On form and transmission:

GUNNEWEG, A. H. J., *Mündliche und schriftliche Tradition der vorexilischen Prophetenbücher als Problem der neueren Prophetenforschung FRLANT*, Neue Folge, 55), Göttingen, 1959.
WESTERMANN, C., *Grundformen prophetischer Rede* (*BET*, 31), München, 1960.
WÜRTHWEIN, E., 'Der Ursprung der prophetischen Gerichtsrede', *ZTK*, xlix, 1952, pp. 1 ff.

On special words and ideas:

BACH, R., *Die Aufforderungen zur Flucht und zum Kampf im Alttestamentlichen Prophetenspruch* (*Wissenschaftliche Monographien zum Alten und Neuen Testament*, 9), Neukirchen, 1962.
GRÖNBAEK, J. H., 'Zur Frage der Eschatologie in der Verkündigung der Gerichtspropheten', *SEÅ*, xxiv, 1959, pp. 5 ff.
HOLLADAY, W. L., *The Root* šûBH *in the Old Testament, with particular Reference to its Usages in covenantal Contexts*, Leiden, 1958.
MARTIN-ACHARD, R., *Israël et les nations, La perspective missionaire de l'Ancien Testament* (*Cahiers théologiques*, 42), Neuchâtel and Paris, 1959. (E. T. *A Light to the Nations: A Study of Israel's Mission to the World*, Edinburgh, 1962.)
MUILENBURG, J., 'The Linguistic and Rhetorical Usages of the Particle *kî* in the Old Testament, *HUCA*, xxxii (*Morgenstern Festschrift*), Cincinnati, 1961, pp. 135 ff.
ROHLAND, E., *Die Bedeutung der Erwählungstraditionen Israels für die Eschatologie der alttestamentlichen Propheten.* Diss. Heidelberg, 1956 (Fotodruck).

I. Reference Index

II. Index of Authors

III. General Index

Aaron, 114, 330
Abraham, 96, 202, 375 f.
Accadian texts, 182, 318, 324, 333
adultery, 349, 357
Aeschylus, 2, 27
Ahab (king), 50, 52, 58, 62, 65, 73 f., 76, 96
Ahab (prophet), 202
'āhaḇ, 'ahᵃḇāh: see 'love'
Ahaz, 150, 194, 221, 276 f., 280, 368
Ahaziah, 49, 56
Ahijah, 49, 52, 54 f., 70 f., 80, 95
Ahura Mazdah, 31 f.
Alexander the Great, 275 f., 284, 294, 420
Amaziah 120, 161, 209, 222, 240
Amos (personality), 98, 120, 182 ff., 209, 218, 280, 363 f.; Book of, 239 ff., 280
anaesthesia, 5, 35, 43
angel; Yahweh's, 56 f.; the guardian, 405, 421
animal sacrifices, 355 f., 358
anointing (of prophets), 64
aphasia, 198 f.
Apocalyptic, 275, 392, 421 f.
apostasy, 320, 332, 347 f., 350, 388, 411
Areopagite, 302
Aristotle, 2
Ashera, 29, 81
Ashima, 353
associations (prophetic), 10, 69 f.
Assurbanipal, 253, 290, 357
Assyria, Assyrians, 245 ff., 253, 281 f., 283, 285, 290, 324, 338, 341, 345, 366 f., 371, 416
audition, 17, 23, 36, 39, 55 f., 121, 135 ff., 309 f.
Augustine, 36, 302, 305
autodramatic vision, 41

Baal, 66, 74, 112, 211, 218, 317, 334, 349, 354, 357; prophets of, 29, 59, 67, 74, 81, 96; priests of, 66, 96; Baal Shamem, 29
Babylon, Babylonia, Babylonians, Chaldaeans, 259, 282, 337, 341, 343, 345, 371, 398, 402, 415 f.
Balaam, 90 ff., 97, 330
bāmôṯ, 352, 354
bārū, 85 f., 89
Baruch, 160, 164, 222, 235, 239, 255, 258, 260, 287, 426
Ben-hadad, 52, 55, 71, 73

bᵉnê hannᵉḇî'îm, 69 f., 184
bᵉrîṯ: see 'covenant'
Blake, William, 2 f.
bliss, prophecies of ('Heilseschatologie'), 315 ff.
book (seen in a vision), 15 f., 18, 23, 190
Book of the Covenant, 358
Brahmans, 302
Bridget (Birgitta of Sweden), 18 ff., 33 f., 37 ff., 58, 61, 64, 72, 75, 144 f., 147 f., 180 f., 190, 193, 303
Bunyan, John, 302

Cain, 67
call (prophetic), 6 f., 13, 18, 21, 45 f., 64 f., 182 ff., 216
Canaanite cult, religion, 66, 319 f., 345, 352, 357, 416; culture, 292, 328, 344 f.
Carmel, the god of, 29, 74, 79
Catherine of Genoa, 305
clairvoyance, 17, 49, 60, 94, 199, 217
classical prophets, 47, 216
coenobium (convent), 9, 69 f., 80
collections, 220 ff.
confessions, prophetic, 137, 162, 195, 214, 220 ff., 235, 298
confidence, trust (in Yahweh), 342 f.
constraint (compulsion), 2, 17 f., 21, 45, 62, 65, 92, 194, 196
contagion, 5, 32, 48
cosmos, 392, 403, 414 f., 421
council (sød), 112 f.
court prophets, 76, 95, 217
court style, 397, 419
covenant, 329 f., 338, 349, 381 f., 392, 404 f.; the New, 373, 382, 389, 391 f., 404, 420
creation, 332, 376 f.
cult, 8, 79 ff., 99, 271, 284, 314, 317 ff., 321, 330, 333 f., 344 f., 349, 351 ff., 383 f., 390, 403, 408 f., 417, 421
cult prophets, 184 f., 206 ff., 215, 218, 277
Cyrus, 176, 199, 234, 267 ff., 285, 376, 398, 402, 420

daʿaṯ Yahwêh, 162, 181, 310, 340 f., 349
dāḇār, 51; *see further* 'word'
dancing, 5, 9, 43, 59 f.
Daniel, Book of, 198, 294, 422
Darius, 145, 272
David, 60 f., 76, 97, 204, 289, 375 f., 382, 401, 405, 412; redivivus, 393 f.

470